W9-BWL-206

Theories of International Relations

Theories of International Relations

Fifth Edition

Scott Burchill
Andrew Linklater
Richard Devetak
Jack Donnelly
Terry Nardin
Matthew Paterson
Christian Reus-Smit
Jacqui True

First edition 1996
Second edition 2001
Third edition 2005
Fourth edition 2009
Fifth edition 2013

Published by
PALGRAVE MACMILLAN
Palgrave Macmillan in the UK is an imprint of Macmillan Publishers Limited, registered in England, company number 785998, of Houndmills, Basingstoke, Hampshire RG21 6XS.

Palgrave Macmillan in the US is a division of St Martin's Press LLC, 175 Fifth Avenue, New York, NY 10010.

Palgrave Macmillan is the global academic imprint of the above companies and has companies and representatives throughout the world.

Palgrave® and Macmillan® are registered trademarks in the United States, the United Kingdom, Europe and other countries

ISBN 978–0–230–36222–2 hardback
ISBN 978–0–230–36223–9 paperback

This book is printed on paper suitable for recycling and made from fully managed and sustained forest sources. Logging, pulping and manufacturing processes are expected to conform to the environmental regulations of the country of origin.

A catalogue record for this book is available from the British Library.

A catalog record for this book is available from the Library of Congress

10   9   8   7   6   5   4   3   2   1
22   21   20   19   18   17   16   15   14   13

Printed and bound in China

Contents

Preface to the Fifth Edition　　　　　　　　　　　　　viii

List of Abbreviations　　　　　　　　　　　　　　　　ix

1.　Introduction　　　　　　　　　　　　　　　　　1
　　Scott Burchill and Andrew Linklater

　　Frameworks of analysis　　　　　　　　　　　　　1
　　Diversity of theory　　　　　　　　　　　　　　2
　　Contested nature　　　　　　　　　　　　　　　5
　　The foundation of the discipline of International Relations　6
　　Theories and disciplines　　　　　　　　　　　　9
　　Explanatory and constitutive theory　　　　　　　16
　　Interdiscplinary theory　　　　　　　　　　　　19
　　What do theories differ about?　　　　　　　　　20
　　Evaluating theories　　　　　　　　　　　　　26

2.　Realism　　　　　　　　　　　　　　　　　　32
　　Jack Donnelly

　　Defining realism　　　　　　　　　　　　　　　32
　　Hobbes and classical realism　　　　　　　　　　34
　　Waltz and structured realism　　　　　　　　　　37
　　Motives matter　　　　　　　　　　　　　　　42
　　System and structure　　　　　　　　　　　　　45
　　Morality and foreign policy　　　　　　　　　　49
　　How to think about realism (and its critics)　　　　54

3.　Liberalism　　　　　　　　　　　　　　　　　57
　　Scott Burchill

　　After the Cold War　　　　　　　　　　　　　　57
　　The liberal view: 'inside looking out'　　　　　　　59
　　War, democracy and free trade　　　　　　　　　60
　　Globalization, the financial system and terrorism　　73
　　Conclusion　　　　　　　　　　　　　　　　　85

4.　The English School　　　　　　　　　　　　　88
　　Andrew Linklater

　　From power to order: international society　　　　　93
　　Order and justice in international relations　　　　　97

The revolt against the West and the expansion of
    international society   103
Progress in international relations   108
Conclusion   112

5. **Marx and Marxism**   **113**
    Andrew Linklater

    Class, production and international relations in Marx's
        writings   116
    Theories of nationalism and imperialism   123
    The changing fortunes of Marxism in International
        Relations   128
    Beyond the paradigm of production: implications for
        the emancipatory project   133
    Conclusion   136

6. **Historical Sociology**   **138**
    Andrew Linklater

    Origins of historical sociology   141
    Power and production in historical sociology   143
    Power and interdependence in international relations   148
    System and society   150
    Morality, culture and the emotions   153
    A higher synthesis?   156
    On grand narratives   158
    Conclusion   160

7. **Critical Theory**   **162**
    Richard Devetak

    Origins of critical theory   163
    The politics of knowledge in international relations theory 166
    Rethinking political community   172
    Conclusion   185

8. **Post-structuralism**   **187**
    Richard Devetak

    Power and knowledge in international relations   187
    Textual strategies of post-structuralism   194
    Problematizing sovereign states   199
    Beyond the paradigm of sovereignty: rethinking the
        political   209
    Conclusion   216

9. **Constructivism**   217
    Christian Reus-Smit

    Rationalist theory   217
    The challenge of critical theory   221
    Constructivism   222
    Constructivism and its discontents   229
    The contribution of constructivism   233
    Recent developments in constructivism   235
    Conclusion   239

10. **Feminism**   241
    Jacqui True

    Empirical feminism   244
    Analytical feminism   251
    Normative feminism   259
    Conclusion   264

11. **Green Politics**   266
    Matthew Paterson

    Theorizing environment within international relations   268
    Beyond IR: Green politics and the challenge to world order   272
    Bioenvironmentalism – authority, scale, and eco-centrism   273
    Social greens – limits to growth and political economy   280
    Greening global politics   284
    Conclusions   287

12. **International Political Theory**   291
    Terry Nardin

    Theorizing international politics   291
    Justice in war   296
    International justice   302
    Global justice   307
    The history of international thought   314

Bibliography   319

Index   358

Preface to the Fifth Edition

Theories of International Relations was first published in 1996. It was designed as a guide for Masters students and upper-level undergraduate students who were encountering theoretical perspectives for the first time. That it has survived into its fifth edition is testimony to the hard work and commitment of our authors who have continued to revise and update their chapters in the face of tight deadlines. Those who have used the book and who have commented on it – some have been teachers, others have been students – have provided advice and encouragement that is greatly appreciated. We are again grateful to the team at Palgrave Macmillan, and particularly to Steven Kennedy, Stephen Wenham and Helen Caunce as well as our copy-editor, Keith Povey – not only for their continuing faith in the volume but for their guidance and patience.

SCOTT BURCHILL
ANDREW LINKLATER

List of Abbreviations

APEC	Asia Pacific Economic Cooperation
CND	Campaign for Nuclear Disarmament
FDI	Foreign direct investment
GAD	Gender and development
ICC	International Criminal Court
ICJ	International Court of Justice
ILO	International Criminal Court
IMF	International Monetary Fund
IR	International Relations
MAI	Multilateral Agreement on Investments
MNC	Multi-national corporation
NAFTA	North American Free Trade Agreement
NATO	North Atlantic Treaty Organization
NGO	Non-governmental organization
NTB	Non-tariff barriers
OECD	Organisation for Economic Co-operation and Development
SAP	Structural adjustment policy
TNC	Transnational corporation
UN	United Nations
UNDP	United Nations Development Programme
UNHCR	United Nations High Commissioner for Refugees
UNICEF	United Nations Children's Fund (formerly: United Nations International Children's Emergency Fund)
UNIFEM	United Nations Development Fund for Women
WCED	World Commission on Environment and Development
WID	Women in international development
WMD	Weapons of mass destruction
WTO	World Trade Organization

1 | Introduction

SCOTT BURCHILL AND ANDREW LINKLATER

Frameworks of analysis

From its inception as a separate field of study, International Relations has been the site of major theoretical debates. (We follow the academic convention of using 'International Relations' to refer to the discipline, and 'international relations' to refer to the structures, processes, episodes and events that the discipline investigates.) Two of the foundational texts in the field, E. H. Carr's *The Twenty Years' Crisis* (first published in 1939) and Hans Morgenthau's *Politics Among Nations* (first published in 1948) were works of theory in three central respects. Each developed a broad framework of analysis which distilled the essence of international politics from disparate events; each sought to provide future analysts with the theoretical tools for understanding general patterns underlying seemingly unique episodes; and each reflected on the forms of political action which are most appropriate in a realm where the struggle for power was pre-eminent. Both thinkers were motivated by the desire to correct what they saw as deep misunderstandings about the nature of international politics lying at the heart of the liberal project – especially the belief that the struggle for power could be tamed by international law and the idea that the pursuit of self-interest could be replaced by the shared objective of promoting security for all. Not that Morgenthau and Carr thought the international political system was condemned for all time to revolve around the relentless struggle for power and security. Their main claim was that all efforts to reform the international system, which ignored the struggle for power, would quickly end in failure. More worrying in their view was the danger that attempts to bring about fundamental change would compound the problem of international relations. They believed the liberal internationalist world-view had been largely responsible for the crisis of the inter-war years.

Many scholars, particularly in the United States during the 1960s, believed that Morgenthau's theoretical framework was too impressionistic in nature. Historical illustrations had been used to support rather than demonstrate ingenious conjectures about general patterns of international relations. Consequently, the discipline lagged significantly behind the study of economics which used a sophisticated methodology drawn from the natural sciences to test specific hypotheses, develop general laws and predict human behaviour. Proponents of the scientific approach attempted to build a new theory of international politics, some for the sake of better explanation and higher levels of predictive accuracy, others in the belief that science held the key to understanding how to transform international politics for the better.

The scientific turn led to a major disciplinary debate in the 1960s in which scholars such as Hedley Bull (1966b) argued that international politics were not susceptible to scientific enquiry. This is a view widely shared by analysts committed to diverse intellectual projects. The radical scholar Noam Chomsky has claimed that in international relations 'historical conditions are too varied and complex for anything that might plausibly be called "a theory" to apply uniformly' (1994: 120). What is generally known as 'post-positivism' in International Relations rejects the possibility of a science of international relations which uses standards of proof associated with the physical sciences to develop equivalent levels of explanatory precision and predictive certainty (Smith, Booth and Zalewski 1996). In the 1990s, a major debate occurred around the claims of positivism. The question of whether there is a world of difference between the 'physical' and the 'social' sciences was a crucial issue, but no less important were disputes about the nature and purpose of theory. The debate centred on whether theories – even those that aim for objectivity – are ultimately 'political' because they generate views of the world which favour some political interests and disadvantage others. That dispute has produced very difficult questions about what theory is and what its purposes are. These questions are now central to the discipline – more central than at any other time in its history. What does it mean it to speak of a theory of international politics?

Diversity of theory

One purpose of this volume is to analyse the diversity of conceptions of theory in the study of international relations. Positivist or 'scientific' approaches remain crucial, and are indeed dominant in the United States, as the success of rational choice analysis demonstrates. But that is not the only type of theory available in the field. An increasingly large number of theorists are concerned with a second category of theory in which the way that observers construct their images of international relations, the methods they use to try to understand this realm, and the social and political implications of their 'knowledge claims', are leading preoccupations. They believe it is just as important to focus on how we approach the study of world politics as it is to try to explain global phenomena. In other words the very process of understanding and explaining world politics itself becomes a vital object of inquiry.

Steve Smith (1995: 26–7) has argued that there is a fundamental division within the discipline 'between theories which seek to offer *explanatory* [our emphasis] accounts of international relations', and perspectives that regard 'theory as *constitutive* [our emphasis] of that reality'. Analysing these two conceptions of theory informs much of the discussion in this introductory chapter. In addition, theory now also embraces cognate fields such as historical sociology and international political theory, which have made their own distinctive marks on the study of international relations.

The first point to make in this context is that constitutive theories have an increasingly prominent role in the study of international relations, but the importance of the themes they address has long been recognized. As early as the 1970s, Hedley Bull (1973: 183–4) argued that:

> the reason we must be concerned with the theory as well as the history of the subject is that all discussions of international politics ... proceed upon theoretical assumptions which we should acknowledge and investigate rather than ignore or leave unchallenged. The enterprise of theoretical investigation is at its minimum one directed towards criticism: towards identifying, formulating, refining, and questioning the general assumptions on which the everyday discussion of international politics proceeds. At its maximum, the enterprise is concerned with theoretical construction: with establishing that certain assumptions are true while others are false, certain arguments valid while others are invalid, and so proceeding to erect a firm structure of knowledge.

This quotation reveals that Bull thought that explanatory and constitutive theory are both necessary in the study of international relations: intellectual enquiry would be incomplete without the effort to increase understanding on both fronts. Although his comments were made in the early 1970s, it was not until later in the decade that constitutive theory began to enjoy a more central place in the discipline, in large part because of the influence of developments in the cognate fields of social and political theory. In the years since, with the growth of interest in international theory, a flourishing literature has been devoted to addressing theoretical concerns, much of it concerned with constitutive theory. This focus on the process of theorizing has not been uncontroversial. Some have argued that the excessive preoccupation with theory represents a withdrawal from an analysis of 'real-world' issues and a sense of responsibility for policy relevance (Wallace 1996). There is a parallel here with a point that Keohane (1988) made against post-modernism, which is that the fixation with problems in the philosophy of social science leads to a neglect of important fields of empirical research.

Critics of that argument maintain that it rests on unspoken or unde-fended theoretical assumptions about the purposes of studying interna-tional relations, and specifically on the belief that the discipline should be concerned with issues which are more vital to states than, for example, to civil society actors aiming to change the international political system (Booth 1997; Smith 1997). Here it is important to recall that Carr and Morgenthau were interested not only in explaining the world 'out there' but in making a powerful argument about what states could reasonably hope to achieve by way of ending the competitive world of international politics. Smith (1996: 113) argues that all theories do this whether inten-tionally or unintentionally: they 'do not simply explain or predict, they tell us what possibilities exist for human action and intervention; they define not merely our explanatory possibilities, but also our ethical and practical horizons'.

Smith questions what he sees as the false assumption that 'theory' stands in opposition to 'reality' – conversely that 'theory' can be tested against a 'reality' which is already 'out there' and knowable without any theoretical assumptions (see also George 1994). The issue is whether what is 'out there' is always theory-dependent and invariably condi-tioned to some degree by the language and culture of the observer and by general beliefs about society that are tied to a particular place and time. And as noted earlier, those who wonder about the purpose of theory cannot avoid the fact that analysis is always theoretically informed and likely to have political implications and consequences (Brown 2002). The growing feminist literature in the field discussed in Chapter 10 has stressed that argument in its claim that many of the dominant traditions are gendered, in that they reflect specifically male experiences of society and politics. Critical approaches to the discipline, which are areas discussed in Chapters 7 and 8 have been equally keen to stress that there is, as Nagel (1986) has argued in a rather different context, 'no view from nowhere'.

To be fair, many exponents of the scientific approach recognized this very problem, but they believed that natural science made it possible for analysts to rise above the social and political world they were investigat-ing. What the physical sciences had achieved could be emulated in social-scientific forms of enquiry. That is a matter to come back to later. But debates about the possibility of a science of international relations, and disputes about whether there has been an excessive preoccupation with theory in recent years at the cost of policy-relevant analysis, demonstrate that scholars do not agree about the nature and purposes of theory or concur about its proper place in the wider field. International Relations is a discipline of theoretical disagreements – a 'divided discipline', as Holsti (1985) once called it.

Contested nature

Indeed it has been so ever since those who developed this comparatively new subject, in the Western academy in the aftermath of World War I, first debated the essential features of international politics. Since then, but more keenly in some periods than in others, almost every aspect of the study of international politics has been contested. What should the discipline aim to study? Relations between states? Growing transnational economic ties, as recommended by early twentieth-century liberals? Increasing international interdependence, as advocated in the 1970s? The global system of dominance and dependence, as claimed by Marxists and neo-Marxists from the 1970s? Globalization, as scholars have argued in more recent times? What role should be the study of gender and the investigation of questions of identity and differences have in the field? These are some examples of how the discipline has been divided on the very basic question of its *subject matter*.

How, in addition, should international political phenomena be studied? By using empirical data to identify laws and patterns of international relations? By using historical evidence to understand what is unique (Bull 1966a) or to identify some traditions of thought which have survived for centuries (Wight 1991)? By using Marxist approaches to explain the influence of production, class and material inequalities on world politics? By emulating, as Waltz (1979) does, the study of the market behaviour of firms to understand systemic forces that allegedly make all states behave in much the same way? By claiming, as Wendt (1999) does in his defence of constructivism, that in the study of international relations it is important to understand that 'it is ideas all the way down?' Those are some illustrations of fundamental differences about the appropriate *methodology* or *methodologies* to use in the field.

Finally, is it possible for scholars to provide neutral forms of analysis, or are all approaches culture-bound and necessarily biased? Is it possible to have objective knowledge of facts but not of values, as advocates of the scientific approach have often argued? Or, as some students of global ethics have claimed, is it possible to have knowledge of the goals that states and other political actors should aim to realize such as the promotion of global justice (Beitz 1979) or ending world poverty (Pogge 2002)? These are some of the *epistemological* debates in the field, debates about what human beings can and cannot know about the social and political world. Many of the 'great debates' and watersheds in the discipline have focused on such questions.

In the remainder of this introductory chapter we will examine these and other issues under the following headings:

- The foundation of the discipline of International Relations
- Theories and disciplines
- Explanatory and constitutive theory
- Interdisciplinary theory
- What do theories of international relations differ about?
- What criteria exist for evaluating theories?

One of our aims is to explain the proliferation of theories since the 1980s, to analyse their different 'styles' and methods of proceeding, and to comment on a recurrent problem in the field which is that theorists often appear to 'talk past' each other rather than engage in productive dialogue that explores areas of convergence and leads to higher-level synthesis in the field. Another aim is to identify ways in which meaningful comparisons between different perspectives of International Relations can be made. It will be useful to bear these points in mind when reading later chapters on several influential theoretical traditions in the field. We begin, however, with a brief introduction to the development of the discipline.

The foundation of the discipline of International Relations

Although historians, international lawyers and political philosophers have written about international politics for centuries, the formal recognition of a separate discipline of International Relations is usually thought to have occurred at the end of World War I with the establishment of the Woodrow Wilson Chair of International Politics at the University of Wales, Aberystwyth. Other Chairs followed in Britain and the United States. International relations were studied before 1919, but there was no discipline as such. Its subject matter was shared by a number of older disciplines; including law, philosophy, economics, politics and diplomatic history – but before 1919 the subject was not studied with the great sense of urgency which was the product of World War I.

It is impossible to separate the foundation of the discipline of International Relations from the larger public reaction to the horrors of the 'Great War', as it was initially called. For many historians of the time, the intellectual question which eclipsed all others and monopolized their interest was the puzzle of how and why the war began. Gooch in England, Fay and Schmitt in the United States, Renouvin and Camille Bloch in France, Thimme, Brandenburg and von Wegerer in Germany, Pribram in Austria and Pokrovsky in Russia deserve to be mentioned in this regard (Taylor 1961: 30). They had the same moral purpose, which was to discover the causes of World War I so that future generations might be spared a similar catastrophe.

The human cost of the 1914–18 war led many to argue that the old assumptions and prescriptions of power politics had been totally discredited. Thinkers such as Sir Alfred Zimmern (the first holder of the Chair at Aberystwyth) and Philip Noel-Baker came to prominence in the immediate post-war years. They believed that peace would come about only if the classical balance of power were replaced by a system of collective security (including the idea of the rule of law) in which states transferred domestic concepts and practices to the international sphere. Central here was a commitment to the nineteenth-century liberal belief that humankind could make political progress by using reasoned debate to develop common interests. That was a view shared by many liberal internationalists, later dubbed 'idealists' or 'utopians' by critics who thought their panaceas were simplistic. Carr (1939/1945/1946) maintained that their proposed solution to the scourge of war had suffered from the major defect of reflecting, albeit unwittingly, the position of the satisfied powers – 'the haves' as opposed to the 'have-nots' in international relations. It is interesting to note that the first complaint about the ideological and political character of such a way of thinking about international politics was first made by a 'realist' such as Carr who was influenced by Marxism and its critique of the ideological nature of the dominant liberal approaches to politics and economics that had become especially prominent in the nineteenth century. Carr thought that the same criticism held with respect to the so-called 'utopians', as he called them.

The war shook the confidence of those who had invested their faith in classical diplomacy and who thought the use of force was necessary at times to maintain the balance of power. At the outbreak of World War I, few thought it would last more than a few months and fewer still anticipated the scale of the impending catastrophe. Concerns about the human cost of war were linked with the widespread notion that the old international order, with its secret diplomacy and secret treaties, was immoral. The belief in the need for a 'clean break' with the old order was bound up with the view that the study of history was an unreliable guide to how states should behave in future, especially given the increasingly destructive forms of violence that were at their disposal. In the aftermath of the war, a new academic discipline was thought essential to understand and prevent international conflict. The first scholars in the field, working within universities in the victorious countries, and particularly in Britain and the United States, were generally agreed that the following three questions should guide their new field of inquiry:

1.   What were the main causes of World War I, and what was it about the old order that led national governments into a war which resulted in misery for millions?
2.   What were the main lessons that could be learned from World War I? How could the recurrence of a war of this kind be prevented?
3.   On what basis could a new international order be created, and how could international institutions, and particularly the League of Nations, ensure that states complied with its defining principles?

In response to these questions, many members of the first 'school' or 'theory' of international relations maintained that war was partly the result of 'international anarchy' and partly the result of misunderstandings, miscalculations and recklessness on the part of politicians who had so clearly lost control of events in 1914. The 'idealists' argued that a more peaceful world order could be created by making foreign policy elites accountable to public opinion and by democratizing international relations (Long and Wilson 1995; Chapter 2). According to Bull (quoted in Hollis and Smith 1990: 20):

> the distinctive characteristic of these writers was their belief in progress: the belief, in particular, that the system of international relations that had given rise to the First World War was capable of being transformed into a fundamentally more peaceful and just world order; that under the impact of the awakening of democracy, the growth of the 'international mind', the development of the League of Nations, the good works of men of peace or the enlightenment spread by their own teachings, it was in fact being transformed; and that their responsibility as students of international relations was to assist this march of progress to overcome the ignorance, the prejudices, and the sinister interests that stood in its way.

Bull brings out the extent to which normative visions animated the discipline in its first phase of development when many thought World War I was the 'war to end all wars'. Only the rigorous study of the phenomenon of war could explain how states could create a world order in which the recurrence of such conflicts would be impossible. Crucially, then, the discipline was born in an era when many believed that the reform of international politics was not only essential but clearly achievable. Whether or not the global order can be radically improved has been a central question in the study of international relations ever since.

The critics' reaction to this liberal internationalism dominated the discipline's early years. Carr (1939; 1945; 1946: Chapter 1), who was one of the more scathing of them, maintained that 'utopians' were guilty of 'naivety' and 'exuberance'. Visionary zeal stood in the way of dispassionate analysis. The realist critique of liberal internationalism launched by Carr immediately before World War II, and continued by various scholars including Morgenthau in the United States in the 1940s and 1950s, led to the so-called first 'great debate'. Whether that debate actually occurred has been contested by recent scholars (Wilson 1998); however the myth of a great debate between the realists and the idealists gave the discipline its identity in the years following World War II. Interestingly Carr (1939; 1945; 1946), who criticized the utopians for their 'naivety' also turned his guns on the realists, accusing them of 'sterility' and 'complacency'. Theories acquire dominance in any discipline for different reasons, such as the extent to which they prevail in debates with their adversaries (sometimes more imagined than real). They can also be the beneficiary of widespread beliefs that they are right for the times or more relevant to the dominant events of the day than are other perspectives. The '20 years' crisis' culminating in World War II and followed by the Cold War era led in any case to the dominance of realism.

The purpose of theory in the early years of the discipline was to change the world for the better by removing the blight of war. A close connection existed between theory and practice: theory was not disconnected from the actual world of international politics. This was true of the liberal internationalists who believed 'the world to be profoundly other than it should be' and who had 'faith in the power of human reason and human action' to change it so 'that the inner potential of all human beings [could] be more fully realized' (Howard 1978: 11). It was no less true of the realists who thought that theory had a stake in political practice, most obviously by trying to understand as dispassionately as possible the constraints on realizing the vision which the 'utopians' had been too anxious to embrace. It was the realist position in the dispute about what could and could not be achieved in a world of competing states that gave the discipline its identity in the 1950s and 1960s.

Theories and disciplines

Over 40 years ago, Wight (1966a) posed the question, 'Why is there no International Theory?' His explanation for the absence of traditions of international theory ('speculation about the society of states, or the family of nations, or the international community') which even begin to match the achievements of political theory ('speculation about the state') was as follows. Domestic political systems had witnessed extraordinary developments over recent centuries including the establishment of public education and welfare systems. But in terms of its basic properties, the international political system had barely changed at all. Wight called it 'the realm of recurrence and repetition' which was 'incompatible with progressivist theory'. Whereas political theory was rich in its characterizations of 'the good life', international theory was confined to questions of 'survival'. The vocabulary of political theory and law – which was a language 'appropriate to man's control of his social life' – had no obvious use for the analysis of international affairs (Wight 1966a: 15, 25–6, 32).

At first glance, Wight sided with the realists in their debate with those with a utopian temperament. But in an influential set of lectures given at the London School of Economics in the 1950s and 1960s, Wight (1991) protested against the reduction of thinking about international relations to two traditions of thought. What was lost in the division of the field into 'realism' and 'idealism' was a long tradition of inquiry (the 'rationalist' or 'Grotian' tradition) which regarded the society of states as its starting point. This perspective, which has come to be known as the English School (Chapter 4), has been especially influential in Britain, Australia and Canada. Its distinguishing quality is that international relations are neither as bleak as realists suggest nor as amenable to change as utopians ('revolutionists', in Wight's language) believe. There is, members of the English School argue, a high level of order and cooperation in the relations between states, even though they live in a condition of anarchy – a condition marked by the absence of a power standing above and able to command sovereign states.

More than four decades on, we can no longer refer, as Wight did, to the 'paucity' of international theory (Chapter 12). As this volume will show, there are now several rich strands of international theory, many of which are not constrained by the problems of state survival or by the apparent absence of a vocabulary with which to theorize global politics. How did this change come about, and where does it leave earlier discussions about the possibility of progress in international relations?

We can begin to answer these questions by noting that the 1960s and 1970s saw the rapid development of the study of International Relations, as new academic departments and centres appeared not only in the United States and Britain but in several other places. This period also saw the rapid proliferation of approaches to the field. The preoccupation with war and conflict remained, the nuclear age leading to the rise of a new sub-field of strategic studies in the 1950s and 1960s. However, the boundaries of the discipline expanded, in the period now under discussion, to include foreign policy analysis, itself divided into several different approaches, one aiming for a predictive science of foreign policy behaviour which might lead to better 'crisis management' (Hill 2003). The 1970s witnessed the emergence of studies of international interdependence – or rather its re-emergence, because liberal internationalists such as Zimmern had identified the expansion of international trade as a crucial level of analysis. Liberal theories of interdependence and the later 'neo-liberal institutionalist' analysis of international regimes argued that the economic and technological unification of the human race required new forms of global international cooperation.

To those influenced by the socialist tradition, however, the term international interdependence was a misnomer. The reality was a system of global dominance and dependence in which the world was divided between 'core' and 'periphery'. The phrase, 'the inter-paradigm debate' was used in the 1970s and 1980s to show that an early consensus about the nature of the discipline (which was always incomplete) had been replaced by a broad spectrum of contending approaches, a condition that survives to this day (Banks 1985; Hoffman 1987). Only some of these approaches (neo-realism being by far the most important – see Chapter 2) continue to regard the international system as a unique 'anarchic' domain which can be analysed in isolation from social and economic developments within and across societies. The influence of other disciplines and cognate fields is now pronounced in the subject, and many strands of International Relations theory deny that the subject has a distinctive subject matter or can proceed without borrowing heavily from languages of inquiry in cognate fields of investigation. The import of various ideas from social and political theory is one development which has become increasingly prominent since the 1980s and 1990s.

In the course of this volume we will examine a number of the more influential theories, including liberal internationalism, realism, neo-realism and the English School, as well as less influential approaches such as Marxism and newer perspectives such as constructivism, feminism and green political thought. We will also consider the established field of international political theory, and the emerging interest in linkages between historical sociology and International Relations which advocates (in ways that will be of special interest to students of Marxism, constructivism and the English School) focusing inquiry on long-term processes of change in international or world politics.

In this way, we hope to provide a snapshot of contemporary debates about the nature and purposes of International Relations theory. We have chosen to call them 'theories', but in the literature over the years they have also been referred to as 'paradigms', 'perspectives', 'discourses', 'schools of thought', 'images' and 'traditions'. What they are called is less important than what they set out to do, and how they differ from one another. The following descriptions of theory capture some of their diverse purposes:

- Theories explain the laws of international politics or recurrent patterns of national behaviour (Waltz 1979).
- Theories draw on history and historical sociology, not least in order to argue that claims about the recurrent nature of international politics should be treated with suspicion and to show that the nature of contemporary events will remain elusive unless they are analysed in conjunction with long-term processes of development (Linklater 2011a; Rosenberg 1994; Teschke 2003).
- Theories attempt either to explain and predict behaviour or to understand the world 'inside the heads' of actors (Hollis and Smith 1990).
- Theories are traditions of speculation about relations between states which focus on the struggle for power, or on the nature of international society, or on the possibility of a world community (Wight 1991).
- Theories use empirical data to test hypotheses about the world such as the absence of war between liberal-democratic states (Doyle 1983).
- Theories analyse and try to clarify the use of concepts such as the balance of power or the idea of causality (Butterfield and Wight 1966; Suganami 1996; Kurki 2008).
- Theories criticize forms of domination and question perspectives which make the socially constructed and changeable seem natural and unalterable (critical theory).
- Theories reflect on how the world ought to be organized and analyse ways in which various conceptions of human rights or global social justice are constructed and defended (international political theory or global ethics).
- Theories reflect on the process of theorizing itself; they analyse epistemological claims about how human beings know the world and ontological claims about what the world ultimately consists of – for example, whether it basically consists of sovereign states or individuals with rights against, and obligations to, the rest of humanity (constitutive theory).

That list shows that practitioners in the field do not agree about what is involved in theorizing international relations. When we compare theories we are comparing different and seemingly incommensurable phenomena. There is no agreement about what counts as the best line of argument in any theory, and no agreement about whether the principal achievements of different standpoints can be combined in a unified grand theory. Post-structuralist theory – or theories, since its advocates would deny there is a single approach to which all faithfully adhere (Chapter 9) – rejects the notion possibility of one total theory of international relations. More basically, and as already noted, there is a good deal of overlap between different theories but no consensus about what the term, 'international relations', actually signifies. Its most obvious meaning is the analysis of relations between nations – more accurately, states, but that is the approach taken by realists and neo-realists and rejected or substantially qualified by exponents of competing perspectives, some of whom think the term 'global politics' or 'world politics' is a better term for describing what the subject should study in the contemporary age (Baylis, Smith and Owens 2011).

Though far from exhaustive, the following list summarizes some disciplinary preoccupations in recent times:

- *Dominant actors* – traditionally this was the sovereign state but the list now includes transnational corporations (TNCs), transnational classes and 'casino capitalists', international organizations such as the World Trade Organization (WTO), international non-governmental organizations (NGOs) such as Amnesty International, new social movements including women's and ecological movements, and international terrorist organizations such as Al-Qaeda.
- *Dominant relationships* – strategic relations between the great powers traditionally but, also in recent years, trade relations between the advanced industrial societies, the 'liberal peace', relations of dominance and dependence between the core and periphery in the capitalist world economy, forms of solidarity within 'global civil society', the gendered nature of global economic and political relations, and distinctions between 'advanced' and 'backward' peoples that have their origins in the age of Western imperialism.
- *Empirical issues* – the distribution of military power, arms control and crisis management but also economic globalization, global inequality, identity politics and national fragmentation, the universal human rights culture, the plight of refugees, gender issues, environmental conservation, transnational crime and the global drugs trade, and HIV/AIDS.
- *Ethical issues* – the just war, the rights and wrongs of humanitarian intervention and human rights, the case for and against the global redistribution of power and wealth, duties to nature, to future generations and to non-human species, respect for cultural differences and the rights of women and children.

- *Issues in the philosophy of the social sciences* – methodological disputes about the possibility of a science of international politics, competing epistemological and ontological standpoints, the nature of causation and the idea of historical narrative.
- *The prospects for multidisciplinarity* – recasting the discipline by using liberal and radical approaches to develop international political economy was the most significant shift towards interdisciplinarity in the 1980s and 1990s. Building links with social theory, historical sociology, international political theory and 'world history', and dismantling barriers between International Relations, Political Theory and Ethics that have been leading developments since the 1990s.

Quite how to deal with such a rich diversity of themes is one of the central questions every theory of international relations must address. Theories have to rely on some principles of selection to narrow their scope of inquiry; they discriminate between actors, relationships, empirical issues and so forth, which they judge most important or regard as trivial. Waltz's neo-realist theory is one of the most-debated illustrations of that process of selectivity. Waltz (1979) maintained that theory must abstract from the myriad forces at work in international politics while recognizing that in reality 'everything is connected with everything else'. But theory must 'distort' reality – and Waltz offers a complex argument about the philosophy of social sciences and the achievements of economics to defend this – if it is to explain what he regards as the central puzzle of world politics: the 'dismaying persistence' of the international states-system and the recurrence of the struggle for power and security over several millennia despite the rise and fall of different kinds of political system, ideologies and so forth. Waltz argued that international economic relations, international law, and so on, are undoubtedly interesting phenomena but they must be ignored by a theory with the purposes he sets for it, namely explaining recurring patterns of behaviour.

It is useful to compare this argument with Cox's (1981; 1983) claim influenced by Marxism that a theory of international relations has to deal with social forces (including class relations), states and world order if it is to understand the nature of global hegemony and identify 'counter-hegemonic' movements which are working to promote realizable visions of a better form of world order. In that approach, the question of what is most important in world politics is not answered by providing a list of the most powerful actors and relationships but by inquiring into the causes of inequalities of power and opportunities between human beings and by identifying the political movements which are spearheading the struggle against these asymmetries – movements which are not as powerful as states but, in Cox's analysis, are more important than them *because of the values they are trying to promote* (for further discussion, see Chapters 6 and 8).

In Cox's argument – and this is a position common to the various strands of radical scholarship in the field – the question of what is important in international relations is not an empirical problem which can be solved by looking at what is 'out there' in the 'real world'; it is fundamentally a political question, one that begins with the issue of whose interests are protected and whose are disadvantaged or ignored by the dominant political and economic structures. Such matters are not resolved by empirical inquiry – first and foremost they are ethical matters which have crept to the centre of the field over the last twenty or so years (see Chapter 12).

This raises important issues about how theories acquire disciplinary dominance or hegemony. The post-positivist turn made such matters prominent in the field, but they have a more ancient lineage. Since the 1960s, for example, scholars in the United States such as Yergin (1990) and Chomsky (1969) have analysed the close connections which have often existed between the academic study of International Relations and the world of government, especially in the United States (for an appraisal of Chomsky's work, see Herring and Robinson 'Forum on Chomsky', 2003). They have stressed how the dominant political needs of the time, as defined by governments, have favoured some theories over others so that one perspective acquires hegemony while others make dissenting claims on the margins of the field. Strategic Studies is a case in point, as many radical scholars such as C. Wright Mills stressed its close connections with the 'military-industrial complex' in the 1960s. Realism was the dominant ideology of the US political establishment in the late 1960s and early 1970s when the Nixon Administration broke with the Cold War ideology which had impeded the development of amicable relations with the Soviet Union and China (Henry Kissinger, Nixon's National Security Advisor and later Secretary of State, had been a leading realist academic prior to 1968). Since the 1980s, the dominant ideology has been neoliberal economics, which has had enormous influence through the 'Washington Consensus' in promoting the deregulation of world markets or in advancing a global 'market civilization' (see Chapter 3). A fascinating illustration of the changing political fortunes of academic theories is that realism came to have a dissenting role with respect to post-9/11 US foreign policy while remaining one of the dominant traditions in the American academy. The phenomenon of 'realists against the war' (many leading realist scholars published their opposition to the prospect of war against Iraq in *The New York Times* in 2002) is an example of how dominance in one domain may not be converted into dominance in the other.

It is necessary to stress the politicized nature of the discipline because the politics of International Relations can determine how broad the spectrum of 'legitimate theoretical opinion' can actually be. For example, Marxist scholars have highlighted the limits of expressible dissent in the discipline's attempt to uncover the cause of World War I. They have pointed to the conceptual and ideological parameters beyond which the investigators into war causes could not, or would not, proceed. For opinion to be considered legitimate, it had to fall within the narrow spectrum of opinion that extends from 'realism' to 'idealism'. According to those Marxists, certain facts were axiomatically excluded as not belonging to the inquiry at all. Tensions within society, such as class struggles and economic competition between colonial powers – during this period a popular Marxist explanation of the origins of war – were not considered seriously within the discipline at the time. One commentator has suggested that the theory of imperialism was deliberately excluded because, by locating the causes of war within the nature of the capitalist system, it posed a direct threat to the social order of capitalist states: 'this false doctrine had to be refuted in the interest of stabilizing bourgeois society ... the [historians] acted and reflected within the social context of the bourgeois university, which structurally obstructed such revolutionary insights' (Krippendorf 1982: 27). Feminists have made a similar claim about the exclusion of their presence and perspectives from the concerns of international relations, arguing that the organization of the academy was designed in ways that occluded inquiry into patriarchal power.

Explanatory and constitutive theory

One reason for studying a wide variety of International Relations theories is to make international politics more intelligible – to make better sense of the actors, structures, institutions, processes and particular episodes mainly, but not only, in the contemporary world. At times, theories may be involved in testing hypotheses, in proposing causal explanations with a view to identifying main trends and patterns in international relations – hence the claim that they are *explanatory* theories.

But why study international relations in this way? Is it obvious that the student of international relations needs theory at all? Is it not more centrally important to investigate the facts which are already out there? Halliday's three answers to this last question are instructive:

First, there needs to be some preconception of which facts are significant and which are not. The facts are myriad and do not speak for themselves. For anyone, academic or not, there need to be criteria of significance. Secondly, any one set of facts, even if accepted as true and as significant, can yield different interpretations: the debate on the 'lessons of the 1930s' is not about what happened in the 1930s, but about how these events are to be interpreted. The same applies to the end of the Cold War in the 1980s. Thirdly, no human agent, again whether academic or not, can rest content with facts alone: all social activity involves moral questions, of right and wrong, and these can, by definition, not be decided by facts. In the international domain such ethical issues are pervasive: the question of legitimacy and loyalty – should one obey the nation, a broader community (even the world, the cosmopolis), or some smaller sub-national group; the issues of inter-vention – whether sovereignty is a supreme value or whether states or agents can intervene in the internal affairs of states; the question of human rights and their definition and universality. (Halliday 1994: 25)

In this view, theories are not 'optional extras' or interesting 'fashion accessories'. They are a necessary means of bringing order to the subject matter of International Relations. Theories are needed to conceptualize contemporary events. As Doyle (1983) argues in his writings on the liberal peace, an explanation of the absence of war between liberal states for almost two centuries has to begin by discussing what it means to describe a state as 'liberal' and what it means to claim there has been 'no war'. As Suganami (1996) has argued, any explanation of what causes war or what makes peace possible between societies, will be unsatisfac-tory unless it deals with the question of what it means to say that 'x' *causes* 'y' (see also Kurki 2008). Conceptual analysis – an inherently philosophical activity – is a necessary part of any attempt to explain or understand world politics.

International relations comprise a multiplicity of events, issues and relationships which are often enormous in scale and bewildering in their complexity. Theories can help the observer to think critically, logically and coherently by sorting these phenomena into manageable categories so that the appropriate units and level of analysis can be chosen and so that, where possible, significant connections and patterns of behaviour are identified.

To the scholar of the 'international', theories are unavoidable. After all, the interpretation of 'reality' is always contingent on theoretical assumptions of one kind or another. To reiterate the point, the events and issues which comprise international relations can be interpreted and understood only by reference to a conceptual framework. The theory of international relations provides us with a choice of such frameworks, all of which have significant limitations (Kolko 2006).

The process we undertake when theorizing is also in dispute and, as Bull insisted, critical, reflective examination is imperative and always required. Gellner (1974: 175) asks whether it is possible or meaningful to distinguish 'between a world of fact "out there" and a cognitive realm of theory that *retrospectively* [our emphasis] orders and gives meaning to factual data'. If, as some post-structuralists maintain, there is no Archimedean standpoint which makes objective knowledge about an external reality possible, then the very process of separating 'theory' from 'practice', or the 'subject' from the 'object' it seeks to comprehend, is deeply problematical. Indeed, the very process of using positivist social science to acquire 'objective knowledge' may be deeply ideological. Far, then, from rising above the 'particular' to produce 'universal' truths about the social world, analysis may simply reflect specific cultural locations and sectional interests, and reproduce existing forms of power and domination (George and Campbell 1990).

Those questions lead to a second category of theory, *constitutive* international theory. Everyone comes to the study of international relations with a specific language, cultural beliefs and preconceptions, as well as specific life-experiences that affect their understanding of the subject. Language, culture, religion, ethnicity, class and gender are a few of the factors which shape world-views. Indeed it is possible to understand and interpret the world only within particular cultural and linguistic frameworks: they are the *lenses* through which we perceive the world. One of the main purposes of studying theory is to enable us to examine these lenses to discover just how distorted and distorting any particular worldview may be. It is important to ask why, for example, realists focus on specific images which highlight states, geopolitics and war while remaining blind to other phenomena such as class divisions or gender and material inequalities or cultural assumptions about the most 'advanced' peoples and those who are deemed to lag behind.

As noted earlier, in the theory of international relations it is important to be as concerned with how we *approach* the study of world politics as we are with events, issues and actors in the global system. It is necessary to examine background assumptions because all forms of social analysis raise important questions about the moral and cultural constitution of the observer. It is important to reflect upon the cognitive interests and normative assumptions which underpin research. The point here is to become acutely aware of hidden assumptions, prejudices and biases about how the social and political world is and what it can be. According to various 'critical' perspectives, it is futile or unrealistic to attempt to dispense with those assumptions. Indeed, post-structuralist approaches have called for the celebration of diverse experiences of the world of international relations while maintaining that all standpoints should be subjected to forms of critical analysis that highlights their closures and exclusions (George and Campbell 1990). We can best do this by developing an awareness of the diversity of images of international relations. The task of constitutive international theory is to analyse the different forms of reflection about the nature and character of world politics and to stress that these forms of knowledge do not simply mirror the world, but also help to shape it.

Interdisciplinary theory

Although at the outset conceived as a separate discipline, International Relations has always been influenced by cognate fields of study. In recent times it has been shaped by interdisciplinary studies which are not easily categorized as either explanatory or constitutive theoretical approaches. Nor are they obviously either normative or empirical. Two of these fields, international political theory and historical sociology, are germane to so many theoretical discussions about global politics today, that they have been given separate chapters in this volume.

Sometimes regarded as empirical theory, international political theory extends a range of ethical, philosophical and historical questions about politics, that were once more or less confined to analyses of relations within domestic settings, into the domain of international politics. Though not necessarily prescriptive, international political theory seeks to understand the grounds on which a range of ethical choices and normative preferences in international politics are made. Issues such as just-war theory, global justice and humanitarian intervention now occupy a central place in the theory of international relations. When is it legitimate to use force? What is the basis of a good international society? Are there any human rights that should be absolutely central to any decent international order? What obligations do affluent peoples have to assist the victims of famine and poverty in other societies? When do our obligations to people in other political communities – and to humanity generally – supersede our duties to fellow nationals? International political theory analyses the arguments that are advanced in attempts to answer such questions, and reflects on the presuppositions and politics which reside in the foundations of these discussions. It also reminds us that international thought has a history which deserves serious consideration by all scholars who deploy theoretical arguments without always being fully aware of how their conceptual tools were first forged.

As its title suggests, historical sociology is concerned with identifying and understanding long-term patterns and processes of change in international relations. They include the changing configurations of power in global politics, the shifting shape and functions of political communities, and rising levels of economic and social interconnectedness between peoples. Historical sociology is also concerned with how normative commitments including attitudes to violence, cruelty and suffering, have influenced the ethical and cultural contours of international politics over time. A central question is whether it is possible to identify specific long-term trends (as opposed to general laws) in world politics; a related issue is how far the contemporary society of states is very similar to earlier eras (as neo-realists have argued) or is radically different from preceding eras (as, for example, Marxist analyses of the relationship between industrial capitalism and the modern states-system have contended).

Like international political theory, historical sociology has many different strands and traditions. Some embrace grand historical narratives with an eye to uncovering distinctive patterns and themes, while others can be considered an antidote to 'presentism' – providing historical context to ensure that the analysis of supposedly unique contemporary events takes account of their relationship with processes that may stretch back for decades or centuries, and in some cases for millennia. Such phenomena as the globalization of capitalism and its implications, democratization after the Cold War, the history of states-systems, and the role of morality and the emotions in the international relations are just a few of the subjects upon which historical sociologists have reflected and significantly contributed to our knowledge of global politics.

What do theories differ about?

Although this volume identifies major perspectives, the authors do not want to give the impression that schools of thought are monolithic and homogeneous theoretical traditions. Although they may share some basic assumptions, the exponents of each perspective can have widely differing, and even conflicting, positions on the issues raised earlier. Feminism and Marxism are examples of very broad 'churches' which display great diversity – and can on occasion seem as different from each other as the main perspectives in the field. Realism has its internal variations; so has the English School, the many branches of critical theory and so on. To someone who is new to the field, this diversity can be frustrating but there is nothing abnormal about differences of perspective within the same broad theoretical tradition. Heterogeneity is a strength and an obstacle to ossification.

It is possible to compare and contrast sub-schools of International Relations because they do have much in common. It is possible to focus on what they generally agree are the issues worth disagreeing about, on what they regard as the principal stakes involved in understanding the world and in striving for more sophisticated modes of analysis. Here it is necessary to proceed with great caution because no account of the main stakes in the debates between theories can do justice to the many debates and controversies in the field. There is bound to be some arbitrariness in any attempt to make sense of the discipline as a whole. However, with that caveat, we believe it is useful to consider what the main perspectives have concluded about the following four issues: certainly a brief summary of where different theories stand on these issues may make it easier to chart a path through the thicket of major controversies in the field.

Object of analysis and scope of the enquiry

The first is the *object of analysis and the scope of the enquiry*. Debates about the object of analysis have been especially important in the discipline since the 'level of analysis' debate that began in the 1960s (Singer 1961; Hollis and Smith 1990: 92–118). One of the best illustrations of what is at stake here is Waltz's discussion of the causes of wars. In *Man, the State and War*, Waltz (1959) argued that three different levels of analysis (or three 'images') had been explored in the literature on this subject: (a) human nature; (b) the structure of political systems; and (c) the nature of the international system. Waltz showed how many psychologists have tried to explain war by looking at the innate aggressiveness of the species; many liberals and Marxists maintained that war is the product of the way in which some political systems are organized. Liberals maintained that war was the result of autocratic government; Marxists saw it as the by-product of capitalism. From each standpoint, war was regarded as a phenomenon which could be abolished – by creating liberal regimes in the first case, and by establishing socialist forms of government in the second. According to students of the 'third level' of analysis, war is a product of the anarchic nature of international politics and the unending competition for power and security. Waltz argued for the primacy of this 'third image of international politics', which stressed that war is inevitable in the context of anarchy (while recognizing that the other two levels of analysis also contribute to the study of war origins).

Thinking back to an earlier part of the discussion, we can see that the dominance of realism was in large part a consequence of its persuasive argument about the most important level of analysis for students of the field. We can also see that some of the main changes in the discipline have been the result of discontent with the realists' concentration on the problem of anarchy to the virtual exclusion of all other domains of world politics. When feminists argue for bringing women within the parameters of discussion, or the English School argues for focusing on international society, when constructivists urge the importance of understanding the social construction of norms, when post-colonial thinkers stress the need to understand imperial ideologies, and so on, they are involved in fundamental disciplinary debates about the appropriate correct *object* (or level) of analysis.

Purpose of social and political enquiry

They are also involved in crucial debates about the *purpose of social and political enquiry*. Returning to Waltz, in his account of the causes of war (and later in his classic work, *Theory of International Politics,* 1979), he maintained that the purpose of analysis is to understand the limits on political change, more specifically to show that states are best advised to work with the existing international order rather than to try to change it radically. Above all else, they should aim to as far as they can the preservation of a *balance of power* which deters states from going to war although it cannot always prevent it. Ambitious projects of global reform are, on that analysis, destined to fail. Members of the English School do not deny the importance of the balance of power, but they stress the need to attend to all the phenomena that make international order possible including the belief that the society of states is legitimate and, in the aftermath of Western colonialism, willing to be responsive to claims for justice advanced by 'Third World' states. Other perspectives include the liberal argument that the purpose of analysis is to promote economic and social interdependence between individuals across the world and, in the case of many radical approaches to the field, to create new forms of political community, or to challenge various notions of cultural superiority, or to promote new forms of human solidarity.

For the neo-realist, the purpose of the analysis is defined by the belief that international anarchy makes many of those visions utopian and dangerous. For many opponents of neo-realism, its purpose of inquiry is too quick to resign to what it regards as unchangeable processes; one of the main purposes of international political inquiry is to resist the perceived fatalism, determinism and conservatism of this position. In this context, the emergence of critical approaches to international relations (whether derived from Marxism and the Frankfurt School or located within developments in French social theory or representing post-colonial standpoints) has been especially important. Their purpose is to criticize neo-realist claims about the 'knowable reality' of international politics. Post-structuralists, for example, maintain that 'reality' is discursively produced (that is, constructed by discourse): it is 'never a complete, entirely coherent "thing", accessible to universalized, essentialist or totalized understandings... [it] is always characterized by ambiguity, disunity, discrepancy, contradiction and difference' (George 1994: 11). Reality can never be contained, in other words, within one grand theory or reduced to one set of forces which are judged to be more important than all others.

Critiques of the neo-realist purpose of inquiry have had huge implications for the scope of inquiry mentioned earlier. One consequence has been to make questions of ontology more central to the field. As Cox (1992b: 132) argued, 'ontology lies at the beginning of any enquiry. We cannot define a problem in global politics without presupposing a certain basic structure consisting of the significant kinds of entities involved and the form of significant relationships among them.' He added that 'ontological presuppositions [are] inherent in ... terms such as "International Relations", which seems to equate nation with state and to define the field as limited to the interactions among states' (Cox 1992b: 132). Cox displayed a preference for focusing on how domestic and transnational class forces, states and powerful international institutions have been combined to form a global hegemonic order. As noted earlier, debates about the 'basic structure of international politics' are not just about what is 'out there' and how we come to know 'reality'; they are also inextricably tied up with different views about the purposes of political inquiry. Cox (1981: 128) emphasized this point in the striking claim that 'theory is always *for* someone and *for* some purpose'.

In one of the most influential distinctions in the field, Cox claimed that neo-realism has a 'problem-solving' purpose, its main task being to ensure that existing political arrangements 'function more smoothly' by minimizing the potential for conflict and war. Of course, Cox did not underestimate the importance of that endeavour, but he challenged its sufficiency. The main problem, as he saw it, is that neo-realism assumes that the world is frozen in particular ways and ultimately unchangeable. But the consequence of taking 'the world as it finds it ... as the given framework for action' is that neo-realism confers legitimacy on that order and the forms of dominance and inequality which are inherent in it. (There is a direct parallel here with one of the central themes in post-structuralist thought – ultimately derived from Foucault's writings – on how forms of knowledge are connected with forms of power (Chapter 9).) On the other hand, critical theory, Cox (1981, 1992b) maintained, had a broader purpose which is to reflect on how a particular order came into being, how it has evolved over time and may change again because of 'counter-hegemonic' struggles in ways that improve the life-chances of the vulnerable people. A broadly similar critical purpose runs through all the main radical approaches to the field, including feminism, green political theory and 'critical constructivism'. All are actively reformist and libertarian in that they are broadly committed to the normative task of exposing constraints upon human autonomy that can in principle be removed.

Appropriate methodology

Debates about the purpose of international political enquiry lead to a third point of difference between approaches which revolves around the *appropriate methodology* for the advancement of discipline. Key questions are best approached by recalling that politically motivated scholarship is deeply controversial and often anathema to many scholars. The main issue is the status of normative claims. Is it possible to provide an objective account of why human beings should value autonomy and rally around a project of promoting universal human emancipation? Exponents of scientific approaches have argued that objective knowledge about the ends of the social and political is unobtainable; post-structuralists have argued that the danger is that any doctrine of ideal ends will become the basis for new forms of power and domination. In the 1990s, debates about what constitutes the 'knowable reality' of international relations (ontological questions) were accompanied by increasingly complex discussions about how knowledge is generated or about how analysts know that they know about the world (epistemological questions). Of course, the 'great debate' in the 1960s was very much concerned with epistemological issues, with the advocates of science such as Kaplan and Singer supporting quantificationist techniques and hypothesis-testing while 'traditionalists' such as Bull believed that the methodologies of history, law, philosophy and other classical forms of academic inquiry were the best way to approach international politics. As noted earlier, that was a debate (with its origins in the late eighteenth century) about the extent to which the methods of the natural sciences can be applied to the study of society and politics. It was also a debate about the possibility of a neutral or 'value-free' study of international relations.

Such debates are far from being resolved – or, at least, there is no consensus in the field as to how to resolve them. Various forms of critical theory joined the critique of scientific approaches, claiming (as Horkheimer and Adorno had done in the 1940s) that they are inseparable from efforts to create new forms of social and political power. However, scientific approaches continue to have the upper hand in the American study of International Relations. They have been central to studies of the liberal peace (see Doyle 1983), and one analyst has claimed that the observation that there has been no war between liberal states for nearly two centuries is the nearest thing to a law in world politics (Levy

1989). It is also important to note the increasing prominence in the United States of 'rational choice' or 'game-theoretical' approaches as applied to studies of cooperation between 'rational egoists' (see the discussion of liberal institutionalism in Keohane 1984). But those methodologies have not been influential in the development of 'traditionalist' perspectives such as the English School, or in constructivist analysis, or in the different branches of critical scholarship that include feminism and post-colonialism.

Distinct area of intellectual endeavour

A fourth point of difference between perspectives revolves around the issue of whether the discipline should be conceived as a *relatively distinct area of intellectual endeavour* or considered as a field which can develop only by drawing heavily on other areas of investigation, such as historical sociology or and the study of world history (see Buzan and Little 2001 and Linklater 2011a, who call for closer ties with the study of world history). The more the analyst sees international politics as a realm of competition and conflict that is inherent in the condition of anarchy, the stronger the tendency to regard it as radically different from other academic fields. Here, its anarchic character is often seen as separating the study of International Relations from other social sciences, and the relevance of concepts and ideas drawn from outside the discipline is assumed to be limited. We have already encountered this theme in Wight's (1966a) paper, 'Why Is There No International Theory?'

Neo-realism is also associated with the view that, like most of the states it studies, International Relations has sharply defined boundaries. Waltz (1979) is explicit on this point, claiming that the international political system should be regarded as a 'domain apart' – although he looks beyond the field to economics and to developments in the philosophy of science to develop his thesis about international anarchy. The more dominant tendency in recent international theory has been to embrace inter- or multidisciplinarity as a way of escaping the perceived insularity of the field. Many theorists have looked to developments in European social theory, post-colonial thinking and sociology, more generally, in order to develop appropriate conceptual frameworks to explore new areas of investigation; some have looked to studies of ethics and political theory for insight. Many of the questions which have fascinated feminist scholars – about patriarchy, gender identity, etc. – can only be answered by going outside classical disciplinary boundaries. That is also manifestly true of thinking about green politics which necessarily looks beyond the conventional discipline (Chapter 11). The most recent phase in the history of globalization has led many to deepen the move

towards multidisciplinarity (Scholte 2000). The upshot of those developments is that the boundaries of International Relations have been keenly
contested, and in many sub-fields substantially redrawn. That does not
mean the end of International Relations as an academic discipline,
although the extent to which it borrows from other fields without having
much influence on the wider humanities and social sciences in return is,
for some, a real cause for concern (see Buzan and Little 2001). On the
other hand, cross-pollination from cognate fields can also enrich the
study of international relations. All theories of international relations
have to deal with the state and nationalism, with the struggle for power
and security, and with the use of force, but they do not deal with these
phenomena in the same way. Different conceptions of the scope of the
inquiry, its purpose and methodology mean that the issues of war and
peace which formed the classical core of the subject have been conceptualized and analysed in increasingly diverse ways.

Evaluating theories

We probably should not expect too much from any empirical theory. No
single theory identifies, explains or understands all the key structures and
dynamics of international politics. International historians such as
Gaddis (1992–3) stressed that none of the major traditions of international theory predicted the collapse of the Soviet Union and its immediate consequences for Europe and the rest of the world. But many
theorists do not believe that their purpose is prediction or concede that
theories should be assessed by how well they can predict events. An
assessment of different theories cannot begin, then, by comparing their
achievements in explaining international political reality 'out there' in
the sense of predicting the future course of events.
  What we have tried to show in this introduction, and what the other
chapters demonstrate, is that some of the most interesting debates
revolve around the question of *what it means to provide a good account*
of any dimension of international politics. We do not claim that this
volume provides an exhaustive survey of the field at the current time, and
we do not deny the claims of other perspectives which lack representation here. But we do believe that a comparison of the nine main theories
considered in this volume, and an examination of interdisciplinary studies such as historical sociology, feminism, green theory and international
political theory, will show why the nature of a good account of international political phenomena is keenly contested and why *debates about
this matter are important*. That is why the great proliferation of theoretical approaches should be applauded rather than lamented as evidence

that the discipline has lost its way or has collapsed into competing 'tribes'. One can begin to decide if one has a good account of any international political phenomenon only by engaging with different theories. In that way, analysts of international relations become more self-conscious about the different ways of practising their craft and more aware of omissions and exclusions which may reflect personal or cultural biases. This theme is crucially important if those of a critical persuasion are broadly right that all forms of inquiry have political implications and consequences, most obviously by creating narratives which privilege certain standpoints and experiences to some degree. That theme is also significant because of the criticism that International Relations has been a Western-dominated discipline rather than a global discipline that integrates Western and non-Western perspectives in a more comprehensive understanding of the world.

There is one final point to make before commenting briefly on the chapters that follow. Here, it is necessary to return to a comment made at the start of this introduction, namely that the realists and the liberal internationalists have been involved in a major controversy about the forms of political action that are most appropriate in a realm in which the struggle for power and security is pre-eminent. It is also worth recalling Steve Smith's claim that theories 'do not simply explain or predict, they tell us what possibilities exist for human action and intervention; they define not merely our explanatory possibilities, but also our ethical and practical horizons' (1996: 113). Now the analyst of any dimension of international politics may not be concerned with the possibilities for 'human action and intervention'; and many theorists of international relations would deny that this is what theory is essentially about. There is no reason to suggest an agenda that all good theories should follow. But to look at the main perspectives and at the debates between them is to see that the issue of whether or not the international political system can be reformed is *one* recurrent question which concerns them all. For those who think global reform is possible, other questions immediately follow. How are different visions of international political life to be assessed, and what are the prospects for realizing them? We suggest that those questions provide one measure of a comprehensive analysis account of world politics. Others will disagree. To decide the merits of different positions on the possibilities for 'human action and intervention' – whether large or small – it is important to be familiar with at least the perspectives which are considered in this volume.

In Chapter 2, Jack Donnelly analyses classical realism which dominated the field for at least the first 50 years of its existence and which remains highly influential in the discipline today. The writings of early realists such as Carr and Morgenthau remain key reference points in contemporary debates many decades after their first publication. Interestingly, as explained in Chapter 2, neo-realism which emerged in the late-1970s and which was at the heart of most debates during the following two decades, was one of the main challenges to classical realism. However, neo-realism was also concerned with the critique of liberal approaches (as well as Marxist and other radical approaches to the field) which it considers guilty of exaggerating the ability of economic and social processes to change the basic structure of international politics.

In Chapter 3, Scott Burchill discusses the development of the liberal tradition, noting in particular how many contemporary neo-liberal accounts of the world market and the defence of free trade, resonate with ideas promoted by economic liberals in the nineteenth century. However, contemporary liberalism contains much more than a particular conception of how freeing trade and global markets from the hands of the state can promote material prosperity and establish the conditions for lasting peace. Other features of the perspective which have been influential in recent years include the defence of the universal human rights culture and the development of international criminal law, the study of 'cooperation under anarchy' associated with neo-liberal institutionalism, and the immensely important discussion of the liberal peace. These features of recent liberal thinking about international relations will also be discussed in Chapter 3.

In Chapters 4 and 5, Andrew Linklater analyses the English School and Marxism. Neither has enjoyed the global influence of realism/neo-realism and liberalism/neo-liberalism, although the English School has been particularly influential in British International Relations. Over the last fifteen years, there has been considerable interest in the English School theory of international society and in its position as a 'third way' between the pessimism of realism and the more idealistic forms of liberalism and various radical perspectives including Marxism. Chapter 4 pays particular attention to the contribution of Wight, Vincent and Bull to the discipline, and notes their special relevance for contemporary discussions about human rights, humanitarian intervention and the use of force in international affairs. Chapter 5 turns to Marxism, which has often been criticized by neo-realists and members of the English School on the grounds that its economic reductionism casts little if any light on the dominant forces in world politics. Whether the rejection of Marxism overlooked its ability to make a significant contribution to the field is a question that Chapter 5 considers in detail. Particular attention will be paid to Marx's writings on globalization, to Marxist analysis of nationalism and internationalism, and to reflections on the importance of forms of production – and specifically the development of modern capitalist forms of production – for global politics. The 'critical' dimensions of

Marxism – its interest not only in explaining the world, but in changing it – are also noted in this chapter.

In Chapter 6 Andrew Linklater explains how important trends within historical sociology have started to influence theoretical debates within International Relations. Historical sociology identifies patterns and processes of change in the broader sweep of history – over the long term. The evolution of the states-system, the spread of capitalism and the changing nature of political communities are just three key themes examined by historical sociologists which are central to contemporary debates within International Relations. The provision of historical context to the contemporary discussion of global politics makes historical sociology an indispensable tool in the hands of theorists in the field.

Marxism provided the intellectual background for the development of critical theory as developed by members of the Frankfurt School such as Horkheimer and Adorno in the 1930s, and by Habermas, Honneth and others in more recent times. In Chapter 7, Richard Devetak explains the central aims of critical theory and their impact on various theorists such as Ashley in the early 1980s, and on Ken Booth (1991a/b, 2008) and Robert Cox who have defended a version of international politics committed to the idea of human security or emancipation (see also the discussion in Brincat, Lima and Nunes 2012). Although the term 'critical theory' was initially associated with the Frankfurt School, which derived many of its ideas from a dialogue with orthodox Marxism, it is also strongly associated with post-structuralism, a perspective which is deeply suspicious of the emancipatory claims of classical Marxism. In Chapter 8, Richard Devetak explains the post-structural turn in the social sciences by considering the writings of Derrida, Foucault and Lyotard, and their influence on International Relations since the 1980s. Its critique of the 'Enlightenment project' of universal human emancipation is an important element of this chapter, as is the stress on the critique of 'totalizing' perspectives which are judged to be a threat to the flourishing of human differences.

Constructivism, which Christian Reus-Smit discusses in Chapter 9, has emerged as a powerful challenge to orthodox perspectives in the field in the past decade and, most crucially, to theories which assume that states derive certain interests from their location in an anarchic condition. In a famous challenge to those approaches, Alexander Wendt (1992) argued that 'anarchy is what states make of it'. The claim was that anarchy is socially constructed, that it is shaped by the beliefs and attitudes of states; it is not an unchanging structure which imposes certain constraints on states and compels all to participate in an endless struggle for power and security. Constructivism which has focused particularly on the relationship between interests and identities encompasses several competing approaches. Some are influenced by post-structuralism, others by critical theory in the Frankfurt School tradition; some share the neo-realist focus on analysing relations between states in isolation from other processes (systemic constructivism) whereas others see the states-system in connection with a range of national and global cultural and political phenomena (holistic constructivism).

In Chapter 10, Jacqui True sheds light on a subject which first came onto the International Relations agenda in the mid-1980s, namely feminism. This perspective is not reducible to a study of the position of women in the global order, although many feminists such as Cynthia Enloe did set out to explain how women are affected by war and by developments in the global economy, including structural adjustment policies (SAPs) in the 1980s and 1990s. The invisibility of women in mainstream approaches and in many critical alternatives was one reason for the development of the feminist literature. However, feminist perspectives have been no more homogeneous than other theoretical standpoints. Some feminists, such as Christine Sylvester (1994a, 2002), have used post-structuralist approaches to question 'essentialist' accounts of women, their interests and rights. One concern has been to challenge claims that the dominant Western conceptions of 'woman' are valid for women everywhere. Other feminists, such as Steans (1995/2006), have been influenced by the Marxist tradition. It is important to repeat that feminism is not simply interested in the place of women in the global political and economic order. It is also preoccupied with constructions of gender including constructions of masculinity, and with how they affect forms of power and inequality and, at the epistemological level, knowledge claims about the world.

Matthew Paterson discusses developments within green political thinking in Chapter 11. Environmental degradation, transnational pollution and climate change have had a significant impact on the study of global politics. Those issues have featured in studies of 'international regimes' with responsibility for environmental issues. Questions of global justice have been at the heart of discussions about the fair distribution of obligations between rich and poor and about moral responsibility for reversing environmental harm. Obligations to non-human species and to future generations have been important themes in environmental ethics. Green political thought has criticized the dominant assumptions, until the 1960s, about infinite economic growth and the faith in the virtues of unbridled capitalism. Questions about the prospects for 'ecologically responsible' states and global environmental citizenship which have been discussed in green political thought have special relevance for students of international relations (Dobson 2003; Eckersley 2004). These are some of the ways in which green political thought and practice have tried to reconfigure the study of international relations so that more attention is devoted to the long-term fate of the planet and the different life forms that inhabit it.

Finally in Chapter 12, Terry Nardin considers the recent impact of international political theory on contemporary theoretical debates in International Relations. Drawing on debates within 'domestic' political theory, international political theory examines the political, philosophical and ethical basis of key concerns within international relations, including assumptions which underwrite the discussion of global justice and the use of force and, as noted earlier, debates over what constitutes a just war, as well as disputes about the merits of humanitarian intervention. International political theory also reminds us of the long history of international thought and the broader intellectual connections between political philosophy and international politics that have not always been properly acknowledged (Walker 1993; Brown, Nardin and Rengger 2002).

Most of the authors in this volume identify with one or other of the perspectives analysed in this book, but none argues that any one theory can solve the many problems which arise for theorists of international relations. We see merit in all the approaches surveyed, and we certainly believe it is essential to engage with all theoretical perspectives from the 'inside', to see the world from different theoretical vantage-points, to learn from them, to test one's own ideas against them, and to think carefully about what others would regard as the vulnerabilities of one's perspective, whatever it may be. Those who teach the theory of international relations are sometimes asked 'what is the correct theory?' We hope our readers will conclude there is no obviously correct theory which solves all the problems listed in this introduction and considered in more detail in the pages below. Some may concur with Martin Wight (1991) that the truth about international relations will not be found in any one of the traditions but in the continuing *dialogue and debate* between them. This is almost certainly the right attitude to adopt when approaching the study of international theory for the first time, and it may still be the best conclusion to draw from one's analysis.

2 | **Realism**

JACK DONNELLY

Political realism, *Realpolitik*, 'power politics,' is the oldest and most frequently adopted theory of international relations. (Smith (1986) and Donnelly (2000) provide book-length introductions. Doyle (1997) and Wight (1992) consider realism in relation to two alternative traditions. Forde (1992), Grieco (1997), Jervis (1998) and Wohlforth (2008) are representative single-chapter introductions.) Every serious student of IR must not only acquire a deep appreciation of political realism but also understand how his/her own views relate to the realist tradition. Therefore, let me lay my cards on the table at the outset. Normatively, I rebel against the world depicted in realist theory and I reject realism as a prescriptive theory of foreign policy. Analytically, however, I am no more an anti-realist than I am a realist. Realism, I will argue, is a limited yet powerful and important approach to and set of insights about international relations.

Like most of the other theories or approaches considered in this volume, realism has two faces. It is a general orientation rooted in a central substantive focus (in this case, power). It also, however, is a body of explanatory theories, models, or propositions (emphasizing anarchy and the balance of power). This chapter begins and concludes by looking at the general character of the realist approach. In between, the focus is on particular realist explanations.

Defining realism

Although definitions of realism differ in detail (see Cusack and Stoll 1990: chapter 2; Donnelly 2000: 6–9), they share a clear family resemblance, 'a quite distinctive and recognizable flavour' (Garnett 1984: 110). Realists emphasize the constraints on politics imposed by human selfishness ('egoism') and the absence of international government ('anarchy'), which require 'the primacy in all political life of power and security' (Gilpin 1986: 305). Emblematic twentieth-century figures include Reinhold Niebuhr, Hans Morgenthau, George Kennan, Kenneth

Waltz, and John Mearsheimer in the United States and E. H. Carr in Britain. In the history of Western political thought, Niccolò Machiavelli and Thomas Hobbes usually are considered realists.

Rationality and state-centrism are frequently identified as core realist premises (e.g. Keohane 1986: 164–5; Lynn-Jones and Miller 1995: ix). But no (reasonably broad) theory of international relations presumes irrationality. And treating 'states' as a shorthand for polities or political 'units,' state-centrism is widely shared across international theories. The core or realism lies in the conjunction of egoism and anarchy and the resulting imperatives of power politics.

Realists recognize that human desires both vary and range widely. They emphasize, however, 'the limitations which the sordid and selfish aspects of human nature place on the conduct of diplomacy' (Thompson 1985: 20). 'It is above all important not to make greater demands on human nature than its frailty can satisfy' (Treitschke 1916: 590). As Machiavelli put it, in politics we must act as if 'all men are wicked and that they will always give vent to the malignity that is in their minds when opportunity offers' (1970: Book I, chapter 3).

A few theorists (e.g. Niebuhr 1932; Tellis 1995/6: 89–94) adopt realism as a general theory of politics. Most, however, treat realism as a theory of *international* politics. This shifts our attention from human nature to political structure.

'The difference between civilization and barbarism is a revelation of what is essentially the same human nature when it works under different conditions' (Butterfield 1949: 31). Within states, egoism usually is substantially restrained by hierarchical political rule. In international relations, anarchy – the absence of government – allows, even encourages, the worst aspects of human nature to be expressed, assuring the centrality of the struggle for power 'even in the absence of aggressivity or similar factors' (Herz 1976: 10; compare Waltz 1979: 62–3). 'Structural realism' is one standard label for such realist accounts, which give predominate emphasis to international anarchy. 'Neo-realism,' the other standard label, distinguishes it from an earlier generation of more complicated and eclectic realists.

These earlier 'classical realists,' without denying the centrality of anarchy, also emphasized human nature. For example, Morgenthau argued that 'the social world [is] but a projection of human nature onto the collective plane' (1948: 7; cf. Niebuhr 1932: 23; 1962: 7). Classical realists saw 'that conflict is in part situationally explained, but ... believe that even were it not so, pride, lust, and the quest for glory would cause the war of all against all to continue indefinitely. Ultimately, conflict and war are rooted in human nature' (Waltz 1991: 35). They also often emphasized the role of statesmanship and the analysis of the attributes of state power.

More recently, some realists have advanced an approach that combines analyses of structures and the internal attributes of states. These 'neo-classical realists' (Rose 1998; Schweller 2003) focus on the ways in which characteristics internal to states interact with international structural forces to produce state behaviour.

Realists can be further distinguished by the intensity and exclusivity of their commitment to core realist premises. Here we can think of a continuum of positions. 'Radical' realists exclude almost everything except power and self-interest from (international) politics. The Athenian envoys to Melos in Thucydides' *History* (Book V, ch. 85–113) express such a view, but it is held by few if any international theorists. 'Strong' realists stress the predominance of power, self-interest, and conflict but allow modest space for politically salient 'non-realist' forces and concerns. Niebuhr, Carr, Morgenthau, Waltz, and Mearsheimer, leading realists of their generations, all lie in this range of the continuum. As Carr put it, 'we cannot ultimately find a resting place in pure realism' (1946: 89). 'Weak' or 'hedged' realists accept the realist analysis of the 'problems' of international politics but are open to a wider range of political possibilities and see more important elements of international relations lying outside the explanatory range of realism.

Weak realism gradually shades into something else. At some point (non-realist) 'hedges' outweigh the (realist) 'core.' Conversely, analysts operating from other perspectives may appeal to characteristically realist forces and explanations that 'hedge' their own theories.

Hobbes and classical realism

Chapter 13 of Thomas Hobbes' *Leviathan*, originally published in 1651, imagines politics in a pre-social 'state of nature.' The result is an unusually clear realist theory that gives roughly equal weight to human nature and international anarchy.

The Hobbesian state of nature

Hobbes makes three simple assumptions:

1. Men are equal. (This language not only reflects standard seventeenth-century usage but a deeply gendered, masculinist perspective. See Tickner (1988); Chapter 10.)
2. They interact in anarchy, understood as the absence of both rulers and rules.
3. They are motivated by competition, diffidence, and glory.

The conjunction of these conditions leads to a war of all against all.

Men, Hobbes argues, are equal in the elemental sense that 'the weakest has strength enough to kill the strongest, either by secret machination or by confederacy with others' (para. 1). 'From this equality of ability ariseth equality of hope in the attaining of our ends' (para. 3). I'm as good as you are and thus ought to have (at least) as much as you. But scarcity prevents each from having as much as he desires – which makes men enemies. (We might want to list scarcity as a fourth assumption, but Hobbes seems to take it as too obvious to merit mention.)

Enmity is exacerbated by the passions of competition, diffidence, and glory (para. 6). 'The first maketh men invade for gain; the second, for safety; and the third, for reputation' (para. 7). Even where one is not seeking gain, fear leads to defensive war, for 'there is no way for any man to secure himself so reasonable as anticipation' (para. 4). And every man's desire 'that his companion should value him at the same rate he sets upon himself' (para. 5) leads to conflict over reputation.

Add the absence of both rules and government and the mixture becomes volatile and vicious. 'During the time men live without a common power to keep them all in awe, they are in that condition which is called war; and such a war as is of every man against every man' (para. 8). Although fighting is not constant, any dispute may degenerate into violence. As a result, human industry has little scope for operation 'and the life of man [is] solitary, poor, nasty, brutish, and short' (para. 10).

It is important to see that this state of war is a necessary logical consequence. The Hobbesian logic of conflict can be evaded only if one or more of the model's assumptions does not hold or if the forces not included in the model intervene. For example, power inequalities may lead to imposed hierarchy, which substantially mitigates conflict and violence even in the absence of government or formal rules. Among countervailing forces, Hobbes identifies 'the passions that incline men to peace' and reason, which 'suggesteth convenient articles of peace upon which men may be drawn to agreement' (para. 14). He has little confidence, however, in their power to overcome the egoistic passions, especially in the absence of government to enforce rules of cooperation.

Assessing Hobbesian realism

Hobbes acknowledges (para. 12) that such a savage state never existed across the entire globe. I would suggest that we go further and abandon any pretence of history or comparative anthropology. Hobbes, in this reading, identifies a logic of interaction, an ideal type model of pressures and tendencies. When equal, competitive, fearful, and vain actors interact in anarchy, generalized violent conflict can be predicted.

Theory is artful abstraction. It directs our attention away from the welter of 'confusing details' towards what is 'most important.' Theories are beacons, lenses, filters. They direct us to what, according to the theory, is essential for understanding (some part of) the world. Much as a good caricature selects, exaggerates, and thus wilfully distorts in order to capture the defining features of its subject, a good theory intentionally over-simplifies in order to highlight forces that are allegedly central to patterned behaviour.

Therefore, the proper question to pose of Hobbes' theory, or any theory, is not whether it accurately describes the world. Of course it does not (except in a very rough, over-simplified first-approximation). We should ask instead where Hobbes' simplifying theoretical assumptions help us to understand important elements of international politics – and where they do not.

Hobbes sees human nature as naturally given and largely unalterable. This certainly is contentious. Most analysts, however, would agree that the prevalence of competition, diffidence, and glory is sufficiently frequent and central to make it an often fruitful simplifying assumption.

As for anarchy, the fact that it has been largely overcome by hierarchical political rule within most states actually increases the likelihood that it will persist internationally. Even vicious and inefficient governments provide considerable security for the lives and property of their citizens. Because people do not face a life that is solitary, poor, nasty, brutish, and short, the pressures to replace the international state of nature with international government are dramatically reduced. Furthermore, international anarchy reflects the strong desire of states and their citizens for autonomy.

The assumption of equality is probably the most problematic aspect of Hobbes model. Material inequality in fact regularly leads to domination, spheres of influence, hegemony, and empire. But among 'great powers' – states with the capacity to inflict punishing damage on any other power in the system – the Hobbesian assumption of equality holds. (Note that this suggests that (Hobbesian) realism is a theory of great power politics, rather than a general theory of international relations. Relations between fundamentally unequal powers reflect another logic of interaction.)

Each of Hobbes' assumptions seems applicable to some important parts of international relations. The crucial question then is the extent to which other factors and forces push in different directions. How much of international relations, in what circumstances, is governed by the Hobbesian conjunction of anarchy, egoism, and equality? To use social scientific jargon, what are the relative impacts of 'endogenous variables' (factors included within the theory) and 'exogenous variables' (those not included)? We will return to this question, recurrently, as we proceed.

Waltz and structural realism

Hobbes' 'classical' realism gives roughly equal emphasis to anarchy and egoism. By contrast, most realist work over the past three decades has been more or less rigorously structural, largely as a result of the influence of Kenneth Waltz. Structural realism aims to set aside those features of international relations that depend on the character of the actors or the nature of their interactions in order to highlight the constraining impact of the structure of the international system.

Waltzian structuralism

Political structures, Waltz argues, are defined by their ordering principle, differentiation of functions, and distribution of capabilities; that is, how units are related to one another, how political functions are allocated, and how power is distributed.

Waltz argues that there are only two basic political ordering principles, hierarchy and anarchy (which he associates with domestic and international politics). Units either stand in relations of authority and subordination (hierarchy) or they do not (anarchy). And this is structurally central because striking qualitative differences exist 'between politics conducted in a condition of settled rules and politics conducted in a condition of anarchy' (Waltz 1979: 61).

Anarchy, Waltz contends, largely eliminates functional differentiation between the units. In anarchic/international orders, every unit must 'put itself in a position to be able to take care of itself since no one else can be counted on to do so' (1979: 107). Differences between states 'are of capability, not function' (1979: 96). 'National politics consists of differentiated units performing specified functions. International politics consists of like units duplicating one another's activities' (1979: 97).

If all international orders are anarchic, and if this implies minimal functional differentiation, then international political structures differ only in their distributions of capabilities. They are defined by the changing fates of great powers. More abstractly, international orders vary according to the number of great powers; that is, the polarity (number of poles of power) of the system.

Balancing

The central theoretical conclusion of structural realism is that in anarchy states 'balance' rather than 'bandwagon' (Waltz 1979: 126).

In hierarchic political orders, actors tend to 'jump on the bandwagon' of a leading candidate or recent victor, because 'losing does not place their security in jeopardy' (Waltz 1979: 126). 'Bandwagoners' attempt to increase their gains (or reduce their losses) by siding with the stronger party.

In anarchy, however, bandwagoning courts disaster by strengthening someone who later may turn on you. The power of others – especially great power – is always a threat when there is no government to turn to for protection. 'Balancers' attempt to reduce their risk by opposing a stronger or rising power.

Weak states have little choice but to guess right and hope that early alignment with the victor will bring favourable treatment. Only foolish great powers, however, would accept such a risk. Instead, they will balance. Realists typically identify both internal balancing, which reallocates resources from other purposes to national security, and external balancing, carried out through alliances and other (formal and informal) agreements.

Structural pressures to balance explain important yet otherwise puzzling features of international relations. Consider Soviet–American relations. The United States opposed the Russian Revolution and for two decades remained implacably hostile to the Soviet Union. Nonetheless, the rise of Hitler's Germany propelled the US and the USSR into alliance in World War II. Notwithstanding their intense internal differences and history of animosity, they balanced against a common threat. After the war, the US and the Soviet Union again became adversaries. In this version of the story, though, internal and ideological differences did not cause renewed rivalry (although they may have increased its virulence and influenced its form). Enmity was structurally induced. In a bipolar world, each superpower is the only serious threat to the security of the other. Each, whatever its preferences or inclinations, must balance against the other.

The Cold War, in this account, was not 'caused' by anyone; it was the 'natural' result of bipolarity. Soviet expansion into Central and Eastern Europe did not arise from either vicious rulers in the Kremlin or rabid anti-communists in Washington (although both may have exacerbated the rivalry). It was the normal behaviour of a country that had been invaded from the West, with devastating consequences, twice in twenty-five years, and once more a century earlier. Cold War conflicts in Southeast Asia, Central America, and Southern Africa likewise were not driven by a global communist (or anti-communist) conspiracy but rather were the ordinary result of ordinary efforts by great powers to increase their international influence.

This example suggests a very important interpretative point. Realism provides a theoretical account of how the world works. It can be used for peaceful purposes – there are a number of Quaker realists – as well as for war. For example, hundreds of thousands of lives might have been saved, and millions of injuries avoided, had the United States pursued a realist bipolar rivalry with the Soviet Union rather than an ideological Cold War. Leading realists such as Niebuhr and Morgenthau were early and vocal critics of the war in Vietnam. Not a single prominent realist supported the American invasion of Iraq in 2003.

Prisoners' Dilemma, relative gain, and cooperation

Anarchy and egoism greatly impede cooperation. Prisoners' Dilemma offers a standard formal representation of this logic.

Imagine two criminal colleagues taken in separately by the police for questioning. Each is offered a favourable plea bargain in return for testimony against the other. Without a confession, though, they can only be convicted of a lesser crime. Each must choose between cooperating (remaining silent) and defecting (testifying against the other). Imagine also that both have the following preference ordering: 1) confess while the other remains silent; 2) both remain silent; 3) both confess; 4) remain silent while the other confesses. Assume finally that their aversion to risk takes a particular form: they want to minimize their maximum possible loss.

If both cooperate (remain silent) both receive their second choice payoff (conviction on the lesser charge). But cooperation leaves each vulnerable to the worst possible outcome (serving a long prison term – and knowing that your partner put you there). Each can assure against disaster by confessing (defecting). The rational choice thus is to defect (confess) *even though both know that they both could be better off by cooperating*. Both end up with their third choice, because this is the only way to assure that each avoids the worst possible outcome.

Conflict here does not arise from any special defect in the actors. They are mildly selfish but not particularly evil or vicious. Far from desiring conflict, both prefer cooperation. They are neither ignorant nor ill informed. Nonetheless, they are pushed by fear towards treating each other as adversaries.

Anarchy, in other words, sometimes can defeat even our best intentions – which realists see as rare enough to begin with. Without insurance schemes that reduce the risk of cooperating – and, as other examples show, without procedures to determine how to divide the gains – even those who want to cooperate may remain locked in a vicious cycle of mutually destructive competition. For example, states may engage in not merely costly but counter-productive arms races because arms control agreements cannot be adequately verified.

Herbert Butterfield calls this 'Hobbesian fear.' 'If you imagine yourself locked in a room with another person with whom you have often been on the most bitterly hostile terms in the past, and suppose that each of you has a pistol, you may find yourself in a predicament in which both of you would like to throw the pistols out of the window, yet it defeats the intelligence to find a way of doing it.' (1949: 89–90) The 'security dilemma' (Glaser 1997; Booth and Wheeler 2008) has a similar logic. 'Given the irreducible uncertainty about the intentions of others, security measures taken by one actor are perceived by others as threatening; the others take steps to protect themselves; these steps are then interpreted by the first actor as confirming its initial hypothesis that the others are dangerous; and so on in a spiral of illusory fears and "unnecessary" defenses' (Snyder 1997: 17).

Anarchic pressures towards balancing and against cooperation are reinforced by the relativity of power. Power is control over outcomes, 'the ability to do or effect something' (*Oxford English Dictionary*). It is less a matter of absolute resources – how much 'stuff' one has – than of relative capabilities. Facing an unarmed man, a tank is pretty powerful. The same tank facing a squadron of carrier-based attack jets is not very powerful at all.

The relativity of power requires states to 'be more concerned with relative strength than with absolute advantage' (Waltz 1979: 106). Bandwagoning seeks absolute gains, aligning early with a rising power to gain a share of the profits of victory. Balancing pursues relative gains.

Actors who focus on relative gains, however, will find it much more difficult to cooperate. They must consider not only whether one gains but, more importantly, whether one's gains outweigh those of others (who, in anarchy, must be seen as potential adversaries). Even predatory cooperation is problematic unless it maintains the relative capabilities of the cooperating parties. In fact, states may be satisfied with conflicts that leave them absolutely worse off – so long as their adversaries are left even worse off.

Polarity

The preceding two sub-sections have considered the principal theoretical implications realists draw from anarchy, the ordering principle of international relations. If, following Waltz, we see minimal functional differentiation in anarchic orders, then the other principal contribution of structural realism should lie in its analysis of the impact of the distribution of capabilities. How does polarity, the number of great powers in a system, structure international relations?

Unipolarity became a hot topic after the end of the Cold War. Waltzian balancing logic (Layne 1993; Mastanduno 1997) suggests that unipolarity is unstable. Unipolarity should provoke near universal balancing that will facilitate the rise of new great powers, much as a rising hegemon (e.g.

Napoleonic France) provokes a 'grand coalition' that unites the other great powers. Other theorists, however, argue that this expectation is overly simplistic (Wohlforth 1999). And recent comparative empirical work suggests that failures to balance against a rising hegemon are at least as common as balancing (Hui 2005; Kaufman *et al.* 2007; Wohlforth *et al.* 2007). But whatever its frequency or resilience, unipolarity (and resistance to it) gives international relations a very different character from systems with two or more great powers.

Schweller (1998) has shown that tripolar systems have a distinctive structural logic. And systems with very many or no great powers – the two are effectively equivalent – have a different structural logic than multipolar systems with a few (four, five, or a couple more) great powers. Systems with a one, two, three, or a few great powers are monopolistic or oligopolistic. Those with many or no great powers are more like competitive markets.

Most attention, however, has focused on the differences between bipolar and multipolar orders; that is, systems with two and a few great powers. For example, conflicts in the periphery pose little threat to the general bipolar balance. In multipolar systems, however, where power is divided among more actors, a change in the periphery of the same absolute magnitude may have a noticeable impact on the general balance. The significance of such a difference, however, is obscure. Should peripheral conflicts be more frequent in bipolar systems because they are less destabilizing and thus 'safer' (for the great powers)? Or should they be less frequent because there are no compelling reasons to become involved?

There is thus considerable disagreement over the relative stability of bipolar and multipolar systems. The classic mid-1960s accounts of Waltz (1964), Deutsch (1964), and Rosecrance (1966) argue, respectively, for bipolarity, multipolarity, and 'bi-multipolarity' (both/neither). More recent and more sophisticated accounts try to incorporate, for example, the impact of different forms of alignment (Christensen and Snyder 1990) and changes across time in the distribution of capabilities (Copeland 1996). Unfortunately, empirical tests are constrained by the fact that in 2,500 years of Western history there have been as few as four bipolar systems (Athens–Sparta in the fifth century BCE, Carthage–Rome in the third century BCE, the Hapsburg–Bourbon rivalry in the sixteenth century, and the US–USSR Cold War).

The nature of structural predictions

Part of the problem with the debate on the relative stability of bipolar and multipolar orders is that posing the question in structural terms is probably misguided. For example, a rising 'revisionist' or 'revolutionary' power with a high propensity for risk poses very different problems than a risk-averse, satisfied, 'status quo' power. Such considerations fall outside the scope of structural realism. Therefore, if their effects characteristically are significant, there can be no answer to the (structural) question of the relative stability of bipolar and multipolar orders.

Structures push states in certain directions. They do not mechanically determine outcomes. The predictions of structural realism are, as Waltz repeatedly notes, 'indeterminate' (1979: 124, 122, 71; 1986: 343). States are also subject to numerous other pressures and influences – which often are decisive in determining outcomes. This does not make polarity or anarchy unimportant. It just happens that other forces often are more powerful – making structural expectations misleading or simply wrong.

It is the job of the analyst, not the theorist, to determine where a particular theoretical logic applies in the world. Whether a 'good theory,' in the sense of a rigorous logic of interaction, is a 'good theory to apply' in any particular case depends not on the theory but on contingent facts about the world.

We can thus identify three types of theoretical failures. If a predicted outcome does not occur because the assumptions of the theory are not satisfied in the case under consideration, the 'failure' is entirely attributable to the analyst. If the underlying assumptions are satisfied but the predicted results do not occur, the failure is attributable to the theory. The most interesting situation, however, is when the theoretically predicted pressures operate but are overwhelmed by other forces.

The significance of this third type of theoretical 'failure' depends on which 'exogenous variables' (explanatory factors not considered within the theory in question) prevail, how often, and in what kinds of cases. We will also want to know how powerful those exogenous forces must be to overcome the effects of the endogenous variables. If endogenous variables almost always hold up against all but the strongest expressions of a few exogenous variables, the theory is relatively powerful; 'robust'. If a wide range of relatively weak exogenous variables regularly swamp the endogenous variables, the theory is not exactly 'wrong' – the predicted pressures do still operate – but it is not very useful.

Many of the disagreements between realists and their critics can be seen as, in effect, disputes about the frequency and significance of realism's failures, and what type of failures they are.

Motives matter

How far we can go with purely structural theories; that is, with anarchy, the distribution of capabilities, and nothing else? Not very far.

Abstracting from versus assuming motives

Waltz claims that his theory 'abstract[s] from every attribute of states except their capabilities' (1979: 99). He thus talks of 'units;' abstract, characterless concentrations of capabilities. In fact, however, Waltz's theory, by his own admission, 'is based on assumptions about states;' 'built up from the assumed motivations of states' (1979: 118; 1996: 54). There is a huge difference between abstracting from all particulars and assuming certain ones. And the substance of realist assumptions about states accounts for much of the distinctive character of the theory.

Hobbes' war of all against all arises not from anarchy alone but also from equal individuals driven by competition, diffidence, and glory. Conversely, 'wars would hardly be likely to occur if all men were Christian saints, competing with one another in nothing, perhaps, save self-renunciation' (Butterfield 1979: 73).

Even Waltz, despite repeated claims to the contrary, admits this. 'Structurally we can describe and understand the pressures states are subject to. We cannot predict how they will react to the pressures without knowledge of their internal dispositions' (1979: 71). To abstract from all attributes of states (other than capabilities) makes prediction impossible. Thus in practice Waltz, like other realists, relies heavily on knowledge of or assumptions about the interests and intentions of states.

This would not be seriously problematic if Waltz had a clear and coherent account of state motivation. He does claim that states 'are unitary actors with a single motive – the wish to survive' (1996: 54). But Waltz also allows that 'some states may persistently seek goals that they value more highly than survival' (1979: 92). He argues that states seek wealth, advantage, and flourishing (1979: 112; 1986: 337; 1993: 54), peaceful coexistence (1979: 144), peace and prosperity (1979: 144, 175), and sovereignty, autonomy, and independence (1979: 204, 107, 104) – and that they act out of pride and feeling put upon (1993: 66, 79). Waltz even claims that states 'at minimum, seek their own preservation and, at maximum, drive for universal domination' (1979: 118). This rules out little beyond charity and beneficence.

(Re-)incorporating the state

Over the past two decades, realists have adopted three principal strategies to incorporate motives in ways that make their predictions more determinate.

The first major move was made by Stephen Walt (1987), who, examining alliance behaviour empirically, concluded that states balance not against power but against threat. Consider, for example, the very different

American behaviour towards British, French, and Chinese (or Israeli, Indian, and North Korean) nuclear arsenals, which weigh about equally in the global distribution of capabilities. Unfortunately, *structural* realism in principle has nothing to say about threat (as opposed to capabilities), leaving the crucial explanatory variable outside the scope of the theory. And Walt never seriously addresses the problems of integrating structural and non-structural variables.

A second strategy has been to make consistent, precise, and determinate motivational assumptions. Survival and domination can be seen as extreme statements of defensive and expansive orientations. Modelling states as driven by one or the other leads to what are typically called defensive and offensive realism (see, for example, Lynn-Jones 1995; Labs 1997: 7–17; Zakaria 1998: 25–42; and Snyder 2002). In effect, the distinction drawn by many classical realists between status quo (or satisfied) and revisionist (or revolutionary) powers has been revived and placed within a structural context. Again, though, structural and non-structural variables are simply thrown together, rather than integrated into a coherent general account. And there is no defence of including *these* particular non-structural variables but not others.

On the defensive realist side, Michael Mastanduno argues that 'realists expect nation-states to avoid gaps that favor their partners, but not necessarily to maximize gaps in their own favor. Nation-states are not 'gap maximizers'. They are, in Joseph Grieco's terms, 'defensive positionalists" (Mastanduno 1991: 79, n. 13). John Mearsheimer, the leading exponent of offensive realism, however, argues that 'states seek to survive under anarchy by maximizing their power relative to other states' (1990: 12). His states are 'short-term power maximizers' (1995: 82): that is, *offensive* positionalists. As Fareed Zakaria puts it, 'the best solution to the perennial problem of the uncertainty of international life is for a state to increase its control over that environment through the persistent expansion of its political interests abroad' (1998: 20).

Whether states are defensive or offensive positionalists, however, is an empirical, not a theoretical, question. And the historical record clearly shows examples of both. Therefore, it would be foolish to 'be' an offensive realist or a defensive realist. Both have some potential value. Both need to be available to analysts as potentially useful tools. But neither is a pure structural theory, in the strict Waltzian sense of that term. And neither is 'the best' realist theory. They are fundamentally different models that are both unquestionably realist.

The third strategy, which has generated some of the most innovative and interesting recent work within the realist tradition, has been to supplement rather than refine structural realism. Neo-classical realists have in effect argued that purely structural theory, no matter how sophisticated, rarely produces sufficiently determinate predictions to offer adequate understanding. 'States often react differently to similar systemic pressures and opportunities, and their responses may be less motivated by systemic-level factors than domestic ones' (Schweller 2006: 6). Realists, therefore, must 'open up' the state, which in structural theories is treated as a 'black box'.

The neo-classical project is to investigate patterns in state behaviour that interact with structural forces. For example, Jack Snyder (1991) has examined the domestic political forces and processes that lead states not to rational balancing but reckless imperial over-reach. Randall Schweller, by looking at variables such as elite cohesion and regime stability, has developed five 'causal schemes' that seek to predict when states will balance in Waltzian (or Waltian) ways and when they are likely to 'under-balance' (2006: chapter 2). Miriam Fendius Elman (2000) argues that parliamentary and presidential systems respond to structural forces in systematically different ways. Jean-Marc Blanchard and Norrin Ripsman (2008) argue that the degree of state autonomy from society systematically alters its response to structural pressures.

Waltz is content to say a 'small number of big and important things' (cf. 1979: 70; 1986: 329) about (all) international systems. Most contemporary realists, however, want to be able to say more things. And they are interested in patterns that apply only in particular types of systems or circumstances. They thus are willing to give up the simplicity and generality of pure structural theories in return not just for greater depth and detail but a much wider range of coverage.

System and structure

Making assumptions about the motives of states does not necessarily remove a theory from the set of systems theories. To appreciate this, we need to distinguish between units and levels of analysis: that is, between the thing (unit) to be explained and the (analytical level of the) thing that does the explaining. The state, for example, is the standard unit of analysis in realist theories, which characteristically seek to explain state behaviour. State behaviour, however, may be explained by forces operating at the level of the state (e.g., national history, ideology, or regime type), in the system (e.g., anarchy induces a balancing pursuit of relative gains), or in individuals (e.g., the impact of a particular national leader).

Neo-classical realism self-consciously combines system-level and state-level explanatory variables. Offensive and defensive realism does the same, although often implicitly. There is another type of structural option, however, that has been largely ignored or rejected by realists:

rather than treat state motives as, (a) determined at the unit level, (b) universal, or (c) matters of assumption, we could look for system-level forces that *variably* shape the behaviour of the unit.

The most striking example is Alexander Wendt's (1999: chapter 6) demonstration that anarchic orders function very differently when actors see each other as 'enemies' out to destroy each other, 'rivals' who compete but do not threaten each other's survival, and 'friends' who have abandoned force in their relations. Realism in effect becomes a special case; what Wendt calls the 'Hobbesian' anarchy of enemies. Sovereignty, understood as rights to territorial integrity and political independence, transforms relations into those among 'Lockean' rivals, who compete, and even fight, without threatening one another's survival.

There are at least two ways to read such a move. We might want to expand the conception of structure to include unit type (e.g., Kaufman 1997: 181–5; Reus-Smit 1999; Donnelly 2012). Alternatively, we might want to keep a narrow definition of structure but refuse to follow Waltz in collapsing systems theory into structural theory. Both options, but especially the second, suggest additional directions for expanding the range of realist thinking.

A system is a bounded space defined by: (a) units that interact differently, and usually much more intensively, with each other than with those outside the system; (b) the structure within which they interact; and (c) the characteristic interactions of the units within that structure. A system involves not only *parts of a particular type* but also *particular relations between the parts*. System-level patterns in the processes of state interaction promise to provide much richer and more determinate realist theories.

Process formations

Glenn Snyder has suggested greater attention to what he calls 'process variables,' patterns of interaction that are neither structural nor at the level of the unit; that is, are systemic but not structural. Operating largely (although not entirely) outside the realist framework, Barry Buzan and Richard Little talk similarly about 'process formations' (cf. Buzan *et al.* 1993: 48–50; Buzan and Little 2000: 79, 379).

Snyder (1997) has developed this idea in relation to alliance politics. Consider alignment. As a rough first approximation, states can be seen to stand in relations of amity or enmity, seeing themselves as allies or adversaries. This has systematic consequences. For example, states are more likely to balance against adversaries than allies. Conversely, relative gains considerations may be substantially muted among allies.

Both allies and adversaries may have common or competing interests, which also help to make predictions more determinate. Common interests facilitate cooperation – although anarchy and relative gains always cut against successful cooperation. Conversely, competing interests may impede or prevent balancing against a common enemy.

Waltzian structural realism allows us only to predict *that* balances will form. Taking alignment and other process variables into account allows us to predict which particular balances are likely or unlikely to develop. 'If, as Waltz says, system structures only 'shape and shove,' [process variables] give a more decided push' (Snyder 1997: 32).

The cost, as with neo-classical realism, is greater complexity and less generality. Structure influences all states. Particular process variables influence only some parts of the system.

Parsimony and scope are great theoretical virtues; to explain everything with a single variable is the theorist's utopia. It is important that we appreciate the attractions of Waltz' aspiration to say some important things about international relations, more or less anywhere and at any time, based only on anarchy and the distribution of capabilities. Such a theory, within the domain of its operation, has considerable power. Snyder, however, argues – correctly in my view – that Waltz is guilty of 'excessive parsimony, in the sense that the explanatory gain from some further elaboration would exceed the costs in reduced generality' (1996: 167).

This does not, however, sacrifice system-level theorizing. Alignment, for example, is about the *distribution* of amity and enmity and thus no less systemic than the distribution of capabilities. The system-level of theorizing is not restricted to structure (which is only one of the defining elements of a system).

Norms and institutions

Snyder also identifies what he calls structural modifiers, 'system-wide influences that are structural in their inherent nature but not potent enough internationally to warrant that description' (1996: 169). He looks at military technology and norms and institutions. On the role of military technology, consider, for example, the special character of nuclear weapons, which Waltz (however inconsistently) uses to explain the Cold War peace between the superpowers. (1990) Or consider the impact on conflict and the propensity to war of the 'offence-defence balance' (the relative advantage of offensive or defensive forces) (e.g. Glaser and Kaufmann 1998; Van Evera 1998). Here I will briefly consider norms and institutions.

Norms and institutions are clearly structural in domestic society. 'They create the hierarchy of power and differentiation of function that are the hallmarks of a well-ordered domestic polity, but that are present only rudimentarily in international society. In principle, they are also structural internationally' (Snyder 1996: 169).

As both this quote and the earlier reference to potency make clear, the actual impact of international norms and institutions is an empirical, not a theoretical, question. Shared values and institutions may in particular cases shape and shove actors even more strongly than (Waltzian) structure. Consider not only the European Union but also the Nordic countries and the US–Canadian relationship. The literature on pluralistic security communities (e.g. Adler and Barnett 1998), in which violence has been completely removed from consideration in politics within the group, emphasizes the potential impact of institutions, values, and identities even in the high politics of international security.

Even at the global level, norms and institutions can have considerable influence. Sovereignty and other rights of states are a matter of mutual recognition. Material resources alone will not even tell us which of their rights states actually enjoy. It simply is untrue that, as the Athenians at Melos put it, 'the strong do what they can, the weak suffer what they must' (Thucydides: V.89). The strong often are constrained by the rights of even weak states. They may, of course, violate the rules of sovereignty. But predictions based on, say, the norm of non-intervention are no more 'indeterminate' than those based on anarchy or polarity. It is an empirical not a theoretical question whether the logic of rights or the logic of power more frequently accounts for international behaviour. And, whatever the general pattern, if a logic of rights matters more in any particular instance, that is the essential point. Our analytical framework should not hide this fact from us.

Consider also the principle of self-determination, which played a central role in creating scores of new, usually weak, states. Most postcolonial states have survived not through their own power or the power of allies but because of international recognition. Their survival – which offensive realists in particular must find inexplicable – has been further enhanced by the effective abolition of aggressive war in the second half of the twentieth century.

Pursuing this line of analysis leads us well into the weak or hedged range of the realist spectrum – or off the scale altogether. Snyder clearly is a realist: he emphasizes anarchy and the struggle for power and is generally sceptical of the power of norms and institutions. But his approach is unusually open.

The typical realist approach is much more sceptical of norms and institutions, as suggested by titles like 'The False Promise of International Institutions' (Mearsheimer 1994/95) and *Sovereignty: Organized Hypocrisy* (Krasner 1999). Institutions and norms are treated as largely reducible to the material interests of the powerful. The furthest most realists are willing to go is to treat them as 'intervening variables' that can be expected to have strong independent effects only in issue areas relatively far removed from the struggle for power. (An interesting, but little explored, alternative is to theorize institutions from within a realist framework (Schweller and Priess (1997) is a rare example).

Constancy and change

A standard complaint about realism is its inability to comprehend fundamental change in international relations. This charge, however, is less damning than critics often imagine.

Realism is a theory 'tuned' to explaining constancy. Realists are more impressed by the repeated occurrence of certain patterns across time than by the undeniable historical and cultural diversity of actors and interactions. They emphasize constancy not accidentally but by self-conscious theoretical choice. Although others may not share this judgement, it is one about which reasonable people may reasonably disagree.

The failure of realism to account for the end of the Cold War is a large part of the explanation of its declining popularity over the past two decades. Ironically, though, realists can fairly claim that they never attempted to explain change. They can even note that no other theory of international relations did a better job. It is understandable, and in some ways appropriate, that dramatic change is held up against a theory that emphasizes constancy. Nonetheless, whatever kind of failure it represents is shared by all other prominent theories of international relations.

Morality and foreign policy

In popular and foreign policy discussions, 'realist' most frequently refers to arguments against pursuing international moral objectives. Although in principle simply a special case of the broader issue of norms and institutions, the place of morality in foreign policy was a central concern of many classical realists. It is also an issue of vital substantive importance. Therefore, it merits discussion here, even though it has been peripheral in the work of academic realists over the past three decades, whose concerns have been more scientific and scholarly.

Do states pursue moral objectives?

The subordination of morality to power often is presented as a descriptive statement of the facts of international political life. 'The actions of states are determined not by moral principles and legal commitments but by considerations of interest and power' (Morgenthau 1970: 382). 'States in anarchy cannot afford to be moral. The possibility of moral behaviour rests upon the existence of an effective government that can deter and punish illegal actions' (Art and Waltz 1983: 6).

Such claims are obviously false. Just as individuals may behave morally in the absence of government enforcement of moral rules, states often can and do act out of moral concerns. Consider, for example, the outpouring of international aid in the wake of natural and political disasters such as the 2004 Indian Ocean tsunami and recurrent famines in Somalia.

It simply is not true, of either men or states, that they 'never do good unless necessity drives them to it;' that 'all do wrong to the same extent when there is nothing to prevent them doing wrong' (Machiavelli 1970: Book I, chapter 2, 58). States sometimes, even frequently, value compliance with ethical and humanitarian norms for reasons that have little or nothing to do with the threat of coercive enforcement. And even when states do violate norms because of the absence of enforcement, the independent ethical force of an infringed norm frequently is a significant part of the calculus of both the state and those who judge it.

The costs of compliance and violation

Even in anarchy, coercive enforcement is possible at times, most obviously through self-help. Furthermore, mechanisms exist to induce, even when they cannot compel, compliance. Public opinion, both national and international, can be a powerful force – as can be the persuasion of friends, allies, and interested parties. In some cases, the power and authority of intergovernmental institutions may be significant. More generally, international law, which includes some obligations that are also moral obligations, is no more frequently violated than domestic law. In any case, violations typically do have costs for states (although not always sufficiently high costs to compel compliance).

Realists rightly emphasize that a powerful state bent on violating a moral or legal norm usually can get away with it – and that when it can't, that usually is because of the power of other states. Nonetheless, states do sometimes comply with moral norms both for their own sake and out of consideration of the costs of non-compliance. As a matter of fact, states regularly conclude that in some instances they *can* afford to be moral, despite international anarchy.

For example, humanitarian interventions in Kosovo, East Timor, and Darfur, however tardy and limited, simply cannot be understood without the independent normative force of the anti-genocide norm and humanitarian principles. Such normative concerns rarely are the sole motive behind foreign-policy action. Often, though, they are an important element of the calculus. And few significant foreign-policy actions reflect just a single self-interested motive. Foreign policy is driven by the intersection of multiple motives, some of which are ethical in a large number of countries.

Pursuing moral objectives such as spreading democracy or combating preventable childhood diseases certainly may be costly but no political goals can be achieved without cost. Just as the cost of pursuing economic objectives is no basis for excluding economic interests from foreign policy, the costs of pursuing moral objectives do not justify categorically excluding them from foreign policy agendas. The proper course is to weigh the costs and benefits of pursuing any and all relevant interests, moral and non-moral interests alike. Moral values are indeed values and therefore must be taken into account in any truly reasonable and realistic political calculus. Thus even Mearsheimer allows that 'there are good reasons to applaud the Christmas Day 1978 Vietnamese invasion of Cambodia, since it drove the murderous Pol Pot from power' (1994/95: 31).

Realists often suggest that ordinary citizens and even politicians, especially in democracies, tend to underestimate the costs of – and thus overestimate the space available for – the pursuit of moral interests. But to the extent this is true, most non-realists would offer the same criticisms. There is nothing distinctively realist about insisting that foreign policy should be based on a rational calculation of costs and benefits.

Realism as a prescriptive theory

Perhaps the strongest realist arguments appeal to the nature of states and statesmanship. The doctrine of *raison d'état* (reason(s) of state) holds that 'where international relations are concerned, the interests of the state predominate over all other interests and values' (Haslam 2002: 12). Because the 'primary obligation' of any government 'is to the *interests* of the national society it represents', 'the same moral concepts are no longer relevant to it' (Kennan 1954: 48; 1985/86: 206). Morgenthau thus talks about 'the autonomy of politics' (1954: 12; 1962: 3).

Such arguments, however, are ethical arguments. They concern *which* values are appropriate in international relations, not whether foreign policy is appropriately subject to normative evaluation. 'Power politics may be defined as a system of international relations in which groups consider themselves to be ultimate ends' (Schwarzenberger 1951: 13). Thus Morgenthau talks of 'the moral dignity of the national interest' (1951: 33). Joel Rosenthal's social history of post-war American realists is nicely titled *Righteous Realists* (1991).

There is also a central ethical dimension to realist arguments that different standards apply to the public actions of national leaders and the actions of private individuals (e.g., Carr 1946: 151; Kennan 1954: 48; Thompson 1985: 8). 'Unlike the solitary individual who may claim the right to judge political action by universal ethical guidelines, the statesman will always make his decision on the basis of the state's interest' (Russell 1990: 51). Like other professionals, statesmen have a professional obligation to give priority to the interests of their 'clients'. Much as a defence lawyer is ethically bound to (within certain limits) give an aggressive defence to a guilty client, and a doctor (within certain limits) is required to do what is best for her patient rather than society as a whole, so a statesman is, by the nature of her office, required to do what is best for his/her state and its interests. The resulting foreign policy, however, although not shaped or directly judged by the principles of ordinary morality, is neither 'value free' nor beyond ethical or other normative limits.

It may be true that when national survival is at stake, responsible national leaders have no choice but to abandon all other considerations, including morality. Even most moralists would agree with Machiavelli that 'when the safety of one's country wholly depends on the decision to be taken, no attention should be paid either to justice or injustice' (1970: Book I, chapter 41). But such an argument applies no less against non-moral objectives, such as pursuing economic interests and supporting an ally. Furthermore, survival rarely is at stake in international relations. And even less rarely does it depend wholly on the decisions of national leaders.

It simply is not true that 'the struggle for power is identical with the struggle for survival' (Spykman 1942: 18). Neither is it true that 'the system forces states to behave according to the dictates of realism, or risk destruction' (Mearsheimer 1995: 91). Many moral foreign policy objectives pose no risk to national survival. And other national interests simply do not have the ethical priority of survival.

There is no compelling theoretical reason why a state should not place a high value on, for example, fighting communism, environmental degradation, or world poverty. Appeals to *raison d'état* and statesmanship cannot determine what interests the state has or ought to have. 'The national interest' is what the term manifestly indicates, namely, those interests/values that are held by the nation. The insistence of some realists (e.g. Morgenthau 1954: 5, 10) that states define their interest in terms of power reflects a deeply contentious, and descriptively inaccurate, prescriptive theory of foreign policy.

Morality and moralism

Realists rightly criticize 'moralism,' the belief that international relations can appropriately be judged *solely* by conventional moral norms. But few if any serious theorists or activists have actually believed that. Even the inter-war peace activists that realists pejoratively dismiss as idealists in fact usually held far more sophisticated views (Lynch 1999).

To the extent that there is a tendency toward moralism in foreign policy, especially in the United States, realists may offer a healthy corrective. Five hundred years ago, it might have been scandalous for Machiavelli to argue that a good statesman must 'learn to be able not to be good, and to use this and not use it according to necessity' (1985: chapter 15). Today, however, almost all students of international relations would agree that sometimes the good statesman ought to act in ways inconsistent with the principles of private morality – for example, to give greater consideration to preserving the lives of her own soldiers than the soldiers of her adversary.

Controversy arises over when, where, and how frequently violating moral norms is truly necessary. Realists suggest that anarchy and egoism so severely constrain the space for the pursuit of moral concerns that it is only a small exaggeration to say that states in anarchy cannot afford to be moral. This, however, is (at most) a contingent empirical fact. It provides no grounds for categorically excluding morality from foreign policy. And even if the primary obligation of the statesman is to the national interest, that is not his/her exclusive obligation. States not only are free to, but in fact often do, include certain moral objectives in their definition of the national interest.

Realists rightly remind us of the dangers of ignoring 'realities' rooted in anarchy and egoism. A narrow vision of 'the national interest defined in terms of power' (Morgenthau 1954: 4, 10) certainly deserves consideration in debates over a state's international objectives. But arguments that 'no ethical standards are applicable to relations between states' (Carr 1946: 153) and that 'universal moral principles cannot be applied to the actions of states' (Morgenthau 1954: 9) not only cannot bear critical scrutiny but prove not even to reflect the considered views of most leading self-identified realists – despite their unfortunate tendency to repeat and emphasize such indefensibly exaggerated claims.

As John Herz notes, 'the mitigation, channeling, balancing, or control of power has prevailed perhaps more often than the inevitability of power politics would lead one to believe' (1976: 11). In fact, on careful examination we find that most leading realists acknowledge that moral and ethical principles are 'operative but not controlling' (Thompson

1985: 22). Carr argues that 'it is an unreal kind of realism which ignores the element of morality in any world order' (1946: 235). Morgenthau talks of 'the curious dialectic of ethics and politics, which prevents the latter, in spite of itself, from escaping the former's judgment and normative direction' and allows that 'nations recognize a moral obligation to refrain from the infliction of death and suffering under certain conditions despite the possibility of justifying such conduct in the light of ... the national interest' (1946: 177; 1948: 177). Niebuhr not only insists that 'an adequate political morality must do justice to the insights of both moralists and political realists' but argues that the 'ultimate purpose' of realist analysis 'is to find political methods which will offer the most promise of achieving an ethical social goal for society' (1932: 233, xxiv).

How to think about realism (and its critics)

Not only are realists prone to rhetorical exaggerations – consider, for example, Nicholas Spykman's claim that 'the search for power is not made for the achievement of moral values; moral values are used to facilitate the attainment of power' (1942: 18) – but even more moderate statements regularly lack the necessary qualifications. Note the absence of an adverb like often, frequently, or even usually in Kennan's claim, quoted above, that non-moral considerations 'must be allowed to prevail.' Likewise, Mearsheimer, although allowing that institutions matter 'on the margins,' on the same page asserts the obviously false claim that institutions 'have no independent effect on state behavior' (1994/95: 7).

Strong adherents of a theory often unthinkingly slide from (justifiable) theoretical simplifications to (unjustifiable) descriptive claims. As I have noted repeatedly, theories must abstract, simplify, and thus exaggerate. Problems arise when these simplified theoretical models are presented as categorical empirical claims. That realists are no less prone to this confusion than adherents of other theories is ironic but not particularly surprising.

Waltz nicely captures the contribution of realism: it identifies a 'a small number of big and important things' (1986: 329; cf. 1979: 70). Were realists, and Waltz himself, always this modest, the discipline, especially in the United States, would be much better off – particularly if realists took to heart the negative implication that realism does not comprehend *most* big and important things. Realism simply cannot even begin to explain the vast majority of what happens in international relations.

The realist response that they explain 'the most important things' is a contentious normative judgement. Furthermore, given the 'indeterminacy' of most realist predictions, it is by no means clear that realism offers deep or satisfying explanations of even the things to which it applies (cf. Wendt 1999: 18, 251–9). But even if realism does adequately explain the few most important things, there is no reason to restrict the discipline to those. Certainly we do not want medicine to restrict itself to studying and treating only the three leading causes of death.

That realism cannot account for most of international relations is no reason to denigrate or marginalize it. Realists, though, must allow the same for other theories. Realism must be an important, even essential, part of a pluralistic discipline of international studies: no less, but no more.

The familiar question 'Are you a realist?' may be appropriate if we understand realism as a moral theory or world-view. A few realists, particularly Augustinian Christians such as Niebuhr (1941; 1943) and Butterfield (1953), have treated realism in such terms. Among contemporary academic realists, Robert Gilpin (1986; 1996) perhaps borders on holding such a view. But world-views – e.g., natural law, Islam, Kantianism, Christianity, Aristotleanism, humanism – are not usually what we have in mind by 'theories of international relations'. If we are talking about analytical or explanatory theory, 'being' (or 'not being') a realist makes little sense.

Unless realist predictions or explanations are almost always correct across something close to the full range of international relations – and neither realism nor any other theory of international relations even vaguely approximates this – no serious student or practitioner of international relations would want to 'be' a realist in the sense of always applying or acting upon realist theory. But unless realism never provided valuable insights or explanations – and even its strongest critics do not suggest this – no reasonable person would want to 'be' an anti-realist in the sense of never using realist theories.

The proper questions are how regularly, in what domains, and for what purposes does realism – or any other theory – help us to understand or act in the world. My general answer is 'a lot less often than most realists claim, but a lot more frequently than many critics would like to allow'. More substantively, realist logics seems most applicable where survival is at stake. As we move away from this overriding interest, the utility of realist explanations tends to degrade rather rapidly. Therefore, depending on one's interests and substantive concerns, one might appropriately use realism regularly, occasionally, or almost never in one's analyses or actions.

Realism *must* be a part of the analytical toolkit of every serious student of international relations. But if it is our only tool – or even our primary tool – we will be woefully under-equipped for our analytical tasks; our vision of international relations will be sadly impoverished; and, to the extent that theory has an impact on practice, the projects we undertake in the world are liable to be mangled and misshapen.

3 | **Liberalism**

SCOTT BURCHILL

Liberalism is the most enduring and influential philosophical tradition to have emerged from the European Enlightenment. It is an approach to politics which champions scientific rationality, freedom and the inevitability of human progress. It is a perspective of government which emphasizes individual rights, constitutionalism, democracy and limitations on the powers of the state. It is also a model of economic organization which argues that market capitalism best promotes the welfare of all by most efficiently allocating scarce resources within society.

Despite its ancient lineage, liberalism's influence today can be measured by its authorship of two profound trends in contemporary international politics – the spread of democracy after the Cold War and the globalization of the world economy.

There are many strands of liberal thought which influence the study of international relations. The chapter will begin by analysing the revival of liberal thought after the Cold War. It will then explain how liberal attitudes to war, the spread of democracy and human rights continue to inform political thinking and government behaviour. The influence of economic liberalism, in particular interdependency theory and liberal institutionalism, will then be assessed before liberal arguments for globalization and the impact of non-state terrorism on liberal thought are measured. The conclusion will judge the contribution of liberalism to the theory of international relations.

After the Cold War

The demise of Soviet Communism at the beginning of the 1990s enhanced the influence of liberal theories of international relations within the academy, a theoretical tradition thought to have been discredited by perspectives such as realism, which emphasize the recurrent features of international relations. In a reassertion of the teleology of liberalism, Fukuyama claimed in the early 1990s that the collapse of the

Soviet Union proved that liberal democracy had no serious ideological competitor: it was 'the end point of mankind's ideological evolution' and the 'final form of human government' (Fukuyama 1992: xi–xii). It is an argument that has been strengthened by recent transitions to democracy in East Asia, East Europe, Latin America, and possibly North Africa and the Middle East.

For Fukuyama, the end of the Cold War saw the triumph of the 'ideal state' and a particular mode of political economy, 'liberal capitalism', which 'cannot be improved upon': there can be 'no further progress in the development of underlying principles and institutions' (Fukuyama 1992, xi–xii). According to Fukuyama, the end of the East–West conflict confirmed that liberal capitalism was unchallenged as a model of, and endpoint for, humankind's political and economic development. There 'is a fundamental process at work that dictates a common evolutionary pattern for *all* human societies – in short, something like a Universal History of mankind in the direction of liberal democracy' (Fukuyama 1992: xi–xii, 48).

Fukuyama's belief that Western forms of government and political economy are the ultimate destination for the entire species poses a number of challenges for the study of international relations. First, his claim that political and economic development terminates at liberal-capitalist democracy assumes that the Western path to modernity will not face a future rival, and will eventually command global consent. Second, Fukuyama's argument assumes that national, religious and cultural distinctions are no barrier to the triumph of liberal democracy and capitalism. Third, Fukuyama's thesis raises vital, unanswered questions about governance and political community. For example, what are the implications of globalization for nation-states and their sovereign powers? What about societies which explicitly reject market capitalism and parliamentary democracy?

The post-Cold War optimism of many liberals has been tempered by a series of unexpected events which, at the very least, suggest the path to modernity remains a rocky one. The rise of Islamist terrorism, democratic reversals in states such as Thailand and Fiji, and resistance to the coercive spread of democracy in Afghanistan and Iraq, suggest Fukuyama's celebration of the end of history may have been premature. Endemic financial crises, which have plagued the global economy continuously since 2007, have similarly shaken the confidence of liberals who believed capitalism was a stable, enduring economic model.

Liberals believe that progress in human history can be measured by the elimination of global conflict and the adoption of principles of legitimacy that have evolved in domestic political orders. This constitutes an *inside-out* approach to international relations, where the behaviour of states can be explained by their endogenous arrangements. It also leads to Doyle's important claim that 'liberal democracies are uniquely willing to eschew the use of force in their relations with one another', a view which rejects the realist contention that the anarchical nature of the international system means states are trapped in a struggle for power and security (Linklater 1993: 29).

Fukuyama's reflections on the end of the Cold War may appear to be of no more than historical interest now but their influence at the time was considerable. They encapsulated many of the core liberal ideas that have been influential especially in the United States and in various international organizations over the last quarter century, including the belief in the liberal-democratic peace and in free market economies that have been critical to the practice of exporting democracy. Fukuyama is now less sanguine about the progressive inevitability of liberalism and he laments the absence of new liberal leaders emerging from the Arab Spring and other recent political transitions. He remains an organic liberal to the extent that he believes liberal-democratic orders must be endogenous if they are to succeed (they can't be exported by violence), but is discouraged by the failure of liberals in the post-Cold War period to organize themselves into viable political parties (Fukuyama 2012).

The liberal view: 'inside looking out'

In the 1990s, Fukuyama revived a long-held view among liberals that the spread of legitimate domestic political orders would eventually bring an end to international conflict. This neo-Kantian position assumes that particular states, with liberal-democratic polities, constitute an ideal which the rest of the world will emulate. Fukuyama was struck by the extent to which liberal democracies have transcended their violent instincts and institutionalized norms which pacify relations between them. He was particularly impressed by the emergence of shared principles of legitimacy among the great powers. The projection of liberal-democratic principles to the international realm provides the best prospect for a peaceful world order because 'a world made up of liberal democracies ... should have much less incentive for war, since all nations would reciprocally recognize one another's legitimacy' (Fukuyama 1992: xx).

This approach is rejected by neo-realists who claim that the moral aspirations of states are thwarted by the absence of an overarching authority which regulates their behaviour towards each other. The anarchical nature of the international system tends to homogenize foreign policy behaviour by socializing states into the system of power politics.

Requirements for strategic power and security are paramount in an insecure world, and override the ethical pursuits of states, regardless of their
domestic political complexions.

In stressing the importance of legitimate domestic orders in explaining
foreign policy behaviour, realists such as Waltz believe that liberals are
guilty of 'reductionism' when they should be highlighting the 'systemic'
features of international relations. The differences between 'inside-out'
and 'outside-in' approaches to international relations is an important
line of demarcation in modern international theory (Waltz 1991a: 667).
The extent to which the neo-realist critique of liberal internationalism
can be sustained will be a major consideration of this chapter.

Fukuyama's argument was more than a celebration of the fact that
liberal capitalism has survived the threat posed by Marxism. It also
implies that neo-realism has overlooked 'the foremost macropolitical
trend in contemporary world politics: the expansion of the liberal zone of
peace' (Linklater 1993: 29). Challenging the view that anarchy conditions international behaviour is Doyle's argument that there is a growing
core of pacific states which have learned to resolve their differences without resorting to violence. The expansion of this pacific realm is a significant feature of the contemporary world. If this claim can be upheld it will
constitute a significant comeback for an international theory widely
thought to have been terminally damaged by Carr in his critique of
liberal utopianism in the late 1930s. It also poses a serious challenge to
theoretical assumptions that war is an endemic feature of international
life (Doyle 1986: 1151–69).

War, democracy and free trade

The foundations of contemporary liberal internationalism were laid in
the eighteenth and nineteenth centuries by liberals proposing precondi-
tions for a peaceful world order. In broad summary they concluded that
the prospects for the elimination of war lay with a preference for democracy over aristocracy and free trade over autarky. This section will examine these arguments in turn, and the extent to which they inform
contemporary liberal thought.

Prospects for peace

For liberals, peace is the normal state of affairs: in Kant's words, peace
can be perpetual. The laws of nature dictated harmony and cooperation
between peoples. War is therefore both unnatural and irrational, an artificial contrivance and not a product of some peculiarity of human nature.

Liberals believe in progress and the perfectibility of the human condition. With faith in the power of human reason and the capacity of human beings to realize their inner potential, they remain confident that the stain of war can be removed from human experience (Gardner 1990: 23–39; Hoffmann 1995: 159–77; Zacher and Matthew 1995: 107–50).

A common thread, from Rousseau, Kant and Cobden, to Schumpeter and Doyle, is that wars were created by militaristic and undemocratic governments for their own vested interests. Wars were engineered by a 'warrior class' bent on extending their power and wealth through territorial conquest. According to Paine in *The Rights of Man* (1791), the 'war system' was contrived to preserve the power and the employment of princes, statesmen, soldiers, diplomats and armaments manufacturers, and to bind their tyranny ever more firmly upon the necks of the people' (Howard 1978: 31). Wars provide governments with excuses to raise taxes, expand their bureaucratic apparatus and increase control over their citizens. The people, on the other hand, were peace-loving by nature, and only plunged into conflict by the whims of their unrepresentative rulers.

War was a cancer on the body politic. But it was an ailment that human beings, themselves, had the capacity to cure. The treatment which liberals began prescribing in the eighteenth century has not changed: the 'disease' of war could be successfully treated with the twin medicines of *democracy* and *free trade*. Democratic processes and institutions would break the power of the ruling elites and curb their propensity for violence. Free trade and commerce would overcome the artificial barriers between individuals and unite them everywhere into one community.

For liberals such as Schumpeter, war was the product of the aggressive instincts of unrepresentative elites. The warlike disposition of these rulers drove the reluctant masses into violent conflicts which, while profitable for the arms industries and the military aristocrats, were disastrous for those who did the fighting. For Kant, the establishment of republican forms of government in which rulers were accountable and individual rights were respected would lead to peaceful international relations because the ultimate consent for war would rest with the citizens of the state (Kant 1991: 100). For both Kant and Schumpeter, war was the outcome of minority rule, though Kant was no champion of democratic government (MacMillan 1995). Liberal states, founded on individual rights such as equality before the law, free speech and civil liberty, respect for private property and representative government, would not have the same appetite for conflict and war. Peace was fundamentally a question of establishing legitimate domestic orders throughout the world – 'When the citizens who bear the burdens of war elect their governments, wars become impossible' (Doyle 1986: 1151).

The dual themes of domestic legitimacy and the extent to which liberal-democratic states exercise restraint and peaceful intentions in their foreign policy have been taken up more recently by Doyle, Russett and others. In a restatement of Kant's argument that a 'pacific federation' (*foedus pacificum*) can be built by expanding the number of states with republican constitutions, Doyle claims that liberal democracies are unique in their ability and willingness to establish peaceful relations among themselves. This pacification of foreign relations between liberal states is said to be a direct product of their shared legitimate political orders based on democratic principles and institutions. The reciprocal recognition of these common principles – a commitment to the rule of law, individual rights and equality before the law, *and* representative government based on popular consent – means that liberal democracies evince little interest in conflict with each other and have no grounds on which to contest each other's legitimacy: they have constructed a 'separate peace' (Doyle 1986: 1161; Fukuyama 1992: xx). This does not mean that they are less inclined to make war with non-democratic states, and Doyle is correct to point out that democracies maintain a healthy appetite for conflicts with authoritarian states, as recent conflicts in the Middle East and Central Asia attest. But it does suggest that the best prospect for bringing an end to war between states lies with the spread of liberal-democratic governments across the globe. The expansion of the zone of peace from the core to the periphery is also the basis of Fukuyama's optimism about the post-Communist era (Doyle 1986, 1995, 1997; Russett 1993).

There are both structural and normative aspects to what has been termed 'democratic peace theory'. Some liberals emphasize the institutional constraints on liberal-democratic states, such as public opinion, the rule of law and representative government. The checks and balances provided by elections, divisions of power and other legal–political restrictions make wars more difficult for liberal states to contrive. Others stress the normative preference for compromise and conflict resolution which can be found in the political processes of many liberal democracies.

A combination of both explanations strengthens the argument that liberal-democratic states do not resolve their differences violently, although realist critics point to definitional problems with the idea of liberal democracy, the question of covert action, and ask why the constraints on war-making don't apply in relations with authoritarian states. Realists argue that at best democratic peace theory identifies a correlation in international politics rather than an 'iron law' or theory (Maoz and Russett 1993; Owen 1994).

The argument is extended by Rawls, who claims that liberal societies are also 'less likely to engage in war with non-liberal outlaw states, except on grounds of legitimate self-defence (or in the defence of their legitimate allies), or intervention in severe cases to protect human rights' (Rawls 1999: 49). Recent US-led wars in Afghanistan and Iraq pose significant challenges to the claim that only self-defence and humanitarianism incline liberal-democratic states to war.

In light of wars in Afghanistan and Iraq, and recent Western intervention in Libya, similar suggestions that democracy can be exported by force are difficult arguments to sustain. Regardless of their ultimate destination, the political revolutions in North Africa beginning in 2011 known collectively as the Arab Spring, were without exception endogenous uprisings and not enthusiastically welcomed by outsiders in the West who normally espouse the virtues of liberal democracy.

A related argument by Mueller (1989) claims that we are already witnessing the obsolescence of war between the major powers. Reviving the liberal faith in the capacity of people to improve the moral and material conditions of their lives, Mueller argues that, just as duelling and slavery were eventually seen as morally unacceptable, war is increasingly viewed in the developed world as repulsive, immoral and uncivilized. That violence is more widely seen as an anachronistic form of social intercourse is not due to any change in human nature or the structure of the international system. According to Mueller, the obsolescence of major war in the late twentieth century was the product of moral learning, a shift in ethical consciousness away from coercive forms of social behaviour. Because war brings more costs than gains and is no longer seen as a romantic or noble pursuit, it has become 'rationally unthinkable' (Mueller 1989).

The long peace between states of the industrialized world is a cause of profound optimism for liberals such as Fukuyama and Mueller, who are confident that we have already entered a period in which war as an instrument of international diplomacy is becoming obsolete. But if war has been an important factor in nation-building, as Giddens, Mann and Tilly have argued, the fact that states are learning to curb their propensity for violence will also have important consequences for forms of political community which are likely to emerge in the industrial centres of the world. The end of war between the great powers may have the effect of weakening the rigidity of their political boundaries and inspiring a wave of sub-national revolts, although the recent wave of anti-Western terror has complicated matters in this regard by encouraging states to solidify their boundaries and make greater demands on the loyalty of citizens.

Far from sharing the post-Cold War optimism of liberals, realists such as Waltz and Mearsheimer argue that the collapse of bipolarity in the early 1990s was a cause for grave concern. Mutual nuclear deterrence maintained a stabilizing balance of power in the world, whereas unipolarity would not last, eventually leading to volatility and war. As Waltz argues, 'in international politics, unbalanced power constitutes a danger even when it is American power that is out of balance' (Waltz 1991a: 670). Accordingly, the expansion of a zone of peace is no antidote to the calculations of raw power in an anarchical world.

Recent conflicts in the Balkans, Central Asia and the Gulf region – all involving major industrial powers – are a reminder that the post-Cold War period remains volatile and suggest that war may not yet have lost its efficacy in international diplomacy. None of these was a conflict between democratic states but they are no less important to the maintenance of world order. These and other struggles in so-called 'failed states' such as Afghanistan and Somalia, are a reminder that the fragmentation of nation-states and civil wars arising from secessionist movements have not been given the same attention by liberals as more conventional inter-state wars.

Democratic peace theory provides few guidelines for how liberal states should conduct themselves with non-liberal states. Rawls, however, is concerned with the extent to which liberal and non-liberal peoples can be equal participants in a 'Society of Peoples'. He argues that principles and norms of international law and practice – the 'Law of Peoples' – can be developed and shared by both liberal and non-liberal or decent hierarchical societies, without an expectation that liberal democracy is the terminus for all. Guidelines for establishing harmonious relations between liberal and non-liberal peoples under a common Law of Peoples, takes liberal international theory in a more sophisticated direction because it explicitly acknowledges the need for utopian thought to be realistic (Rawls 1999: 11–23).

As the number of East Asian and Islamic societies which reject the normative superiority of liberal democracy consolidates, doubt is cast on the belief that the non-European world is seeking to imitate the Western route to political modernization. This has also been illustrated by the wave of anti-Western Islamist terror since 2001. Linklater suggests that it is not so much the spread of liberal democracy *per se* which has universal appeal, 'but the idea of limited power which is present within, but not entirely synonymous with, liberal democracy' (Linklater 1993: 33–6; Rawls 1999). The notion of limited power and respect for the rule of law contained within the idea of 'constitutionalism' may be one means of solving the exclusionary character of the liberal zone of peace. It is a less ambitious project and potentially more sensitive to the cultural and political differences among states in the current international system. It may avoid the danger of the system bifurcating into a privileged inner circle and a disadvantaged, disaffected outer circle (Linklater 1993: 33). The greatest barrier to the expansion of the zone of peace from the core is the perception within the periphery that this constitutes little more than the domination of one culture by another.

The spirit of commerce

Eighteenth and nineteenth-century liberals felt that the spirits of war and commerce were mutually incompatible. Wars were often fought by states to achieve their mercantilist goals. According to Carr, 'the aim of mercantilism ... was not to promote the welfare of the community and its members, but to augment the power of the state, of which the sovereign was the embodiment ... wealth was the source of power, or more specifically of fitness for war'. Until the Napoleonic wars, 'wealth, conceived in its simplest form as bullion, was brought in by exports; and since, in the static conception of society prevailing at this period, export markets were a fixed quantity not susceptible of increase as a whole, the only way for a nation to expand its markets and therefore its wealth was to capture them from some other nation, if necessary by waging a trade war' (Carr 1945: 5–6).

Free trade, however, was a more peaceful means of achieving national wealth because, according to the theory of comparative advantage, each economy would be materially better off than if it had been pursuing nationalism and self-sufficiency (autarky). Free trade would also break down the divisions between states and unite individuals everywhere in one community. Artificial barriers to commerce distorted relations between individuals, thereby causing international tension. Free trade would expand the levels of understanding between the peoples of the world and encourage international friendship and understanding. According to Kant, unhindered commerce between the peoples of the world would unite them in a common, peaceful enterprise. 'Trade ... would increase the wealth and power of the peace-loving, productive sections of the population at the expense of the war-orientated aristocracy, and ... would bring men of different nations into constant contact with one another; contact which would make clear to all of them their fundamental community of interests' (Howard 1978: 20; Walter 1996). Similarly Ricardo believed that free trade 'binds together, by one common tie of interest and intercourse, the universal society of nations throughout the civilized world' (Ricardo 1911: 114).

Conflicts were often caused by states erecting barriers which distorted the natural harmony of interests commonly shared by individuals across the world. The solution to the problem, argued Adam Smith and Tom Paine, was the free movement of commodities, capital and labour. 'If commerce were permitted to act to the universal extent it is capable, it would extirpate the system of war and produce a revolution in the uncivilized state of governments' (Howard 1978: 29). Writing in 1848, John Stuart Mill also claimed that free trade was the means to bring about the end of war: 'it is commerce which is rapidly rendering war obsolete, by strengthening and multiplying the personal interests which act in natural opposition to it' (Howard 1978: 37). The spread of markets would place societies on an entirely new foundation. Instead of conflicts over limited resources such as land, the industrial revolution raised the prospect of unlimited prosperity for all: material production, so long as it was freely exchanged, would bring human progress. Trade would create relations of mutual dependence which would foster understanding between peoples and reduce conflict. Economic self-interest would then be a powerful disincentive for war.

Liberals believe unfettered commercial exchanges would encourage links across frontiers and shift loyalties away from the nation-state. Leaders would eventually come to recognize that the benefits of free trade outweighed the costs of territorial conquest and colonial expansion. The attraction of going to war to promote mercantilist interests would be weakened as societies realized that war can only disrupt trade and therefore the prospects for economic prosperity. Interdependence would replace national competition and defuse unilateral acts of aggression and reciprocal retaliation.

Interdependence and liberal institutionalism

Free trade and the removal of barriers to commerce is at the heart of modern interdependency theory. The rise of regional economic integration in Europe, for example, was inspired by the belief that conflict between states could be reduced by creating a common interest in trade and economic collaboration among members of the same geographical region. This would encourage states, such as France and Germany, which traditionally resolved their differences militarily, to cooperate within a commonly agreed economic and political framework for their mutual benefit. States would have a joint stake in each other's peace and prosperity. The European Union is a good example of economic integration engendering closer economic and political cooperation in a region historically bedevilled by national conflicts.

As Mitrany argued, initial cooperation between states would be achieved in technical areas where it was mutually convenient, but once successful it could 'spill over' into other functional areas where states found that mutual advantages could be gained (Mitrany 1948: 350–63). In a development of this argument, Keohane and Nye have explained how, via membership of international institutions, states can significantly broaden their conceptions of self-interest in order to widen the scope for cooperation. Compliance with the rules of these organizations not only discourages the narrow pursuit of national interests, it also weakens the meaning and appeal of state sovereignty (Keohane and Nye 1977). This suggests that the international system is more normatively regulated than realists believe, a position further developed by English School theorists such as Wight and Bull, as discussed in Chapter 4.

A development of this argument can be found in liberal institutionalism which shares with neo-realism an acceptance of the importance of the state and the anarchical condition of the international system, though liberal institutionalists argue that the prospects for cooperation, even in an anarchical world, are greater than neo-realists allow (Young 1982; Nye 1988; Powell 1994). Liberal institutionalists claim that cooperation between states can be organized in institutions. 'Institutions' in this sense means sets of rules which govern state behaviour in specific policy areas, such as the Law of the Sea.

Accepting the broad structures of neo-realism, but employing rational choice and game theory to anticipate the behaviour of states, liberal institutionalists demonstrate that cooperation between states can be enhanced even without the presence of a hegemonic player which can enforce compliance with agreements. For them, anarchy is mitigated by regimes and institutional cooperation which brings higher levels of regularity and predictability to international relations. Regimes – sets of principles, norms, rules and decision-making procedures – constrain state behaviour by formalizing the expectations of each party to an agreement where there is, for example, a pandemic, drug trafficking or organized crime. They reflect the inability of individual states to solve global issues without broader cooperation. They enhance trust, continuity and stability in a world of otherwise ungoverned anarchy.

Neo-realists and neo-liberals disagree about how states conceive of their own interests. Whereas neo-realists, such as Waltz, argue that states are concerned with 'relative gains' – meaning gains assessed in comparative terms (who will gain more?), neo-liberals claim that states are concerned with maximizing their 'absolute gains' – an assessment of their own welfare independent of their shared interests (what will gain me the most?). Institutions then assume the role of encouraging cooperative habits, monitoring compliance, enforcement where possible, and sanctioning cheaters and defectors.

Today, regimes are said to exist in a growing range of policy areas, including environmental regulation (e.g. climate change), global finance and trade (through the G20), and counter-terrorism.

Neo-realists argue that states will baulk at cooperation if they expect to gain less than their rivals. Liberal institutionalists, on the other hand, believe international relations need not be a zero-sum game, as many states feel secure enough to maximize their own gains regardless of what accrues to others. Mutual benefits arising out of cooperation are possible because states are not always preoccupied with relative gains – hence the opportunities for constructing regimes around issues and areas of common concern.

Liberal institutionalists acknowledge that cooperation between states is likely to be tenuous and limited, particularly where enforcement procedures are weak and cheating brings advantages. However, in an environment of growing regional and global integration, states can often discover – with or without the encouragement of a hegemon – a coincidence of strategic and economic interests which can be turned into a formalized agreement determining the rules of conduct. In areas such as environmental degradation, financial crises and the threat of terrorism, the argument for formalized cooperation between states is compelling. Keohane has recently acknowledged the strain on liberal institutionalism from new centres of political and economic power in the world, as well as the continuing relevance of the realist critique. Nonetheless he maintains that institutions offer a source of hope for those liberals who remain committed to progress in international politics whilst being concerned by the dangers of unchecked power (Keohane 2012).

According to Rosecrance (1986), the growth of economic interdependency has been matched by a corresponding decline in the value of territorial conquest for states. In the contemporary world the benefits of trade and cooperation among states greatly exceed those of military competition and territorial control. In their mercantilist phase, nation-states regarded the acquisition of territory as the principal means of increasing national wealth. More recently it has become apparent that additional territory does not necessarily help states to compete in an international system where the 'trading state' rather than the 'military state' is becoming dominant. In the 1970s, state elites began to realize that wealth is determined by their share of the world market in value-added goods and services. This understanding had two significant effects. First, the age of the independent, self-sufficient state is over. Complex layers of economic interdependency ensure that states cannot act aggressively without risking economic penalties imposed by other members of the international community, a fate even for great powers. It also makes little sense for a state to threaten its commercial partners, whose markets and capital investment are essential for its own economic growth. Second, territorial conquest in the nuclear age is both dangerous and costly for rogue states. The alternative – economic development through trade and foreign investment – is a much more attractive and potentially beneficial strategy (Rosecrance 1986; Strange 1991).

Neo-realists have two responses to the liberal claim that economic interdependency is pacifying international relations (Grieco 1988). First, they argue that in any struggle between competing disciplines, the anarchic environment and the insecurity it engenders will always take priority over the quest for economic prosperity. Economic interdependency will never take precedence over strategic security because states must be primarily concerned with their precarious survival. Their capacity to explore avenues of economic cooperation will be limited by how secure they feel, and the extent to which they are required to engage in military competition with others. Second, the idea of economic interdependence implies a misleading degree of equality and shared vulnerability to economic forces in the global economy. Interdependence does not eliminate hegemony and dependency in inter-state relations because power is unevenly distributed throughout the world's trade and financial markets. Dominant players such as the United States have usually framed the rules under which interdependency has flourished. Conflict and cooperation is therefore unlikely to disappear, though it may be channelled into more peaceful forms.

Human rights

The advocacy of democracy and free trade foreshadows another idea which liberal internationalism introduced to international theory. Liberals believe the legitimacy of domestic political orders is contingent upon upholding the rule of law and the state's respect for the human rights of its citizens. If it is wrong for an individual to engage in socially unacceptable or criminal behaviour, it is also wrong for states.

References to essential human needs are implicit in some of the earliest written legal codes from ancient Babylon, as well as early Buddhist, Confucian and Hindu texts, though the first explicit mention of universal principles governing common standards of human behaviour can be found in the Western canon.

The idea of universal human rights has its origins in the Natural Law tradition, debates in the West during the Enlightenment over the 'rights of man' and in the experience of individuals struggling against the arbitrary rule of the state (Donnelly 2003). The Magna Carta in 1215, the development of English Common Law and the Bill of Rights in 1689 were significant, if evolutionary, steps along the path to enshrining basic human rights in law, as were intellectual contributions from Grotius (the law of nations), Rousseau (the social contract) and Locke (popular consent, limits of sovereignty). An early legal articulation of human rights can be found in the American Declaration of Independence in 1776 ('we take these truths to be self-evident, that all men are created equal, and that they are endowed by their Creator with certain unalienable Rights, that amongst these are Life, Liberty and the pursuit of Happiness') and in France's Declaration of the Rights of Man and the Citizen in 1789 ('all men are born free and equal in their rights').

The development of human rights occurred as cultural and legal practices in the Western world changed. These included the expansion of moral communities as empathy for human suffering spread beyond the confines of particularist locales, the rejection of torture as an instrument for establishing the truth in legal processes, and the redefinition of human relationships, including greater respect for the autonomy of the body, found in literature and art from the late eighteenth century (Hunt 2007).

Human beings are said to be endowed – purely by reason of their humanity – with certain fundamental rights, benefits and protections. These rights are regarded as inherent in the sense they are the birthright of all, inalienable because they cannot be given up or taken away and universal since they apply to all regardless of nationality, status, gender or race. Liberals have a normative commitment to human rights, believing certain values and standards should be universally applied.

The extension of these rights to all peoples has a particularly important place in liberal thinking about foreign policy and international relations for two reasons. First, these rights provide a legal foundation to emancipation, justice and human freedom. Their denial by state authorities is an affront to the dignity of all and a stain on the human condition. Second, states which treat their own citizens ethically and allow them meaningful participation in the political process are thought to be less likely to behave aggressively internationally. The task for liberals has been to develop moral standards which would command universal consent, knowing that in doing so states may be required to jeopardize the pursuit of their own national interests. This has proven to be a difficult task, despite evident progress on labour rights, the abolition of slavery, the political emancipation of women in the West, the treatment of indigenous peoples and the end of white supremacy in South Africa (Dunne and Wheeler 1999; Donnelly 2003).

The creation of important legal codes, instruments and institutions in the post-World War II period is a measure of achievement in the area. The most important instruments are the Universal Declaration of Human Rights (1948), the International Covenant on Civil and Political Rights (1966) and the International Covenant on Economic, Social and Cultural Rights (1966), while the International Labour Organization (ILO) and the International Court of Justice (ICJ) play a significant institutional and symbolic role in the protection of human rights. A greater concern about genocidal crimes, the outlawing of cruel and inhuman punishment and the rights of detainees apprehended on the battlefield are a reflection of ongoing progress in the area.

In his seminal account, Vincent (1986) identified the right of the individual to be free from starvation as the only human right which is likely to become a global consensus. The world community, regardless of religious or ideological differences, agrees that a right to subsistence was essential to the dignity of humankind. Beyond this right, nation-states struggle to find agreement, not least because the developing world is suspicious that human rights advocacy from metropolitan centres is little more than a pretext for unwarranted interference in their domestic affairs. Most states are reluctant to give outsiders the power to compel them to improve their ethical performance, although there is a growing belief that the principle of territorial sovereignty should no longer be used by governments as a credible excuse for avoiding legitimate international scrutiny – hence the growing concern with international humanitarian intervention (Wheeler 2000).

Marxists have dismissed liberal human rights as mere bourgeois freedoms which fail to address the class-based nature of exploitation contained within capitalist relations of production. Realists would add that 'conditions of profound insecurity for states do not permit ethical and humane considerations to override their primary national considerations' (Linklater 1992b: 27). It is interests which determine political action and in the global arena, politics is the amoral struggle for power to advance these interests. Other critics claim that the implementation of these rights, for example the abolition of child labour on the sub-continent, would consign millions to greater levels of poverty.

Liberals struggle to avoid the charge that their conceptions of democracy and human rights are culturally specific, ethnocentric and therefore largely irrelevant to societies which are not Western in cultural orientation. To many societies, appeals to universality merely conceal the means by which one dominant society imposes its culture upon another, infringing on its sovereign independence. The promotion of human rights from the core to the periphery assumes a degree of moral superiority – that the West not only possesses moral truths which others are bound to observe, but that it can sit in judgement on other societies.

The issue is further complicated by the argument that economic, social and cultural rights should precede civil and political rights – one made earlier by Communist states and more recently by a number of East Asian governments. Sometimes this is characterized as a struggle between first and second generation rights. This claim is a direct challenge to the idea that human rights are indivisible and universal, and may be part of what Bull called a revolt against the West. It implies that the alleviation of poverty and economic development in some societies depends on the initial denial of political freedoms and human rights to the citizen. However, the claim that rights can be prioritized in this way – that procedural and substantive freedoms are incompatible – is problematic and widely seen, with justification, as a rationalization by governments for authoritarian rule.

An increasing number of conservative political leaders in East Asia have also argued that there is a superior Asian model of political and social organization comprising the principles of harmony, hierarchy and consensus (Confucianism) in contrast to what they regard as the confrontation, individualism and moral decay which characterizes Western liberalism. Regardless of how self-serving this argument is – and it is rarely offered by democratically elected rulers – it poses a fundamental challenge to Fukuyama's suggestion that in the post-Cold War period liberal democracy faces no serious universal challenges. It is clear that a number of states, including those self-consciously Islamic societies, are not striving to imitate the Western route to political modernization. Some reject it outright.

Recent years have also seen considerable slippage in the Western world's commitment to universal human rights. The 'war on terror' led by the United States provided a more permissive attitude to the use of torture, the incarceration without trial of enemy combatants and the rendition of enemy suspects to third countries for more coercive interrogation than would be permitted in the West. The exposure of these practices weakened any moral force the West may have invoked for the universal spread of human rights.

Even if universal rules and instruments could be agreed upon, how could compliance with universal standards be enforced? Liberals are divided over this issue, between non-interventionists who defend state sovereignty, and those who feel that the promotion of ethical principles can justify intervention in the internal affairs of other states (see Bull 1984a; Wheeler 2000).

Examples of so-called humanitarian intervention in Cambodia, Rwanda, Serbia, Somalia, East Timor and Libya pose a growing challenge to the protection from outside interference traditionally afforded by sovereignty claims. This also applies to the prosecution of those suspected of committing war crimes and crimes against humanity by international tribunals such as the ICJ (Forbes and Hoffman 1993). The embryonic International Criminal Court established in 2002 (ICC) may be seen as a further expression of liberal sentiments which oppose the arbitrary cruelty of political leaders and the use of agencies of the state to inflict harm on minorities and opponents. However, its very structure and functions limit the sovereign right of a government to administer the internal affairs of their state free from outside interference. States like the

United States and Russia, which refuse to ratify the ICC for reasons of sovereignty, are likely to come under increasing pressure in the years ahead to conform with what appears to be a growing global consensus.

Celebrated trials (Milosevic, Saddam, Mubarak) and attention given to non-trials (Pinochet, Suharto, Gaddafi) indicate a significant shift away from the traditional provision of sovereign immunity to heads of state and others guilty of war crimes and crimes against humanity. Whereas in the past, justice, if dispensed at all, would come from within the state, the establishment of international legal fora and the further development of international law in this area are largely due to the influence of liberal internationalism and its emphasis on the importance of global benchmarks and the rule of law. It is true that cases like these never truly escape the political atmosphere of the day, in particular the domestic political climate in each country directly involved, however the fact that they arise at all within international legal jurisdictions indicates significant progress towards a system of global justice.

Modern forms of humanitarian intervention follow a pattern established in the middle of the eighteenth century when the British and Dutch successfully interceded on behalf of Prague's Jewish community, which was threatened with deportation by authorities in Bohemia. The protection of Christian minorities at risk in Europe and in the Orient in the eighteenth and nineteenth centuries by the Treaty of Kucuk-Kainardji (1774) and the Treaty of Berlin (1878) are also part of the same legal precedent, as is the advocacy of British Prime Minister Gladstone in the second half of the nineteenth century and US President Wilson early in the twentieth century. Vietnam's invasion of Cambodia in 1978, when refracted through the ideological prism of the Cold War, highlighted the politically contingent nature of humanitarian intervention in the modern period. This explains why the articulation of a 'right to protect' (R2P) still awaits political support across the globe. Liberals who support both the sovereign rights of independent states and the right of external intervention in cases where there is an acute humanitarian crisis, find it difficult to reconcile both international norms (Chomsky 1999).

Globalization, the financial system and terrorism

Fukuyama's post-Cold War optimism is on firmer ground if we consider the extent to which economic liberalism has become the dominant ideology of the contemporary period. The move towards a global political economy organized along neo-liberal lines is a trend as significant as the likely expansion of the zone of peace. Early in the twenty-first century, the world economy more closely resembles the prescriptions of Smith and Ricardo than at any previous time. As MacPherson forecast, this development is also a measure of 'how deeply the market assumptions about the nature of man and society have penetrated liberal-democratic theory' (MacPherson 1977: 21). Two dark clouds which appeared on the horizon, however, were as serious as they were unexpected. A wave of anti-Western Islamist terror beginning in 2001 became a significant blockage on the path to globalization and confronted liberals with a range of intellectual dilemmas and policy reversals for which they were unprepared. And the global financial crisis which broke in 2007 shook the confidence of those espousing the virtues of market forces in the sector.

Before examining the extent to which liberalism has shaped the contours of the world economy today and the impacts of economic crises and Islamist terror, it is important to recognize that the experience of laissez faire capitalism in the nineteenth century challenged many liberal assumptions about human beings, the market and the role of the state.

Critics such as Polanyi highlighted the extent to which material self-gain in a market society was necessary for survival in an unregulated market economy, rather than a reflection of the human condition in its natural state. It is unwise for liberals to generalize from the specific case of market capitalism – to believe that behaviour enforced as a result of a new and presumably transient form of political economy was a true reflection of a human being's inner self (Polanyi 1944; Block and Somers 1984).

State intervention in the economic life of a society was in fact an act of community self-defence against the destructive power of unfettered markets which, according to Polanyi, if left unregulated, threatened to annihilate society. However, state intervention in the economy was also necessary for markets to function – free trade, commercial exchanges and liberal markets have always been policies of the state and have not emerged organically or independently of it.

As List and many since have explained, the state plays a crucial role in the economic development of industrial societies, protecting embryonic industries from external competition until they are ready to win global market shares on an equal footing. There are few, if any examples of states emerging as industrial powerhouses by initially adopting a policy of free trade. Protectionism and state coordinated economic development have been key early ingredients of economic success in the modern world, as the post-war experience of East Asia suggests.

Liberalism and globalization

To a significant extent, the globalization of the world economy coincided with a renaissance of neo-liberal thinking in the Western world. The political triumph of the 'New Right' in Britain and the United States in particular during the late 1970s and 1980s was achieved at the expense of Keynesianism, the first coherent philosophy of state intervention in economic life. According to the Keynesian formula, the state intervened in the economy to smooth out the business cycle, provide a degree of social equity and security, and maintain full employment. Neo-liberals, who favoured the free play of 'market forces' and a minimal role for the state in economic life, wanted to 'roll back' the welfare state, in the process challenging the social-democratic consensus established in most Western states during the post-war period.

Just as the ideological predilection of Western governments became more concerned with efficiency and productivity and less concerned with welfare and social justice, the power of the state to regulate the market was eroded by the forces of globalization, in particular the de-regulation of finance and currency markets. The means by which domestic societies could be managed to reduce inequalities produced by inherited social structures and accentuated by the natural workings of the market, declined significantly. In addition, the disappearance of many traditional industries in Western economies, the effects of technological change, increased competition for investment and production and the mobility of capital, undermined the bargaining power of labour. The sovereignty of capital began to reign over both the interventionary behaviour of the state and the collective power of organized working people.

There is a considerable debate over globalization, between liberals who believe it constitutes a fundamentally new phase of capitalism and statists who are sceptical of such claims (Held *et al.* 1999; Held and McGrew 2000). Liberals point to the increasing irrelevance of national borders in the conduct and organization of economic activity. They focus on the growth of free trade, the capacity of transnational corporations (TNCs) to escape political regulation and national legal jurisdictions, and the liberation of capital from national and territorial constraints (Ohmae 1995; Friedman 2000; Micklewait and Wooldridge 2000). Sceptics, on the other hand, claim that the world was less open and globalized at the end of the twentieth century than it was in the nineteenth. They suggest that the volume of world trade relative to the size of the world economy is much the same at the end of the twentieth century as it was at the beginning, though they concede that the enormous explosion of short-term speculative capital transfers since the collapse of the Bretton Woods system in the early 1970s has restricted the planning options for national governments. Significantly, sceptics want to distinguish between the idea of an international economy with growing links between separate national economies, which they concede, and a single global political economy without meaningful national borders or divisions, which they deny (Weiss 1998; Chomsky 1999; Hirst and Thompson 1996; Hobsbawm 2000).

The next section will examine the extent to which liberal ideas have shaped the current economic order. It will focus on the contemporary nature of world trade, the questions of sovereignty and foreign investment and the challenges to liberal ideas recently posed by Islamic terrorism.

The nature of 'free trade'

For neo-liberals, the principles of free trade first enunciated by Smith and Ricardo continue to have contemporary relevance. Commercial traders should be allowed to exchange money and goods without concern for national barriers. There should be few legal constraints on international commerce, and no artificial protection or subsidies constraining the freedom to exchange. An open global market, where goods and services can pass freely across national boundaries, should be the objective of policy makers in all nation-states. Only free trade will maximize economic growth and generate the competition that will promote the most efficient use of resources, people and capital.

Conversely, protectionism is seen as a pernicious influence on the body politic. Policies which protect uncompetitive industries from market principles corrupt international trade, distort market demand, artificially lower prices and encourage inefficiency, while penalizing fair traders. Protection is the cry of 'special' or 'vested' interests in society and should be resisted by government in 'the national interest'. It penalizes developing nations by excluding them from entry into the global marketplace where they can exploit their domestic advantage in cheap labour.

The cornerstone of the free trade argument is the theory of comparative advantage, which discourages national self-sufficiency by advising states to specialize in goods and services they can produce most cheaply – their 'factor endowments'. They can then exchange their goods for what is produced more cheaply elsewhere. As everything is then produced most efficiently by the discipline of the price mechanism, the production of wealth is maximized and everyone is better off. For Smith, the 'invisible hand' of market forces directs every member of society in every state to the most advantageous position in the global economy. The self-interest of one becomes the general interest of all.

The relevance of the theory of comparative advantage in the era of globalization has come under question (Strange 1985; Bairoch 1993; Daly and Cobb 1994; Clairmont 1996). The first difficulty is that it was devised at a time when there were national controls on capital movements. Ricardo and Smith assumed that capital was immobile and available only for national investment. They also assumed that the capitalist was first and foremost a member of a national political community, which was the context in which he established his commercial identity: Smith's 'invisible hand' presupposed the internal bondings of community, so that the capitalist felt a 'natural disinclination' to invest abroad. Smith and Ricardo could not have foreseen 'a world of cosmopolitan money managers and TNCs which, in addition to having limited liability and immorality conferred on them by national governments, have now transcended those very governments and no longer see the national community as their context' (Daly and Cobb 1994: 215). The emergence of capitalists who freed themselves from community obligations and loyalties, and who had no 'natural disinclination' to invest abroad, would have appeared absurd. Highly mobile and volatile capital markets are a major challenge for the theory of comparative advantage.

The second problem is that the forms of international trade have changed dramatically over recent decades. The idea of national, sovereign states trading with each other as discrete economic units is becoming an anachronism. Intra-industry or intra-firm trade dominates the manufacturing sector of the world economy. Over 40 per cent of all trade now comprises intra-firm transactions, which are centrally managed interchanges within TNCs (that cross international borders) guided by a highly 'visible hand'. Intra-firm trade runs counter to the theory of comparative advantage which advises nations to specialize in products where factor endowments provide a comparative cost advantage. The mobility of capital and technology, and the extent to which firms trade with each other, means that 'governments in virtually all industrial societies now take an active interest in trying to facilitate links between their own domestic firms – including offshoots of multinationals – and the global networks' in strategic industries. They can no longer remain at arm's length from business as neo-liberal economic theory demands (Emy 1993: 173).

Similarly, the globalization of the world economy has seen the spread of manufacturing industries to many developing countries and the relocation of transnational manufacturing centres to what are often low-wage, high-repression areas – regions with low health and safety standards where organized labour is frequently suppressed or illegal. TNCs are becoming increasingly adept at circumventing national borders in their search for cheap labour and access to raw materials, and few states can refuse to play host to them. The creation of new centres of production occurs wherever profit opportunities can be maximized because investment decisions are governed by absolute profitability rather than comparative advantage. For liberals, this is the best way of encouraging much-needed foreign investment in the developing world and establishing a trade profile for countries which might otherwise be excluded from world trade altogether.

Modern trading conditions have diverged significantly from the assumptions which underpin the neo-liberal analysis of how markets and trade actually work. The internationalization of production, the mobility of capital and the dominance of transnational corporations are just three developments which render theories of comparative advantage some-what anachronistic. The idea of national sovereign states trading with each other as discrete economic units is steadily becoming the exception rather than the rule. Neo-mercantilist theory, which stresses the maxi-mization of national wealth, also fails to explain contemporary trade realities. A more accurate description is 'corporate mercantilism', with 'managed commercial interactions within and among huge corporate groupings, and regular state intervention in the three major Northern blocs to subsidize and protect domestically-based international corpora-tions and financial institutions' (Chomsky 1994: 95). If there is such a thing as a nation's comparative advantage it is clearly a human achieve-ment and certainly not a gift of nature, though this view remains unorthodox within powerful economic circles.

The third challenge to the relevance of the theory of comparative advantage is the steady erosion of the rules which have underpinned multilateral trade in the post-war era. While there has been a reduction in barriers to trade *within* blocs such as the European Union and the North American Free Trade Agreement (NAFTA), they have been raised *between* blocs. Tariffs have come down but they have been replaced by a wide assortment of non-tariff barriers (NTBs), including import quotas and voluntary restraint agreements. This is a concern to small, 'fair' traders which are incapable of matching the subsidies provided by Europeans and North Americans. States which unilaterally adopt free market doctrines while leading industrial societies head in the opposite direction place themselves in a vulnerable position in the world economy. But regardless of whether tariff barriers and NTBs are dismantled, the world market would not be 'free' in any meaningful sense, because of the power of the TNCs to control and distort markets through transfer pric-ing and other devices.

The proliferation of free trade agreements and organizations such as NAFTA, Asia Pacific Economic Cooperation (APEC) and the WTO and the growing importance of international organizations such as the G8, the International Monetary Fund (IMF) and the World Bank is indicative of the influence of neo-liberalism in the post-Cold War period. These are powerful transnational bodies which embody free trade as their govern-ing ideology. To their supporters, they provide developing societies with the only opportunity to overcome financial hardship and modernize their economies. To their critics, however, they impose free market strictures on developing societies. They are organizations which institutionalize market relationships between states. By locking the developing world into agreements which force them to lower their protective barriers, NAFTA and the WTO, for example, prevent the South from developing trade profiles which diverge from the model dictated by their supposed 'comparative advantage'. The IMF and the World Bank, on the other hand, make the provision of finance (or, more accurately, 'debt') to developing societies conditional on their unilateral acceptance of free market rules for their economies – the 'conditionality' of the so-called 'structural adjustment policies' or SAPs.

Critics attack these institutions for legitimizing only one kind of global order, based on unequal market relations. Specifically, the institutions are criticized for imposing identical prescriptions for economic development on all countries, regardless of what conditions prevail locally. Developing societies are expected to adopt the free market blueprint (sometimes called the 'Washington Consensus') – opening their economies up to foreign investment, financial de-regulation, reductions in government expenditure and budgetary deficits, the privatization of government-owned enterprises, the abolition of protection and subsidies, developing export orientated economies – or risk the withholding of much-needed aid and finance. And because they are required to remove national controls on capital movements – which make it possible for states to reach their own conclusions about investment and spending priorities – the direction of their economic development is increasingly set by amorphous financial markets which act on profit opportunities rather than out of any consideration of national or community interest.

Arguments for free trade are powerfully made on the grounds of economic efficiency and as the only way of integrating the developing world into the wider global economy. Protectionism within the North disadvantages the South by pricing their economies out of markets in the industrialized world, thus denying them the opportunity to modernize their economies. For economic liberals, free trade is a battle which must be fought within and outside the industrialized world.

Sovereignty and foreign investment

The enormous volumes of unregulated capital liberated by the collapse of the Bretton Woods system in the early 1970s, have transformed the relationships between states and markets. Credit (bonds and loans), investment (Foreign Direct Investment, or FDI) and money (foreign exchange) now flow more freely across the world than commodities. The resulting increase in the power of transnational capital and the diminution of national economic sovereignty is perhaps the most impressive realization of liberal economic ideas (Strange 1996, 1998).

The relationship between a nation's economic prosperity and the world's money markets is decisive. Because most states are incapable of generating sufficient endogenous wealth to finance their economic development, governments need to provide domestic economic conditions which will attract foreign investment into their countries. In a world where capital markets are globally linked and money can be electronically transferred around the world in microseconds, states are judged in terms of their comparative 'hospitality' to foreign capital: that is, they must offer the most attractive investment climates to relatively scarce supplies of money. This gives the foreign investment community significant leverage over policy settings and the course of a nation's economic development generally, and constitutes a diminution in the country's economic sovereignty.

The power of transnational finance capital in the modern period can scarcely be overestimated. The volume of foreign exchange trading in the major financial centres of the world, estimated at over $US1.5 trillion per day, has come to dwarf international trade by at least 60 times. UN statistics suggest that the world's 100 largest TNCs, with assets of over $US5 trillion, account for a third of the total FDI of their home states, giving them increasing influence over the economies of host countries.

The brokers on Wall Street and in Tokyo, the clients of the 'screen jockeys' in the foreign exchange rooms, and the auditors from credit ratings agencies such as Moody's and Standard & Poor's, pass daily judgements on the management of individual economies, and signal to the world's financial community the comparative profit opportunities to be found in a particular country. Inappropriate interventionary policies by government can be quickly deterred or penalized with a (threatened) reduction in the nation's credit rating, a 'run' (sell off) on its currency or an investment 'strike'. The requirements of the international markets can be ignored only at a nation's economic peril. Not only have nation-states lost direct control over the value of their currencies and the movements of capital around the world, they can no longer determine the institutional settings in which capital markets operate. Neo-liberals regard this development as a positive change, believing that on the question of allocating resources, markets rather than the governments know what is in peoples' best interests.

Finance markets, dominated by large banks and financial institutions, insurance companies, brokers and speculators, exist only to maximize their own wealth. There is no compelling reason for them to act in the interests of the poor, the homeless, the infirm or those who are deprived of their basic human rights by their own governments. States which cede economic sovereignty to these global players in the name of free trade and commerce therefore run the risk of elevating private commercial gain to the primary foreign policy objective of the state.

When the foreign investment community is freed from state barriers and controls, and able to choose the most profitable location for its capital, it has the effect of homogenizing the economic development of nation-states across the globe. In what is effectively a bidding war for much-needed infusions of capital, states are driven by the lowest common denominator effect to reduce their regulations, standards, wages and conditions, in order to appear attractive to the investor community. Priority is given to the drive for efficiency and profits. The threat of disinvestment becomes the stick for markets to wield over the heads of government. For liberals, this is a pleasing reversal of modern history which they see as a struggle for liberation from the clutches of arbitrary state power. Ironically, in many instances the key to attracting overseas investment is for the host government to provide the transnational investor with subsidies and protection from market forces. In some cases, this is the only way states can win and maintain the confidence of global markets.

The ill-fated 1995–8 Multilateral Agreement on Investments (MAI) was a vivid illustration of just how far governments in the developed world have been prepared to follow liberal advice and surrender their discretionary economic power to the markets. In this case Organisation for Economic Co-operation and Development (OECD) members were offering voluntarily to restrict their own ability to discriminate against foreign capital. The MAI is a reminder that, as with the establishment of national markets in the nineteenth century, globalization is not the result of the gradual and spontaneous emancipation of the economic sphere from government control. On the contrary, it has been the outcome of conscious and sometimes violent state intervention by advanced capitalist states. Just as domestically the labour market can be 'freed' only by legislative restrictions placed on trades unions, the creation of the postwar liberal trading regime and the de-regulation of the world's capital markets in the 1970s required deliberate acts by interventionary states.

During the current phase of globalization, national economic sovereignty has not so much been lost but either enthusiastically given away or begrudgingly surrendered. The state's capacity to direct the national economy has been deliberately and significantly undercut by the globalization of relations of production and exchange. Significant sovereign power has been ceded to bond holders, fund managers, currency traders, speculators, transnational banks and insurance companies – groups that by definition are democratically unaccountable in any national jurisdiction. In effect, the world economy has come to resemble the global strategic environment. It has become anarchic in character and, as a consequence, the competition for economic security is as intense as the search for strategic security.

The irony in liberal economic thinking was exposed by the global financial crisis which began in 2007. Irresponsible lending practices by financial institutions and complex financial instruments few could understand, almost brought the global financial system to its knees. Ultimately only massive taxpayer-funded government bailouts prevented a great unwinding of the entire system in many leading economies, though many have still not recovered from the shock. The state, acting as lender of last resort, considered the largest investment banks to be too big to fail, a view paradoxically shared by the managers of private capital within them who, until this point, had trumpeted the virtues of free market policies. Although the bankers successfully thwarted moves to re-regulate the financial system after the peak of the crisis, in rescuing the global financial system the state clarified to all but the most devout free market liberals that the unstable, crisis-prone global economy of the twenty-first century is most accurately described as state capitalism (Mason 2010; Johnson and Kwak 2010; Baker 2010; Stiglitz 2010).

Unsurprisingly, concern about a growing 'democratic deficit' has arisen within and outside liberal political philosophy. According to Eric Hobsbawm, economic globalization is undermining liberal democracy as participation in the market replaces participation in politics: the voter in elections is being displaced by the consumer in the market.

Hobsbawm identifies three areas where the power and authority of the state has been undermined by globalization. The first sees the state's monopoly of coercive force being eroded by non-state actors, such as terrorists, who seek weapons of mass destruction. Second, the commitment and loyalty of citizens to the state is weakening. The capacity for states to conscript citizens for military service, to administer colonial rule, and to compel people to abide by the law (e.g. speed cameras, computer hacking and viruses, music downloading), has significantly reduced. It is becoming more difficult for democratic governments to mobilize their populations for war, regardless of their ruling ideology. Finally, the ability of governments to provide public goods – arbitration, law and order, personal security, etc. – has been damaged by the liberation of market forces, such as the privatization of state services and the de-regulation of capital markets. The state as an essential unit of liberal democracy is weakening while public antipathy to globalization grows (Hobsbawm 2007).

David Held's (1995) advocacy of cosmopolitan democracy is seen as utopian by hard-nosed realists, however it is a serious attempt to bring some of the forces of globalization under a degree of popular control.

Proposals such as regional parliaments and the devolution of sovereign power to regional bodies, universal human rights benchmarks entrenched in domestic jurisdictions and monitored by international courts, radical reform of the United Nations (UN) and the promotion of a global civil society are serious suggestions for extending and modernizing democratic politics. The work of Held and his colleagues is an important reminder that as well as rendering significant economic change, globalization has important political challenges and implications which liberals cannot ignore (Archibugi *et al.* 1998; Held 1995; Archibugi 1998).

Non-state terrorism

Whether or not the most recent wave of Islamic militancy is the latest chapter in a long-standing revolt against the West, there can be little doubt that it represents a direct challenge to both the claim that liberal democracy is the universal destination for the species and the assumption that globalization is inexorable. However incoherent and unlikely it is as a political programme, Islamic terrorism is profoundly anti-secular and an opponent of liberal modernity (Gray 2004).

It seems premature and misleading for liberals to claim that the emergence of Al-Qaeda and affiliated groups which perpetrate transnational terrorism constitutes a victory for the deterritorialization of world politics (Buzan 2003: 297, 303). Rather as David Harvey notes, 'the war on terror, swiftly followed by the prospect of war with Iraq ... [has] allowed the state to accumulate more power,' a claim difficult to refute and one that poses an unexpected challenge to liberals who believed that globalization was finally eroding the sovereign significance of the state (Harvey 2003: 17). The national security state has been revived.

The resuscitation of state power across the industrialized world after the 9/11 attacks has taken numerous forms, including new restrictions on civil liberties, greater powers of surveillance and detention, increased military spending and the expansion of intelligence services. The threats posed by Islamic terror and the dangers of weapons of mass destruction (WMD) have also been matched by an increase in state intervention around the world, in particular by US-led coalitions acting in Afghanistan and Iraq. With each subsequent terrorist assault, states which consider themselves innocent victims have been emboldened to interfere in each others' internal affairs – even pre-emptively.

Pre-emption, the disarmament of states alleged to possess WMD, regime change, humanitarianism and the spread of democracy have all been invoked as public justifications for these interventions, although critics have pointed to traditional geo-strategic rationales beneath the surface. Many states, such as China, Israel and Russia, have also used the cover provided by the 'war against terror' to settle domestic scores with secessionists, dissidents and those resisting their territorial occupations. Others seem to be victims of 'blowback', reaping disastrous and unintended consequences from earlier foreign policy actions. Regardless of what the true motives of these interventions are, the irony of socially conservative, economically neo-liberal governments expanding the reach and size of government should not be lost on anyone (Johnson 2002).

The return of the overarching state is perhaps an unsurprising response to community calls for protection from non-state terrorism. When citizens of a state require emergency medical relief, as many victims of the Bali bombings did in October 2002, there is little point appealing to market forces for help. Nor can those responsible for attacks such as the Beslan school atrocity in September 2004 be hunted down, disarmed and prosecuted by privately owned TNCs. Even if the state remains ambivalent about insulating its citizens from the vicissitudes of the world economy, it is still expected to secure them from the threat of terrorism. Only the state can meet these and many other challenges such as 'border protection' and transnational crime. There are no market-based solutions to the dangers posed by what seems to be the latest chapter in the revolt against the West.

Since the end of the Cold War, realists such as Kenneth Waltz have argued that in the absence of effective countervailing pressures, the United States is likely to become increasingly unilateral in seeking to secure its foreign policy interests, and in so doing rely on military power to realize its vision of a new world order. The 'war against terror' has seemingly changed little in this regard. If anything, these events have enhanced a trend which some liberals had either believed or hoped had passed into history.

Historian Eric Hobsbawm has observed that 'the basic element to understanding the present situation is that 9/11 did not threaten the US. It was a terrible human tragedy which humiliated the US, but in no sense was it any weaker after those attacks. Three, four or five attacks will not change the position of the US or its relative power in the world' (Hobsbawm 2002).

This view is similar to Waltz's claim that the problem of terrorism does not challenge the continuities of international politics. 'Although terrorists can be terribly bothersome', says Waltz, 'they hardly pose threats to the fabric of a society or the security of the state ... Terrorism does not change the first basic fact of international politics – the gross imbalance of world power' in favour of the United States. 'Instead, the effect of September 11 has been to enhance American power and extend its military presence in the world' (Waltz 2002: 348–53).

Realists in the United States also led the intellectual opposition to Washington's attack on Iraq in March 2003, arguing that Saddam Hussein had been successfully contained, that he was prevented from using his WMD against the West because of the likely consequences to him and that for similar reasons he couldn't risk passing these weapons – if he in fact possessed them – to groups such as Al-Qaeda. As during the Second Cold War in the Reagan era, realists found themselves in the unusual position of being at the limits of respectable dissent in debates over the Iraq war as a consequence of the influence of the misnamed neo-conservatives, whose muscular liberalism underwrote the administration of George W. Bush (Mearsheimer and Walt 2002; Hobsbawm 2007).

Conclusion

At the beginning of this chapter, it was argued that liberalism was an 'inside-out' approach to international relations, because liberals favour a world in which the endogenous determines the exogenous. Their challenge is to extend the legitimacy of domestic political arrangements found within democratic states to the relationships between all nation-states. To put it another way, liberals believe that democratic society, in which civil liberties are protected and market relations prevail, can have an international analogue in the form of a peaceful global order. The domestic free market has its counterpart in the open, globalized world economy. Parliamentary debate and accountability is reproduced in international fora such as the United Nations. And the legal protection of civil rights within liberal democracies is extended to the promotion of human rights across the world. With the collapse of Communism as an alternative political and economic order, the potential for continuity between the domestic and the international became greater than in any previous period.

Fukuyama had reason to be optimistic. The spread of liberal democracies and the zone of peace was an encouraging development, as is the realization by states that trade and commerce is more closely correlated with economic success than territorial conquest. The number of governments enjoying civilian rather than military rule has increased, and ethical considerations of human justice have a permanent place on the diplomatic agenda. There can be little doubt that the great powers are now much less inclined to use force to resolve their political differences with each other and it appears that liberal democracies are in the process of constructing a separate peace.

The globalization of the world economy means that there are few obstacles to international trade. Liberals want to remove the influence of the state in commercial relations between businesses and individuals, and the decline of national economic sovereignty is an indication that the influence of the state is diminishing. TNCs and capital markets wield significant influence over the shape of the world economy, in the process homogenizing the political economies of every member state of the international community.

Globalization has undermined the nation-state in other ways that have pleased liberals. The capacity of each state to direct the political loyalties of its citizens has been weakened by an increasing popular awareness of the problems faced by the entire human species. The state cannot prevent its citizens turning to a range of sub-national and transnational agents to secure their political identities and promote their political objectives. Sovereignty is no longer an automatic protection against external interference called 'humanitarian intervention'. And decision making on a range of environmental, economic and security questions has become internationalized, rendering national administration less important than transnational political cooperation.

Despite these important changes, there are also counter-trends which can be identified. Realists would argue that liberals such as Ohmae are premature in announcing the demise of the nation-state. They would remind the enthusiasts for globalization that as a preferred form of political community, the nation-state still has no serious rival. There are currently around 200 nation-states in the world asserting their political independence, and the figure grows each year.

Realists cite a number of important powers retained by the state despite globalization, including monopoly control of the weapons of war and their legitimate use, and the sole right to tax its citizens. They would argue that only the nation-state can still command the political allegiances of its citizens or adjudicate in disputes between them. And it is still only the nation-state which has the exclusive authority to bind the whole community to international law.

They would question the extent to which globalization today is an unprecedented phenomenon, citing the nineteenth century as a period when similar levels of economic interdependence existed. They would also point to the growing number of states which reject the argument that Western modernity is universally valid or that political development always terminates at liberal-capitalist democracy. More recently realists have highlighted the expanding reach of the state as a result of the latest wave of anti-Western Islamic militancy – a significant reversal for liberals who anticipated the imminent demise of the nation-state. Islamism is a direct challenge to liberal assumptions about economics and politics terminating at a liberal-capitalist consensus.

Those who welcome the demise of the state in international commerce will similarly be perplexed by the need for extensive government intervention to prevent a greater financial catastrophe after 2007. When markets fail, virtually all eyes look to the state for a rescue, including those champions of market forces who drove the financial system to the precipice. An increasingly crisis-prone global economy has dented the confidence of those who believe capitalism can be successfully managed without government regulation.

Unpredictable challenges have left liberalism on the back foot, questioning whether the linear path to improving the human condition is as straight and as inexorable as they thought only a few short years ago.

4 | The English School

ANDREW LINKLATER

The 'English School' is a term that was coined in the 1970s to describe a group of predominantly British, or British-inspired, writers for whom 'international society' is the primary object of analysis (Jones 1981; Linklater and Suganami 2006). Its most influential early members include Hedley Bull, Martin Wight, John Vincent and Adam Watson whose main publications appeared between the mid-1960s and the late 1980s (see Bull 1977; Wight 1977; 1991; Watson 1982; Bull and Watson 1984; Vincent 1986). Robert Jackson, Tim Dunne and Nicholas Wheeler have been among the most influential members of the English School in more recent years (Dunne 1998; Jackson 2000; Wheeler 2000). Since the late 1990s, the English School has enjoyed a renaissance in large part because of the efforts of Barry Buzan, Richard Little, Andrew Hurrell and other UK-based scholars (Little 2000; Buzan 2001; 2003; Hurrell 2007). The English School remains one of the most important approaches to international politics although its influence is probably greater in Britain than in most other societies where International Relations is taught.

The foundational claim of the English School is that sovereign states form a society, but an anarchical one since they do not submit to a higher monopoly of power that can force them to comply with global rules. That states have succeeded in creating a society of sovereign equals is regarded as one of the most fascinating dimensions of world politics. There is, it is argued, a very high level of order, and surprisingly little interstate violence, in the absence of a higher coercive authority. Readers are invited to reflect on the probable level of violence, fear, insecurity and distrust in even the most stable of domestic societies should sovereign authority collapse. A condition of fear and chaos would most likely ensue, but that is not the defining feature of international relations.

That is not to suggest that the English School underestimates the importance of force in relations between states. Its members regard violence as an endemic feature of the 'anarchical society' (the title of

Hedley Bull's most famous work, 1977) but they add that international law and morality restrain it to a significant extent. Confusion about the main purpose of the School can result from the fact that some members seem unreservedly realist at times. That is particularly apparent in Wight's essay, 'Why is there no International Theory?', which contended that domestic politics is the sphere of the good life whereas international politics is the realm of security and survival (Wight 1966a: 33). Realist convictions are also evident in his observation that international relations are 'incompatible with progressivist theory'. In a statement that seems to place him squarely in the realist camp, Wight (1996a: 26) maintained that the sixteenth-century thinker, Sir Thomas More, would have recognized the basic features of world politics in the 1960s since so much had remained constant over the centuries. Some have contended that the English School is a British variant on state-centric realism that underestimates how far appeals to defend international society simply protect the interests of the dominant powers (for a critical discussion, see Wheeler and Dunne 1996).

English School analysts are attracted by elements of realism and idealism, yet gravitate towards the middle ground, never wholly reconciling themselves to either point of view. In an influential series of lectures delivered at the London School of Economics in the 1950s, Wight (1991) described what he called the 'rationalist' or 'Grotian tradition' in those terms. The variety of terms can be confusing here, but suffice it to add that English School thinking is usually regarded as a modern twist on older patterns of thought (see Jeffery 2006 for a critique of the notion of a Grotian tradition). Wight cited Grotius' statement in his magnum opus, *De Jure Belli ac Pacis* first published in 1625, that those who believe that anything goes in war are as deluded as those who think that force is never justified. On that argument, Grotius envisaged an international society in which violence between Catholic and Protestant states was replaced by a condition of relatively amicable co-existence. Wight argued that the tradition to which Grotius belonged was the '*via media*' or middle way between realism and 'revolutionism' which was a term used to describe the medley of utopian perspectives which hold that world peace is realizable, if not imminent (also Wight 1966a: 91). In the lectures, Wight lamented the way in which the tensions between realism and idealism or utopianism in the inter-war years had obscured the existence of a third path that focused on international society.

In short, the English School (which is best regarded as a diverse grouping of scholars rather than a homogeneous community) maintain that the international system is more orderly and civil than realists and neo-realists suggest. But since violence is probably ineradicable in their view, they are critical of 'utopians' who believe that a condition of perpetual peace can be realized. There is no expectation, they maintain, that the international political system will ever enjoy a level of cooperation that is comparable with what exists in stable national societies. If there is more to international politics than realists suggest, there will always be less than the idealist or cosmopolitan desires.

The idea of the '*via media*' can be explored further by considering points of contrast with realism and 'revolutionism', and by developing the theme that the English School offers a limited progressivist account of world politics. As shown in Chapter 2, realism emphasizes the unending struggle for power and security in the world of states. Sovereignty, anarchy and the security dilemma are crucial terms in its lexicon; the idea of progress is largely absent from its vocabulary. Moral principles and social progress are held to be important for descriptions of domestic politics where trust prevails and where security is provided by the state. But cosmopolitan projects are thought to have little relevance for international relations where states must provide their own security, and where distrust and suspicion are pervasive. In that domain, moral principles serve to justify national interests and to stigmatize competitors: they are not the basis for a radical experiment in creating a world political organization that supersedes the sovereign nation-state.

The more or less unbridgeable gulf between domestic and international politics is a central theme in realist and neo-realist thought. By contrast, utopian or cosmopolitan thinkers envisage a world order – but not necessarily a world government – where universal moral principles are observed, and the gulf between domestic and international politics is narrowed. The tensions between those approaches were central to the so-called 'first debate' between realists and idealists. The characteristics of that debate need not detain us, but it is useful to note that liberal internationalists believed that realism was 'unrealistic' about the feasibility of radical change while realists countered by maintaining that liberals were naive about the prospects for a new world order based on the rule of law, open diplomacy and collective security. Reflecting on the recent history of international thought, Wight's protégé, Hedley Bull, argued that both perspectives contain valuable insights, but neither recognized that the international system is far from a state of war, despite the fact that states possess a monopoly of the instruments of violence. Common interests in restraining force have led states to develop the art of diplomatic accommodation and compromise that made international society possible. Success on that front undermined what he described as the 'domestic analogy' – the belief that order between states could only be established by building, as world government thinkers supposed, the same institutions that uphold order within stable sovereign territories (Suganami 1989).

Adam Watson (1987: 151) argued that a 'strong case can be made out, on the evidence of past systems as well as the present one, that the regulatory rules and institutions of a system usually, and perhaps inexorably, develop to the point where the members become conscious of common values and the system becomes an international society'. That observation suggests that an international society is likely to develop wherever independent political communities co-exist. It was not the basis for arguing that international society is merely a stepping-stone to a world community. However, English School thinkers argued that it is impossible to make sense of relations between states without understanding the recurrent appeal of utopian visions of international politics. While recognizing the merits of realist observations about the dangers inherent in international anarchy, those scholars are far more prepared to analyse arguments for global reform that led to the universal culture of human rights and, more recently, to support for humanitarian intervention and to radical innovations in international criminal law. English School analysts maintain that debates about the merits of humanitarian intervention reveal much about their object of analysis (international society) and about its internal divisions. The realist contention that states are locked in struggles for power and security only partly explains the tensions that arise over intervention. States also have different conceptions of fundamental human rights and conflicting beliefs about how such ideals should be realized. Since the end of the bipolar era, several societies including China have not shared the enthusiasm of many Western powers for military intervention to protect human rights in Kosovo and, more recently, in Libya. China, Russia and others have opposed what they regard as dangerous Western interference in Syria. Such fears were intensified by the neo-conservative experiment during the recent Bush Administration and specifically by the flawed intervention to secure regime change in Iraq. If post-colonial states are troubled by decisions to undermine sovereignty it is because memories of struggles to free themselves from the Western imperial powers remain strong, and because they believe that a 'new imperialism' will further entrench global inequalities of power and status (Mayall 2000). English School analysts regard such divisions, which are anchored in differences of culture and ideology, as central features of international society in its 'post-European' phase. Significantly, members of the School disagree amongst themselves about whether the time is ripe to build new principles of humanitarian intervention into international society or whether such noble aspirations will create unnecessary rivalries that damage what they regard as the only arrangement that has the capacity to preserve order between states with different levels of military power and diverse cultures (see the references to the differences between Jackson and Wheeler on pages 100–2).

Members of the English School insist that the survival of that fragile society can never be taken for granted. It can be undermined by realist struggles for power and by anti-status quo or expansionist powers that thought, as in the case of Napoleon's France or Nazi Germany, that they can only realize their objectives by using force. But international society can also be undermined by breaches of international law, and by failures to use diplomacy to reach global agreements that respect diverse outlooks and orientations. English School theorists maintain that there is no guarantee that the modern society of states will survive indefinitely; it is therefore essential to understand its foundations and to ask how it can be strengthened. That does not rule out support for 'utopian' aspirations. Observing that demands for morality and justice have always influenced international relations, Wight (1977: 192) argued that 'the fundamental political task at all times [is] to provide order, or security, from which law, justice and prosperity may afterwards develop'. But that comment rested on the assumption that justice would not benefit from a politics that underestimated the difficulties of preserving international order – that had to be in place before 'higher' aspirations could be promoted. In the age of superpower rivalries that ended with the collapse of the Soviet Union, English School writers reflected the prevailing diplomatic realities by emphasizing the priority of maintaining order and stability. In the mid-1980s, Vincent argued that global support for the right to be free from starvation could at one and the same time promote justice and strengthen international society (see Cox and Rengger 2011). In the post-bipolar era, Dunne and Wheeler argued for a more explicitly normative English School stance on human rights and humanitarian intervention. They defended a 'critical international society' approach that considered ways in which states could act as 'good international citizens' to promote cosmopolitan values (Dunne 1998; Wheeler and Dunne 1998). But as already noted, others within the English School have been critical of their belief that international society had reached the point where new efforts to secure justice for *individuals* could be added to the traditional emphasis on creating and preserving order between *states*. Such tensions have been core elements of Western responses to the 'humanitarian challenge' of the 'Arab Spring'.

English School writings have long maintained that international society largely depends on how far the great powers are 'great responsibles' that are restrained in the pursuit of self-interest and willing to use their influence to promote global values of the kind that Vincent, Dunne and Wheeler have defended. Underlying that standpoint is the belief that it is the great powers that usually pose the most serious threat to international society (Wight 1991: 130). How far they accept 'special responsibilities' is critical to the maintenance of that society, and the key to the legitimacy of its fundamental institutions (Bukovanski *et al.* 2012; Clark and Reus-Smit 2007). The recent phase of American hegemony – and the conduct of the 'war against terror' in particular – led English School analysts to return to the question of whether the survival of international society ultimately rests on the balance of power. Dunne (2003) fore-grounded that question in his discussion of the Bush doctrine of 'preventive war' against hostile regimes that were believed to be willing to share weapons of mass destruction with terrorist groups. Such discussions reveal how great powers rewrite the rules of international society to suit their perceived interests (see Holmes 2007) – or, as in the case of the US position on the International Criminal Court, refuse to be restrained by what they see as unnecessary obligations and entanglements (Ralph 2007). Other English School writers have explored new lines of investigation into the extent to which great power hegemony can be a basic 'institution' of international society – as was the case in the ancient Greek city-states system (Wight 1977: chapter 1) – contrary to those who believe that the balance of power is central (Clark 2011). The issue has arisen in conjunction with the recent 'unipolar moment'; it may assume even greater importance if China's rise to power continues. Efforts continue to build on earlier support for introducing a principle of humanitarian intervention into international society – and on analyses of how efforts to improve the position of the world's indigenous peoples can reduce the 'moral backwardness of international society' (see Keal 2003). Indeed, one would expect proponents of an approach that is positioned between the poles of realism and utopianism to continue to develop distinctive debates about the prospects for improving international society and about the main obstacles that stand in the way.

The remainder of this chapter is in four sections. The first focuses on the idea of order and society in the foundational English School texts. The second considers English School analyses of the relative importance of order and justice in the traditional European society of states. That is followed by a discussion of the 'revolt against the West' and the emergence of the first universal society of states in which demands for justice have been more frequently heard. The fourth section returns to the question of English School reflections on the limited progress that has occurred in international relations, and it offers some final observations about the idea that its position as the *via media* gives it an advantage over other positions in the field.

From power to order: international society

We have seen that the English School analyses begin with the surprisingly high level of order that exists between independent political communities in the condition of anarchy. Some such as Wight (1977: 43) were intrigued by the small number of international societies that have existed in human history and by their short life-spans, all previous examples having been destroyed by empire after four or five centuries. Wight (1977: 35–9) also noted the propensity for internal schism in the form of international revolutions that brought transnational forces and ideologies rather than sovereign states into conflict. He posed the interesting question of whether commerce first brought different societies into contact, and created the context in which a society of states later developed (1977: 33). In his remarks about the three international societies about which most is known (the Ancient Chinese, the Graeco-Roman and the modern society of states) he maintained (1977: 33–5) that each emerged in a region that possessed a high level of linguistic and cultural unity. Independent political communities felt they belonged to a superior civilization. A sense of their 'cultural differentiation' from allegedly semi-civilized and barbaric peoples facilitated communication between them, and made it easier to define the rights and duties that bound them together in an exclusive international society. They did not believe that 'uncivilized' peoples had the same rights. In the case of the modern society of states, the commitment to sovereign equality as a principle of 'civilized' international relations co-existed with assumptions about the right to use force to colonize those who were regarded as social inferiors.

Writing on the evolution of modern international society, Hedley Bull (1977: 82) observed that in 'the form of the doctrine of natural law, ideas of human justice historically preceded the development of ideas of inter-state or international justice and provided perhaps the principal intellectual foundations upon which these latter ideas at first rested'. Those words appear to echo Wight's position that some sense of cultural unity is essential before an international society can develop. But Bull's position was different because he argued that a society of states can exist in the absence of linguistic, cultural or religious solidarities. To clarify the point, he distinguished between an international system and an international society. A 'system of states (or international system)', he maintained, 'is formed when two or more states have sufficient contact between them, and have sufficient impact on one another's decisions to cause them to behave – at least in some measure – as parts of a whole' (1977: 9–10). A society of states can be said to exist 'when a group of states, conscious of certain common interests and common values, form a society in the sense that they conceive themselves to be bound by a common set of rules in their relations with one another, and share in the working of common institutions' (1977: 13). That important distinction underpinned Bull's efforts to provide a more detailed account of how international societies develop.

As we have seen, Bull maintained that order can exist between states that do not regard themselves as members of the same civilization. A pragmatic need to co-exist was all that was needed to give rise to what Bull (1977: 316) called a 'diplomatic culture' – a web of conventions and institutions that preserves order between states that are divided by culture and ideology. He added that a diplomatic culture is likely to be stronger if it is anchored in an 'international political culture' – it is more likely to flourish if states share the same general way of life and have similar beliefs. Illustrating the point, Bull and Watson argued that, in the nineteenth century, the European society of states rested on an international political culture, but with the expansion of that society to embrace the non-European regions of the world, the sense of being part of a common civilization has declined. Even so, the basic rules of the international order that first developed in Europe have been accepted by an overwhelming majority of its former colonies, now equal sovereign members of the first universal society of states. No international political culture currently underpins the diplomatic culture; however Bull (1977: 316–17) thought that condition might change if different elites across the world come to identify with an emergent 'cosmopolitan culture' of modernity.

Bull (1977: 53–5) provided the most detailed analysis of the foundations of international order. He stated that all societies – domestic and international – have arrangements for protecting three 'primary goals'. They are placing restraints on violence, upholding property rights, and ensuring that contracts and agreements are kept. The fact that those primary goals are common to domestic and international society explains Bull's rejection of 'the domestic analogy' which, it will be recalled, is the idea that a peaceful international order will only come into being when states surrender their powers to centralized institutions similar to those at the national level. As we have seen, English School writers break with realism because they believe that states can enjoy the benefits of society without transferring sovereign prerogatives to a higher authority. Bull's approach was that states are usually committed to limiting the use of force, to ensuring respect for property, and to preserving trust in their relations with one another. Those shared interests – rather than any common culture or shared way of life – are the ultimate foundation of international society.

As members of that society, sovereign nation-states have similar commitments to protecting primary goals, but the interstate order is distinctive because of its 'anarchical' nature. The citizens of each state are governed by 'primary rules' that specify how they should behave, and by 'secondary rules' that determine how such primary rules are created, interpreted and enforced (Bull 1977: 133). Central institutions have the authority to make primary and secondary rules within sovereign communities. But in international society, states create their own primary rules as well as the secondary rules that govern their creation, interpretation and enforcement. In addition, international society has a set of unique primary goals (Bull 1977: 16–20). The traditional idea that only sovereign states can be members of international society (and not individuals or business corporations) is one such distinguishing feature – so is the conviction that the society of states is the only legitimate form of global political organization, and the understanding that states should respect one another's sovereignty. Those goals may conflict with one another, as Bull observed in his reflections on order and justice which will be discussed below.

Societies of states exist because most political communities want to constrain the use of force and to bring a measure of civility to their external relations. An interesting question is whether some states are more likely than others to attach special value to international society and to protect its core institutions such as diplomacy, international law and the practice of balancing the power of states that aspire to dominate others. English School writers argue that international society can be multidenominational and include states that have radically different cultures and philosophies of government. Indeed, one of the central aims of diplomacy is to promote mutual understanding and to find the common ground between very different cultures that often fail to comprehend each other's intentions. Wight argued that those European societies that had a strong commitment to constitutional government played a key role in the formation of an international society that was also concerned with restraining power struggles (Linklater 1993). The crucial issue here is how far the 'inside' affects the 'outside' – how far domestic beliefs contribute to the development of international order. Wight's essay on international legitimacy showed how the principles of international society that included the rules of admission and right conduct changed as the dynastic system of government was replaced by the idea that sovereignty resides in the people or nation (Wight 1977; see also Clark 2005). He added that 'these principles of legitimacy mark the region of approximation *between* international and domestic politics. They are principles that prevail (or are at least proclaimed) *within* a majority of the states that form international society, as well as in the relations between them' (Wight 1977: 153 emphasis in original).

From that perspective it is unsurprising that certain regimes have tried to force others to comply with their vision of the good society. Examples include competing forces in the religious wars of the seventeenth century, the French revolutionary wars and the Bolshevik efforts to export socialism. More recent attempts to export democracy, for instance, through the

US–UK led intervention to promote regime change in Iraq are part of a longer-term trend that Wight regarded as 'revolutionist' in orientation (or as combining revolutionist aspirations with a realist focus on the importance of military power). English School thinkers have been unconvinced by those who think that the members of the society of states must subscribe to the same political ideology (Wight 1991: 41–2). They have advised against efforts to impose one set of values on others, when the real challenge is how to build international society in the midst of cultural diversity. But they recognize that such endeavours have surfaced many times in the history of the modern society of states, and provide evidence of profound struggles over the nature of that society – over its rightful members, organizing principles and future direction. That emphasis makes the English School a natural ally of more recent constructivist analyses of principles of legitimacy and global norms in international affairs (Edelman 1990; Clark and Reus-Smit 2007; Philpott 2001; see Chapter 8). However, English School analysis has been distinguished by its long-standing investigation into the 'normative' and 'institutional' factors that give international society its distinctive 'logic' and identity (Bull and Watson 1984: 9). The increasingly multicultural and multi-religious character of world society only serves to underline the value of its approach to understanding the complex interplay between domestic ideologies, social and political forces, and the configuration of international society.

Order and justice in international relations

English School writers have been interested in the processes that transform systems of states into societies of states, and in the norms and institutions that prevent the collapse of civility and erode the constraints on military power. They have been concerned with whether societies of states can develop ways of ensuring justice for individuals in their own right. We have seen that Bull distinguished between international societies and international systems, but in order to understand the tensions between order and justice in world affairs, he introduced an important distinction between the 'pluralist' and the 'solidarist' (or 'Grotian') conceptions of international society that has been a major influence on English School in the intervening decades (Bull 1966a).

The 'central Grotian assumption', Bull (1966a: 52) maintained, 'is that of the solidarity, or potential solidarity, of the states comprising international society, with respect to the enforcement of the law'. That standpoint was apparent in the Grotian conviction that there is a clear difference between just and unjust wars, and in the parallel assumption 'from which [the] right of humanitarian intervention is derived ... that individual human beings are subjects of international law and members of international society in their own right' (1966a: 64). The contrasting pluralist approach, as expounded by the eighteenth-century international lawyer, Emmeric de Vattel, contended that 'states do not exhibit solidarity of this kind, but are capable of agreeing only for certain minimum purposes which fall short of that of the enforcement of the law' (1966a: 52). From that standpoint, order between states is more likely to exist if they recognize that they have different conceptions of justice and diverse understandings of what counts as a just war. A related argument was that the basic members of international society are states rather than individuals. Moreover, as sovereign equals, they can have no legitimate interest in matters that fall within each other's domestic jurisdiction, and no right of intervention to protect individuals (1966a: 68). Having made that distinction, Bull asked whether there was any evidence for the view that international society was developing in a more solidarist direction. The answer in Bull (1977: 73) was that expectations of greater solidarity were seriously 'premature'. How far that is correct has been a major bone of contention in more recent disputes between pluralists such as Jackson (2000) and solidarists such as Wheeler (2000).

To understand Bull's reasoning, it is necessary to recall his discussion of primary goals in international society (1977: 16–18, chapter 4). Bull argued that the interest in preserving the balance of power has often clashed with the notion of the equal sovereignty of each state. On three separate occasions in the eighteenth century, Polish independence was sacrificed for the sake of equilibrium between the great powers. In the 1930s, the League of Nations decided not to defend Abyssinia from Italian aggression because Britain and France needed Italy's support to balance Nazi Germany. In such cases, order took priority over justice that insists that sovereign states deserve to be treated equally. There were many examples of the tension between order and justice in the bipolar era. Order and stability demanded that the superpowers prevent nuclear proliferation, but justice suggested that all states – and not just the great powers – have the right to acquire weaponry that they regard as central to their defence (1977: 227–8). Moreover, the value that was attached to order between the superpowers meant that justice for individuals – in the form of protecting human rights – had low priority. The dominant assumption was that international society would be weakened if each superpower attempted to export its particular conception of justice on its members. But with the collapse of the Soviet Union, the United States and its key Western allies were free to promote the human rights culture and to attempt to export liberal democracy and 'market civilization' (Bowden and Seabrooke 2006; Donnelly 1998; Hobson 2008; Stivachtis 2010).

They did so in the belief that global support for certain visions of liberal democracy is critical for global governance. But that conviction has often been linked with the 'revolutionist' supposition that the members of international society should have similar political systems and ideological perspectives.

As Bull (1977: 89) argued with respect to the war crimes tribunals at the end of World War II, efforts to apply principles of justice to international relations are often highly selective, and breed opposition and discontent. What some regard as legitimate international punishment is 'Victor's justice' for others. That point has arisen in conjunction with the trials of Slobodan Milosevic and Saddam Hussein in recent years. Bull did not live to analyse debates about humanitarian intervention and the prosecution of 'war criminals' that have been particularly prominent since NATO's military action against Serbia in 1999. It is possible that he would have supported such developments. However, Bull believed that it was essential to remind Western liberals that their conception of fundamental human rights did not automatically appeal to all non-Western peoples. As in the case of contemporary China, many groups believe it is more important to preserve political stability and ensure economic growth rather than promote Western-style democracies. The point was that liberals had to appreciate that tensions over the meaning of such rights were unavoidable in a multicultural society of states; liberals and non-liberals alike had to try to understand other cultural perspectives rather than dismiss them as manifestations of less rational ways of life (1977: 126; see also Bull 1979a). Such tolerance of diversity was crucial for the survival of international society – and never more so than in the post-European society of states.

Bull maintained that states often disagree about the meaning of justice, and can more easily concur about how to maintain international order. Most agree that each state should respect each other's sovereignty, and observe the principle of non-intervention. Each society can then promote its idea of the good life within its own territory, secure in the knowledge that others recognize it as an equal. Bull repeatedly emphasized the difficulties that were involved in resolving the tension between order and justice, but he was also insistent that the purpose of international society is to promote 'order in human society as a whole'. It is 'order among all mankind', he claimed, that has 'primary value, not order within the society of states' (1977: 22). That apparent cosmopolitanism sat awkwardly alongside his conviction that there is little evidence that societies are converging on what it would mean to build a world community. But the key point was that states should try to promote world order (and justice for individuals) whenever circumstances allow, while recognizing that progress in this domain is likely to be slow, and can easily be thrown into reverse (see also Buzan 2004 and Clark 2007 on the relationship between world and international society).

Wight's claim that the analysis of international society is the *via media* between realism and revolutionism is worth recalling at this point. Considered alongside Bull's writings on order and justice, that idea draws attention to the belief that the society of states is evidence of political progress, at least in agreeing on basic principles of co-existence. Tensions between order and justice are a reminder that progress has not advanced very far, so that 'revolutionists' understandably condemn what they regard as deeply flawed arrangements even though they may fail to appreciate the achievement of international society and the difficulty that states have in initiating and implementing programmes of radical reform. It follows that English School analysis necessarily concentrates on how naked power struggles or the lack of prudence in foreign policy can undo the progress that has occurred in creating an international society; but it must also be interested in whether there are any signs that states are making real progress (or are capable of making more progress) in creating a more just world order.

The development of English School thinking about human rights is fascinating in this regard. Bull (1977: 83) argued that pluralism has had the upper hand over solidarism in the history of modern international society. Prior to the twentieth century, the solidarist belief in the primacy of individual human rights clung on, but 'underground' as if states had entered into 'a conspiracy of silence ... about the rights and duties of their respective citizens' (1977: 83). As noted earlier, many states that have thrown off imperial rule in recent decades fear that human rights law will be used as a pretext for great power interference in their internal affairs. However, the long-term trend over recent decades has been the rise of solidarist measures to promote the global protection of human rights and to disseminate liberal values (Bull 1984a; Buzan 2004).

That is the starting-point for the recently revisited argument that the right of the individual to be free from starvation and malnutrition is one human entitlement on which most states can agree despite deep political and ideological differences (Vincent 1986; see the contributions to Cox and Rengger 2011). Vincent argued that the lack of the basic means of subsistence should shock the conscience of humankind and lead to global action. Consensus on that matter would represent a significant advance in relations between the Western world (which has traditionally been concerned with order rather than justice) and the non-Western world (which has stressed the need for global justice). Vincent (1974) had argued that non-intervention is one of the foundations of international order. But in his later writings, which are often regarded as the starting-point for the solidarist turn in the English School, he observed that states are increasingly under pressure to comply with global human rights norms. Moreover, some violations might be so serious that states should consider setting aside the usual prohibition on military intervention while recognizing the need to balance 'principle and prudence' (Vincent and Wilson 1994; Linklater 2011c). Whether, and how, they should do so have been central questions since the implosion of the former Yugoslavia and the Rwandan genocide (Dunne and Wheeler 1999). The fact remains that there is no global consensus about when sovereignty can be overridden to protect human rights. However, there have been important advances in support of the principle that sovereign governments have a 'responsibility to protect' their citizens (Bellamy 2008; Evans 2008; Welsh 2011).

Divisions within the English School have echoed those differences. Dunne and Wheeler (1999) argued that the end of bipolarity made it possible for the aspiring 'good international citizen' to intervene where there is a 'supreme humanitarian emergency', even though the states involved might breach existing international law. Jackson (2000: 291ff) stressed the danger that intervention might create great power rivalries that weakened international order. If it was necessary to choose between them, preserving restraints on the use of force should therefore take priority over 'humanitarian' wars.

The 'revolt against the West' is a subject for the next section, but one of its dimensions, namely the demand for racial equality, is pertinent to this discussion. Bull (in Bull and Watson 1984) and Vincent (1984b) argued that the rejection of white supremacism has been a central feature of the transition from a European to a universal society of states. The demand for racial equality demonstrated that international order would not endure unless Third World peoples realized their aspirations for justice. International society had been remarkably agreed on the need for global action to end the evil of apartheid. That aspect of the revolt against the West adds force to Wight's point that modern international society has been unusual in making the legitimacy or illegitimacy of systems of government a matter of great moral importance for the international community (Wight 1977: 41). In the aftermath of 9/11, US concerns about tyrannical regimes in the Middle Eastern societies sought to extend such considerations, but clearly without the earlier consensus about the immorality of apartheid (Bull 1982: 266).

The revolt against white supremacism revealed that progress towards solidarism is perfectly possible, but also quite limited. As Bull (1977: 95) maintained, such advances depend on a broad consensus that change is needed to promote justice, that it will strengthen international society, and contribute to order. Crucially, they depend on the backing of the great powers which have the capacity to obstruct global action. Despite the obstacles, Watson (1987: 152) stated that Bull and he 'inclined [towards the] optimistic view' that modern states are 'consciously working out, for the first time, a set of transcultural values and ethical standards'. The growth of the human rights culture to include the responsibility to protect and recent developments in international criminal law support that view. We have to remember that societies are still in an early phase of dealing with the economic, environmental and military issues that have arisen as a result of unprecedented levels of global interconnectedness (see Chapter 6). Whether they can make further progress in such domains depends in part on how far the great powers demonstrate the requisite 'moral vision' in their foreign policy (see Bull 1983: 127–31). But crucially with the rise of world society, much depends on how far non-governmental organizations can influence public opinion and government action, and not least by altering principles of international legitimacy so that greater importance is attached to freeing humanity from unnecessary suffering (Heins 2008; also Clark 2007).

It is hard to tell whether Bull and Watson believed that the expansion of international society to include the West's former colonies would lead to greater solidarism or demonstrate that hopes for global political progress are still 'premature' (see Mayall 1996; Wheeler 2000). Pursuing the theme, Jackson (2000: 181) argued that the diverse nature of international society in the post-colonial era makes support for the pluralist image all the more essential. He contended that pluralism is the best arrangement that societies have devised thus far for reconciling the demand for political independence with the desire for order (see also Nardin 1983). Bull was perhaps equivocal on this point. The emergence of an elite 'cosmopolitan culture of modernity' was encouraging (Bull 1977: 317). However, that culture was heavily 'weighted in favour of the dominant cultures of the West' (Bull 1977: 317). More seriously, and here the increased importance of religious fundamentalism immediately comes to mind, there was clear evidence that various groups were drifting further apart. It was important to remember, Bull (1984b: 6) argued, that when Third World groups first issued demands for justice, they did so as 'supplicants' in a world dominated by the Western powers, where it was vital to use Western terms in order to elicit a sympathetic response. But the revival of indigenous cultures and the emergence of new elites in non-Western societies set new processes in motion. Many groups placed 'new interpretations' on 'Western values', and some dispensed with them entirely, thereby raising large questions about whether many of the demands issuing from non-Western groups were 'compatible with the moral ideas of the West' (Bull 1984b).

Those comments invite some remarks about the alleged coming 'clash of civilizations' that have been debated since the early to mid-1990s, and especially following the attacks on the US, Spain, Britain, Bali and so forth by Islamic terrorists (Huntington 1993). As we shall see in the next section, Bull believed in the 1980s that the great majority of new states had accepted the Western idea of international society with its principles of sovereignty and non-intervention. There is no obvious reason to depart from that conclusion. Cultural and religious differences between many Western and non-Western groups may have increased over the last 25 years, and the gulf may widen in future. However, the 'Arab Spring' is widely regarded as a rejection of 'radical Islamist' hostility to Western values, and as evidence of strong popular demands for political representation and the rule of law that augurs well for the Middle East. But it is impossible to predict how political and cultural change in post-colonial regions will affect the future of international society. Although some members such as Wight had a deep interest in the relationship between politics and religion (see Thomas 2001; Hall 2006; Jackson 2008), the English School more generally has focused most of its attention on understanding the development of a secular Western international society. A recurrent claim is that the survival of international society has depended on a consensus to keep 'faith' out of 'politics'. Whether that agreement is likely to survive in the long-run is one of the most interesting questions raised by the revolt against the West (see Phillips 2011 for an analysis of such issues from a constructivist standpoint).

The revolt against the West and the expansion of international society

The impact of the revolt against the West upon the modern society of states was a central theme in Bull and Watson's writings in the 1980s. The question was whether the diverse civilizations that had been brought together by Europe's overseas conquests have a common desire to belong to an international society as opposed to an international system. It was necessary to recall that the world of the late eighteenth century was dominated by four regional international orders (the Chinese, European, Indian and Islamic). Most 'governments in each group had a sense of being part of a common civilization' that was superior to all others (Bull and Watson 1984: 87). European states were committed to the principle of sovereign equality within their continent, but refused to extend such rights to non-Europeans. How Europeans should behave towards the colonized peoples was always a matter of dispute. Some claimed the right to enslave or exterminate them, while others defended their equal membership of the society of humankind and their entitlement to humane treatment. The dominant theories of empire in the twentieth century, as expressed in the League of Nations mandate system and in the United Nations trusteeship system maintained that the colonial powers had a moral duty to prepare non-European peoples for their eventual admission into the society of states on equal terms with the founding members (Bain 2003).

Most Europeans believed such a transition would take decades if not centuries to complete, in large part because other civilizations had to divest themselves of the hegemonial conception of international society in which they placed themselves at the centre of the world. Traditional China defined itself as the 'Middle Kingdom' which deserved tribute from other societies that were thought to be at a lower stage of cultural development. Traditional Islamic views of international relations distinguished between the House of Islam (*Dar al Islam*) and the House of War (*Dar al Harb*) – between believers and infidels – though the possibility of a temporary truce (*Dar al Suhl*) with non-Islamic powers was acknowledged. Also committed to a hegemonial view of international order, the European powers believed that societies that had yet to reach their 'standard of civilization' should be barred from international society (Gong 1984).

In short, those different civilizations belonged to an international system. With the expansion of Europe, other peoples were forced to comply with its conception of world politics. Gradually, most of those societies came to accept European principles of international society. But they only came to enjoy equal membership of that society after a long battle to weaken Europe's confidence in its moral and political superiority and to erode its belief in its right to determine their fate.

Bull (1984c: 220–4) in Bull and Watson (1984) called this process, 'the revolt against the West'. He divided it into five elements. The first was 'the struggle for equal sovereignty' undertaken by societies such as China and Japan that 'retained their formal independence' in the age of imperialism. Those societies were governed by unequal treaties 'concluded under duress'. As a result of the principle of 'extra-territoriality', they were denied the right to settle any disputes involving foreigners according to domestic law. Following the legal revolt against the West, Japan joined the society of states in 1900, Turkey in 1923, Egypt in 1936 and China in 1943.

The political revolt against the West was a second dimension of the process in which the colonies demanded freedom from imperial domination. The racial revolt which included the struggle to abolish slavery and the slave trade as well as all forms of white supremacism was the third dimension. A fourth was the economic revolt against the forms of inequality and exploitation that are inherent in a Western-dominated global commercial and financial system. The fifth revolt, the cultural revolt, was a protest against cultural imperialism, including the West's assumption that it was entitled to decide how other peoples should live, not least by globalizing liberal-individualistic conceptions of human rights. That process of 'modernization' has some of the hallmarks of the 'Requirement' – the assumption on the part of the Spanish colonists in Central and South Americas that Christians had the right to stand in judgment of other societies and to remake them in their own image (Brown 1988).

Bull maintained that the first four dimensions of the revolt of the Third World attempted to persuade the colonial powers to take their own principles seriously in their relations with non-European peoples. Together, they appeared to signify a desire to follow the Western path of economic and political development. But, as noted earlier, the cultural revolt was different because it was often 'a revolt against Western values as such' (Bull 1984c: 223) in Bull and Watson (1984). The inevitable question was whether the expansion of international society would lead to new forms of disharmony and possibly conflict. As noted earlier, the importance of that question has been underlined by the religious revolt, and specifically by radical Islamist reactions against the West, embodied in Al-Qaeda, that vigorously oppose American support for Israel, its policy of supporting what are held to be corrupt pro-Western elites in the Middle East, as well as the spread of Western secular values that they regard as incompatible with, and as a threat to, their conception of Islamic society. Significantly, the terrorist attacks on the United States were not accompanied by diplomatic demands that are invariably compromised as part of the 'give and take' of politics.

That might seem to be a new form of revolt against the West in which the use of force does not observe Clausewitz's famous dictum that war is the continuation of politics by other means, although terrorist attacks have sought to compel the US and others to withdraw from the Islamic world as well as to humiliate the enemy and to build self-respect amongst the members of a transnational faith community. 'Radical Islam' which has been the most violent form of 'revolt against the West' has been highlighted to defend the conviction that the main divisions in world politics are increasingly 'civilizational' (Huntington 1993; Holmes 2007). Such interpretations have been used to reinforce realist assumptions about the inevitability of conflict and about the need to be prepared to use force against radical challenges to core security interests. It is important to contrast that standpoint with English School orientations towards increasing cultural diversification that stress the imperative of understanding the reasons for the revolt against the West and reconstructing international society so that it is more responsive to the needs of 'post-colonial' peoples. That view of the long-term development of international society is not incompatible with support for the use of force in response to violent challenges but it emphasizes the deeper problem of building bridges between peoples through patient diplomacy. The perspective is also at odds with post-colonial thinkers who argue that international society was an instrument of colonial domination until recently, and remains suffused with distinctions between 'advanced' and 'backward' peoples that go back to the imperial era. They criticize a tendency in the English School to regard the society of states as the custodian of 'neutral' principles of co-existence, and they doubt whether it can secure the advances in global justice that Bull and others have called for (Seth 2011). Recent popular accounts of the 'revolt against the West' stress that the critique of Western values has a long history (Mishra 2012). They invite more attention than one will find in most English School writings to the non-Europeans' traumatic experience of European expansion. Post-colonial writings more generally point to the need for more sophisticated analyses of the diverse ways in which non-European societies and governments have been influenced by, incorporated within, and responded to Western modernity (Pasha 2009; Pasha 2012).

Where that revolt will lead, and what it will mean for the future of international society, will attract scholarly interest for years to come. An obvious issue is whether an agreement about the merits of the pluralist idea of international society is all that radically different cultures can accomplish, and all they should expect to attain. But even that cannot be taken for granted if, for example, radical Islamic movements in Middle Eastern societies succeed in rallying support for the conviction that the 'solidarism of faith' is far more important than observing Western concepts of sovereignty and non-intervention that developed hand-in-hand with the secularization of society. As noted earlier, the first phase of the Arab Spring did not demonstrate widespread support for the more militant forms of Islam. The main patterns of development are consistent with the view that Bull and Watson expressed in the mid-1980s that an international order that reflected the interests of non-Western states is at least partly constructed. Not that they were complacent about the nature of that society. They were adamant that it would only command the support of many non-Western peoples if radical changes took place (Bull and Watson 1984: 429). A substantial redistribution of power and wealth from North to South was essential (Bull 1977: 316–17), as was a greater openness to non-Western values. As far as the latter point is concerned, large issues arise about the extent to which international society can ensure justice between cultures (Shapcott 2001). They remain central to the most recent discussions about the 'revolt against the West' (Mishra 2012), and underline the need for closer English School engagement with the expanding post-colonial literature (Pasha 2008, 2009, 2012; Seth 2009, 2011).

Several new states have appeared as a result of the fragmentation of the Soviet bloc and the disintegration of several Third World societies in the period since Bull and Watson analysed the expansion of international society. Unforeseen problems have been created by 'failed states' such as Afghanistan and Somalia (Helman and Ratner 1992–3; also Jackson (1990) on the fact that several new states acquired 'negative sovereignty' – freedom from external interference – but they failed to achieve 'positive sovereignty' – the ability to satisfy the basic needs of their populations). Unexpected challenges have arisen because of gross violations of human rights in civil conflicts, because of regimes that are in a state of war with sections of their own population, because of chaotic or troubled regions such as Somalia and Yemen that might provide a safe haven for terrorist organizations, and because of fears that the disintegration of nuclear powers (Pakistan is often mentioned in this context but the possibility of a nuclear Iran creates the same anxieties) could deliver weapons of mass destruction into the hands of terrorist organizations. Old debates about Western intervention and about the legitimacy of foreign occupation have arisen in this context, and familiar tensions between the 'pluralist' and 'solidarist' conceptions of international society have become prominent (Roberts 1993). At this juncture, such disputes point to an international society in transition – unable to wholeheartedly embrace solidarism but incapable of moving back to what was in many ways the simpler reality of a world governed by pluralist principles (Hurrell 2002, 2007; Mayall 2000; Welsh 2011). What is clear is that Western powers no longer have a virtual monopoly of power in deciding how international society should respond to human rights violations, weapons proliferation, climate change, the management of global economic management and so forth (Hurrell 2006b). The rise of new centres of power such as China, India and Brazil represents a new stage in the evolution of the society of states that was born in Europe and which was – although this is now changing – dominated by the West. With respect to the question of order and justice, on some accounts, a new era of 'post-colonial donors' may be emerging in which development assistance does not depend on 'civilizational hierarchies' based on old distinctions between the 'modern North' and the 'pre-modern South'; support for the pluralist conception of international society may check the temptation to echo the West in demanding that the recipients follow the path taken by the allegedly most civilized peoples (Vieira 2012). But much will depend on how new centres of power resolve tensions between 'developing country' and 'aspiring great power' identities (Hurrell 2006b: 19).

Progress in international relations

Quite how far progress in world politics is possible is one of the most intriguing questions in International Relations. Wight (1966b: 26) maintained that the international system is 'the realm of recurrence and repetition', a formulation that can also be found in Waltz's classic statement of neo-realism (Waltz 1979: 66). The argument of this chapter is that the English School points to limited progress in the shape of agreements about how to maintain order and, to a lesser degree, about how to promote global justice. Bull's writings often suggested that order is prior to justice, not least because states find it easier to agree on basic principles of co-existence. On those occasions, Bull seems to be aligned with what Wight described as the 'realist' wing of rationalism but, elsewhere, he is closer to its 'idealist' side (Wight 1991: 59). Towards the end of his life, Bull seemed more sympathetic to the solidarist point of view and stimulated important reflections on the prospects for internationalism and the significance of world society (see Dunne 1998: chapter 7; Buzan 2004).

That shift is most pronounced in the Hagey Lectures delivered at the University of Waterloo in Canada in 1983 (Bull 1984b). It is illustrated by the comment that 'the idea of sovereign rights existing apart from the rules laid down by international society itself and enjoyed without qualification has to be rejected in principle'; that was because 'the idea of the rights and duties of the individual person has come to have a place, albeit an insecure one' within the society of states 'and it is our responsibility to seek to extend it' (Bull 1984b: 11–12). The 'moral concern with welfare on a world scale' was evidence of a 'growth of ... cosmopolitan moral awareness' which represented 'a major change in our sensibilities' (1984b: 13). With the evolving global agenda, it was essential that states became the 'local agents of a world common good' (1984b: 14). Such ideas have lost none of their importance in a period in which international society has struggled to reach a consensus on how to deal with global environmental politics, a sphere that the English School has largely neglected with the notable exception of Hurrell (1994; 2006b; 2007: chapter 9).

It would be a mistake to suggest that Bull had come to think that solutions to global problems would be any easier to find, or that the point would soon be reached where states would no longer face 'terrible choices' (1984b: 14). Scepticism invariably blunted the visionary impulse. That is evident from his observation that new, post-sovereign political institutions and loyalties might yet develop in Western Europe, but such a world would not be free from danger. Medieval international society, with its complex structure of overlapping jurisdictions and multiple loyalties, had been more violent than the modern states-system (Bull 1977: 255, 267). Bull (1979b) therefore advanced a qualified defence of the society of states which emphasized that most states play a 'positive role in world affairs'. Despite its numerous defects, international society was unlikely to be bettered by any other form of world political organization in the foreseeable future.

We have considered how the English School differs from realism, but it is also necessary to consider its assessment of 'revolutionism' and the criticisms of international society that have been advanced by advocates of that perspective. Bull (1977: 22) argued that the essence of that doctrine can be found in the Kantian belief in 'a horizontal conflict of ideology that cuts across the boundaries of states and divides human society into two camps – the trustees of the immanent community of mankind and those who stand in its way, those who are of the true faith and the heretics, the liberators and the oppressed'. He believed that the Kantian conception of world politics held that diplomatic conventions should be swept to one side in the quest to unify humanity. 'Good faith with heretics' had no intrinsic merits; it had no more than 'tactical convenience' because 'between the elect and the damned, the liberators and the oppressed, the question of mutual acceptance of rights to sovereignty or independence does not arise' (1977:24).

Such orientations have been present in, for example, the relationship between the US and the threat posed by Al-Qaeda, but they have little to do with Kant's thought (Hoffmann 1990: 23–4). Indeed, for all his cosmopolitanism (which included his belief in a duty of hospitality to strangers and the conviction that peoples should cooperate to promote international law and world peace), Kant defended a society of sovereign states based on principles of sovereignty and non-intervention. What troubled English School thinkers such as Bull and Wight was the 'revolutionist' belief that peace or order cannot exist until all societies share the same ideology – a belief that Wight (1991: 421–2) wrongly imputed to Kant (see MacMillan 1995). That concern was also evident in the earlier realist critique of the dangers of crusading mentalities in world politics (Chapter 3). Common to realism and the English School is a fear of proponents of ideologies that are intolerant of different views, and impatient to remove the imperfections of international society by force if necessary. All those sentiments were supposedly present in Kant's revolutionism, but the reality was rather different (see Linklater and Suganami 2006: chapter 5).

Wight stressed that 'rationalism' overlapped with realism and revolutionism. We have seen one point of convergence between realism and the English School. A degree of overlap between the English School and revolutionism can also be found in Wight's lectures where he compared

Kant to the rationalist who was, first and foremost, 'a reformist, the practitioner of piecemeal social engineering' (Wight 1991: 29). The principal works of the English School shied away from visions of how humanity should be organized: there was a certain reluctance to engage with what has come to known as global ethics and international political theory (see however Vincent 1986; also Chapter 11). Bull spoke for many in the English School when he maintained that there was no reason to think that political philosophers will succeed where diplomats have repeatedly failed, namely in identifying moral principles which all or most societies can regard as the foundation for an improved international order. On the other hand, a basic humanism informed Bull's argument that international order must be judged by what it contributes to the lives of individual people, as well as Wight's claim that the function of politics is to promote order and security 'from which law, justice and prosperity may afterwards develop'; it is evident in the thesis that, despite noble intentions, the advocates of humanitarian intervention may increase suffering that could have been avoided by the prudent reliance on the tried and tested conventions in international relations that often seem disappointing from a 'utopian' point of view (Bain 2003; Jackson 2000). A concern with what Dunne and Wheeler (1999) have called 'suffering humanity' runs through English School approaches, whether pluralist or solidarist, whether supportive of efforts to embed a principle of humanitarian intervention in international society or opposed to it, and whether keen to defend human rights or quick to stress the danger that cosmopolitan projects will become entangled in interstate struggles for power and prestige.

Before concluding this section, it is useful to consider how the English School stands in relation to some other branches of international relations theory. There is a clear parallel between the English School analysis of international society and neo-liberal institutionalist empirical theories of cooperation in the context of anarchy. However, members of the English School have not followed neo-liberal institutionalists by using game theory to explain how cooperation can exist between rational egotists (Keohane 1989a). In general orientation, they are closer to constructivists but they have not shared their interest in epistemological and methodological issues, an omission has been described as explaining a certain confusion in the US about its research programme (Finnemore 2001; also Buzan 2004; Linklater and Suganami 2006: part one; and Chapter 8 below). Members of the English School agree with the notion that anarchy is 'what states make of it' (Wendt 1992). They share the belief that sovereignty is not an unchanging reality but has acquired different meanings in accordance with shifting ideas about, for example, the place of human rights in international society. As Bull argued, states can create an international system or an international society out of anarchy, and in more stable times they may be able to make some progress in building support for principles of justice (see also Wight 1977 and Reus-Smit 1999). Nothing is pre-ordained here; everything depends on how states think of themselves as separate political communities, how they understand their rights against, and duties to, the rest of humanity, and how far they are prepared to use diplomacy, patiently and prudently, to discover common ground. That is why the English School has been especially interested in the legal and moral dimensions of world politics, why constructivist discussions of global norms and international legitimacy have special relevance for English School inquiry, and why the 'international society approach' has much to offer constructivist scholarship (Edelman 1990; Clark 2005, 2007; Clark and Reus-Smit 2007; Raymond 1997).

The idea of 'critical international society', as defended by Dunne and Wheeler, has made important connections between critical theory and the English School (see also Heins 2008: Introduction). But in the main, English School writers have been sceptical of partisan social inquiry, arguing that attempts to understand world politics should strive for detachment from moral and political standpoints. For their part, critical theorists of different persuasions have drawn extensively on the English School's contribution (see Der Derian 1987; Linklater 1998, 2011b). Certainly, Wight's lectures contain a wealth of insight on questions of cultural diversity in international politics that have been central to post-structuralist and post-colonial inquiry (Wight 1991). Analyses of the expansion of international society and the development of world society may be incomplete without a discussion of the principles that should be used to assess global arrangements that can be found in the literature on international political theory and global ethics. With some notable exceptions, members of the English School have not been especially active in that area (Williams 2006; Dunne 2008). It probably remains the case that the majority share Bull's standpoint that the task is to understand international society rather than reflect on how to change it. To that end they have been especially active in studying the history of political thought (see Chapter 12).

The English School has devoted most attention to the 'diplomatic dialogue' between states (Watson 1982), noting in particular its importance for restraining force, promoting understanding between different cultures, resolving major political differences and examining the prospects for cooperation and for promoting global justice. How international society should be organized has been less important than considering how that diplomatic community has developed, and examining what it has achieved in the way of taming the competition for power and security, as well as in bridging cultural differences and responding to the demands of the 'have-nots' in international society. Through such inquiries, the English School continues to develop its unique contribution to the study of world politics.

Conclusion

In *The Twenty Years' Crisis 1919–1939*, E. H. Carr (1939/1945/1946: 12) argued that international theory should avoid the 'sterility' of realism and the 'naivety' of idealism. The English School can claim to have passed that test of an effective international theory. Its members have analysed elements of society and civility which have been of little interest to realists and neo-realists. Although they have been principally concerned with understanding international order, the English School has also considered the prospects for global justice. Few of its members are persuaded by utopian or revolutionist arguments which maintain that states can settle their most basic differences about morality and justice. That is the key to the claim that the English School is the *via media* between realism and revolutionism.

The English School argues that international society is a precarious achievement whose survival is far from guaranteed, and it stresses that, without it, more radical political developments are unlikely to take place. It is to be expected that there will always be two sides to the English School: the realist side that is quick to detect threats to international society and the more cosmopolitan side that identifies possibilities for making that society more responsive to the needs of the weak and vulnerable. The relationship between those different orientations will continue to change in response to historical circumstances. The Cold War years did little to encourage forward-looking interpretations of world order. The passing of bipolarity was more conducive to the development of solidarism. Developments in the immediate aftermath of 9/11 showed how the resurgence of national security politics can quickly weaken restraints on military force. Fears about the proliferation of weapons of mass destruction have raised the question of whether a new phase of geo-political rivalry is emerging. Of growing importance is the question of how new centres of power such as China, India and Brazil will transform international society in the 'post-colonial' or 'post-Western' era. Whatever the future holds, the ideas of 'system', 'society' and 'community' which are central to the study of the diplomatic dialogue will provide analysts with important conceptual tools for understanding continuity and change in world politics.

5 | Marx and Marxism

ANDREW LINKLATER

In the mid-1840s Marx and Engels wrote that capitalist globalization was transforming the international states-system. They believed that conflict and competition between nation-states had yet to come to an end, but the main fault-line in the future would revolve around the divisions between the two dominant social classes: the national bourgeoisie in each country and an increasingly international proletariat. The outline of a new social experiment based on the Enlightenment ideals of liberty, equality and fraternity was already contained within the most advanced political movements of the industrial working class. Through revolutionary action, the international proletariat would embed those ideals in a form of global cooperation that would free all human beings from poverty, exploitation and oppression (Marx and Engels 1977).

Many traditional theorists of international relations have stressed the failings of Marxism or the 'materialist interpretation of history'. Marxism has been the foil for realist arguments that international politics have long revolved around power struggles between independent political communities that will continue well into the future. In particular, Kenneth Waltz argued that Marxism was a 'second-image' account of international relations which believed that the rise of socialist *regimes* would eliminate conflict between states. Its utopian aspirations were dashed by the struggle for power and security which is inherent in international anarchy – the subject of what Waltz (1959; 1979) called 'third-image' analysis. English School thinkers such as Martin Wight maintained that Lenin's *Imperialism: The Highest Stage of Capitalism* (1916) might appear to be a study of international politics, but it was too preoccupied with the economic aspects of human affairs to be regarded as a serious contribution to the field (Wight 1966a). Marxists had underestimated the crucial importance of nationalism, the state, geo-politics and war, and the role of the balance of power, international law and diplomacy in world politics.

New interpretations of Marxism have appeared since the 1980s: the perspective has been an important weapon in the critique of realism, and there have been many innovative attempts to harness its ideas to develop a more complex, political economy approach to international relations where the aim is to understand the interplay between states and markets, the states-system and the capitalist world economy, power and production (Ayers 2008; Bieler and Morton 2006; Cox 1981; 1983; Gill 1993a; 2003; Halliday 1994; Rosenberg 1994, 2000; Teschke 2003, van der Pijl 2007, 2010). Mediated by the Frankfurt School, its impact on critical international theory has also been immense (see Chapter 6). For some, the collapse of the Soviet Union and the triumph of capitalism marked the death of Marxism. But in the 1990s, a number of scholars argued that the relevance of Marxism had increased with the passing of bipolarity and with accelerating economic globalization (Gamble 1999). A biography of Marx in the late 1990s argued that his analysis of how capitalism had broken down Chinese walls and unified the human race finally came of age with the collapse of the Soviet Union (Wheen 1999). For others, the resurgence of national security politics since 9/11, coupled with the increasing importance of religion in international affairs, provided a reminder that Marxism has little grip on the most basic realities of international politics. In American IR – matters are different in Europe where the 'Left Academy' has always been stronger – the mood shifted from the 'mild' resistance to Marxism of the Cold War years to the condition in which it 'virtually disappeared as a serious strand of academic inquiry' (Falk 1999: 37). But historical materialism remains an important strand of thought in Canada, especially because of the writings of Robert Cox and Stephen Gill, and in Britain, particularly as a result of the contributions of Rosenberg, Teschke and van der Pijl.

Since Marx's writings in the 1840s, the main strength of historical materialism has been its analysis of how capitalism has become the dominant system of production world-wide. The recent global financial crisis has provided a salutary reminder of the power of global capital and the need for historical-materialist explorations of the relationship between states and capitalism, or between government, society and the 'financial aristocracy'. Many Marxists conceded in the 1970s and 1980s that materialist approaches had paid insufficient attention to the nation-state and violence in the modern world. Since then, few have kept faith with Marx's belief that the triumph of capitalism would be short-lived, or subscribed to his belief that inexorable laws would lead to its destruction and replacement by Communism. But the financial crisis has borne out Marx's contention that unregulated capitalism is prone to, and will undergo, crises that have major consequences for society and politics. The global financial crisis has breathed new life into historical materialism which may only increase in importance in the years ahead, particularly in societies where the influence of the Left Academy continues to be strong.

Interesting questions have also been raised by the reality that modern forms of globalization have been accompanied by renewed ethnic violence and national fragmentation. Insightful though they were about the advance of capitalist globalization and growing economic inequalities, Marx and Engels did not foresee the influential role that nationalism would play in the coming decades. Marxists such as Lenin argued that globalization and national fragmentation are two consequences of the spread of the capitalist mode of production. Perspectives such as dependency theory and world-systems theory, which will be considered later in this chapter, have offered complex accounts of the transformative role of the spread of capitalism to all regions of the world over the last few centuries. Furthermore, particular Marxist writers such as Gramsci have been major influences on attempts over the past 25 years to understand the nature of global hegemony and counter-hegemonic struggles not only in the conventional core areas of the world economic and political systems but also in regions that were once regarded as the inconsequential periphery (Cox 1983).

For the moment, it is necessary to set aside the question of how far classical Marxism ignored geo-political competition and war, and ask whether mainstream approaches to IR have been wrong to ignore or dismiss Marxist analyses of capitalist globalization. It is also important to consider whether its project of constructing a critical theory of global politics is one respect in which Marxism advanced beyond the dominant Anglo-American approaches to international relations (see Chapter 7). It is worth recalling that, in the 1930s, members of the Frankfurt School maintained that the challenge for the social sciences was to preserve the 'spirit' but not the 'letter' of classical Marxism (Friedman 1981: 35–6). Although his work over approximately the past 30 years has had little direct connection with Marxism, Habermas famously called for the 'reconstruction of historical materialism', for preserving the strengths and cancelling the weakness of Marxist scholarship (Linklater 1990a; see also Chapter 6). Researchers that draw on the historical-materialist perspective continue to explore ways of reconstructing its approach to politics and history in order to cast light on structures and processes that are neglected by mainstream approaches to the field. As noted, a recurrent tendency in the mainstream is to analyse the international states-system in isolation, and neglect to examine its relationship with the development of industrial capitalism. The great exception was E. H. Carr's Marxian-inspired analysis of the interplay between the economic crisis of the 1920s and 1930s, the rise of violent nationalism, and the increased tolerance of force to settle great power differences (see Carr 1945).

It is impossible to discuss the varieties of Marxism in a short chapter which surveys the significance of historical materialism for International

Relations (see Joseph 2006 for a broad-ranging survey of Marxist perspectives). The approach taken here begins by describing the main features of historical materialism and by explaining how international relations were discussed within that framework. Section two summarizes key themes in the Marxist analysis of nationalism and imperialism. Those sections on the history of Marxist ideas are followed by a brief overview of the orthodox critique of Marxism in International Relations and its rehabilitation since the 1980s as political economy and critical theory became central to debates. The final section evaluates the Marxist tradition in the light of recent developments in international relations theory.

Class, production and international relations in Marx's writings

One of Marx's ambitions was to provide an overview of the history of human development from the earliest phases of social existence to the contemporary era. Human history, he argued, had been a laborious struggle to satisfy basic material needs, to understand and tame nature, to resist class domination and exploitation, and to overcome fear and distrust of other communities. Societies had succeeded in mastering hostile natural forces that had once been beyond their understanding and control. They had transformed their relationship with the physical environment with the result that it had become possible to imagine a world in which there is no material scarcity. But Marx's view was that human history, and specifically since the rise of capitalism, had unfolded in a tragic manner. Power over nature had increased to unprecedented levels, but individuals were trapped within a global division of labour, exposed to unregulated market forces, and exploited by new forms of factory production that turned workers into 'appendages to the machine' (Marx 1977a: 477). Marx also maintained that capitalism had produced levels of global interconnectedness that removed many of the cultural differences between societies. Nationalism, he observed, had little or no place in the political imagination of the international proletariat. But capitalism was a system of largely unchecked human exploitation in which the bourgeoisie controlled and profited from the labour-power of the subordinate classes. It was the root cause of an alienating condition in which the human species – the bourgeoisie as well as the proletariat – was at the mercy of global structures and forces which it had created, but not in a planned way. Crucially, the point was not only to describe those conditions with maximum detachment. Marx (1977b: 158) wrote that philosophers had interpreted the world; the point was to change it. An end to alienation, exploitation and estrangement was the ideal that drove the attempt to understand the laws of capitalism and the course of human history. This concern with human emancipation is a major part of the Marxist legacy that recent critical approaches to international relations continue to develop.

Marx believed that the historical role of the forces of production (technology) and the relations of production (class relations) had been neglected by the Hegelian movement with which he was allied in his formative intellectual years. Hegel had focused on the evolution of the forms of self-consciousness (political, historical, religious and so forth) that the species had experienced in the course of coming to understand more about itself. After his death, the Left Hegelians criticized religion, believing it was a form of 'false consciousness' that prevented humans from comprehending what they are and can become. For Marx, religious belief was not an intellectual error that had to be corrected by philosophical analysis but an expression of the frustrations and aspirations of people in their struggles with the material conditions of everyday life. Religion was 'the opium of the masses' – the 'sigh of an oppressed creature' (Marx 1977c: 64). Revolutionaries had to understand and challenge the social conditions that generated the need for religious solace. The 'critique of heaven', as Marx put it, had to evolve into 'the critique of earth' (1977c).

Here it might be added that Marx was wedded to the belief that the long-term trend in human history was towards the secularization of society, a conviction that seems obsolete given the recent religious revival. Perhaps the failings of Marxism as a secular theory should be added to those listed earlier – although questions always arise about how far religious beliefs should be regarded as a response to economic and political frustrations, as Marx had emphasized. Those who believe that the religious revival amounts to a return to the ignorance and superstition that the Enlightenment looked certain to overcome need look no further than Marx's writings for support. Those who think that religion satisfies spiritual needs that are quintessentially human will find the Marxist belief in the ideal of secularization entirely alien to their beliefs. That is not to imply that all forms of Marxism have been antagonistic to religion. Liberation theology in Latin America, for instance, sought to combine Marxism and Christianity in the struggle against oppression.

The pivotal theme in the materialist conception of history is that people must satisfy their most basic physical needs before they can do anything else. In short, humans have bodies that need to be sustained through labour, or through profiting from the labour of others. The main practical consequence is that for millennia the mass of humanity has had to surrender control of its labour-power simply to survive. Those who owned the means of production – feudal lords, slave-owners, factory owners and so on – have exploited subordinate classes but that has often led to class conflict in the form of slave revolts, peasant rebellions and working-class struggles in more recent times. Class struggle for Marx had been the principal form of conflict in human history. Political revolution had been the agent of historical development; technological innovation had been the driving force behind social change.

Marx (1977d: 105) wrote that history was the continuous transformation of human nature. Put differently, humans have not only modified the natural world by working on it; they have also changed themselves, acquiring new needs and aspirations in the process. From that perspective, the history of the species could be understood by tracing the development of different modes of production which, in the West, included primitive communism, slave societies, feudalism and capitalism, soon to be replaced – so Marx thought – by socialism on a world scale. The fact that Marx believed that socialism would be a global phenomenon deserves further comment. War, imperialism and commerce had destroyed the isolation of the earliest societies, but capitalism forced all social systems within a single stream of universal history and made them aware of their global interconnectedness. Few mainstream students of international relations have recognized the importance of this interest in the economic and technological unification of the human species that has been central to recent accounts of globalization, which historical materialists have criticized because they overlook the forms of power and inequality that are inherent in what should be the object of analysis – the process of *capitalist* globalization that has been spearheaded by dominant class forces in association with powerful states (see Halliday 1988a; Gill 1993a; Lacher 2006: chapter 1; Rosenberg 2000). One might also note how Marxist concerns with such long-term processes that have affected humanity as a whole have parallels in contemporary approaches to world history and international relations (see Chapter 7).

In his reflections on capitalism, Marx argued that universal history came into being when the social relations of production and exchange became global and when more cosmopolitan tastes emerged, as illustrated by the desire to consume the products of distant societies and to enjoy an emergent 'world literature'. But the forces that unified humanity also prevented the rise of universal solidarity by pitting members of the bourgeoisie against the proletariat, and by forcing members of the working class to compete for scarce employment. Marx's belief was that new forms of solidarity between the exploited classes were emerging as part of the resistance to growing inequalities, and because of the disjuncture between the extraordinary wealth that capitalism produced and the poverty of individual lives. International working class solidarity was triggered by the remarkable way in which capitalist societies used the language of freedom and equality to justify their existence, while systematically denying real freedom and equality to subordinate classes.

Large normative claims are raised by the question of what it means to be truly free and equal. In general, Marx and Engels were dismissive of the study of ethics, but they were far from dispassionate in their analysis of industrial capitalism (Lukes 1985; Brown 1992b; Rengger 2008). Indeed, Marx's own purpose was made clear in *The Eighteenth Brumaire of Louis Bonaparte* where he wrote that people make their history but not under conditions of their own choosing (Marx 1977e: 300). His point was that they create their history because they possess the power of self-determination, which other species either do not have or cannot exercise to the same degree, and yet people cannot make history just as they please because class structures exploit them and constrain their freedom of action. A distinctive political project is contained within that observation, namely building the conditions in which people gain control over unregulated processes and make more of their history – global history in the modern era – under conditions they have chosen for themselves.

Although Marx rejected Hegel's study of history and politics, he kept faith with one of Hegel's central themes which is that, in the course of their history, people acquire a deeper appreciation of what it means to be free and a better understanding of how society must be changed to promote freedom. In line with his belief that history revolves around the labour process, Marx observed that freedom and equality under capitalism meant that members of the bourgeoisie and the proletariat entered into labour contracts as legal equals, but power asymmetries placed workers at the mercy of the bourgeoisie, and exposed them to the effects of growing inequalities and the disastrous effects of periodic capitalist economic crises. He held the view that proletarian organizations understood that socialist planning was necessary to realize the ideals of freedom and equality that capitalist societies defended. Marx's condemnation of capitalism has to be seen in that light. The critique of the capitalist order rested on a distinctive methodology that was derived from Hegel's writings and focused on the tensions and contradictions within any society that may lead to its destruction and to the emergence of new ways of life.

The society in question was no longer national but global in scope. Marx shared Kant's conviction that efforts to realize freedom within sovereign states were ultimately futile since they could be undermined in a moment by external events. For Kant, war was the dominant threat to the creation of the perfect society; hence his belief in the priority of working for perpetual peace. For Marx, global capitalist crisis was the main danger, and the reason for rejecting what would later be known as 'social-ism in one country'. Human freedom could be only achieved by universal cooperation to re-make world society as a whole. The fascination with globalization and its political effects is one reason why Marx had little to say about relations between states. Marx and Engels (the latter had a keen interest in strategy and war) were perfectly aware of the role of geo-poli-tics in human history. They knew that war and conquest had forced social groups into ever larger political associations, but their main goal was to understand the role that capitalism had played in creating global social and political relations, the assumption being that capitalism would not last forever but would be destroyed by internal crises and contradictions. For that reason, some have referred to the 'geo-political deficiency' in the foundational writings and, specifically to the failure to explain *'why* polit-ical power constitutes itself territorially in the shape of a world system of multiple sovereign states and *how* the dynamics between these political jurisdictions relate to the national and international reproduction of capi-talism' (Teschke 2008: 166; also Lacher 2006).

Some of the most striking passages in Marx and Engels' writings predicted the rising levels of human interconnectedness that have appeared in recent decades. The essence of capitalism was to 'strive to tear down every barrier to intercourse', to 'conquer the whole earth for its market', and to annihilate the tyranny of distance by reducing 'to a minimum the time spent in motion from one place to another' (Marx 1973: 539). In a classic passage in *The Communist Manifesto,* Marx and Engels claimed that:

> The bourgeoisie has through its exploitation of the world market given a cosmopolitan character to production and consumption in every country ... All old-fashioned national industries have been destroyed or are daily being destroyed ... In place of the old wants, satisfied by the productions of the country, we find new wants, requir-ing for their satisfaction the products of different lands and climes. In place of the old local and national seclusion and self-sufficiency, we have [the] universal interdependence of nations ... The bourgeoisie, by the rapid improvement of all instruments of production, by the immensely facilitated means of communication, draws all, even the most barbarian nations, into civilisation. The cheap prices of its commodities are the heavy artillery with which it batters down all Chinese walls, with which it forces the barbarians' intensely obstinate hatred of foreigners to capitulate. It compels all nations, on pain of extinction, to adopt the bourgeois mode of production ... i.e. to become bourgeois themselves. In one word, it creates a world after its own image. (Marx and Engels 1977: 224–5)

As noted earlier, that remarkably prescient statement had clear implications for revolutionary strategy. The sense of 'nationality' might already be 'dead' among the enlightened proletariat, but national bourgeoisies remained in control of state structures, and used nationalism to dampen down class conflict. Marx and Engels believed that each proletariat would first have to settle scores with its own national bourgeoisie, but revolutionary struggle would be national only in form. The capture of state power was a stepping-stone to realizing cosmopolitan ideals (1977: 230, 235).

Realists such as Waltz have argued that, at the outbreak of World War I, national proletariats realized that they had more in common with their bourgeoisies than with each other. The realist argument was that no-one with an understanding of nationalism, the state and war should have been remotely surprised, yet many socialists were astonished by divisions between Europe's working classes. For realists, the failure to anticipate that outcome demonstrates the central flaw in Marxism – its economic reductionism, as manifested in the belief that capitalism is the key to understanding the nature of the modern world (Waltz 1959). That is one of the most influential interpretations of Marxism in International Relations. There are three points to make about it.

Marx and Engels were amongst the first thinkers to reflect on the new era of rapid economic and social globalization. They believed that class conflict within particular nation-states would trigger the decisive revolutions of the time that would spread quickly, so they believed, from the region in which they first erupted to all other capitalist societies. It has been pointed out that the relatively peaceful international system in the middle of the nineteenth century encouraged such beliefs. Theories of the state and war were replaced by theories of society and the economy (Gallie 1978). Reflecting that shift in political thought, Marx (1973: 109) argued that relations between states were undoubtedly important but of 'secondary' or 'tertiary' importance compared with the dynamics of the capitalist system of production. In a letter to Annenkov, he asked whether 'the whole organisation of nations, and all their international relations [is] anything else than the expression of a particular division of labour. And must not these change when the division of labour changes?' (Marx 1966: 159). That is a question rather than an answer, and a rhetorical one perhaps. It might be regarded as evidence that realists have been correct to stress that historical materialism casts no light on international politics because of its economic reductionism. But on another level, Marx's point is instructive. Relations between states have their own autonomy, or relative autonomy, but one cannot understand them in long-term perspective without taking account of larger patterns of change that include economic development and technological innovation. But the analysis of the interplay between those phenomena across the generations is largely absent from mainstream approaches to international relations.

Second, Marx and Engels reconsidered their ideas about the impending demise of the nation in response to the power of nationalist sentiments during the 1848 revolutions. They wrote that the Irish and the Poles were the victims of national rather than class domination, and they added that freedom from national oppression was critical if a world-wide proletarian organization was to develop (Marx and Engels 1971; Benner 1995). They took account of the persistence of national animosities while remaining convinced that national differences would probably decline and even disappear over the coming decades or centuries (Halliday 1999: 79). The end of the long peace that developed after the Napoleonic wars led to other adjustments to their position. Stressing the role of force throughout human history, Engels predicted unprecedented violence and suffering in the next major European war, and thought that military competition rather than capitalist crisis might be the spark that ignited the long-awaited proletarian revolution. Interestingly, Engels recognized that the possibility of major war meant that the socialist movement had to be seen to take matters of national security and the defence of the homeland seriously (Gallie 1978; also Carr 1953).

Third, as Gallie (1978) has noted, those intriguing comments about nationalism, the state and war did not lead Marx and Engels to rework their early statements about the explanatory power of historical materialism. An unhelpful distinction between the economic base of society and the legal, political and ideological superstructure remained central to summaries of the perspective. Too often, the state was regarded as little more than an instrument of the ruling class, although it was realized that, in some circumstances, it could acquire significant autonomy from the dominant class forces. Marx and Engels' political writings revealed greater subtlety than their summations of historical materialism ever did. The latter continued to regard class and production as central, to claim that economic power is the dominant form of power in society, and to reduce the emancipatory project to the liberation of the working class that would occur with the transition from capitalism to socialism.

Marx's analysis of modern capitalism is exemplary because it considered the emergence of that revolutionary mode of production in very long-term perspective. Similarly long-term standpoints that regard contemporary realities as the product of patterns of change that stretch back over many centuries or millennia are uncommon in International Relations – and the link with an interest in the emancipation of humanity as a whole from needless suffering is very rare indeed. However, the preoccupation with class exploitation obscured other forms of domination and exploitation that critical social theory should address. They include racial and gender-based oppression. Others were left with the challenge of re-orientating critical social analysis. Something of the kind is evident in Austro-Marxist writings that provided a richer inquiry into the relationship between nationalism and globalization. In the early part of the twentieth century, Karl Renner and Otto Bauer contended that Marx and Engels had seriously underestimated the importance of cultural differences in human history, the enduring appeal of national loyalties, and the need to develop a socialist vision that would satisfy demands for national-cultural autonomy (Bottomore and Goode 1978). Whereas Marx and Engels had been vague about whether national differences would endure in post-capitalist societies, the Austro-Marxists were clear that cultural differences should survive and indeed flourish under socialism. They offered a broader conception of human emancipation that was anchored in a more complex sociology of the relationship between class loyalties and national identities.

Those were controversial ideas that clashed with the socialist doctrine that emerged in Soviet Russia under Lenin and Stalin; however, they indicated one way of reworking the spirit of Marxism that continues to this day (see in particular van der Pijl 2007, 2010). With the rise of Marxism–Leninism, the various anomalies and contradictions within the Marxist tradition were lost in a doctrinaire system of supposed scientific truths; the latent possibilities for developing a more sophisticated understanding of society and politics were not explored (Gouldner 1980). It would be several decades before 'Western Marxism' would release historical materialism from the stifling effect of the Soviet period (Anderson 1983).

Theories of nationalism and imperialism

Marx and Engels' writings raised key questions about the tensions between centrifugal and centripetal forces in the modern world, and they began to grapple with the peculiar paradox that human societies were becoming more closely interconnected, and indeed internationalist to a degree, and yet national loyalties were often untouched by those changes. Assumptions about how capitalist globalization would be replaced by socialist internationalism had to be rethought as a result of the increased importance of nationalism and geo-political rivalries in the late nineteenth century. The theory of capitalist imperialism should be seen in that light.

Lenin (1968) and Bukharin (1972) developed a distinctive explanation of the causes of World War I. They argued that the conflict was the result of a desperate need for new outlets for surplus capital that had been accumulated by the leading capitalist societies. The approach has been largely discredited on familiar grounds – for assuming the primacy of economic forces. But, despite its flaws, it was an attempt to understand how political communities became more violently nationalistic in that period – a necessary preoccupation given the earlier confidence that the dominant historical trend was towards closer cooperation between national proletariats (Linklater 1990a: chapter 4).

The theory of capitalist imperialism remains interesting as an attempt to develop a more complex historical-materialist interpretation of globalization and nationalism, capitalism and warfare. A central aim was to criticize the liberal proposition that industrial capitalism was committed to free trade internationalism that would bring an end to war. The analysis combined the Marxian claim that capitalism was destined to experience frequent crises with the observation that such instabilities led not only to class conflict but also to dangerous international rivalries. (It is worth pausing to note that in the 1930s Carr drew the conclusion that global market forces had be brought under control so that future disturbances did not result in the dissolution of international order.) Lenin and Bukharin maintained that the dominant tendency of the era was the rise of new mercantilist states that were willing to use force to achieve their economic and political objectives. National accumulations of surplus capital were regarded as the main reason for the demise of a relatively peaceful international system, but Lenin did at least recognize that the decline of British hegemony and the changing balance of military power contributed to the relaxation of constraints on the use of force in relations between societies.

Lenin and Bukharin maintained that nationalist and militarist ideologies had blurred class loyalties and stymied class conflict in that changing environment. In *Imperialism: The Highest Stage of Capitalism*, Lenin (1968: 102) claimed that no 'Chinese wall separates the [working class] from the other classes'. Indeed, a labour aristocracy bribed by colonial profits and closely aligned with the bourgeoisie had developed in monopoly capitalist societies. With the outbreak of World War I, the working classes, which had become 'chained to the chariot of … bourgeois state power', were quick to answer the nationalist call to defend the homeland (Bukharin 1972: 166). It was assumed, however, that the shift of the 'centre of gravity' from class conflict to inter-state rivalry would not last indefinitely. The horrors of war would reveal that the working classes' 'share in the imperialist policy [was] nothing compared with the wounds inflicted' by it (1972: 167). Instead of 'clinging to the narrowness of the national state', and succumbing to the patriotic ideal of 'defending or extending the boundaries of the bourgeois state', the proletariat would finally resume its mission of 'abolishing state boundaries and merging all the peoples into one Socialist family' (1972: 167).

Few now support the theory of capitalist imperialism, but it had the virtue of focusing on the tensions between globalization and fragmentation in world politics. That theme (which has been important in the social sciences over recent decades) was central to Lenin's thought:

> Developing capitalism knows two historical tendencies in the national question. The first is the awakening of national life and national movements, the struggle against all national oppression, and the creation of national states. The second is the development and growing frequency of international intercourse in every form, the breakdown of national barriers, the creation of the international unity of capital, of economic life in general, of politics, science, etc. (Lenin 1964: 27)

It is useful to compare that passage with Marx's observation about the relationship between global capitalism and cosmopolitanism (see page 120), and not least because it foreshadowed neo-Marxist analyses of the uneven development of the capitalist world economy, as well as Marxist studies of how capitalism takes different forms in different parts of the world (Morton 2007). The contention that globalization and fragmentation advance in tandem was central to Lenin's account of how capitalism spreads unevenly across the world. That theme was taken further by Trotsky in his discussion of the 'combined and uneven development' of capitalism, and by what came to be known as Third World Marxism (Knei-Paz 1978). That account of how elements of capitalist and precapitalist social relations have been fused in many parts of the non-Western world is the starting-point for one important historical-materialist explanation of long-term processes of change in international relations that draws explicitly on Trotsky's perspective on social and political change (Rosenberg 2006, 2007; also Morton 2007, and Linklater 1990a: chapter 4, on the emergence of Third World Marxist analyses of the relationship between distinctive forms of capitalism and autonomous state structures in post-colonial societies). Moreover, the idea of the 'labour aristocracy' introduced a theme that would become fundamental to neo-Marxist dependency theory and world-systems analysis. The contention was that the proletariat in capitalist societies was as implicated as the bourgeoisie in exploiting peripheral peoples in the global capitalist system. Subordinated peoples across the world endeavoured to escape economic exploitation not by forging alliances with the Western proletariats but by embracing the politics of national independence. The question for Marxists (who were in the main hostile to, or suspicious of, nationalism) was how far, and whether, Marxism should regard nationalist movements as a worthy ally in the struggle for universal emancipation.

Lenin recognized that particular groups such as the Jews were oppressed because of their religion or ethnicity, and that demands for national self-determination were hardly surprising. Although he believed that socialists should support progressive national movements, he rejected the Austro-Marxists' suggested solution to the 'national question'. They advocated a federal approach that would grant national groups significant autonomy within existing states. Lenin's position was that national movements should be forced to choose between complete secession and continued membership of the state, but with exactly the same rights as all other citizens. Lenin's speculation was that most nationalist groups would decide against secession, realizing that they would forfeit the levels of material prosperity that were provided by economies of scale in larger social systems. Movements that did opt for secession would gain freedom from the forms of domination that had bred national enmity or distrust. In time, Lenin thought, closer links between separate national proletariats would develop. The point was to avoid the compromise with nationalism that Austro-Marxists had favoured. Proletarian internationalism was more important than creating multicultural political communities.

The approaches that have been surveyed shared Marx's conviction that capitalism was progressive in that it would bring industrial development and wealth to the rest of the world (along with liberation from what Marx regarded as the slavish superstition that pervaded pre-capitalist societies in the periphery). It was assumed that non-Western societies would follow the European course of development. Post-World War II neo-Marxist theories of global development and underdevelopment broke with such ideas. Dependency theorists argued that exploitative alliances between the dominant class interests in core and peripheral societies blocked the latter's industrialization (Frank 1967). On that argument, secession from the capitalist world economy was essential if the periphery was to industrialize. Building on dependency theory, but avoiding too crude a division between core and peripheral nations, world-systems theory, as developed by Wallerstein in the 1970s and 1980s, challenged the classical Marxist view that industrial capitalism will, in the long run, promote economic development everywhere (for a summary of world-systems theory see Wallerstein 1979).

Frank and Wallerstein's positions have been described as neo-Marxist because they shift the emphasis from relations of *production* to relations of *exchange* or trade in a world market (see also Emmanuel 1972). The intricacies of such discussions need not detain us here. Suffice it to add that the term, neo-Marxist, points to certain continuities with earlier Marxist ideas, specifically the belief that economic factors are the driving force behind long-term patterns of change, and the tendency to underestimate the autonomy or relative autonomy of the state and geo-politics (Linklater 1990a: chapter 6). However, a crucial difference was that neo-Marxists argued that the unprecedented material wealth of capitalist societies cannot be explained as the result of the transition from feudalism to capitalism *within* Europe. It was crucial to understand that capitalist prosperity was achieved by incorporating colonized and peripheral peoples in an exploitative global capitalist economy and by forcing them to produce raw materials and other commodities that were in short supply in the capitalist West. Marx and classical Marxists argued that the capitalist mode of production developed in Western Europe in the eighteenth and nineteenth centuries, and then spread to other regions. Frank and Wallerstein contended that a capitalist world-economic system with the attributes that have just been noted had existed for several centuries (see also Frank and Gills 1993).

As noted above, Western Marxists disagreed profoundly about whether or not to support Third World national liberation movements, and many feared that the compromise with nationalism would sacrifice the internationalism of classical Marxism (Warren 1980; Nairn 1981). Important questions arise about how far any such global vision is not universal at all because it is tied to particular cultural biases and interests, and can easily give rise to new forms of power. Sensitivities to those issues became prominent in International Relations as a result of the influence of post-structuralism and post-colonialism (see Chapter 8). They are clearly pertinent to the interpretation of Marxism as an outgrowth of the European Enlightenment. It emerged in a phase of European overseas dominance in which confidence in the superiority of Western civilization and certainty in the need for a civilizing mission to elevate Europe's 'social inferiors' was at its height. Dependency theory and world-systems analysis, and Third World Marxism in the 1960s and 1970s, challenged those assumptions. Those shifting orientations are not only interesting manifestations of how scholars have endeavoured to understand long-term processes of global change from Marxist or neo-Marxist perspectives. They shaped broader developments in the social sciences and in International Relations. Dependency theory in the 1970s encouraged a broadening of horizons so that the discipline focused on 'North–South' relations as well as 'East–West' relations and the connections between them. The aim was to construct more global perspectives that moved beyond the attempts by nineteenth-century European thinkers to understand *their* world, and to suppose that outlying regions had only marginal importance. Efforts to construct a 'global' social science that considers social and political developments in long-term perspective without the Eurocentrism of old appeared in an era when non-Western peoples were engaged in struggles to reduce injustices in world politics. Neo-Marxist analyses of patterns of uneven development within the capitalist world economy, and reflections on the plight of the 'periphery', reflected those changes. They enlarged the study of international relations that had been largely preoccupied with strategic relations between the great powers and narrowly focused on questions of order and stability at the expense of issues of global justice (see Chapter 4).

The changing fortunes of Marxism in International Relations

We have seen that the consensus within the mainstream approaches has been that Marxism has little, if anything, to offer the student of international relations – apart from a catalogue of errors that the serious analyst will avoid. Realists maintained that Marxism was largely concerned with how humans acted on nature, and only secondarily with how societies interacted with each other. The importance of the state, geo-politics and war was obscured by a conceptual framework that invested all resources in analysing systems of production, class structures and class conflict. A largely unspoken assumption was that moral and political commitments prevented Marxists from providing a more detached and realistic understanding of world politics – an interpretation that plainly neglected the pioneering role that historical materialism has played in investigating the long-term trend towards the economic and technological integration of the species (and the distinctive role that industrial capitalism has played in accelerating that process over the last two centuries). Marxist scholarship over approximately the last four decades has concentrated on developing more sophisticated explanations of world politics. Rather less energy has been devoted to reflecting on the meaning of universal emancipation today. In fact, historical materialists have not engaged with the normative issues that have been explored within global ethics and international political theory (see Chapter 11). The central task has been to extend, refine or qualify 'the paradigm of production'.

Prior to discussing some recent developments on that front, it is useful to note that realist assessments of historical materialism have invariably emphasized the record of Marxism in power. For example, Waltz (1959) argued that Marxists were unprepared for the realities of promoting socialism in a anarchic world of sovereign nation-states – and especially for the exercise of promoting 'socialism in one country'. Trotsky's remark that he would issue a few revolutionary proclamations as Russia's Commissar for Foreign Affairs before closing shop has often been cited as evidence of dismaying naivety. Moreover, the speed with which the Soviet regime resorted to classical power politics to ensure its security and survival has been highlighted as evidence of the superiority of realist explanation. Lenin stressed in 1919 that 'we are living not merely in a state, but in a system of states' (quoted in Halliday 1999: 312) – yet far from changing the international system, 'Marxism in power' was transformed by it. The Soviet domination of Eastern Europe provoked demands for national self-determination that swept socialist internationalism aside. Conflicts between socialist states demonstrated that the demise of capitalist regimes made little impression on the 'logic of anarchy' (Kubalkova and Cruickshank 1980).

Failures to anticipate those events have often been regarded as evidence that historical materialism had a flawed theory of the state. Many Marxists conceded as much in the 1970s and 1980s in the course of moving away from Marx's thesis that the capitalist state is nothing other than 'the executive committee of the bourgeoisie' (Marx and Engels 1977: 223). Many argued that the capitalist state had to have some autonomy from the ruling class simply to ensure that capitalism survived. State structures had to protect capitalists from themselves by ensuring that short-term competition for profit did not drive down wages to such a degree that mass poverty and social unrest became inevitable. By providing access to welfare, the state played a critical role in reproducing the capitalist mode of production. Following the Italian Marxist, Antonio Gramsci, several historical materialists argued that the state played a vital role in placating subordinate class forces. The state ensured what Gramsci called the hegemony of the dominant class interests by incorporating some lower-class aspirations in national ideologies. Hegemony was preserved as much by consent as by coercion.

Other historical materialists took a different path by recognizing the importance of Max Weber's claim that the state has considerable power and autonomy from class forces because of its monopoly control of the instruments of violence – and it claims domestic legitimacy by virtue of the responsibility it has for protecting society from internal and external threats. A large literature in the 1970s and 1980s sought to reorient the 'paradigm of production' so that it had a more sophisticated understanding of what was described at the time as 'the relative autonomy of the state' as well as a deeper appreciation of how the state in capitalist societies could free itself from the grip of the dominant class forces, as had occurred in Nazi Germany (Anderson 1974; Block 1980; see also Skocpol 1979; and Linklater 1990a: chapter 7).

Just as historical materialism was absorbing ideas that are more often associated with realism, the study of international relations became more open to Marxist and neo-Marxist interpretations of world politics. As explained earlier, dependency theory was influential in persuading IR scholars to consider the inter-relations between 'realist' power struggles and the evolution of the modern capitalist world economy. As far as historical materialists were concerned, the objective was to demonstrate that radical forms of international political economy that preserved the critical ethos of classical Marxism surpassed the realist explanation with its impoverished commitment to geo-political reductionism.

Robert Cox's analysis of social forces, states and world order remains one of the most ambitious attempts to use historical materialism to move beyond conventional international relations theory. Cox analysed the relationship between those three levels, stressing that states and the international institutions that preserve world order do not simply express the will of the dominant social classes. Systems of production could be as much the cause as the effect of developments at those other levels. The point was that one had to understand how their inter-relations found expression in what Gramsci called the 'historic blocs' that govern national societies. Echoing the latter's interest in how hegemony operates through coercion and consent, Cox argued for analysing world hegemony not in conventional terms, as one power's military domination over the others, but as a constellation of class forces, state structures and international organizations that ensured the dominance of the capitalist mode of production. Crucially important was the role of 'counter-hegemonic movements', and the extent to which their efforts to change the global distribution of political and economic power were thwarted by hegemonic strategies to co-opt and divide opponents of the current world order (Cox 1983).

The neo-Gramscian school has actively developed the study of the origins, development and possible transformation of global hegemony (Ayers 2008; Bieler and Morton 2006; Gill 1993b, 2012). It has analysed how hegemony is preserved by forms of cooperation between powerful elites inside and outside the core regions of the world system, and by a web of international economic and political institutions that are responsible for global governance (Gill 1993b; see also Bromley 1999; Cox 1983; Gamble 1999; and Hay 1999). The idea of 'disciplinary neo-liberalism' has extended that investigation as has the notion of the 'new constitutionalism' which refers to international institutions that have pressed national governments to accept neo-liberal conceptions of the state, society and markets (Gill 1995; 2003). Also important are pressures on national governments – some internal in origin, some external and expressing the power of a transnational capitalist class that is actively involved in transforming the global economic and political system. Crucial manifestations of its hegemonic free market vision are efforts to deregulate major sectors of national economies and to facilitate transnational corporate activity (see Morton 2007; Robinson and Harris 2000; van der Pijl 1998). Free market ideologies, it is argued, remove the 'economic' domain from the principles of 'democratic deliberation' that capitalist societies regard as essential in the 'political' sphere; however, capitalist social relations leave individuals, who are often torn from traditional communities, powerless in the face of advancing global forces (Robinson and Harris 2000). Chapter 2 has shown that neo-realism emphasizes how states are compelled to comply with the dictates of anarchy. Historical materialists have analysed similar pressures that have forced more and more societies to submit to the competitive logic of the capitalist world economy that has led to monopolies of productive and (inadequately regulated) financial power and to growing inequalities between those who own or control labour-power or investment and those who belong to the subordinate classes. Those monopolies are supported by national and transnational institutions, by domestic and international law, and by forms of cultural hegemony that promote 'common sense' understandings of the legitimacy of current arrangements – or at least of the absence of viable alternatives (Cutler 2006).

Contemporary formulations of historical materialism have provided innovative analyses of the consolidation of such global power structures but, in keeping with Marx's Hegelian claim that all societies contain the seeds of their own destruction, they have also focused on 'the resistances these engender' and the conceptions of different forms of social and political organization that run through the practice of counter-hegemonic movements (Rupert 2003: 181; also Rupert 2000, 2006; Rupert and Solomon 2005). Reflecting broader movement within Marxism in the twentieth century, the emphasis falls on what Cox calls the 'counter-hegemonic' elements in the global order that challenge those power arrangements and the dominant role of neo-liberal conceptions of society and politics. Here it is valuable to note the differences with Marx's understanding of how capitalism had become a global system in the first part of the nineteenth century. Not only are states, geo-politics and war accorded greater importance in recent investigations, but the stress has shifted to how internationalization has occurred more rapidly and more extensively amongst the ruling elites than amongst the world's diverse and internally divided counter-hegemonic movements. No claims are made about the privileged social forces – the modern counterpart of Marx's conception of the historical mission of the industrial proletariat – that are poised to transform the world system in part or in whole.

Some analysts have identified the importance of the 'anti-globalist Far Right', the 'progressive elites and national movements' in Latin America and elsewhere, and the elements that comprise 'the global justice movement' (Robinson 2006). In some accounts, one of the challenges is to

understand the nature and potential of resistance movements in the traditional 'periphery' – that is, the struggles of 'subaltern groups' in the
regions outside the centres where industrial capitalism and socialist
projects first developed (Pasha 2008, 2009 and Jones 2008). Such struggles can be regarded as part of an ongoing 'revolt against the West'. They
point to ways in which English School analyses of that phenomenon (see
Chapter 4) are relevant to – and can learn from – historical-materialist
reflections on changing relations between 'core' and 'periphery'. They
draw attention to the importance of debate and discussion between
historical materialists and 'post-colonial' scholars whose studies act as a
counterweight to the Eurocentrism of traditional Marxism (Hobson
2012), as well as post-structuralist analyses of the politics of identity
(Bieler and Morton 2010; see Chapter 8).

Explorations of those struggles and patterns of resistance indicate that
historical materialists do not believe it is possible to predict the outcome
of such phenomena as the global financial crisis. Much will depend on
the extent to which states can restore economic stability or make
advances in 'the taming of economic aristocracies' (Blomert 2012), and
on how far the dominant elites in the realms of finance and production
can reclaim authority and entrench existing powers and privileges
(Robinson 2006). Efforts to rescue the banks have shown that states are
locked into a financial system that they do not control; they have raised
difficult questions about whether states can organize forms of 'global
leadership' to prevent future 'neo-liberal' crises (Gill 2012). Whether or
not they come within the tradition of historical materialism, analyses of
the global financial crisis and studies of national and international
responses can profitably engage with largely forgotten Marxist sociological studies of state and class that were at the centre of important debates
in the social sciences three to four decades ago (see Linklater 1990a:
chapter 4). Historical materialists are well-placed to explain the current
phase in the development of the world capitalist system, but they do so
without Marx and Engels' confidence that counter-hegemonic resistance
reveals that the transition from capitalism to socialism is under way, and
without a plausible vision of a future world order. Significantly, many
strands of historical materialism offer sophisticated accounts of global
economic and political structures but they have not tried to develop the
ethical dimensions of Marx's thought and classical Marxism (see
Rengger 2008 on profound tensions within 'the ethics of Marxism').

The discussion in this section has shown that historical materialists
have constructed a distinctive approach to studying world politics.
Halliday (1994: 61) summarizes the dominant tendency by arguing that
'the modern inter-state system emerged in the context of the spread of
capitalism across the globe, and the subjugation of pre-capitalist soci-

eties. This socio-economic system has underpinned both the character of individual states and ... their relations with each other: no analysis of international relations is possible without reference to capitalism, the social formations it generated and the world system they comprise' (see also Rosenberg 1994). That summation is perfectly compatible with the realist thesis that states often act independently of dominant class forces, but the contention is that it is impossible to understand long-term trends in international relations by focusing on geo-political interaction alone – or by regarding that sphere, in Waltz's words, as a 'domain apart' (see Chapter 2).

The latter's way of representing international politics raises large questions for historical materialists who maintain that a crucial issue is neglected, namely explaining how the 'economic' and the 'political' became separated from each other in the modern period (Rosenberg 1994). The argument is that they were not separable in pre-capitalist societies and international systems; they became so with the emergence of the capitalist era. In the preceding centuries and millennia, coercion was central to the appropriation of wealth. In classical antiquity, for example, force was used to acquire slaves, the majority of whom were captured in war. But with industrial capitalism, wealth is accumulated through the operation of markets rather than through the use of physical force (Anderson 1974). The political sphere comes to be regarded as separate from the economic domain. But, in reality, the two are bound together and increasingly inter-related. From that perspective, it is not historical materialism that is guilty of reductionism but neo-realism which commits the error of assuming that international relations in all periods and places can be explained in terms of a timeless 'logic of anarchy' (see Teschke 2003).

Beyond the paradigm of production: implications for the emancipatory project

Several developments in historical materialism in the recent period, including the increased emphasis on the role of the state, geo-politics and war, represent a move beyond the classical paradigm with its focus on the determining role of modes of production and class conflict. The question inevitably arises of how far historical materialism can extend that focus to include, for instance, investigations into the significance of race and gender distinctions in the organization of society, and at the same time remain distinctively Marxist. Enlarging the object of analysis in that way raises large questions about the contemporary significance of classical Marxist conceptions of universal emancipation that were anchored in the belief that the industrial proletariat was the social force that would free humanity from surplus constraints and unnecessary suffering.

Habermas's reflections on the 'reconstruction of historical material-ism', which were developed in the 1980s, warrant attention in this context and not least because they combined the quest for a more comprehensive approach to politics and history with an explicit norma-tive position that was geared towards the promotion of human emanci-pation and understanding. He argued that Marxism had overestimated the influence of 'labour' on social organization and on human history, and underestimated the role of 'interaction' – the forms of communica-tion that have facilitated the search for levels of agreement and under-standing that make it possible for people to live together in viable societies. That was not to claim that the 'paradigm of production' was worthless. Historical materialism had been correct to make the struggle to satisfy basic material needs, and the relationship between society and nature, central to social explanation. But the analysis was limited with-out considering developments in the realm of morality and culture that had less to do with interaction with the natural world and more to do with the interaction between people and the recurring challenge to discover principles that made it easier for them to live side-by-side in peaceful ways. Extending the point, Habermas maintained that Marxism had been right to draw attention to forms of social learning that had led to greater understanding and mastery of the natural world. But learning in that domain did not ensure that people could live together amicably in viable societies. As the first generation of Frankfurt School theorists had argued, greater control over nature had not ushered in a new era of enlightenment and emancipation. The same instruments that had been used to dominate the physical environment – namely increased state power and bureaucratic controls – made it easier for people to dominate each other, as had occurred in Nazi Germany and Soviet Russia (see Horkheimer and Adorno 1972). It also enabled them to inflict greater destruction on each other in times of war.

Habermas added that historical materialism had failed to provide a robust philosophical defence of its vision of universal emancipation. Marx and Engels had highlighted the tension between bourgeois commitments to freedom and actual social realities, and they argued that, under socialism, the aspiration to freedom would finally be realized. But they did not make the philosophical case for the socialist conception of freedom. Moreover, Marxism in the first part of the twentieth century had no ethical response to the distortion of the socialist ideal in the Soviet Union and no moral critique of the totalitarian rule in Nazi Germany. Habermas's conception of learning in the sphere of interaction was linked with the argument that societies have developed more complex means of assessing the worth of social and political institutions. Habermas stated that, as a result of social learning, moral codes had developed that upheld the principle that all people have an equal right to be consulted about any decisions that might affect them. He contended that the notion of discourse ethics – or the discourse theory of morality – provided the most advanced defence of that standpoint, a cosmopolitan standpoint that required the democratization of institutions at all levels – local, national and international (Habermas 1979).

The discourse theory of morality is clearly linked with Marx's vision of a world where people make their history without the burden of unnecessary constraints. But that conception of universal emancipation was not dependent on the 'paradigm of production'; nor was it reliant on the belief that the global proletariat was the privileged social force that would lead humanity towards the 'kingdom of freedom'. That standpoint is untenable, Habermas argued, given the many different forms of exploitation and domination in some societies. Some are undoubtedly class-based, but others are not: most obviously those that are anchored in the distinctions of gender, ethnicity, or race. That is not to imply that the politics of race and gender develop independently of class relations (or vice versa). But it is to underline the point that one of the purposes of critical theory is to explain how the relations between those phenomena have shaped human societies.

Some of the developments that have been discussed in the last few paragraphs have clear parallels in the theory of international relations. There are broad similarities between Habermas's idea of a reconstructed historical materialism and Cox's writings in the 1990s. They analysed what has come to be known as 'identity politics' or the struggles for recognition that have been initiated by minority nations, indigenous peoples and other marginal groups in society. Cox drew attention to the sense of identification with particular civilizations, and he defended a vision of 'a post-hegemonic order ... in which different traditions of civilization ... coexist through advances in 'mutual recognition and mutual understanding' (Cox 1992b, 1993: 265). That point brings to mind Habermas's stress on forms of social learning that are oriented towards establishing principles that enable people to co-exist more amicably than in the past. As already noted, Habermas maintained that the discourse theory of morality is the key to promoting 'mutual understanding'. The theme has been explored in other critical approaches that follow the spirit but not the letter of historical materialism (Linklater 1998).

A similar theme can be found in the writings of the deconstructionist theorist, Jacques Derrida (see Chapter 7). In a discussion of the contemporary relevance of Marx and Engels' *Communist Manifesto*, Derrida (1994a; 1994b) made the case for a 'new International' that responds to the reality that 'violence, inequality, exclusion, famine, and thus economic oppression [have never] affected as many human beings in the history of the Earth and of humanity'. He called for freeing Marx's vision of the 'withering away of the state' from its association with socialist internationalism and the dictatorship of the proletariat (Derrida 1994a: 56). The aim of the 'new International' should be to criticize 'the state of international law' and 'the concepts of state and nation' that under-pinned particularistic sovereign states and national conceptions of citizenship (Derrida 1994a: 58).

Such an inquiry, Derrida added, should be undertaken, in the 'spirit of Marxism', a claim that may not command much support amongst the advocates of other critical perspectives such as feminism and post-colonial theory. They are more inclined to regard historical materialism as an approach that has not been 'on their side'. In short, the traditional emphasis was on understanding and eradicating class exploitation rather than patriarchy or imperial ideologies that were suffused with notions of Western cultural and racial superiority. With the rise of those standpoints, historical materialism lost its position at the centre of critical theory. Advocates of post-structuralism and post-colonialism rarely turn to the perspective for inspiration and insight. They are more likely to perceive it as a specialist form of international political economy that has reconstructed rather than transcended the paradigm of production in the quest for a comprehensive study of society and politics. But as Derrida's comments reveal, non-Marxist or 'post-Marxist' critical theory is deficient unless it engages with, and attempts to develop, the Marxian legacy.

Conclusion

Marxism was the dominant version of critical theory until recently, one that combined the analysis of the long-term trend towards the globalization of social relations with a political economy of the revolutionary impact of industrial capitalism and a vision of universal emancipation. No previous approach to politics and history had operated on such an ambitious scale. That conception of social inquiry has no counterpart within the study of international relations where the recurrent criticism has been that historical materialism shed little or no light on the state, nationalism and war, on diplomacy, or on the balance of power and international law. Few have recognized that Marx's writings set out a vision of the whole of human history, of the rise and development of industrial capitalism, of internal crises and social struggles that may lead to new forms of social organization – in short, a vision of what the social sciences should aspire for that remains standard-setting to this day.

In one crucial respect, mainstream standpoints have largely failed to deal with historical materialism on its terms. There is an important contrast with the neo-realist interest in explaining the persistence of geopolitical rivalries across many millennia. Marxists have emphasized the necessity of placing those recurrent forces in their historical context – the latter do not operate in exactly the same way in all eras, but interact with the dominant power structures and forms of political resistance. As a version of critical theory, Marxism has been especially interested in understanding areas of resistance that realists and neo-realists do not regard as central dimensions of world politics. But what is marginally interesting from the vantage point of those perspectives is highly significant from critical-theoretical perspectives such as Marxism. They are most interested in 'counter-hegemonic' struggles that give rise to new conceptions of society and visions of freedom. Central to that focus is the conviction that first appeared in Marx's critique of bourgeois political economy, that explanations of the social world are never as neutral or as objective as they may appear. Albeit unintentionally, they may promote forms of knowledge that entrench existing forms of power and domination rather than contest them as part of an exercise in understanding how society can be organized to free people from unnecessary constraints (see Chapter 7).

For such reasons, historical materialism has been a key resource in the critique of realism and neo-realism, in efforts to explain the inter-relations between the development of the modern states-system and the evolution of industrial capitalism, and in analyses of capitalist globalization and the national and other divisions and conflicts that have developed alongside it. In the main, rival approaches that investigate the politics of gender, ethnicity or race do not draw on historical materialism or its classical vision of universal emancipation. However, that perspective has a range that is unusual in the social sciences, since it combined the empirical analysis of long-term social and political processes with an emancipatory vision and the aspiration to understand how it can be realized in practice. One must doubt that critical theory can be based entirely around historical materialism, but there is still much to be said for the thesis that it should proceed in the 'spirit of Marxism', and aim to understand (from an emancipatory standpoint) the processes that have drawn societies into longer webs of interconnectedness over the millennia, and especially over the last few centuries and decades.

6 | Historical Sociology

ANDREW LINKLATER

Chapter 5 explained that Marx's analysis of industrial capitalism was part of a larger inquiry into the evolution of human society from the most distant times to the modern era. Marx emphasized the increased power of the species over the natural world and the globalization of social and economic relations. By analysing the impact of large-scale structural change on collective action and everyday life, Marx pioneered historical sociology which has been defined as that 'tradition of research devoted to understanding the character and effects of large-scale structures and fundamental processes of change' (Kelly 2003; Skocpol, quoted in Hobden 1998: 3). Several overviews of historical sociology have maintained that studies of long-term changes in social and political structures also investigate their relationship with such features of everyday existence as emotional attitudes to violence and suffering (Abrams 1982: chapter 1; Skocpol 1984: chapter 1; Smith 1990: 3). Its breadth and scope distinguishes historical sociology from approaches that focus on short-term intervals and contemporary events. It also marks it off from historical writings that cast light on the distinctive or exceptional character of particular eras, episodes or events, but do not reflect on how they were connected with longer-term social directions.

Historical sociologists therefore focus on what has been called '*la longue durée*', a term coined by the French historian, Braudel, to refer to slow-moving, and often barely perceptible, trends that are frequently ignored by students of high-profile contemporary problems (Burke 2003). Many scholars of international relations have been attracted to historical sociology precisely because it offers an alternative to 'presentism', or 'the retreat into the present' – that is, the concentration on problems of immediate interest (Buzan and Little 2000; Elias 1998b). Invariably, the focus on promoting long-term perspectives is motivated by the belief that the distinctive and possibly unique features of the modern world will remain opaque unless they are placed in broad historical context. Some perspectives do that by analysing dominant trends over the last few centuries. Others reach further back in time by using different disciplines to explain the extraordinary development of the human species from the small and relatively isolated societies with populations of only a few dozen that were the norm for most of human history to the large territorial states and high levels of global interconnectedness that exist today. The objective, which also animated Marx's thought, is to comprehend 'the long-term trend towards the globalization of human society' (Mennell 1990; also Buzan and Little 2000).

It is intriguing to consider how relations between states have influenced, and been influenced by, that overall process. That is one reason for recent efforts to build connections between International Relations and historical sociology (which is not a theory of international relations *per se* but a group of diverse perspectives that are increasingly influential reference points in explanatory theory). With respect to building new links between those areas, most of the initiative has come from students of international relations who have turned to historical sociology in the attempt to take the subject to new levels of sophistication. In short, 'ready-made' approaches to international relations do not exist in most branches of historical-sociological inquiry. The latter provide concepts and perspectives that can be used to develop International Relations. Such efforts can also enrich historical sociology. But there is a larger issue at stake which is contributing to the social sciences more generally by taking a long-term perspective on the changing relations between domestic social and political structures and their international contexts.

The plain desire to understand social and political change is often the primary motivation for engaging in historical-sociological inquiry. But some have claimed that comprehending long-term developments can provide knowledge that may be used one day to bring unregulated processes under greater control (Elias 1998a). As the last chapter explained, in Marx's thought, the interest in understanding the development of human society from the earliest times was linked with the political aspiration of not only interpreting but also changing the course of history. For the most part, historical sociologists have been concerned with explaining the world and not with harnessing inquiry to one or other normative project. But it is interesting on reflect on how their investigations can support cosmopolitan social and political thought. The latter endeavour can be strengthened by acquiring a deeper understanding of such processes as the overall long-term trend towards the globalization of human society.

Whatever its form, historical sociology has been entangled in various methodological controversies about its capacity to add to the stock of knowledge about society and politics (see Kiser and Hechter 1991, 1998). Some scholars are suspicious of large-scale narratives that depend heavily on detailed works of scholarship that have used archives, interviews and similar sources to understand their specialist object of analysis. By comparison, the argument is, the former are likely to be selective, highly personalized and impressionistic. The criticism or reservation is that pre-conceived ideas about overall historical directions may lead to oversim-plified accounts of the human past, and give rise to distorted images of the particular areas studied by specialists. The main response to that crit-icism is that academic specialization brings its own liabilities such as the sacrifice of the broader historical overview that makes specific develop-ments intelligible (see the illuminating exchange between Goldthorpe 1991 and Mann 1994a on those matters). From that angle, historical sociologists aim to integrate the findings of particular studies in an attempt to uncover patterns and directions stretching back over many centuries or millennia that specialists may not detect. In that way, the grand overview can stimulate more specialized inquiries and learn from, and build on, them in a mutually profitable exchange of ideas.

It is possible to distinguish between three general approaches to historical sociology that are often combined in particular areas of inves-tigation. The first is comparative in nature. Examples include Eisenstadt's study of empires and, in International Relations, Wight's conception of a comparative sociology of international states-systems. The second aims to explain the development of the modern world, and concentrates on the central directions of the last few centuries. Examples include Wallerstein's analysis of the capitalist world-system, Elias's explanation of the evolution of the modern state and the 'civilizing process' and, in International Relations, Teschke's critical examination of the rise of the so-called 'Westphalia' era. A third approach extends the inquiry to cover the entire course of recorded history. Examples include Mann's analysis of changing configurations of 'social power' over approximately the last five millennia and, in International Relations, studies of relations between political communities in very long-term perspective that include Ferguson and Mansbach (1996), Watson (1992), Buzan and Little (2000) and, more recently, van der Pijl (2007, 2010).

One final point needs to be added before proceeding further. As part of the academic division of labour that appeared in the nineteenth-century academy, the emergent field known as sociology focused on changes within 'modern' societies. Relations between states were usually placed to one side; they would fall under the purview of the new disci-pline of International Relations in the following century as a reaction to the historical neglect of peace and war. But especially over the last 25–30 years, sociologists have made international relations more central to their inquiry. It is lower case rather than upper case 'international relations' that has commanded their attention. As already noted, the broadening of sociological horizons has been a major influence on recent studies of international relations. For example, scholars in the latter field have had a particular interest in considering how historical sociology can contribute to the attempt to supersede the belief, which neo-realism has championed, that in some fundamental respects international relations have barely changed over the millennia (see Chapters 2 and 5 above). It is important to add that very few IR scholars have set out to contribute directly to historical sociology, just as few historical sociologists have been concerned with advancing IR. Indeed, the fact that many write about international relations without consulting the IR literature has been described as evidence of 'the failure of IR as an academic project' – its peculiar lack of influence on the humanities and the social sciences more generally (Buzan and Little 2001). The question remains of how elements from sociology and International Relations can be integrated in a more synoptic perspective on society and politics that transcends disciplinary boundaries (see Lawson 2007; also Linklater 2011a, c). Engaging with historical sociology is one way in which International Relations scholars can contribute to that goal as well as to their specialist areas of inquiry.

The rest of this chapter provides an overview of some leading approaches to historical sociology. Section one explains the rise of historical sociology in the nineteenth century. Sections two and three analyse influential approaches in twentieth-century thought, noting how relations between states moved to the foreground of the discussion in that period. Most of those perspectives have stressed the primacy of material forces such as struggles for power or competition for economic resources. Sections four and five consider approaches that focus on the part that moral and cultural forces and collective emotions have played in the development of human societies. The final sections consider the quest for 'higher-level synthesis' in the social science, and the contribution that IR can make to the creation of new 'grand narratives'.

Origins of historical sociology

European sociology arose in response to fundamental patterns of social and political change in the late eighteenth and early nineteenth centuries – industrialization, democratization, urbanization, bureaucratization and individualization which have been described as the core features of the 'the great transformation' of modernity (Nisbet 1966; Mazlish 1989; Dean 1994; Skocpol 1984). To characterize the direction in which modern societies were heading, social thinkers referred to the shift from 'community' to 'association' (Ferdinand Toennies), from 'status' to 'contract' (Henry Maine), from feudalism to capitalism (Karl Marx), from 'mechanical' to 'organic' solidarity (Émile Durkheim), and from traditional to legal forms of domination (Max Weber). A common theme was that the traditional social bonds and status hierarchies of the countryside were being dissolved by the advance of what Marx, following Carlyle, called the impersonal 'cash nexus' between increasingly individuated people in urbanizing, industrializing societies (Mazlish 1989).

Two of the dominant sources of historical sociology illustrate that last point. Marx's account of the move from feudalism to capitalism emphasized that the ties between lord and serf had been replaced by contractual relationships that exposed individuals to market forces that were transforming the world as a whole. Weber argued that traditional social relations were being replaced by the more abstract 'legal-rational' ties of bureaucratized societies. The personal ties that had bound together the lord and the serf were giving way to impersonal laws that applied to citizens in general. Reacting against Marxist reductionism, Weber stressed the need to understand the influence of religious ideas on social and political change. His analysis of the Calvinist ethic identified 'elective affinities' between its religious outlook and the capitalist mentality that was one of the driving forces behind the patterns of economic and political change that have distinguished the modern West from all other eras. Whereas Marx thought that the dominant social tendencies pointed towards the triumph of socialism, Weber predicted that future societies including any socialist order would not escape the levels of bureaucratic domination that signified the advancing 'iron cage' of modernity. One purpose of historical sociology is to endeavour to identify such long-term trends that may continue into the future.

Unlike the majority of nineteenth-century sociologists who were wedded to 'endogenous models of social development', or to inside-out theories of change (see Giddens 1985: 22–31), Weber was acutely aware of the influence of nationalism and power politics on the modern world, but there is a simple reason for the neglect of those phenomena in sociological thought in the preceding century. Sociology emerged in a period of relative international tranquillity when many leading thinkers believed that the spread of industry and commerce would promote perpetual peace. They emphasized what has come to be known as globalization. As with the optimistic interpretations of the globalization of society in recent times, many believed that the overall trend favoured internationalism as well as prosperity. The nineteenth-century social thinker, Saint-Simon, for example, contended that history had been a journey from the tribe to the state that would be replaced by new forms of political association that would embrace humanity as a whole. War and conquest were not central themes in the dominant sociological voices of the nineteenth century. That would come later. The Frankfurt School thinker, Theodor

Adorno, observed that history is a journey from 'the slingshot to the a-bomb', a contention that reflected the twentieth-century experience of the horrors of industrialized war and mechanized killing that few had anticipated a few decades earlier.

Nineteenth-century sociologists such as August Comte linked their new discipline with the normative conviction that greater knowledge of the social world could be used to improve social arrangements. As noted earlier, that is not a central theme in historical sociology today, nor has it influenced efforts in IR to build links with that area of investigation. In general, the purpose is explanatory. It is important to add that many nineteenth-century studies of the 'great transformation' regarded the triumph of the West as evidence of irreversible historical progress. That delusion was undermined as a result of the unprecedented violence of modern technological warfare and the rise of totalitarian rule in the USSR and Nazi Germany that made the twentieth century one of the most destructive in human history. Some have maintained that the critique of theories of progress was necessary and correct, but it made the mistake of throwing 'the baby out with the bathwater' by discarding the analysis of long-term patterns of change (Norbert Elias, cited in van Krieken 1998: 66). Contemporary strands of historical sociology have tried to rehabilitate the focus on long-term trajectories of development without perpetuating the Eurocentrism and progressivism of the nine-teenth-century philosophies of history advanced by Hegel, Marx and Comte (see Hobson 2012). The question is whether such approaches express greater intellectual detachment from particular cultures and from the contemporary era, and contribute to an understanding of human history that is free from the nineteenth-century interest in explaining the triumph of Europe or the West. The grand historical overview may then become part of a 'cosmopolitan education' that explains how different societies have been forced together by long-term processes of change, and contends that a broadening of cultural horizons is now critical for *human* security and survival (Diamond 1997 and 2005; Camilleri and Falk 2009).

Power and production in historical sociology

It is unsurprising that much twentieth-century historical sociology focused on developments at the level of coercive power and systems of production. The spread of industrial capitalism and the expansion of state power – including the capacity to wage ever more destructive forms of warfare over larger areas – explain that intellectual preoccupation. It is hardly astonishing that historical sociologists now emphasize the influence of geo-politics and war on social and political change over centuries or millennia. It was a short step from sociological accounts of the state's monopoly control of the instruments of violence, as stressed by Weber, to the analysis of how states are locked in struggles for power and security that have transformed social and political structures and relations. As noted earlier, that greater focus on the state, geo-politics and war encouraged students of international relations to follow developments in historical sociology and to build connections with that field of inquiry (see the pioneering studies of Hobden 1998; Hobden and Hobson 2002).

To explain how those areas of investigation have begun to converge in recent years, it is useful to consider how Perry Anderson and Immanuel Wallerstein extended Marxist and neo-Marxist perspectives. As Chapter 5 showed, Marx's principal object of analysis had been the rise of industrial capitalism and its rapid spread to other continents. During the 1970s, Wallerstein, building on Braudel's study of the evolution of capitalism, provided a detailed historical account of how the capitalist world economy had emerged in the sixteenth century. Wallerstein criticized mainstream sociological studies that treated societies as self-contained entities that developed independently of each other. Along with dependency theorists such as Gunder Frank, Wallerstein replaced those assumptions with an examination of how the economic and political development of different societies depended on their location in the capitalist world-system. To explain those differences, his writings distinguished between core, peripheral and semi-peripheral positions. They traced the rise of hegemonic powers – including Spain, Holland, Britain and the United States – that had organized the world economy to promote their specific interests. The writings in question argued that the great powers have enjoyed temporary dominance, not only because of challenges to their position but because of the tendency for production to shift from the core regions to peripheral and semi-peripheral societies where labour costs are significantly lower.

Wallerstein argued that the capitalist system differs from ancient empires by virtue of its division into separate states. The study of the world-system described state structures as instruments that were designed to influence the functioning of the global economy. To improve their own position and disadvantage others, successive great powers imposed free trade arrangements on less competitive societies and on possible rivals. As with dependency theory before it, the approach commanded attention in IR because it was regarded as an important counterweight to the preoccupation with geo-politics and the general neglect of global economic structures and processes that were clearly important for understanding changes in the international distribution of military and political power. But in IR, critics argued that Wallerstein ignored the relatively autonomous sphere of geo-politics and warfare. Similar criticisms were advanced in sociology (see Zolberg 1981 on the fact that the capitalist world economy might not have survived at all but for the strategic alliance between France and the Ottoman Empire in the sixteenth century that was designed to thwart Spain's imperial ambitions).

Such accusations of economic reductionism do not apply to Anderson's discussion of the transition from feudalism to capitalism which was critical of the orthodox Marxist view that class struggle was the driving-force behind that seismic development. Historical materialist analysis had failed to recognize the crucial part that rivalries between 'absolutist states' in the seventeenth and eighteenth centuries had played in that transition. Beginning with the claim that states in early modern Europe were essentially feudal – and not capitalist as classical Marxism had believed – Anderson argued that geo-political rivalries forced the ruling aristocratic strata to ally with emerging bourgeoisies to finance the preparation and conduct of war. In short, geo-political rivalries between absolutist states were a decisive factor in the revolutionary shift from feudalism to capitalism (Anderson 1974; see also Teschke 2003).

Earlier comments about Marx and Weber have shown that the precise relationship between 'political' and 'economic' forces has long been a bone of contention in historical sociology. Debates about their relative importance continue, but disputes about causal primacy have largely been settled in favour of 'multi-causal explanation'. Marxist approaches to the economic and the political domains remain important, however, for understanding how the modern states-system differs from its predecessors. As explained in Chapter 5, Marxist historical sociology has argued that the state in capitalist societies is not directly involved in using force to promote economic development. As Anderson argued, the 'typical medium of inter-feudal rivalry' was 'military' whereas with the rise of 'inter-capitalist competition' it is primarily 'economic' (1974: 33). To put that another way, force was regarded as a legitimate way of seizing wealth in the feudal era, but it is not so regarded in the capitalist world where force and geo-politics are thought to be separate from the economic domain (even though the reality is very different).

Here it is worth noting an important debate between neo-realist and historical-materialist interpretations of whether international relations between medieval political units were significantly different from the relations between modern states. Drawing on neo-realism, Fischer (1992) argued that the anarchic nature of the medieval and modern international systems compelled political entities to adopt similar ways of ensuring their security and survival. In short, throughout history, external forces have forced societies to behave in much the same manner despite radically different belief-systems, regime-types and forms of social and political organization. Criticizing that interpretation from a historical-materialist perspective, Teschke (1998) maintained that the feudal nobles' assumed right to use force to appropriate wealth and to settle disputes holds the key to understanding political behaviour in the medieval period. The neo-realist argument about the effects of anarchy on state action in different eras had failed to comprehend deeper structural relations between 'economic' and 'political' phenomena that made violence endemic throughout much of that era. Instead of assuming that the same logic of anarchy explains the relations between political entities in all periods, it is necessary, on Teschke's argument, to analyse the interdependencies between what came to be regarded as the separate realms of economic and politics (see Rosenberg 1994 for a similar critique of the ahistorical nature of neo-realist approaches to international politics, and Latham 2012 for a constructivist critique of both historical materialist and neo-realist interpretations of the medieval states-system).

It is a short step from that argument to the contention that it is impossible to understand the evolution of the modern states-system, and its geopolitical rivalries and tensions, without analysing one of the major revolutions of the last two centuries – the rise and spread of industrial capitalism (Halliday 1994; Teschke 2003). As explained in Chapter 5, recent approaches to analysing long-term trends have stressed the importance of the 'uneven and combined development' of that system of production. They have emphasized different rates of capitalist development across the world as well as the complex social and political arrangements that have resulted from the fusion or co-existence of pre-capitalist and capitalist social relations (Chapter 5; Rosenberg 1994; 2006). Such analyses do not argue that relations between states lack all autonomy but stress that they reflect processes at the level of the forces and relations of production. The argument is that analysts of international relations in the modern era – just like students of international politics in the medieval period – cannot explain long-term tendencies and trends unless they trace the connections between the separate spheres of power and production.

Virtually all sociological studies of the modern world recognize the decisive influence of the interplay between modern industrial capitalism, geo-politics and war, although that is not to imply that they agree on how to explain the relationship between class power and state structures, or between capitalism and international politics. Influential approaches have shown how the interaction between increasing coercive capabilities and higher levels of capital accumulation made it possible for the modern territorial state to eliminate the other forms of political association (small city-states and aspiring empires) that competed for power in early modern Europe (see Tilly 1992 and Nexon 2009: chapter 3). Some have argued that relations between four processes have shaped the modern world – state-building, warfare, capitalism and industrialization (Giddens 1985). A study of the revolutions in France in 1789, Russia in 1917 and China in 1949 argued that geo-political rivalries created enormous pressures on the ruling elites to extract more wealth from the dominant class which then exploited subordinate classes more intensively, triggering social and political revolution. The result was not only a shift in the balance of power between different strata within such societies, but a new phase in an age-old struggle to create powerful state structures in a world of potentially lethal geo-political rivalries (Skocpol 1979). Similar trends have transformed societies outside Europe. Indeed, the export of the modern European army and the 'Western way of warfare' along with the emulation of Western-style state structures has been one of the defining features of the recent global era (Ralston 1990).

Similarly multi-causal approaches have endeavoured to explain long-term trends over the last five millennia. Especially notable is Mann's account of the development of social power since the emergence of city-states in Mesopotamia and the rise of the first empires such as Assyria, Persia and Rome (Mann 1986, 1994b). Using what he called the 'IEMP model', Mann (1994) traces the impact of relations between *ideological, economic, military and political* power on the organization of society. It is impossible to summarize that ambitious work here, but two features deserve the attention of students of international relations. The first is the focus on the long-term trend towards societies with greater 'intensive' and 'extensive' capabilities – with an increased ability to govern the social world within their borders, and with the related capacity to project their political and military power well beyond their frontiers (Mann 1986: 7). A second important theme is Mann's rejection of the tendency in sociology until quite recently to regard societies as largely self-contained, bounded entities. Throughout his analysis of social power, Mann stresses the impact of transnational influences such as universal religions and international phenomena such as war on the configuration of societies. As noted earlier, more recent works such as Buzan and Little (2000) have also analysed the impact of 'economic' and 'political' phenomena on international systems in world history. Also notable but from the standpoint of historical materialism are the first and second parts of a major three-volume study that traces the connections between systems of production and modes of conducting foreign relations from nomadic societies through successions of empires and states to the contemporary era (van der Pijl 2007, 2010). There are major differences between those works, but what they have in common – and what marks them out as major innovations in the discipline – is their interest in analysing contemporary international relations in long-term perspective.

Power and interdependence in international relations

The emphasis on how state-building and warfare have interacted to shape the modern world is central to 'realist' historical sociology as defended by Hintze (1975: 159) almost a century ago in a critique of Marxist economic reductionism. To realists and neo-realists, that shift of orientation within sociology may signify the belated recognition of themes that have long been central to state-centric approaches, though largely neglected elsewhere in the social sciences. But it is far from clear that those movements within sociology signify a victory for neo-realism. Many IR scholars are attracted to historical sociology because of its sensitivity to the existence of long-term processes of change. As we have seen, they have been critical of 'presentism' in the field, and they have challenged 'anarchocentrism' – the belief that the 'logic of anarchy' has dictated that states behave in similar ways as part of the struggle for survival, and ensured that international relations in different eras are more or less the same. They have opposed the way in which neo-realism derives bold claims about long-term trends in world politics from theoretical distinctions between anarchic and hierarchic systems that are detached from historical inquiry. Many have objected to projecting features of the modern 'Westphalian' international era back onto earlier systems, a practice that obscures the distinctive features of the modern world just as it distorts the past and assumes that there will be little fundamental change in world politics in the future (Buzan, Jones and Little 1993; Buzan and Little 2000).

A leading alternative approach provides a 'historical and multicultural perspective' on the interaction between different types of polity (including tribes, states and empires) over the millennia (Ferguson and Mansbach 1996: introduction). That perspective highlights a theme that is largely missing from the dominant theories of international relations, namely how the capabilities of political associations are constrained by cross-cutting identities and competing objects of loyalty (Ferguson and Mansbach 1996). Similar sensitivities to historical context are evident in some realist accounts of power and interdependence. Of particular importance is the stress on how successive great power hegemonies have entangled human beings in ever-wider structures and processes, an emphasis that echoes sociological writings on the role that states have played in promoting the long-term towards 'the globalization of human society' (Mennell 1990). As with Tilly's analysis of the rise of the modern sovereign state, a central aim is to explain how that peculiar European invention became the dominant political organization across the whole world, an outcome that could not have been predicted in the late medieval or early modern period when states first emerged. The encroachment of Western influences led many peripheral societies to create modern state structures in the hope of resisting external influences (Modelski 1978; Gilpin 1981: chapter 3). Some realists have argued that there is no reason to think that modern territorial states and the international system to which they belong will survive forever – just as there was little reason for people five centuries ago to believe that those emerging arrangements would dominate the political architecture of the modern world. The realities of the last few centuries must be considered in the broadest historical context. On that argument, the 'succession of hegemonies' that has defined world politics over the last few centuries may be replaced by the return of the norm in human history, which is the rise and fall of empires (Gilpin 1981: 144ff). Such issues have acquired special significance because of the rise of China, with analysts continuing to debate whether the modern states-system is in the process of escaping the hegemonic rivalries and wars that have been at the heart of international relations for millennia (see Buzan 2011, Clark 2011, Jervis 2011; Lebow 2010; also Elias 2010a).

Many analysts argue that there are important similarities between different international systems, as Waltz stated, but they are more inclined to look for realist 'generalizations' that are 'based on observations of historical experience' (Gilpin 1981; also Kaufman, Little and Wohlforth 2007 on balance of power in world history). In the attempt to explain international political change, they focus not only on war and geo-politics but also on such diverse phenomena as technological innovation, the relationship between the 'scale' of political organization and the 'loyalty' that political institutions can command, and levels of international economic competitiveness. A revised structural realist approach to international systems in world history attached special importance to changes in 'interaction capacities' over long-term intervals – that is, shifts in how political units are connected to each other and in the intensity of those connections (Buzan and Little 2000; 2002: 104–5.) In a direct challenge to Waltz's stress on the primacy of geo-political forces, the perspective highlights developments in 'sector integration', and notes how economic linkages have come to acquire unprecedented influence in recent times, in large part because of a more peaceful international environment. Growing interconnectedness has made it increasingly necessary to promote the collective management of world politics. A key contention is that the modern states-system surpasses its predecessors in the extent of its institutional refinement, as exemplified not only by joint efforts to preserve a balance of power but by the importance attached to other underpinnings of international society such as diplomacy, the plethora of international organizations and international law (Linklater and Suganami 2006; also Hurrell 2007). The question is whether rising levels of interconnectedness in recent decades have created unusual pressures (when considered in long-term perspective) to cooperate to restrain the use of force and to collaborate in order to deal with, for example, the challenges of climate change and global economic instability.

The final point to make in this section is that the structural realist approach has drawn attention to a 'wholly new departure in human history' which is 'the widespread acceptance of a universal norm of human equality' (Buzan and Little 2000: 340; see also Crawford 2000: 393). Such changes in the normative domain have found expression in the peculiarly modern phenomena of the universal human rights culture and international criminal law. They have also been regarded as the key to understanding other distinctive episodes in the modern states-system such as the delegitimation of colonialism and chattel slavery, two prevalent phenomena in international relations over the millennia (Crawford 2002). The 'Arab Spring' is a manifestation of widespread discontent with authoritarian or autocratic systems of government, although whether Egypt, Libya, Syria and other Middle Eastern societies will become Western-style liberal democracies is an open question. Suffice it to add that changes in principles of political legitimacy – including the dissemination of democratic norms – deserve pride of place in efforts to build bridges between historical sociology and International Relations. But they have not been discussed at length in 'structural' approaches that have analysed the influence of material production and/or coercive power on world politics (see Watson 1992: 208–9; Buzan and Little 2002: 29; Clark 2005, 2009).

System and society

To summarize the discussion thus far – various historical sociologists have attempted to explain phenomena that neo-realists have been accused of failing to examine: how the sovereign, territorial states that now dominate modern world politics replaced the complex webs of local and transnational authorities and loyalties that existed in the medieval era; how such associations acquired their prominence in Europe and then spread across the whole world; how those developments are connected with the evolution of a global capitalist economy and the rise of industrial capitalism and, increasingly, how shifts in power and production are linked with changing ideas about legitimacy in domestic and international politics, and with changing global standards or norms.

The English School of international relations and constructivism have been especially concerned with counteracting realism by underlining the importance of the ideational sphere, and specifically the role of law, morality and culture. Bull's distinction between international systems and societies which was discussed in Chapter 4 clarifies the point. Whereas systems are shaped by geo-political competition and by frequent outbreaks of war, international societies are constituted by common values, interests and institutions. Recent efforts in IR to build bridges with historical sociology have often ignored 'home grown' historical sociology which has analysed those features of international society. That neglect is partly because the British Committee for the Study of International Politics did not complete the project of comparing states-systems that had the potential to be a major contribution to historical-sociological investigation (Dunne 1998: 124ff). Wight (1977) provides the best summary of that enterprise. The first chapter of that collection of essays outlined the approach to analysing interdependencies between struggles for power, conceptions of international order, and visions of world community in different international societies – and particularly in the ancient Greek, ancient Chinese, and modern examples. It speculated that such an inquiry might reveal similar long-term patterns of development, namely the trend towards the concentration of military power in the hands of a declining number of states and the struggles for total dominance that transformed the relevant states-system into a universal empire. Without underestimating the importance of war and geo-politics in every historical era, the approach also emphasized the crucial role of moral and cultural forces in international societies (Chapter 4).

The main legacy of the British Committee's proposed comparative sociology is Watson (1992). The analysis provides a panoramic overview of international relations from the rise of the first city-state system in Mesopotamia around five and a half millennia ago to the current global economic and political order. The 'pendulum effect' which is central to that approach to international history emphasizes the alternation between monopolizing tendencies in systems of states and disintegrative forces in world empires (Watson 1992: 252ff). The theme is linked with the claim that the neo-realist distinction between 'anarchic' and 'hierarchic' systems obscures central features of international configurations of power. Those have ranged from the unusual condition in which the world is divided between *separate states* that respect one another's equality, to *hegemony* where one state or group of states determines the external conduct of all others, and *dominion,* where one state or group of states shapes the internal as well as the external affairs of other societies. Empires complete the spectrum (Watson 1992: 13ff). Watson adds that, in general, the distribution of power has fallen between the polar opposites of empire and a multi-state system in which the constituent parts recognize one another's sovereign equality.

The focus on different configurations of power represents the move towards a more structuralist version of the English School that downplays traditional concerns with moral and cultural forces in world politics (see Buzan 2004). But earlier questions about the evolution of principles of legitimacy have been revived in studies of the interpenetration of international and world society, and in constructivist writings (Clark 2005, 2007; Clark and Reus-Smit 2007; also Chapter 4 above). Two traditional themes have been central to those developments – the criteria that define legitimate members of international society, and the norms that codify what counts as 'rightful' and 'wrongful' conduct (Reus-Smit 1999: 30). Investigations into the 'moral purpose of the state' in different international systems, and analyses of how modern conceptions of sovereignty have shifted in response to changing principles of legitimacy, are important constructivist developments of Wendt's thesis that 'anarchy is what states make of it' (Reus-Smit 1999; Philpott 2001; Wendt 1992). Such explanations take issue with studies of structural constraints that neglect ideational forces and global norms.

More recent works are evidence of a reconsideration of the relationship between realism and constructivist sociology. In a comparison of the reasons for the collapse of two international orders – Latin Christendom and the Sinosphere – Phillips (2011) argues that constructivists must pay more attention to the interplay between the coercive foundations of international order and the ideational factors that have dominated their analysis thus far. In so doing, it becomes possible to understand how international orders have collapsed as a result of challenges to legitimacy and it becomes easier to comprehend the challenge posed by jihadist terrorism in the contemporary era. A similar shift towards synthesizing realism and constructivism (see Barkin 2010) is also evident in the critique of the orthodox assumption that the modern states-system emerged as part of a major rupture with the political architecture of the Middle Ages. The contention is that the outlines of the modern states-system were already present in the 1300s. The so-called medieval and modern periods should therefore be regarded as phases of one long developmental process that stretches back over approximately eight hundred years (Latham 2012). Along with Hui (2005) which compares the early modern and Chinese international orders, those recent works mark the revival of interest in comparative inquiry although none draws on, or aims to develop, the comparative sociology of states-systems that was outlined by Wight (1977: chapter 1).

Morality, culture and the emotions

Reference has been made to changes in large structures that historical sociologists analyse. The idea of structure suggests the brute realities of economic power and coercive capabilities that form major external constraints on human action. However, morality and culture are also important in many accounts of the structured worlds in which humans live – indeed from their standpoints, it is impossible to understand structures without considering their suffusion with values or norms. The critique of Weber's belief that ideas are like 'switchmen' that determine the tracks along which interests travel makes this point clear (Reus-Smit 2002b). The objection is that interests and norms cannot be separated in the manner suggested by the 'switchmen' metaphor. Interests are not formed in isolation from social principles and ideas. Indeed norms are part of their constitution. In International Relations, that conception of interdependencies between norms, identities and interests informs efforts to transcend the neo-realist assumption that anarchy dictates the interests that rational actors must pursue in order to survive. That is at the core of the attempt to move beyond ahistorical generalizations about core interests that are the assumed product of the logic of anarchy towards the historical analysis of the interplay between power struggles and normative frameworks in different phases of international history (Latham 2012; Phillips 2011; Reus-Smit 1999; and earlier Wight 1977).

European sociologists have long recognized the importance of developing a sociology of morals. Durkheim (1993: 32) called for 'a science of ethics' that placed 'moral facts' on the same level as all other social phenomena, and added that it is possible to 'observe them, describe them, classify them, and look for the laws explaining them'. Parallel themes ran through Weber's sociology of religion which, following the belief that Calvinism had been a major influence on the rise of Western capitalism, investigated the forms of economic life that had most affinity with the world-views of Hinduism, Confucianism and other major faith traditions. Weber's continuing importance approach is evident in Mann's reflections on how universal religions have often been the 'tracklayer of history' (1986: 342, 363). Especially important for the student of international relations are Weber's comments on the relationship between world religions and a phenomenon that is central to relations between human groups – namely 'the dualism of in-group and out-group morality'. Weber observed that from the earliest times, respect for the maxim, 'as you do unto me, I shall do unto you', has found most support in visions of how those who belong to the same community should behave towards each other. The group's right to depart from that ethic in its relations with other communities was often taken for granted, although,

Weber (1948: 329ff) stressed that Islamic, Christian and other religions defended a conception of 'universal brotherhood' which held that the 'do unto others' principle should be observed in relations with all other people, including enemies.

Weber's ideas have been regarded as laying the basis for a contemporary sociology of civilizations (Nelson 1973). Claims about the importance of civilizations became central to International Relations as a result of Huntington's controversial thesis in the early 1990s that world politics may be heading towards a 'clash of civilizations' – or to a reawakening of old civilizational identities that survived the rise of nationalism and the state but were obscured by the importation of those indicators of 'modernity'. The approach has been criticized for underestimating political and other divisions within Islamic and other civilizations, for suggesting that each civilization has an unchanging essence, and for neglecting such points of convergence between civilizations as the belief in 'universal brotherhood' that can be found in many world religions. Such debates have rekindled interest in the sub-field of civilizational analysis that appeared in the United States in the 1970s (Mandalios 2003; Katzenstein 2010, 2012a/b). Some approaches built on Weber's perspective, not least by paying more attention than his writings did to relations between civilizations, including the influence of Islamic scientific and theological ideas on early modern European social and political development (Nelson 1973). Understanding what Europe borrowed or learned from China and civilizations in its rise to global dominance has become a central theme in recent studies of world history (Hobson 2004 and McNeill 1995). Such analyses reflect the search for a post-colonial explanation of the interweaving of peoples that breaks with the widespread Eurocentrism of earlier narratives (Hobson 2012).

A related theme is what different civilizations have contributed to universal brotherhood, or to creating 'wider universalities of discourse' that promote sensitivity to the needs of other communities and greater accountability to distant strangers (Nelson 1973: 96). That focus is an important extension of Weber's emphasis on 'the dualism of in-group and out-group morality'. It raises questions about the potentials for more cosmopolitan orientations to relations between groups that require further research on the sociology of morals and, more specifically, on the role of emotions in world politics. Those questions need to be seen in conjunction with the central features of historical sociology that were described in the first paragraph of this chapter – namely the interest in explaining long-term processes of change and the relationship between social and political structures and everyday life. Approaches to power and production invariably analyse long-term structural change but do not explain how it is mirrored in the lives of the people involved. The idea of the sociology of morals provides a bridge between micro- and macro-social processes, particularly by considering the part that moral emotions play in binding 'agents' to 'structures'. The statement that social norms are literally embodied in the individual's emotional life, and are followed almost instinctively, captures the crucial point that shame, guilt and compassion and other emotions are not residual phenomena that are assigned their role once social structures are in place (Barbalet 2002). They are as much cause as effect of structural changes in the spheres of power and production.

Innovative developments in historical sociology have cast light on different aspects of the emotional life. Prominent among them is the study of mentalities that was advanced by the French *Annales* historians, and particularly by Lucien Febvre. In the 1920s, Febvre made the case for a new mode of inquiry called historical psychology that would investigate 'the emotional life of the past'. One aim was to discover how far basic emotions such as fear, pity and compassion have changed over time (Burke 1973). The sub-field of emotionology has extended that project by analysing 'the attitudes or standards that society, or a definable group within a society, maintains towards basic emotions and their appropriate expression' (Stearns and Stearns 1985).

Although this is changing, little attention has been paid to the emotions in mainstream IR – in large part because of the dominance of interest-based explanation (Crawford 2000; also Bleiker and Hutchison 2008). In recent years, constructivists and others have discussed the ways in which guilt, shame, compassion and other emotions have influenced how states behave in international society (Edelman 1990; Raymond 1997). Some approaches have analysed global 'campaigns of compassion' (Sznaider 2001), and they have shown how changing attitudes to cruelty and suffering contributed to the abolition of the Atlantic slave trade and colonialism, and led to support for the protection of minority peoples and indigenous peoples (Edelman 1990; Crawford 2002; Rae 2002; Keal 2003). Explorations of global norms have emphasized the causal role of moral beliefs and collective emotions as well as material interests, and they have argued that the challenge for explanatory theory is to understand their inter-relatedness (Raymond 1997). Attention has been drawn to the role of 'transnational moral entrepreneurs' in spearheading efforts to alleviate human suffering, and in seeking to find allies amongst the most powerful states (Edelman 1990). Such studies raise the question of whether moral concerns with reducing suffering are more influential in the modern states-system than in any of its predecessors.

Whatever the answer to that question may be, studies of emotions provide an essential counterweight to the neo-realist view that beliefs and emotions need not feature in a 'parsimonious' theory of international politics (Chapter 2). The former can contribute to understanding 'we-images' in security communities, that underpin the 'democratic peace', and facilitate or block the development of trust between independent political communities (Adler and Barnett 1998; MacMillan 1998; Booth and Wheeler 2007). By stressing the importance of ideas and agency in world politics, those approaches do more than criticize what they regard as the one-sided focus on structural constraints in traditional analyses of production and power. They take issue with the pessimism that runs through many of those approaches, and explore what may be unique opportunities for embedding humanitarian norms in international society. That is a major reason for replacing the focus on the supposedly immutable 'logic of anarchy' with more historically aware investigations of possibilities for new departures.

A higher synthesis?

The last two sections invite the question of whether a higher level of theoretical synthesis can integrate insights about how the interaction between material power, systems of production, culture and identity, morality and the emotions have shaped long-term developments in the relations between societies. With that issue in mind, the following turns to Elias's conception of 'process sociology' which suggests how such a synthesis can be constructed.

The nature of process sociology is evident in his explanation of the transformation of Western European societies between the fifteenth and twentieth century. Elias was primarily interested in understanding the relationship between state-formation and the 'civilizing process' in which Europeans came to see themselves as superior to their medieval forebears and to peoples in the non-European world. It is essential to add that Elias did not use the notion of the civilizing process to support some doctrine of European cultural superiority. The aim was to understand the long-term processes of change that led to such collective self-images (for a summary of Elias's argument, see Linklater and Mennell 2010).

Elias described medieval Europe as a zone of conflict in which lords were compelled to compete for power and security in the absence of a higher monopoly of force. 'Elimination contests' led to territorial concentrations of power. The development of state monopolies of power contributed to internal pacification, to urbanization and to higher levels of economic interdependence. More and more people became interconnected in a complex social division of labour. The fear of the state's power became less critical for the preservation of order; the individual's capacity for self-restraint grew in importance. Social constraints on violence became more deeply embedded in the lives of people, among the 'the secular upper classes' at first, and then across the remainder of society (Elias 1983: 55–6).

From the standpoint of process sociology, changes in the emotional life were as central as the rise of state monopolies of power and longer chains of interdependence for long-term patterns of development. The need for coercion did not lose its importance, but the instruments of violence 'retreated to the barracks', only to reappear when there were challenges to the state or threats to public order. Different groups came to think that cruel and violent acts were incompatible with their 'civilization'. The public execution and the violent punishment of criminals were eliminated in most of the societies involved; cruelty to animals and children was outlawed. Those changes were evidence of closer emotional identification between the members of modern societies. In governing those societies, ruling elites are as a result less violent than their medieval predecessors who had few inhibitions in injuring, exploiting or humiliating those who were deemed to be their social inferiors.

The analysis of the civilizing process operated at a high level of synthesis that brought the competition for power and security, increasing levels of interconnectedness, and shifting moral sensibilities that included changing emotional attitudes to cruelty and violence together within a single framework. The approach is relevant to attempts to understand such central questions in International Relations as 'How did the state get to the state? What is sovereignty, who has it, and over what? If the state is sovereign, how did it get sovereignty? Why is sovereignty exerted territorially rather than on some other basis?' (Thomson 1994: 153): Of particular interest in this regard is the fact that Elias was unusual among sociologists of his generation in integrating domestic and international politics within one perspective. A recurrent theme in his writings is that, throughout human history, most people have identified with the relevant 'survival unit' – the kinship group, city-state, modern nation-state or whatever entity protected them from internal and external threats. Echoing Weber's emphasis on insider/outsider distinctions, Elias argued that most societies have had a double standard of morality, developing strict taboos against killing members of the in-group while tolerating, and at times encouraging and rewarding, violence against other communities. As a result, there has been no counterpart to the civilizing process in the relations between independent communities. In the absence of a higher monopoly of power, there has been limited success in taming violent struggles for power and in widening the scope of emotional identification between people. What had changed over time, Elias argued, is the size of the viable 'survival unit'. Elimination contests had led to ever-larger territorial monopolies of power, a social dynamic that might only end when humanity is brought under the dominion of a world state.

Elias believed that there was more to human history than an overall trend towards ever larger concentrations of power with the capacity to inflict more devastating forms of harm on more and more people over greater distances. An important overall long-term trend was the development of higher levels of interconnectedness within and between societies. Within the more pacified societies, the greater interweaving of peoples' lives had created pressures to establish national institutions to steer the future course of development (Mennell 2007). As noted earlier, the scope of emotional identification had widened between members of the same society, particularly where the dominant groups depended on less powerful social strata for the satisfaction of their interests (De Swaan 1995, 1997). A central question in Elias's writings is whether similar developments will take place globally in the absence of political institutions that have a monopoly control of the instruments of violence (see Linklater 2011a for further details).

Elias maintained that an 'immense process of integration' has forced societies into global webs of interdependence, introducing the need to exercise greater self-restraint (not least with respect to the most destructive instruments of violence) and to become more attuned to the interests of others 'over wider areas' and 'over longer chains of action'. A sense of moral responsibility for suffering strangers had grown to some extent, but there are no guarantees that societies will become more cosmopolitan. Many groups resent the encroachment of alien influences and fear that globalization will lead to the loss of power and status. Nationalist or xenophobic 'counter-thrusts' to the growing interweaving of societies exist, Elias argued, and may increase in future. Violent struggles for power and security have not come to an end, nor has the temptation to set aside 'civilized' constraints on force when communities believe that security or survival are threatened. Those observations about long-term social processes did not display much optimism about the prospects for a global civilizing process, but at least some progress had been made in eliminating hegemonic wars. Elias observed that current levels of interconnectedness have appeared in what is still an early stage in humanity's history. Major advances in learning how to co-exist amicably might occur over the thousands or millions of years that lie ahead, assuming that the species does not destroy itself first (Elias 2010b).

On grand narratives

Process sociology has analysed long-term processes both in the European context and with respect to developments that have affected humanity as a whole. It is the heir to the nineteenth-century theories of history, but shorn of the belief in the inevitability of social progress that the post-modern thinker, Lyotard, condemned in his influential critique of the 'grand meta-narratives' (see Chapter 8). Elias (2007) maintained that those narratives were premature because they relied on what is now known to be unreliable evidence and rested on a discredited faith in Western superiority. They were best regarded as preliminary efforts to understand long-term trends towards the globalization of social and economic life that can now be analysed with greater detachment.

Such approaches to historical sociology overlap with accounts of world history (see Mann 1986, 1994b; McNeill 1979) and McNeill and McNeill 2003). Also noteworthy is the sub-field of 'new global history' that analyses the history of globalization (Mazlish and Irigye 2005; Mazlish 2006; also Denemark *et al.* 2000 and Gills and Thompson 2006). Parallel ventures in IR can be found in works by Buzan and Little (2000), Camilleri and Falk (2009), Ferguson and Mansbach (1996), van der Pijl (2007, 2010), and Watson (1992). In the main, those approaches have developed independently of each other, and it is unclear that they add up to a coherent narrative. But there is merit in the idea that they have a common interest in understanding the history of interconnected-ness between societies over the centuries and millennia (Manning 2003). That shared perspective is evidence of the need to incorporate an analy-sis of encounters between strangers (in the form of trade, cultural exchange, migration, war and geo-politics) in a more comprehensive conception of world history (McNeill 1995). As noted earlier, the main purpose is explanatory. But there is a normative dimension to some approaches which is evident in the claim that understanding 'the trials and tribulations of humanity as a whole' may help to foster a sense of identification between peoples, contribute to diminishing 'the lethality of group encounters', and encourage more cooperative responses to the interlocked challenges that affect, however unevenly, the whole species (McNeill 1986: 16).

Confidence in the normative value of studying world history raises standard questions about the principles that should underpin some future world political organization. A related issue is whether such explanatory projects can avoid the dangers of earlier grand narratives, and specifically the nineteenth-century philosophies of history that inter-preted the human past as a journey that led inexorably to the global ascendancy of Western civilization. Such concerns owe much to the influ-ence of post-colonial writings that have explored how those narratives legitimated the imperial domination of colonized peoples (Said 1979). The issue is whether future analyses of long-term processes that have shaped the development of humanity as a whole can become more detached, thereby avoiding the reinvention of similar divisions between the 'civilized self' and the 'backward other'. To date, such analyses have developed without much engagement with the post-colonial literature (see Chakrabarty 2003; Patomaki 2007 and Seth 2011). Suffice it to add that attempts to revive grand narratives will need to be conscious of post-colonial warnings of the dangers of producing interpretations of the past that celebrate some peoples' accomplishments while diminishing others' achievements (Burke 2003).

Conclusion

Efforts to build new bridges between historical sociology and International Relations have increased in the past few years. Various scholars in IR have turned to historical sociology to cast light on the changing features of international politics that are obscured by neo-realist analysis, and to provide a counterweight to 'presentism'. However, historical sociology is a 'post-disciplinary' web of approaches that have different objects of analysis and methodological commitments (Delanty and Isin 2003). Some attach more importance to power or production than to ideational forces; some make moral and cultural developments central to the analysis; some seek to unite, albeit in different ways, those phenomena within one overarching framework. In addition, some perspectives focus on the development of the modern world; some compare international systems in different eras, and others are concerned with long-term historical trends that have affected the whole of humanity. But common to many is the desire to understand the development of interconnections between societies and to explain the overall trend towards the integration of the species.

Students of international relations have much to gain from engaging with those diverse approaches. They can acquire a deeper understanding of the reasons for the rise and spread of the modern territorial state, of the relationship between capitalism and the state system, and of the influence of different conceptions of morality and legitimacy on world politics. They can derive insights into the respects in which the modern system of states is similar to, and different from, earlier forms of world political organization. That is where the study of international relations can also contribute to the development of historical sociology. The discipline has a unique capacity to reveal how relations between independent communities have shaped the expanding human web over centuries and millennia. Current levels of global interconnectedness make it all the more important to understand how societies responded to the challenges of interdependence in earlier times. Comprehending past achievements and failures in developing solidarities between communities has its intrinsic value, but it can also contribute to efforts to deal with the challenges of rising levels of human interconnectedness in the contemporary era.

7 | Critical Theory

RICHARD DEVETAK

One of the defining characteristics of critical theory is its insistence on self-reflection, including an account of how knowledge emerges out of and is situated in particular contexts. It should come as little surprise then that critical theory should cast a backwards glance not only at its intellectual origins and evolution, but also its achievements and failures in application to the study of international relations. In the years since 1981, according to these self-reflective accounts (Rengger and Thirkell-White 2007, Brincat, Lima and Nunes 2012), the discipline of International Relations has been transformed, not least because of the theory's critical interventions across a broad range of topics in the study of international relations.

While guided by the long-term project of an emancipatory politics, critical theories of international relations take problems and issues in the present as their point of departure. Among the most pressing issue areas addressed by critical theorists of international relations in recent years are: international security (Fierke 2007), ballistic missile defence (Peoples 2010), the war on terror (Burke 2004, 2005), humanitarian intervention (Bjola 2005; Devetak 2007; Head 2008) and the global trade regime (Kapoor 2004), just to name a few. On a broader scale, Andrew Linklater (2011b), one of the foremost proponents of critical theory in International Relations, has published the first of a projected three-volume study of harm in international relations, and has been joined by other critical theorists in pursuit of a cosmopolitan politics (Beardsworth 2011; Benhabib 2006; Fine 2007). Still others have restated and advanced the case for a critical theory of international relations in general (Anievas 2005; Haacke 2005; Roach 2010; Weber, 2002, 2005, 2007). Perhaps one of the most interesting developments over the past decade or so has been the increasing interest taken in international relations by the world's leading critical theorist, Jürgen Habermas. In his recent writings he has intervened in the debate on NATO's humanitarian war over Kosovo (1999), articulated a forthright critique of the Iraq War (2003a), reflected on the terrorist attacks of September 11 (2003b), continued his support for Europe as a constitutional 'counter-power' (Habermas and Derrida 2003), and comprehensively outlined an alternative vision of cosmopolitan global governance (2006: chapter 8).

This chapter will show how critical theories of international relations have come to achieve this position in the discipline. The first part sketches the origins of critical theory; the second offers an examination of the political nature of knowledge claims in international relations; and the third details critical international theory's attempt to place questions of community at the centre of the study of international relations. Differences will emerge among critical theorists, but if there is one thing that holds together the disparate group of scholars who subscribe to 'critical theory', it is the idea that the study of international relations should be oriented by an emancipatory politics.

Origins of critical theory

Critical theory has its roots in a strand of thought which is often traced back to the Enlightenment and connected to the writings of Kant, Hegel and Marx. While this is an important lineage in the birth of critical theory it is not the only one that can be traced, as there is also the imprint of classical Greek thought on autonomy and democracy to be considered, as well as the thinking of Nietzsche and Weber. However, in the twentieth century critical theory became most closely associated with a distinct body of thought known as the Frankfurt School (Jay 1973). It is in the work of Max Horkheimer, Theodor Adorno, Walter Benjamin, Herbert Marcuse, Erich Fromm, Leo Lowenthal and, more recently, Jürgen Habermas and Axel Honneth that critical theory acquired a renewed potency and in which the term *critical theory* came to be used as the emblem of a philosophy which questions modern social and political life through a method of immanent critique. It was largely an attempt to recover a critical and emancipatory potential that had been overrun by recent intellectual, social, cultural, political, economic and technological trends.

Essential to the Frankfurt School's critical theory was a concern to comprehend the central features of contemporary society by understanding its historical and social development, and tracing contradictions in the present which may open up the possibility of transcending contemporary society and its built-in pathologies and forms of domination. Critical theory intended 'not simply to eliminate one or other abuse', but to analyse the underlying social structures which result in these abuses with the intention of overcoming them (Horkheimer 1972: 206). It is not difficult to notice the presence here of the theme advanced by Marx in his eleventh thesis on Feuerbach: 'philosophers have only interpreted the world in various ways; the point is to change it' (Marx 1977a: 158). This normative interest in identifying immanent possibilities for social transformation is a defining characteristic of a line of thought which extends, at least, from Kant, through Marx, to contemporary critical theorists such as Habermas and Honneth. This intention to analyse the possibilities of realizing emancipation in the modern world entailed critical analyses of both obstructions to, and intrinsic tendencies towards, 'the rational organization of human activity' (Horkheimer 1972: 223). Indeed, this concern extends the line of thought back beyond Kant to the classical Greek conviction that the rational constitution of the *polis* finds its expression in individual autonomy and the establishment of justice and democracy. Politics, on this understanding, is the realm concerned with realizing the just life.

There is, however, an important difference between critical theorists and the Greeks, which relates to the conditions under which knowledge claims can be made regarding social and political life. There are two points worth recalling in this regard: first, the Kantian point that reflection on the limits of what we can know is a fundamental part of theorizing and, second, a Hegelian and Marxian point that knowledge is always, and irreducibly, conditioned by historical and material contexts; in Mark Rupert's words (2003: 186), it is always 'situated knowledge'. Since critical theory takes society itself as its object of analysis, and since theories and acts of theorizing are never independent of society, critical theory's scope of analysis must necessarily include reflection on theory. In short, critical theory must be *self-reflective*; it must include an account of its own genesis and application in society. By drawing attention to the relationship between knowledge and society, which is so frequently excluded from mainstream theoretical analysis, critical theory recognizes the political nature of knowledge claims.

It was on the basis of this recognition that Horkheimer distinguished between two conceptions of theory, which he referred to as 'traditional' and 'critical' theories. Traditional conceptions of theory picture the theorist at a remove from the object of analysis. By analogy with the natural sciences, they insist that subject and object must be strictly separated in order to theorize properly. Traditional conceptions of theory assume there is an external world 'out there' to study, and that an inquiring subject can study this world in a balanced and objective manner by withdrawing from the world it investigates, and leaving behind any ideological beliefs, values, or opinions which would invalidate the inquiry. To qualify as theory it must at least be value-free. On this view, theory is possible only on condition that an inquiring subject can withdraw from the world it studies (and in which it exists) and rid itself of all biases. This contrasts with critical conceptions that deny the possibility of value-free social analysis.

By recognizing that theories are always embedded in social and political life, critical conceptions of theory allow for an examination of the purposes and functions served by particular theories. However, while such conceptions of theory recognize the unavoidability of taking their orientation from the social context in which they are situated, their guiding interest is one of emancipation from, rather than legitimation and consolidation of, existing social forms. The purpose underlying critical, as opposed to traditional, conceptions of theory is to improve human existence by abolishing injustice (Horkheimer 1972). As articulated by Horkheimer (1972: 215), this conception of theory does not simply present an expression of the 'concrete historical situation', it also acts as 'a force within [that situation] to stimulate change'. It allows for the intervention of humans in the making of their history.

It should be noted that while critical theory had not directly addressed the international level until recently, this in no way implies that international relations is beyond the limits of its concern. The writings of Kant and Marx, in particular, have demonstrated that what happens at the international level is of immense significance to the achievement of universal emancipation. It is the continuation of this project in which critical international theory is engaged. The Frankfurt School, however, never addressed international relations in its critiques of the modern world, and Habermas made only scant reference to it until recently (see Habermas 1998, 2003a, 2006; Habermas and Derrida 2003). The main tendency of critical theory is to take individual society as the focus and to neglect the dimension of relations between and across societies. For critical international theory, however, the task is to extend the trajectory of Frankfurt School critical theory beyond the domestic realm to the international – or, more accurately, global – realm. It makes a case for a theory of world politics which is 'committed to the emancipation of the species' (Linklater 1990a: 8). Such a theory would no longer be confined to an individual state or society, but would examine relations between and across them, and reflect on the possibility of extending the rational, just and democratic organization of political society across the globe (Neufeld 1995: chapter 1; Shapcott 2001).

To summarize, critical theory draws upon various strands of Western social, political and philosophical thought in order to erect a theoretical framework capable of reflecting on the nature and purposes of theory and revealing both obvious and subtle forms of injustice and domination in society. Critical theory not only challenges and dismantles traditional forms of theorizing, it also problematizes and seeks to dismantle entrenched forms of social life that constrain human freedom. Critical international theory is an extension of this critique to the international domain. The next part of the chapter focuses on the attempt by critical international theorists to dismantle traditional forms of theorizing by promoting more self-reflective theory.

The politics of knowledge in international relations theory

It was not until the 1980s, and the onset of the so-called 'third debate', that questions relating to the politics of knowledge were taken seriously in the study of international relations. Epistemological questions regarding the justification and verification of knowledge claims, the methodology applied and the scope and purpose of inquiry, and ontological questions regarding the nature of the social actors and other historical formations and structures in international relations, all carry normative implications that had been inadequately addressed. One of the important contributions of critical international theory has been to widen the object domain of International Relations, not just to include epistemological and ontological assumptions, but to explicate their connection to prior political commitments.

This section outlines the way in which critical theory brings knowledge claims in international relations under critical scrutiny. First, it considers the question of epistemology by describing how Horkheimer's distinction between traditional and critical conceptions of theory has been taken up in international relations; and second, it elaborates the connection between critical theory and emancipatory theory. The result of this scrutinizing is to reveal the role of political interests in knowledge formation. As Robert Cox (1981: 128) succinctly and famously said, 'theory is always *for* someone and *for* some purpose'. As a consequence, critical international theorists reject the idea that theoretical knowledge is neutral or non-political. Whereas traditional theories would tend to see power and interests as *a posteriori* factors affecting outcomes in interactions between political actors in the sphere of international relations, critical international theorists insist that they are by no means absent in the formation and verification of knowledge claims. Indeed, they are *a priori* factors affecting the production of knowledge, hence Kimberly Hutchings' (1999: 69) assertion that 'international relations theory is not only about politics, it also is itself political'.

Problem-solving and critical theories

In his pioneering 1981 article, Robert Cox distinguished critical from problem-solving theory. Despite appearances, Cox (2012: 18) insists that he had been unaware of the Frankfurt School's work in general, or Horkheimer's distinction in particular, when he devised the distinction (see Leysens 2008 and Devetak 2012: 116). Nonetheless, parallels exist. Problem-solving theories, like Horkheimer's traditional theories, are marked by two main characteristic theoretical tendencies: by a positivist methodology, and by a tendency to legitimize prevailing social and political structures. Critical theories, again like Horkheimer's, oppose problem-solving theories by rejecting both these theoretical tendencies.

Heavily influenced by the methodologies of the natural sciences, problem-solving theories suppose that positivism provides the only legitimate basis of knowledge. Positivism is seen, as Steve Smith (1996: 13) remarks, as the 'gold standard' against which other theories are evaluated. There are many different characteristics that can be identified with positivism, but two are particularly relevant to our discussion. First, positivists assume that facts and values can be separated; second, that it is possible to separate subject and object. This results in the view not only that an objective world exists independently of human consciousness, but that objective knowledge of social reality is possible insofar as values are expunged from analysis.

Problem-solving theory, as Cox (1981: 128) defines it, 'takes the world as it finds it, with the prevailing social and power relationships and the institutions into which they are organized, as the given framework for action. It does not question the present order, but has the effect of legitimizing and reifying it.' Its general aim, says Cox (1981: 129), is to make the existing order 'work smoothly by dealing effectively with particular sources of trouble'. Neo-realism, *qua* problem-solving theory, takes seriously the realist dictum to work with, rather than against, prevailing international forces. By working within the given system it has a stabilizing effect, tending to preserve the existing global structure of social and political relations. Cox points out that neo-liberal institutionalism also partakes of problem solving. Its objective, as explained by its foremost exponent, is to 'facilitate the smooth operation of decentralized international political systems' (Keohane 1984: 63). Situating itself between the states-system and the liberal capitalist global economy, neo-liberalism's main concern is to ensure that the two systems function smoothly in their co-existence. It seeks to render the two global systems compatible and stable by diffusing any conflicts, tensions, or crises that might arise between them (Cox 1992b: 173). As critical theorist James Bohman (2002: 506) says, such an approach 'models the social scientist on the engineer, who masterfully chooses the optimal solution to a problem of design'. In summary, traditional conceptions of theory tend to work in favour of stabilizing prevailing structures of world order and their accompanying inequalities of power and wealth.

The main point that Cox wishes to make about problem-solving theory is that its failure to reflect on the prior framework within which it theorizes means that it tends to operate in favour of prevailing ideological priorities. Its claims to value-neutrality notwithstanding, problem-solving theory is plainly 'value-bound by virtue of the fact that it implicitly accepts the prevailing order as its own framework' (Cox 1981: 130). As a consequence, it remains oblivious to the way power and interests precede and shape knowledge claims.

By contrast, critical international theory starts from the conviction that because cognitive processes themselves are contextually situated and therefore subject to political interests, they ought to be critically evaluated. Theories of international relations, like any knowledge, are necessarily conditioned by social, cultural and ideological influence, and one of the main tasks of critical theory is to reveal the effect of this conditioning. As Richard Ashley (1981: 207) asserts, 'knowledge is always constituted in reflection of interests', so critical theory must bring to consciousness latent interests, commitments, or values that give rise to, and orient, any theory. We must concede therefore that the study of international relations 'is, and always has been, unavoidably normative' (Neufeld 1995: 108), despite claims to the contrary. Because critical international theory sees an intimate connection between social life and cognitive processes, it rejects the positivist distinctions between fact and value, object and subject. By ruling out the possibility of objective knowledge, critical international theory seeks to promote greater 'theoretical reflexivity' (1995: chapter 3). Cox (1992a: 59) expresses this reflexivity in terms of a double process: the first is 'self-consciousness of one's own historical time and place which determines the questions that claim attention'; the second is 'the effort to understand the historical dynamics that brought about the conditions in which these questions arose'. Similarly, Bohman (2002: 503) advocates a form of theoretical reflexivity based on the 'perspective of a critical-reflective participant'. By adopting these reflexive attitudes critical theory is more like a meta-theoretical attempt to examine how theories are situated in prevailing social and political orders, how this situatedness impacts on theorizing, and, most importantly, the possibilities for theorizing in a manner that challenges the injustices and inequalities built into the prevailing world order.

Critical theory's relation to the prevailing order needs to be explained with some care. For although it refuses to take the prevailing order as it finds it, critical theory does not simply ignore it. It accepts that humans do not make history under conditions of their own choosing, as Marx observed in *The Eighteenth Brumaire of Louis Bonaparte* (1977e), and so a detailed examination of present conditions must necessarily be undertaken. Nevertheless, the order which has been 'given' to us is by no means natural, necessary or historically invariable. Critical international theory takes the global configuration of power relations as its object and asks how that configuration came about, what costs it brings with it and what alternatives remain immanent in history.

Critical theory is essentially a critique of the dogmatism it finds in traditional modes of theorizing. This critique reveals the unexamined assumptions that guide traditional modes of thought, and exposes the complicity of traditional modes of thought in prevailing political and social conditions. To break with dogmatic modes of thought is to 'denaturalize' the present, as Karin Fierke (1998: 13) puts it, to make us 'look again, in a fresh way, at that which we assume about the world because it has become overly familiar'. Denaturalizing '[allegedly] objective realities opens the door to alternative forms of social and political life'. Implicitly, therefore, critical theory *qua* denaturalizing critique serves 'as an instrument for the delegitimisation of established power and privilege' (Neufeld 1995: 14). The knowledge critical international theory generates is not neutral; it is ethically charged by an interest in social and political transformation. It criticizes and debunks theories that legitimize the prevailing order and affirms progressive alternatives that promote emancipation.

This immediately raises the question of how ethical judgements about the prevailing world order can be formed. Since there are no objective theoretical frameworks there can be no Archimedean standpoint outside history or society from which to engage in ethical criticism or judgement. It is not a matter of drafting a set of moral ideals and using them as a transcendent benchmark to judge forms of political organization. There is no utopia to compare to facts. This means that critical international theory must employ the method of immanent critique rather than abstract ethics to criticize the present order of things (Linklater 1990a: 22–3; Fierke 2007: chapter 8).

The task, therefore, is to 'start from where we are', in Rorty's words (quoted in Linklater 1998: 77), and excavate the principles and values that structure our political society, exposing the contradictions or inconsistencies in the way our society is organized to pursue its espoused values. This point is endorsed by several other critical international theorists, including Karin Fierke and Kimberly Hutchings. Immanent critique is undertaken in the absence of 'an independently articulated method' or 'an ahistorical point of reference' (Hutchings 1999: 99; Fierke 2007: 167). Following Hegel's advice, critical international theory must acknowledge that the resources for criticizing and judging can be found only 'immanently', that is, in the already existing political societies from where the critique is launched. The critical resources brought to bear do not fall from the sky, they issue from the historical development of concrete legal and political institutions and social movements. The task of the political theorist is therefore to explain and criticize the present political order in terms of the principles presupposed by and embedded in its own legal, political and cultural practices and institutions (Fierke 1998: 114; Hutchings 1999: 102).

Fiona Robinson (1999) similarly argues that ethics should not be conceived as separate from the theories and practices of international relations, but should instead be seen as embedded in them. In agreement with Hutchings she argues for a 'phenomenology of ethical life' rather than an 'abstract ethics about the application of rules' (Robinson 1999: 31). On her account of a 'global ethics of care', however, it is necessary also to submit the background assumptions of already existing moral and political discourses to critical scrutiny. Fierke, Hutchings and Robinson agree with Linklater that any critical international theory must employ a mode of immanent critique. This means that the theorist must engage critically with the background normative assumptions that structure our ethical judgements in an effort to generate a more coherent fit between modes of thought and forms of political organization, and without relying on a set of abstract ethical principles.

Critical theory's task as an emancipatory theory

If problem-solving theories adopt a positivist methodology and end up reaffirming the prevailing system, critical theories are informed by the traditions of hermeneutics and *Ideologiekritik* (ideology critique). Critical international theory is concerned not only with understanding and explaining the existing realities of world politics, it also intends to criticize and transform them. It is an attempt to comprehend essential social processes for the purpose of inaugurating change, or at least knowing whether change is possible. In Hoffman's words (1987: 233), it is 'not merely an expression of the concrete realities of the historical situation, but also a force for change within those conditions'. Neufeld (1995: chapter 5) also affirms this view of critical theory. It offers, he says, a form of social criticism that supports practical political activity aimed at societal transformation.

Critical theory's emancipatory interest is concerned with 'securing freedom from unacknowledged constraints, relations of domination, and conditions of distorted communication and understanding that deny humans the capacity to make their future through full will and consciousness' (Ashley 1981: 227). This plainly contrasts with problem-solving theories which tend to accept what Linklater (1997) calls the 'immutability thesis'. Critical theory is committed to extending the rational, just and democratic organization of political life beyond the level of the state to the whole of humanity.

The conception of emancipation promoted by critical international theory is largely inherited from a strand of thought which finds its origin in the Enlightenment project. This was generally concerned to break with past forms of injustice to foster the conditions necessary for universal freedom (Devetak 1995b). To begin with, emancipation, as understood by Enlightenment thinkers and critical international theorists, generally expresses a negative conception of freedom which consists in the removal of unnecessary, socially created constraints. This understanding is manifest in Booth's (1991b: 539) definition of emancipation as 'freeing people from those constraints that stop them carrying out what freely they would choose to do'. The emphasis in this understanding is on dislodging those impediments or impositions which unnecessarily curtail individual and collective freedom. Emancipation is a quest for autonomy, for self-determination (Linklater 1990a: 10, 135), but one that 'cannot be gained at the expense of others' (Fierke 2007: 188). It is also an open-ended 'process rather than an end-point, a direction rather than a destination' (Fierke 2007: 190).

In Linklater's account of critical international theory two thinkers are integral: Immanuel Kant and Karl Marx. Kant's approach is instructive because it seeks to incorporate the themes of power, order *and* emancipation (Linklater 1990a: 21–2). As expressed by Linklater (1992b: 36), Kant 'considered the possibility that state power would be tamed by principles of international order and that, in time, international order would be modified until it conformed with principles of cosmopolitan justice'. Kant's theory of international relations is an early attempt to map out a critical international theory by absorbing the insights and criticizing the weaknesses – in what would later be called realist thought – under an interest in universal freedom and justice. While Linklater believes Marx's approach to be too narrow in its focus on class-based exclusion, he thinks it nevertheless provides the basis of a social theory on which critical international theory must build. As Linklater observed (1990b: 159), both Marx and Kant share 'the desire for a universal society of free individuals, a universal kingdom of ends'. Both held strong attachments to the Enlightenment themes of freedom and universalism, and both launched strong critiques of particularistic life-forms with the intention of expanding moral and political community.

To conclude this part of the chapter, critical international theory makes a strong case for paying closer attention to the relations between knowledge and interests. One of critical international theory's main contributions in this regard is to expose the political nature of knowledge formation. Underlying all this is an explicit interest in challenging and removing socially produced constraints on human freedom, thereby contributing to the possible transformation of international relations (Linklater 1990b: 1, 1998).

Rethinking political community

Informing critical international theory is the spirit, if not the letter, of Marx's critique of capitalism. Like Marx, critical international theorists seek to develop a social theory with emancipatory intent (Haacke 2005; Linklater 2007a: chapter 11). Since the mid-1990s one of the core themes that has grown out of critical international theory is the need to develop more sophisticated understandings of community as a means of identifying and eliminating global constraints on humanity's potential for freedom, equality and self-determination (Linklater 1990b: 7). Linklater's approach to this task, which has set the agenda is first, to analyse the way in which inequality and domination flow from modes of political community tied to the sovereign state, second, to develop a social theory of the states-system, and third, to consider alternative forms of political community which promote human emancipation.

This section elaborates the three dimensions on which critical international theory rethinks political community (see Linklater 1992a: 92–7). The first dimension is normative, and pertains to the philosophical critique of the state as an exclusionary form of political organization. The second is sociological, and relates to the need to develop an account of the origins and evolution of the modern state and states-system and their accompanying harms. The third is the praxeological dimension concerning practical possibilities for reconstructing international relations along more emancipatory and cosmopolitan lines. The overall effect of critical international theory, and its major contribution to international relations, is to focus on the normative foundations of political life.

The normative dimension: the critique of ethical particularism and social exclusion

One of the key philosophical assumptions that has structured political and ethical thought and practice about international relations is the idea that the modern state is the natural form of political community. The sovereign state has been 'fetishized', to use Marx's term, as the normal mode of organizing political life. Critical international theorists, however, wish to problematize this fetishization and draw attention to the 'moral deficits' that are created by the state's interaction with the capitalist world economy. In this section, I outline critical international theory's philosophical inquiry into the normative bases of political life and its critique of ethical particularism and the social exclusion it generates.

The philosophical critique of particularism was first, and most systematically, set out in Andrew Linklater's *Men and Citizens* (1990b). His main concern there was to trace how modern political thought had constantly differentiated ethical obligations due to co-citizens from those due to the rest of humanity. In practice, this tension between 'men' and 'citizens' has always been resolved in favour of citizens. Even if it was acknowledged, as it was by most early modern thinkers, that certain universal rights were thought to extend to all members of the human community, they were always residual and secondary to particularistic ones. Indeed, as Linklater (2007a: 182) observes, this tension has often been exploited for the purposes of devaluing the 'suffering of distant strangers' and sometimes even celebrating their suffering.

Men and Citizens is, among other things, a work of recovery. It seeks to recover a political philosophy based on universal ethical reasoning which has been progressively marginalized in the twentieth century, especially with the onset of the Cold War and the hegemony of realism. That is, it seeks to recover and reformulate the Stoic-Christian ideal of human community. While elements of this ideal can be found in the natural law tradition, it is to the Enlightenment tradition that Linklater turns to find a fuller expression of this ideal. Linklater here is strongly influenced by the thought of Kant, for whom war was undeniably related to the division of humankind into separate, self-regarding political units, Rousseau, who caustically remarked that in joining a particular community individual citizens necessarily made themselves enemies of the rest of humanity, and Marx who saw in the modern state a contradiction between general and private interests.

The point being made here is that particularistic political associations lead to inter-societal estrangement, the perpetual possibility of war and social exclusion. This type of argument underlies the thought of several Enlightenment thinkers of the eighteenth century, including Montesquieu, Rousseau, Paine and Kant among others, for whom war was simply an expression of *ancien régime* politics and a tool of state. Marx extended the critique of the modern state by arguing that, in upholding the rule of law, private property and money, it masks capitalism's alienation and exploitation behind bourgeois ideals of freedom and equality. Marx, of course, viewed the separation of politics and economics as a liberal illusion created to mask capitalism's power relations. In Rupert's words (2003: 182), one of Marx's enduring insights is 'that the seemingly apolitical economic spaces generated by capitalism – within and across juridical states – are permeated by structured relations of social power deeply consequential for political life'. From this Marxian perspective, modern international relations, insofar as they combine the political system of sovereign states and the economic system of market capitalism, are a form of exclusion where particular class interests parade themselves as universal. The problem with the sovereign state therefore is that as a 'limited moral community' it promotes exclusion, generating estrangement, injustice, insecurity and violent conflict between self-regarding states by imposing rigid boundaries between 'us' and 'them' (Cox 1981: 137; Linklater 1990b: 28).

Such arguments have led in recent times, and especially after a century which saw genocides and unprecedented flows of stateless peoples and refugees, to more general and profound questions about the foundations on which humanity is politically divided and organized. In particular, as Hutchings (1999: 125) notes, it has led critical international theory to a 'questioning of the nation-state as a normatively desirable mode of political organisation'. Consistent with other critical international theorists Hutchings (1999: 122, 135) problematizes the 'idealised fixed ontologies' of nation and state. Hutchings goes further than Linklater, however, by also problematizing the individual 'self' of liberalism. Her intention is to examine the status of all normative claims to self-determination, whether the 'self' is understood as the individual, nation, or state. But insofar as her critique is aimed at placing the 'self' in question as a self-contained entity, Hutchings' analysis complements and extends the philosophical critique of particularism undertaken by Linklater.

Richard Shapcott (2000b, 2001) also continues this critique by inquiring into the way different conceptions of the 'self' shape relations to 'others' in international relations. Shapcott's main concern is with the possibility of achieving justice in a culturally diverse world. Although more influenced by Hans-Georg Gadamer and Tzvetan Todorov than Habermas, Shapcott's critique of the self is consistent with Linklater's and Hutchings'. He rejects both liberal and communitarian conceptions of the self for foreclosing genuine communication and justice in the relationship between self and other. Liberal conceptions of the self, he says, involve a 'significant moment of assimilation' because they are incapable of properly recognizing difference (2000b: 216). Communitarians, on the other hand, tend to take the limits of political community as given and, as a consequence, refuse to grant outsiders or non-citizens an equal voice in moral conversations. In other words, 'liberals underestimate the moral significance of national differences, while communitarians overestimate them. Both, in short, fail to do justice to difference' (Shapcott 2001: chapter 1).

The common project of Hutchings, Linklater and Shapcott here is to question the boundedness of identity. A less dogmatic attitude towards national boundaries is called for by these critical international theorists, as national boundaries are recognized as 'neither morally decisive nor morally insignificant' (Linklater 1998: 61). They are probably unavoidable in some form. The point, however, is to ensure that national boundaries do not obstruct principles of openness, recognition and justice in relations with the 'other' (Linklater 1998: chapter 2; Hutchings 1999: 138; Shapcott 2000a: 111).

Critical international theory has highlighted the dangers of unchecked particularism which can too readily deprive 'outsiders' of certain rights. This philosophical critique of particularism has led critical international theory to criticize the sovereign state as one of the foremost modern forms of social exclusion and therefore as a considerable barrier to universal justice and emancipation. In the following section we outline critical international theory's sociological account of how the modern state came to structure political community.

The sociological dimension: states, social forces and changing world orders

Rejecting realist claims that the condition of anarchy and the self-regarding actions of states are either natural or immutable, critical international theory has always been a form of small-'c' constructivism. One of its essential tasks is therefore to account for the social and historical production of both the agents and structures taken for granted by traditional theories.

Against the positivism and empiricism of various forms of realism, critical international theory adopts a more hermeneutic approach, which conceives of social structures as having an inter-subjective existence. 'Structures are socially constructed' – that is, says Cox (1992a: 138), 'they become a part of the objective world by virtue of their existence in the inter-subjectivity of relevant groups of people'. Allowing for the active role of human minds in the constitution of the social world does not lead to a denial of material reality, it simply gives it a different ontological status. Although structures, as inter-subjective products, do not have a physical existence like tables or chairs, they nevertheless have real, concrete effects (1992b: 133). Structures produce concrete effects because humans act *as if* they were real (Cox 1986: 242). It is this view of ontology which underlies Cox's and critical international theory's attempts to comprehend the present order.

In contrast to individualist ontologies which conceive of states as atomistic, rational and possessive, and as if their identities existed prior to or independently of social interaction (Reus-Smit 1996: 100), critical international theory is more interested in explaining how both individual actors and social structures emerge in, and are conditioned by, history. For example, against the Westphalian dogma that 'the state is a state is a state' (Cox 1981: 127), critical international theory views the modern state as a distinctive form of political community, bringing with it particular functions, roles, and responsibilities that are socially and historically determined. Whereas the state is taken for granted by realism, critical international theory seeks to provide a social theory of the state.

Crucial to critical international theory's argument is that we must account for the development of the modern state as the dominant form of political community in modernity. What is therefore required is an account of how states construct their moral and legal duties and how these reflect certain assumptions about the structure and logic of international relations. Using the work of Michael Mann and Anthony Giddens in particular, Linklater (1998: chapters 4–5) undertakes what he calls an historical sociology of 'bounded communities'.

Linklater's *Beyond Realism and Marxism* (1990a) had already begun to analyse the interplay of different logics or rationalization processes in the making of modern world politics. But in *Transformation of Political Community* (1998), he carried this analysis further by providing a more detailed account of these processes and by linking them more closely to systems of inclusion and exclusion in the development of the modern state. His argument is that the boundaries of political community are shaped by the interplay of four rationalization processes: state-building, geo-political rivalry, capitalist industrialization and moral-practical learning (Linklater 1998: 147–57). Five monopoly powers are acquired by the modern state through these rationalization processes. These powers, which are claimed by the sovereign state as indivisible, inalienable and exclusive rights, are: the right to monopolize the legitimate means of violence over the claimed territory, the exclusive right to tax within this territorial jurisdiction, the right to demand undivided political allegiance, the sole authority to adjudicate disputes between citizens and the sole subject of rights and representation in international law (1998: 28–9).

The combining of these monopoly powers initiated what Linklater refers to as the 'totalizing project' of the modern, Westphalian state. The upshot was to produce a conception of politics governed by the assumption that the boundaries of sovereignty, territory, nationality and citizenship must be coterminous (1998: 29, 44). The modern state concentrated these social, economic, legal and political functions around a single, sovereign site of governance that became the primary subject of international relations by gradually removing alternatives. Of crucial concern to Linklater is how this totalizing project of the modern state modifies the social bond and consequently changes the boundaries of moral and political community. Though the state has been a central theme in the study of international relations there has been little attempt to account for the changing ways that states determine principles which, by binding citizens into a community, separate them from the rest of the world.

Linklater's focus on the changing nature of social bonds has much in common with Cox's (1999) focus on the changing relationship between state and civil society. The key to rethinking international relations, according to Cox, lies in examining the relationship between state and civil society, and thereby recognizing that the state takes different forms, not only in different historical periods, but also within the same period.

Lest it be thought that critical international theory is simply interested in producing a theory of the state alone, it should be remembered that the state is but one force that shapes the present world order. Cox (1981: 137–8) argues that a comprehensive understanding of the present order and its structural characteristics must account for the interaction between social forces, states and world orders. Within Cox's approach the state plays an 'intermediate though autonomous role' between, on the one hand, social forces shaped by production, and on the other, a world order which embodies a particular configuration of power determined by the states-system and the world economy (1981: 141).

There are two fundamental and intertwined presuppositions upon which Cox founds his theory of the state. The first reflects the Marxist–Gramscian axiom that 'World orders ... are grounded in social relations' (Cox 1983: 173). This means that observable changes in military and geo-political balances can be traced to fundamental changes in the relationship between capital and labour. The second presupposition stems from Vico's argument that institutions such as the state are historical products. The state cannot be abstracted from history as if its essence could be defined or understood as *prior to* history (Cox 1981: 133). The end result is that the definition of the state is enlarged to encompass 'the underpinnings of the political structure in civil society' (Cox 1983: 164). The influence of the church, press, education system, culture and so on, has to be incorporated into an analysis of the state, as these 'institutions' help to produce the attitudes, dispositions and behaviours consistent with, and conducive to, the state's arrangement of power relations in society. Thus the state, which comprises the machinery of government, plus civil society, constitutes and reflects the 'hegemonic social order' (1983).

This hegemonic social order must also be understood as a dominant configuration of 'material power, ideology and institutions' that shapes forms of world order (Cox 1981: 141). The key issue for Cox, therefore, is how to account for the transition from one world order to another. He devotes much of his attention to explaining 'how structural transformations have come about in the past' (Cox 1986: 244). For example, he has analysed in some detail the structural transformation that took place in the late nineteenth century from a period characterized by craft manufacture, the liberal state and *pax Britannica,* to a period characterized by mass production, the emerging welfare-nationalist state and imperial rivalry (Cox 1987). In much of his recent writing, Cox has been preoccupied with the restructuring of world order brought about by globalization. In brief Cox, and his colleague Stephen Gill, have offered extensive examinations of how the growing global organization of production and finance is transforming Westphalian conceptions of society and polity. At the heart of this current transformation is what Cox calls the 'internationalization of the state', whereby the state becomes little more than an instrument for restructuring national economies so that they are more responsive to the demands and disciplines of the capitalist global economy. This has allowed the power of capital to grow – 'relative to labour and in the way it reconstitutes certain ideas, interests, and forms of state' – and given rise to a neo-liberal 'business civilization' (Gill 1995, 1996: 210; see also Cox 1993, 1994).

Drawing upon Karl Polanyi, Cox and Gill see the social purposes of the state being subordinated to the market logics of capitalism, disembedding the economy from society, and producing a complex world order of increasing tension between principles of territoriality and interdependence (Cox 1993: 260–3; Gill 1996). Some of the consequences of this economic globalization are, as Cox (1999) and Gill (1996) note, the polarization of rich and poor, increasing anomie, a stunted civil society and, as a result, the rise of exclusionary populism (extreme right, xenophobic and racist movements).

The point of reflecting on changing world orders, as Cox (1999: 4) notes, is to 'serve as a guide to action designed to change the world so as to improve the lot of humanity in social equity'. After all, as both Cox (1989) and Maclean (1981) argue, an understanding of change should be a central feature of any theory of international relations. So it is with the express purpose of analysing the potential for structural transformations in world order that critical international theory identifies and examines 'emancipatory counter-hegemonic' forces. Counter-hegemonic forces could be states, such as a coalition of 'Third World' states which struggles to undo the dominance of 'core' countries, or the 'counter-hegemonic alliance of forces on the world scale', such as trade unions, non-governmental organizations (NGOs) and new social movements, which grow from the 'bottom-up' in civil society (Cox 1999; Maiguaschca 2003; Eschle and Maiguaschca 2005).

The point of critical international theory's various sociological analyses is to illuminate how already existing social struggles might lead to decisive transformations in the normative bases of global political life. This has prompted Linklater (2002a, 2011c) to undertake an ambitious three-volume study of the problem of harm in world politics. Linklater's objective in the first volume is to theorize harm by setting the theoretical foundations for sociologically informed historical enquiries in subsequent projected volumes. 'A central aim of the overall project', Linklater (2011c: 5) explains, 'is to understand whether, or how far, the modern world has made progress in making harm a key moral and political question for humanity as a whole'. More specifically, Linklater wishes to compare states-systems across time on the basis of how they deal with international and transnational harms. What kinds of harm are generated in particular states-systems, and to what extent are rules and norms against harm built into these states-systems? Drawing upon the work of sociologist Norbert Elias, Linklater has explored the impact of the 'civilizing process' on the modern states-system. Changing attitudes to violence and suffering have generated greater sensitivity towards emotions such as embarrassment, guilt, shame and disgust (Linklater 2011b: chapter 5). This return to emotions is consistent with some early Frankfurt School writings, not least by Adorno, and with recent trends in post-structuralism, but it is a move away from the cold rationalism associated with Kant's Categorical Imperative. For Linklater, the larger point of returning to emotions is to place suffering and solidarity at the heart of the theoretical enterprise. It is an attempt to understand the way in which cosmopolitanism might be grounded in compassion, sympathy and other emotional attachments.

Whatever civilizing gains may have been made by the modern states-system, de-civilizing threats persist. Though there have been different responses to the terrorist attacks perpetrated by al-Qaeda, Linklater (2002b, 2007b) was concerned that the dominant White House rhetoric of a civilizational war against evil and relaxation of the global anti-torture norm threatened to unleash 'de-civilizing' potentials. The US-led 'war on terrorism', by privileging military means, putting more innocent lives at risk, suspending the rule of international law and employing 'constitutional torture', raised the question of 'whether the vision of a world in which fewer human beings are burdened with preventable suffering has been dealt a blow from which it will not easily recover' (Linklater 2002b: 304). Implicit in Linklater, and explicit in the writings of others, is the argument that the greatest threat to world order may not be the terrorists who perpetrated such inexcusable harm, but the reaction by the United States. By placing itself outside the rules, norms and institutions of international society in its prosecution of its war on terrorism, the United States was not only diminishing the prospects of a peaceful and just world order, but undermining the very 'civilizing' principles and practices on which it was founded (Booth and Dunne, 2011; Devetak 2005; Habermas 2003a, 2006).

The praxeological dimension: cosmopolitanism and discourse ethics

One of the main intentions behind a sociology of the states-system is to assess the possibility of dismantling the modern state's totalizing project and moving towards more open, inclusive forms of community. This reflects critical international theory's belief that while totalizing projects have been tremendously successful, they have not been complete in colonizing modern political life. They have not been able to 'erode the sense of moral anxiety when duties to fellow-citizens clash with duties to the rest of humankind' (Linklater 1998: 150–1). In this section, I outline critical international theory's attempt to rethink the meaning of community in the light of this residual moral anxiety and an accumulating 'moral capital' which deepens and extends cosmopolitan citizenship. This involves not simply identifying the forces working to dismantle practices of social exclusion, but also identifying those working to supplant or at least supplement the system of sovereign states with cosmopolitan structures of global governance. For Thomas Diez and Jill Steans (2005: 132) this means facilitating institutional developments that concretize the dialogic ideal; for Hauke Brunkhorst and Habermas it means facilitating 'global governance without global government', and 'post-national democracies without post-national states' (Scheuerman 2008 and 2011).

Linklater's work forms the most sustained and extensive interrogation of political community in international relations. In *Transformation of Political Community* (1998), Linklater elaborates his argument in terms of a 'triple transformation' affecting political community. The three transformational tendencies Linklater identifies are: a progressive recognition that moral, political and legal principles ought to be universalized, an insistence that material inequality ought to be reduced and greater demands for deeper respect for cultural, ethnic and gender differences. The triple transformation identifies processes that open the possibility of dismantling the nexus between sovereignty, territory, citizenship and nationalism and moving towards more cosmopolitan forms of governance. In this respect, the praxeological dimension closes the circle with the normative dimension by furthering the critique of the modern state's particularism. However, we should note a slight revision of this critique. Modern states are not just too particularistic for Linklater's liking, they are also too universalistic (Linklater 1998: 27). He here finesses his earlier critique of particularism by acknowledging the feminist and post-modern arguments that universalism runs the risk of ignoring or repressing certain marginalized or vulnerable groups unless it respects legitimate differences. Nonetheless, it remains consistent with the Enlightenment critique of the system of sovereign states, and the project to universalize the sphere in which human beings treat each other as free and equal.

If critical international theory's overall objective is to promote the reconfiguration of political community, not just by expanding political community beyond the frontiers of the sovereign state, but also by deepening it within those frontiers, then it must offer a more complex, multi-tiered structure of governance. Ultimately, it depends on reconstituting the state within alternative frameworks of political action that reduce the impact of social exclusion and enlarge democratic participation.

The key to realizing this vision is to sever the link between sovereignty and political association which is integral to the Westphalian system (Devetak 1995a: 43). A post-exclusionary form of political community would, according to Linklater, be post-sovereign or post-Westphalian. It would abandon the idea that power, authority, territory and loyalty must be focused around a single community or monopolized by a single site of governance. The state can no longer mediate effectively or exclusively among the many loyalties, identities and interests that exist in a globalizing world (see Devetak 2003). Fairer and more complex mediations can be developed, argues Linklater (1998: 60, 74), only by transcending the 'destructive fusion' achieved by the modern state and promoting wider communities of dialogue. The overall effect would thus be to 'de-centre' the state in the context of a more cosmopolitan form of political organization.

This requires states to establish and locate themselves in overlapping forms of international society. Linklater (1998: 166–7) lists three forms. First, a pluralist society of states in which the principles of co-existence work 'to preserve respect for the freedom and equality of independent political communities'. Second, a 'solidarist' society of states that have agreed to substantive moral purposes. Third, a post-Westphalian framework where states relinquish some of their sovereign powers so as to institutionalize shared political and moral norms (see Habermas 2006). These alternative frameworks of international society would widen the boundaries of political community by increasing the impact which duties to 'outsiders' have on decision-making processes and contribute to what Linklater (1998) and Shapcott (2001) call 'dialogical cosmopolitanism'.

Linklater and Shapcott make the case for what they refer to as 'thin cosmopolitanism'. A 'thin cosmopolitanism' would need to promote universal claims yet do justice to difference (Shapcott 2000b, 2001). Within such a setup, loyalties to the sovereign state or any other political association cannot be absolute (Linklater 1998: 56; Devetak 2003). In recognizing the diversity of social bonds and moral ties, a 'thin cosmopolitan' ethos seeks to multiply the types and levels of political community (for critical engagements with Linklater's 'thin' cosmopolitanism, see

Geras 1999; and Walker 1999). It should be noted, however, that this does not mean that duties to humanity override all others. There is no fixed 'moral hierarchy' within a 'thin cosmopolitan' framework (Linklater 1998: 161–8, 193–8). This version of 'thin cosmopolitanism' places the ideals of dialogue and consent at the centre of its project, and, to use Habermas' (2006) language, seeks to *juridify,* rather than moralize, international relations. That is, Habermas' cosmopolitan critical international theory wants to extend the progressive 'constitutionalization of international law' so as to realize a 'global domestic politics without a world government' (Habermas 2006: 135–7). The purpose of this multilevel global framework would be limited to securing international peace and protecting human rights (Habermas 2006: chapter 8; see also Beardsworth 2011: 32–40).

Another version of cosmopolitanism has been advanced, individually and collectively, by David Held and Daniele Archibugi (Archibugi and Held 1995; Archibugi 2002, 2004a). Their work stems from an appreciation of the dangers and opportunities globalization presents to democracy. It seeks to globalize democracy even as it democratizes globalization (Archibugi 2004a: 438). The thrust of *cosmopolitan* democracy is captured by the question Archibugi asks (2002: 28): 'why must the principles and rules of democracy stop at the borders of a political community?' As he explains, it is not simply a matter of 'replicating, *sic et simpliciter,* the model we are acquainted with across a broader sphere' (2002: 29). It is a matter of strengthening the rule of law and citizens' participation in political life through differentiated forms of democratic engagement. Archibugi (2004b) has gone so far as to outline cosmopolitan principles governing humanitarian intervention. This controversial proposal stems from post-Cold War developments and a growing willingness on the part of international society to suspend sovereignty when extreme, large-scale cases of human suffering occur. Though difficult practical questions remain about 'who is authorized to decide when a humanitarian intervention is needed', Archibugi (2004b) strongly rejects the idea that states can unilaterally intervene under the humanitarian cause (see also Devetak 2002, 2007).

In this final section I outline briefly how the emphasis on dialogue is utilized in critical international theory. Linklater employs Habermas's notion of discourse ethics as a model for his dialogical approach. Discourse ethics is essentially a deliberative, consent-oriented approach to resolving political issues within a moral framework. As elaborated by Habermas (1984b: 99), discourse ethics builds upon the need for communicating subjects to account for their beliefs and actions in terms which are intelligible to others and which they can then accept or contest. It is committed to the Kantian principle that political decisions or norms must be generalizable and consistent with the normative demands of public scrutiny if they are to attain legitimacy. At such moments when an international principle, social norm, or institution loses legitimacy, or when consensus breaks down then, ideally, discourse ethics enters the fray as a means of consensually deciding upon new principles or institutional arrangements. According to discourse ethics, newly arrived at political principles, norms, or institutional arrangements can be said to be valid only if they can meet with the approval of all those who would be affected by them (Habermas 1993: 151).

There are three features worthy of note for our purposes. First, discourse ethics are *inclusionary*. It is oriented to the establishment and maintenance of the conditions necessary for open and non-exclusionary dialogue. No individual or group which will be affected by the principle, norm, or institution under deliberation should be excluded from participation in dialogue. Second, discourse ethics are *democratic*. It builds on a model of the public sphere which is bound to democratic deliberation and consent, where participants employ an 'argumentative rationality' for the purpose of 'reaching a mutual understanding based on a reasoned consensus, challenging the validity claims involved in any communication' (Risse 2000: 1–2). Combining the inclusionary and democratic impulses, discourse ethics provide a method that can test which principles, norms, or institutional arrangements would be 'equally good for all' (Habermas 1993: 151). Third, discourse ethics are a form of *moral-practical reasoning*. As such, it is not simply guided by utilitarian calculations or expediency, nor is it guided by an imposed concept of the 'good life'; rather, it is guided by *procedural fairness*. It is more concerned with the method of justifying moral principles than with the substantive content of those principles.

It is possible to identify three general implications of discourse ethics for the reconstruction of world politics which can only be briefly outlined here. First, by virtue of its consent-oriented, deliberative approach, discourse ethics offers procedural guidance for democratic decision-making processes. In light of social and material changes brought about by the globalization of production and finance, the movement of peoples, the rise of indigenous peoples and sub-national groups, environmental degradation and so on, the 'viability and accountability of national decision-making entities' is being brought into question (Held 1993: 26). Held highlights the democratically deficient nature of the sovereign state when he asks: 'Whose consent is necessary and whose participation is justified in decisions concerning, for instance, AIDS, or acid rain, or the use of non-renewable resources? What is the relevant constituency: national, regional or international?' (1993: 26–7). Under globalizing conditions it is apt that discourse ethics raise questions not only about 'who' is to be involved in decision-making processes, but also 'how' and 'where' these decisions are to be made. The key here, in Linklater's (1999: 173) words, is 'to develop institutional arrangements that concretize the dialogic ideal' at all levels of social and political life; or, in Hauke Brunkhorst's (2002) words, to facilitate multiple levels of deliberative democracy by developing strong public spheres framed by norms of global constitutionalism. Apart from the constitutionalization of international law, this directs attention to an emerging global or international public sphere where 'social movements, non-state actors and "global citizens" join with states and international organizations in a dialogue over the exercise of power and authority across the globe' (Devetak and Higgott 1999: 491). As Marc Lynch (1999, 2000) has shown, this network of overlapping, transnational publics not only seeks to influence the foreign policy of individual states, it seeks to change international relations by modifying the structural context of strategic interaction. The existence of a global public sphere ensures that, as Risse (2000:21) points out, 'actors have to regularly and routinely explain and justify their behaviour'. Neta Crawford (2009) has corroborated this argument by demonstrating that 'talk', as the dominant characteristic of world politics, has contributed to further institutionalization and the growth of venues where argument and persuasion may take the place of coercive force. In other words, the institutionalization of talk – arguing, persuading and other forms of communicative action – enable global governance institutions to attain greater legitimacy by providing 'voice opportunities to various stakeholders' and improved 'problem-solving capacity' through deliberation (Risse 2004). The growing interest in Axel Honneth's work on 'struggles for recognition' is salient here. Jürgen Haacke (2005) and Martin Weber (2007) have argued convincingly that Honneth's account of the sources of social conflict, social identity and solidarity may be fruitfully explored for the study of international relations. His approach offers one way of thinking about how experiences of denigration, domination and exclusion may spur struggles for recognition which carry inherent moral claims.

Second, discourse ethics offer a procedure for regulating violent conflict and arriving at resolutions which are acceptable to all affected parties. The cosmopolitan democratic procedures are geared towards removing harm from international relations as far as possible. The invasion of Iraq by the United States and United Kingdom in March 2003 led Habermas (2003: 369) to pronounce that 'multilateral will-formation in interstate relations is not simply one option among others'. By giving up its role as guarantor of international rights, violating international law and disregarding the United Nations, Habermas (2003: 365) says, 'the normative authority of the United States of America lies in ruins'. Even though the fall of a brutal regime is a great political good, Habermas condemned the war and rejected comparisons with the Kosovo war to which he and other critical theorists lent their qualified support as a humanitarian intervention. Habermas' reasons for condemning the Iraq War are that it failed to satisfy any of the criteria of discourse ethics. Not only did the United States and United Kingdom base their arguments on questionable intelligence, they also contravened established norms of dispute resolution and showed a less than convincing commitment to 'truth-seeking' aimed at mutual understanding and reasoned consensus.

Third, discourse ethics offer a means of criticizing and justifying the principles by which humanity organizes itself politically. By reflecting on the principles of inclusion and exclusion, discourse ethics can reflect on the normative foundations and institutions which govern global political life. From the moral point of view contained within discourse ethics, the sovereign state as a form of community is unjust because the principles of inclusion and exclusion are not the outcome of open dialogue and deliberation where all who stand to be affected by the arrangement have been able to participate in discussion. Against the exclusionary nature of the social bond underlying the sovereign state, discourse ethics have the inclusionary aim 'to secure the social bond of all with all' (Habermas 1987: 346). In a sense, it is an attempt to put into practice Kant's ideal of a community of co-legislators embracing the whole of humanity (Linklater 1998: 84–9). As Linklater (1998: 10) argues, 'all humans have *a prima facie* equal right to take part in universal communities of discourse which decide the legitimacy of global arrangements'. In sum, discourse ethics promotes a cosmopolitan ideal where the political organization of humanity is decided by a process of unconstrained and unrestricted dialogue.

Conclusion

There can be little doubt that critical theory has made a major contribution to international relations theory since its emergence in the early 1980s. One of these contributions has been to heighten awareness of the link between knowledge and politics. Critical international theory rejects the idea of the theorist as objective observer or detached bystander. Instead, the theorist is enmeshed in social and political life; and theories of international relations, like all theories, are informed by prior interests and convictions, whether they are acknowledged or not. A second contribution critical international theory makes is to rethink accounts of the modern state and political community. Traditional theories tend to take the state for granted, but critical international theory analyses the changing ways in which the boundaries of community are formed, maintained and transformed. It not only provides a sociological account, it provides a sustained normative analysis of the practices of inclusion and exclusion. Critical theory's aim of achieving an alternative theory and practice of international relations rests on the possibility of overcoming the exclusionary dynamics associated with the modern system of sovereign states and establishing a cosmopolitan set of arrangements that will better promote peace, freedom, justice, equality and security across the globe. It is thus an attempt to rethink the normative foundations of international relations for the purpose of enhancing a global emancipatory politics.

8 | Post-structuralism

RICHARD DEVETAK

Post-structuralism remains one of the most controversial theories in the human and social sciences. Things are no different in International Relations where critics continue to censure the theory for a wide range of alleged intellectual misdemeanours; including accusations of moral relativism and irrationalism (Halliday 1994; Spegele 1992), imputations of flawed interpretation, 'bowdlerization', or 'pillaging' of post-structuralism's 'founding figures' (Blair 2011; Jarvis 2000; Selby 2007; Spegele 1992), and fulminations against purported discursive idealism and disregard for 'the real' (Halliday 1994). In the words of one recent critic, post-structuralism has 'failed to establish any authentic theoretical innovations capable of providing us with a viable framework for furthering our understanding of international relations' (Blair 2011: 828). The very fact that post-structuralism has generated so much heated argument and controversy makes it an interesting theory to study. It has ruffled more than a few feathers. While this chapter makes no attempt to defend post-structuralism against the myriad charges in any direct way, it does respond to the claim that post-structuralism has failed to make any substantial 'theoretical innovations'. This chapter contends that a more sympathetic account of the theory – one that engages with post-structuralism on its own conceptual and methodological terms – will allow for a fairer judgement of post-structuralism's contribution to the study of international relations.

The chapter is divided into four main sections. The first deals with the relationship between power and knowledge in the study of international relations. The second outlines the textual strategies employed by post-structuralist approaches. The third is concerned with how post-structuralism deals with the state. The final part of the chapter outlines post-structuralism's attempt to rethink the concept of the political.

Power and knowledge in international relations

Within orthodox social scientific accounts, knowledge ought to be immune from the influence of power. The study of international relations, or any scholarly study for that matter, is thought to require the suspension of values, interests and power relations in the pursuit of objective knowledge – knowledge uncontaminated by external influences and based on pure reason. Kant's (1970: 115) caution that 'the possession of power inevitably corrupts the free judgement of reason', stands as a classic example of this view. It is this view that post-structuralism problematizes by drawing upon the writings of thinkers such as Friedrich Nietzsche and Michel Foucault.

Rather than treat the production of knowledge as simply a cognitive matter, post-structuralism treats it as an aesthetic, normative and political matter (Shapiro 1999: 1). Nietzsche, for example, argued that 'when we say something about the world we also inevitably say something about our conception of the world – something that is linked not to the facts and phenomena we try to comprehend but to the assumptions and conventions of knowing that we have acquired over time and that have become codified in language' (Bleiker and Chou 2010: 9). For this reason, as Roland Bleiker and Mark Chou (2010) show admirably, Nietzsche places great emphasis on language, and particularly style and metaphor, in the production of knowledge. On this understanding, language is less a neutral, pure medium of communication, than a mediating set of habits, conventions, values and prejudices enabling us to make sense of the world.

Though less concerned with the question of style than Nietzsche, Foucault was no less concerned to debunk the idea that knowledge was neutral. In particular, he wanted to see if there was a common matrix that tied together the fields of knowledge and power. According to Foucault, there is a general consistency, which cannot be reduced to an identity, between modes of interpretation and operations of power. Power and knowledge are mutually supportive; they directly imply one another (Foucault 1977: 27). The task therefore is to see how operations of power fit with the wider social and political matrices of the modern world. For example, in *Discipline and Punish* (1977), Foucault investigates the possibility that the evolution of the penal system is intimately connected to the human sciences. His argument is that a 'single process of "epistemologico-juridical" formation' underlies the history of the prison on the one hand, and the human sciences on the other (1977: 23). In other words, the prison is consistent with modern society and modern modes of apprehending 'man's' world.

This type of analysis has been attempted in international relations by various thinkers. Richard Ashley has exposed one dimension of the power-knowledge nexus by highlighting what Foucault calls the 'rule of immanence' between knowledge of the state and knowledge of 'man'. Ashley's (1989a) argument, stated simply, is that, '[m]odern statecraft is modern mancraft'. He seeks to demonstrate how the 'paradigm of sovereignty' simultaneously gives rise to a certain epistemological disposition and account of modern political life. On the one hand, knowledge is thought to depend on the sovereignty of 'the heroic figure of reasoning man who knows that the order of the world is not God-given, that man is the origin of all knowledge, that responsibility for supplying meaning to history resides with man himself, and that, through reason, man may achieve total knowledge, total autonomy, and total power' (1989a: 264–5). On the other hand, modern political life finds in sovereignty its constitutive principle. The state is conceived by analogy with sovereign man as a pre-given, bounded entity which enters into relations with other sovereign presences. Sovereignty acts as the 'master signifier' as Jenny Edkins and Veronique Pin-Fat (1999: 6) put it. Both 'man' and the state are marked by the presence of sovereignty, which contrasts with international relations which is marked, and violently so, by the absence of sovereignty (or alternatively stated, the presence of multiple sovereignties). In short, the theory and practice of international relations are conditioned by the constitutive principle of sovereignty.

Genealogy

It is important to grasp the notion of genealogy, as it has become crucial to many post-structuralist perspectives in international relations. Genealogy is a style of historical thought which exposes and registers the significance of power-knowledge relations. It is perhaps best known through Nietzsche's radical assault on the concept of origins. As Roland Bleiker (2000: 25) explains, genealogies 'focus on the process by which we have constructed origins and given meaning to particular representations of the past, representations that continuously guide our daily lives and set clear limits to political and social options'. It is a form of history which historicizes those things which are thought to be beyond history, including those things or thoughts which have been buried, covered, or excluded from view in the writing and making of history.

In a sense, genealogy is concerned with writing counter-histories which expose the processes of exclusion and covering-over which make possible the teleological idea of history as a unified story unfolding with a clear beginning, middle and end. History, from a genealogical perspective, does not evidence a gradual disclosure of truth and meaning. Rather, it stages 'the endlessly repeated play of dominations' (Foucault 1987: 228); or at least 'the diversity and specificity of battles' between rival interpretations (Vucetic 2011: 1300). History proceeds as a series of dominations and impositions in knowledge and power, and the task of the genealogist is to unravel history to reveal the multifarious trajectories that have been fostered or closed off in the constitution of subjects, objects, fields of action and domains of knowledge. Moreover, from a genealogical perspective there is not one single, grand history, but many interwoven histories varied in their rhythm, tempo, and power-knowledge effects.

Genealogy affirms a perspectivism which denies the capacity to identify origins and meanings in history objectively. A genealogical approach is anti-essentialist in orientation, affirming the idea that all knowledge is situated in a particular time and place and issues from a particular perspective. The subject of knowledge is situated in, and conditioned by, a political and historical context, and constrained to function with particular concepts and categories of knowledge. Knowledge is never unconditioned. As a consequence of the heterogeneity of possible contexts and positions, there can be no single, Archimedean perspective which trumps all others. There is no 'truth', only competing perspectives. David Campbell's analysis of the Bosnian war in *National Deconstruction* (1998a) affirms this perspectivism. As he rightly reminds us, 'the same events can be represented in markedly different ways with significantly different effects' (1998a: 33). Indeed, the upshot of his analysis is that the Bosnian war can be known only through perspective.

In the absence of a universal frame of reference or overarching perspective, we are left with a plurality of perspectives. As Nietzsche (1969: III, 12) put it: 'There is *only* a perspective seeing, *only* a perspective "knowing"'. The modern idea, or ideal, of an objective or all-encompassing perspective is displaced in post-structuralism by the Nietzschean recognition that there is always more than one perspective and that each perspective embodies a particular set of values. Moreover, these perspectives do not simply offer different views of the same 'real world'. The very *idea* of the 'real world' has been 'abolished' in Nietzsche's thought (1990: 50–1), leaving *only* perspectives, *only* interpretations of interpretations, or in Derrida's (1974: 158) terms, *only* 'textuality'.

Perspectives are thus not to be thought of as simply optical devices for apprehending the 'real world', like a telescope or microscope, but also as the very fabric of that 'real world'. For post-structuralism, following Nietzsche, perspectives are integral to the constitution of the 'real world', not just because they are our only access to it, but because they are basic and essential elements of it. The warp and woof of the 'real world' is woven out of perspectives and interpretations, none of which can claim to correspond to reality-in-itself, to be a 'view from nowhere', or to be exhaustive. Perspectives are thus component objects and events that go towards making up the 'real world'. In fact, we should say that there is no object or event outside or prior to perspective or narrative. As Campbell explains, after Hayden White, narrative is central, not just to understanding an event, but to constituting that event. This is what Campbell (1998a: 34) means by the 'narrativizing of reality'. According to such a conception, events acquire the status of 'real' not because they occurred but because they are remembered and because they assume a place in a narrative (1998a: 36). Narrative is thus not simply a re-presentation of some prior event, it is the means by which the status of reality is conferred on events. But historical narratives also perform vital political functions in the present; they can be used as resources in contemporary political struggles (1998a: 84; 1999: 31).

The event designated by the name 'September 11' is a case in point. Is it best conceived as an act of terrorism, a criminal act, an act of evil, an act of war, or an act of revenge? (Devetak 2009). Perhaps it is best thought of as an instance of Islamo-fascism' or the clash of civilizations? Or perhaps as 'blowback'? Furthermore, which specific acts of commission and omission constitute this event? Did 'September 11' begin at 8.45 a.m. when American Airlines flight 11 crashed into the north tower of the World Trade Centre? Or at 7.59a.m. when the plane departed from Boston? Did it commence when the perpetrators began planning and training for the attack? Or did it begin even earlier, as a reaction (however unjustified) to US Middle East policy? These questions show that the event of 'September 11' is only constituted in a narrative that integrates it into a sequence of other events and thereby confers significance upon it.

It may be that, as Jenny Edkins (2002: 245–6) says, events like 'September 11' cannot be experienced in any normal sense. Rather, they exceed experience and our normal social and linguistic frameworks. Nevertheless, there will be, as Campbell (2002a: 1) notes, struggles over the meaning of 'September 11'. He, like Edkins, cautions against a hasty attempt to fix the meaning of 'September 11'. In particular he shows that, despite the White House asserting the unprecedented nature of the September 11 attacks, the 'war on terrorism' has returned to past foreign policy practices; in his words, it has morphed into the Cold War (1999: 17; see also Walker 1999). 'This return of the past means that we have different objects of enmity, different allies, but the same structure for relating to the world through foreign policy' (2002a: 18). Cynthia Weber (2002) makes a similar argument, suggesting instead that the Pearl Harbor attacks of 7 December 1941 provide an interpretive framework for the US military response today. 'September 11' is thus read as if it had the same meaning as 'December 7'. For post-structuralism, the representation of any political event will always be susceptible to competing interpretations.

Genealogy is a reminder of the essential agonism in the historical constitution of identities, unities, disciplines, subjects and objects. From this perspective, 'all history, including the production of order, [is comprehended] in terms of the endless power-political clash of multiple wills' (Ashley 1987: 409). Metaphors of war and battle are central to genealogy. In a series of lectures given at the Collège de France in 1975–6 under the title 'Society Must be Defended', Foucault employed genealogy to analyse power relations in the state. He explored a historico-political discourse dating from the end of the civil and religious wars of the sixteenth century that understood war to be 'a permanent social relationship, the ineradicable basis of all relations and institutions of power' (Foucault 2003: 49). This discourse, found in Sir Edward Coke, John Lilburne and Henri Comte de Boulainvilliers among others, challenged the prevailing assumption of the day that society is at peace. Instead, beneath the calm, peaceful order of law-governed society posited by philosophico-juridical discourses, this discourse perceives 'a sort of primitive and permanent war', according to Foucault (2003: 47).

Foucault (2003: 15) characterized this discourse through an inversion of Clausewitz's famous proposition: 'politics is the continuation of war by other means'. Foucault meant to analyse how war became viewed as an apt way of describing politics. He wanted to know when political thought began to imagine, perhaps counter-intuitively, that war serves as a principle for the analysis of power relations within political order. This conflictual understanding of society is equally at odds with Kantian liberalism and Hobbesian realism. If anything, it seemed to pre-empt Nietzsche's emphasis on struggle. Political power, instituted and legitimized in the sovereign state, does not bring war to an end; rather, 'In the smallest of its cogs, peace is waging a secret war' (2003: 50). This 'war discourse' posited a binary structure that pervades civil society, wherein one group is pitted against another in continuing struggle.

Foucault (1987: 236) claimed as one of genealogy's express purposes the 'systematic dissociation of identity', challenging the givenness of individual or group identity. There are two dimensions to this purpose. First, it has a purpose at the ontological level: to avoid substituting causes for effects (metalepsis). It does not take identity or agency as given but seeks to account for the forces which underwrite this apparent agency. Identity or agency is an *effect* to be explained, not assumed. This means resisting the temptation to attribute essences to agents, things or events in history, and requires a transformation of the question 'what is?' into 'how is?' For Nietzsche, Foucault and thus post-structuralism, it is more important to determine the forces that give shape to an event or a thing than to attempt to identify its hidden, fixed essence. Second, it has an ethico-political purpose in problematizing prevailing identity formations which appear normal or natural. It refuses to use history for the purpose of affirming present identities, preferring to use it instead to disturb identities that have become dogmatized, conventionalized or normalized.

A good example of this genealogical method is to be found in Maja Zehfuss's (2003) analysis of 'September 11' and the war on terrorism. She challenges assumptions about unified agency and about the relationship between causes and effects. As she points out, to imply that the events of 'September 11' were an attack on 'the West', as the US and UK governments did, is to ignore the ambiguous character of Western identity. At a minimum, it is to ignore the fact that Western nations are complicit with the technologies and perpetrators, but it also ignores political dissent from those who do not wish the memory of the dead to be used to perpetuate further violence (2003: 524–5). Following Nietzsche, Zehfuss (2003: 522) also questions cause-and-effect thinking; 'cause and effect are ... never as easily separated' as they appear to be. For example, governments leading the so-called war on terrorism imply that 'September 11' *caused* the war on terrorism. It is as if 'September 11' were 'an "uncaused" cause' (Zehfuss 2003: 521), or as if, in Judith Butler's (2004: 6) words, 'There is no relevant prehistory to the events of September 11.' But this ignores a good deal of prior political history which is essential to any adequate understanding.

It would be a mistake, however, to think that genealogy focuses only on what is forgotten. Zehfuss draws our attention to the politics of memory also. She points out that both Osama bin Laden and President George W. Bush wanted the world to remember the events of September 11. Bin Laden wanted the world to remember the humbling of a hyperpower, Bush wanted the world to remember the loss of innocent life. Both, says Zehfuss (2003: 514), 'have an interest in our memory of the events'. Zehfuss's (2003: 525) argument is that a 'certain way of using memory has become politically powerful', especially in the United States, where the White House exploited the memory of 'September 11' to justify the curtailment of civil liberties at home, and an aggressive military response abroad. Her point is that we need to forget the dominant narratives before we can understand what made 'September 11' a distinctive event.

It is in view of such genealogical analyses as these that we can understand Foucault's (1977: 31) attempt at 'writing the history of the present'. A history of the present asks: How have we made the present seem like a normal or natural condition? What has been forgotten and what has been remembered in history in order to legitimize the present and present courses of action?

One of the important insights of post-structuralism, with its focus on the power-knowledge nexus and its genealogical approach, is that many of the problems and issues studied in international relations are not just matters of epistemology and ontology, but of *power* and *authority;* they are struggles to impose authoritative interpretations of international relations. As Jacques Derrida (2003: 105) said in an interview conducted after September 11: 'We must also recognize here the strategies and relations of power. The dominant power is the one that manages to impose and, thus, to legitimate, indeed to legalize ... on a national or world stage, the terminology and thus the interpretation that best suits it in a given situation.' The following section outlines a strategy which is concerned with destabilizing dominant interpretations by showing how every interpretation systematically depends on that for which it cannot account.

Textual strategies of post-structuralism

James Der Derian (1989: 6) contends that post-structuralism is concerned with exposing the 'textual interplay behind power politics'. It might be better to say it is concerned with exposing the textual interplay *within* power politics, for the effects of textuality do not remain behind politics, but are intrinsic to them. The 'reality' of power politics (like any social reality) is always already constituted through textuality and inscribed modes of representation. It is in this sense that David Campbell (1992) refers to 'writing' security, Gearóid Ó Tuathail (1996) refers to 'writing' global space, and Cynthia Weber (1995) refers to 'writing' the state. Two questions arise: first, what is meant by textual interplay? Second, how does post-structuralism seek to disclose this textual interplay?

Textuality is a common post-structuralist theme. It stems mainly from Derrida's redefinition of 'text' in *Of Grammatology* (1974). It is important to clarify what Derrida meant by 'text'. He did not restrict its meaning to literature and the realm of ideas, as some have mistakenly thought, rather, he implied that the world is *also* a text, or better, the 'real' world is constituted like a text, and 'one cannot refer to this "real" except in an interpretive experience' (Derrida 1988: 148). Post-structuralism firmly regards interpretation as necessary and fundamental to the constitution of the social world. But as Roland Bleiker (2001) and Michael J. Shapiro (2005, 2007) have shown extensively, matters of interpretation are also aesthetic matters.

Recognition of the relationship between interpretation and aesthetics, what Bleiker (2001, 2009) calls the 'aesthetic turn', does not mean reducing politics and international relations to works of art that can be measured against an ideal of beauty. Rather, it means analysing the relationship between forms of representation and the things represented, and the irreducible interpretive choices that are required. Not unlike artists, international relations students have to make choices in how they represent or depict an event. Painters, for example, need to choose the time of day, the angle of view, the level of detail, the type of paint, the palette of colours, the brush sizes, and so on. International relations students have similar choices to make: the time frame, the perspective, the selection of relevant data or facts, the key concepts, and so on. All of these decisions are necessary, but the individual choices are not self-evident; they vary from one student to the next. And this is why political events are susceptible to different interpretations. There is nothing inherent in events or objects in the world which determines how they must be represented in either words or paintings. Instead, it is the structures of human consciousness and the various interpretive choices we make that shape how we perceive and depict the world around us (Bleiker 2001: 513; Shapiro 2005: 233–4). The important point for us, as Bleiker (2001: 510) shows, is that aesthetic insight compels us to recognize the politics involved in representation itself; that it is not a natural or neutral reflection of reality. This is another way of making Campbell's point about the narrativization of reality.

To tease out the textual interplay mentioned above, let us review two strategies employed by post-structuralism: *deconstruction* and *double reading*. These will show how 'textual interplay' is a mutually constitutive relationship between different interpretations in the representation and constitution of the world.

Deconstruction

Deconstruction is a general mode of radically unsettling what are taken to be stable concepts and conceptual oppositions. Its main point is to demonstrate the effects and costs produced by the settled concepts and oppositions, to disclose the parasitical relationship between opposed terms and to attempt a displacement of them. According to the inventor of deconstruction, the Franco-Maghrebian philosopher of Sephardic Jewish heritage, Jacques Derrida, conceptual oppositions are never simply neutral but are inevitably hierarchical. One of the two terms in opposition is privileged over the other. This privileged term supposedly connotes a presence, propriety, fullness, purity, or identity which the other lacks (for example, sovereignty as opposed to anarchy, metropolitan centre as opposed to colonial periphery). Deconstruction attempts to show that such oppositions are untenable, as each term *always already* depends on the other. Indeed, the prized term gains its privilege only by disavowing its dependence on the subordinate or debased term.

From a post-structuralist perspective, the apparently clear opposition between two terms is neither clear nor oppositional. Derrida often spoke of this relationship in terms of a structural parasitism and contamination, as each term is structurally related to, and already harbours, the other. Difference *between* the two opposed concepts or terms is always accompanied by a veiled difference *within* each term. Neither term is pure, self-same, complete in itself, or completely closed off from the other, though so much is feigned. This implies that totalities, whether conceptual or social, are never fully present and properly established. Moreover, there is no pure stability, only more or less successful stabilizations as there is a certain amount of 'play', or 'give', in the structure of the opposition.

As a general mode of unsettling, deconstruction is particularly concerned with locating those elements of instability or 'give' which ineradicably threaten any totality. Nevertheless, it must still account for stabilizations (or stability-effects). It is this equal concern with undoing or de-constitution (or at least their ever-present possibility) which marks off deconstruction from more familiar modes of interpretation. To summarize, deconstruction is concerned with both the constitution and de-constitution of any totality, whether a text, theory, discourse, structure, edifice, assemblage, institution or regime of practices.

Interestingly, there has been some discussion recently about deconstruction's colonial origins (Ahluwalia 2005; Sajed 2012). Robert Young (2004: 32) has argued that the single most important moment in the rise of post-structuralism, including Derrida's deconstruction, is the Algerian War of Independence. Certainly the Algerian War provides a crucial context for understanding Derrida's philosophy of deconstruction (Baring 2010). But Young (2004: 50) makes the stronger point that 'deconstruction involves the decentralization and decolonization of European thought'. On this reading, deconstruction holds a natural affinity with post-colonialism insofar as they both offer a critique of the authority and grounds of European or Western forms of knowledge and politics. At the heart of post-colonialism – which grew out of the experience of anti-colonial struggles of the twentieth century – is the rejection of binary oppositions which privilege the Western or European 'self' at the expense of the non-Western 'other'. Like post-structuralism, post-colonialism deconstructs commonplace oppositions between the civilized and uncivilized, modern and primitive, colonizer and colonized by revealing them to be 'intimate enemies' rather than mutually exclusive oppositions (Nandy 1983).

Double reading

Derrida sought to expose the relationship between stability-effects and destabilizations by passing through two readings in any analysis. As expressed by Derrida (1981: 6), double reading is essentially a duplicitous strategy which is 'simultaneously faithful and violent'. The first reading is a commentary or repetition of the dominant interpretation – that is, a reading which demonstrates how a text, discourse or institution achieves the stability-effect. It faithfully recounts the dominant story by building on the same foundational assumptions, and repeating conventional steps in the argument. The point is to demonstrate how the text, discourse, or institution appears coherent and consistent. It is concerned, in short, to elaborate how the identity of a text, discourse, or institution is constituted. Rather than yield to the monologic first reading, the second, counter-memorializing reading unsettles it by applying pressure to those points of instability within a text, discourse, or institution. It exposes the internal tensions and how they are (incompletely) covered over or expelled. The text, discourse, or institution is never completely at one with itself, but always carries within it elements of tension and crisis which renders it less than stable.

The task of double reading as a mode of deconstruction is to understand how a discourse or social institution is put together, but at the same time to show how it is always already threatened with its undoing. It is important to note that there is no attempt in deconstruction to arrive at a single, conclusive reading. The two mutually inconsistent readings, which are in a performative (rather than logical) contradiction, remain permanently in tension. The point is not to demonstrate the truthfulness of a story, but to expose how any story depends on the repression of internal tensions in order to produce a stable effect of homogeneity and continuity.

Ashley's double reading of the anarchy problématique

Richard Ashley's double reading of the *anarchy problématique* was one of the earliest and most important deconstructions in the study of international relations. His main target was the conception of anarchy and its theoretical and practical effects. The *anarchy problématique* is the name Ashley gives to the defining moment of most inquiries in international relations. It is exemplified by Oye's (1985: 1) assertion that: 'Nations dwell in perpetual anarchy, for no central authority imposes limits on the pursuit of sovereign interests.' Most importantly, the *anarchy problématique* deduces from the absence of a central, global authority, not just an empty concept of anarchy, but a description of international relations as power politics, characterized by self-interest, *raison d'état*, the routine resort to force, and so on.

The main brunt of Ashley's analysis is to problematize this deduction of power politics from the lack of central rule. Ashley's many analyses of the *anarchy problématique* can be understood in terms of double reading. The first reading assembles the constitutive features, or 'hard core' of the *anarchy problématique,* while the second reading disassembles the constitutive elements of the *anarchy problématique,* showing how it rests on a series of questionable theoretical suppositions or exclusions.

In the first reading, Ashley outlines the *anarchy problématique* in conventional terms. He describes not just the absence of any overarching authority, but the presence of a multiplicity of states in the international system, none of which can lay down the law to the others. Further, the states which comprise this system have their own identifiable interests, capabilities, resources and territory. The second reading is interruptive (Weber 2011), questioning the self-evidence of international relations as an anarchical realm of power politics. The initial target in this double reading is the opposition between sovereignty and anarchy, where sovereignty is valorized as a regulative ideal, and anarchy is regarded as the absence or negation of sovereignty. Anarchy takes on meaning only as the antithesis of sovereignty. Moreover, sovereignty and anarchy are taken to be mutually exclusive and mutually exhaustive. Ashley demonstrates, however, that the *anarchy problématique* works only by making certain assumptions regarding sovereign states. If the dichotomy between sovereignty and anarchy is to be tenable at all, then inside the sovereign state must be found a domestic realm of identity, homogeneity, order and progress guaranteed by legitimate force; and outside must lie an anarchical realm of difference, heterogeneity, disorder and threat, recurrence and repetition. But to represent sovereignty and anarchy in this way (that is, as mutually exclusive and exhaustive), depends on converting differences *within* sovereign states into differences *between* sovereign states (Ashley 1988: 257). Sovereign states must expunge any traces of anarchy that reside within them in order to make good the distinction between sovereignty and anarchy. Internal dissent and what Ashley (1987, 1989b) calls 'transversal struggles', which cast doubt over the idea of a clearly identifiable and demarcated sovereign identity, must be repressed or denied to make the *anarchy problématique* meaningful. In particular, the opposition between sovereignty and anarchy rests on the idea of a 'well-bounded sovereign entity possessing its own "internal" hegemonic centre of decision-making capable of reconciling "internal" conflicts and capable, therefore, of projecting a singular presence' (Ashley 1988: 245).

The general effect of the *anarchy problématique* is to confirm the opposition between sovereignty and anarchy as mutually exclusive and exhaustive. This has two particular effects: (1) to represent a domestic domain of sovereignty as a stable, legitimate foundation of modern political community, and (2) to represent the domain beyond sovereignty as dangerous and anarchical. These effects depend on what Ashley (1988:

256) calls a 'double exclusion'. They are possible only if, on the one hand, a single representation of sovereign identity can be imposed and, on the other hand, if this representation can be made to appear natural and indisputable. The double reading interrupts and problematizes the *anarchy problématique* by posing two questions: first, what happens to the *anarchy problématique* if it is not so clear that fully present and completed sovereign states are ontologically primary or unitary? And, second, what happens to the *anarchy problématique* if the lack of central global rule is not overwritten with assumptions about power politics?

Problematizing sovereign states

States, sovereignty and violence are long-standing themes in the established traditions of international relations that gained renewed importance after the September 11 terrorist attacks. They are also central themes in post-structuralist approaches to international relations. However, rather than adopt them uncritically from traditional approaches, post-structuralism revises them in view of insights gained from genealogy and deconstruction.

Post-structuralism addresses a crucial issue regarding interpretations and explanations of the sovereign state that state-centric approaches have obscured – namely, its historical constitution and reconstitution as the primary mode of subjectivity in world politics. This returns us to the type of question posed by Foucault's genealogy: how, and by virtue of what political practices and representations, is the sovereign state instituted as the normal mode of international subjectivity? Posing the question in this manner directs attention, in Nietzschean fashion, less to what is the essence of the sovereign state than to how the sovereign state is made possible, how it is naturalized and how it is made to appear as if it had an essence.

To the extent that post-structuralism seeks to account for the conditions which make possible the phenomenon of the state as something which concretely affects the experience of everyday life, it is phenomenological. Yet this is no ordinary phenomenology. It might best be called a 'quasi-phenomenology' for, as already noted, it is equally concerned with accounting for those conditions which destabilize the phenomenon or defer its complete actualization. In this section, post-structuralism's quasi-phenomenology of the state will be explained. This comprises four main elements: (1) a genealogical analysis of the modern state's 'origins' in violence, (2) an account of boundary inscription, (3) a deconstruction of identity as defined in security and foreign policy discourses and (4) a revised interpretation of statecraft. The overall result is to rethink the ontological structure of the sovereign state in order to respond properly to the question of how the sovereign state is (re)constituted as the normal mode of subjectivity in international relations.

Violence

Modern political thought has attempted to transcend illegitimate forms of rule (such as tyranny and despotism) where power is unconstrained, unchecked, arbitrary and violent, by founding legitimate, democratic forms of government where authority is subject to law. In modern politics, it is *reason* rather than power or violence which has become the measure of legitimacy. However, as Campbell and Dillon (1993: 161) point out, the relationship between politics and violence in modernity is deeply ambiguous for, on the one hand, violence 'constructs the refuge of the sovereign community' and, on the other hand, it is 'the condition from which the citizens of that community must be protected'. The paradox here is that violence is both poison and cure.

The link between violence and the state is revealed in Bradley Klein's genealogy of the state as strategic subject. Klein's (1994; 139) broad purpose in *Strategic Studies and World Order* was to analyse 'the violent making and remaking of the modern world'. His more particular purpose was to explain the historical emergence of war-making states. Rather than assume their existence, as realists and neo-realists tend to, Klein examined how political units emerge in history which are capable of relying upon force to distinguish a domestic political space from an exterior one. Consistent with other post-structuralists, he argued that 'states rely upon violence to constitute themselves as states', and in the process, 'impose differentiations between the internal and external' (1994: 38). Strategic violence is constitutive of states; it does not merely 'patrol the frontiers' of the state, it 'helps constitute them as well' (1994: 3).

The point made by post-structuralism regarding violence in modern politics needs to be clearly differentiated from traditional approaches. In general, traditional accounts take violent confrontation to be a normal and regular occurrence in international relations. The condition of anarchy is thought to incline states to war as there is nothing to stop wars from occurring. Violence is not constitutive in such accounts as these, but is 'configurative', or 'positional' (Ruggie 1993: 162–3). The ontological structure of the states is taken to be set up already before violence is undertaken. Violence merely modifies the territorial configuration, or is an instrument for power-political, strategic manoeuvres in the distribution or hierarchy of power. Post-structuralism, however; exposes the constitutive role of violence in modern political life. Violence is fundamental to the ontological structuring of states, and is not merely something to which already fully formed states use for power-political reasons. Violence is, according to post-structuralism, inaugural as well as augmentative.

This argument about the intimate and paradoxical relationship between violence and political order is taken even further by Jenny Edkins, who places the Nazis and NATO, concentration camps and refugee camps on the same continuum. All, she claims, are determined by a sovereign power that seeks to extend control over life. She argues that even humanitarianism can be placed on the spectrum of violence since it, too, is complicit with the modern state's order of sovereign power and violence, notwithstanding claims to the contrary. Indeed, she says that famine-relief camps are like concentration camps since they are both sites of 'arbitrary decisions between life and death, where aid workers are forced to choose which of the starving they are unable to help' (Edkins 2000: 13). Famine victims appear only as 'bare life' to be 'saved'; stripped of their social and cultural being, they are depoliticized, their political voices ignored (2000: 13–14). In different language, Campbell (1998b: 506) affirms this view by arguing that prevailing forms of humanitarianism construct people as victims, 'incapable of acting without intervention'. This insufficiently political or humane form of humanitarianism, therefore, 'is deeply implicated in the production of a sovereign political power that claims the monopoly of the legitimate use of violence' (Edkins 2000: 18). Mick Dillon and Julian Reid offer a similar reading of humanitarian responses to 'complex emergencies', but rather than assume an equivalence between humanitarianism and sovereign power, they see a susceptibility of the former to the operations of the latter. Global governance, they say, 'quite literally threatens nongovernmental and humanitarian agencies with recruitment into the very structures and practices of power against which they previously defined themselves' (Dillon and Reid 2000: 121).

Edkins and Dillon and Reid draw upon an influential and richly textured argument advanced by the Italian philosopher Giorgio Agamben in *Homo Sacer: Sovereign Power and Bare Life* (1998). Following Carl Schmitt, Agamben posits sovereignty as the essence of the political. The sovereign claims the right to decide the exception. This leads, among other things, to the sovereign's right to decide who is in and who is out of a political community. If one of the main concerns of critical theory (as outlined in Chapter 7) is examining the possibilities for more inclusive forms of community, Agamben focuses on exclusion as a condition of possibility of political community. He argues that 'In Western politics, bare life has the peculiar privilege of being that whose exclusion founds the city of men' (Agamben 1998: 7). 'Bare life', most basically, is the simple biological fact of not being dead. But Agamben assigns a further meaning to bare life, a meaning captured in the term *homo sacer* (sacred man), which refers to a life that can be taken but not sacrificed, a holy but damned life. Banished from society, *homo sacer* acts as the 'constitutive outside' to political life. But, in truth, *homo sacer* is neither inside nor outside political community in any straightforward sense. Instead, he occupies a 'zone of indistinction' or 'no-man's land'. Indeed, as Agamben (1998: 74, 80) points out, the Roman concept of *homo sacer* precedes the distinction between sacred and profane, which is why, paradoxically, a so-called '*sacred* man' can be killed. The clearest expression of this was the system of camps established under the Nazis before and during World War II. But similar systems were established during the Bosnian war. As David Campbell (2002b: 157) spells out, the Bosnian Serb camps at Omarska and Trnopolje were 'extra-legal spaces' integrated into an 'ethnic-cleansing strategy based on an exclusive and homogeneous' political community.

Judith Butler, in an essay titled 'Indefinite Detention' (in Butler 2004), applies Agamben's arguments in her reflections on America's 'war on terrorism'. Drawing from Agamben's writing on sovereign power, she notes how states suspend the rule of law by invoking a 'state of emergency'. There can be no more significant act demonstrating the state's sovereignty than withdrawing or suspending the law. Referring to the controversial detainment of terrorism suspects at Guantánamo Bay, Butler says: 'It is not just that constitutional protections are indefinitely suspended, but that the state (in its augmented executive function) arrogates to itself the right to suspend the Constitution or to manipulate the geography of detentions and trials so that constitutional and international rights are effectively suspended' (Butler 2004: 63–4). The detainees are thus reduced to bare life in a no-man's land beyond the law. Butler (2004: 68) observes that 'to be detained indefinitely ... is precisely to have no definitive prospect for a reentry into the political fabric of life, even as one's situation is highly, if not fatally, politicized'.

One of the most impressive attempts to deal with these issues in International Relations is to be found in the work of Andrew Neal (2009). Engaging with the writings of Schmitt, Agamben and Foucault, Neal provides a persuasive account of why arguments about compromising principles of liberty under necessitous conditions remain so powerful politically. He shows that 'exceptionalism' – the array of practices by which states suspend liberty and the rule of law to confront a threat – is a well-established part of political discourse. Far from being an anomaly or aberration, the 'state of exception' is symptomatic of liberal political discourses, constituting the limit of liberal practices of state sovereignty. By engaging with Agamben, Foucault and, more critically, Schmitt, these post-structuralist works seek to show how sovereign states, even liberal democratic ones, constitute themselves through exclusion and violence justified by exceptionalism.

Boundaries

To inquire into the state's (re)constitution, as post-structuralism does, is partly to inquire into the ways in which global political space is partitioned. The world is not naturally divided into differentiated political spaces, and nor is there a single authority to carve up the world. This necessarily leads to a focus on what Dillon and Everard (1992: 282) call the 'boundary question', and what Nick Vaughan-Williams (2009) calls 'border politics'.

Post-structuralism is less concerned with *what* sovereignty is, than *how* it is spatially and temporally produced and how it is circulated. How is a certain configuration of space and power instituted? And with what consequences? The obvious implication of these questions is that the prevailing mode of political subjectivity in international relations (the sovereign state) is neither natural nor necessary. As Gearóid Ó Tuathail (1996: 1) affirms, '[g]eography is about power. Although often assumed to be innocent, the geography of the world is not a product of nature but a product of histories of struggle between competing authorities over the power to organize, occupy, and administer space'. There is no necessary reason why global political space has to be divided as it is, and with the same bearing. Of crucial importance in this differentiation of political space is the inscription of *boundaries*. Marking boundaries is not an innocent, pre-political act. It is a political act with profound political implications as it is fundamental to the production and delimitation of political space.

There is no political space in advance of boundary inscription. As a 'central feature of the architecture of global politics' (Vaughan-Williams 2009: 3) and the modern geo-political imaginary, boundaries function to divide an interior, sovereign space from an exterior, pluralistic, anarchical space. The opposition between sovereignty and anarchy rests on the possibility of clearly dividing a domesticated political space from an undomesticated outside. It is in this sense that boundary inscription is a defining moment of the sovereign state. Indeed, neither sovereignty nor anarchy would be possible without the inscription of a boundary to divide political space. This 'social inscription of global space', to use Ó Tuathail's (1996: 61) phrase, produces the effect of completed, bounded states, usually built around what Campbell (1998a: 11) calls the 'nationalist imaginary'.

However, as Connolly (1994: 19) points out, boundaries are highly ambiguous since they 'form an indispensable protection against violation and violence; but the divisions they sustain in doing so also carry cruelty and violence'. At stake here is a series of questions regarding boundaries: how boundaries are constituted, what moral and political status they are accorded, how they operate simultaneously to include and exclude, and how they simultaneously produce order and violence. Clearly, these questions are not just concerned with the location of cartographic boundaries, but with how these cartographic boundaries serve to represent, limit, and legitimate a political identity. But how, through which political practices and representations, are boundaries inscribed? And what are the implications for the mode of subjectivity produced?

Identity

There is, as Rob Walker (1995a: 35–6) notes, a privileging of spatiality in modern political thought and practice. By differentiating political spaces, boundaries are fundamental to the modern world's preference for the 'entrapment of politics' within discrete state boundaries (Magnusson 1996: 36). Post-structuralism asks: How has political identity been imposed by spatial practices and representations of domestication and distancing? And how has the concept of a territorially defined self been constructed in opposition to a threatening other?

Of utmost importance here are issues of how security is conceived in spatial terms and how threats and dangers are defined and articulated, giving rise to particular conceptions of the state as a secure political subject. Debbie Lisle (2000) has shown how even modern tourism participates in the reproduction of this spatialized conception of security. By continuously reaffirming the distinction between 'safety here and now' and 'danger there and then' tourist practices help sustain the geo-political security discourse. Her reading suggests that war and tourism, rather than being two distinct and opposed social practices, are actually intimately connected by virtue of being governed by the same global security discourse.

A detailed account of the relationship between the state, violence and identity is to be found in David Campbell's post-structuralist account of the Bosnian war, in *National Deconstruction* (1998a). His central argument is that a particular norm of community has governed the intense violence of the war. This norm, which he calls 'ontopology', borrowing from Derrida, refers to the assumption that political community requires the perfect alignment of territory and identity, state and nation (Derrida 1994a: 82; Campbell 1998a: 80). It functions to disseminate and reinforce the supposition that political community must be understood and organized as a single identity perfectly aligned with and possessing its allocated territory. The logic of this norm, suggests Campbell (1998a:

168–9), leads to a desire for a coherent, bounded, monocultural community. These 'ontopological' assumptions form 'the governing codes of subjectivity in international relations' (1998a: 170). What is interesting about Campbell's (1998a: 23) argument is the implication that the outpouring of violence in Bosnia was not simply an aberration or racist distortion of the ontopological norm, but was in fact an exacerbation of this same norm. The violence of 'ethnic cleansing' in pursuit of a pure, homogeneous political identity is simply a continuation, albeit extreme, of the same political project inherent in any modern nation-state. The upshot is that all forms of political community, insofar as they require boundaries, are given to some degree of violence (Campbell 1998a: 13).

Post-structuralism focuses on the discourses and practices which substitute threat for difference in the constitution of political identity. Simon Dalby, for instance (1993), explains how cold wars result from the application of a geo-political reasoning which defines security in terms of spatial exclusion and the specification of a threatening other. 'Geopolitical discourse constructs worlds in terms of Self and Others, in terms of cartographically specifiable sections of political space, and in terms of military threats' (1993: 29). The geo-political creation of the external other is integral to the constitution of a political identity (self) which is to be made secure. But to constitute a coherent, singular political identity often demands the silencing of internal dissent. There can be internal others that endanger a certain conception of the self, and must be necessarily expelled, disciplined, or contained. Identity, it can be surmised, is an effect forged, on the one hand, by disciplinary practices which attempt to normalize a population, giving it a sense of unity and, on the other, by exclusionary practices which attempt to secure the domestic identity through processes of spatial differentiation, and various diplomatic, military and defence practices. There is a supplementary relationship between the containment of domestic and foreign others, which helps to constitute political identity by expelling 'from the resultant "domestic" space ... all that comes to be regarded as alien, foreign and dangerous' (Campbell 1992: chapters 5, 6, 1998a: 13).

If it is plain that identity is defined through difference, and that a self requires an other, it is not so plain that difference or otherness necessarily equates with threat or danger. Nevertheless, as Campbell (1992) points out, the sovereign state is predicated on discourses of danger. The constant articulation of danger through foreign policy is thus not a threat to a state's identity or existence', says Campbell (1992: 12), 'it is its condition of possibility'. The possibility of identifying the United States as a political subject, for example, rested, during the Cold War, on the ability to impose an interpretation of the Soviet Union as an external threat, and the capacity of the US government to contain internal threats

(1992: chapter 6). Indeed, the pivotal concept of containment takes on a Janus-faced quality as it is simultaneously turned inwards and outwards to deal with threatening others, as Campbell (1992: 175) suggests. The end result of the strategies of containment was to ground identity in a territorial state.

It is important to recognize that political identities do not exist prior to the differentiation of self and other. The main issue is how something which is different becomes conceptualized as a threat or danger to be contained, disciplined, negated, or excluded. There may be an irreducible possibility that difference will slide into opposition, danger, or threat, but there is no necessity. Political identity need not be constituted against, and at the expense of, others, but the prevailing discourses and practices of security and foreign policy tend to reproduce this reasoning. Moreover, this relation to others must be recognized as a morally and politically loaded relation. The effect is to allocate the other to an inferior moral space, and to arrogate the self to a superior one. As Campbell (1992: 85) puts it, 'the social space of inside/outside is both made possible by and helps constitute a moral space of superior/inferior'. By coding the spatial exclusion in moral terms it becomes easier to legitimize certain politico-military practices and interventions which advance national security interests at the same time that they reconstitute political identities. As Shapiro (1988: 102) puts it, 'to the extent that the Other is regarded as something not occupying the same moral space as the self, conduct toward the Other becomes more exploitive'. This is especially so in an international system where political identity is so frequently defined in terms of territorial exclusion.

But the process of 'Othering' is not only spatial. As Sergei Prozorov (2011) argues, it may also be temporal. He shows how Europe today engages in 'temporal Othering', casting its own particularistic and conflictual past as the Other against which it must delimit and identify itself. By virtue of its transformative capacity, Europe seeks to fashion for itself an identity as progressive and peaceful. This also entailed Europe representing itself as the sovereign subject that speaks in the name of history and modernity in contrast to non-Western peoples whose histories are presented in terms of lack, incompletion, and failure (Chakrabarty 2000: chapter 1). Dipesh Chakrabarty's project of 'provincializing Europe' seeks to de-centre Europe and question its claims to political modernity. Though his post-colonial approach draws predominantly from post-Marxist theories, Chakrabarty's recovery of subaltern history as inseparable from European history shares common ground with genealogy and deconstruction insofar as he reclaims subjugated knowledge and challenges the authority and universality of dominant European modes of political thought and practice (see Seth 2011).

Statecraft

The above section has sketched how violence, boundaries and identity function to make possible the sovereign state. This only partly deals with the main genealogical issue of how the sovereign state is (re)constituted as a normal mode of subjectivity. Two questions remain if the genealogical approach is to be pursued: how is the sovereign state naturalized and disseminated? And how is it made to appear as if it had an essence?

Post-structuralism is interested in how prevailing modes of subjectivity neutralize or conceal their arbitrariness by projecting an image of normalcy, naturalness, or necessity. Ashley has explored the very difficult question of how the dominant mode of subjectivity is normalized by utilizing the concept of hegemony. By 'hegemony' Ashley (1989b: 269) means not an 'overarching ideology or cultural matrix', but 'an ensemble of normalized knowledgeable practices, identified with a particular state and domestic society ... that is regarded as a practical paradigm of sovereign political subjectivity and conduct'. 'Hegemony' refers to the projection and circulation of an 'exemplary' model, which functions as a regulative ideal. Of course the distinguishing characteristics of the exemplary model are not fixed but are historically and politically conditioned. The sovereign state, as the currently dominant mode of subjectivity, is by no means natural. As Ashley (1989b: 267) remarks, sovereignty is fused to certain 'historically normalized interpretations of the state, its competencies, and the conditions and limits of its recognition and empowerment'. The fusion of the state to sovereignty is, therefore, conditioned by changing historical and cultural representations and practices which serve to produce a particular form of political subjectivity. This is an idea explored by Derrida in one of his last books, *Rogues* (2005). He there explored the way that state sovereignty presupposes a particular form of self-hood that is the function of a distinctively modern kind of self-positing or self-positioning (Derrida 2005: 11–12). Derrida's last ruminations on subjectivity include analysis of how the state's autonomy is inseparable from its auto-immune or suicidal tendencies (Derrida 2003: 94–109; 2005: 45). That is, states carry the potential to threaten the very things that can help sustain or secure their subjectivity.

A primary function of the exemplary model is to negate alternative conceptions of subjectivity or to devalue them as underdeveloped, incomplete or deviant. Anomalies are contrasted with the 'proper', 'normal', or 'exemplary' model. For instance, 'failed states', 'rogue states' and 'terrorist states' represent empirical cases of 'pathological' states which deviate from the norm by failing to display the recognizable or preferred signs of sovereign statehood (Constantinou 2004: 17; Bleiker 2005). In this failure, they help to reinforce hegemonic modes of subjectivity, and to reconfirm not just the sovereignty/anarchy opposition, but the presumed superiority of the North (Devetak 2008).

In order for the model of sovereign subjectivity to have any power at all, though, it must be replicable; it must be seen as a universally effective mode of subjectivity which can be invoked and instituted at any site. The pressures applied on states to conform to normalized modes of subjectivity are complex and various, and emanate both internally and externally. Some pressures are quite explicit, such as military intervention, others less so, such as conditions attached to foreign aid, diplomatic recognition and general processes of socialization. The point is that modes of subjectivity achieve dominance in space and time through the projection and imposition of power.

How has the state been made to appear as if it had an essence? The short answer to this question is that the state is made to appear as if it had an essence by the performative enactment of various domestic and foreign policies, or what might more simply be called 'statecraft', with the emphasis on 'craft'. Traditionally, 'statecraft' refers to the various policies and practices undertaken by states to pursue their objectives in the international arena. The assumption underlying this definition is that the state is already a fully formed, or bounded, entity before it negotiates its way in this arena. The revised notion of statecraft advanced by poststructuralism stresses the on- going political practices which found and maintain the state, having the effect of keeping the state in perpetual motion.

As Richard Ashley (1987: 410) stressed in his path-breaking article, subjects have no existence prior to political practice. Sovereign states emerge on the plane of historical and political practices. This suggests it is better to understand the state as performatively constituted, having no identity apart from the ceaseless enactment of the ensemble of foreign and domestic policies, security and defence strategies, protocols of treaty making, and representational practices at the United Nations, among other things. The state's 'being' is thus an effect of performativity. By 'performativity' we must understand the continued iteration of a norm or set of norms, not simply a singular act, which produces the very thing it names. As Weber (1998: 90) explains, 'the identity of the state is performatively constituted by the very expressions that are said to be its result'.

It is in this sense that David Campbell (1998a: ix–x), in his account of the war in Bosnia, focuses on what he calls 'metaBosnia', by which he means 'the array of practices through which Bosnia … comes to be'. To help come to terms with the ceaseless production of Bosnia as a state or subject, Campbell recommends that we recognize that we are never dealing with a given, *a priori* state of Bosnia, but with metaBosnia – that is, the performative constitution of 'Bosnia' through a range of entraining and differentiating practices. 'Bosnia', like any other state, is always under a process of construction.

To summarize then, the sovereign state, as Weber (1998: 78) says, is the 'ontological effect of practices which are performatively enacted'. As she explains, 'sovereign nation-states are not pre-given subjects but subjects in process' (1998), where the phrase 'subjects in process' should also be understood to mean 'subjects on trial' (as the French *'en procès'* implies). This leads to an interpretation of the state (as subject) as always in the process of being constituted, but never quite achieving that final moment of completion (Edkins and Pin-Fat 1999: 1). The state thus should not be understood as if it were a prior presence, but instead should be seen as the simulated presence produced by the processes of statecraft. It is never fully complete but is in a constant process of 'becoming-state'. Though 'never fully realized, [the state] is in a contin-ual process of concretization' (Doty 1999: 593). The upshot is that, for post-structuralism, there is statecraft, but there is no completed state (Devetak 1995a).

Lest it be thought that post-structuralist theories of international rela-tions mark a return to realist state-centrism, some clarification will be needed to explain its concern with the sovereign state. Post-structuralism does not seek to explain world politics by focusing on the state alone, nor does it take the state as given. Instead, as Ashley's double reading of the *anarchy problématique* testifies, it seeks to explain the conditions which make possible such an explanation and the costs consequent on such an approach. What is lost by taking a state-centric perspective? And most importantly, to what aspects of world politics does state-centrism remain blind?

Beyond the paradigm of sovereignty: rethinking the political

One of the central implications of post-structuralism is that the paradigm of sovereignty has impoverished our political imagination and restricted our comprehension of the dynamics of world politics. In this section, we review post-structuralist attempts to develop a new conceptual language to represent world politics beyond the terms of state-centrism in order to rethink the concept of the political. For Walker (2010: 184) this means confronting sovereignty as 'a problem' rather than a 'permanent or disappearing condition'.

Campbell (1996: 19) asks the question: 'can we represent world poli-tics in a manner less indebted to the sovereignty problematic?' The chal-lenge is to create a conceptual language that can better convey the novel processes and actors in modern (or post-modern) world politics.

Campbell (1996: 20) recommends 'thinking in terms of a *political prosaics* that understands the *transversal* nature' of world politics. To conceptualize world politics in that way is to draw attention to the multitude of flows and interactions produced by globalization that cut across nation-state boundaries. It is to focus on the many political, economic and cultural activities that produce a 'de-territorialization' of modern political life; activities that destabilize the paradigm of sovereignty.

The argument here draws heavily upon the philosophical work of Gilles Deleuze and Felix Guattari (1977, 1987). They have developed a novel conceptual language which has been deployed by post-structural theorists of international relations to make sense of the operation and impact of various non-state actors, flows and movements on the political institution of state sovereignty. The central terms are re-territorialization and de-territorialization (see Patton 2000; Reid 2003). The former is associated with the totalizing logic of the paradigm of sovereignty, or 'State-form' as Deleuze and Guattari say, whose function is defined by processes of capture and boundary-marking. The latter, de-territorialization, is associated with the highly mobile logic of nomadism whose function is defined by its ability to transgress boundaries and avoid capture by the State-form. The one finds expression in the desire for identity, order and unity, the other in the desire for difference, flows and lines of flight.

The 'political prosaics' advocated by Campbell and others utilize this Deleuzian language to shed light on the new political dynamics and demands created by refugees, immigrants, and new social movements as they encounter and outflank the State-form. These 'transversal' groups and movements not only transgress national boundaries, they call into question the territorial organization of modern political life. As Roland Bleiker (2000: 2) notes, they 'question the spatial logic through which these boundaries have come to constitute and frame the conduct of international relations'. In his study of popular dissent in international relations, Bleiker argues that globalization is subjecting social life to changing political dynamics. In an age of mass media and telecommunications, images of local acts of resistance can be flashed across the world in an instant, turning them into events of global significance. Globalization, Bleiker suggests, has transformed the nature of dissent, making possible global and transversal practices of popular dissent (2000: 31). No longer taking place in a purely local context, acts of resistance 'have taken on increasingly transversal dimensions. They ooze into often unrecognized, but nevertheless significant grey zones between domestic and international spheres', blurring the boundaries between inside and outside, local and global (2000: 185). By outflanking sovereign controls and crossing state boundaries, the actions of transversal dissident groups can be read as 'hidden transcripts' that occur 'off-stage', as it were, behind and alongside the 'public transcript' of the sovereign state. The recent 'Arab Spring' might be considered in this context. The 'hidden transcripts' of transversal movements are therefore de-territori-alizing in their function, escaping the spatial codes and practices of the dominant actors and making possible a critique of the sovereign state's modes of re-territorialization and exclusion (2000: chapter 7).

This is also the case with refugees and migrants. They hold a different relationship to space than citizens do. Being nomadic rather than seden-tary, they are defined by movement across and between political spaces. They problematize and defy the 'territorial imperative' of the sovereign state (Soguk and Whitehall 1999: 682). Indeed, their wandering move-ment dislocates the ontopological norm which seeks to fix people's iden-tities within the spatial boundaries of the nation-state (1999: 697). As a consequence they disrupt our state-centric conceptualizations, prob-lematizing received understandings of the character and location of the political.

Similar arguments are advanced by Peter Nyers and Mick Dillon regarding the figure of the refugee. As Nyers (1999) argues, the figure of the refugee, as one who cannot claim to be a member of a 'proper' polit-ical community, acts as a 'limit-concept', occupying the ambiguous zone between citizen and human. Dillon (1999) argues that the refugee/stranger remains outside conventional modes of political subjec-tivity which are tied to the sovereign state. The very existence of the refugee/stranger calls into question the settled, sovereign life of the polit-ical community by disclosing the estrangement that is shared by both citi-zens and refugees. As Soguk and Whitehall (1999: 675) point out, refugees and migrants, by moving across state boundaries and avoiding capture, have the effect of rupturing traditional constitutive narratives of international relations.

Sovereignty and the ethics of exclusion

Post-structuralism's ethical critique of state sovereignty needs to be understood in relation to the deconstructive critique of totalization and the de-territorializing effect of transversal struggles. Deconstruction has already been explained as a strategy of interpretation and criticism that targets theoretical concepts and social institutions which attempt total-ization or total stability. It is important to note that the post-structural critique of state sovereignty focuses on *sovereignty*.

The sovereign state may well be the dominant mode of subjectivity in international relations today, but it is questionable whether its claim to be the primary and exclusive political subject is justified. The most thoroughgoing account of state sovereignty's ethico-political costs is offered by Rob Walker in *Inside/Outside* (1993). Walker sets out the context in which state sovereignty has been mobilized as an analytical category with which to understand international relations, and as the primary expression of moral and political community. Walker's critique suggests that state sovereignty is best understood as a constitutive political practice which emerged historically to resolve three ontological contradictions. The relationship between time and space was resolved by containing time within domesticated territorial space. The relationship between universal and particular was resolved through the system of sovereign states which gave expression to the plurality and particularity of states on the one hand, and the universality of one system on the other. This resolution also allowed for the pursuit of universal values to be pursued within particular states. Finally, the relationship between self and other is also resolved in terms of 'insiders' and 'outsiders', friends and enemies (Walker 1995a: 320–1, 1995b: 28). In deconstructive fashion, Walker's (1993: 23) concern is to 'destabilise [these] seemingly opposed categories by showing how they are at once mutually constitutive and yet always in the process of dissolving into each other'. The overall effect of Walker's inquiry into state sovereignty, consistent with the 'political prosaics' outlined above, is to question whether it is any longer a useful descriptive category and an effective response to the problems that confront humanity in modern political life.

The analysis offered by Walker suggests that it is becoming increasingly difficult to organize modern political life in terms of sovereign states and sovereign boundaries. He argues that there are 'spatiotemporal processes that are radically at odds with the resolution expressed by the principle of state sovereignty' (1993: 155). For both material and normative reasons, Walker refuses to accept state sovereignty as the only, or best, possible means of organizing modern political life. Modern political life need not be caught between mutually exclusive and exhaustive oppositions such as inside and outside. Identity need not be exclusionary, difference need not be interpreted as antithetical to identity (1993: 123), and the trade-off between men and citizens built into the modern state need not always privilege the claims of citizens above the claims of humanity (Walker 2000: 231–2).

To rethink questions of political identity and community without succumbing to binary oppositions is to contemplate a political life beyond the paradigm of sovereign states. It is to take seriously the possibility that new forms of political identity and community can emerge which are not predicated on absolute exclusion and spatial distinctions between here and there, self and other (Walker 1995a: 307).

Connolly delivers a post-structuralist critique which brings the question of democracy to bear directly on sovereignty. His argument is that the notion of state sovereignty is incompatible with democracy, especially in a globalized late modernity. The point of his critique is to challenge the sovereign state's 'monopoly over the allegiances, identifications and energies of its members' (Connolly 1991: 479). The multiple modes of belonging and interdependence, and the multiplication of global risks that exist in late modernity, complicate the neat simplicity of binary divisions between inside and outside. His point is that obligations and duties constantly overrun the boundaries of sovereign states. Sovereignty, Connolly says, 'poses too stringent a limitation to identifications and loyalties extending beyond it', and so it is necessary to promote an ethos of democracy which exceeds territorialization by cutting across the state at all levels (1991: 480). He calls this a 'disaggregation of democracy', or what might better be called a 'de-territorialization of democracy'. 'What is needed politically', he says, 'is a series of cross-national, nonstatist movements organized across state lines, mobilized around specific issues of global significance, pressing states from inside and outside simultaneously to reconfigure established convictions, priorities, and policies' (Connolly 1995: 23).

A similar argument is advanced by Campbell. According to Campbell (1998a: 208), the norm of ontopology produces a 'moral cartography' that territorializes democracy and responsibility, confining it to the limits of the sovereign state. But Campbell, like Connolly, is interested in fostering an ethos of democratic pluralization that would promote tolerance and multiculturalism within and across state boundaries. By promoting an active affirmation of alterity it would resist the sovereign state's logics of territorialization and capture.

Post-structuralist ethics

Post-structuralism asks, what might ethics come to mean outside a paradigm of sovereign subjectivity? There are two strands of ethics which develop out of post-structuralism's reflections on international relations. One strand challenges the ontological description on which traditional ethical arguments are grounded. It advances a notion of ethics which is not predicated on a rigid, fixed boundary between inside and outside. The other strand focuses on the relation between ontological grounds and ethical arguments. It questions whether ontology must precede ethics.

The first strand is put forward most fully by Ashley and Walker (1990) and Connolly (1995). Fundamental to their writing is a critique of the faith invested in boundaries. Again, the main target of post-structuralism is the sovereign state's defence of rigid boundaries. Territorial boundaries, which are thought to mark the limits of political identity or community, are taken by post-structuralism to be historically contingent and highly ambiguous products (Ashley and Walker 1990). As such, they hold no transcendental status. As a challenge to the ethical delimitations imposed by state sovereignty, post-structuralist ethics, or the 'diplomatic ethos', as Ashley and Walker call it, is not confined by any spatial or territorial limits. It seeks to 'enable the rigorous practice of this ethics in the widest possible compass' (1990: 395). No demarcatory boundaries should obstruct the universalization of this ethic which flows across boundaries (both imagined and territorial):

> Where such an ethics is rigorously practised, no voice can effectively claim to stand heroically upon some exclusionary ground, offering this ground as a source of a necessary truth that human beings must violently project in the name of a citizenry, people, nation, class, gender, race, golden age, or historical cause of any sort. Where this ethics is rigorously practised, no totalitarian order could ever be. (Ashley and Walker 1990: 395)

In breaking with the ethics of sovereign exclusion, post-structuralism offers an understanding of ethics which is detached from territorial limitations. The diplomatic ethos is a 'de-territorialized' ethics which unfolds by transgressing sovereign limits. This transgressive ethics complements the de-territorialized notion of democracy advanced by Connolly. Underlying both ideas is a critique of state sovereignty as a basis for conducting, organizing and limiting political life.

The other ethical strand is advanced by Campbell. He follows Derrida and Levinas by questioning traditional approaches which deduce ethics from ontology, specifically an ontology or metaphysics of presence (Campbell 1998a: 171–92; and see Levinas 1969: section 1A). It does not begin with an empirical account of the world as a necessary prelude to ethical consideration. Rather, it gives primacy to ethics as, in a sense, 'first philosophy'. The key thinker in this ethical approach is Emmanuel Levinas who has been more influenced by Jewish theology than Greek philosophy. Indeed, the differences between these two styles of thought are constantly worked through in Levinas's thought as a difference between a philosophy of alterity and a philosophy of identity or totality.

Levinas overturns the hierarchy between ontology and ethics, giving primacy to ethics as the starting point. Ethics seems to function as a condition which makes possible the world of beings. Levinas offers a re-description of ontology such that it is inextricably tied up with, and indebted to, ethics, and is free of totalizing impulses. His thought is antagonistic to all forms of ontological and political imperialism or total-itarianism (Levinas 1969: 44; Campbell 1998a: 192). In Levinas's schema, subjectivity is constituted through, and as, an ethical relation. The effect of the Levinasian approach is to recast notions of subjectivity and responsibility in light of an ethics of otherness or alterity (see Campbell 1994: 463, 1998a: 176). This gives rise to a notion of ethics which diverges from the Kantian principle of generalizability and symmetry that we find in critical theory. Rather than begin with the Self and then generalize the imperative universally to a community of equals, Levinas begins with the Other. The Other places certain demands on the Self, hence there is an asymmetrical relationship between Self and Other. The end result is to advance a 'different figuration of politics, one in which its purpose is the struggle *for* – or *on behalf of* – alterity, and not a struggle to efface, erase, or eradicate alterity' (Campbell 1994: 477, 1998a: 191). But, as Michael Shapiro (1998: 698–9) has shown, this ethos may not be so different from a Kantian ethic of hospitality that encourages universal tolerance of difference as a means of diminishing global violence.

Campbell (2005: 224) believes that post-structuralism adopts an 'ethos of political criticism' that seeks to disturb settled practices and expose the contingently constructed character of political structures and practices. In this respect, post-structuralism is not so far removed from the Kantian-inspired tradition of critical theory. As Richard Beardsworth (2005: 224) has rightly noted, post-structuralism, as a 'critical philoso-phy', should not underestimate 'how much good work reason can do, how much reason can shape contingencies of history, and how much reason can release difference'. This is in part what Derrida (2005) explores in his book *Rogues,* which is subtitled *Two Essays on Reason.*

The consequence of taking post-structuralism's critique of totality and sovereignty seriously is that central political concepts such as commu-nity, identity, ethics, democracy, and civilization are re-thought to avoid being persistently re-territorialized by the sovereign state or claimed by and for European political modernity. Indeed, de-linking these concepts from territory and sovereignty underlies the practical task of a post-structuralist – and perhaps post-colonial – politics or ethics. As Anthony Burke (2004: 353) explains in a forceful critique of Just War theory after September 11, post-structuralism's conception of an 'ethical peace' would refuse 'to channel its ethical obligations solely through the state, or rely on it to protect us violently'. It should be noted, however, that post-structuralism, as a critique of totalization, opposes concepts of iden-tity, community and civilization only to the extent that they are tied dogmatically to notions of territoriality, boundedness, exclusion and supremacy. The thrust of post-structuralism has always been to challenge both epistemological and political claims to totality and sovereignty and thereby open up questions about the location and character of the political (Walker 2010: 19).

Conclusion

Notwithstanding the myriad accusations and charges levelled against post-structuralism, this chapter has shown that post-structuralism makes a substantial contribution to the study of international relations with innovative theoretical methods and insights. First, through its genealogical method it seeks to expose the intimate connection between claims to knowledge and claims to political power and authority. Second, through aesthetic insight and the textual strategy of deconstruction it seeks to problematize all claims to epistemological and political totalization by revealing the inherently political choices behind competing interpretations. This has especially significant implications for how we conceptualize the sovereign state; not least because dominant understandings are predicated on practices of capture and exclusion. A more comprehensive account of contemporary world politics must therefore include an analysis of those transversal actors and movements that operate outside and across state boundaries. Third, post-structuralism seeks to rethink concepts of the political and responsibility without invoking assumptions of sovereignty and re-territorialization. By challenging the idea that the character and location of the political must be determined by the sovereign state, post-structuralism seeks to broaden the political imagination and the range of political possibilities for transforming international relations in innovative ways. These contributions seem as important as ever a decade after the events of September 11.

9 | Constructivism

CHRISTIAN REUS-SMIT

During the 1980s, two debates structured International Relations scholarship, particularly within the American mainstream. The first was between neo-realists and neo-liberals, both of which sought to apply the logic of rationalist economic theory to international relations, but reached radically different conclusions about the potential for international cooperation. The second was between rationalists and critical theorists; the latter challenging the epistemological, methodological, ontological and normative assumptions of neo-realism and neo-liberalism, and the former accusing critical theorists of having little of any substance to say about 'real-world' international relations. Since the end of the Cold War, these axes of debate have been displaced by two new debates: between rationalists and constructivists, and between constructivists and critical theorists. The catalyst for this shift was the rise of a new constructivist approach to international theory, an approach that challenged the rationalism and positivism of neo-realism and neo-liberalism while simultaneously pushing critical theorists away from metatheoretical critique to the empirical analysis of world politics.

This chapter explains the nature and rise of constructivism in international theory, situating it in relation to both rationalist and critical theories. Constructivism is characterized by an emphasis on the importance of normative as well as material structures, on the role of identity in shaping political action and on the mutually constitutive relationship between agents and structures. When using the terms rationalism or rationalist theory, I refer not to the 'Grotian' or 'English' School of international theory, discussed by Andrew Linklater in Chapter 4 in this volume, but to theories that are explicitly informed by the assumptions of rational choice theory, principally neo-realism and neo-liberalism. I use the term 'critical theory' broadly to include all post-positivist theory of the Third Debate and after, encompassing both the narrowly defined critical theory of the Frankfurt School and post-modern international theory, discussed by Richard Devetak in Chapters 7 and 8, respectively (note that Devetak uses the term 'post-structural' in preference to 'post-modern'). After revisiting the rationalist premises of neo-realism and neo-liberalism, and reviewing the broad-based critique of those premises mounted by critical theorists during the 1980s, I examine the origins of constructivism and its principal theoretical premises. I then distinguish between three different forms of constructivist scholarship in International Relations: systemic, unit-level and holistic. This is followed by some reflections on the emergent discontents that characterize constructivism as a theoretical approach, a discussion of the contribution of constructivism to international relations theory, and a consideration of recent developments in constructivism, including the recent emphases on civilization and religion, power, social practices, and the turn to ethics.

Rationalist theory

After World War II, realism became the dominant theory of international relations. Yet this dominance did not go unchallenged, with new theoretical perspectives emerging, forcing revisions in realist theory. In the 1970s, the classical realism of Claude, Carr, Morgenthau, Niebuhr and others was challenged by liberals, such as Robert Keohane and Joseph Nye, who emphasized interdependence between states, transnational relations and non-state actors, particularly multinational corporations (MNCs). International relations was not to be conceived as a system of 'colliding billiard balls', but as a cobweb of political, economic and social relations binding sub-national, national, transnational, international and supranational actors (Keohane and Nye 1972). This view was subsequently modified to pay greater attention to the role and importance of sovereign states, with Keohane and Nye re-conceiving state power in the light of 'complex interdependence' (Keohane and Nye 1977). States were acknowledged to be the principal actors in world politics, but pervasive interdependence was thought to alter the nature and effectiveness of state power, with the balance of military power, so long emphasized by realists, no longer determining political outcomes, as sensitivity and vulnerability to interdependence produced new relations of power between states.

This challenge to realism did not go unanswered. As Jack Donnelly explains, in Chapter 2 of this volume, in 1979 Kenneth Waltz published the *Theory of International Politics* (1979), in which he advanced a radically revised realist theory, subsequently labelled 'neo-realism' or 'structural realism'. Waltz drew on two sources of intellectual inspiration: the philosopher of science Imre Lakatos' model of theory construction, and macroeconomic theory. The first led him to devise a theory with minimal assumptions, a parsimonious set of heuristically powerful propositions that could generate empirically verifiable hypotheses about international relations; the second encouraged him to emphasize the structural determinants of state behaviour. The resulting neo-realist theory built on two assumptions: that the international system is anarchical, in the sense that it lacks a central authority to impose order; and that in such a system states are primarily interested in their own survival. Waltz went on to argue that to ensure their survival, states must maximize their power, particularly their military power. Because such power is zero-sum – with an increase in the military power of one state necessarily producing a decrease in the relative power of another – Waltz argued that states are 'defensive positionalists'. They are conscious of their position within the power hierarchy of states, and at a minimum seek to maintain that position, at a maximum to increase it to the point of domination. For this reason, Waltz claimed that the struggle for power is an enduring characteristic of international relations, and conflict is endemic. In such a world, he argued, cooperation between states is at best precarious, at worst non-existent.

Theory of International Politics reinvigorated realism, giving realists a new identity – as neo- or structural realists – and a new confidence. Not all were convinced, though, and criticisms mounted on several fronts. The most moderate of these came from a new school of neo-liberal institutionalists, led by the repositioned Robert Keohane. Moving away from his previous concern with transnational relations and interdependence, Keohane took up the task of explaining cooperation under anarchy. Realists had long argued that if international cooperation was possible at all, it was only under conditions of hegemony, when a dominant state was able to use its power to create and enforce the institutional rules necessary to sustain cooperation between states. By the end of the 1970s, however, America's relative power was clearly on the wane, yet the framework of institutions it had sponsored after World War II to facilitate international economic cooperation was not collapsing. How could this be explained? In his 1984 book, *After Hegemony,* Keohane proposed a neo-liberal theory of international cooperation, a theory that embraced three elements of neo-realism: the importance of international anarchy in shaping state behaviour, the state as the most important actor in world politics, and the assumption of states as essentially self-interested. He also endorsed the Lakatosian model of theory construction that informed neo-realism (Keohane 1984, 1989a).

Despite this common ground with neo-realism, neo-liberalism draws very different conclusions about the potential for sustained international cooperation. As noted above, neo-liberals accept that states have to pursue their interests under conditions of anarchy. In Axelrod and Keohane's words, anarchy 'remains a constant' (1993: 86). Nevertheless, anarchy alone does not determine the extent or nature of international cooperation. Neo-realists are closest to the mark, neo-liberals argue, when there is low interdependence between states. When economic and political interactions between states are minimal, there are few common interests to spur international cooperation. When interdependence is high, however, as since World War II, states come to share a wide range of interests, from the management of international trade to global environmental protection. The existence of mutual interests is a prerequisite for international cooperation, but neo-liberals insist that the existence of such interests does not itself explain the extent and nature of cooperative relations between states – international cooperation remains difficult to achieve. Even when states have interests in common, the lack of a central world authority often deters them from incurring the reciprocal obligations that cooperation demands. Without a central authority, states fear that others will cheat on agreements; they can see cooperation as too costly, given the effort they would have to expend; and often they lack sufficient information to know that they even have common interests with other states. This not only explains why states fail to cooperate even when they have common interests, it explains how they cooperate when they do. According to neo-liberals, states construct international institutions, or regimes, to overcome these obstacles to cooperation (Keohane 1984: 57, 85–109).

In spite of these differences, neo-realism and neo-liberalism are both rationalist theories; they are both constructed upon the choice-theoretic assumptions of microeconomic theory. Three such assumptions stand out. First, political actors – be they individuals or states – are assumed to be atomistic, self-interested and rational. Actors are treated as *pre-social*, in the sense that their identities and interests are autogenous. In the language of classical liberalism, individuals are the source of their own conceptions of the good. Actors are also *self-interested*, concerned primarily with the pursuit of their own interests. And they are *rational*, capable of establishing the most effective and efficient way to realize their interests within the environmental constraints they encounter. Second, and following from the above, actors' interests are assumed to be exogenous to social interaction. Individuals and states are thought to enter social relations with their interests already formed. Social interaction is not considered an important determinant of interests. Third, and following again from the above, society is understood as a strategic realm in which individuals or states come together to pursue their predefined interests. Actors are not, therefore, inherently social; they are not products of their social environment, merely atomistic rational beings that form social relations to maximize their interests.

The challenge of critical theory

While neo-realists and neo-liberals engaged in a rationalist family feud, critical theorists challenged the very foundations of the rationalist project. Ontologically, they criticized the image of social actors as atomistic egoists, whose interests are formed prior to social interaction, and who enter social relations solely for strategic purposes. They argued, in contrast, that actors are inherently *social,* that their identities and interests are socially constructed, the products of intersubjective social structures. Epistemologically and methodologically, they questioned the neo-positivism of Lakatosian forms of social science, calling for interpretive modes of understanding, attuned to the unquantifiable nature of many social phenomena and the inherent subjectivity of all observation. And normatively, they condemned the notion of value-neutral theorizing, arguing that all knowledge is wedded to interests, and that theories should be explicitly committed to exposing and dismantling structures of domination and oppression (Hoffman 1987; George and Campbell 1990).

Beneath the umbrella of this broad critique, modern and post-modern critical theorists stood united against the dominant rationalist theories. Just as the rationalists were internally divided, though, so too were the critics. The post-modernists, drawing on the French social theorists, particularly Jacques Derrida and Michel Foucault, adopted a stance of 'radical interpretivism'. They opposed all attempts to assess empirical and ethical claims by any single criterion of validity, claiming that such moves always marginalize alternative viewpoints and moral positions, creating hierarchies of power and domination. The modernists, inspired by the writings of Frankfurt School theorists such as Jürgen Habermas, assumed a position of 'critical interpretivism'. They recognized the contingent nature of all knowledge – the inherent subjectivity of all claims and the connection between knowledge and power – but they insisted that some criteria were needed to distinguish plausible from implausible knowledge claims, and that without minimal, consensually grounded ethical principles, emancipatory political action would be impossible. Mark Hoffman characterized this difference between modernists and post-modernists in terms of a distinction between 'anti-foundationalism' and 'minimal foundationalism' (1991: 169–85).

Despite these important differences, the first wave of critical theory had a distinctive meta-theoretical or quasi-philosophical character. Critical international theorists roamed broadly over epistemological, normative, ontological and methodological concerns, and their energies were devoted primarily to demolishing the philosophical foundations of the rationalist project. Noteworthy empirical studies of world politics were certainly published by critical theorists, but the general tenor of critical writings was more abstractly theoretical, and their principal impact lay in the critique of prevailing assumptions about legitimate knowledge, about the nature of the social world, and about the purpose of theory (Cox 1987; Der Derian 1987). This general orientation was encouraged by a widely shared assumption among critical theorists about the relationship between theory and practice. This assumption was evident in the common refrain that realism constituted a 'hegemonic discourse', by which they meant two things. First, that realist assumptions, particularly dressed up in the garb of rationalism and neo-positivism, as was neo-realism, defined what counts as legitimate knowledge in the field of International Relations. And, second, that the influence of these assumptions extended far beyond the academy to structure policy making, particularly in the United States. Rationalist theories were thus doubly insidious. Not only did they dominate the discourse of International Relations, to the exclusion of alternative perspectives and forms of knowledge, they informed Washington's Cold War politics, with all the excesses of power these engendered. From this standpoint, theory was seen as having a symbiotic relationship with practice, and critiquing the discourse of International Relations was considered the essence of substantive analysis (Price and Reus-Smit 1998).

Constructivism

The end of the Cold War produced a major reconfiguration of debates within the dominant American discourse of international relations theory, prompted by the rise of a new 'constructivist' school of thought. While constructivism owes much to intellectual developments in sociology – particularly sociological institutionalism (see Finnemore 1996) – it also drew heavily on critical international theory, with many of its pioneers employing insights from critical scholarship to illuminate diverse aspects of world politics (see Price and Reus-Smit 1998). Constructivism differs from first-wave critical theory, however, in its emphasis on *empirical analysis*. Some constructivists have continued to work at the meta-theoretical level (Onuf 1989; Wendt 1999), but most have sought conceptual and theoretical illumination through the systematic analysis of empirical puzzles in world politics. The balance of critical scholarship has thus shifted away from the previous mode of abstract philosophical argument toward the study of human discourse and practice beyond the narrow confines of international relations theory. Where first-wave critical theorists had rejected the rationalist depiction of humans as atomistic egoists and society as a strategic domain – proffering an alternative image of humans as socially embedded, communicatively constituted and culturally empowered – constructivists have used this alternative ontology to explain and interpret aspects of world politics that were anomalous to neo-realism and neo-liberalism. And where earlier theorists had condemned the neo-positivist methodology of those perspectives, calling for more interpretive, discursive and historical modes of analysis, constructivists have employed these latter techniques to further their empirical explorations.

The rise of constructivism was prompted by four factors. First, motivated by an attempt to reassert the pre-eminence of their own conceptions of theory and world politics, leading rationalists challenged critical theorists to move beyond theoretical critique to the substantive analysis of international relations. While prominent critical theorists condemned the motives behind this challenge, constructivists saw it as an opportunity to demonstrate the heuristic power of non-rationalist perspectives (Walker 1989). Second, the end of the Cold War undermined the explanatory pretensions of neo-realists and neo-liberals, neither of which had predicted, nor could adequately comprehend, the systemic transformations reshaping the global order. It also undermined the critical theorists' assumption that theory drove practice in any narrow or direct fashion, as global politics increasingly demonstrated dynamics that contradicted realist expectations and prescriptions. The end of the Cold War thus opened a space for alternative modes of understanding and prompted critically inclined scholars to move away from a narrowly defined meta-theoretical critique. Third, by the beginning of the 1990s a new generation of young scholars had emerged who embraced many of the propositions of critical international theory, but who saw potential for innovation in conceptual elaboration and empirically informed theoretical development (Klotz 1995: 20; Kier 1997; Price 1997; Hall 1999; Lynch, M., 1999; Reus-Smit 1999; Tannenwald 1999; Rae 2002). Not only had the end of the Cold War thrown up new and interesting questions about world politics (such as the dynamics of international change, the nature of basic institutional practices, the role of non-state agency, and the problem of human rights), the rationalist failure to explain recent systemic transformations encouraged this new generation of scholars to revisit old questions and issues long viewed through neo-realist and neo-liberal lenses (including the control of WMD, the role and nature of strategic culture and the implications of anarchy). Finally, the advance of the new constructivist perspective was aided by the enthusiasm that mainstream scholars, frustrated by the analytical failings of the dominant rationalist theories, showed in embracing the new perspective, moving it from the margins to the mainstream of theoretical debate (Katzenstein 1996; Ruggie 1993).

Echoing the divisions within critical international theory, constructivists are divided between modernists and post-modernists. They have all, however, sought to articulate and explore three core ontological propositions about social life, propositions that they claim illuminate more about world politics than rival rationalist assumptions. First, to the extent that structures can be said to shape the behaviour of social and political actors, be they individuals or states, constructivists hold that *normative* or *ideational* structures are as important as material structures. Where neo-realists emphasize the material structure of the balance of military power, and Marxists stress the material structure of the capitalist world economy, constructivists argue that systems of shared ideas, beliefs and values also have structural characteristics, and that they exert a powerful influence on social and political action. There are two reasons why they attach such importance to these structures. Constructivists argue that 'material resources only acquire meaning for human action through the structure of shared knowledge in which they are embedded' (Wendt 1995: 73). For example, Canada and Cuba both exist alongside the United States, yet the simple balance of military power cannot explain the fact that the former is a close American ally, the latter an enemy. Ideas about identity, the logics of ideology and established structures of friendship and enmity lend the material balance of power between Canada and the United States and Cuba and the United States radically different meanings (and hence implications for behaviour). Constructivists also stress the importance of normative and ideational structures because these are thought to shape the social identities of political actors. Just as the institutionalized norms of the academy shape the identity of a professor, the norms of the international system condition the social identity of the sovereign state. For instance, in the Age of Absolutism (1555–1848) the norms of European international society held that Christian monarchies were the only legitimate form of sovereign state, and these norms, backed by the coercive practices of the community of states, conspired to undermine Muslim, liberal or nationalist polities.

Second, constructivists argue that understanding how non-material structures condition actors' identities is important because identities inform interests and, in turn, actions. As we saw above, rationalists believe that actors' interests are exogenously determined, meaning that actors, be they individuals or states, encounter one another with a preexisting set of preferences. Neo-realists and neo-liberals are not interested in where such preferences come from, only in how actors pursue them strategically. Society – both domestic and international – is thus considered a *strategic domain,* a place in which previously constituted actors pursue their goals, a place that does not alter the nature or interests of those actors in any deep sense. Constructivists, in contrast, argue that understanding how actors develop their interests is crucial to explaining a wide range of international political phenomenon that rationalists ignore or misunderstand. To explain interest formation, constructivists focus on the social identities of individuals or states. In Alexander Wendt's words, 'Identities are the basis of interests' (Wendt 1992: 398). To return to the previous examples, being an 'academic' gives a person certain interests, such as research and publication, and being a Christian monarch in the age of Absolutism brought with it a range of interests, such as controlling religion within your territory, pursuing rights of succession beyond that territory, and crushing nationalist movements. Likewise, being a liberal democracy today encourages an intolerance of authoritarian regimes and a preference for free-market capitalism. Constructivists are not opposed to the idea that actors might be 'self-interested', but they argue that this tells us nothing unless we understand how actors define their 'selves' and how this informs their 'interests'.

Third, constructivists contend that agents and structures are *mutually constituted*. Normative and ideational structures may well condition the identities and interests of actors, but those structures would not exist if it were not for the knowledgeable practices of those actors. Wendt's emphasis on the 'supervening' power of structures, and the predilection of many constructivists to study how norms shape behaviour, suggest that constructivists are structuralists, just like their neo-realist and Marxist counterparts. On closer reflection, however, one sees that constructivists are better classed as structurationists, as emphasizing the impact of non-material structures on identities and interests but, just as importantly, the role of practices in maintaining and transforming those structures. Institutionalized norms and ideas 'define the meaning and identity of the individual actor and the patterns of appropriate economic, political, and cultural activity engaged in by those individuals' (Boli, Meyer and Thomas 1989: 12), and it 'is through reciprocal interaction that we create and instantiate the relatively enduring social structures in terms of which we define our identities and interests' (Wendt 1992: 406). The norms of the academy give certain individuals an academic identity which brings with it an interest in research and publication, but it is only through the routinized practices of academics that such norms exist and are sustained. Similarly, the international norms that uphold liberal democracy as the dominant model of legitimate statehood, and which license intervention in the name of human rights and the promotion of free trade, exist and persist only because of the continued practices of liberal democratic states (and powerful non-state actors).

Normative and ideational structures are seen as shaping actors' identities and interests through three mechanisms: imagination, communication and constraint. With regard to the first, constructivists argue that non-material structures affect what actors see as the realm of possibility: how they think they should act; what the perceived limitations on their actions are, and what strategies they can imagine, let alone entertain, to achieve their objectives. Institutionalized norms and ideas thus condition what actors consider necessary and possible, in both practical and ethical terms. A president or prime minister in an established liberal democracy will only imagine and seriously entertain certain strategies to enhance his or her power, and the norms of the liberal democratic polity will condition his or her expectations. Normative and ideational structures also work their influence through communication. When an individual or a state seeks to justify their behaviour, they will usually appeal to established norms of legitimate conduct. A president or prime minister may appeal to the conventions of executive government, and a state may justify its behaviour with reference to the norms of sovereignty – or, in the case of intervention in the affairs of another state, according to international human rights norms. As the latter case suggests, norms may conflict with one another in their prescriptions, which makes moral argument about the relative importance of international normative precepts a particularly salient aspect of world politics (Risse 2000). Finally, even if normative and ideational structures do not affect an actor's behaviour by framing their imagination or by providing a linguistic or moral court of appeal, constructivists argue that they can place significant constraints on that actor's conduct. Realists have long argued that ideas simply function as rationalizations, as ways of masking actions really motivated by the crude desire for power. Constructivists point out, though, that institutionalized norms and ideas work as rationalizations only because they already have moral force in a given social context. Furthermore, appealing to established norms and ideas to justify behaviour is a viable strategy only if the behaviour is in some measure consistent with the proclaimed principles. The very language of justification thus provides constraints on action, though the effectiveness of such constraints will vary with the actor and the context (Reus-Smit 1999: 35–6).

Given the preceding discussion, constructivism contrasts with rationalism in three important respects. First, where rationalists assume that actors are atomistic egoists, constructivists treat them as deeply *social*: not in the sense that they are 'party animals', but in the sense that their identities are constituted by the institutionalized norms, values and ideas of the social environment in which they act. Second, instead of treating actors' interests as exogenously determined, as given prior to social interaction, constructivists treat interests as *endogenous* to such interaction, as a consequence of identity acquisition, as learned through processes of communication, reflection on experience and role enactment. Third, while rationalists view society as a strategic realm, a place where actors rationally pursue their interests, constructivists see it as a *constitutive realm,* the site that generates actors as knowledgeable social and political agents, the realm that makes them who they are. From these ontological commitments, it is clear why constructivists are called 'constructivists', for they emphasize the social determinants of social and political agency and action.

In the 1990s, three different forms of constructivism evolved: systemic, unit-level and holistic constructivism. The first of these follows neo-realists in adopting a 'third-image' perspective, focusing solely on interactions between unitary state actors. Everything that exists or occurs within the domestic political realm is ignored, and an account of world politics is derived simply by theorizing how states relate to one another in the external, international domain. Wendt's influential writings provide the best example of systemic constructivism. In fact, one could reasonably argue that Wendt's writings represent the only true example of this rarefied form of constructivism (Wendt 1992, 1994, 1995, 1999). Like other constructivists, Wendt believes that the identity of the state informs its interests and, in turn, its actions. He draws a distinction, though, between the social and corporate identities of the state: the former referring to the status, role or personality that international society ascribes to a state; the latter referring to the internal human, material, ideological, or cultural factors that make a state what it is. Because of his commitment to systemic theorizing, Wendt brackets corporate sources of state identity, concentrating on how structural contexts, systemic processes, and strategic practices produce and reproduce different sorts of state identity. Though theoretically elegant, this form of constructivism suffers from one major deficiency: it confines the processes that shape international societies within an unnecessarily and unproductively narrow realm. The social identities of states are thought to be constituted by the normative and ideational structures of international society, and those structures are seen as the product of state practices. From this perspective, it is impossible to explain how fundamental changes occur, either in the nature of international society or in the nature of state identity. By bracketing everything domestic, Wendt excludes by theoretical fiat most of the normative and ideational forces that might prompt such change.

Unit-level constructivism is the inverse of systemic constructivism. Instead of focusing on the external, international domain, unit-level constructivists concentrate on the relationship between domestic social and legal norms and the identities and interests of states, the very factors bracketed by Wendt. Here Peter Katzenstein's writings on the national security policies of Germany and Japan (1996, 1999) are emblematic.

Setting out to explain why two states, with common experiences of military defeat, foreign occupation, economic development, transition from authoritarianism to democracy and nascent great-power status, have adopted very different internal and external national security policies, Katzenstein stresses the importance of institutionalized regulatory and constitutive national social and legal norms. He concludes that:

> In Germany the strengthening of state power through changes in legal norms betrays a deep-seated fear that terrorism challenges the core of the state. In effect, eradicating terrorism and minimizing violent protest overcome the specter of a 'Hobbesian' state of nature ... In Japan, on the other hand, the close interaction of social and legal norms reveals a state living symbiotically within its society and not easily shaken to its foundation. Eliminating terrorism and containing violent protest were the tasks of a 'Grotian' community ... Conversely, Germany's active involvement in the evolution of international legal norms conveys a conception of belonging to an international 'Grotian' community. Japan's lack of concern for the consequences of pushing terrorists abroad and its generally passive international stance is based on a 'Hobbesian' view of the society of states. (Katzenstein 1996: 153–4)

While not entirely disregarding the role of international norms in conditioning the identities and interests of states, Katzenstein draws attention to the internal, domestic determinants of national policies. Unit-level constructivism of this sort has the virtue of enabling the explanation of variations of identity, interest and action across states, something that systemic constructivism obscures. It follows, though, that this form of constructivism has difficulty accounting for similarities between states, for patterns of convergence in state identity and interest.

Where systemic and unit-level constructivists reproduce the traditional dichotomy between the international and the domestic, holistic constructivists seek to bridge the two domains. To accommodate the entire range of factors conditioning the identities and interests of states, they bring the corporate and the social together into a unified analytical perspective that treats the domestic and the international as two faces of a single social and political order. Concerned primarily with the dynamics of global change – particularly the rise and possible demise of the sovereign state – holistic constructivists focus on the mutually constitutive relationship between this order and the state. This general perspective has spawned two distinctive, yet complementary, analyses of international change: one focusing on grand shifts between international systems, the other on recent changes within the modern system. The former is typified by John Ruggie's path-breaking work on the rise of sovereign states out of the wreck of European feudalism, work that emphasizes the importance of changing social epistemes, or frameworks of knowledge (1986, 1993). The latter is exemplified by Friedrich Kratochwil's writings on the end of the Cold War, which stress the role of changing ideas of international order and security (Kratochwil 1993; Koslowski and Kratochwil 1995). Though less parsimonious and elegant than systemic constructivism, holistic scholarship has the merit of being able to explain the development of the normative and ideational structures of the present international system, as well as the social identities they have engendered. The more concerned this form of constructivism becomes with grand tectonic transformations, however, the more structuralist it tends to become, and human agency tends to drop out of the story. Ideas change, norms evolve, and culture transforms, but these seem to move independently of human will, choice, or action.

Constructivism and its discontents

The articulation of a constructivist theoretical framework for the study of international relations has significantly altered the axes of debate within the field. The internecine debate between neo-realists and neo-liberals, which, until the middle of the 1990s was still being hailed as *the* contemporary debate, has been displaced as rationalists have haphazardly joined forces to confront a common constructivist foe. The rise of constructivism has also displaced the debate between rationalists and critical international theorists. The veracity of the epistemological, methodological and normative challenges that critical theorists levelled at rationalism has not diminished, but the rise of constructivism has focused debate on ontological and empirical issues, pushing the meta-theoretical debate of the 1980s off centre stage. The core debate now animating the field revolves around the nature of social agency, the relative importance of normative versus material forces, the balance between continuity and transformation in world politics and a range of other empirical-theoretical questions. This does not mean, though, that rationalism and constructivism constitute unified, unproblematic or fully coherent theoretical positions, standing pristine in opposition to one another. We have already seen the significant differences within the rationalist fold, and I now turn to the discontents that characterize contemporary constructivism. Four of these warrant particular attention: the disagreements among constructivists over the nature of theory, the relationship with rationalism, the appropriate methodology, and the contribution of constructivism to a critical theory of international relations.

It has long been the ambition of rationalists, especially neo-realists, to formulate a general theory of international relations, the core assumptions of which would be so robust that they could explain its fundamental characteristics, regardless of historical epoch or differences in the internal complexions of states. For most constructivists, such ambitions have little attraction. The constitutive forces they emphasize, such as ideas, norms and culture, and the elements of human agency they stress, such as corporate and social identity, are all inherently variable. There is simply no such thing as a universal, transhistorical, disembedded, culturally autonomous idea or identity. Most constructivists thus find the pursuit of a general theory of international relations an absurdity, and confine their ambitions to providing compelling interpretations and explanations of discrete aspects of world politics, going no further than to offer heavily qualified 'contingent generalizations'. In fact, constructivists repeatedly insist that constructivism is not a theory, but rather an analytical framework. The one notable exception to this tendency is Wendt, who has embarked on the ambitious project of formulating a comprehensive social theory of international relations, placing himself in direct competition with Waltz. In pursuit of this goal, however, Wendt makes a number of moves that put him at odds with almost all other constructivists: namely, he focuses solely on the systemic level, he treats the state as a unitary actor and he embraces an epistemological position called 'scientific realism' (Wendt and Shapiro 1997). While these represent the theoretical proclivities of but one scholar, Wendt's prominence in the development of constructivism makes them important sources of division and disagreement within the new school. His *Social Theory of International Politics* (1999) is the most sustained elaboration of constructivist theory yet, and for many in the field defines the very nature of constructivism. However, the vision of theory it presents has been vigorously contested by other constructivists, thus forming one of the principal axes of tension within constructivism over the coming years.

The second discontent within constructivism concerns the relationship with rationalism. Some constructivists believe that productive engagement is possible between the two approaches, engagement based on a scholarly division of labour. We have seen that constructivists emphasize how institutionalized norms shape the identities and interests of actors, and that rationalists, treating interests as unexplained givens, stress how actors go about pursuing their interests strategically. The first focuses on interest formation, the second on interest satisfaction. Seeking to build bridges instead of fences between the two approaches, some constructivists see in this difference a possible division of labour, with constructivists doing the work of explaining how actors gain their preferences and rationalists exploring how they realize those preferences.

Constructivism is thus not a rival theoretical perspective to rationalism at all, but rather a complementary one. 'The result', Audie Klotz argues, 'is a reformulated, complementary research agenda that illuminates the independent role of norms in determining actors' identities and interests. Combined with theories of institutions and interest-based behaviour, this approach offers us a conceptually consistent and more complete understanding of international relations' (1995: 20). As attractive as this exercise in bridge-building appears, not all constructivists are convinced. Reus-Smit has demonstrated that the institutionalized norms that shape actors' identities help define not only their interests but also their strategic rationality (1999). Attempts to confine constructivist scholarship to the realm of interest formation, and to concede rationalists the terrain of strategic interaction, have thus been criticized for propagating an unnecessarily 'thin form of constructivism' (Laffey and Weldes 1997).

Another discontent within constructivism involves the question of methodology. Critical theorists have long argued that the neo-positivist methodology championed by neo-realists and neo-liberals is poorly suited to the study of human action, as the individuals and groups under analysis attach meanings to their actions: these meanings are shaped by a pre-existing 'field' of shared meanings embedded in language and other symbols, and the effect of such meanings on human action cannot be understood by treating them as measurable variables that cause behaviour in any direct or quantifiable manner (Taylor 1997: 111). This led early constructivists to insist that the study of ideas, norms and other meanings requires an interpretive methodology, one that seeks to grasp 'the relationship between "intersubjective meanings" which derive from self-interpretation and self-definition, and the social practices in which they are embedded and which they constitute' (Kratochwil and Ruggie 1986; Kratochwil 1988/9; Neufeld 1993: 49). Curiously, these arguments have been forgotten by a number of constructivists, who defend a position of 'methodological conventionalism', claiming that their explanations 'do not depend exceptionally upon any specialized separate "interpretive methodology"' (Jepperson, Wendt and Katzenstein 1996: 67). They justify this position on the grounds that the field has been bogged down for too long in methodological disputes and, at any rate, the empirical work of more doctrinaire constructivists such as Kratochwil and Ruggie does not look all that different from that of conventional scholars. Neither of these grounds addresses the substance of the original constructivist argument about methodology, nor do the advocates of methodological conventionalism recognize that the similarity between mainstream empirical work and that of interpretive constructivists may have more to do with the failure of rationalists ever to meet their own neo-positivist standards. The gap between these rival methodological standpoints within constructivism is most clearly apparent in the contrast between those studies that employ quantitative methodological techniques and those that adopt genealogical approaches (Johnston 1995; Price 1997).

The final discontent concerns the relationship between constructivism and critical international theory. It is reasonable, we have seen, to view constructivism as influenced, in significant measure, by critical theory, and Price and Reus-Smit (1998) have argued that its development has great potential to further the critical project. Andrew Linklater (1992a) has identified three dimensions of that project: the normative task of critically assessing and revising how political organization, particularly the sovereign state, has been morally justified; the sociological task of understanding how moral community – locally, nationally and globally – expands and contracts; and the praxeological task of grasping the constraints and opportunities that bear on emancipatory political action (1992a: 92–4). Nowhere is the second of these tasks being undertaken with greater energy and rigour than within constructivism. Exploring the development and the impact of the normative and ideational foundations of international society is the constructivist stock in trade, and dialogue between constructivists and those engaged in the more philosophical project of normative critique and elaboration is the most likely path toward true praxeological knowledge. Constructivism is divided, however, between those who remain cognizant of the critical origins and potentiality of their sociological explorations, and those who have embraced constructivism simply as an explanatory or interpretive tool. Both standpoints are justifiable, and the work of scholars on both sides of this divide can be harnessed to the critical project, regardless of their individual commitments. It is imperative, though, that the former group of scholars work to bring constructivist research into dialogue with moral and philosophical argument, otherwise constructivism will lose its ethical veracity and critical international theory one of its potential pillars.

It is tempting to explain these discontents in terms of differences between modern and post-modern constructivists, differences outlined earlier. Yet disagreements over the nature of theory, the relationship to rationalism, the appropriate method and the contribution to critical international theory do not map neatly onto the divide between minimal and anti-foundationalism. While post-modern constructivists would never advocate the development of a general theory of international relations, task-sharing with rationalists, methodological conventionalism, or pure explanation, neither would many modern constructivists. Here Ted Hopf's (1998) distinction between 'conventional' and 'critical' constructivisms may be more fruitful: 'To the degree that constructivism creates theoretical and epistemological distance between itself and its origins in critical theory, it becomes "conventional" constructivism' (1998: 181). The discontents outlined above reflect the differences between those who have consciously or unconsciously created such distance and those who wish to stay in touch with constructivism's roots. Among the latter group, important differences remain between modernists and post-modernists. The most important of these differences concerns the questions they address, with the former focusing on *why* questions, the latter on *how* questions. For instance, Reus-Smit (1999) takes up the question of why different international societies have evolved different institutional practices to solve cooperation problems and facilitate coexistence among states, while Cynthia Weber asks 'How is the meaning of sovereignty fixed or stabilized historically via practices of international relations theorists and practices of political intervention?' (1995: 3).

The contribution of constructivism

In spite of these discontents, which are as much a sign of dynamism as division, the rise of constructivism has had several important impacts on the development of international relations theory and analysis. Thanks largely to the work of constructivists, the social, historical and normative have returned to the centre stage of debate, especially within the American core of the discipline.

Until the late 1980s, two factors conspired to marginalize societal analysis in International Relations scholarship. The first was the overwhelming materialism of the major theoretical perspectives. For neo-realists, the principal determinant of state behaviour is the underlying distribution of material capabilities across states in the international system, a determinant that gives states their animating survival motive, which in turn drives balance of power competition. To the extent that they discussed it, neo-liberals also saw state interests as essentially material, even if they did posit the importance of international institutions as intervening variables. The second factor was the prevailing rationalist conception of human action. As we have seen, both neo-realists and neo-liberals imagined humans – and, by extension, states – as atomistic, self-interested, strategic actors, thus positing a standard form of instrumental rationality across all political actors. When combined, the materialism and rationalism of the prevailing theories left little room for the social dimensions of international life, unless of course the social is reduced to power-motivated strategic competition. Materialism denied the causal significance of shared ideas, norms and values, and rationalism reduced the social to the strategic and ignored the particularities of community, identity and interest. By re-imagining the social as a constitutive realm of values and practices, and by situating individual identities and interests within such a field, constructivists have placed sociological inquiry back at the centre of the discipline. Because of the prominence of the 'international society' (or 'English') school, such inquiry had never disappeared from British International Relations scholarship. Constructivists, however, have brought a new level of conceptual clarity and theoretical sophistication to the analysis of both international and world society, thus complementing and augmenting the work of the English School.

By resuscitating societal analysis, the rise of constructivism has also sparked a renewed interest in international history. So long as International Relations theorists were wedded to the idea that states are driven by context-transcendent survival motives or universal modes of rationality, the lessons of history were reduced to the proposition that nothing of substance ever changes. Such assumptions denied the rich diversity of human experience and the possibilities of meaningful change and difference, thus flattening out international history into a monotone tale of 'recurrence and repetition'. Historical analysis became little more than the ritualistic recitation of lines from the celebrated works of Thucydides, Machiavelli and Hobbes, all with aim of 'proving' the unchanging nature of international relations, licensing the formulation of increasingly abstract theories. Such history had the paradoxical effect of largely suffocating the study of international history in the American core of the discipline. Aided by the momentous changes that attended the end of the Cold War, and also by the on-going processes of globalization, the constructivist interest in the particularities of culture, identity, interest and experience created space for a renaissance in the study of history and world politics. If ideas, norms, and practices matter, and if they differ from one social context to another, then history in turn matters. Not surprisingly, in their efforts to demonstrate the contingency of such factors and their impact on the conduct of world politics, constructivists have sought to re-read the historical record, to re-think what has long been treated as given in the study of international relations. While a similar impulse came from International Relations scholars inspired by the re-birth of historical sociology, constructivists have dominated the new literature on international history (Ruggie 1986, 1993; Welch 1993; Thomson 1994; Kier 1997; Hall 1999; Reus-Smit 1999; Philpott 2001; Rae 2002; Phillips 2011).

Finally, constructivism may be credited with helping to re-invigorate normative theorizing in International Relations. Not because constructivists have been engaged in philosophical reflection about the nature of the good or the right, a project that has itself been re-energized by the multitude of ethical dilemmas thrown up by the end of the Cold War and the march of globalization, but because they have done much to demonstrate the power of ideas, norms and values in shaping world politics. While talk of the 'power of ideas' has at times carried considerable rhetorical force outside of academic International Relations, such talk within the field has long been dismissed as naive and even dangerous idealism. Material calculations, such as military power and wealth, have been upheld as the motive forces behind international political action, and ideational factors have been dismissed as mere rationalizations or instrumental guides to strategic action. Through sustained empirical research, constructivists have exposed the explanatory poverty of such materialist scepticism. They have shown how international norms evolve, how ideas and values come to shape political action, how argument and discourse condition outcomes and how identity constitutes agents and agency, all in ways that contradict the expectations of materialist and rationalist theories. While this 'empirical idealism' provides no answers to questions probed by international ethicists, it contributes to more philosophically oriented normative theorizing in two ways: it legitimizes such theorizing by demonstrating the possibility of ideas driven international change; and it assists by clarifying the dynamics and mechanisms of such change, thus furthering the development of E. H. Carr's proposed 'realistic utopianism'.

Recent developments in constructivism

In the past two decades constructivism has moved from being the new kid on the block to one of the principal theoretical approaches in the field. Prior to the end of the Cold War, North American textbooks spoke of three great paradigms: realism, liberalism, and Marxism. Today, they speak of realism, liberalism, and constructivism. But as we have seen, constructivism is a broad church, encompassing several different varieties and a host of tensions and disagreements. Despite all of this, however, constructivism remains a vibrant, constantly evolving, perspective on international relations, spawning some of the most important innovations in international theory. In this final section I explore, in a necessarily brief fashion, four of these innovations.

The first concerns the study of power, a staple of international relations theory. Traditionally, discussions of power in international relations have been seen as a realist preserve. 'Absolute power', 'relative power', 'structural power' and 'the balance of power' are all considered realist conceptions, as are notions of 'the struggle for power', 'power-maximization', 'power transition', and hegemonic stability. Yet as Wendt argues persuasively, the 'proposition that the nature of international politics is shaped by power relations ... cannot be a *uniquely* Realist claim' (1999: 96–7). What is uniquely realist is the 'hypothesis that the effects of power are constituted primarily by brute material forces' (1999: 97). Events in world politics cast serious doubt on this hypothesis, however. For much of the post-Cold War period the United States has been cast as a 'unipol' or a 'hyperpower', a state with a greater degree of material preponderance than perhaps any other state in history. Well before the onset of the current global financial crisis, however, there was strong evidence to suggest that America's impressive material capacities were not producing commensurate levels of 'power', understood as sustained political influence. The George W. Bush Administration was not shy about flexing America's military muscle to achieve political ends. Yet time and again the results were at best mixed: unintended consequences were as common as intended. Partly in response to this gap between America's material preponderance and ambiguous and inconsistent political influence, constructivists have sought more complex, and heuristically useful, understandings of power in world politics (see Reus-Smit 2004a). One approach has been to develop a more holistic understanding of power, and to locate the realist conception as but one of a number of different forms. Michael Barnett and Raymond Duvall, for example, have distinguished between compulsory, institutional, structural, and productive power, showing that realists are really only concerned with the first (Barnett and Duvall 2004). Another approach stresses the non-material sources of power, particularly the importance of legitimacy. From this perspective, an actor's power is not merely determined by the material resources it commands, but by the degree to which other actors perceive its identity, interests, and actions as legitimate, as rightful in relation to prevailing social norms and expectations (Bukovansky 2002; Hurd 2005, 2007; Clark and Reus-Smit 2007). Related to this work is the growing corpus of constructivist work on international law, an institution intimately related to the politics of norms, legitimacy and power (Brunnee and Toope 2000; Finnemore and Toope 2001; Reus-Smit 2004b; Brunnee and Toope 2010).

The second innovation concerns culture in world politics. The study of culture and international relations is closely related to constructivism, an association reinforced by book titles such as *Cultural Realism* (by Alastair Iain Johnston) and *The Culture of National Security* (by Peter J. Katzenstein). Until recently, however, constructivists have taken 'culture' to mean social and legal norms, and they have confined their studies to how these are constructed and then deployed, through argument and communication, to constitute actors' identities and interests. Culture, understood more holistically as the broader framework of intersubjective meanings and social practices that give a society its distinctive character, has been largely neglected. Yet things have changed since September 11, 2001. Culture suddenly assumed centre stage in world politics, with arguments about religious and civilizational difference deployed as master lenses through which configurations of power and axes of conflict could be understood. This new terrain of debate was ready made for constructivist engagement, and over time two powerful responses have emerged. The first makes a comprehensive assault on Samuel Huntington's essentialist understanding of civilizations, articulated in his best seller *The Clash of Civilizations*. In a recent trilogy of edited volumes, Katzenstein and his contributors advance a radically different understanding of the nature of civilizations as cultural phenomena, and the nature of intra- and inter-civilizational engagement (see Katzenstein 2010, 2012a, 2012b). Instead of being coherent, unitary cultural entities, civilizations are understood here as loose, inherently pluralist cultural constellations. In contrast to much contemporary discourse, they are not political actors with agential qualities; though they can contain within them multiple actors: states, polities, and empires. Equally importantly, civilizations evolve and exist in the context of other civilizations; indeed, they are deeply interpenetrated and constituted by one another. The second response concerns the study of religion in world politics. International Relations, as a field of study, had largely written religion out of existence: great founding moments like the Peace of Westphalia were assumed to have domesticated religion, religious belief came to be seen as an extra-rational (if not irrational) form of consciousness, and secularization was considered the natural course of social evolution, in which religion was effectively relegated to the private sphere. The apparent return of religion to world politics thus came as a shock to International Relations, and the overwhelming tendency has been to understand it in essentialist terms ('Islam is like this', 'Christianity is like that') and to see it as a 'problem'. Yet recent constructivist research, of which Elizabeth Shakman Hurd's writings are emblematic, approaches the issue from an entirely different direction, asking how the secularist division of politics and religion has constituted modern regimes of political authority, how it has handicapped international relations thought, and, most importantly, how it structures contemporary political responses to religion in world politics (see Shakman Hurd 2004; 2008).

A third important innovation relates to the more explicit constructivist concern with normative theory, instead of just the study of norms. Constructivists have been criticized for having a merely empirical project; for studying the role that moral norms play in shaping actors' identities, interests, and behaviour, but having little to say about ethics of the norms in question. For conventional or mainstream constructivists this critique has little bite, as they are content with constructivism remaining a largely explanatory endeavour. But for those with more critical inclinations, constructivism should, and does, have something of value to contribute to normative international theory. Their response to the criticism has been twofold. First, a key volume edited by Richard Price (2008) argues that ethical reasoning is not merely about what constitutes appropriate moral ends or rightful means to achieve such ends. It also involves assumptions about what is morally possible in world politics; about the nature and limits of moral action. Such assumptions, however, are often empirically unsustainable, akin to the primitive anthropologies that informed much classic moral and political philosophy. Second, Price and others argue that constructivism's contribution to normative international theory lies in its ability to provide robust, empirically sustainable understandings of the nature and limits of moral action in world politics, thus helping us to unravel complex moral dilemmas in world politics. In Price's words, constructivism can help determine on what

> ethically defensible action depends exactly, when the deductive integrity of eminently necessary ethical guideposts of general moral rules frays under the strain of concrete application. A chief contribution here is the identification of different sources and types of moral dilemmas, which carry different implications for moral limit and possibility. There are clashes between ethics and interests, and there are conflicts between moral norms. Some of the latter do appear to be genuine conflicts for which there is no good solution, but many upon close analysis reveal themselves not to be immutable dilemmas but rather predicated upon (1) social constructions amenable to change, and (2) ethical positions underpinned by unwarranted empirical propositions. (Price 2008: 283)

The value of constructivism is that it can help us think through these complex issues.

The final innovation concerns what has been termed 'the practice turn' in International Relations. As explained above, although constructivism often appears structuralist, with intersubjective norms and beliefs constituting actors' identities, interests, and behaviour, it is in fact better understood as structurationist. Norms may shape actors and actions in important ways, but these norms only exist by virtue of the routinized practices of knowledgeable human agents. Practices, or what actors do, are thus crucially important to production and reproduction of social structures. This insight, long left undeveloped in constructivism, has now become a major site of theoretical innovation and empirical inquiry. Building on the work of social theorists such as Michel De Certeau and

Pierre Bourdieu, constructivists argue that not only are practices central to social and political life, but that a focus on practices can enable International Relations scholars to move beyond a number of important theoretical impasses: principally, between agency and structure, and between the ideational and the material. Practices, Emanuel Adler and Vincent Pouliot argue, 'are patterned actions that are embedded in particular organized contexts' (2011: 6). The social practice of the wedding is a good example, as is the practice of diplomacy. When understood in this way, practices entwined both agency and structure: they are things done by agents, but take a structural form as well. Similarly, practices also stand between ideas and materiality. Practices are always informed by, and embed, ideas and values, but when they are performed they become material phenomena: concrete things actors do. A focus on practices, it is claimed, thus enables us to move beyond a series of conceptual dichotomies that have ossified debate in the field. More than this, practice theory is proving a particularly illuminating way of understanding key phenomena in world politics. Pouliot has employed the concept to understand the nature and development of security communities (2010), Bially Mattern the social nature of emotions (2011), and Brunnee and Toope the sources of international legal obligation (2010). (On the practice turn more generally in International Relations scholarship, see the special issue of the journal *Millennium*: 'Out of the Ivory Tower', 40(3), 2012.)

Conclusion

The rise of constructivism has heralded a return to a more sociological, historical and practice oriented form of International Relations scholarship. Where rationalists had reduced the social to strategic interaction, denied the historical by positing disembedded, universal forms of rationality and reduced the practical art of politics to utility maximizing calculation, constructivists have re-imagined the social as a constitutive domain, reintroduced history as realm of empirical inquiry and emphasized the variability of political practice. In many respects, constructivism embodies characteristics normally associated with the 'English School', discussed by Linklater in Chapter 4 in this volume. Constructivists have taken up the idea that states form more than a system – that they form a society – and they have pushed this idea to new levels of theoretical and conceptual sophistication. Their interest in international history also represents an important point of convergence with the English School, as does their stress on the cultural distinctiveness of different societies of states. Finally, their initial emphasis on interpretive methods of analysis echoes Hedley Bull's call for a classical approach, 'characterized above all by explicit reliance upon the exercise of judgement' rather than neo-positivist standards of 'verification and proof' (1969/1995: 20–38).

These similarities, as well as constructivism's roots in critical international theory, appeared to pose a challenge to conventional understandings of the field. An 'Atlantic divide' has long structured understandings of the sociology of International Relations as a discipline, with the field seen as divided between North American 'scientists' and European (mainly British) 'classicists'. Two of the defining 'great debates' of the discipline – between realists and idealists and positivists and traditionalists – have been mapped onto this divide, lending intellectual divisions a cultural overtone. At first glance, constructivism appears to confuse this way of ordering the discipline. Despite having taken up many of the intellectual commitments normally associated with the English School, constructivism has its origins in the United States. Its principal exponents were either educated in or currently teach in the leading American universities, and their pioneering work has been published in the premier journals and by the leading university presses. The United States also spawned much of the earlier wave of critical international theory, especially of a post-modern variety, but that work never achieved the same centrality within the American sector of the discipline. One of the reasons for constructivism's success in the United States has been its emphasis on empirically informed theorizing over meta-theoretical critique, an orientation much less confronting to the mainstream. With success, however, has come normalization, and this has seen the neglectful forgetting, or active jettisoning, of theoretical commitments that were central to constructivism in the early years. Disappearing, in the American discipline, are the foundational ideas that constructivism rests on a social ontology radically different from rationalism's, that studying norms, as social facts, demands an interpretive methodology, and that constructivism was linked, in important ways, to the emancipatory project of critical theory. The continued importance of these commitments to non-American constructivism suggests that a new manifestation of the 'Atlantic divide' may now be emerging.

10 Feminism

JACQUI TRUE

Breaking with the powerful bond among men, states and war, feminist theories of international relations have flourished since the mid 1980s. These theories have introduced *gender* as an empirical category and analytical tool for understanding global power relations as well as a normative position from which to consider alternative world orders. Like other constitutive theories such as constructivism, critical theory, post-modernism, and green theories, feminism shifts the study of international relations away from a singular focus on interstate relations toward a comprehensive analysis of transnational actors and structures and their transformations. But with their focus on non-state actors, marginalized peoples and alternative conceptualizations of power and relationships, feminist perspectives bring fresh thinking and action to world politics.

In the new millennium, especially since the events of September 11, there has been a proliferation of research on gender and international security (see Al-Ali and Pratt 2009a; Sjoberg 2010; Wibben 2011), including feminist analysis of the gendered impacts of war and peace and quantitative analysis using gender as a variable to explain aspects of state behaviour and international conflict (Carpenter 2005; Nayak and Suchland 2006; Shepherd 2007). With this growth and range of gender and International Relations scholarship, feminists have recently given explicit accounts of their alternative methodological approaches to research on global politics (Ackerly, Stern and True 2006; Ackerly and True 2008b, 2010). The application of feminist International Relations 'ethical principles' to the global practices of policy makers and advocates is still relatively underdeveloped. But increasingly scholars are bringing the insights of feminist praxis to bear on discussions of peace and democratization processes, security operations, the meaning of universal human rights, and more just economic globalization policies. Within feminist practices there are resources for developing normative guidelines about the possibility for global dialogue across ethnic, cultural, national, racial, sexual and gender differences.

Until the 1980s, the field of International Relations studied the causes of war and conflict and the global expansion of trade and commerce with no particular reference to people. Indeed the use of abstract categories such as 'the state', 'the system', strategic security discourses such as nuclear deterrence and positivist research approaches effectively removed people as agents embedded in social and historical contexts from theories of international relations. This is ironic since the scholarly field emerged, following the end of World War I, to democratize foreign policy making and empower people as citizen-subjects rather than mere objects of elite statecraft (Hill 1999). So where does the study of people called 'women' and 'men' or the social construction of masculine and feminine genders fit within International Relations? How are the international system and the study of International Relations gendered? To what extent do feminist perspectives help us to explain, understand and improve global politics? This chapter explores these questions as they have been addressed by a growing and diverse community of feminist scholars in and outside the International Relations field.

The chapter starts with a brief overview of the development of feminist International Relations. It differentiates three overlapping forms of feminist scholarship that represent a useful heuristic for discussing the varied contributions to International Relations. These are: (1) *empirical feminism*, that focuses on women and/or explores gender dynamics as an empirical dimension of international relations; (2) *analytical feminism*, that uses gender as a theoretical category to reveal the gender bias of International Relations concepts and explain constitutive aspects of international relations; and (3) *normative feminism*, that reflects on the process of theorizing and the role of scholarship in a normative agenda for global social and political change. These forms do not prefigure or suggest any particular feminist epistemology. For example, Jacqueline Berman's (2003) analysis of the way in which European states secure their borders through anti-sex trafficking policies is an example of an empirical feminist approach informed by post-structuralist attention to the politics of domination involved in all efforts to categorize and 'protect' human subjects. Empirical, analytical and normative feminist approaches that challenge the assumptions of explanatory theories of International Relations and help to construct new constitutive theories of global politics are discussed in the second, third and fourth sections of the chapter.

Transformations in the structure of international relations have greatly altered patterns of gender relations just as gender dynamics have influenced processes of militarization and economic globalization (see Gray, Kittleson and Sandholtz 2006). If the first wave of feminism mobilized for women's equal access to the public sphere of civil and political rights, and the second wave of the world-wide feminist movement struggled to make visible inequalities between men and women in the private sphere that shape public economic and political inequalities, then feminist scholars of International Relations have built on both waves to argue that 'the personal which is political' is also 'international'. In *Bananas, Beaches, and Bases* (1989), Cynthia Enloe exposed how international politics frequently involves intimate relationships, personal identities and private lives. These informal politics are less transparent, less straightforward to study methodologically than the stuff of official politics and as such, International Relations scholars typically ignore them. Taking the view from 'below', feminists have sought to demonstrate that gender relations are an integral part of international relations: diplomatic spouses smooth over the workings of power among states and statesmen (sic); opaque but trustworthy marital contracts have historically facilitated empire-building – in contemporary politics they facilitate transnational money laundering and sex trafficking; global media icons such as *Cosmopolitan* conquer foreign cultures and prepare them for the onslaught of Western capitalism; and women and men organize in kitchens, churches and kin-communities to overthrow authoritarian regimes and make peace in the face of brutal conflict (Ali-Ali and Pratt 2009b; Cockburn 1998; True 2003; Domett 2005).

Focusing on politics at the margins dispels the assumption that power is what comes out of the barrel of a gun or ensues from the declarations of world leaders. Indeed, feminist efforts to reinterpret power suggest that International Relations scholars have underestimated the pervasiveness of power and precisely what it takes, at every level and every day, to reproduce a grossly uneven and hierarchical world order (Enloe 1997). Feminist reconceptualizations of power and attention to the margins of global politics have allowed International Relations scholars to recognize and comprehend new political phenomena and, importantly, from new angles, the experience of non-elites.

A first generation of feminist International Relations in the late 1980s challenged the conventional focus of the field, engaging in the 'third debate' about the impossibility of objectivity in International Relations and the embeddedness of scholarship in global power relations discussed in the Introduction, Chapter 8 (post-structuralism) and Chapter 9 (constructivism). In this debate, feminist scholars contested the exclusionary, state-centric and positivist nature of the discipline primarily at a meta-theoretical level. Many of these feminist contributions sought to deconstruct and subvert *realism,* the dominant 'power politics' explanation of post-war International Relations. Often implicit in their concern with gender relations was the assumption of a feminist standpoint epistemology. Such a standpoint maintains that women's lives on the margins of world politics afford us a more critical and comprehensive understanding of international relations than the objectivist view of the realist theorist or foreign policy lens of the statesman since they are less biased by existing institutions and elite power (Keohane 1989a: 245; Sylvester 1994a: 13; see also Harding 1986; Runyan and Peterson 1991; Tickner 1992; Zalewski 1993).

These first-generation feminist challenges opened the space for critical International Relations scholarship but they begged the question of what a feminist perspective on world politics would look like substantively, and how distinctive it would be (Zalewski 1995). More than two decades after the first journal in the field devoted a special issue to 'women and international relations' (*Millennium* 1988), this question is less challenging to answer, although there is no univocal feminist International Relations perspective. Most courses on International Relations theory world-wide now consider gender issues or feminist perspectives due to the publication of a growing number of texts and monographs by feminist International Relations scholars, including this chapter (Peterson and Runyan 2009, Pettman 1996; Sylvester 1994a, 2000; Peterson 2003; Shepherd 2010; Steans 2006; Tickner 1992, 2001; True 2012). Many disciplinary journals have published special issues on the subjects of women, gender and feminism in international relations, and in 1999 the *International Feminist Journal of Politics* was established to promote dialogue among scholars of feminism, politics and international relations.

A second-generation of feminist research has further developed feminist International Relations by making gender a central analytic category in studies of foreign policy, security and global political economy that explore a range of historical and geographical contexts (Chin 1998; Hooper 2000; Moon 1997; Mackenzie 2012; Prügl 2000; Stern 2005; True 2003; Whitworth 2004). Often analysing the intersection of gender, class, race, ethnicity, sexuality and nationality, second-generation feminist scholarship is closely tied to developments in feminist methodologies, critical international theory, constructivist social science, and post-Marxist political economy. This feminist scholarship provides empirical support for first-generation theoretical challenges, while also generating new insight on the gendering of global politics, as the rest of the chapter illustrates.

Empirical feminism

Empirical feminism turns our attention to women and gender relations as empirical aspects of international relations. Feminist challenges to

International Relations contend that women's lives and experiences have been, and still are, often excluded from the study of international relations. This 'sexist' exclusion has resulted in research that presents only a partial, masculine view in a field in which the dominant theories claim to explain the reality of world politics (Halliday 1988b). Empirical feminism corrects the denial or misrepresentation of women in world politics due to false assumptions that male experiences can count for both men and women, and that women are either absent from international political activities or not relevant to global processes. It is not that women have not been present or their experiences relevant to international relations. Rather, as Cynthia Enloe's (1989, 1994, 2000) scholarship demonstrates, women are and have always been part of international relations – if we choose to see them there. Moreover, it is in part because women's lives and experiences have not been empirically researched in the context of world politics, as Grant and Newland (1991: 5) argue, that International Relations has been largely 'focused on conflict and anarchy and a way of practising statecraft and formulating strategy that is excessively focused on competition and fear'. Studies of the norms and ideas that make the reproduction of the state system possible and of the structural violence (poverty, environmental injustice, socio-political inequality) that underpins direct state-sanctioned violence are seen as secondary to the 'manly' study of war and conflict in international relations due to their association with domestic 'soft' (read: feminine) politics. As a result, neo-realist and neo-liberal International Relations scholars theorize politics and the international realm 'in a way that guarantees that women will be absent from their inquiry, and that their research agendas remain unaltered' (Steurnagel 1990: 79–80).

Feminist research is not a form of empiricism since feminist scholars need conceptual clarity and thus to engage in theoretical debates about the ontology of gender and international relations in order to conduct empirical research. For instance, to make abstract concepts and relationships amenable to empirical exploration the feminist researcher must identify those which can be seen to exist and are the most important for closer study, while also developing a research methodology for translating and analysing them empirically (see Caprioli 2004; Ackerly, Stern and True 2006; Ackerly and True 2010).

Empirical feminist International Relations addresses different questions and employs a variety of methodologies. Research under the rubric of 'women in international development' (WID), and more recently gender and development (GAD), have documented how male bias in the development process has led to poor implementation of projects and unsatisfactory policy outcomes in terms of eradicating global poverty and empowering local communities (Newland 1988; Goetz 1991;

Kardam 1991; Kabeer 1994; Rathergeber 1995). These studies make visible the central role of women as subsistence producers and providers of basic needs in developing countries (Beneria 1982; Charlton, Everett and Staudt 1989). They reveal that the most efficient allocation of international development aid is often to provide women with appropriate agricultural technology, credit financing, education and health resources. For example, the United Nations (2000) estimates that while women's farming accounts for one-half of the food production in the developing world, it provides three-quarters of domestic food supply for family households. Gender-sensitive researchers have found that investing in girls' education is one of the most cost-effective international development policies, resulting in positive gains for a whole community by raising incomes and lowering population rates (see Sen 2001; Marchand and Parpart 1995).

Economic globalization has intensified social and economic polarization, both within and across states. Feminist International Relations scholars document how globalization processes have increased the world-wide inequality between men and women. Their research has revealed 'the feminization of poverty', that is, the disproportionate numbers of women compared with men in poverty – due to Third World debt and financial crises, structural adjustment policies (SAPs) in the South and state restructuring in the North (Afshar and Dennis 1992; Sparr 1994; Porter and Judd 2000). As economic policy has become increasingly governed by the global imperatives of export earnings, financial markets and comparative labour costs, states have struggled to meet their commitments to full employment and citizen well-being. Empirical feminist research shows how this shift from a largely domestic state to global market provision of services has imposed a disproportionate burden on women to pick up the slack of the state (United Nations Development Programme 1999; Marchand and Runyan 2000; Hoskyns and Rai 2007).

In the global context also, an internationalized gender division of labour has been created by the disproportionate employment of migrant Third World women as a cheap and flexible source of labour for multinational corporations in free trade zones (Mitter 1986; Standing 1992; Ong 1997). Saskia Sassen's (1991, 1998a, b) research on global cities shows how they have become the nodal points for global financial markets and economic transactions, dependent on a class of women workers. Like 'intimate others' of economic globalization, domestic workers, typically immigrant women of colour, service the masculinized corporate elite in these urban centres (Boris and Prügl 1996; Stasilius and Bakan 1997; Chin 1998; Chang and Ling 2000). Feminist research reveals an even darker 'underside' of globalization, however, in the phenomenal growth of sex-tourism, 'male-order' brides and transnational trafficking of women and girls for prostitution (Pettman 1996; Prügl and Meyer 1999; Berman 2003). For subordinate states in the world system, these economic activities are key sources of foreign exchange and national income (Jeffrey 2002; Hanochi 2003). For example, Chin (1998) shows how Malaysian political elites maintained the legitimacy of their export-oriented development strategy in the 1980s and 1990s by importing female domestic servants from the Philippines and Indonesia.

Global processes of structural change do not only victimize women however; in many cases, they are empowered by these processes. Feminist researchers explore how global trade and financial liberalization reshapes women's subjectivities and local gender relations as material conditions are transformed. These researchers highlight how new credit and employment opportunities have brought cultural changes in the lives of poor women in rural, developing areas (Gibson, Law and McKay 2001). Naila Kabeer (1994), for example, has investigated how changing material incentives provided by the re-siting of multinational corporations' garment production, opened up possibilities for young Bangladeshi women to make a better living and at the same time to challenge patriarchal gender arrangements. Angela McCracken (2011) shows how the spread of global consumption, beauty culture and information in post-NAFTA Mexico has enabled different groups of Mexican women to challenge traditional gender identities and create feminist identities (see also True 2003).

Feminist studies reveal the gendered processes and organizational cultures of international institutions, which to an even greater extent than nation-state institutions are dominated by elite men (Prügl, Çaglar and Zwingel 2012; Rai and Waylen 2008). Gender mainstreaming initiatives have allowed more women to join the policy-making ranks and created the momentum for the establishment of the mega-gender equality and women's empowerment agency, UN Women, in 2011 (True and Mintrom 2001; True and Parisi 2012). For instance, women now head many of the United Nations' agencies, including UN Women (headed by former Chilean President, Michele Bachelet) the United Nations Development Programme (UNDP) (headed by former New Zealand Prime Minister, Helen Clark), the World Health Organisation (WHO), the United Nations Children's Fund (UNICEF), the Office of the High Commissioner for Refugees (UNHCR), UNESCO, the World Food Programme and the World Population Fund. The Deputy Secretary General and the High Commissioner for Human Rights are also both women, but there has never been a female UN Secretary General despite the intense advocacy campaigns by global women's movements. Yet, as these feminist studies point out, in institutions like the United Nations, women continue to be ghettoized in less powerful agencies and in administrative rather than decision-making positions (Reanda 1999; Whitworth 2004). UN Women, which combines four smaller agencies previously devoted to addressing gender inequalities and the advancement of women, now has a targeted budget of US $500 million per annum. This is nonetheless a paltry sum compared with the estimated US $3.4 billion budget of the agency dedicated to children (UNICEF) in 2009, even though the plight of girl and boy children in the world is very much dependent on the relative status of their mothers.

International organizations also institutionalize gender-based policies and priorities. In her study of the International Labour Organization (ILO) Sandra Whitworth (1994) shows how assumptions about gender relations shaped ILO policies that have had discriminatory effects in national and international labour markets, reinforcing women's inequality. Elisabeth Prügl (2000), employing a feminist constructivist approach in her study of home-workers, shows how the gendered rules and regimes of the ILO and the global solidarity networks that emerged to change them have been powerful forces in determining the plight of these mainly women workers around the world, most recently in 2011 in adopting a landmark international convention (189) concerning decent work for domestic workers. At the regional level, Catherine Hoskyns (1996) shows how women's movements in member states have successfully used the European Union's supranational body of equal opportunities law and policy to address gender disparities at the national level. Hoskyns' gender-sensitive analysis shows how the process of European integration has had the effect of extending women's social citizenship rights in member states, although the European Union is only beginning to play a global role through development, trade and human rights policies in advocating gender equality beyond its borders (Prügl 2007; True 2009).

In the realm of foreign policy, feminist analyses have revealed the dominant masculine gender of policy makers and the gendered assumption that these policy makers are strategically rational actors who make life and death decisions in the name of an abstract conception of the 'national interest'. As Nancy McGlen and Meredith Sarkees (1993) have assessed in their study of the foreign policy and defence establishment, women are rarely 'insiders' of the actual institutions that make and implement foreign policy and conduct war. In 2008, the fact that 28 women were foreign ministers suggests that this male dominance of global diplomacy is undergoing some change; as do the establishment of the Council of Women World Leaders (currently headed by former Irish President and UN Human Rights Commissioner Mary Robinson) and the Nobel Women's Initiative (led by women winners of the Nobel Peace prize) that seek to leverage women leaders' collective strengths to bring about global peace and security (Stiehm 2006). Feminist scholars analyse the persistent 'gender gap' in the foreign policy beliefs of men and women foreign-policy-making elites and citizens; women leaders and citizens in Western states are consistently more likely to oppose the use of force in international actions and are typically more supportive of humanitarian interventions (Rosenau and Holsti 1982; Tessler, Nachtwey and Grant 1999). People's attitudes toward gender equality and sexual liberty also affect their attitudes toward tolerance, human rights and democracy and are good predictors of more pacific attitudes to international conflict (Tessler and Warriner 1997).

States with greater domestic gender inequality are also more likely to go to war or to engage in state-sanctioned violence according to feminist International Relations scholars (Goldstein 2001). Domestic gender equality also reduces the likelihood that a state will use force first in inter-state disputes, limits the escalation of violence and decreases the severity of violence during international crises (Caprioli 2000; Caprioli and Boyer 2001). By the same token, those states that come closest to gender parity tend also to be more pacific in their relations, more generous aid donors and generally good citizens in the international realm (Regan and Paskeviciute 2003). However, our preoccupation with states can prevent us from seeing the multiple non-state actors who also play significant roles in foreign policy making. Feminist researchers such as Enloe (1989, 2000) make visible the women who provide support services for military activities (domestic, psychological, medical and sexual). If we see militarization as a social process consisting of many gendered assignments that make possible those ultimate acts of state violence then, she argues, the official provision of sexual services on military bases for instance can be seen as a central factor in a foreign intervention. In *Sex Among Allies,* Katherine Moon (1997) argues that the exploitative sexual alliances between Korean prostitutes (*kijich'on* women) and US soldiers defined and supported the similarly unequal military alliance between the United States and South Korea in the post-war era. Among other things, under the Nixon Doctrine, *kijich'on* women as personal ambassadors became the main indicator of Seoul's willingness to accommodate US military interests (see also Zimelis 2009).

Women are more likely to be among the group of non-state actors in global politics. Feminist researchers highlight the activism of women, who are often marginalized, poor and vulnerable: whether in networks of sex workers, home workers, mothers or civil activists, in counter-cultural campaigns and performances. As well as highlighting local activism, however, feminist researchers have observed new forms of cross-border solidarity and identity formation. In recent years, women have played key roles in the global anti-violence movements including the movement to ban landmines, the Campaign for Nuclear Disarmament (CND), and the network protesting against sexual and gender-based violence globally (Cockburn 2012; Stienstra 1994; Friedman 1995; Rupp 1997; Williams and Goose 1998). For example, in two troubled conflict zones of the world, Israel/Palestine and the former Yugoslavia, groups known as 'Women in Black' have protested against the escalation of militarism, weaponry and war, and men's violence against women and children (Sharoni 1993; Cockburn 1998; Korac 1998; Jacoby 1999). Feminist researchers highlight peace activists and mothers protesting against their sons being conscripted in international conflicts such as the post-Soviet conflicts in Chechyna and Georgia (Eichler 2011). They also investigate female suicide bombers and other 'violent women' who transgress gendered social norms to take their own lives and others with them as a global political statement (Alison 2004; Gentry and Sjoberg 2008).

Noting how new female subjectivities create the momentum for new forms of collective action, feminist researchers trace the growth of transnational women's networks, the alliances forged between women's organizations, governments and inter-governmental actors, and the development of international legal and policy mechanisms promoting gender justice. For example, due to these alliances, human rights instruments and global declarations increasingly acknowledge the gender-specificity of human rights (Peters and Wolper 1995; Philapose 1996; Ackerly and Okin 1999; Ackerly 2000). In 1990, Amnesty International, the global human rights NGO, recognized women's human rights by adding gender persecution to its list of forms of political persecution. Governments and international organizations have followed suit. For example, until the 1990s Yugoslav conflict, states and international agencies interpreted the persecution of women as a matter of personal privacy and cultural tradition (Rao 1995). However, as a result of the lobbying by transnational feminist networks and the widespread media coverage of rape as a specific war strategy in Yugoslavia, rape and other egregious sexual violence have now been prosecuted as a war crime under the Geneva Convention Against War Crimes (1949) and the International Criminal Court (Niarchos 1995; Philapose 1996; Chappell 2008).

Bringing women's lives and gender relations into view through empirical research has policy-relevant and material effects. Indeed, feminist scholars argue that only when women are recognized by states and international institutions to be fundamental players in economic and political processes with relevant and distinctive perspectives to offer that can improve international negotiations and policy decisions will they expand the opportunities for women to participate equally with men. That recognition or equal participation has yet to be achieved. By redressing the empirical neglect of women and gender relations, feminist International Relations scholarship not only improves our understanding of global politics, it helps to put women's equal voice and gender-specific concerns on the global agenda. However, in order to make gender an important dimension of the study of international relations, it is necessary to challenge the conceptual framework which has excluded women from this study in the first place. Empirical feminism is thus complemented by analytical feminism that reveals the theoretical exclusions of the International Relations field and seeks to revision International Relations from a gender-aware perspective.

Analytical feminism

Analytical feminism deconstructs the theoretical framework of International Relations, revealing the gender bias that pervades key concepts and inhibits an accurate and comprehensive understanding of international relations. The feminist concept of 'gender relations' refers to the asymmetrical social constructs of masculinity and femininity as opposed to ostensibly evolutionary 'biological' male–female differences (although feminist post-modernists contend that both sex and gender are socially constructed categories, see Butler 1990; Gatens 1991). The hegemonic Western brand of masculinity is associated with autonomy, sovereignty, the capacity for reason and objectivity and universalism, whereas the dominant notion of femininity is associated with the absence or lack of these characteristics. For example, the routine practices of militaries replicate these hegemonic gender identities by training soldiers, including female soldiers (MacBride and Wibben 2012), both to protect 'women-children' through killing and to suppress (feminine) emotions associated with bodily pain and caring (Goldstein 2001). Military training, in Barbara Roberts' (1984) words is 'socialization into masculinity carried to the extremes'. A common assumption is that gender identities are natural or 'human nature' and not subject to social constitution or human agency. When this assumption about gender is applied to social and political phenomena such as war, terrorism, financial crisis, or mass sexual violence in armed conflict, however, it has political effects in terms of reproducing the status quo or existing power relations. As Joan Scott (1988: 48) has stated, 'the binary opposition and the social process of gender relationships [have] both become part of the meaning of power itself' and thus 'to question or alter any aspect of [them], threatens the entire [international] system'.

International Relations' key concepts are neither natural nor gender neutral: they are derived from a social and political context where masculine hegemony has been institutionalized. Feminist scholars argue that notions of power, sovereignty, autonomy, anarchy, security and the levels of analysis typology in International Relations are inseparable from the gender division of public and private spheres institutionalized within and across states. These concepts are identified specifically with masculinity and men's experiences and knowledge derived from an exclusive, male-dominated public sphere. Theorizing, as Burchill and Linklater state in the Introduction to this volume (Chapter 1), is 'the process by which we give meaning to an allegedly objectified world "out there"'. A feminist analysis reveals that the dominant International Relations conceptual framework is but one, partial, attempt to make sense of world politics.

The discursive separation of domestic and international politics, together with the neo-realist aversion to domestic explanations for inter-state relations, obscures the prior gendered public–private division within states and masculine aversion to the latter's association with emotion, subjectivity, reproduction, the body, femininity and women. Both explanatory and constitutive theories of world politics overlook this private sphere because it is submerged within domestic politics and state forms (Walker 1992; Sylvester 1994a). The ontology of realist International Relations theory conceives the private sphere, like the international sphere, as a natural realm of disorder. The lower being, represented by women, the body and the anarchical system, must be subordinated to the higher being, represented by men, the rational mind and state authority. Jean Elshtain (1992) insists that the realist narrative of International Relations, in particular, pivots on this public–private division and its essentialist construction of femininity and masculinity as the respective cause of disorder and bringer of order. Within this order, non-hegemonic states with rigid patriarchal hierarchies that systematically repress women may also be conceived by neo-realists, neo-liberal institutionalists and hegemonic states as part of international anarchy (and therefore justifying international war or intervention). We need only recall in the United States, the Bush Administration's stated reasons for military intervention to depose the Taliban regime in Afghanistan.

For feminist analysts, the independence of domestic politics from international politics and the separation of public from private spheres cannot be the basis for a disciplinary boundary, since anarchy outside and gender hierarchy at home may be mutually reinforcing – and indeed a key cause of war and conflict. Throughout modern history, for example, women have been told that they will receive equality with men, after the war, after the revolution, and when democracy has been consolidated or the national economy has been rebuilt and so on: but after all of these 'outside' forces have been conquered and the political or post-conflict transition is over, governments and dominant groups in society call for things to go back to normal, and women to their subordinate place in the family, home and private sphere. As Cynthia Enloe (1989: 131) has observed 'states depend upon particular constructions of the domestic and private spheres in order to foster smooth[er] relationships at the public/international level'. But this political ordering too often results in a regression in women's status and rights as has been the case following the 'Arab Spring' revolutions and political upheavals in the Middle East and North Africa regions in which women were notable participants. Politically engaged women citizens have been subject to gender-based violence including sexual harassment, abuse, rape and murder when seeking an equal voice in the public sphere. At the very time when there is a crucial political opening for women's rights advocates to influence the 'rules of the game' the leading institutions in the public realm, and political processes, especially those relating to peace, security and political transition have systematically marginalized them.

Feminists seek to theorize the relationships between gender relations, domestic and international politics despite International Relations' conventional levels of analysis that treats the individual, the state and the international system as distinct analytic units. This theoretical schema has become 'the most influential way of classifying explanations of war, and indeed of organising our understanding of inter-state relations in general' (Walker 1987: 67). Gender analysis undermines the divisions between the individual, state and international system by showing how each level is preconditioned by an image of rational man that excludes women and femininity (Tickner 1992; Sylvester 1994a; True 2008b). For instance, much feminist theorizing rejects neo-realist structural theory, examining how gender is constructed within states and individual behaviour that has implications for international relations. However, Laura Sjoberg (2012) asserts that the international system is itself gender-hierarchical; that assumptions about gender underlie the structure and ordering principles of the international system that affects the function of states, the distribution of capabilities among states, and the political processes shaping their interaction. But because dominant discourses conceptualize international structure as gender neutral, gender, being a relational factor, is difficult to see when only the 'masculine' (characteristics of institutions and of individual male and female actors) is present. Sjoberg (2012: 14) argues 'this makes the structural nature of gender hierarchy "invisible" to scholars like Waltz who are not looking for it'. This is also why the increasing presence of the 'feminine' in international politics (including feminine characteristics represented by some women world leaders as well as feminized issues and approaches) are perceived to unsettle international structure for better or worse, depending on the political ideology deployed (see Fukuyama 1998; Nye 2012).

In International Relations theory, Kenneth Waltz (1959: 188) applies the analogy between man and the state as proof of the hostile reality that he observes in the anarchical system as a whole: '[a]mong men as among states there is no automatic adjustment of interests. In the absence of a supreme authority there is then the constant possibility that conflicts will be solved by force'. Reductionist arguments explaining international conflict through conceptions of 'evil' human nature are frequently used in realist International Relations. Hans Morgenthau argued that the objective 'national interest' is rooted deeply in human nature and thus, in the actions of statesmen (Tickner 1988). Even the neo-realist Waltz (1959: 238), who prefers systemic explanations, embraces Alexander Hamilton's polemic set forth in the 1788 *Federalist Papers*: 'to presume a lack of hostile motives among states is to forget that men are ambitious, vindictive and rapacious'. From a feminist perspective, the implication of this man/state analogy is that rationality is equated with men's behaviour and the state as a rational actor bears a male-masculine identity (Sylvester 1990).

Most feminist theorists analyse the state as the centralized, main organizer of gendered power, working in part through the construction of public–private, production–reproduction, domestic–international boundaries (Connell 1990). Feminist constructivist scholar, Ann Towns (2011) reveals how the position of states today in the interstate hierarchy is partly based on how they rank or outrank other states on the achievement of domestic gender equality in educational, political and economic outcomes. States' reputational status in the international system is also affected by the extent to which states' implementation of international gender norms that prohibit violence against women, promote the mainstreaming of gender in public policies, and establish parity quotas in legislatures and other decision-making bodies (see Krook and True 2012). Thus, state identity is not a 'coherent identity subordinate to the gaze of a single interpretative centre' (Ashley 1988: 230) as in neo-realist theories but has many gendered dimensions reflecting the corporate as well as the social identity of the state (see Chapter 9 on constructivism) This notion reflects, rather, an idealized model of hegemonic masculinity and the patriarchal foundations of the state form. International Relations feminists argue that the state manipulates gender identities and gender equality and inequality for its own internal unity and external legitimacy. Although this is changing in some contexts, albeit not globally, men are socialized to identify with constructions of masculinity which emphasize autonomy, male superiority, fraternity, strength, public protector roles and ultimately the bearing of arms. Women, on the other hand, while traditionally taught to defer to the protection and stronger will of men, and provide the emotional, economic and social support systems for masculine war activities, are increasingly expected to contribute to the economic prosperity of a nation in the paid labour force and to promote security through official peace-building activities. Nonetheless, feminist scholars view states as deeply implicated in the production and reproduction of various forms of violence against women. For instance, many states support inter-personal gender-based and state-sanctioned violence through their stance of non-intervention in the private 'family' or community religious or cultural group. This also occurs when states fail the 'due diligence' international law standard with respect to gender discrimination in the private 'market' sphere, and in the justice system by employing legal definitions of rape and victimhood from a male standpoint (Pateman 1989). Both 'liberal' and 'illiberal' states have assumed that the absence of overt coercion implies female consent despite prevailing economic, social and political gender inequalities that constrain women's choice and exit options, let alone their opportunities for voice (True 2012; Peterson 1992b: 46–7).

In conventional International Relations theories, the rational, self-interested actor is a metaphor for state behaviour in an anarchical international system. Abstracted from a place in time and space, from particular prejudices, interests and needs, feminist theorists claim that the model of rational man cannot be generalized: he is a masculine agent derived from a context of unequal gender relations, where women's primary care work supports the development of autonomous male selves, making cooperation for them a daily reality and relieving men of these necessities. Consequently, the vast majority of people, social relationships, and institutions that cannot be interpreted as coherent rational selves are thus denied agency in international politics. Feminist analysts Grant and Newland (1991: 1) argue that the study of International Relations is 'constructed overwhelmingly by men working with mental models of human activity seen through a[n elite] male eye and apprehended through a[n elite] male sensibility'.

Some feminists posit an alternative *female* model of agency as connected, interdependent and interrelated (Gilligan 1982; Tronto 1989), However, most feminist International Relations scholars are sceptical of positing a nurturing account of feminine nature to correct the gender bias of Waltzian man/state (cf. Elshtain 1985: 41). International Relations feminists search for richer, alternative models of agency that take account of both production and reproduction, redefine rationality to be less exclusive and instrumental and respect human relationships (across all levels) as well as the interdependence of human beings with nature (Tickner 1991: 204–6). For example, some scholars posit a feminist ethic of care as an ontological claim about 'the central role of care and other relational moral practices in the everyday lives of people in all settings' rather than an epistemological stance (Robinson 2006: 225). Other feminist scholars look for emancipatory models of agency at the margins – among Third World women and human rights activists (Ackerly 2000). Feminist alternatives to International Relations' levels of analysis reject universal abstractions. They demand greater historical and cultural contextualization in order to reflect more adequately the complexity and indeterminacy of human agency and social structure.

Feminist scholars use gender analysis to uncover potential gender biases in particular International Relations conceptualizations of 'power' and 'security'. Such bias not only limits the theoretical application of these concepts, it has detrimental effects on the practice of international relations. *Power* in International Relations theory has been almost exclusively conceived of as 'power-over': the power to force or influence someone to do something that they otherwise would not (Jaquette 1984). An individual's or individual state's power rests on his or her autonomy from the power of others. In this view, power cannot be shared nor can power be readily increased by relationships with others in the context of interdependent or common interests. The accumulation of power capabilities and resources, according to Morgenthau, is both an end and a means to security. In the context of an anarchical state system, which is interpreted as necessarily hostile and self-helping, states that act 'rationally' instinctively deduce their national interests as their maximization of 'power-over' other states. The Waltzian notion of power is only mildly different. Waltz conceptualizes power as a means for the survival of a state but not as an end-goal in itself, to the extent that a stable, bipolar, balance of power configuration exists between states. Consequently, in the Waltzian world-view, the only power that really matters is the power-capability of 'Great Powers', whose bipolar or multipolar arrangement brings limited order to an anarchic international realm.

Tickner (1988) shows how the realist concept of power is based on masculine norms through her analysis of Hans Morgenthau's six principles of power politics. It reflects male self-development and objectivist ways of knowing in patriarchal societies where men's citizenship and personal authority has traditionally relied on their head-of-household power-over women's sexuality and labour. This concept of power also rests on a particularly gender-specific notion of autonomous agency that makes human relationships and affective connections invisible. If the human world is exhaustively defined by such gendered constructions of 'power-over', as in realist accounts, feminists ask, why do some leaders and regimes retreat from power non-violently, how do people cooperate and mobilize in collective movements (Weldon 2006) and how is post-conflict peace sustained? Sylvester (1992: 32–8) argues that it is incoherent to posit self-help as the essential feature of world politics when many 'relations international' go on within households and other institutions. These relations include diplomatic negotiations, trade regimes and the socialization of future citizens, which are not based on self-help alone, but which take interdependent relations between self and other as the norm. The neo-realist International Relations' assumption that men and states are 'like units' presents power politics as a self-fulfilling prophecy. Power politics, however, is a gendered and, therefore, biased account of world politics because its conceptualization of power depends upon the particular not the universal agency of rational man.

For feminists, power is a complex phenomenon of creative social forces that shape our personal gendered identities as men, women and national citizens rather than just the deployment of brute force. As such, Enloe (1997) argues that paying attention to women can expose how much 'power' it takes to maintain the international political system in its present form. To understand the nature of power at the international or global levels, feminists together with other critical, constructivist, green politics and post-modernist theorists urge that we study the domestic and transnational social relations that not only support the foreign policies of states but also constitute the state as the territorial authority with a monopoly over the use of legitimate force.

Security as conventionally conceived in International Relations is also a gender-biased concept when seen from a feminist perspective. Rather than bringing security to individual women, men and children, it is equated with a situation of stability provided by militaristic states whose nuclear proliferation, ironically, is seen to prevent total war (if not the many 'small wars'). Security is examined only in the context of the presence and absence of war, because the threat of war is considered endemic to the sovereign state system. This reactive notion of security is zero-sum and by definition 'national'. It presupposes what Peterson (1992a: 47–8) terms a 'sovereignty contract' established between states. According to this imaginary contract the use of military force is a necessary evil to prevent the outside – difference, irrationality, anarchy and potential conflict – from conquering the inside of homogeneous, rational and orderly states. States, in this feminist analysis, are a kind of 'protection racket' that by their very existence as bully 'protectors' create threats outside and charge for the insecurity that they bring to the 'protected' population 'inside' the state. In the name of protection, states and citizens demand the sacrifice of their members, including that of soldiers – historically men but increasingly men and women – through military conscription and that of families – historically mothers but increasingly fathers – who devote their lives to socializing these dutiful citizens for the state/nation (Elshtain 1992; Goldstein 2001).

Feminists use gender analysis to critique gendered identities and security discourses (see Shepherd 2008). Employing a feminist approach, Helen Kinsella (2005; Sjoberg 2006) explores how the ostensibly gender-neutral distinction between civilians and combatants in the laws of war is produced by gendered discourses that naturalize sex and gender difference. This categorical distinction has been deployed in gendered ways such as in the 1990s war in the former Yugoslovia – where male civilians were treated as inherently combatants and women civilians were assumed to be always victims (Kinsella 2005: 253). Kinsella argues that neither women nor men are protected by the gendered immunity principle that extends from the laws of war. Moreover, the gender stereotypes on which the just war tradition is based 'affect the meaning of gender and the subordination of women outside wartime', re-inscribing gender hegemonies within domestic (familial) and international (civilized) orders (Barnett and Duvall 2005: 31).

In the post-9/11 global 'war on terror' feminist scholars have deconstructed American discourses of security that looked for 'manly men' to protect 'us' from 'them' and blamed feminism and homosexuality for weakening the resolve of the West to stamp out Islamic fundamentalism and other 'threats' (Bar On 2003: 456; Agathangelou and Ling 2004). Feminists also scrutinized the gendered discourses in the Islamic fundamentalist groups behind the terrorist acts of violence against the West and among the US occupation forces in Iraq (Kaufman-Osborn 2005). Differences in attitudes about gender and sexuality, not toward democracy or capitalism, are the most statistically significant divide in the public opinions of Western and non-Western publics according to the World Values Survey (Norris and Ingelhart 2003). These salient differences are deployed by Western and anti-Western actors to incite and to justify violence (Khalid 2011). The statements of Osama Bin Laden and the diary account left behind by the 9/11 terrorists suggest that their actions were directed not merely against the West but against the Western gender identities perceived to be so threatening to their vision of an Islamic and/or pan Arabic culture (Tickner 2002). When Islamic fundamentalists deride the depraved morals of the West, referring to sexual equality and women's rights norms, they heighten the potential for conflict between non-Western and Western states, although international alliances are still possible as in the Libyan intervention (True 2004).

Gender analysis reveals masculine identities and states, domestic and international violence, to be inextricably related. The limited security they provide allows them to consolidate their authority over other men and states, but importantly also over women and territory, on which they depend for a source of exploitable resources, and for the socio-cultural and biological reproduction of power relations. Paying attention to women's as well as men's experiences in peace and war, feminist analysts urge that security must be redefined. In particular, what is called 'national security' is profoundly endangering to human survival and sustainable communities (Tickner 1992). State military apparatuses create their own security dilemmas by purporting control and power-over to be the name of the game; a game we are persuaded to play in order to achieve the absolute and relative gains of state security.

Concepts such as 'rationality', 'security' and 'power' could be building-blocks of explanation for a feminist theory of international politics (Tickner 1991). There is nothing inherent in the terms, which suggests that they must be discarded, rather it is their narrow, gendered meanings in mainstream International Relations theory and practice which is problematic for feminist analysts. Runyan and Peterson (1991: 70) claim that dichotomous thinking – inside–outside, sovereignty–anarchy, domestic–international – prevents International Relations theory from being able to 'conceptualise, explain, or deliver the very things it says it is all about – security, power and sovereignty'. For International Relations feminists, these conceptual opposites reproduce the self-fulfilling security dilemma and reinforce masculine power politics, thus limiting the possibility for creating a more just and equal world order.

Normative feminism

Normative feminism reflects on the process of International Relations theorizing as part of a normative agenda for global change. 'All forms of feminist theorising are normative, in the sense that they help us to question certain meanings and interpretations in IR theory' (Sylvester 2001: 248). Feminists are self-consciously explicit about the position from which they are theorizing, how they enter the International Relations field and go about their research (Ackerly and True 2008b). They view their social and political context and subjectivity as part of theoretical explanation. Gender is a *transformative* category from a normative perspective not because we can deconstruct or do away with it, but because once we understand it as a social construction we can transform how it works at all levels of social and political life.

Feminist empirical research and gender analysis are important contributions, but they are only starting points for feminist goals of transforming global social hierarchies (Persram 1994; Ship 1994; Hutchings 2000; Robinson 2006). Normative feminist theorists bring the experiences of women's activism to bear on debates about international ethics, humanitarian aid and intervention and human rights instruments (Cochran 1999; Robinson 1999; Ackerly 2000; Hutchings 2004). Care ethics is one example of how feminist theory can inform ethical guidelines for humanitarian intervention, multilateral peacekeeping, development aid, foreign security policy, and human rights protection among other practical global issues and dilemmas (see Hutchings 2000: 122–3). Joan Tronto (2006), for example, analyses the normative framework supporting multilateral peacekeeping from a feminist perspective. She stresses that the shift from the right to intervene in a sovereign state to a responsibility to protect citizens not protected by their own state, is a shift from liberal to care ethics, from the masculine assumption of an autonomous self – sovereign man or state – to the assumption of a relational self with responsibilities to others. The emergent '1325: women, peace and security' norm and subsequent United Nations Security Council Resolutions since 2000 also embrace state responsibilities to protect against and prevent armed conflict, including sexual and gender-based violence and the distinctive impacts of war on women (see Davies and Stamnes 2012).

Linklater (Chapter 4) argues that the prospects for moral and political universals and for respect for difference are central to the debate among normative international theorists. Seen in this context, the different feminist epistemologies most commonly identified in International Relations' writings as feminist empiricism, feminist standpoint and feminist post-modernism are not discreet or contradictory approaches to gender-sensitive knowledge in International Relations (see Keohane 1989b; Weber 1994). On the contrary, these epistemologies are interrelated feminist challenges to the masculine universalism of science (McClure 1992: 359) that suggest feminist alternatives for including or embracing different forms of knowledge (for example, indigenous knowledges, Smith 1999). Feminist empiricism, standpoint and post-modernism share a *normative* struggle to produce knowledge that is accountable to diverse women's movements and that sustain connections to practical feminist politics and the concrete workings of gendered power.

Feminist scholars problematize the defining dichotomies of the International Relations field that are reinforced through their association with the masculine–feminine gender dichotomy: for example, the association of women and femininity with peace, cooperation, subjectivism and 'soft' domestic politics and men and masculinity with war, competition, objectivity and 'hard' international politics (Elshtain 1987; Sylvester 1987, 1994a, 2002). They question how these gender hierarchies are reproduced in International Relations theories and how they serve to naturalize other forms of power and domination in world politics. From a normative feminist perspective attentive to the politics of knowledge, gender difference is not merely about the relations between masculine and feminine identities, it is about how and from what position in the hierarchy we can know.

Cynthia Enloe's research radically subverts conventional ways of knowing and doing International Relations. To make sense of international politics, she analyses the (extra)ordinary lives of women from below – which the history of the discipline would tell us is the least likely place for 'high politics'. Enloe reveals constructions of masculinity and femininity at the heart of international processes. She considers the withdrawal of Russian mothers' support for the Soviet army, due to the gross and unaccountable sacrifice of their sons in the USSR–Afghanistan war, as one of many personal expressions of gendered power that led to the delegitimization of the Soviet regime and the end of the Cold War. And in *Nimmo's War, Emma's War*, she considers the various gendered experiences of the war in Iraq through the everyday lives of four American women and four Iraqi women (Enloe 1994; 2010). Enloe's standpoint epistemology encourages us to broaden our ways of knowing 'the truth' of international politics, and to consider from whose perspective interstate 'legitimate' force is the most significant expression of violence and potent explanation for war.

However, if asking questions about women's location in world politics, addressed by empirical feminist International Relations, is dependent upon bringing gender in as an analytical construct in order to account for the patterns of women's marginalization at every level of state and global politics then, normative feminism questions the binary concept of gender itself. The mutually exclusive opposition of masculinity and femininity is not 'the essence from which social organization can be explained' as in evolutionary socio-biology or psychology accounts (Scott 1988: 2); rather, it is a social construction that must itself be explained before it can be transformed. While analytical feminist theories created the category of gender to reveal the social construction of women's oppression, normative feminist theories contextualize gender as an analytical device that harbours its own exclusions and, like International Relations theories, must also be critically interrogated (Sylvester 2001).

Since the 1990s there has been some controversy over the application of gender in International Relations, and across feminist studies. In International Relations, two main criticisms of gender as a concept have arisen. The first criticism is that the analytic use of gender masks other forms of oppression prevalent in global politics. Speaking to a Western women's studies' audience in the 1980s from a Third World feminist standpoint, Chandra Mohanty (1991) criticized Western feminism for constructing the victimized 'Third World woman' based on universal, Western assumptions of gender, emptied of all historical, cultural and geographical specificity, including realities of race and class oppression. As in the adage, 'the master's tools won't bring down the master's house',

Mohanty made the point that Western categories cannot be used to challenge the imposition of Western categories and imperialist structures in non-Western societies. Post-colonial feminists in International Relations employ this analysis to scrutinize the liberal feminist 'women's rights' norms used as justification for the US intervention in Afghanistan (Hunt 2002; Khalid 2011).

The implication of the Third World feminist challenge for feminist International Relations is that a universal concept of gender cannot be applied. Indeed, if, as feminist scholars argue, gender relations are culturally and historically constructed, then it also follows that they cannot be the same everywhere. International Relations feminists seek to understand gender constructions at the global level and how they shape and are shaped by myriad local gender discourses and norms that have impacts on women and men's lives (Miller 1998; Baines 1999; Prügl 2000; True 2003).

Recognizing the potential for Western imperialism when universal categories of 'woman' or 'man' are deployed, feminist scholarship explores a dynamic intersectional relationship between the global political economy, the state and culturally, geographically race- and class-specific gender relations (Chan-Tierberghien 2004; Agathangelou and Ling 2004). Feminist researchers analysing the global sex trade, for example, address this complexity of global power relations (Mackie 2001; Whitworth 2001; Berman 2003; Agathangelou 2004). They explore the specific constructions of gender and sexuality in the sending and receiving countries, which in turn depend upon particular constructions of class, ethnicity, nationality, and race. Feminist scholars begin their analysis of the sex trade with the observation that women are the core labourers in this multi-billion-dollar global business. However, as they engage in further research, drawing on non-elite knowledge and practice (such as that of the sex workers themselves) they are led to an understanding of the multiple and interlocking nature of oppressions, and of women's agency even in situations of physical coercion and other, more structural, forms of violence (see True 2012).

Normative feminism recognizes that there is no feminist 'high ground' from which to theorize about international relations. Sylvester (1994a: 12) argues that 'all places to speak and act as women are problematic', because they are socially and historically constructed and exclude other identities. She destabilizes the feminist standpoint position that women's experience can constitute the ground(s) for a more critical and universal theory of international relations, in favour of multiple feminist standpoints that question the discipline's hegemonic knowledge. Feminism, 'is the research posture of standing in many locations, illuminating important relations and practices darkened by the long shadows of official IR, of painting International Relations differently ... Feminism has many types and shifting forms. It is non-uniform and non-consensual; it is a complex matter with many internal debates' (Sylvester 2001: 269). International Relations feminism demonstrates that it is possible to do research and make normative claims, despite there being no given and many different ontological starting points for theories of international relations.

Feminist identity and solidarity are problematic insofar as achieving feminism's normative goal of un-gendering social and political relations depends on politically organizing on the basis of gender 'as women'. Contrary to the tenets of 1970s radical feminisms, there is no easily realized, readily mobilized, global sisterhood. Rather, feminist cooperation, as Christina Gabriel and Laura Macdonald (1994) show in their analysis of women's transnational organizing in the context of NAFTA, and Laurel Weldon (2006) reveals in her analysis of the global movement to eradicate violence against women, must be created by acknowledging and confronting, not ignoring, the differences among women. The very tension between positivist and post-positivist epistemologies that has divided contemporary theorists, including International Relations theorists, is the source of feminisms' theoretical dynamism and political relevancy. International Relations feminism acknowledges the lack of a foundational collective subject 'woman', and a relatively bounded realm of the international or the political. Feminist perspectives also seek to make a difference to women's daily lives, with the realization that gendered categories including some feminist categories have historically served to marginalize many women and men, silencing their experiences of violence and agency.

Empirical and analytical feminist approaches challenge given ways of thinking about and doing International Relations, especially dominant rationalist approaches. But feminism does more than this. Feminist questions about why agents – statesmen and soldiers – typically discussed in International Relations theories tend to be men leads us to consider the normative status of International Relations, including the gendered identity of the knowers and the intersection of these identities with particular, so-called 'objective' ways of knowing that have been institutionalized in the International Relations field (see Ackerly and True 2008a). Introducing the world-views of women who are differently situated in the present world order exemplifies the normative feminist perspective that there are multiple standpoints from which to view global politics, and that each may reveal diverse realities and relationships.

Conclusion

The three forms of feminism discussed in this chapter – empirical feminism, analytical feminism and normative feminism – all suggest that the theory and practice of international relations has suffered from its neglect of feminist perspectives. Feminists argue that conventional International Relations theories distort our knowledge of both 'relations' and the ongoing transformations of the 'international'. These International Relations theories overlook the political significance of gendered divisions of public and private spheres institutionalized within states, and by extension the state system. As a result, they ignore the political activities and activism of women: whether they are mobilizing for war, protesting against state stockpiles of nuclear weapons or organizing for the international recognition of women's human rights. Moreover, the objectivist approach of much International Relations theory produces relatively superficial knowledge and tends to reproduce the dichotomies which have come to demarcate the field. These dichotomies are gendered: they define power as power-over 'others', autonomy as reaction rather than relational, international politics as the negation of domestic, 'soft' politics and the absence of women, and objectivity as the lack of (feminine or feminized) subjectivity. In sum, approaches to international relations that fail to take gender seriously overlook critical aspects of world order and abandon a crucial opening for effecting change.

Feminist International Relations contributes to expanding and strengthening existing theories and analyses including liberal, critical theory, post-modern, constructivist and green theories of international relations. As well as introducing new questions and political phenomena to the traditionally narrowly defined study of International Relations, feminist research has re-conceptualized non-feminist research questions on state behaviour, international norms and law, and global civil society, and adapted non-feminist methodologies such as quantitative analysis, frame analysis and institutional analysis for feminist purposes. Engaging with other International Relations theories has allowed feminism to contest and expand the criteria for what counts as good scholarship to include ethical self-reflection on research processes as well as research findings. Feminists have also been able to share with proponents of other critical theories the illuminating effects that can come from viewing global social and political processes from a gender perspective.

This chapter began by asking, how do feminist perspectives help us understand and improve international relations? Addressing that question it explored the empirical, analytical and normative contributions of feminism. Feminists in and outside the field of International Relations are continually adding to our empirical and normative knowledge, while advancing the tools of gender analysis. But it is the feminist commitment to self-reflexivity, to attending to the power of epistemology, of boundaries and relationships in the very practice of theorizing and research that contributes most to the study of International Relations (Ackerly, Stern and True 2006). This critical feminist methodology rather than any single empirical approach or theory makes feminist International Relations distinctive among International Relations theories. Efforts to forge a unitary neo-feminist approach (Caprioli 2004) or non-feminist gender standpoint (Carpenter 2002) seek to mainstream gender analysis without this self-reflexive methodology, not unlike the World Bank or the World Economic Forum with their focus on gender equality as the key ingredient for advancing economic growth and competition but often forgetting the most marginalized women surviving outside of the capitalist market. Such attempts to use gender to empirically and analytically examine aspects of international relations without being 'tainted' by normative content may be fruitful from neo-realist or neo-liberal perspectives, but they hinder efforts to advance feminist perspectives on international relations.

International Relations theories have been shown to have major blind spots with respect to global social and political change. This conceptual blindness frequently leads to empirical blindness. It is not surprising then that International Relations analysts are often caught off-guard by events in world politics. Clearly, a re-thinking of the basic assumptions of this discipline remains urgent if scholars want to understand global politics in the twenty-first century. Feminist scholarship of the sort reviewed in this chapter offers a way out of the darkness. If scholars want to gain fresh insights into the dynamics of world order, they need to take into account gendered social processes and marginalized subjects. Feminist perspectives reveal that, in many instances, the sites of global power and transformation are not just the domain of political and economic elites; such sites also exist in the invisible, under-appreciated nooks and crannies of societies. Traditional expectations about the nature of states and international relations are both disrupted when a gender perspective is brought to bear. Feminism helps us to recognize power shifts within nation-states and internationally, not least of all women's political leadership and the growing movement for achieving gender balance in decision making, that have ramifications for world order. Surely, observing and interpreting such power shifts as they arise in a variety of global and local venues constitute core functions of contemporary and future-oriented International Relations scholarship.

11 | **Green Theory**

MATTHEW PATERSON

The past 40 years of global politics have been punctuated by cycles of concern about the basic sustainability of the trajectory on which human societies are headed, cycles which have been provoked by particular environmental scares but which have frequently been articulated as presaging a more systemic crisis. We moved thus from concerns about pesticides in the early 1960s, to those about 'limits to growth' and the 'population bomb' by the early 1970s. In a later cycle in the 1980s we moved from regional concerns about acid rain or nuclear fallout to 'global' concerns like ozone depletion, deforestation, biodiversity loss, or climate change. In the present cycle, climate change has again loomed large and is increasingly understood through a lens of its potential to cause industrial civilization to 'collapse'.

As a cycle of concern returns, the systemic character of the crisis becomes more apparent, and the implications for the way that global politics is organized become more evident. In recent years, we have seen numerous examples of this. The persistent problems in negotiating a treaty to replace the UN's 1977 Kyoto Protocol on Climate Change, notably the near-collapse of talks in Copenhagen in 2009, combined with the weakness of the Kyoto Protocol in the first place, all occurred at the same time as societies realized ever more clearly the depth of the crisis that climate change poses and the apparent inability of existing political structures to respond adequately (e.g. Bodansky 2010; Dubash and Rajamani 2010). At the same time, even partial responses to the crisis generate their own problems. The rapid emergence of crises over food prices and scarcity provoked in part by the pursuit of biofuels, themselves ostensibly promoted as a response to climate change, suggest the complex and systemic character of the global socio-ecological crisis (e.g. Clapp 2009). While often this calls attention to the contradictions between the organization of global politics and the ecological predicament societies face (however such contradictions are conceptualized), there are also glimmers of changes in political practice and perhaps even structure, which may prefigure some more substantial transformations.

Theorists have approached the political character of the ecological crisis in a variety of ways. Not all accept that such a crisis may produce profound systemic change; indeed not all accept that an overall 'crisis', understood as a set of interlocking problems that require a 'holistic' response, even exists. But the *raison d'être* of this chapter is that such radical accounts – which I will group under the heading 'Green theory' – deserve to be taken seriously, and thus the potential for ecological crises to reshape global politics should be thought through. Indeed, as one strand of ecological IR theory now suggests (Eckersley 2004), as much as engaging in normative theory as to how global politics *ought* to be reshaped to meet the goal of sustainability, the challenge is to understand political transformations that are *already* under way. It should also be understood that for such accounts, the ambition of Green theory goes way beyond the narrow understanding of 'environmental issues'. The classic questions of International Relations – the search for peace, the operations of power politics, the question of global governance, normative questions such as global justice – all undergo a thorough rethinking in the light of the ecological challenge.

Jennifer Clapp and Peter Dauvergne (2005) provide us with a useful way to understand the range of theoretical approaches to global ecological politics. They distinguish between four principal variants of thought: free-market environmentalism, institutionalism, bio-environmentalism, and social ecology. (I should say at the outset that while I think their categories are very useful, I apply them here with a number of differences to their accounts of each approach. I will also use the term Greens (with a capital G) to refer to proponents of both bio-environmentalist and social green arguments, since these two types of arguments frequently coexist among activists in Green movements.) Anyway, these extend distinctions frequently made (e.g. Dobson 1990) between environmentalism and ecologism, and provide considerably more nuance about the variants of environmental ideology. I will however say little about free-market environmentalism, not because it is not important in the field of environmental ideology (indeed its practitioners dominate much of global environmental political practice), but rather because its proponents have nothing to say specifically about international relations. The key debate then is between institutionalists, who tend to eschew discussion of any broad 'environmental crisis', and focus on how international institutions deal with specific issue areas, and bio-environmentalists and social greens, who insist on such a crisis and the need for political transformation to deal effectively with it. The former provide the bulk of the literature within IR on environmental questions – if you read articles on the environment in journals such as *International Organization,* or even the main journal in the field *Global Environmental Politics,* a solid majority will be written from an institutionalist perspective. This chapter starts with a discussion of institutionalist approaches to global environmental politics, before moving on to what I argue are two variants of a properly Green approach to global politics.

Theorizing environment within international relations

From the earliest accounts of the global political character of environmental problems, they have been understood on the one hand as problems of collective action, and on the other through lenses of 'security'. Perhaps the founding metaphor for both of these is that of Garrett Hardin's 'Tragedy of the Commons' (1968). This suggests that the structural incentives of actors (states) operating in relation to open-access resources (Hardin's misnamed commons) both lead to the overuse and abuse of those resources, and impede collective efforts to mitigate such abuse. Hardin's argument can also be seen as a basis for the notion of 'environmental security'. The actors themselves in the situation he describes (and by extension, in relation to a whole range of 'real world' environmental problems) come to view both the environmental problem itself (land degradation) and the actions of the other actors as a threat to the security of their livelihood. Out of this observation, as well as out of more obviously problematic accounts of a 'population bomb' (Ehrlich 1968; for an updated version, Kaplan 1994), a whole industry has emerged focusing on 'environmental security', specifically examining various sorts of environmental change, notably resource shortages (water, oil) but also climate change, soil erosion, as sources either of interstate conflict or of social instability which then generates international instability. Much of this literature is clearly realist in inspiration; thus there are no specific ecological–theoretical insights to be developed about global politics. Some (notably Dalby 2002) do develop specific claims from a notion of ecological (as opposed to environmental) security that contribute to a rethinking of global politics from an ecological point of view, points I will elaborate below (for a broad selection of writings on this topic, see Myers 1993; Homer-Dixon 1999; Deudney and Matthew 1999; Barnett 2000; Klare 2001; Dalby 2002).

Hardin's argument proceeds from an ideal-type of a village commons, where herders from the village have the right to graze cows. The land can only support a fixed number of cows, but each herder has an incentive to graze more than their share on the land. They gain the income from the extra cow, while the damages are shared across all the herders. Hardin's initial motivation is to show that there is no technological solution to this problem (indeed, new technologies may simply accelerate the rate of destruction), but that the problem is rather structural – in the authority structure over the land which permits open access to all, and in the incentives herders face which lead to them over-using resources.

Hardin's conclusion, and that of some following his logic, is that the tragedy is insurmountable without an overarching change in the authority structure. William Ophuls (1977) elaborated this logic most fully, arguing explicitly for a world state with sufficient power to impose ecological restraint on actors across the world. His reasoning was precisely that the logic of collective action elaborated by Hardin would lead to ruin.

Institutionalist accounts of environmental politics

Hardin's claim is actually significantly milder. Having argued that 'freedom in a commons brings ruin to all' (Hardin 1968: 1244), his other catchphrase in the article is his call for 'mutual coercion, mutually agreed upon' (Hardin 1968: 1247). While much has been made of his term 'coercion', leading to him being called (along with Ophuls and others) 'eco-authoritarian', the logic of his claim is also shared by the liberal institutionalist school in IR and the way it analyses international environmental politics. I use institutionalist to refer to approaches across the social sciences which emphasize the role that social and political institutions play in shaping the behaviour of actors and in mediating the outcomes such behaviour produces (for a general overview, see Hall and Taylor 1996). In IR, this translates to the liberal institutionalist perspective most closely associated with Robert Keohane (1989a). I leave out the 'liberal' qualifier in what follows, but when I use the term institutionalist I use it to refer to this perspective in IR.

Hardin's logic mirrors much analysis of what are more often called 'collective action problems' across the social sciences. These refer to situations where actors recognize the necessity of acting in concert with others in the pursuit of specific goals, but where such collaboration may not be easy to achieve, for many of the reasons Hardin identifies. Collective action problems are usually understood through the lens of rational choice theory – that actors pursue their individual preferences in a systematic fashion.

In rational choice terms, Hardin's tragedy of the commons is similar to a game of Prisoner's Dilemma (PD). In that game, where (classically) two prisoners are held by the police and offered more lenient sentences in return for information which will lead to the conviction of their colleague for a more serious crime, the best outcome is that both keep quiet (cooperate) but in fact each is likely to spill the beans (defect). Similarly the best outcome in Hardin's commons is that all limit themselves to ten cows (cooperate) but the dominant dynamic is that each puts an extra cow on the land (defects), thus undermining the interests of all.

Institutionalists argue that a number of features of 'real world' situations mean that such catastrophic outcomes are less likely than Hardin would anticipate. Specifically, the PD metaphor suggests that there are only two actors, they only play the game once, and cannot communicate with each other. It is not hard to understand how if these conditions are relaxed, cooperation might in general become more feasible. If the game is played over and over, actors can generate strategies to elicit cooperation from the others (a process outlined classically by Taylor 1976, or Axelrod 1984). If the actors can communicate with each other directly, they may then also be able to build the trust and confidence that each will cooperate. The numbers question is more ambiguous – while some increases in the number of actors may help cooperation, as actors may be able to use a third party to get round a stalemate between just two, once you get to large numbers of actors, the transaction costs of simply negotiating become high, while the possibilities of miscommunication and lack of confidence also increase.

On the basis of these arguments, institutionalists suggest that, (a) the possibilities of cooperation are significantly greater than that allowed by Hardin (or in IR, by realists), and (b) international organizations and institutions may therefore play a significant role in fostering cooperation (see Young 1994). The concept of an international regime (Krasner 1983) is the central concept here elucidating research on the consequences of this – the development of a set of interlocking norms, rules, principles, which govern how states interact.

Not all institutionalists proceed from rational choice assumptions about state behaviour. Others, notably Oran Young (1989b, 1994, 1999a) or Peter Haas (1989, 2000) are more 'constructivist' in orientation (see Chapter 9). For Young, international institutions are constitutive of international politics, not simply the outcomes of state strategic interaction, and they build on each other – earlier institutions provide general norms which guide practice and thus create new norms, and so on. (The argument is also rather like the English School; see Chapter 4.) For an account of international regimes that draws on environmental politics for its material and which explicitly compares institutionalist and English School approaches see Hurrell (1993, and for the same author's elaboration of environmental politics in English School terms, see Hurrell 2007: chapter 9).) At a most basic level, institutions construct not only how states interact, but also what states are. In addition, as Young shows (1989a) in the environmental field in particular, states face contradictory motivations and considerable ambiguity about outcomes, meaning that even if states could in other situations act according to the premises of rational choice theory, in this instance it is simply impossible. Finally, non-rationalist institutionalists also suggest that environmental regimes involve novel actors and processes, specifically concerning the role of scientists and scientific discourse in regime formation; the origin of 'cognitivist' accounts of international regimes is in analysis of environmental politics (Haas 1990, 1992).

To simplify things somewhat, institutionalists tend to ask one of two types of question. First, they ask what affects how regimes are established, to explain why regimes form in some circumstances and not others. Some of this literature is pitched at a broad theoretical level, typically outlining a threefold account of theories based on power (realist explanations), interests (liberal, rational choice explanations) or knowledge ('cognitive', or constructivist explanations) of regime formation (e.g. Young 1994: 84–98; Vogler 1992; Hansenclever, Mayer and Rittberger 1996), for an application to the ozone and climate cases, see Rowlands 1994). Others (e.g. Hahn and Richards 1989, Young 1989a) focus rather on a series of more discrete factors, such as the number of actors, the problem structure of the issue at hand, the question of uncertainty, or notions of fairness.

Second, institutionalists attempt to explain the effectiveness of regimes (e.g. Bernauer 1995; Victor, Raustiala and Skolnikoff 1998; Young 1999b; Mitchell 2006). Under what conditions do they contribute to successful responses to the problem at hand? Haas (1990, 1992), Haas, Keohane and Levy (1993) outline three sorts of key elements, what they call the three Cs – concern, the contractual environment and capacity. That is, international institutions can contribute to the articulation of concern about particular problems and an understanding of their implications, they can reduce transaction costs and help identify possible sites of interstate agreement, and they can help states build their capacity to respond to environmental challenges, for example through the building of monitoring capacity. Most studies agree with these claims, but nevertheless a further link is necessary in order to deal with the normative question of effectiveness.

For our purposes here, two aspects of the institutionalist literature are worth emphasizing. First, when discussing the effectiveness of environmental regimes, analysts often withdraw to a more limited account of effectiveness – for example, along the lines of 'does the institution affect state behaviour?' or 'are emissions lower than they would have been without the institution?'. Asking the question 'have they contributed to a reversal of unsustainable trends?', would lead to a rather pessimistic assessment. Only in the ozone depletion case is a clear reversal of trends identifiable, with some more modest claims that could be made in the case of sulphur emissions and perhaps one or two other cases. More generally, as Princen eloquently establishes (2003, 2005), we have witnessed over the last 30 years an extraordinary process of cooperation and institution building, and *at the same time* a significant increase in the throughput of resources and pollution, and in corresponding environmental degradation. Returning to the starting metaphor, one could use this to suggest that Hardin's original logic was correct, that this is indeed a tragedy (in the sense, as he suggests, of a remorseless logic unfolding with its disastrous consequences). Alternatively, one could conclude that the problem has been mis-specified – that in fact the political origins of environmental problems are less to do with the problem of open-access resources, but rather have their origins in other causes. The bio-environmentalists and social greens outlined below start with different analyses of the origins of environmental problems.

We could, however, take institutionalist conclusions in a different direction. Institutionalists start with the premise, shared with many perspectives in IR that international politics is to be characterized as a number of sovereign states interacting in an anarchic environment. But to the extent that environmental institution building becomes ever more complex, shaping more and more deeply state behaviour, increasingly involving a wide range of actors other than states, the utility of the international anarchy metaphor in explaining what happens declines. Institutionalists occasionally acknowledge this problem, and usually reject it, insisting that the world is still first and foremost an interstate world (e.g. Young 1997). But at least the potential for what has become known as 'global environmental governance' to create possible post-sovereign politics exists (Paterson 2000: chapter 7).

Beyond IR: Green politics and the challenge to world order

There are a number of limits to institutional analyses of global environmental politics. (For a fuller elaboration of these points, see Paterson 2000: chapter 2.) The problem of establishing the ecological effectiveness of regimes is one, already alluded to. The limitation of focusing only on the interstate aspect of global politics, to the neglect of various phenomena (MNCs, global civil society, globalization, private governance, for example), is another. Most important perhaps is the lack of a sustained account of why environmental degradation occurs in the first place. Sometimes they deploy the metaphor of Hardin's tragedy of the commons (e.g. Vogler 1992: 118; Young 1994). But whereas these analyses tend to treat the metaphor in terms of obstacles to cooperation, Hardin developed it to explain the origins of environmental degradation. At other times, institutionalists offer a discussion of discrete, secular trends – in population, consumption, technology, individual behaviour (e.g. Choucri 1993; Homer-Dixon 1993). These however are treated as ad hoc explanations, and the phenomena are not considered as part of a broad structural whole – a set of imperatives for economic growth for example. The two perspectives elaborated below specifically start from a basis of insisting on this structural character of environmental degradation.

Perhaps most obviously, however, if all there was to the study of global environmental politics was the institutionalist approach or the notion of environmental security, there would be little novel theoretically to say. All of the theoretical propositions entailed in the above discussion come from one or another variant of mainstream IR theory – realism, liberalism or constructivism in particular. However, a much more radical tradition exists in Green ideology, out of which a more distinctive Green theory of global politics can be fashioned. Clapp and Dauvergne (2005: 9–15) usefully distinguish between two broad types of radical approach to environmental politics – radical both in the sense that they properly try to 'get to the root of the political origins of environmental degradation as suggested above, and in the more common sense usage of proposing far-reaching political changes in response to such degradation. They label proponents of these two approaches 'bio-environmentalists' and 'social greens' respectively.

Bio-environmentalism – authority, scale, and eco-centrism

Bio-environmentalists tend to focus on the aggregate impact of human activity on the 'natural' environment. They couch their arguments in terms of a humanity–nature dualism, and that the objective is to reorganize human societies in order that they live 'in harmony' with nature. The approach is often developed in highly quantitative terms – in terms of increases in resource use, emissions levels, ecosystem tolerance, and so on. Key terms such as 'carrying capacity' and 'limits to growth' have been articulated principally within this framework. Both refer to an idea that the earth has definite biophysical limits in terms of the numbers of people and the level of economic activity that can be supported without undermining the life-support systems (water, air, etc.) that the planet provides. Bio-environmentalists suggest that two key trends in human societies – population growth and economic growth, both which are growing exponentially – are in the process of moving rapidly towards, or even going beyond those limits.

The classic study *The Limits to Growth* (Meadows, Randers and Behrens 1972) argued that the exponential economic and population growth of human societies was producing an interrelated series of crises. Exponential growth was producing a situation where the world was rapidly running out of resources to feed people or to provide raw material for continued industrial growth (exceeding *carrying capacity* and *productive capacity*), and simultaneously exceeding the *absorptive capacity* of the environment to assimilate the waste products of industrial production (Meadows *et al.* 1972; Dobson 1990: 15). Meadows, Randers and Behrens (1972) produced their arguments based on computer simulations of the trajectory of industrial societies. They predicted that, at current rates of growth, many raw materials would rapidly run out, pollution would quickly exceed the absorptive capacity of the environment, and human societies would experience 'overshoot and collapse' some time before 2100.

The details of their predictions have been fairly easily refuted. But it does not follow that their basic logic, that infinite growth in a finite system is impossible, is faulty. Most Greens have taken this principle to be a central plank of their position (e.g. Spretnak and Capra 1984; Trainer 1985; Porritt 1986), and this limits to growth argument has been recently revived and popularized (see in particular Victor 2008; Jackson 2009). Dobson (1990: 74–80) suggests there are three arguments that are important here. First, technological solutions will not work – they may postpone the crisis but cannot prevent it occurring at some point. Second, the exponential nature of growth means that 'dangers stored up over a relatively long period of time can very suddenly have a catastrophic effect' (Dobson 1990: 74). Recent developments in climate change have underscored this point very effectively. Many things that are regarded as both significant impacts of climate change, but also positive feedbacks that make it worse and take it away from potential human control, were thought to be in the medium-term future but have already arrived on us – the decline in Arctic sea ice and melting of Greenland's ice sheets, both of which are occurring much faster than climate scientists and their computer models thought possible (Stroeve *et al.* 2012). Finally, the problems associated with growth are all interrelated. Simply dealing with them issue by issue will mean that there are important knock-on effects from issue to issue; solving one pollution problem alone may simply change the medium through which pollution is carried, or the scale over which it extends, not reduce pollution overall. The problem of biofuels and food prices mentioned in the introduction to this chapter is a classic example of this.

The idea of 'ecological footprints' (Wackernagel and Rees 1996) is a more recent version of this type of argument. Many analysts argue on this basis that human societies have already gone beyond the limits of the planet to absorb the impacts of human activity without irreversible damage. For example the WWF's *Living Planet Report* (WWF 2010) argues that we are already in a situation of 'ecological debt', using more of the planet's resources than can be replenished. (For elaborations of the data in these reports, updated periodically, see the WWF's website at http://wwf.panda.org/about_our_earth/all_publications/living_planet_report/, accessed 12 October 2011.)

Politically speaking, the bio-environmentalist approach tends to go in one of three directions. One possibility is that the logic requires highly authoritarian solutions to environmental problems. As noted above, Hardin's logic has an authoritarian reading, and his metaphor was used to generate an argument that centralized global political structures would be needed to force changes in behaviour to reach sustainability (e.g. Hardin 1974; Ophuls 1977). In some versions, this involved the adoption of what were called 'lifeboat ethics' (Hardin 1974), where ecological scarcity meant that rich countries would have to practise triage on a global scale – to 'pull up the ladder behind them'. This argument, largely an ecological version of the world-government proposals of 'Idealist' versions of liberal internationalism (see Chapter 3) has, however, been for the most part rejected by Greens.

Others suggest that authoritarianism may be required, but reject the idea that this can be on a global scale. The vision here is for small-scale, tightly knit communities run on hierarchical, conservative lines with self-sufficiency in their use of resources (*The Ecologist* 1972; Heilbroner 1974). It shares with the above position the idea that it is freedom and egoism which has caused the environmental crisis, and that these tendencies need to be curbed to produce sustainable societies.

A second type of political response to environmental degradation from this perspective is one focusing on the question of scale. There is a spatial dimension to the world-government proposals, but the spatial character of environmental problems does not necessarily lead to proposals for world government or authoritarianism. Some bio-environmentalists tend to argue for a position known as bio-regionalism (e.g. Sale 1980). Here, the argument for 'living within nature's limits' takes the form of suggesting that the spatial character of ecosystems should determine the spatial scale of social, political and economic activity. Particularly important is water, such that watersheds become the key spatial category.

But the most common spatial argument by bio-environmentalists is to argue for radical decentralization of power. This is the position O'Riordan long ago termed the 'anarchist solution' (1981: 303–7). Most Greens argue that this is the best interpretation of the implications of limits to growth. For many, it is also regarded as a principle of Green politics in its own right (for example, as one of the four principles of

Green politics in the widely cited *Programme of the German Green Party* 1983). The term 'anarchist' is used loosely in this typology. It means that Greens envisage global networks of small-scale self-reliant communities. This position would for example be associated with people like E. F. Schumacher (1976). It shares the focus on small-scale communities with the previous position, but has two crucial differences. First, relations within communities would be libertarian, egalitarian and participatory. This reflects a very different set of assumptions about the origins of the environmental crisis; rather than being about the 'tragedy of the commons', it is seen to be about the emergence of hierarchical social relations and the channelling of human energies into productivism and consumerism (Bookchin 1982). Participatory societies should provide means for human fulfilment that do not depend on high levels of material consumption. Second, these communities, while self-reliant, are seen to be internationalist in orientation. They are not cut off from other communities, but in many ways conceived of as embedded in networks of relations of obligations, cultural exchanges and so on.

However, whether or not one shares such anarchist leanings, the decentralist impulse is nevertheless the most important theme coming out of Green politics for IR. One of the best-known Green political slogans is 'think globally, act locally'. While obviously fulfilling rhetorical purposes, it is often seen to follow from the two above principles. It stems from a sense that while global environmental and social/economic problems operate on a global scale, they can be successfully responded to only by breaking down the global power structures which generate them through local action and the construction of smaller-scale political communities and self-reliant economies.

One of the best-developed arguments for decentralization within Green theory is given in John Dryzek's *Rational Ecology* (1987). Dryzek summarizes the advantages of decentralization thus; small-scale communities are more reliant on the environmental support services in their immediate locality and therefore more responsive to disruptions in that environment (Dryzek 1987: chapter 16). Self-reliance and smallness shortens feedback channels, so it is easier to respond quickly before disruptions become severe. Dryzek also suggests that they are more likely to develop a social ontology which undermines pure instrumental ways of dealing with the rest of nature, commonly identified as a cause of environmental problems (Dryzek 1987: 219; see also *The Ecologist* 1993 for extended discussions of similar arguments).

The advocacy of radical decentralization has been widely criticized both within academic debates and by some within green movements. On the one hand, it is seen as politically 'unrealistic', and Green parties have certainly scaled back their commitments to decentralization in response to electoral success and the corresponding need for 'realism' (Doherty and de Geus 1996: 4). Beyond this pragmatic concern, the principal criticisms of proposals are threefold (see earlier editions of this chapter; and Carter 1999). First, some claim that small-scale anarchistic communities would be too parochial and potentially self-interested to provide atmospheres conducive to cross-community cooperation. Part of this argument is therefore that it would be stultifying or oppressive for those within the community, but it also suggests that they would be unconcerned with effects across their borders (e.g. Dobson 1990: 101, 124). Second, decentralized small-scale communities, it is claimed, will have little chance of developing effective mechanisms for resolving global environmental problems (see in particular Goodin 1992). While small-scale communities might be able to deal better with local environmental problems, for the reasons Dryzek (1987) outlines, the coordination problems would escalate beyond control with a massive increase in the number of actors at the international level. A third critique is rather different. Rather than arguing that Greens' attempts to abandon sovereignty and decentralize power means that there is insufficient coordinating capacity, many in fact suggest that Green politics remains committed to a sovereign model of politics (e.g. Kuehls 1996, Wapner 1996, Lipschutz 1997 or Dalby 1998). Part of this argument takes us back to the spatial character of ecological problems, which some of these authors (in particular Dalby 1998, 2002) suggest should be understood as about flows and networks, not closed spaces. Part also starts from the observation that contemporary global politics is also now organized through flows and networks, thus creating possibilities for political engagement without relying on the metaphor of territorial sovereignty (see in particular Spaargaren, Mol and Buttel 2006 for an attempt to think through environmental governance in terms of flows).

The third bio-environmentalist account of politics is that the environmental crisis requires a new ethical sensibility to guide political practice. Most refer to this through the notion of *eco-centrism*; Greens reject anthropocentric ethics (with humans at the centre of the moral world) in favour of an eco-centric approach. For Eckersley (1992), eco-centrism has a number of central features. Empirically, it involves a view of the world as ontologically composed of *inter-relations* rather than individual entities (1992: 49). All beings are fundamentally 'embedded in ecological relationships' (1992: 53). Consequently, there are no convincing criteria that can be used to make a hard and fast distinction between humans and non-humans (1992: 49–51). Ethically, therefore, since there is no good reason to make rigid distinctions between humans and the rest of nature, a broad emancipatory project, to which Eckersley allies herself, ought to be extended to non-human nature. Eco-centrism is about 'emancipation writ large' (1992: 53). All entities are endowed with a relative autonomy, within the ecological relationships in which they are embedded, and therefore humans are not ethically free to dominate the rest of nature.

Politically, Eckersley (1992) argues against the decentralist emphasis in much Green thought. On the basis of her reading of the implications of eco-centrism, she develops a political argument from this that is statist in orientation. Although she does not adopt the position of the 'eco-authoritarians' mentioned above, she suggests, in direct contradiction to the eco-anarchism that is widespread in Green political thought, that the modern state is a necessary political institution from a Green point of view. She suggests that eco-centrism requires that we both decentralize power down within the state, but also centralize power up to the regional and global levels. She argues that a 'multi-tiered' political system, with dispersal of power both down to local communities and up to the regional and global levels is the approach that is most consistent with eco-centrism (Eckersley 1992: 144, 175, 178).

This position could be developed within a conventional perspective in International Relations (such as liberal institutionalism) to look at the character of a wide variety of interstate treaties and practices. The most obvious would be those regarding biodiversity, acid rain, or climate change. But it could also be developed for global economic institutions such as the World Bank, or the military practices of states.

Eckersley's account could also be developed in the context of the literature on 'global environmental governance', which implies forms of governance emerging which do not rely solely on sovereign states (Paterson 1999a; Humphreys, Paterson and Pettiford 2003). One view of this is that we are currently witnessing a simultaneous shift of authority up to international/transnational institutions, and down to local organizations (Rosenau 1992; Hempel 1996). Rosenau makes this claim concerning patterns of authority in global politics in general, but also specifically in relation to global environmental politics (Rosenau 1993). More recent literature has documented a dramatic expansion in forms of governance that cross scales from global to local in all sorts of different ways. Bulkeley *et al.* (forthcoming) discuss 60 different such governance initiatives on climate change, such as the Carbon Disclosure Project, the Transition Towns movement, the Renewable Energy and Energy Efficiency Partnership or the Climate Change and Biodiversity Alliance. These are organized by various actors – city or regional governments, companies, institutional investors, environmental or development NGOs, often working in novel collaborative arrangements, but what they have in common is an attempt to work transnationally – across the globe at the sites where they think interventions are needed, not according to the logic of state sovereignty, and at times precisely to fill the gap left by the inadequacy of state-led responses to climate change. For Hempel, such forms of global environmental governance are emerging because the spatial scale of the state is inadequate for dealing with the scales of environmental change. The state is simultaneously too small and too big to deal effectively with such change and thus, in response, practices of governance move towards regional and global levels and at the same time towards local levels. Many of the current transnational or multi-level governance initiatives (see below), where environmental governance is a leading sphere of activity, can be seen in this light, as can more general attempts to situate global environmental politics in terms of global–local interactions (e.g. Kütting and Lipschutz 2009). Eckersley's position in her (1992) book is a normative claim justifying such shifts in authority.

A core problem with this argument is that the interpretation of eco-centrism, which underpins Eckersley's (1992) book, is challengeable. Eco-centrism is in itself politically indeterminate. It can have many variants, ranging from anarchist to authoritarian, with Eckersley's version in the middle of the continuum. The predominant alternative interpretation within Green thinking suggests that it is the emergence of modern modes of thought which is the problem from an eco-centric point of view. The rationality inherent in modern Western science is an instrumental one, where the domination of the rest of nature (and of women by men) and its use for human instrumental purposes have historically, at least, been integral to the scientific project on which industrial capitalism is built (e.g. Merchant 1980; Plumwood 1993). In other words, environmental ethics are given a historical specificity and material base – the emergence of modern forms of anthropocentrism is located in the emergence of modernity in all its aspects.

This interpretation argues, therefore, that since modern science is inextricably bound up with other modern institutions such as capitalism, the nation-state and modern forms of patriarchy, it is inappropriate to respond by developing those institutions further, centralizing power through the development of global and regional institutions. Such a response will further entrench instrumental rationality that will undermine the possibility for developing an eco-centric ethic. An eco-centric position therefore leads to arguments for scaling down human communities, and in particular for challenging trends towards globalization and homogenization, since it is only by celebrating diversity that it will be possible to create spaces for eco-centric ethics to emerge. More importantly, thinking through this logic suggests that talking about environmental politics as if the character of human societies is more or less irrelevant has severe limits. It is this gap which social greens fill.

Social greens – limits to growth and political economy

Clapp and Dauvergne's (2005) final category is that of social greens. These tend to agree with bio-environmentalists about the existence of physical limits to growth, particularly economic growth (they at least downplay, and often reject, arguments about population, as patriarchal and/or imperialist). But they insist that such an observation must be understood in terms of the social systems which generate such growth, and thus of the complex interactions between social and ecological problems. At a general level, social greens are united in a claim that the power structures – capitalist, statist, patriarchal – of contemporary societies, are at the same time highly exploitative, unjust or oppressive, and systematically generate environmental degradation.

In terms specifically of global politics, these arguments can be most clearly seen in those writers who identify global inequalities as key to understanding global (environmental) politics (e.g. Parks and Roberts 2010; Okereke 2008), and also who often suggest that dominant political forces deploy environmental concerns to extend their global control, a process exemplified by Vandana Shiva's phrase (1993) 'the greening of global reach'. We can best understand their arguments on the one hand through their critique of the discourse of sustainable development (which shows their distinct take on limits to growth), and on the other through their reinterpretation of the notion of the commons (which gives Greens a distinct political economy). There is also, however, another emerging literature which could be regarded as an extension of key social-ecological insights to global politics – that which deploys theories of complex open systems to global environmental politics, theories which were developed in part in ecological contexts, and which can be used to analyse both social and ecological systems, and their interactions, with a view to identifying potential system disruptions and transformations (see in particular Harrison 2006; Hoffmann 2011).

Social limits to growth

As the notion of sustainable development became fashionable in the 1980s, and as the specific predictions of Meadows *et al.* concerning resource exhaustion proved inaccurate, belief in limits subsided. But in the 1990s, a politics rejecting economic growth as the primary purpose of governments and societies re-emerged. It came, however, less out of the computer-modelling methods of Meadows *et al.* (although her team did produce a twenty-year-on book, *Beyond the Limits*, Meadows and Randers 1992) than out of emerging critiques of development in the South from the 1980s onwards. Such 'post-development' perspectives draw heavily on post-modernism, post-colonialism and feminism (e.g. Escobar 1995; Shiva 1988), and have been used by Greens in the North to develop what might be called a 'global ecology' perspective. Through the critique of 'development', economic growth again became the subject of critique, although in this vein critics made much closer connections between its ecological and its social consequences (Douthwaite 1992; Wackernagel and Rees 1996; Booth 1998).

One reason why the 'global ecology' writers object to development is because of limits to growth arguments, abandoned by much of the environmental movement during the 1980s. Implicit throughout their work is a need to accept the limits imposed by a finite planet, an acceptance ignored by the planet's managers and mainstream environmentalists (e.g. Sachs 1993). They are also sceptical of the idea that it is possible to decouple the concept of development from that of growth. While many environmentalists try to distinguish the two by stating that 'growth is quantitative increase in physical scale while development is qualitative improvement or unfolding of potentialities' (Daly 1990; Ekins 1993), others would suggest that in practice it is impossible to make such neat distinctions. For the practitioners of sustainable development, 'sustainable growth' and 'sustainable development' are in practice usually conflated, and certainly the Brundtland Commission regarded the pursuit of economic growth as essential for sustainable development (WCED 1987).

However, their arguments are more subtle than simply re-asserting limits to growth arguments. They focus on a number of *anti-ecological* elements of development. One of the central features of development is the enclosure of commons in order to expand the realm of commodity production and thus of material throughput (*The Ecologist* 1993). A second is the way such enclosure redistributes and concentrates resources, which has direct ecological consequences and creates a growth-supporting dynamic as growth mitigates the effects of enhanced inequality. A third is the concentrations of power that are involved in enclosure, as smaller numbers of people are able to control the way that land is used (and often able to insulate themselves from the ecological effects of the way land is used, for example by reserving for themselves privileged access to uncontaminated water sources). A fourth is the way such enclosure and the concentrations of power and wealth it effects produce shifts in knowledge relations and systems, typically involving the marginalization of 'indigenous knowledges' and the empowerment of 'experts'(*The Ecologist* 1993: 67–70; Appfel-Marglin and Marglin 1990). Finally, such a set of shifts in property systems, distribution of resources and power-knowledge relations entrenches the world-view which regards the non-human world in purely instrumental terms, thus legitimizing the destructive use of non-human nature.

The global ecology writers present a powerful set of arguments as to how development is inherently anti-ecological. This is not only because of abstract limits to growth-type arguments, but because they show in a subtler fashion how development in practice undermines sustainable practices. It takes control over resources away from those living sustainably in order to organize commodity production, it empowers experts with knowledge based on instrumental reason, it increases inequality which produces social conflicts and so on. Otherwise put, development is conceptualized as inherently colonial. The perspective's close connections to post-colonial thought are well illustrated by how a number of post-colonial writers (e.g. Escobar 1995) form part of this perspective.

Back to the commons

While adding in a socio-ecological critique of growth to the bio-environmentalists techno-scientific one, social greens do something similar for arguments about decentralization of power. On the one hand, for many Greens, much of the decentralist impulse has its origins in a rejection of the state similar to that of anarchists. For example, Spretnak and Capra (1984) suggest that it is the features identified by Max Weber as central to statehood that are the problem from an ecological point of view (1984: 177). Bookchin (1980) gives similar arguments, suggesting that the state is the ultimate hierarchical institution that consolidates all other hierarchical institutions. Carter (1993) suggests that the state is part of the dynamic of modern society that has caused the present environmental crisis. He outlines a 'environmentally hazardous dynamic, where [a] centralized, pseudo-representative, quasi-democratic state stabilizes competitive, inegalitarian economic relations that develop "non-convivial", environmentally damaging "hard" technologies whose productivity supports the (nationalistic and militaristic) coercive forces that empower the state' (Carter 1993: 45). Thus the state is not only unnecessary from a Green point of view, it is positively undesirable.

The decentralist impulse is also expressed in the re-appropriation of the notion of the commons. The 'global ecology' writers reinforce a political-theoretic argument for decentralization by giving it a political economy. By this I mean they make it so that it is not only a question of the scale of political organization and the authoritarian character of the state, but also a reorganization of the structural form of political institutions, and in particular a re-conceptualization of how economic production, distribution and exchange – the direct way in which human societies transform 'nature' – is integrated into political life. Their positive argument is that the most plausibly Green form of political economy is the 'commons'. This argument is most fully developed by the editors of

The Ecologist magazine in their book *Whose Common Future? Reclaiming the Commons* (1993).

The argument is essentially that common spaces are sites where the most sustainable practices currently operate. They are under threat from development that continuously tries to enclose them in order to turn them into commodities (the most recently notable effort at this is in efforts to enclose the global carbon cycle via the establishment of carbon markets – see in particular Lohmann 2006). Therefore a central part of Green politics is resistance to this enclosure. But it is also a (re)constructive project – creating commons where they do not exist.

What are commons? First, they are not the commons as suggested by Hardin, which is rather an 'open access' resource (*The Ecologist* 1993: 13). They are not 'public' in the modern sense, which connotes open access under control by the state, while commons are often not open to all, and the rules governing them do not depend on the hierarchy and formality of state institutions. Nor are they 'private' – no one person owns and controls the resource. They are rather resources held in common, where the relevant community collectively develops rules governing the use of the resources. This has been a widespread form of resource governance throughout human history, and as *The Ecologist* (1993) show, still persists in many places today.

Commons, therefore, are not 'anarchic' in the sense of having no rules governing them. They are spaces whose use is closely governed, often by informally defined rules, and by the communities that depend on them. They depend for their successful operation on a rough equality between the members of the community, as imbalances in power would make some able to ignore the rules of the community. They also depend on particular social and cultural norms prevailing – for example, the priority of common safety over accumulation, or distinctions between members and non-members (although not necessarily in a hostile sense, or one which is rigid and unchanging over time) (*The Ecologist* 1993: 9).

The key point is that they are typically organized for the production of use values rather than exchange values – that is, they are not geared to commodity production and are not susceptible to the pressures for accumulation or growth inherent in capitalist market systems. Commons are therefore held to produce sustainable practices, for a number of reasons. First, the rough equality in income and power means that none can usurp or dominate the system (*The Ecologist* 1993: 5). Second, the local scale at which they work means that the patterns of mutual dependence make cooperation easier to achieve. Third, this also means that the culture of recognizing one's dependence on others, and therefore having obligations, is easily entrenched. Finally, commons make practices based on accumulation difficult to adopt, usufruct being more likely.

The idea of the commons is clearly very consistent with the arguments about the necessity of decentralization of power, and grassroots democracy. It should be obvious that from this perspective the term 'global commons', in widespread use in mainstream environmental discussions or in institutionalist literature to refer to problems such as global warming or ozone depletion (e.g. Vogler 1995; Buck 1998), is literally nonsensical. However it supplements the decentralist argument by showing how small-scale democratic communities, working with particular sorts of property systems, are the most likely to produce sustainable practices within the limits set by a finite planet.

Both bio-environmentalists and social greens propose concrete analyses of the origins of environmental degradation and unsustainability, and make far-reaching normative claims about the political changes that responding to such a crisis entails. They differ in their analysis broadly between a dualistic account of 'humanity' versus 'nature', as opposed to a social analysis of the origins of unsustainability in particular social systems and the intertwining of social and ecological crises. But they share a sense of the radical nature of the changes required.

Greening global politics

How then might global politics be 'Greened'? One of the things that the proponents of all of Clapp and Dauvergne's (2005) positions tend to share, is a rather static account of the relationship between political systems and environmental degradation. For example, for bio-environmentalists there is an ahistorical 'naturalizing' account of population and economic growth, or in Ophuls (1997) a reification of the states-system as having a 'timeless' logic that never changes. For some social greens (Bookchin 1980, for example) there is equally an identification of 'the state' as the problem, as if 'the state' is not itself undergoing constant change. Given that political systems are in constant flux, this may create possibilities as well as obstacles to the pursuit of sustainability. We might want to ask what an *immanent* Green critique of global politics might look like, as opposed to a *transcendental* Green critique of the (reified) states-system.

It is in this light that Eckersley's *The Green State* (2004) comes to the fore. (I use Eckersley's book as the point of departure for this discussion as it remains the fullest expression of what can now be termed an emerging literature on 'the greening of the state' (see also Dryzek *et al.* 2003; Barry and Eckersley 2005; or Spaargaren, Mol and Buttel 2006; for an exchange on Eckersley's book, see the forum published in *Politics and Ethics Review* 2006). In this book, Eckersley ends up with similar conclusions to those she draws from eco-centrism in her earlier book. But the argument is developed in much greater detail, and is based not on the transcendental claims of eco-centric ethics but on the importance of an immanent critique of contemporary global politics. That is, she starts from an analysis both of the contemporary anti-ecological tendencies and structures within global politics (for her, these are interstate anarchy, global capitalism, the limits of liberal democracy) *and* the contemporary trends that create the possibility of countering these tendencies (environmental multilateralism, ecological modernization, deliberative/discursive democracy).

Collectively, Eckersley argues that these three elements create the possibility of an ecological world order which works from existing practices, rather than having to develop a world order anew. Thus she draws heavily on constructivist accounts of international politics (see also Reus-Smit, Chapter 9 in this volume, or Williams 2006), particularly on the notion of 'cultures of anarchy' (Wendt 1999) to argue that sovereignty need not simply mean relentless hostility and competition between states (as assumed in both eco-authoritarian arguments for world government and in eco-anarchist arguments against the state), but can entail the development of mutual obligations and extensive cooperation, and suggests that the development of environmental multilateralism to date is evidence for the possibilities here. Eckersley draws on accounts of ecological modernization (e.g. Hajer 1995; Christoff 1996; Mol 1996) to suggest that the growth and globalization dynamic of global capitalism is only one possible future for the world economy, while remaining highly critical of the 'weak' nature of most actually existing ecological modernization. Finally, she draws on work on deliberative and transnational democracy (Held 1995; Dryzek 1990, 1992, 1999; Linklater 1998) and implicitly at least on ecological citizenship (Dobson 2003) both to suggest that the former would enable the move to 'strong' ecological modernization which would properly ecologize economic processes, and the latter could embed properly the transformations of sovereignty away from the Hobbesian image.

Once Green critiques of international politics are understood this way, the door is open for a critical but constructive re-engagement with other International Relations traditions thinking similarly about the way that the states-system is undergoing transformation and how such transformations might be pushed in a radical direction. In the environmental sphere, work such as that by Hurrell on challenges to sovereignty and the states-system (1994), Shue on global justice and global environmental politics (1992), or Dobson on ecological citizenship (2003) all suggest, in differing ways, how Green conceptions of necessary global political reforms could fruitfully engage with specific existing elements of global politics in the manner indicated at a more general level by Eckersley. Most recently, the rapidly emerging literature on multi-level and transnational environmental governance mentioned above offers many illustrative examples of the sorts of transformations Eckersley envisages. These typically entail complex sorts of partnership arrangements between different sorts of actors, attempting to govern specific aspects of environmental degradation in novel ways (see for example Pattberg 2007; Dingwerth 2007; Bulkeley *et al.* 2012). Paradigmatic examples include the Forest Stewardship Council that engages in transnational certification of timber operations (Cashore *et al.* 2004), or the Cities for Climate Protection network that involves many cities around the world collaborating to reduce greenhouse gas emissions (Bulkeley and Betsill 2005).Outside the environmental sphere, Linklater's account of critical theory (Linklater 1998; Chapter 6 in this volume) in terms of the possible transformations of forms of political community, or related debates about cosmopolitan or transnational democracy (Held 1995; Dryzek 1999) would be obvious sites of potential engagement.

An objection to this argument would be to question the focus on democratic deliberation in the arguments of Eckersley and others (see in particular Dryzek 1999; Bäckstrand *et al.* 2010). Fundamentally, she assumes that it is the character of *democratic deliberation* that underpins (un)sustainable polities. That is, while in *Environmentalism and Political Theory* (1992), it was eco-centric ethics which underpinned political claims about sustainability, in *The Green State* (2004) what sustainability requires politically is that 'all those potentially affected by ecological risks ought to have some meaningful opportunity to participate, or be represented, in the determination of policies or decisions that may generate risks' (2004: 243). This assumption generates the focus both on the weak nature of deliberative processes in liberal democracy, and the need to enable deliberative processes that do not exclude those beyond the borders of individual states. The main Green criticism here could come from the lines of argument developed by the 'global ecology' writers. Eckersley's account of democratic deliberation rightly questions the uncritical nature of 'individual preferences' as invoked by liberal democratic rhetoric – or, if you like, the separation of public and private, but fails to question also its (related) separation of politics and economics. Thus in the 'reclaiming the commons' literature, what is evident is that it is the embeddedness of political institutions in concrete socio-economic forms which engenders sustainable practices, whereas in Eckersley's account of ecological democracy it is clear that the practices of democratic deliberation and the practices of the production of daily life are much more clearly removed from each other, disembodied if you will (see also Luke 2009). This line of argument could be extended to a broader discussion of the relationship between capitalism and the state, and thus the implications for the character of political transformations implied by 'greening the state' (for discussions of this question, see for example Paterson 2007; Paterson *et al.* 2006; Meadowcroft 2006). However, at the same time, what is clear is that Eckersley's arguments concerning ecological democracy, if given a 'decentralist' twist – that is, if her insistence on the national state as the starting point for thinking about the site of political activity is dropped – then become significantly more attractive for most Greens, and an enormously sophisticated and valuable addition to Green arguments.

What is perhaps also at stake is Eckersley's account of contemporary global political developments that inform therefore the 'limits of the possible' out of which her immanent critique can then be developed. To repeat, this is for her the emergent potential of environmental multilateralism, ecological modernization and deliberative democracy arising out of interstate anarchy, global capitalism and liberal democracy. What is interesting in this context is perhaps the lack of a discussion of 'anti-globalization' movements, in which Greens have played prominent roles, as well as an acknowledgement that the commons as a form of political economy that Greens want to promote *already exists* in many areas around the world. If one adds this dimension of contemporary global developments to those Eckersley discusses, then this transforms what one thinks of the potential by decentralism as argued by Greens. These movements can, of course, be analysed as pressures that support more reformist movements developing environmental multilateralism, ecological modernization and discursive democracy. But they can also be analysed as movements generating political change in their own right, embedded in a broader pattern of Green social and political change which challenge the power of global capital, the centralization of power and so on, and act as the agents that help to forge and sustain ecological democracy and citizenship.

Conclusions

My main aim in this chapter has been to show that between the two approaches that Clapp and Dauvergne (2005) label 'bio-environmentalist' and 'social green', there is a set of theories which can properly be called a Green approach to global politics. While these theories certainly arise out of the *problématique* of the environmental crisis, it would be a mistake to limit their import to that 'issue area'. Rather, their character as theories entails claims about the whole range of 'issues' that make up the global political agenda, as well as calling into question the basic character of global politics.

Greens make claims about peace and war (both that environmental problems result from militarism but more broadly that war-like practices result from the same world-view based on accumulation, domination, exploitation, which lead to unsustainability), about development (not only about its environmental unsustainability but its dominating character) and about global governance (in various, at times contradictory, ways as we have seen in the chapter). These claims are not add-on extras to a Green approach, but logical extensions of the character of the claims Greens make.

In the introduction to the book (Chapter 1) some of the central questions and distinctions concerning theoretical traditions in International Relations were outlined. Green politics should clearly be regarded as a critical rather than problem-solving theory. It is one, however, which aims to be both explanatory and normative – it tries both to explain a certain range of phenomena and problems in global politics and provide a set of normative claims about the sorts of global political changes necessary to respond to such problems. Writers within this tradition have to date spent less time engaging in constitutive-theoretical activity – reflecting on the nature of their theorizing *per se,* although there is attention, in particular among the writers in what I have called the 'global ecology' school to power/knowledge questions (but cf. Doran 1995).

For Greens, the central object of analysis and scope of enquiry is the way in which contemporary human societies are *ecologically unsustainable.* Such a destructive mode of existence is deplored both because of the independent ethical value held to reside in organisms and ecosystems, and because human society ultimately depends on the successful function of the biosphere as a whole for its own survival. Regarding International Relations specifically, Greens focus on the way in which prevailing political structures and processes contribute to this destruction. This is the root of their rejection of institutionalist accounts that suggest institutions can be built to 'tame' international anarchy or global capitalism. The purpose of enquiry is thus explicitly normative – to understand how global political structures can be reformed to prevent such destruction and provide for a sustainable human relationship to the planet and its inhabitants. Like Idealism, the normative imperative is the original impulse in Green politics – the explanation of environmental destruction comes later. Methodologically, while Greens are hostile to positivism, not least because of its historical connection to the treating of 'nature' (including humans) as objects, purely instrumentally, there is no clearly identifiable 'Green' methodology. Eckersley (2004: 8–10) proposes 'critical political ecology' as a method for Green politics. But this turns out to be the method of immanent critique of Frankfurt School critical theory, with an ecological focus. Finally, Greens share with many other perspectives a rejection of any claimed separation of International Relations from other disciplines. As Chapter 1 suggests, the possibility of the emergence of a distinct Green perspective in International Relations has seen the breaking down of disciplinary boundaries.

Regarding other International Relations traditions, Green politics has a number of features in common with many other critical approaches. First, it shares the rejection of a hard and fast fact/value distinction with feminism, critical theory and post-structuralism, by making clear attempts to integrate normative and explanatory concerns. Its conception of theory is clearly incompatible with positivist conceptions that have such a clear distinction. Second, it shares an interest in resisting the concentration of power, the homogenizing forces in contemporary world politics and the preservation of difference and diversity with post-structuralism and feminism. Third, it shares a critique of the states-system with critical theory and others, although it adopts a position that rejects the idea of global power structures emerging in correspondence with some idea of a 'global community' in favour of decentralizing power away from nation-states to more local levels. (For an account with many similarities to that of Linklater in relation to environmental politics, see Low and Gleeson 1998: chapter 7. For a critique of such universalist thinking along the lines of the 'global ecology' writers discussed above, see Esteva and Prakash 1997). While for critical theorists such as Linklater (1998), the idea of community at the global level is about balancing unity and diversity rather than one which wishes to create a homogeneous global identity, there is a much stronger sense in Green politics that community only makes sense at the very local level – the idea of a 'global community' is for Greens nonsensical, if not potentially totalitarian (Esteva and Prakash 1997). Nevertheless, there is a shared sense that the purpose of theory is to promote emancipation (Laferriere 1996; Laferriere and Stoett 1999, 2006). Allied to this normative rejection of the states-system is a rejection of a clear empirical split between domestic and international politics shared in particular with pluralists but also with Marxists, critical theorists and feminists. Greens would not believe it useful therefore to think in terms of 'levels of analysis', a form of thinking still prevalent in realism, as it arbitrarily divides up arenas of political action which should be seen as fundamentally interconnected. The emergence of various 'multi-level' or 'transnational' governance projects to deal in particular with climate change in recent years could be seen by Greens as vindication of this logic – that the states-system is too locked up in the pursuit of security, economic growth, and competitive relations with each other, and novel arrangements enable us to deal more adequately with the spatial and political characteristics of the global ecological crisis. Finally, there is a clear focus on political economy, and the structural inequality inherent in modern capitalist economies also focused on by Marxists and dependency theorists.

However, in contrast to post-structuralism, it shares to an extent an element of modernist theorizing, in the sense that Greens are clearly trying to understand the world in order to make it possible to improve it. For Hovden (1999; 2006) or Weber (2006), this makes it more compatible with Frankfurt School-type critical theory and feminism than with post-structuralism, as these both have a clear emancipatory normative goal, and in particular a clearer sense that their explanations or interpretations of the world are connected to a clear political project. This is linked to post-structuralism's rejection of foundationalism, which marks a clear difference from Green politics that necessarily relies on fairly strong foundational claims, of both the epistemological and ethical variety. However, this argument should not be pushed too far, as there are also tensions with the way in which critical theory tries to reconstruct Enlightenment rationality. Eckersley, for example (1992: chapter 5), makes much of attempts by Habermas in particular (she contrasts Habermas to Marcuse) to reclaim science for radical political purposes, suggesting that it necessarily ends up justifying human domination of nature. I would ultimately concur with Mantle (1999), who argues that the closest connections that Green theory has to other approaches in International Relations are to feminism.

Green theory therefore clearly has its own distinctive perspective. The focus on humanity–nature relations and the adoption of an eco-centric ethic with regard to those relations, the focus on limits to growth, the particular perspective on the destructive side of development and the focus on decentralization away from the nation-state are all unique to Green politics. This chapter has illustrated how the purpose of Green theory within International Relations is to provide an explanation of the ecological crisis facing humanity, to focus on that crisis as possibly the most important issue for human societies to deal with, and to provide a normative basis for dealing with it.

12 | **International Political Theory**

TERRY NARDIN

Nothing stands still in the world of international politics and that is also true of theories about international politics. This chapter examines some of the ideas that compose the domain of international political theory, with the aim, as in other chapters in this book, of presenting an up-to-date overview and guide to further study. I give special attention to ideas about global justice because they are increasingly central to that domain. And because the history of international political thought continues to be a lively area of inquiry, I give some attention to recent work in that area as well.

Theorizing international politics

Readers of this book might be puzzled by the title of Martin Wight's famous essay, 'Why is There No International Theory?' Published on the eve of a vast expansion of academic theorizing on international relations, the essay is often used as a point of departure in discussing the field. The present book is no exception. As Scott Burchill and Andrew Linklater suggest in their introduction, we can no longer assume – or as Wight did, even provocatively assert – that there is no international relations theory. The theorizing of the past 50 years, which is covered in this book and to which Wight himself contributed, invites us to re-examine his verdict that 'international theory is marked, not only by paucity but also by intellectual and moral poverty' (Wight 1966a: 20). No one who has read the preceding chapters will complain that there is too little of it! But what of Wight's charge of intellectual and moral poverty?

I can imagine readers voicing a complaint often brought against theory in any field: that international relations theory is arcane, obscure, and irrelevant to practical concerns. But the complaint says more about misplaced expectations than about theory itself. Theorizing, by digging beneath the surface to question presuppositions, demands new ways of thinking and yields unfamiliar conclusions. Thinking about an activity, including political activity, is not the same as engaging in it. Because the aims of theorizing are different from the practical aims of making decisions and taking actions, the theories that are most relevant to practice may be the least genuinely theoretical (Brown 2010). Much of what is called political theory is no more than ordinary opinion turned into a doctrine or ideology, which is in turn applied to conduct. If theorizing criticizes ordinary ways of thinking, it cannot be the criterion of successful theorizing that its conclusions are validated by common sense.

Wight found examples of international theory in the writings of statesmen and diplomats, international lawyers, peace advocates, theorists of reason of state, philosophers and historians. If we survey the half century that has passed since his essay was published, we can find additional examples in each of these categories, but it is the writings of those he calls 'philosophers and historians' that have altered the theoretical landscape most. Moral and political philosophers have written extensively on international affairs during this period, as have historians of political thought, and their work has been critical and illuminating. We must also consider a body of writing that Wight does not mention, in what appears to be a deliberate snub: the writing of academic international relations specialists. Wight found little to admire in the emerging discipline of International Relations, which seemed to him to combine a misguided scientism with mere journalism (Hall 2006: 88–97). Although that charge would be harder to sustain today, it is the work of the philosophers and historians whose efforts have shaped what is now called 'international political theory', not that of mainstream international relations theorists, that has done most to refute the charge of intellectual and moral poverty.

The philosophers who wrote on international affairs in the 1960s addressed practical questions arising from nuclear deterrence, the Vietnam War, and famines in Africa. Attention to such questions marked a turn away from the moral philosophy of the 1950s, which had focused on the definition and foundation of moral judgement. Whatever its origins, the turn to 'applied ethics' soon became self-perpetuating as philosophers responded to each other's arguments and as issues like nationalism and terrorism were added to the agenda. Today, it is hard even for specialists to keep up with the flood of writing on human rights, humanitarian intervention, economic inequality, and other ethically significant topics. Philosophers writing on these topics see themselves as contributing to 'ethics and international affairs' or 'international ethics', though many would acknowledge that the subject has a distinctly *political* character that is sometimes overlooked when the focus is on *ethics* (Williams 2005; Geuss 2008). We neglect the political when we assume that principles of interpersonal ethics can be applied without change to relations between states (Graham 2008: 35–8). 'The domestic analogy', which treats international relations as analogous to relations between persons, can result in arguments that ignore its institutional aspects. Rescuing a community from poverty is not the same as pulling a child from a pond. 'International ethics' is therefore a misleading name for inquiry into the rights and wrongs of international affairs, which requires that we distinguish between moral and institutional duties and recognize, with philosophers from Aristotle onwards, that politics (which certainly includes international politics) is a distinct sphere of activity whose principles are not necessarily those of individual conduct (Kant 1999: 22–7). Institutions create special obligations that can modify, even if they do not erase, general or non-institutional ('natural') duties, which means that justice in civil or international society cannot be reduced to natural justice but must include duties imposed by civil and international law.

Because it acknowledges the claims of politics as well as morality, the expression 'international political theory' is preferable to 'international ethics' as a way of identifying the subject. The former also implies a bit more distance between theory and practice: whereas international ethics is often understood to be normative or applied ethics – the practical activity of guiding and judging action – international political theory puts the emphasis on *theorizing* as distinct from judging and acting. Instead of using moral principles, whose validity is presupposed, to reach a practical conclusion (a decision or a prescription), the theorist questions those principles to uncover the assumptions underlying them. Theorizing aims not at approving or disapproving choices, or recommending or dissuading action, but at understanding the grounds on which choices are made, defended and judged.

Many today would reject both expressions, however, arguing that politics is increasingly global in a world in which transnational networks and other modes of 'global governance' are replacing traditional inter-state diplomacy. For them, globalization involves changes that will eventually erase the subject of this book by transforming the international system into a global one. But even if states retain their identity and independence, one can question conventional understandings of sovereignty or the moral significance of national boundaries. International political theory must be understood to include 'cosmopolitan' theorizing that challenges state-centric assumptions (Beardsworth 2011). We need, then, to consider the implications of globalization for international political theory, paying particular attention to the emergence of 'global justice' as a focus of debate (Nardin 2011c).

Historians as well as philosophers have contributed to international political theory in recent decades by bringing professional standards to the study of past ideas. Many scholars in the field of international relations, in contrast, have had little interest in the past except as a source of ideas for present use. Some claim legitimacy for their own views by linking them to those of an adopted canonical ancestor, as when political realists appeal to the authority of Thucydides and Hobbes or internationalists and cosmopolitans invoke Grotius and Kant. But attention to the past can be strikingly unhistorical when a discipline looks for founders or seeks to recruit past thinkers to current causes. Although efforts to find a useable past continue, there is emerging within the discipline of International Relations a genuinely historical concern with both the discipline itself and the ideas of those who thought about international affairs before there was a discipline. Historical scholarship is revising our understanding of just war theory, the realism–idealism debate, the tension between states systems and empires as ways of organizing regional and world politics, and many other topics. Such scholarship challenges the assumptions about sovereignty and the belief in progress that Wight thought were characteristic of international theorizing and that have distorted many previous efforts to write the history of international thought. Historians today do not write progressive or other meta-narratives, despite the persistence of such narratives in the popular literature under titles like 'the end of history' or 'the clash of civilizations'. A more sophisticated approach to intellectual history has led to the recovery of forgotten texts and greater attention to particular ideas, thinkers and discourses in place of comprehensive histories of international thought, as detailed in the final section of this chapter.

The approaches that I have distinguished are not entirely separate from one another. There is no sharp line between the ethical and the political, the international and the global, or the philosophical and the historical. Nor are these approaches entirely separate from those treated in preceding chapters. As Burchill and Linklater suggest, theories can be critical as well as explanatory. Realism and liberalism are concerned to prescribe as well as to describe foreign policy. Marxists and feminists criticize as well as explain class and gender systems. Green theory has both ethical and explanatory concerns. Wight and other members of the English School emphasized the moral and historical aspects of international relations at a time when American scholars were reinventing the discipline in scientific terms. In seeing the subject through humanistic rather than scientific lenses, they have received support from constructivism, which pays attention to norms. But constructivists have on the whole been more concerned with how norms shape choices than with the ethical content of those norms, and some have been unable to avoid sliding back into scientism. And though ethical concerns appear in the writings of critical theorists and post-structuralists, both claim to reject common moral ideas such as that moral conduct rests on rational judgement or that moral principles are universal (Hutchings 2010: 54–82). In short, the character of international political theory remains contested, as do the boundaries that divide it from other approaches to international relations.

Although international political theory has emerged in recent years as an approach, it is only slowly coming into focus as a domain of inquiry distinct from international *relations* theory. One way of distinguishing the two is to say that the concerns of international political theory are 'normative' and those of international relations theory 'empirical'. But this way of making the distinction equivocates between whether it is the *object of inquiry* or the *inquiry itself* that is 'normative'. If the former, political theory is the disengaged *study* of norms; if the latter, it is an engagement to *use* norms to judge and guide conduct. The word 'empirical' is equally problematic, echoing a discredited view of science as resting on the accumulation of theory-independent facts that is in tension with the idea of empirical *theory*. International relations theory is identified in mainstream (in fact, until recently largely American) thought with scientific theorizing. But this identification is misleading because much of the discourse that goes on under that label – in this book, for example – has abandoned the scientific paradigm. It is interpretative rather than quantitative and epistemologically plural rather than wedded to the idea of a single, unshakeable foundation for knowledge. The distinction between international relations theory and international political theory is eroding along with the normative versus empirical distinction formerly accepted by theorists on both sides of the divide (Snidal and Wendt 2009), as evidenced by the establishment of a new, broad church 'Theory Section' within the International Studies Association. Also eroding is the assumption that the study of international relations can ignore past theorizing, which sought to explain as well as to prescribe, and generated explanations that are not necessarily inferior to our own. Nor can it ignore ideas from societies beyond the West. In short, international political theory connects mainstream international relations theorizing with moral questions, with the political issues posed by globalization, and with the history of international thought, including that of non-Western peoples. Its concerns – ethical, institutional and historical – are central to the activity of theorizing about international relations.

International political theory is most genuinely theoretical when it moves beyond making moral judgements or offering policy prescriptions to question the assumptions on which such judgements or prescriptions rest. Political theorists do many sorts of things, but the vocation of the theorist is not that of a citizen or politician in academic dress but of an observer who stands back from politics to understand it better. The political theorist, *qua* theorist, is a spectator, not a participant in the theatre of events, and in that sense is closer to the scientist or historian than to the practitioner. This is not a prescriptive claim but rather an effort to capture what distinguishes theoretical from other kinds of investigation and, especially, theorizing from advocacy. But such detachment is hard to achieve, and one must be prepared to acknowledge one's own commitments and biases or risk hypocrisy and self-deception.

Justice in war

Theories are the outcome of theorizing, and theorizing often starts with ordinary experience, which may raise questions about received beliefs or invite efforts to give those beliefs a stable foundation. Plato captures this aspect of theorizing well in his parable of the cave, in which through an effort of 'turning around' its prisoners learn that what they had assumed were real figures are only shadows projected on the wall in front of them. When, unchained, they rise and walk through the cave and then out into the sunlight, they see things from new angles and with sharper clarity. It is the same for the theorist of international relations who, by questioning the idea of sovereignty or the distinction between foreign and domestic affairs, gains a fresh view of the subject. Whether we start by examining naive experience or sophisticated interpretation, our aim in theorizing is to question the beliefs that are the subject of our inquiry so that we can better understand and possibly transcend them.

What has come to be called just war theory illustrates this activity of theorizing. In some cases, it begins with a simple judgement ('they are the aggressor, our cause is just'), in others with a complex proposition like the so-called principle of double effect ('it is permissible to harm non-combatant civilians provided the harm done is not one's end, nor a means to that end, and does not unfairly distribute costs between those inflicting and those suffering the harm'). Examining such arguments, we refine or reject them or come to understand how they are related to other arguments by uncovering their presuppositions. A theoretical inquiry seldom ends by simply affirming the original judgement.

It makes sense to discuss justice in war before turning to international or global justice, for several reasons. First, war is 'pre-international', by which I mean that it antedates the modern states system and occurs within as well as between states (Keegan 1993; Keeley 1996). Second, unlike the distributive principles that are contested in debates over economic or social justice, the principles of just war theory are clear, consistent, and relatively stable, even if those principles are often misunderstood or deliberately misused. And third, thinking about war allows us to begin not with a theory but with the actual or vicarious experience of fighting. The reader of military history or war memoirs, or even someone who watches war movies or plays video games, acquires some knowledge of war and its *mores,* and that knowledge, however vicarious, selective and distorted, can invite critical reflection – even if it often doesn't. Thinking about who fights or plays war games, for example, suggests that war is a highly gendered experience and invites reflection on how far gender categories might pervade the larger field of international relations. Memoirs or biographies not only of soldiers but of citizens forced to respond to the exigencies of wartime provide another path into the subject (Zahn 1986; Hallie 1994). There is a phenomenology of war, moving from the experience of combat or resistance to reflections on cruelty, loyalty, friendship and guilt, unmediated by the abstractions of just war ethics that can provide a useful corrective to those abstractions (Gray 1959).

Let's start with an intuitive judgement and work toward the principles that can explain and justify it. The word 'atrocity' comes pre-packaged with the judgement that any act so described is morally wrong. The 1940 Katyn Forest massacre, in which the Soviets killed 8,000 Polish officers together with twice that number of civilians, would have been hard to justify – the murders were, in fact, covered up. Efforts have been made to *excuse* those who killed at least 400 civilians, including many children, at My Lai in Vietnam in 1968, but it is not seriously argued that the killings were morally *justified*. In every war women are the victims of rape, but the rationalizations that are occasionally offered merely highlight the atrocity. Implicit in the idea of atrocity is the principle that innocent people should not be deliberately killed or abused. But this principle can be examined as well as used. What, for example, is meant by the words 'innocent' and 'deliberately'? One answer is that 'innocent', in this context, means not *nocentes* (Latin), not 'engaged in harming' (as the victims at My Lai certainly were not), and therefore not properly subject to violence (Finnis 1996: 27). 'Deliberately' means that the deaths were not inadvertent but were planned and carried out as a matter of policy, either as an end in itself or a means to an end. The idea that innocents should not be deliberately harmed – that doing so is always wrong – was part of the laws of war long before 1940 or 1968 and is basic not only to just war ethics but to morality itself, as morality is often understood. Those laws forbid deliberately killing unarmed and unresisting soldiers and civilians, thereby formalizing a basic moral idea as the principle of 'non-combatant immunity' (Walzer 1977: 133–7; Koontz 1997). By clarifying the grounds for calling something an atrocity, we come to understand some important principles of just war theory.

All principles are provisional, however. They can be criticized, modified or rejected. If we allow that it is wrong to kill civilians and non-combatant soldiers (such as prisoners of war), does this mean that killing soldiers in combat is *not* an atrocity? Because they are fighting, soldiers are not 'innocent' (as that word is defined by the laws of war), and for that reason we do not usually regard their deaths in combat as murder. But some philosophers have questioned that judgement along with the definition of innocence on which it rests, arguing that conscripts or child soldiers (for example) are forced labourers unjustly pushed into combat by their superiors. Such soldiers become 'innocent attackers' whose deaths in battle are as atrocious as the deaths of non-combatants. Others defend the conventional view that soldiers lose their immunity to harm, arguing, for example, that their actions pose a material threat to those they are attacking which the latter are entitled to resist in self-defence, and that killing them in the course of that resistance is therefore not murder. Still others argue that the deaths of soldiers are a foreseeable, even if not wished-for, effect of resisting an enemy state whose unwilling agents they sometimes happen to be. On this view, if the principle of double effect can justify the deaths of bystanders it can also justify the deaths of combatants. In the course of the debate, which in recent years has grown increasingly abstruse, it has become evident that principles of national defence are different from those of individual self-defence and that the analogy between states and persons can take one only so far (Rodin 2002; McMahan 2009). Whatever its outcome, the debate illustrates the theorist's characteristic inclination to *not* take conventional distinctions for granted.

Conscription or the use of child soldiers raises the issue of culpability. People are sometimes excused from responsibility for wrongs they commit if they acted in ignorance or under duress. Those who fight are sometimes lied to, threatened, drugged or brainwashed. So questions of responsibility and culpability cannot be avoided in war any more than in other areas of life. Such questions are distinct from questions of justification. Arguing that a soldier who deliberately kills civilians on the orders of a superior is not guilty of murder might excuse the killer from responsibility but it cannot justify the killing. There is a difference between justifying an action as right and excusing the perpetrator of an action admitted to be wrong. Just how responsibility for war crimes (and, more generally, crimes against humanity) should be conceived and enforced has been a matter of great practical and theoretical interest since the Nuremberg trials following the Second World War (Robertson 2006).

What we call 'the just war tradition' is simply the record of an ongoing discussion about how just and unjust uses of military force should be distinguished. It is often contrasted with two other traditions, pacifism and political realism, that question the distinction between just and unjust wars. The three traditions – pacifism, just war, and political realism – comprise a continuum of progressively more permissive attitudes toward the use of military force.

For many pacifists, war means killing and killing is inherently wrong. All wars are unjust. But not all versions of pacifism reach this conclusion. The one that comes closest we might call 'moral pacifism': it is morally wrong for *me* to kill, which means I cannot serve in any war. This, however, is an individual ethic, not a policy. It is the view of early pre-Constantine Christians and in modern times of Mennonites and Quakers (Koontz 1996). It should be distinguished from a commitment to abolish the institution of war. Abolitionism is based not only on moral revulsion against war but also on doubts about its utility. But unlike moral pacifists, abolitionists don't refuse on principle to fight. Instead they focus on transformation by emphasizing the moral duty to establish arrangements that will make war less likely (Bok 1989). Finally, there is a kind of pacifism, sometimes called 'non-violence', that urges passive resistance to aggression as an alternative to armed force. Non-violent power is regarded as being morally superior to using military force and sometimes as being more effective as well (Sharp 1973).

Political realism marks the other end of the continuum, and it, too, comes in several flavours. One is moral scepticism, the view that war is essentially outside the realm of moral judgement. Another is reason of state, the view that war is an instrument of national policy, which implies confidence in the utility of armed force, properly used. The decision to make war should be dictated by prudence, in the sense of the ability to anticipate consequences, not morality. A prudent weighing of costs and benefits suggests that force should be necessary and proportionate. But no method of violence is absolutely forbidden if it meets these criteria. Realism should not be confused with militarism, which glorifies war or defends it on religious or ideological grounds without appealing to necessity or national defence. The line between realism and militarism can nevertheless be hard to discern. 'Glory' for the ancient Romans and for Renaissance humanists like Machiavelli could be a means of defence as well as an end in itself: the glorious victor, like the breast-pounding gorilla, ensures his dominance by overawing potential rivals. How these various kinds of realism are related to one another as well as to other theories identified as realist (such as the explanatory theories or epistemologies of 'structural', 'neo' or 'critical' realism) remains a matter of ongoing discussion (Jørgensen 2010).

Unlike pacifism, just war thinking does not reject the use of force in principle or deny its efficacy. Unlike realism, it does not exclude war from the jurisdiction of morality and law. Decisions to use force must respond to considerations of moral principle as well as to those of prudential calculation. Interest alone cannot dictate when and how a state makes war. There are justified and unjustified uses of force and therefore just and unjust wars. And just as there are different versions of pacifism and realism, there are also different strands within the just war tradition, each a historically distinguishable discourse of war.

One strand of just war thinking descends from medieval Christian theories of natural law, most influentially expressed in the writings of St Thomas Aquinas. Aquinas distilled a complex debate about the ethics of war down to three principles: just cause, proper authority and right intention (Barnes 1982; Russell 2010). The just cause requirement is that a war must aim at righting a wrong – for example, defending a community against aggression – or punishing that wrong. But the Thomistic tradition has moved away from the idea that one state can lawfully punish another, for that would make the punishing state both a party to the dispute and its judge (Finnis 1996: 20–4; Boyle 2006: 38–41). As this implies, having a just cause is not enough; one must also be authorized to fight. A government can ask its citizens to defend the community, but the government of one state has no authority to punish the government or people of another. And because Thomistic just war theory is a moral theory, not merely a theory of external law, it adds a third criterion, right intention, which refers to the internal motive or spirit in which one fights. It is implicit in this principle not only that one must not be motivated by hatred or the pleasures of battle but also that the innocent must not be intentionally harmed.

A second strand of just war thinking treats international law as a distinct legal order. When international law was linked to natural law, legal and moral arguments were not clearly distinguished. But from the beginning of the nineteenth century, international law has had its own sources and modes of argument. International lawyers and just war moralists agree that self-defence by states against foreign aggression is justifiable but sometimes disagree on the question of humanitarian intervention. The lawyers feel compelled to argue that international law forbids humanitarian intervention because coercive intervention – the exercise of authority by one state within the jurisdiction of another without the latter's permission – violates its sovereignty (Byers 2005: 89–111). The moralists, in contrast, are inclined to defend humanitarian intervention because they see sovereignty as justified only to the degree that it protects the rights and well-being of the subjects of a sovereign state (Walzer 1977: 108; Nardin 2012). This principle of responsible sovereignty also undergirds many accounts of self-defence: a state may defend itself against aggression because it provides an order that protects its inhabitants. Not everyone shares this understanding of the modern state, however. There are Jews who do not recognize the state of Israel because it was founded by human force before the coming of the Messiah. Medieval Muslim theory, embraced by

Islamists today, does not recognize territorial states on the European model. Instead, it distinguishes the realm of faith from the realm of worldly affairs, which is one of discord and war (Hashmi 2002). The statist (or 'legalist') strand of just war thinking therefore presumes a view of the proper ordering of human affairs that differs from other views, within and beyond the West (Brekke 2006).

Statism pulls just war theory toward political realism, but there is a limit to convergence. For the political realist, every state is entitled to preserve itself, which means that a war can be just on both sides because even an aggressor might fight to preserve its independence. This 'relativism of patriotism', as it has been called (Tuck 1999: 31–4), is not the claim that each side thinks its cause is just. It is the more radical claim that a war can actually *be* just on both sides. It is in denying this claim that even statist versions of just war theory are distinguished from political realism. In just war theory, one side is an aggressor, the other a defender. The aggressor is a criminal whom the defender can justly resist. But the aggressor does not always strike first, for aggression can occur without force having been used. A state should be able to defend itself against the threat of imminent attack but it cannot justly wage preventive war against a powerful but not (yet) aggressive neighbour. The distinction between pre-emption and prevention is a relative one – the line between them shifts its position depending on contingencies – but there is still some distance between a limited doctrine of pre-emption and the claim that a government can do whatever it thinks is necessary to deal with security threats (Shue and Rodin 2007). The tilt of 'political' just war theory toward political realism is most evident in arguments for overriding just war limits in situations of supreme emergency or where nuclear deterrence, which rests on the threat to kill innocent people, is concerned. Here the theory comes close to, or collapses into, reason of state (Walzer 2004: 33–50; Finnis, Boyle, and Grisez 1987).

The argument that moral limits must give way in emergencies is often advanced to justify extreme measures in response to suicide bombing attacks and other kinds of terrorism. Consequentialist arguments for choosing 'the lesser evil' in what has been construed after 9/11 as 'the global war on terrorism', including arguments for violating basic civil rights or legalizing torture in 'ticking bomb' situations, have been revived and also challenged (Ramraj 2008; Cohen 2012). Such debates, apart from their practical importance, not only force us to rethink the relationship between justice and expediency but reveal different understandings of justice itself.

International justice

As just war theory illustrates, one way to understand justice in the international system is by means of an analogy with the idea of the state as an association of citizens. Just as citizens must avoid interfering in one another's affairs, states too must practice non-interference. States are politically independent or 'sovereign' and must not interfere forcibly in one another's affairs except to thwart unjustified interference. International law forbids 'aggression' (the wrongful use of force against another state) and 'intervention' (the wrongful use of force within the territory of another state). But there is also a significant disanalogy: unlike civil society, the society of states is without a superior to define and enforce the rights of its members. It is, in the words of Hedley Bull, an 'anarchical society' – anarchical in that it is without a central authority but still a society ordered by common interests and rules (Bull 1977). Framed in this way, the theory of international society, like just war theory, can be seen as rejecting both statist political realism and a state-denying cosmopolitanism in favour of a middle ground ethics that takes the power and rights of states into account while prescribing limits on what states can do internally as well as externally (Nardin 2011b). The revived fashion for political realism in international political thought does not necessarily challenge this view (Bell 2008).

The idea of international society continues to provide a point of departure for theorists, generating a debate between 'pluralists', who argue that international society presupposes only common rules that states agree to respect, and 'solidarists', who argue that international society rests (or should rest) on shared goals that states cooperate to promote. The standard charge of pluralism against solidarism is that it improperly suppresses cultural differences and limits the liberty of states by imposing religious or political uniformity (Nardin 1983: 309–24). The standard charge of solidarism against pluralism is that it arbitrarily privileges sovereignty and offers an unacceptably thin concept of global justice. Solidarists argue that the pluralist idea of international co-existence on the basis of common rules might have been acceptable in the past but 'cannot be applied satisfactorily to the conditions of global political life in the twenty-first century, which require the identification of substantive collective goals and the creation of institutionalized structures of governance to implement them' (Hurrell 2007: 298).

A much-discussed defence of the pluralist conception of international justice is that advanced by John Rawls in *The Law of Peoples* (1999). Rawls thinks political, economic and cultural differences among nations are tolerable, provided such differences are consistent with principles that all can accept as a reasonable basis for public order. These principles, which are incorporated into contemporary international law, require states to respect one another's political sovereignty and territorial integrity, observe treaty obligations and limits on the conduct of war, and cooperate in assisting 'burdened' states to become more just internally by alleviating poverty, corruption and other problems. States may use force only in self-defence or for generally acknowledged humanitarian ends. This principle reflects the moral imperative to suppress both international and internal violence: states should not tolerate aggression or internal crimes against humanity if they can deter or suppress such conduct. The pluralism that remains when such violence has been thwarted is the pluralism of a just international order. Global justice does not require that states disappear. Nor, Rawls argues, does it require that every state observe liberal democratic principles. What it does require is that states with different political traditions must co-exist on the basis of principles (roughly those of international law) that respect such differences within reasonable limits.

Against this pluralism, Rawls's critics argue that a morally legitimate international order is one whose members are morally legitimate states (Buchanan 2004). If liberal principles are valid internally, they apply internationally as well (Beitz 1979; Barry 1998). A morally legitimate international society cannot tolerate morally illegitimate states as members. And a legitimate state violates its own principles if it accepts illegitimate ones as equal members of international society (Tan 2000). The critics differ, however, on what they mean by liberal principles. Some think a morally legitimate state is one that protects basic human rights, others that only liberal democratic states are morally legitimate. For Rawls and other pluralists, such arguments rest on an indefensibly narrow definition of legitimacy. The principles that provide the basis for civil order in one society are not necessarily appropriate for other societies. For Rawls, liberal democratic principles constitute a 'comprehensive doctrine' suitable for ordering a liberal democracy. But the liberalism that is appropriate to international society – 'political liberalism' – respects the right of people in different societies to live according to their own comprehensive doctrines. Just as liberal democracy prescribes respect for non-liberal persons and groups internally, provided they obey the law, so political liberalism at the international level prescribes respect for non-liberal societies, provided those societies obey international law (which now requires that they respect and protect certain human rights internally). The principles of political liberalism rest on the idea of 'public reason', which requires that when arguing across doctrinal lines liberals must frame their arguments so as to find the common ground. In this, Rawls is not far from Jürgen Habermas and others who connect justice with principles that emerge in discussion within a free public realm (Linklater 1998). To insist that all peoples govern themselves according to liberal democratic principles is at best parochial and at worst barbaric.

Framing the dispute between pluralists and solidarists as a debate over the definition of moral legitimacy helps us to see that a central issue is the limits of international toleration. Both sides draw a line beyond which a state can be forcibly resisted, but they draw that line in different places. The pluralist would rule out aggression or crimes against humanity but thinks it is permissible to tolerate less serious moral breaches. The solidarist thinks that violating a wider range of human rights or democratic principles puts a regime beyond the pale. Today, in short, a broad consensus exists that a defensible theory of global justice must locate itself in the middle ground between the extremes of statism and cosmopolitanism (Ypi 2011; Valentini 2011).

There is a long tradition of seeking to accommodate pluralism and solidarism (or statism and cosmopolitanism) through an ascending scale of political orders. Kant, for example, distinguishes between two kinds of international association. The first is composed of states that recognize the principle of national self-determination, are willing to renounce aggression, intervention, and atrocities in war, and are committed to reducing the influence of what would later be called 'the military-industrial complex' by avoiding standing armies and a huge military debt. The second – a subset of the first, composed of states that meet a higher standard – is an international association whose members uphold the rule of law internally and in their relations with one another (Kant 1991: 93–108). Kant's distinction is reflected in the contrast between the European Union, a confederation of rule-of-law states, and the United Nations, a looser association whose members are not necessarily rule-of-law states, though all are committed (or pretend to be committed) to co-existence. Rawls offers a similar typology, in which what he calls 'well-ordered peoples' are capable of achieving a level of justice in their relations with one another that cannot be achieved in their relations with societies that are not well-ordered. The well-ordered category includes, besides liberal democracies, societies with consultative hierarchical regimes that respect religious freedom and other basic human rights and give people some input into governing. Societies that are not well-ordered are absolutist, corrupt, ineffective or violent. Like Kant, who sees minimal co-existence being replaced by cooperation among states committed to the rule of law (Kant 1991: 108–14), Rawls envisions an expanding community of well-ordered states (Rawls 1999: 44–54) that might gradually replace less just forms of international association.

Rawls's theory of international justice has renewed the debate on the limits of pluralism (Martin and Reidy 2006), but has not significantly altered it. What Rawls has done is provide a new vocabulary to augment the existing discourse of human rights, which is also concerned with the moral legitimacy of states and the limits of sovereignty. That discourse is based not on the domestic analogy but on a more nuanced understanding of the state that distinguishes between governments and citizens and holds governments accountable for how they treat citizens as well as other persons – resident aliens, refugees or prisoners of war, for example – over whom they have jurisdiction.

The idea of humanitarian intervention illustrates this point. Some dismiss the idea of intervening to protect the inhabitants of another state as impractical, even if morally justified, in a world ordered by the pursuit of national interests. But this dismissal overlooks the moral and theoretical significance of that idea. Humanitarian intervention can be defined as the use of force by one state within the territory of another without the latter's consent, with the aim of protecting people who are not nationals of the intervening state from violence committed or permitted by the government of the target state. One question about humanitarian intervention is whether it is permissible under international law. Those who rely on the UN Charter say 'no'; others, who look to customary international law, are less certain (Weiss 2007). Another question is whether, leaving international law aside, humanitarian intervention is morally permissible. When does a state have the right to use military force inside the territory of another state? The question challenges both the non-intervention principle and the domestic analogy on which it rests. According to that analogy, if citizens must respect one another's autonomy and bodily integrity, states must respect one another's political sovereignty and territorial integrity. If one state has the right to manage its own affairs free of interference by other states, other states have no right to exercise their authority, which includes using force, inside its territory. On this view, intervention, for any purpose, is an act of aggression. But this blanket ban on intervention forgets the justification of political sovereignty and territorial integrity: that states exist to protect security and well-being. If a state violates basic human rights, or allows them to be violated, this justification ceases and the offending state forfeits its immunity to foreign intervention. It cannot invoke its sovereignty to justify violence or incompetence.

When a government fails to protect those it governs from violence, their rights do not disappear. The duty to defend those rights falls on others, and intervention can be a way to perform it. This duty rests in part on the principle of beneficence, which prescribes assisting others when one can do so without disproportionate inconvenience, and especially when the need is great – as in situations of natural disaster or collective violence. It also rests on the duty to resist injustice when one can. We cannot simply transplant these principles from the interpersonal to the international level, but neither can we plausibly deny that they ground a general duty to protect others from violence, and that fulfilling this duty might sometimes require international action. One of the challenges of humanitarian intervention is to decide who has a duty to intervene. Does the duty fall on certain states, on every state equally, or on organizations representing the international community? How can an abstract general duty become the special duty of a particular agent? Some argue that the duty to protect people from violence can be performed only by agencies that have been authorized and equipped to perform it. In that case, a general duty to resist violence becomes the specific duty of that agency to intervene militarily (Tan 2006). Today, it is increasingly recognized that each state has a 'responsibility to protect' which, if it is unable to perform, passes to the international community and its representatives for action (Evans 2008; Bellamy 2008).

The debate over humanitarian intervention illustrates how the ideas of sovereignty and non-intervention change when we look beneath the surface of state sovereignty to discover its moral rationale. When we qualify the non-intervention principle to make it consistent with that rationale we prescribe not only a duty to respect human rights but also a duty to prevent others from violating them. International justice therefore requires not only that states treat other states justly, as the domestic analogy would imply, but also that they concern themselves with the rights and well-being of people even against their own governments. This formula makes explicit the 'cosmopolitan' basis of 'international' justice. A politically legitimate state is one that can claim immunity from intervention because it does not grossly abuse the rights of those it governs, even if it fails to meet a higher moral standard.

Pluralists as well as solidarists, then, are concerned with the moral character of states, which they do not dismiss as irrelevant (as a moral sceptic would) or take as given (as would a defender of reason of state). Those who hold either of those positions are called political realists, but the positions are distinct and in fact incompatible. Political realism as an ethical doctrine challenges the view that those who govern may not do evil for the sake of good. It is distinguished by the claim that defending a state justifies its government in violating moral limits. Realist ethics is consequentialist because it makes consequences alone the criterion of whether an action is right. But unlike utilitarianism, which focuses on the welfare of humanity as a whole, realism is concerned with the welfare of a particular state. It does not follow, however, that political realists must reject morality. They may grant it provisional authority yet argue that moral considerations must yield to necessity. Most realists distinguish between situations in which moral principles obligate and those in which they may be violated, but they differ on where the boundary lies. Some suggest it separates private from public affairs, others domestic from foreign affairs – as Wight does when he writes that 'international theory is the theory of survival' (Wight 1966a: 33). But some realists do allow a place for morality in foreign affairs: in the 'low politics' of economic policy in contrast to the 'high politics' of national defence, for example, or in the ordinary conduct of war as opposed to the conduct of war in situations of 'supreme emergency' that invite leaders to act immorally.

Realist views can also be distinguished according to whether they hold that expediency in defending a state makes an action 'just' or that justice must simply yield to expediency. Arguably the latter is the more consistent view. Where prudential judgements estimate the probability and value of outcomes, moral judgements interpret the meaning of principles. Clear-headed realists distinguish between justice and policy, that is, between acting on the basis of principle and acting expediently to promote national or international interests. A policy of pursuing the balance of power can be moralized by presenting it as a response to aggression, but statesmen from Pitt the Younger to Churchill have understood it with more honesty as a necessarily ruthless way to preserve the states system from imperial hegemony.

Global justice

The word 'global' seems to be displacing the word 'international' in many contexts, but there is little agreement on what it means. Global can be a synonym for universal or cosmopolitan, but its spatial and temporal connotations, which evoke this planet in our epoch, undercut the claim to universality. These ambiguities carry over into the expression 'global justice', which has yet to acquire an agreed meaning. In some cases, it identifies a residual category that includes everything pertaining to justice in world affairs except justice in war, a topic often and perplexingly excluded from books with global justice in the title (Jones 1999; Pogge and Moellendorf 2008). In others, it marks a debate about the limits of cultural difference or the moral significance of national boundaries (Tan 2000). For many, global justice is distributive justice or, more broadly, a moral duty to relieve poverty. For others it is retributive justice administered through a regime of international criminal law under which people are held accountable for war crimes and other human rights abuses (Robertson 2006). Efforts have been made to link the themes of just war, humanitarian duty, economic inequality, cultural diversity and political order (e.g. Caney 2005) but, in the absence of a precise definition of justice and a systematic theoretical framework, the global justice project must be regarded as unfinished. The obscurity of the words 'global' and 'justice' is not lessened simply by putting them together. The question, then, is whether the expression 'global justice' is something other than a catchall.

Two ideas are necessary if the idea of global justice is to be made coherent. One is the idea of universal moral principles prescribing how people should treat one another as human beings, not as members of a particular community. These principles constitute what was once called natural law and is now called human rights, though the two ideas or traditions are in many ways distinct (Beattie 2010). As these expressions imply, principles of global justice prescribe obligations for everyone whether or not everyone acknowledges their authority: it is not permissible to violate them, regardless of local norms. If this reasoning is sound, a theory of global justice must be 'cosmopolitan' in the sense that it is based on universal moral principles.

The second idea we need is the idea of duty. To say that something is a matter of justice is to say that it involves a duty, which implies a body of law – moral or positive – on which the duty is based. This law also grounds the rights of those to whom the duty is owed. Justice is a virtue and implies a standard of conduct but it is not the only virtue or standard. We need to distinguish what is just from what is virtuous or desirable on other grounds. Not all moral principles, even universal ones, are properly enforceable and therefore a matter of 'justice' – some are principles of utility, humanity, generosity, compassion, courage, honour, or other values. An act may be desirable as a matter of personal virtue or public policy, yet fall outside the realm of justice. Principles of justice prescribe moral duties that could properly be prescribed by positive law as well (Nardin 2005, 2006). Central to any effort to theorize global justice in this way must be a theory of morally permissible coercion. One theorist who has explored this path is Immanuel Kant (Ripstein 2009).

Principles of global justice, then, are universal moral principles that could, without moral impropriety, be enforced as part of civil, international or supranational law. An old debate is whether global justice can be achieved through international law or requires supranational institutions whose authority would supersede that of states. Some argue that global justice can only be secured by moving toward a global order. States are no longer able to respond effectively to problems that affect them because these problems are now global rather than local, or because justice can be realized only within a legal order, which means that global justice requires a global legal order. Others argue that achieving global justice will require new political arrangements because states as we know them are morally illegitimate. Whether global justice is achievable on the basis of international law is a question that depends in part on contingent judgements that are not the job of the theorist to make. Whether a legal order is morally legitimate is a question that does, however, concern the theorist. Provided its laws are reasonably just, a state can be morally legitimate even though those laws are coercive because they are the outcome of collective choices, just as the state itself is the product of such choices. The requirement that the state be just arises from the coercive character of political association, for to enforce unjust laws would be to violate the freedom of the associates. A theory of global justice therefore cannot ignore the rights of states, for these rights are grounded on the moral rights of those who choose to live according to their laws. Nor can it ignore international law, whose authority derives from the rights of states. A society of states is no less legitimate than a single global society. To put it differently, if territorial states are illegitimate, it is hard to see how a global state could be legitimate.

The tension between state-centric and global frameworks for international justice is evident in the debate over economic inequality. A generation ago, that debate centred on the gap between rich and poor countries, the 'haves' and the 'have-nots', and on demands for a 'new international economic order' in which wealth would be redistributed from one country to another. Developed states would acknowledge the sovereign right of less-developed states to own their natural resources, seize foreign-owned assets and settle compensation claims under local law. They would agree to terms of trade more favourable to commodity-exporting countries, share their knowledge and technology, and increase their levels of foreign aid. Distributive justice in the context of this debate meant redistributing wealth and power from rich to poor countries, which is not the same as redistributing wealth within a country. Foreign aid can even increase inequality in poor countries if it is misappropriated by corrupt elites. The proposals for a new international economic order that were advanced by former colonies in the sixties and seventies did not challenge the state-centric premises of the existing international order.

Theorists of international distributive justice from the seventies onwards have argued that redistribution must be global, not international. Here once again, Rawls has been at the centre of the debate. As the leading theorist of justice after publishing *A Theory of Justice*, he disappointed those, like Brian Barry and Charles Beitz, who thought he should have applied the principles articulated in that book internationally. But Rawls never advanced principles of distributive justice beyond the liberal democratic state. (His arguments in *The Law of Peoples* for assisting burdened societies are not based on principles of distributive justice.) Rawls's original reason for ignoring the topic was that in a theory of justice as fairness, which is all that he claimed his theory was, distributive justice means the fair allocation of benefits and burdens in a society understood to be a 'cooperative venture for mutual advantage' (Rawls 1971: 4). International society is not such a venture, he argued. This claim provoked the rejoinder that economic interdependence was transforming the international system into a scheme of social cooperation by linking national economies in a single global economy. If principles of distributive justice apply within a national economy, it is inconsistent to hold that they do not apply in the world economy (Beitz 1979). But this argument had the perverse result of implying that principles of distributive justice apply most strongly between countries with tightly integrated economies, like those of Western Europe, and least between rich and poor countries with few economic ties. Instead of challenging the proposition that there is no injustice in ignoring those with whom we have minimal contact, it seemed to reinforce it. The idea that a society is a scheme of social cooperation for the production of collective benefits is in any case a highly contentious idea, one that is at odds with the liberal conception of the state as a framework for enabling the coexistence of individual wills: a civil order, not a collective enterprise. That the world might be a single society does not settle the question of what kind of society it is or ought to be.

Some argue that global distributive justice requires 'shared meanings' as the basis for an agreed 'scheme of global social cooperation' and a 'meaningful global justice community' (Walzer 1983: 29–30; Hurrell 2007: 317). For them, the ideal of global distributive justice is either a mirage or an invitation to construct the global community it requires. Others regard shared meanings as less relevant in determining duties of global justice than the consideration that human needs know no borders. If people are impoverished, those who are affluent have a duty to assist them that is independent of economic relationships or cultural affinities. The degree to which people share meanings or feel sympathy with one another may explain their willingness to help one another. It is not relevant, however, to whether they should treat each other justly (Van Parijs 2007: 644). The duty to relieve poverty is not a special obligation, like the obligation to care for our children or elderly parents; it is a general obligation premised on our common humanity. We have a duty to assist the 'distant needy' (Chatterjee 2004) as well as duties to assist those closer to home. This debate, sometimes cast as a debate between 'communitarians' and 'cosmopolitans' (Brown 1992a), has a long history and, probably, a long future.

Rawls's reply, in *The Law of Peoples*, seeks the middle ground. There is a duty to help economically burdened societies establish just and effective institutions. But principles of distributive justice that apply within a liberal state do not apply globally because they assume a comprehensive doctrine, liberal egalitarianism, that is accepted in some societies but not in others and that cannot be made a doctrine for all if legitimate cultural differences are to be respected (Rawls 1999: 105–20). As mentioned in the preceding section, the key idea for Rawls is public reason, which requires that the principles for evaluating and ameliorating global poverty should be principles acknowledged by all, not those particular to the views of liberal egalitarians (Rawls 1999: 121–8). This amounts to saying that principles of economic distribution are, within wide limits, principles of choice, not justice. They may represent a desirable goal but, unlike basic human rights and rules against violence, they do not prescribe enforceable duties.

The argument that global poverty is a matter of distributive justice presupposes a relative standard. When theorists of global justice emphasize the gap between rich and poor, they imply that injustice arises from inequality or unfair benefits (Pogge 2008) rather than from the mere fact of poverty. If everyone in the world were equally poor, there would (on this theory) be much suffering but no injustice. This has led some to conclude that relieving poverty is better viewed as a matter of humanity or beneficence than of justice (Campbell, T., 2007), a point also made by feminists who approach the topic from the standpoint of an ethics of care. The global poverty debate may be turning away from the idea of distributive justice to the ideas of freedom, capability, harm, non-domination and human rights, which may be better suited to the topic (Shapcott 2010).

As a result of efforts to replace the idea of humanitarian intervention with that of a broader 'responsibility to protect' on the part of governments and the international community, the suggestion has gained acceptance that everyone is responsible for supporting policies to reduce violence and suffering (Barry and Pogge 2005; Young 2011). David Miller relies on the concept of responsibility in framing a theory of global justice, but although he distinguishes 'moral responsibility' (by which he means culpability for wrongdoing) from responsibility in the causal sense, he does not consistently distinguish culpability from duty (Miller 2007). Arguably these are distinct: one can have a duty to do something yet not be held culpable for failing to do it on grounds of ignorance, duress, insanity, or some other condition that is believed to excuse or mitigate blame. We judge the rightness of actions considered objectively in relation to rules that prescribe duties and support claims to rights. But we also judge the responsibility of agents for actions considered subjectively, with respect to motive and the extent to which the actions are voluntary. Agents cannot be blamed for actions, no matter how wrong, unless they are responsible in this sense. Using the word 'responsibility' to encompass judgements of duty and of culpability obscures the distinction between them.

Those who debate the duty to protect are puzzled by the so-called 'agency problem': if there is an international duty to protect people from harm, whose duty is it? Duties based on capacity to protect or on ties of community are obvious candidates (Miller 2007: 103–4) but they do not resolve the agency problem when there are many agents meeting the criterion (Tan 2006: 97–102). Internationalists think that states have duties to maintain order, protect human rights, relieve poverty, settle international disputes and deal with common problems like terrorism and global warming. Globalists apportion those duties among a wider range of participants, including individuals acting through international advocacy groups in an emerging global 'civil society', state officials coordinating their activities in transnational networks, and those who make decisions in international organizations. Paralleling a concern with 'responsibility' in the discourse of global justice is a concern with 'institutions', though whether the institutions in question are legal ones is sometimes unclear (Weinstock 2005). In the past, theorists of global order took a universal legal system as the ideal toward which the world should move. Theorists of global order now talk less of law and more of 'governance', by which they mean the management of global policies in the absence of a central government.

The idea of global governance is that both public and private decisions contribute to the 'norms' – not 'laws' – that regulate world affairs. The outcome is a system of horizontal interactions in which officials in different branches of government work with counterparts in other countries and with bankers, scientists, activists and others outside government. Those who are optimistic about global governance think it can solve global problems more effectively than traditional diplomacy (Slaughter 2004). Pessimists worry that, under the conditions of complexity and speed that characterize globalization, the effect will be to weaken democracy and the rule of law (Scheuerman 2004). They argue that the idea of global governance blurs the distinction between law and non-law by relying on ideas like regulatory regimes, soft law and private authority, and that it treats law as an instrument of policy while overlooking its importance as a constraint on policy making. The distinction between law and policy vanishes when public deliberation is replaced by administrative decision making or when procedural constraints are ignored for the sake of executive efficiency. The rule of law is most starkly challenged when emergency powers are asserted, but it also suffers erosion when law is displaced by policy ('deformalization') or divided into functionally distinct regulatory regimes managed to advance particular interests ('fragmentation'). Both practices weaken the public realm and the legal order on which it depends (Koskenniemi 2007).

Mirroring the idea of the public realm within modern states is the idea of a global public realm as a space for discussing the laws of an emergent global polity (Dryzek 2011). That discussion must be theorized so as to link the idea of global justice to ideas about democracy and the rule of law. Advocates for global governance sometimes fail to grasp the importance of law for democracy, justice and rational deliberation. Democracy presupposes deliberation within a legally constituted association. Public deliberation is discussion focused on the laws of a state or other political association. Because law involves obligations, public deliberation concerns the obligations that should be imposed by law (Nardin 2011a). Theorists of global democracy overlook this point when they detach deliberation from making decisions about law, as if 'democracy' were only a matter of talk, not a legally constituted mode of government. Deliberative democracy makes sense only when what is being deliberated are the laws according to which citizens are to live together (Archibugi 2008).

The global justice debate seems to be moving beyond the claim that justice must be global *as opposed to* international. It is widely understood that universal obligations can be implemented locally, that states can have moral legitimacy, and that even if globalization is eroding sovereignty, states continue to engage the loyalty of their citizens and to do business with one another. For better or worse, international law provides a framework for ordering the globe whose rationale is both moral and pragmatic. And this means that a theory of global justice cannot ignore the rights and duties of states. Instead of choosing between the global and the international, the theorist of justice needs to consider both. And if law is to be kept in the picture, the proper focus of theorizing is not 'global governance' but global *government* through formal agreements, supranational institutions and perhaps (as theorists from Kant to Rawls have imagined) an expanding confederation of rule-of-law states, for which the European Union remains a model. The financial crisis of 2008 provides a reminder of the importance of oversight and accountability in global systems.

For the moment, global justice is the centre of attention in international political theory. One cannot help thinking, however, that from the standpoint of theory, there is less here than meets the eye. To the extent that one emphasizes the global over the international, the global justice debate risks becoming a debate about 'justice' without qualification. Too often, those who write on global justice advance familiar ideas about social justice without explaining how they are supposed to work at the global level. Or, focusing on injustice, they descend into distinctly untheoretical advocacy. Lacking historical perspective, they fail to see how their arguments are related to those of previous generations. One way forward, then, might be to gain a better understanding of the history behind current debates.

The history of international thought

Many questions prominent in the current global justice debate – the relationship between universal principles and local practices, the problem of poverty, the responsibility to protect victims of oppression, and the emergence of a global public realm – invite inquiry into earlier debates such as those over the Spanish conquest of America, international socialism, the civilizing mission of empire and the dependence of peace on enlightened public opinion. Historians of political thought have paid more attention to internal politics than to world affairs, for the most part touching on ideas about international relations only at the margins of their inquiries. But significant studies of international themes, thinkers and texts have appeared in recent years. International political thought is no longer a marginal concern.

Intellectual history in a given field depends in part on identifying relevant texts, though ideas and arguments are equally important. Shortly before World War I, the Carnegie Institution began a project of editing and translating what it saw, not always correctly, as the foundational texts of international law, and although one can question their selection and scholarship these editions remain useful. The writings of Vattel, Kant, Burke, Mill and many other thinkers on international affairs were dusted off and anthologized on both sides of the Atlantic (Wolfers and Martin 1956; Forsyth, Keens-Soper and Savigear 1970), and by the end of the century new editions of the recognized classics had begun to appear. Another sign that the history of international thought had become an accepted academic subject was the appearance of textbooks (Boucher 1998; Pangle and Ahrensdorf 1999; Keene 2005) and anthologies (Brown, Nardin and Rengger 2002; Reichberg, Syse and Begby 2006). But such books depend on primary historical scholarship, which includes the recovery and translation of non-canonical texts.

Theorists of international relations often draw inspiration from their predecessors, as Hobbes did from Thucydides or Rousseau from Saint-Pierre. But one cannot learn from a text without wondering whether one has understood it correctly, and to do that one must notice that words change their meaning over time and in translation. One must know not only the texts but their contexts and idioms as well (Skinner 1969). Yet the more one focuses on meaning and context, the less one is concerned with using a text and the more with simply understanding it. That effort encompasses investigating its author's intention, the conventions or shared meanings he or she could draw upon, how the text came to be written and rewritten and other matters we would understand to be 'historical' rather than theoretical. These points, which have assumed the status of orthodoxy in the study of the history of political thought, are often ignored by international relations scholars. It is all too easy for those interested in current affairs to read old authors as if they were dealing with current questions rather than questions of their own. But to understand their meaning one must know the questions they were trying to answer, and this means understanding the discourses that are the context of their texts. Those discourses do not determine what can or cannot be said – an author can, and good authors do, challenge conventional meanings – but they provide evidence about what he or she might have been thinking. Similarly, to locate a text within a tradition or lineage one must know how the author's contemporaries and successors understood it, and this too requires historical evidence and judgement (Jahn 2006: 12-17; Holland 2010).

Making sense of past thought about international relations in a genuinely historical manner requires that we avoid reading our own concerns back into the past. It is tempting to recruit luminaries like Thucydides or Grotius to one's cause, but there are dangers in doing so. The historian of international thought cultivates a detached and critical attitude toward the field's intellectual inheritance. Against familiar claims that Thucydides was a political realist, for example, historical scholarship has given us studies of the relevant texts and contexts that support a far more complex portrait (White 1984; Johnson 1993). Instead of honouring Grotius as the father of international law or making him stand for a constructed tradition of international theorizing, we can now read him in his own context as a theologian, humanist, and politician who was in some ways more medieval than modern and in others closer to Hobbes than is usually thought (Tierney 1997; Tuck 1993). It is anachronistic to treat Grotius as a theorist of 'international society' when there is scant evidence that he held any such idea (Jeffery 2006) and misleading to emphasize his remarks on sociability while ignoring those on self-preservation, especially when there is evidence that the former were politically motivated. Nor does it make sense to call Grotius an 'international lawyer' when the idea of international law, as we understand it today, had not yet been invented and when he wrote his most famous book not as a lawyer, which he was not, but as a propagandist for the Dutch East India Company (Borschberg 2011).

Received views of Thomas Hobbes as an archetypical political realist and theorist of international anarchy are also being reconsidered. The first view, Hobbes as realist, neglects the contradictory forms that realism can take, conflating moral scepticism with political realism and leaving the character of Hobbes's alleged realism unresolved. It also fails to acknowledge that Hobbes, like Thucydides, is a brilliant ironist and trenchant moralist. The second view, Hobbes as theorist of international anarchy, was undercut by Murray Forsyth thirty years ago in a perceptive article (Forsyth 1979); Noel Malcolm has now assembled additional evidence to refute it (Malcolm 2002). Hobbes was identified as a theorist of international anarchy only in the twentieth century with the invention of 'anarchy' as an organizing idea for the emerging discipline of international relations (Schmidt 1998; Armitage 2006).

Instead of using interpretative categories inspired by current concerns, the historian reads early modern thinkers who concerned themselves with war, diplomacy and trade in relation to categories appropriate to their time and place. In discussing the sixteenth and seventeenth centuries, for example, a distinction between humanism and scholasticism (Tuck 1999) makes more sense than the distinction between realism and internationalism. In place of timeless 'traditions' of political and international thought like realism and idealism, historians have advanced the idea of contextually specific 'languages' (Pagden 1987), such as Spanish Thomism in the debate over the Indies, modern (or Protestant) natural law in the seventeenth century German thought and the language of commerce in eighteenth-century Britain. This approach has proven productive because it enables the scholar to see that a language of ideas, like a natural language, can be used to say different things – to disagree as well as to agree. The word 'language' lends itself less easily than the word 'tradition' to the idea of doctrinal unity, though any tradition must be a tradition of debate (questions) as well as of doctrine (answers): even those who agree about many things cannot agree about everything. The traditions of just war and reason of state, for example, contain multiple strands and internal disagreements. And from another point of view, they themselves might be seen as having developed in conversation with one another and as strands in a more inclusive tradition of discourse concerning the relationship between morality and prudence in public affairs. Traditions or discursive languages can be defined more or less broadly according to our explanatory purpose.

The category of 'international relations' is itself historically specific. It best suits the period between the emergence of the European territorial state in the seventeenth century and the emergence of global institutions in the twentieth. The word 'international' (like comparable words in other languages) was not available to Europeans living before the middle of the seventeenth century, so to read Vitoria or Grotius as a theorist of international relations, as we understand that subject, is to risk anachronism. But if the word 'international' presumes a world organized on the basis of territorial states, some other word is needed for relations between tribes, cities, kingdoms, colonies and other political communities that are not exactly 'states' in the modern sense of the term. The word 'foreign' (or its equivalent) is probably as old as the idea of a distinct people, making an expression like 'foreign affairs' suitable for use across broad swaths of time and space. The same can be said for words like war, trade and diplomacy, which can be defined in ways independent of the institutional forms they have acquired in particular times and places. Diplomatic representation does not depend on the institution of the resident ambassador, which was invented in the Renaissance and is therefore specifically modern (Mattingly 1956). The balance of power as a practice of resisting imperial conquest may have a long history, but 'the balance of power' as a self-conscious policy of combining to preserve the states system by preserving the independence of its members is, once again, a distinctly modern idea.

At the end of the modern period, the category 'international' is being reconsidered in what many regard as a world being transformed by globalization. Whether the disappearance of international relations is real or illusory remains controversial and globalist arguments are part of that controversy. It would, however, be a mistake to overlook the globalist discourses of earlier periods. The claim that we live in 'one world' (Singer 2002) – that political, military, economic and physical events around the world are now so interconnected as to constitute 'a closed system' – was a commonplace of geo-politics a century ago (Mackinder 1919: 29–30). At the moral level, the idea that people everywhere are citizens of a universal moral community goes back to the Stoics. This might not count as 'globalism' if we view that idea as distinctly modern, but it is certainly universalist or cosmopolitan in discounting the moral significance of the political boundaries and loyalties. Pre-modern conceptions of natural law (comprising moral precepts binding on all rational beings) and the law of nations (comprising rules common to the laws and customs of different peoples) live on in many of today's 'cosmopolitan' theories of human rights and global justice.

It has been argued that the category 'international' is misleading even for the modern period because in concentrating on an intra-European international order it neglects patterns of order that prevailed elsewhere in the world. The pluralist understanding of international society paints a picture of world order in which states co-exist with one another on the basis of international law, but outside Europe the order has historically been one in which European states conquered and ruled non-European peoples in the name of 'civilization' (Keene 2002). In their preoccupation with diplomatic equality and the balance of power within the European system, international relations theorists overlook the unequal and unbalanced relationship between Europe and the rest of the world. They assume that the anarchical pattern is normal and that the imperial pattern is an aberration; in fact, international society displays both. There was certainly an international element in the competition among European imperial powers for trade and territory, starting with the search for gold and spices in the Indies in the sixteenth century and ending with the 'scramble for Africa' at the end of the nineteenth. But the *idea* of empire is a denial of international relations, for each empire imagines itself the guardian of a unitary order governed not horizontally by international law but vertically through imperial administration. One might find this argument overstated or not especially novel but the politics of imperial imagination has nevertheless proven a fruitful area for historical inquiry (Pitts 2006; Bell 2007).

The solution to the categorical problem in writing the history of international thought is to resist broad generalizations by narrowing the focus of inquiry to topics that can be securely grounded on historical evidence. Sometimes that focus is achieved by examining a particular text, like Kant's *Perpetual Peace*, or the writings of a particular thinker, like Hannah Arendt or Hans Morgenthau (Owens 2007; Scheuerman 2009). It can also be achieved by studying a tradition or attitude, like English idealism in the first half of the twentieth century or American realism in the second. With a well-defined thematic focus the historian can cover an extended historical period without anachronism: a history of world government or international law from the Greeks to the present is a non-starter, historically speaking, but a history of international legal theory from 1870 to 1960 or even a history of confederation in modern Europe can be successfully carried off (Koskenniemi 2001; Forsyth 1981).

Theorizing international justice can be difficult for philosophers because in discussing justice in a world that is their own, defining it theoretically and advocating it practically are hard to keep separate. The danger is that theorizing will be distorted by advocacy. This fate is more easily avoided by the historian, who contemplates a world that can never be other than it is – a past that can be understood but cannot be improved. The danger of covert advocacy still exists, however, because the historian does not passively contemplate a given past but is actively engaged in constructing it, and in doing so can succumb to partisanship. The historical profession has canons of inquiry that serve to limit that partisanship, though they are not always observed. But the historian may have an easier time than the philosopher when the latter is reflecting on the politics of his own time. For that reason, if no other, the history of international thought has an important place in international political theory, and Martin Wight was right to insist on its importance.

Bibliography

Abrams, P. (1982) *Historical Sociology* (Shepton Mallet).

Ackerly, B.A. (2000) *Political Theory and Feminist Social Criticism* (Cambridge).

— (2001a) *Political Theory and Feminist Social Criticism* (Cambridge).

— (2001b) Women's Human Rights Activists as Cross-Cultural Theorists', *International Journal of Feminist Politics*, 3(3).

Ackerly, B.A. and Okin, S. M. (1999) 'Feminist Social Criticism and the International Movement for Women's Rights as Human Rights', in I. Shapiro and C. Hacker-Cordon (eds), *Democracy's Edges* (Cambridge).

Ackerly, B. and True, J. (2006) 'Studying the Struggles and Wishes of the Age: Feminist Theoretical Methodology and Feminist Theoretical Methods', in B. Ackerly, M. Stern and J. True (eds), *Feminist Methodologies for International Relations* (Cambridge).

— (2008a) 'An Intersectional Analysis of International Relations: Recasting the Discipline', *Politics and Gender*, 4(1).

— (2008b) 'Reflexivity in Practice: Power and Ethics in Feminist Research on International Relations', *International Studies Review* 10(4): 581–600.

— (2010) *Doing Feminist Research in the Political and Social Sciences* (New York).

Ackerly, B.A., Stern, M. and True, J. (eds) (2006) *Feminist Methodologies for International Relations* (Cambridge).

Adler, E. and Barnett, M. (1998) *Security Communities* (Cambridge).

Adler, E. and Pouliot. V. (eds) (2011) *International Practices* (Cambridge).

Afshar, H. and Dennis, C. (1992) *Women and Adjustment in the Third World* (London).

Agamben, G. (1998) *Homo Sacer: Sovereign Power and Bare Life* (Stanford).

Agathangelou, A. (2004) *The Global Political Economy of Sex: Desire, Violence and Insecurity in Mediterranean Nation States* (New York).

Agathangelou, A. M. and Ling, L. H. M. (2004) 'Power, Borders, Security, Wealth: Lessons of Violence and Desire from September 11', *International Studies Quarterly*, 48(3).

Ahluwalia, P. (2005) 'Out of Africa: Post-Structuralism's Colonial Roots', *Postcolonial Studies*, 8(2).

Al-Ali, N. and Pratt N. (eds) (2009a) *What Kind of Liberation? Women and the Occupation of Iraq* (Berkeley).

— (eds) (2009b) *Women and War in the Middle East* (London).

Alison, M. (2004) 'Women as Agents of Political Violence: Gendering Security', *Security Dialogue*, 35(4).

Amnesty International (1990) *Women in the Front Lines: Human Rights Violations Against Women* (London).

Anderson, P. (1974) *Lineages of the Absolutist State* (London).

— (1983) *In the Tracks of Historical Materialism* (London).

Anievas, A. (2005) 'Critical Dialogues: Habermasian Social Theory and International Relations', *Politics*, 25(3).

Apel, K.-O. (1980) *Towards a Transformation of Philosophy* (London).

Appfel-Marglin, F. and Marglin, S. (eds) (1990) *Dominating Knowledge: Development, Culture and Resistance* (Oxford).

Arblaster, A. (1984) *The Rise and Decline of Western Liberalism* (Oxford).

Archibugi, D. (2002) 'Demos and Cosmopolis', *New Left Review*, 13.

— (2004a) 'Cosmopolitan Democracy and its Critics: A Review', *European Journal of International Relations*, 10(3).

— (2004b) 'Cosmopolitan Guidelines for Humanitarian Intervention', *Alternatives*, 29(1).

— (2008) *The Global Commonwealth of Citizens: Toward Cosmopolitan Democracy* (Princeton).

Archibugi, D. and Held, D. (eds) (1995) *Cosmopolitan Democracy: An Agenda for a New World Order* (Cambridge).

Archibugi, D., Held, D. and Köhler, M. (eds) (1998) *Re-Imagining Political Community: Studies in Cosmopolitan Democracy* (Cambridge).

Armitage, D. (2006) 'Hobbes and the Foundations of Modern International Thought', in A. Brett and J. Tully, with H. Hamilton-Bleakley (eds), *Rethinking the Foundations of Modern Political Thought* (Cambridge).

Art, R. J. and Waltz, K. N. (1983) 'Technology, Strategy, and the Uses of Force', in R. J. Art and K. N. Waltz (eds), *The Use of Force* (Lanham).

Ashley, R. K. (1981) 'Political Realism and Human Interests', *International Studies Quarterly*, 25(2).

— (1987) 'The Geopolitics of Geopolitical Space: Toward a Critical Social Theory of International Politics', *Alternatives*, 12(4).

— (1988) 'Untying the Sovereign State: A Double Reading of the *Anarchy Problématique*', *Millennium*, 17(2).

— (1989a) 'Living on Border Lines: Man, Poststructuralism and War', in J. Der Derian and M. J. Shapiro (eds), *International/Intertextual Relations: Postmodern Readings of World Politics* (Massachusetts).

— (1989b) 'Imposing International Purpose: Notes on a Problematic of Governance', in E.-O. Czempiel and J. Rosenau (eds), *Global Changes and Theoretical Challenges: Approaches to World Politics for the 1990s* (Massachusetts).

Ashley, R. K. and. Walker, R. B. J. (1990) 'Speaking the Language of Exile: Dissidence in International Studies', *International Studies Quarterly*, 34(3).

Axelrod, R. (1984) *The Evolution of Cooperation* (New York).

Axelrod, R. and Keohane, R. O. (1993)[1986] 'Achieving Cooperation under Anarchy: Strategies and Institutions', in K. A. Oye (ed.), *Cooperation under Anarchy* (Princeton). Reprinted in D. Baldwin (ed.) (1993), *Neorealism and Neoliberalism: The Contemporary Debate* (New York).

Ayers, A. (ed.) (2008) *Gramsci, Political Economy and International Relations Theory: Modern Princes and Naked Emperors* (Basingstoke).

Bäckstrand, K., Khan, J., Kronsell, A. and Lövbrand, E. (eds) (2010) *Environmental Politics and Deliberative Democracy: Examining the Promise of New Modes of Governance* (Cheltenham).

Bain, W. (2003) *Between Anarchy and Society* (Oxford).

Baines, E. K. (1999) 'Gender Construction and the Protection Mandate of the UNHCR: Responses from Guatemalan Women', in E. Prügl and M. K. Meyer (eds), *Gender Politics and Global Governance* (Lanham).

Bairoch, P. (1993) *Economic and World History* (Chicago).

Baker, D. (2010) *False Profits: Recovering From The Bubble Economy* (PoliPoint).

— (2011) *The End of Loser Liberalism* (Centre for Economic and Policy Research – eBook).

Bakker, I. (ed.) (1994) *The Strategic Silence: Gender and Economic Policy* (London).

Banks, M. (1985) 'The Inter-Paradigm Debate', in M. Light and A. J. R. Groom (eds), *International Relations: A Handbook of Current Theory* (London).

Bar On, B. (2003) 'Manly After-Effects of 11 September 2001: Reading William J. Bennett's Why We Fight: Moral Clarity and the War on Terrorism', *International Feminist Journal of Politics* 5(3).

Barbalet, J. (ed.) (2002) *Emotions and Sociology* (Oxford).

Baring, E. (2010) 'Liberalism and the Algerian War: The Case of Jacques Derrida', *Critical Inquiry*, 6.

Barkin, J. S. (2010) *Realist Constructivism: Rethinking International Relations Theory* (Cambridge).

Barnes, J. (1982) 'The Just War', in N. Kretzmann, A. Kenny and J. Pinborg (eds), *The Cambridge History of Late Medieval Philosophy* (Cambridge).

Barnett, J. (2000) 'Destabilizing the Environment-Conflict Thesis,' *Review of International Studies,* 26(2).

Barnett, M. and Duvall, R. D. (2004) 'Power in World Politics', *International Organization,* 59(1).

— (eds) (2005) 'Power in Global Governance', in M. Barnett and R. D. Duvall (eds), *Power in Global Governance* (Cambridge).

Barnett, M. and Finnemore, M. (2004) *Rules for the World: International Organizations in Global Politics* (Ithaca).

Barry, B. (1998) 'International Society from a Cosmopolitan Perspective', in D. R. Mapel and T. Nardin (eds), *International Society: Diverse Ethical Perspectives* (Princeton).

Barry, C. and Pogge, T. W. (eds) (2005) *Global Institutions and Responsibilities: Achieving Global Justice* (Malden).

Barry, J. (1995) 'Towards a Theory of the Green State', in S. Elworthy *et al.* (eds), *Perspectives on the Environment* 2 (Aldershot).

— (1999) *Rethinking Green Politics: Nature, Virtue and Progress* (London).

Barry, J. and Eckersley, R. (eds) (2005) *The Global Ecological Crisis and the Nation-State* (Cambridge).

Baylis, J., Smith, S. and Owens, P. (eds) (2011) *The Globalisation of World Politics* (Oxford).

Beardsworth, R. (2005) The Future of Critical Philosophy and World Politics', *Millennium,* 34(1).

— (2011) *Cosmopolitanism and International Relations Theory* (Cambridge).

Beattie, A. (2010) *Morality and Justice: International Relations and the Tradition of Natural Law* (Burlington, VT).

Beitz, C. (1979) *Political Theory and International Relations* (Princeton).

Bell, D. (ed.) (2007) *Victorian Visions of Global Order: Empire and International Relations in Nineteenth-Century Political Thought* (Cambridge).

— (2008) *Political Thought and International Relations: Variations on a Realist Theme* (Oxford).

Bellamy, A. J. (2008) *A Responsibility to Protect: The Global Effort to End Mass Atrocities* (Cambridge).

Beneria, L. (ed.) (1982) *Women and Development: The Sexual Division of Labor in Rural Societies* (New York).

Benhabib, S. (1986) *Critique, Norm and Utopia: A Study of the Foundations of Critical Theory* (New York).

— (2006) *Another Cosmopolitanism* (New York).

Benner, E. (1995) *Really Existing Nationalisms: A Post-Communist View from Marx and Engels* (Oxford).

Berman, J. (2003) '(Un)popular Strangers and Crises (Un)bounded: Discourses of Sex Trafficking, the European Political Community and the Panicked State of the Modern State', *European Journal of International Relations,* 9(1).

Bernauer, T. (1995) 'The Effectiveness of International Environmental Institutions: How We Might Learn More', *International Organization,* 49(2).

Bially Mattern, J. (2011) 'A Practice Theory of Emotion for International Relations', in E. Adler and V. Pouliot (eds), *International Practices* (Cambridge).

Bieler, A. and Morton, A. D. (eds) (2006) *Images of Gramsci: Connections and Contentions in Political Theory and International Relations* (Abingdon).

— (2010) 'The Deficit of Discourse in IPE: Turning Base Metal into Gold', *International Studies Quarterly,* 52(1).

Bjola, C. (2005) 'Legitimating the Use of Force in International Politics: A Communicative Action Perspective', *European Journal of International Relations,* 11(2).

Blair, B. (2011) 'Revisiting the "Third Debate" (Part I)', *Review of International Studies,* 37(2).

Blanchard, J.-M. F, and Ripsman, N. R. (2008) 'A Political Theory of Economic Statecraft', *Foreign Policy Analysis,* 4(4).

Bleiker, R. (2000) *Popular Dissent, Human Agency and Global Politics* (Cambridge).

— (2001) 'The Aesthetic Turn in International Political Theory', *Millennium,* 30(3).

— (2005) *Divided Korea: Toward a Culture of Reconciliation* (Minnesota).

— (2009) *Aesthetics and World Politics* (London).

Bleiker, R. and Chou, M. (2010) 'Nietzsche's Style: On Language, Knowledge and Power in International Relations', in C. Moore and C. Farrands (eds), *International Relations Theory and Philosophy: Interpretive Dialogues* (London).

Bleiker, R. and Hutchison, E. (2008) 'Fear no More: Emotions and World Politics', *Review of International Studies,* (34, special issue).

Bleiker, R. and Leet, M. (2005) 'From the Sublime to the Subliminal: Fear, Awe and Wonder in International Politics', *Millennium,* 34(3).

Block, F. (1980) 'Beyond State Autonomy: State Managers as Historical Subjects', *Socialist Register.*

Block, F. and Somers, M. (1984) 'Beyond the Economistic Fallacy: The Holistic Social Science of Karl Polanyi', in T. Skocpol (ed.), *Vision and Method in Historical Sociology* (Cambridge).

Blomert, R. (2012) 'The Taming of Economic Aristocracies', *Human Figurations: Long-Term Perspectives on the Human Condition,* available at 'http://www. norberteliasfoundation.nl/ blog'.

Bodansky, D. (2010) 'The Copenhagen Climate Change Conference: A Postmortem', *American Journal of International Law* 104(2).

Bohman, J. (2002) 'How to Make a Social Science Practical: Pragmatism, Critical Social Science and Multiperspectival Theory', *Millennium,* 31(3).

Bok, S. (1989) *A Strategy for Peace: Human Values and the Threat of War* (New York).

Boli, J., Meyer, J. and Thomas, G. (1989) 'Ontology and Rationalization in the Western Cultural Account', in G. Thomas *et al.* (eds), *Institutional Structure: Constituting State, Society, and the Individual* (London).

Bookchin, M. (1980) *Toward an Ecological Society* (Montreal).

— (1982) *The Ecology of Freedom: The Emergence and Dissolution of Hierarchy* (Palo Alto).

— (1992) 'Libertarian Municipalism: An Overview', *Society and Nature,* 1(1).

Booth, D. (1998) *The Environmental Consequences of Growth: Steady-State Economics as an Alternative to Ecological Decline* (London).

Booth, K. (1991a) 'Security and Emancipation', *Review of International Studies,* 17(4).

— (1991b) 'Security in Anarchy: Utopian Realism in Theory and Practice', *International Affairs,* 67(3).

— (1997) 'A Reply to Wallace', *Review of International Studies,* 22(3).

— (2008) *Theory of World Security* (Cambridge).

Booth, K. and Dunne T. (eds) (2002) *Worlds in Collision: Terror and the Future of Global Order* (London).

— (2011) *Terror in our Time* (London).

Booth, K. and Wheeler, N. J. (2007) *The Security Dilemma: Fear, Security and Distrust* (Basingstoke).

Boris, E. and Prügl, E. (eds) (1996) *Homeworkers in Global Perspective* (New York).

Borschberg, P. (2011) *Hugo Grotius, the Portuguese and Free Trade in the Indies* (Singapore).

Bottomore, T. B. and Goode, P. (eds) (1978) *Austro-Marxism* (Oxford).

Boucher, D. (1998) *Political Theories of International Relations: From Thucydides to the Present* (Oxford).

Bowden, B. and Seabrooke, L. (eds) (2006) *Global Standards of Market Civilization* (Abingdon).

Boyle, J. (2006) 'Traditional Just War Theory and Humanitarian Intervention' in T. Nardin and M. S. Williams (eds), *Humanitarian Intervention* (New York).

Brekke, T. (ed.) (2006) *The Ethics of War in Asian Civilizations: A Comparative Perspective* (London).

Brewer, A. (1990) *Marxist Theories of Imperialism: A Survey* (London).

Brincat, S., Lima, L. and Nunes, J. (eds) (2012) *Critical Theory in International Relations and Security Studies: Interviews and Reflections* (Abingdon).

Bromley, S. (1999) 'Marxism and Globalisation', in A. Gamble *et al.* (eds), *Marxism and Social Science* (London).

Brown, C. J. (1988) 'The Modern Requirement: Reflections on Normative International Theory in a Post-European World', *Millennium*, 17(2).

— (1992a) *International Relations Theory: New Normative Approaches* (New York).

— (1992b) 'Marxism and International Ethics', in T. Nardin and D. R. Napel (eds), *Traditions of International Ethics* (Cambridge).

— (2002) *Understanding International Relations*, 2nd edn (Basingstoke).

— (2010) 'Bob Dylan, Live Aid, and the Politics of Popular Cosmopolitanism', in C. Brown, *Practical Judgment in International Political Theory: Selected Essays* (Abingdon).

Brown, C., Nardin, T. and Rengger, N. (eds) (2002) *International Relations in Political Thought: Texts from the Ancient Greeks to the First World War* (Cambridge).

Brunkhorst, H. (2002) 'Globalising Democracy without a State: Weak Public, Strong Public, Global Constitutionalism', *Millennium*, 31(3).

Brunnee, J. and. Toope, S. J. (2000) 'International Law and Constructivism: Elements of an International Theory and of International Law', *Columbia Journal of Transnational Law*, 39(1).

— (2010) *Legitimacy and Legality in International Law* (Cambridge).

Bryant, R. and Bailey, S. (eds) (1997) *Third World Political Ecology* (London).

Buchanan, A. (2004) *Justice, Legitimacy, and Self-Determination: Moral Foundations for International Law* (Oxford).

Buck, S. J. (1998) *The Global Commons: An Introduction* (London).

Bukharin, N. (1972) *Imperialism and World Economy* (London).

Bukovansky, M. (2002) *Legitimacy and Power Politics* (Princeton).

Bukovansky, M., Clark, I., Eckersley, R., Price, R., Reus-Smit, C. and Wheeler, N. (2012) *Special Responsibilities and American Power* (Cambridge).

Bulkeley, H. and Betsill, M. (2005) *Cities and Climate Change. Urban Sustainability and Global Environmental Governance* (London).

Bulkeley, H., Andonova, L., Bäckstrand, K., Betsill, M., Compagnon, D., Duffy, R., Kolk, A., Hoffmannn, M., Levy, D., Newell, P., Milledge, T., Paterson, M., Pattberg, P. and VanDeveer, S. (2012) 'Governing Climate Change Transnationally: Assessing the Evidence from a Database of Sixty Initiatives', *Environment and Planning C: Government and Policy*.

Bull, H. (1966a) 'The Grotian Conception of International Society', in H. Butterfield and M. Wight (eds), *Diplomatic Investigations: Essays in the Theory of International Relations* (London).

— (1966b) 'International Theory: The Case for a Classical Approach', *World Politics*, 18. Reprinted in K. Knorr and J. N. Rosenau (eds) (1969), *Contending Approaches to International Relations* (Princeton).

— (1969/1995) 'The Theory of International Politics, 1919–1969', in B. Porter (ed.), *The Aberystwyth Papers* (London). Reprinted in J. Der Derian (ed.) (1995), *International Theory: Critical Investigations* (Basingstoke).

— (1973) 'Foreign Policy of Australia', *Proceedings of Australian Institute of Political Science*, (Sydney).

— (1977) *The Anarchical Society: A Study of Order in World Politics* (London).

— (1979a) 'Human Rights and World Politics', in R. Pettman (ed.), *Moral Claims in World Affairs* (London).

— (1979b) 'The State's Positive Role in World Affairs', *Daedalus*, 108.

— (1982) 'The West and South Africa', *Daedalus*, 111.

— (1983) 'The International Anarchy in the 1980s', *Australian Outlook*, 37(3).

— (ed.) (1984a) *Intervention in World Politics* (Oxford).

— (ed.) (1984b) 'Justice in International Relations', *The Hagey Lectures*, The University of Waterloo (Ontario).

— (ed.) (1984c) 'The Revolt Against the West', in H. Bull and A. Watson (eds), *The Expansion of International Society* (Oxford).

Bull, H. and Watson, A. (eds) (1984) *The Expansion of International Society* (Oxford).

Bunyard, P. and Morgan-Grenville, F. (eds) (1987) *The Green Alternative* (London).

Burguiere, A. (1982) 'The Fate of the History of Mentalities in the Annales', *Comparative Studies in Society and History*, 24(4).

Burke, A. (2004) 'Just War or Ethical Peace? Moral Discourses of Strategic Violence After 9/11', *International Affairs*, 80(2).

— (2005) 'Against the New Internationalism', *Ethics and International Affairs*, 9(2).

Burke, P. (ed.) (1973) *A New Kind of History: From the Writings of Lucien Febvre* (London).

— (2003) 'The Annales, Braudel and Historical Sociology', in G. Delanty and E. Isin (eds), *Handbook of Historical Sociology* (London).

— (2005) *History and Social Theory* (Cambridge).

Butler, J. (1990) *Gender Trouble: Feminist Subversions of Identity* (New York).

— (2004) *Precarious Life: The Powers of Mourning and Violence* (London).

Butterfield, H. (1949) *Christianity and History* (London).

— (1953) *Christianity, Diplomacy, and War* (London).

— (1979) *Herbert Butterfield: Writings on Christianity and History* (New York).

Butterfield, H. and Wight, M. (eds) (1966) *Diplomatic Investigations* (London).

Buzan, B. (2001) 'The English School: An Underexploited Resource in IR', *Review of International Studies*, 27(3).

— (2003) 'Implications for the Study of International Relations', in M. Buckley and R. Fawn (eds), *Global Responses to Terrorism* (London).

— (2004) *From International Society to World Society? English School Theory and the Social Structure of Globalization* (Cambridge).

— (2011) 'A World Order without Superpowers: Decentred Globalism', *International Relations*, 25(1).

Buzan, B. and Little, R. (2000) *International Systems in World History: Remaking the Study of International Relations* (Oxford).

— (2001) 'Why International Relations Has Failed as a Project and What to Do About It', *Millennium*, 31(1).

— (2002) 'International Systems in World History: Remaking the Study of International Relations', in S. Hobden and J. M. Hobson (eds), *Historical Sociology and International Relations* (Cambridge).

Buzan, B. and Waever, O. (2003) *Regions and Powers: The Structure of International Security* (Cambridge).

Buzan, B., Jones, C. A. and Little, R. (1993) *The Logic of Anarchy: Neorealism to Structural Realism* (New York).

Byers, M. (2005) *War Law: Understanding International Law and Armed Conflict* (New York).

Calhoun, C. (2003) 'Afterword: Why Historical Sociology?', in G. Delanty and E. Isin (eds), *Handbook of Historical Sociology* (London).

Camilleri J. A. and Falk, R. (2009) *Worlds in Transition: Evolving Governance Across a Stressed Planet* (London).

Campbell, D. (1992) *Writing Security: United States Foreign Policy and the Politics of Identity* (Minneapolis).

— (1994) 'The Deterritorializing of Responsibility: Levinas, Derrida and Ethics after the End of Philosophy', *Alternatives*, 19(4).

— (1996) 'Political Prosaics, Transversal Politics, and the Anarchical World', in M. J. Shapiro and H. Alker (eds), *Challenging Boundaries: Global Flows, Territorial Identities* (Minneapolis).

— (1998a) *National Deconstruction: Violence, Identity, and Justice in Bosnia* (Minneapolis).

— (1998b) 'Why Fight? Humanitarianism, Principles, and Post-Structuralism', *Millennium*, 27(3).

— (1999) 'Violence, Justice and Identity in the Bosnian Conflict', in J. Edkins, N. Persram and V. Pin-Fat (eds), *Sovereignty and Subjectivity* (Boulder).

— (2002a) 'Time is Broken: The Return of the Past in the Response to September 11', *Theory and Event*, 5(4).

— (2002b) 'Atrocity, Memory, Photography: Imaging the Concentration Camps of Bosnia – the Case of ITN versus Living Marxism, Part 1', *Journal of Human Rights*, 1(1).

— (2005) 'Beyond Choice: The Onto-Politics of Critique', *International Relations*, 19(1).

— (2007) 'Poststructuralism', in T. Dunne, M. Kurki and S. Smith (eds), *International Relations Theory: Discipline and Diversity* (Oxford).

Campbell, D. and Dillon, M. (1993) 'Introduction', in D. Campbell and M. Dillon (eds), *The Political Subject of Violence* (Manchester).

Campbell, T. (2007) 'Poverty as a Violation of Human Rights: Inhumanity or Injustice?' in T. Pogge (ed.), *Freedom from Poverty as a Human Right: Who Owes What to the Very Poor?* (Oxford).

Caney, S. (2005) *Justice Beyond Borders: A Global Political Theory* (Oxford).

Caprioli, M. (2000) 'Gendered Conflict', *Journal of Peace Research*, 37(1).

— (2004) 'Feminist IR Theory and Quantitative Methodology', *International Studies Review*, 6(2).

Caprioli, M. and Boyer, M. (2001) 'Gender, Violence, and International Crisis', *Journal of Conflict Resolution*, 45(4).

Carpenter, R. C. (2002) 'Gender Theory in World Politics: Contributions of a Nonfeminist Standpoint?', *International Studies Review*, 4(3).

— (2005) 'Women, Children and Other Vulnerable Groups: Gender, Strategic Frames and the Politics of Civilian Immunity', *International Studies Quarterly*, 49(2).

— (2006) *Innocent Women and Children: Gender, Norms and the Protection of Civilians* (London).

Carr, E. H. (1939/1945/1946) *The Twenty Years' Crisis: 1919–1939: An Introduction to the Study of International Relations* (London).

— (1945) *Nationalism and After* (New York).

— (1953) 'The Marxist Attitude to War', in E. H. Carr, *A History of Soviet Russia, 3, The Bolshevik Revolution, 1917–23* (London).

Carter, A. (1993) 'Towards a Green Political Theory', in A. Dobson and P. Lucardie (eds), *The Politics of Nature: Explorations in Green Political Theory* (London).

— (1999) 'Game Theory and Decentralization', *Journal of Applied Philosophy*, 16(3).

Carver, T. (1998) *The PostModern Marx* (Manchester).

Cashore, B., Auld, G. and Newsom, D. (2004) *Governing Through Markets: Forest Certification and the Emergence of Non-State Authority* (New Haven).

Chakrabarty, D. (2000) *Provincializing Europe: Postcolonial Thought and Historical Difference* (Princeton).

— (2003) 'Subaltern Studies and Postcolonial Historiography', in G. Delanty and E. Isin (eds), *Handbook of Historical Sociology* (London).

Chan-Tiberghien, J. (2004) 'Gender Scepticism or Gender Boom? Poststructural Feminisms, Transnational Feminisms and the World Conference Against Racism', *International Feminist Journal of Politics*, 6(3).

Chang, K. and Ling, L. H. M. (2000) 'Globalization and its Intimate Other: Filipina Domestic Workers in Hong Kong', in M. Marchand and A. S. Runyan (eds), *Gender and Global Restructuring: Sites, Sightings and Resistances* (New York).

Chappell, L. (2008) 'The International Criminal Court: A New Arena for Transforming Justice' in S. M. Rai and G. Waylen (eds), *Global Governance: Feminist Perspectives* (New York).

Charlton, S. E., Everett, J. and Staudt, K. (eds) (1989) *Women, the State, and Development* (Albany).

Chatterjee, D. K. (ed.) (2004) *The Ethics of Assistance: Morality and the Distant Needy* (Cambridge).

Chatterjee, P. and Finger, M. (1994) *The Earth Brokers: Power, Politics and World Development* (London).

Chayes, A. and Chayes, A. H. (1993) 'On Compliance', *International Organization,* 47(2).

Chin, C. B. (1998) *In Service and Servitude: Foreign Female Domestic Workers and the Malaysian Modernity Project* (New York).

Chomsky, N. (1969) *American Power and the New Mandarins* (Harmondsworth).

— (1994) *World Orders, Old and New* (London).

— (1999) *Profit Over People: Neoliberalism and the Global Order* (New York).

Choucri, N. (1993) 'Introduction: Theoretical, Empirical, and Policy Perspectives', in N. Choucri (ed.), *Global Accord: Environmental Challenges and International Responses* (Cambridge).

Christensen, T. J. and Snyder, J. (1990) 'Chain Gangs and Passed Bucks: Predicting Alliance Patterns in Multipolarity', *International Organization,* 44(2).

Christoff, P. (1996) 'Ecological Modernisation, Ecological Modernities', *Environmental Politics,* 5(3).

Clairmont, F. F. (1996) *The Rise and Fall of Economic Liberalism* (Penang).

Clapp, J. (2009) 'Food Price Volatility and Vulnerability in the Global South: Considering the Global Economic Context', *Third World Quarterly,* 30(6).

Clapp, J. and Dauvergne, P. (2005) *Paths to a Green World: The Political Economy of the Global Environment* (Cambridge).

Clark, A. M., Friedman, E. J. and Hochstetler, K. (1998) 'The Sovereign Limits of Global Civil Society: A Comparison of NGO Participation in UN World Conferences on the Environment, Human Rights, and Women', *World Politics,* 51(1).

Clark, I. (1989) *The Hierarchy of States* (Cambridge).

— (2005) *Legitimacy and International Society* (Oxford).

— (2007) *International Legitimacy and World Society* (Oxford).

— (2009) 'Bringing Hegemony Back In: The United States and International Order', *International Affairs,* 85(1).

— (2011) *Hegemony in International Society* (Oxford).

Clark, I., and Reus-Smit, C. (eds) (2007) 'Resolving International Crises of Legitimacy', *International Relations,* 44(2/3).

Cochran, M. (1999) *Normative Theory in International Relations: A Pragmatic Approach* (Cambridge).

Cockburn, C. (1998) *The Space Between Us: Negotiating Gender and National Identity in Conflict Zones* (London).

— (2012) *Antimilitarism: Political and Gender Dynamics of Movements to End War and Redefine Peace* (New York).

Cohen, J. (1990) 'Discourse Ethics and Civil Society', in D. Rasmussen (ed.), *Universalism vs Communitarianism* (Massachusetts).

— (2012) *Globalization and Sovereignty: Rethinking Legality, Legitimacy and Constitutionalism* (Cambridge).

Connell, R. J. (1990) 'The State, Gender and Sexual Politics', *Theory and Society,* 19(5).

Connolly, W. (1991) 'Democracy and Territoriality', *Millennium,* 20(3).

— (1994) 'Tocqueville, Territory and Violence', *Theory, Culture and Society,* 11(1).

— (1995) *The Ethos of Pluralization* (Minneapolis).

Constantinou, C. (2004) *States of Political Discourse: Words, Regimes, Seditions* (London).

Copeland, D. C. (1996) 'Neorealism and the Myth of Bipolar Stability: Toward a New Dynamic Realist Theory of Major War', *Security Studies,* 5(3).

Cox, M. and Rengger, N. (eds) (2011) 'Fred Halliday, John Vincent and the Idea of Progress in International Relations', *International Affairs,* 87(5).

Cox, R. W. (1981) 'Social Forces, States and World Orders: Beyond International Relations Theory', *Millennium,* 10(2).

— (1983) 'Gramsci, Hegemony and International Relations', *Millennium,* 12(2).

— (1986) 'Postscript 1985', in R. O. Keohane (ed.), *Neorealism and Its Critics* (New York).

— (1987) *Production, Power and World Order: Social Forces in the Making of History* (New York).

— (1989) 'Production, the State, and Change in World Order', in E.-O. Czempiel and J. Rosenau (eds), *Global Change and Theoretical Challenges* (Cambridge).

— (1992a) 'Towards a Post-Hegemonic Conceptualization of World Order: Reflections on the Relevancy of Ibn Khaldun', in J. N. Rosenau and E.-O. Czempiel (eds), *Governance Without Government: Order and Change in World Politics* (Cambridge).

— (1992b) 'Multilateralism and World Order', *Review of International Studies,* 18(2).

— (1993) 'Structural Issues of Global Governance: Implications for Europe', in S. Gill (ed.), *Gramsci, Historical Materialism and International Relations* (Cambridge).

— (1994) 'Global Restructuring: Making Sense of the Changing International Political Economy', in R. Stubbs and G. Underhill (eds), *Political Economy and the Changing Global Order* (London).

— (1999) 'Civil Society at the Turn of the Millennium: Prospects for an Alternative World Order', *Review of International Studies,* 25(1).

— (2012) '*For* Someone and *for* Some Purpose: An Interview with Robert W. Cox', in S. Brincat, L. Lima and J. Nunes (eds) *Critical Theory in International Relations and Security Studies* (Abingdon).

Crawford, N. C. (2000) 'The Passions of World Politics: Propositions on Emotions and Emotional Relationships', *International Security,* 24(4).

— (2002) *Argument and Change in World Politics: Ethics, Decolonization, and Humanitarian Intervention* (Cambridge).

— (2009) '*Homo Politicus* and Argument (Nearly) All the Way Down: Persuasion in Politics', *Perspectives on Politics,* 7(1).

Cronin, B. (1999) *Community under Anarchy: Transnational Identity and the Evolution of Cooperation* (New York).

— (2001) 'The Paradox of Hegemony: America's Ambiguous Relationship with the United Nations', *European Journal of International Relations,* 7(1).

Cusack, T. R. and Stoll, R. J. (1990) *Exploring Realpolitik: Probing International Relations Theory with Computer Simulation* (Boulder).

Cutler, C. (2006) 'Gramsci, Law and the Culture of Global Capitalism', in A. Bieler and A. D. Morton (eds) *Images of Gramsci: Connections and Contentions in Political Theory and International Relations* (Abingdon).

Dalby, S. (1993) *Creating the Second Cold War: The Discourse of Politics* (London).

— (1998) 'Ecological Metaphors of Security: World Politics in the Biosphere', *Alternatives,* 23(3).

— (2002) *Environmental Security* (Minneapolis).

— (2004) 'Ecological Politics, Violence, and the Theme of Empire', *Global Environmental Politics,* 4(2).

Daly, H. E. (1990) 'Toward Some Operational Principles of Sustainable Development', *Ecological Economics,* 2(1).

Daly, H. E. and Cobb, J. B., Jr (1989) *For the Common Good* (Boston), 2nd edn (1994).

Davies, S. E. and Stamnes, E. (2012) 'GR2P Special Issue: The Responsibility to Protect and Sexual and Gender Based Violence (SGBV)', *Global Responsibility to Protect* 4(1).

De Geus, M. (1995) 'The Ecological Restructuring of the State', in B. Doherty and M. de Geus (eds), *Democracy and Green Political Thought* (London).

De Swaan, A. (1995) 'Widening Circles of Identification: Emotional Concerns in Sociogenetic Perspective', *Theory, Culture and Society,* 12(2).

— (1997) 'Widening Circles of Disidentification: On the Psycho- and Sociogenesis of the Hatred of Distant Strangers: Reflections on Rwanda', *Theory, Culture and Society,* 14(2).

Dean, M. (1994) *Critical and Effective Histories: Foucault's Method and Historical Sociology* (London).

Delanty, G. and Isin, E. (2003) 'Introduction: Reorienting Historical Sociology', in G. Delanty and E. Isin (eds) *Handbook of Historical Sociology* (London).

Deleuze, G. and Guattari, F. (1977) *Anti-Oedipus: Capitalism and Schizophrenia* (New York).
— (1987) *A Thousand Plateaus: Capitalism and Schizophrenia* (Minneapolis).
Denemark, R., Friedman, J., Gills, B. K. and Modelski, G. (eds) (2000) *World System History: The Social Science of Long-Term Change* (London).
Der Derian, J. (1987) *On Diplomacy: A Genealogy of Western Estrangement* (Oxford).
— (1989) 'The Boundaries of Knowledge and Power in International Relations', in J. Der Derian and M. J. Shapiro (eds), *International/Intertextual Relations: Postmodern Readings of World Politics* (Lexington).
— (2002) 'The War of Networks', *Theory and Event,* 5(4).
Derrida, J. (1974) *Of Grammatology* (Baltimore).
— (1978) *Writing and Difference* (Henley).
— (1981) *Positions* (Chicago).
— (1988) *Limited Inc.* (Evanston).
— (1994a) 'Spectres of Marx', *New Left Review,* (205).
— (1994b) *Spectres of Marx: The State of the Debt, the Work of Mourning and the New International* (London).
— (2003) 'Autoimmunity: Real and Symbolic Suicides – A Dialogue with Jacques Derrida', in G. Borradori (ed.), *Philosophy in a Time of Terror: Dialogues with Jürgen Habermas and Jacques Derrida* (Chicago).
— (2005) *Rogues: Two Essays on Reason* (Stanford).
Deudney, D. (2007) *Bounding Power: Republican Security Theory from the Polis to the Global Village* (Princeton).
Deudney, D. and Matthew, R. (eds) (1999) *Contested Grounds: Security and Conflict in the New Environmental Politics* (Albany).
Deutsch, K. W. and Singer, J. D. (1964) 'Multipolar Power Systems and International Stability', *World Politics,* 16(3).
Devetak, R. (1995a) 'Incomplete States: Theories and Practices of Statecraft', in J. MacMillan and A. Linklater (eds), *Boundaries in Question: New Directions in International Relations* (London).
— (1995b) 'The Project of Modernity and International Relations Theory', *Millennium,* 24(1).
— (2002) 'Signs of a New Enlightenment? Concepts of Community and Humanity after the Cold War', in S. Lawson (ed.), *The New Agenda for International Relations: From Polarization to Globalization in World Politics* (Cambridge).
— (2003) 'Loyalty and Plurality: Images of the Nation in Australia', in M. Waller and A. Linklater (eds), *Political Loyalty and the Nation-State* (London).
— (2005) 'Violence, Order and Terror', in A. Bellamy (ed.), *International Society and Its Critics* (Oxford).
— (2007) 'Between Kant and Pufendorf: Humanitarian Intervention, Statist Anti-Cosmopolitanism and Critical International Theory', *Review of International Studies,* (33 special issue).
— (2008) 'Failures, Rogues and Terrorists: States of Exception and the North/South Divide', in A. Bellamy, R. Bleiker, S. Davies and R. Devetak (eds), *Security and the War on Terror* (London).
— (2009) 'After the Event: Don DeLillo's *White Noise* and September 11 Narratives', *Review of International Studies,* 35(4).
— (2012) 'Vico contra Kant: The Competing Critical Theories of Cox and Linklater', in S. Brincat, L. Lima and J. Nunes (eds) *Critical Theory in International Relations and Security Studies* (Abingdon).
Devetak, R. and Higgott, R. (1999) 'Justice Unbound? Globalization, States and the Transformation of the Social Bond', *International Affairs,* 75(3).
Diamond, J. (1997) *Guns, Germs and Steel: A Short History of Everybody for the Last Thirteen Thousand Years* (London).
— (2005) *Collapse: How Societies Choose to Fail or Succeed* (New York).

DiCicco, J. M. and Levy, J. S. (1999) 'Power Shifts and Problem Shifts: The Evolution of the Power Transition Research Program', *Journal of Conflict Resolution,* 43(6).

Diez, T. and Steans, J. (2005) 'A Useful Dialogue? Habermas and International Relations', *Review of International Studies,* 31(1).

Dillon, M. (1999) 'The Sovereign and the Stranger', in J. Edkins, N. Persram and V. Pin-Fat (eds), *Sovereignty and Subjectivity* (Boulder).

Dillon, M. and Everard, J. (1992) 'Stat(e)ing Australia: Squid Jigging and the Masque of State', *Alternatives,* 17(3).

Dillon, M. and Reid, J. (2000) 'Global Governance, Liberal Peace, and Complex Emergency', *Alternatives,* 25(1).

Dingwerth, K. (2007) *The New Transnationalism: Transnational Governance and Democratic Accountability* (Basingstoke).

Dobson, A. (1990) *Green Political Thought* (London).

— (2003) *Citizenship and the Environment* (Oxford).

Doherty, B. and de Geus, M. (1996) 'Introduction', in B. Doherty and M. de Geus (eds), *Democracy and Green Political Thought* (London).

Domett, T. (2005) 'Soft Power in Global Politics? Diplomatic Partners as Transversal Actors', *Australian Journal of Political Science,* 40(2).

Donnelly, J. (1992) 'Twentieth Century Realism', in T. Nardin and D. Mapel (eds), *Traditions of International Ethics* (Cambridge).

— (1995) 'Realism and the Academic Study of International Relations', in J. Farr, J. S. Dryzek and S. T. Leonard (eds), *Political Science in History: Research Programs and Political Traditions* (Cambridge).

— (1998) 'Human Rights: A New Standard of Civilization?', *International Affairs,* 74(1).

— (2000) *Realism and International Relations* (Cambridge).

— (2003) *Universal Human Rights in Theory and Practice,* 2nd edn (Cornell).

— (2012) 'The Differentiation of International Societies: An Approach to Structural International Theory,' *European Journal of International Relations* 18(1).

Doran, P. (1993) 'The Earth Summit (UNCED): Ecology as Spectacle', *Paradigms,* 7(1).

— (1995) 'Earth, Power, Knowledge: Towards a Critical Global Environmental Politics', in J. MacMillan and A. Linklater (eds), *New Directions in International Relations* (London).

Doty, R. L. (1999) 'Racism, Desire, and the Politics of Immigration', *Millennium,* 28(3).

Douthwaite, R. (1992) *The Growth Illusion* (Dublin).

Doyle, M. (1983) 'Kant, Liberal Legacies and Foreign Affairs', *Philosophy and Public Affairs,* 12(3).

— (1986) 'Liberalism and World Politics', *American Political Science Review,* 80(4).

— (1995) 'Liberalism and World Politics Revisited', in C. W. Kegley Jr (ed.), *Controversies in International Relations Theory* (New York).

— (1997) *Ways of War and Peace: Realism, Liberalism and Socialism* (New York).

Dryzek, J. (1987) *Rational Ecology: Environment and Political Economy* (Oxford).

— (1990) *Discursive Democracy: Politics, Policy, and Political Science* (Cambridge).

— (1992) 'Ecology and Discursive Democracy: Beyond Liberal Capitalism and the Administrative State', *Capitalism, Nature, Socialism,* 3(2).

— (1999) 'Transnational Democracy', *Journal of Political Philosophy,* 7(1).

— (2011) *Foundations and Frontiers of Deliberative Governance* (Oxford).

Dryzek, J., Downes, D., Hunold, C., Schlosberg, D. and Hernes, H.-K. (2003) *Green States and Social Movements: Environmentalism in the United States, United Kingdom, Germany, and Norway* (Oxford).

Dubash, N.K. and Rajamani, L. (2010) 'Beyond Copenhagen: Next Steps', *Climate Policy* 10.

Dunne, T. (1998) *Inventing International Society: A History of the English School* (Basingstoke).

— (2003) 'Society and Hierarchy in International Relations', *International Relations,* 17(3).

— (2008) 'Good Citizen Europe', *International Affairs,* 84(1).

Dunne, T. and Wheeler, N. J. (eds) (1999) *Human Rights in Global Politics* (Cambridge).

Durkheim, É. (1993) *Ethics and the Sociology of Morals* (New York).

Eckersley, R. (1992) *Environmentalism and Political Theory: Towards an Ecocentric Approach* (London).

— (2004) *The Green State: Rethinking Democracy and Sovereignty* (Massachusetts).

Edelman, N. (1990) 'Global Prohibition Regimes: The Evolution of Norms in International Society', *International Organisation,* 44(4).

Edkins, J. (1999) *Poststructuralism and International Relations: Bringing the Political Back In* (Boulder).

— (2000) 'Sovereign Power, Zones of Indistinction, and the Camp', *Alternatives,* 25(1).

— (2002) 'Forget Trauma? Responses to September 11', *International Relations,* 16(2).

— (2007) 'Poststructuralism', in M. Griffiths (ed,), *International Relations Theory for the Twenty-First Century: An Introduction* (London).

Edkins, J. and Pin-Fat, V. (1999) 'The Subject of the Political', in J. Edkins, N. Persram and V. Pin-Fat (eds), *Sovereignty and Subjectivity* (Boulder).

Ehrlich, P. (1968) *The Population Bomb* (New York).

Eichler, Maya (2011) *Militarizing Men: Gender, Conscription and War in Post-Soviet Russia.* (Stanford).

Eisenstadt, S. N. (1963) *The Political Systems of Empires* (London).

Ekins, P. (1993) 'Making Development Sustainable', in W. Sachs (ed.), *Global Ecology* (London).

Elias, N. (1983) *The Court Society* (Oxford).

— (1994) *Reflections on a Life* (Cambridge).

— (1998a) 'An Interview in Amsterdam', in J. Goudsblom and S. Mennell (eds), *The Norbert Elias Reader* (Oxford).

— (1998b) 'The Retreat of Sociologists into the Present', in J. Goudsblom and S. Mennell (eds), *The Norbert Elias Reader* (Oxford).

— (2000) *The Civilizing Process: Sociogenetic and Psychogenetic Investigations* (Oxford).

— (2007) *Involvement and Detachment* (Dublin).

— (2010a) *The Loneliness of the Dying and Humana Conditio,* (Dublin).

— (2010b) *The Symbol Theory* (Dublin).

Elman, M. F. (2000) 'Unpacking Democracy: Presidentialism, Parliamentarism, and Theories of Democratic Peace', *Security Studies* 9(4).

Elshtain, J. B. (1985) 'Reflections on War and Political Discourse: Realism, Just War, and Feminism in a Nuclear Age', *Political Theory,* 13(1).

— (1987) *Women and War* (New York).

— (1992) 'Sovereignty, Identity, Sacrifice', in M. V. S. Peterson (ed.), *Gendered States: Feminist (Re)visions of International Relations Theory* (Boulder).

Emmanuel, A. (1972) *Unequal Exchange: A Study of the Imperialism of Trade* (New York).

Emy, H. V. (1993) *Remaking Australia* (Melbourne).

Enloe, C. (1989) *Bananas, Beaches and Bases: Making Feminist Sense of International Politics* (London).

— (1994) *The Morning After: Sexual Politics at the End of the Cold War* (Berkeley).

— (1997) 'Margins, Silences, and Bottom-Rungs: How to Overcome the Underestimation of Power in the Study of International Relation', in S. Smith, K. Booth and M. Zalewski (eds), *International Theory: Positivism and Beyond* (Cambridge).

— (2000) *Manoeuvers: The International Politics of Militarizing Women's Lives* (Berkeley).

— (2010) *Nimmo's War, Emma's War: Making Feminist Sense of the War in Iraq* (Berkeley).

Eschle, C. and Maiguaschca, B. (eds) (2005) *Critical Theories, World Politics, and the 'Anti-Globalization Movement'* (London).

Escobar, A. (1995) *Encountering Development: The Making and Unmaking of the Third World* (Princeton).

Escudé, C. (1997) *Foreign Policy Theory in Menem's Argentina* (Gainesville).

Esteva, G. and Prakash, M. S. (1997) 'From Global Thinking to Local Thinking', in M. Rahnema (ed.) with V. Bawtree, *The Post-Development Reader* (London), originally in *Interculture*, 29(2) (1996).

Evans, G. (2008) *The Responsibility to Protect: Ending Mass Atrocity Crimes Once and for All* (Washington, DC).

Falk, R. (1999) *Predatory Globalization: A Critique* (Cambridge).

Ferguson, Y. H., and Mansbach, R. W. (1996) *Polities: Authorities, Identities and Change* (South Carolina).

Fierke, K. M. (1998) *Changing Games, Changing Strategies: Critical Investigations in Security* (Manchester).

— (2007) *Critical Approaches to International Security* (Cambridge).

Fine, R. (2007) *Cosmopolitanism* (London).

Finger, M. (1993) 'Politics of the UNCED Process', in W. Sachs (ed.), *Global Ecology* (London).

Finnemore, M. (1996) 'Norms, Culture, and World Politics: Insights from Sociology's Institutionalism', *International Organization*, 50(2).

— (2001) 'Exporting the English School?', *Review of International Studies*, 27(3).

Finnemore, M. and Toope, S. J. (2001) 'Alternatives to "Legalization": Richer Views of Law and Politics', *International Organization*, 55(3).

Finnis, J. (1996), The Ethics of War and Peace in the Catholic Natural Law Tradition', in T. Nardin (ed.), *The Ethics of War and Peace: Religious and Secular Perspectives* (Princeton).

Finnis, J., Boyle, J. M. and Grisez, G. (1987) *Nuclear Deterrence, Morality and Realism* (Oxford).

Fischer, M. (1992) 'Feudal Europe, 800–1300: Communal Discourse and Conflictual Practices', *International Organisation*, 46(2).

Forbes, I. and Hoffman, M. (eds) (1993) *Political Theory, International Relations and the Ethics of Intervention* (Basingstoke).

Forde, S. (1992) 'Classical Realism', in T. Nardin and D. Mapel (eds), *Traditions of International Ethics* (Cambridge).

Forsyth, M. (1979) 'Thomas Hobbes and the External Relations of States', *British Journal of International Studies*, 5(3).

— (1981) *Unions of States: The Theory and Practice of Confederation* (New York).

Forsyth, M., Keens-Soper, H. M. A. and Savigear P. (eds) (1970) *The Theory of International Relations: Selected Texts from Gentili to Treitschke* (New York).

Foucault, M. (1977) *Discipline and Punish* (Harmondsworth).

— (1987) 'Nietzsche, Genealogy, History', in M. T. Gibbons (ed.), *Interpreting Politics* (London).

— (2003) 'Society Must be Defended': Lectures at the Collège de France, 1975–1976 (New York).

Frank, A. G. (1967) *Capitalism and Underdevelopment in Latin America* (New York).

Frank, A. G., and Gills, B.K. (eds) (1993) *The World System: Five Hundred Years or Five Thousand?* (London).

Friedman, E. (1995) Women's Human Rights: The Emergence of a Movement', in J. Peters and A. Wolper (eds), *Women's Rights/Human Rights: International Feminist Perspectives* (New York).

Friedman, G. (1981) *The Political Philosophy of the Frankfurt School* (New York).

Friedman, T. (2000) *The Lexus and the Olive Tree* (London).

Fukuyama, F. (1992) *The End of History and the Last Man* (London).

— (1998) 'Women and the Evolution of World Politics', *Foreign Affairs*, 77(5): 24–40.

— (2002) 'History and September 11', in K. Booth and T. Dunne (eds), *Worlds in Collision* (London).

— (2012) 'The Failures of the Facebook Generation in the Arab Spring', *The Daily Beast* (21 May).

Gabriel, C. and Macdonald, L. (1994) 'Women's Transnational Organizing in the Context of NAFTA: Forging Feminist Internationality', *Millennium*, 23(3).

Gaddis, J. (1992–3) 'International Relations Theory and the End of the Cold War', *International Security*, 17(3).

Gallie, W. B. (1978) *Philosophers of Peace and War* (Cambridge).

Gamble, A. (1981) *An Introduction to Modern Social and Political Thought* (London).

— (1999) 'Marxism after Communism: Beyond Realism and Historicism', *Review of International Studies*, 25(5).

Gardner, R. N. (1990) 'The Comeback of Liberal Internationalism', *The Washington Quarterly*, 13(3).

Garnett, J. C. (1984) *Commonsense and the Theory of International Politics* (London).

Gatens, M. (1991) *Feminism and Philosophy* (Bloomington).

Gellner, E. (1974) *Legitimation of Belief* (Cambridge).

Gentry, C. and Sjoberg, L. (2008) *Mothers, Monsters, Whores: Women's Violence in Global Politics* (London).

George, J. (1994) *Discourses of Global Politics: A Critical (Re)Introduction* (Boulder).

George, J. and Campbell, D. (1990) 'Patterns of Dissent and the Celebration of Difference: Critical Social Theory and International Relations', *International Studies Quarterly*, 34(3).

Geras, N. (1999) 'The View from Everywhere', *Review of International Studies*, 25(1).

Geuss, R. (2008) *Philosophy and Real Politics* (Princeton).

Gibson, K., Law, L. and McKay, D. (2001) 'Beyond Heroes and Victims: Filipina Contract Migrants, Economic Activism and Class Transformations', *International Feminist Journal of Politics*, 3(3).

Giddens, A. (1985) *The Nation-State and Violence* (Cambridge).

Gill, S. (ed.) (1993a) *Gramsci, Historical Materialism and International Relations* (Cambridge).

— (1993b) 'Gramsci and Global Politics: Towards a Post-Hegemonic Research Agenda', in S. Gill, *Gramsci, Historical Materialism and International Relations* (Cambridge).

— (1995) 'Globalization, Market Civilisation and Disciplinary Neo-Liberalism', *Millennium*, 24(4).

— (1996) 'Globalization, Democratization, and the Politics of Indifference', in J. Mittelman (ed.), *Globalization: Critical Reflections* (Boulder).

— (2003) *Power and Resistance in the New Global Order* (London).

— (2012) *Global Crises and the Crisis of Global Leadership* (Cambridge).

Gilligan, C. (1982) *In a Different Voice: Psychological Theory and Women's Development* (Cambridge).

Gills, B. K., and Thompson, W. R. (eds) (2006) *Globalization and Global History* (Abingdon).

Gilpin, R. (1981) *War and Change in World Politics* (Cambridge).

— (1986) 'The Richness of the Tradition of Political Realism', in R. O. Keohane (ed.), *Neo-Realism and Its Critics* (New York).

— (1996) 'No One Loves a Political Realist', *Security Studies*, 5(3).

Glaser, C. L. (1997) 'The Security Dilemma Revisited', *World Politics*, 50(1).

Glaser, C. L. and Kaufmann, C. (1998) 'What is the Offense-Defense Balance and Can We Measure It?', *International Security*, 22(4).

Goetz, A.-M. (1991) 'Feminism and the Claim to Know: Contradictions in Feminist Approaches to Women in Development', in R. Grant and K. Newland (eds), *Gender and International Relations* (London).

Goldstein, J. (2001) *War and Gender* (Cambridge).

Goldthorpe, J. (1991) 'The Uses of History in Sociology: Reflections on Some Recent Tendencies', *British Journal of Sociology*, 42(2).

Gong, G. (1984) *The Standard of Civilisation in International Society* (Oxford).

Goodin, R. (1992) *Green Political Theory* (Cambridge).

Gouldner, A. (1980) *The Two Marxisms: Contradictions and Anomalies in the Development of Theory* (New York).

Graham, G. (2008) *Ethics and International Relations*, 2nd edn (Malden).

Grant, R. and Newland, K. (eds) (1991) *Gender and International Relations* (London).

Gray, J. G. (1959) *The Warriors* (New York).

— (2004) *Al Qaeda and What It Means To Be Modern* (London).

Gray, M. M., Kittleson, M. C. and Sandholtz, W. (2006) 'Women and Globalization: A Study of 180 Countries, 1975–2000', *International Organization,* 60(2).

Grieco, J. M. (1988) 'Anarchy and the Limits of Cooperation', *International Organization,* 42(3).

— (1997) 'Realist International Theory and the Study of World Politics', in M. W. Doyle and G. J. Ikenberry (eds), *New Thinking in International Relations Theory* (Boulder).

Gulick, E. V. (1967) *Europe's Classical Balance of Power: A Case History of the Theory and Practice of One of the Great Concepts of European Statecraft* (New York).

Guzzini, S. (1998) *Realism in International Relations and International Political Economy: The Continuing Story of a Death Foretold* (London).

Haacke, J. (2005) 'The Frankfurt School and International Relations: On the Centrality of Recognition', *Review of International Studies,* 31(1).

Haas, P. (1989) 'Do Regimes Matter? Epistemic Communities and Mediterranean Pollution Control', *International Organization,* 43(3).

— (1990) *Saving the Mediterranean: The Politics of International Environmental Cooperation* (New York).

— (1992) 'Introduction: Epistemic Communities and International Policy Coordination', *International Organization,* 46(1).

— (2000) 'Social Constructivism and the Evolution of Multilateral Environmental Governance', in A. Prakash and J. Hart (eds), *Globalization and Governance* (London).

Haas, P. M., Keohane, R. O. and Levy, M. A. (1993) *Institutions for the Earth: Sources of Effective Environmental Protection* (Massachusetts).

Habermas, J. (1979) *Communication and the Evolution of Society* (Boston).

— (1984a) *Communication and the Evolution of Society* (London).

— (1984b) *The Theory of Communicative Action, 1: Reason and the Rationalization of Society* (Cambridge).

— (1987) *The Philosophical Discourse of Modernity: Twelve Lectures* (Cambridge).

— (1990) *Moral Consciousness and Communicative Action* (Cambridge).

— (1993) *Justification and Application: Remarks on Discourse Ethics* (Cambridge).

— (1994) *The Past as Future* (Cambridge).

— (1997) 'Kant's Idea of Perpetual Peace, with the Benefit of Two Hundred Years' Hindsight', in J. Bohman and M. Lutz-Bachmann (eds), *Perpetual Peace: Essays on Kant's Cosmopolitan Ideal* (London).

— (1998) *The Inclusion of the Other: Studies in Political Theory* (Cambridge).

— (1999) 'Bestiality and Humanity: A War on the Border between Legality and Morality', *Constellations,* 6(3).

— (2003a) 'Interpreting the Fall of a Monument', *Constellations,* 10(3).

— (2003b) 'Fundamentalism and Terror – A Dialogue with Jürgen Habermas', in Giovanni Borradori (ed.), *Philosophy in a Time of Terror: Dialogues with Jürgen Habermas and Jacques Derrida* (Chicago).

— (2006) *The Divided West* (Cambridge).

Habermas, J. and Derrida, J. (2003) 'February 15, or What Binds Europeans Together: A Plea for a Common Foreign Policy, Beginning in the Core of Europe', *Constellations,* 10(3).

Hahn, R.W. and Richards, K.R. (1989) 'The Internationalisation of Environmental Regulation', *Harvard International Law Journal,* 30(2).

Hajer, M. (1995) *The Politics of Environmental Discourse: Ecological Modernisation and the Policy Process* (Oxford).

Hall, I. (2006) *The International Political Thought of Martin Wight* (Basingstoke).

Hall, P. A. and Taylor, R. C. R. (1996) 'Political Science and the Three New Institutionalisms', *Political Studies,* 44(5).

Hall, R. B. (1999) *National Collective Identity: Social Constructs and International Systems* (New York).

Hall, R. B., and Kratochwil, F. (1993) 'Medieval Tales: Neorealist "Science" and the Abuse of History', *International Organisation*, 47(3).

Halliday, F. (1983) *The Making of the Second Cold War* (London).

— (1988a) 'Three Concepts of Internationalism', *International Affairs*, 64(2).

— (1988b) 'Hidden from International Relations: Women and the International Arena', *Millennium*, 17(3).

— (1990) 'The Pertinence of International Relations', *Political Studies*, 38(1).

— (1994) *Rethinking International Relations* (London).

— (1999) *Revolution and World Politics: The Rise and Fall of the Fifth Great Power* (Basingstoke).

Hallie, P. (1994) *Lest Innocent Blood Be Shed: The Story of the Village of Le Chambon and How Goodness Happened There* (New York).

Hanochi, S. (2003) 'Constitutionalism in a Modern Patriarchal State: Japan, the Sex Sector and Social Reproduction', in I. Bakker and S. Gill (eds), *Power, Production and Social Reproduction* (Basingstoke).

Hansenclever, A., Mayer, P. and Rittberger, V. (1996) 'Interests, Power, Knowledge: The Study of International Regimes', *Mershon International Studies Review*, 40(2).

Hardin, G. (1968) 'The Tragedy of the Commons', *Science*, 162.

— (1974) Commentary: Living on a Lifeboat', *BioScience* 24(10).

Harding, S. (1986) *The Science Question in Feminism* (Ithaca).

— (1987) *Feminism and Methodology* (Bloomington).

Harrison, N. (2006)'From Economics to Ecology: Toward New Theory for International Environmental Politics', in E. Laferrière, and P. Stoett, (eds) *International Ecopolitical Theory: Critical Approaches* (Vancouver).

Harvey, D. (2003) *The New Imperialism* (Oxford).

Hashmi, S. H. (ed.) (2002) *Islamic Political Ethics: Civil Society, Pluralism, and Conflict* (Princeton).

Haslam, J. (2002) *No Virtue Like Necessity: Realist Thought in International Relations since Machiavelli* (New Haven).

Hay, C. (1999) 'Marxism and the State', in A. Gamble *et al.* (eds), *Marxism and Social Science* (London).

Hayward, T. (1995) *Ecological Thought: An Introduction* (Cambridge).

— (1998) *Political Theory and Ecological Values* (Cambridge).

Head, N. (2008) 'Critical Theory and its Practices: Habermas, Kosovo and International Relations', *Politics*, 28(3).

Heilbroner, R. (1974) *An Inquiry into the Human Prospect* (New York).

Heins, V. (2008) *Non Governmental Organizations in International Society: Struggles over Recognition* (Basingstoke).

Held, D. (ed.) (1993) *Prospects for Democracy: North, South, East, West* (Cambridge).

— (1995) *Democracy and the Global Order: From the Modern State to Cosmopolitan Democracy* (Cambridge).

Held, D. and McGrew, A. (eds) (2000), *The Global Transformations Reader* (Cambridge).

Held, D., McGrew, A., Goldblatt, D. and Perraton, J. (1999) *Global Transformations* (Cambridge).

Helleiner, E. (1996) 'International Political Economy and the Greens', *New Political Economy*, 1(1).

— (2000) 'New Voices in the Globalization Debate: Green Perspectives on the World Economy', in R. Stubbs and G. Underhill (eds), *Political Economy and the Changing Global Order*, 2nd edn (Oxford).

Helman, G. B. and Ratner, S. R. (1992–93) 'Saving Failed States', *Foreign Policy*, 89 (Winter).

Hempel, L. (1996) *Environmental Governance: The Global Challenge* (Washington).

Herring, E. and Robinson, P. (eds) (2003) 'Forum on Chomsky', *Review of International Studies*, 29(4).

Herz, J. H. (1976) *The Nation-State and the Crisis of World Politics: Essays on International Politics in the Twentieth Century* (New York).

Hildyard, N. (1993) 'Foxes in Charge of the Chickens', in W. Sachs (ed.), *Global Ecology* (London).

Hill, C. J. (1999) 'Where are we Going? International Relations, the Voice from Below', *Review of International Studies*, 25(1).

— (2003) *The Changing Politics of Foreign Policy* (Basingstoke).

Hintze, O. (1975) *The Historical Essays of Otto Hintze* (edited with an introduction by Felix Gilbert), (Oxford).

Hirst, P. and Thompson, G. (1996) *Globalization in Question: The International Economy and the Possibilities of Governance* (Cambridge).

Hobden, S. (1998) *International Relations and Historical Sociology: Breaking Down Boundaries* (London).

Hobden, S. and Hobson, J. M. (eds) (2002) *Historical Sociology and International Relations* (Cambridge).

Hobsbawm, E. (2000) *The New Century* (London).

— (2002) *The Observer*, 22 September, http://www.observer.co.uk/comment/ story/ 0,6903,796531,00.html

— (2007) *Globalization, Democracy and Terrorism* (Boston).

Hobson, C. (2008) 'Democracy as Civilization', *Global Society* 22(1).

Hobson, J. (2004) *The Eastern Origins of Western Civilisation* (Cambridge).

— (2012) *The Eurocentric Conception of World Politics: Western International Theory 1760–2010* (Cambridge).

Hoffman, M. (1987) 'Critical Theory and the Inter-Paradigm Debate', *Millennium*, 16(2).

— (1991) 'Restructuring, Reconstruction, Reinscription, Rearticulation: Four Voices in Critical International Theory', *Millennium*, 20(2).

— (1992) 'Third-Party Mediation and Conflict-Resolution in the Post-Cold War World', in J. Baylis and N. Rengger (eds), *Dilemmas of World Politics* (Oxford).

— (1993) 'Agency, Identity and Intervention', in I. Forbes and M. Hoffman (eds), *Political Theory, International Relations and the Ethics of Intervention* (London).

Hoffmann, S. (1990) 'International Society', in J. D. B. Miller and R. J. Vincent (eds), *Order and Violence: Hedley Bull and International Relations* (Oxford).

— (1995) 'The Crisis of Liberal Internationalism', *Foreign Policy*, 98 (Spring).

Hoffmann, M. J. (2011) *Climate Governance at the Crossroads: Experimenting with a Global Response after Kyoto* (Oxford).

Holland, B. (2010) 'Sovereignty as *Dominium*? Reconstructing the Constructivist Roman Law Thesis', *International Studies Quarterly* 54(2).

Hollis, M. and Smith, S. (1990) *Explaining and Understanding International Relations* (Oxford).

Holmes, S. (2007) *The Matador's Cape: America's Reckless Response to Terror.* (Cambridge).

Holsti, K. (1985) *The Dividing Discipline: Hegemony and Diversity in International Theory* (Boston).

Homer-Dixon, T. (1993) 'Physical Dimensions of Global Change', in N. Choucri (ed.), *Global Accord: Environmental Challenges and International Responses* (Cambridge).

— (1999) *Environment, Scarcity and Violence* (Princeton).

Hooper, C. (2000) *Manly States: Masculinities, International Relations, and Gender Politics* (New York).

Hopf, T. (1998) 'The Promise of Constructivism in International Relations Theory', *International Security*, 23(1).

Horkheimer, M. (1972) *Critical Theory* (New York).

Horkheimer, M. and Adorno, T. (1972) *Dialectic of Enlightenment* (New York).

Hoskyns, C. (1996) *Integrating Gender: Women, Law and Politics in the European Union* (London).

Hoskyns, C. and Rai, S. (2007) 'Recasting the Global Political Economy: Counting Women's Unpaid Work', *New Political Economy,* 12(3).

Hovden, E. (1999) 'As If Nature Doesn't Matter: Ecology, Regime Theory and International Relations', *Environmental Politics,* 8(2).

— (2006) 'Ecology and Critical Theories: A Problematic Synthesis', in E. Laferrière, and P. Stoett, (eds) *International Ecopolitical Theory: Critical Approaches* (Vancouver).

Howard, M. (1978) *War and the Liberal Conscience* (Oxford).

Hui, V. T.-B. (2005) *War and State Formation in Ancient China and Early Modern Europe* (Cambridge).

Humphreys, D., Paterson, M. and Pettiford, L. (eds) (2003) 'Global Environmental Governance for the 21st Century', *Global Environmental Politics,* Special Issue, 3(2).

Hunt, K. (2002) 'The Strategic Cooptation of Women's Rights: Discourse in the "War on ... Afghanistan and Iraq"', *International Feminist Journal of Politics,* 4(1).

Hunt, L. (2007) *Inventing Human Rights: A History* (Norton).

Huntington, S. (1993) 'The Clash of Civilisations', *Foreign Affairs,* 72(3).

— (1996) *The Clash of Civilizations and the Remaking of World Order* (New York).

Hurd, I. (2005) 'The Strategic Use of Liberal Internationalism: Libya and Sanctions, 1992–2003', *International Organization,* 59(3).

— (2007) *After Anarchy: Legitimacy and Power in the United Nations Security Council* (Princeton).

Hurrell, A. (1993) 'International Society and the Study of International Regimes: A Reflective Approach', in V. Rittberger (ed.), *Regime Theory and International Relations* (Oxford).

— (1994) 'A Crisis of Ecological Viability – Global Environmental Change and the Nation-State', *Political Studies,* 42 (Special Issue).

— (2002) '"There Are No Rules" (George W. Bush): International Order after September 11', *International Relations,* 16(2).

— (2006a) 'The State', in A. Dobson and R. Eckersley (eds), *Political Theory and the Ecological Challenge* (Cambridge).

— (2006b) 'Hegemony, Liberalism and Global Order: What Space for Would-Be Great Powers', *International Affairs,* 82(1).

— (2007) *On Global Order: Power, Values and the Constitution of International Society* (Oxford).

Hurrell, A. and Kingsbury, B. (1992) *The International Politics of the Environment* (Oxford).

Hutchings, K. (1999) *International Political Theory: Rethinking Ethics in a Global Era* (London).

— (2000) 'Towards a Feminist International Ethics', *Review of International Studies,* Special Issue, 26.

— (2004) 'From Morality to Politics and Back Again: Feminist International Ethics and the Civil Society Argument', *Alternatives,* 29(3).

— (2010) *Global Ethics: An Introduction* (Cambridge).

Ikenberry, J. G. (2000) *After Victory* (Princeton).

IUCN (1980) *World Conservation Strategy* (Gland).

Jackson, R. (1990) *Quasi-States: Sovereignty, International Relations and the Third World* (Cambridge).

— (2000) *The Global Covenant: Human Conduct in a World of States* (Oxford).

— (2008) 'From Colonialism to Theology: Encounters with Martin Wight's International Thought', *International Affairs,* 84(2).

Jackson, T. (2009) *Prosperity without Growth: Economics for a Finite Planet* (London).

Jacoby, T. (1999) 'Feminism, Nationalism and Difference: Reflections on the Palestinian Women's Movement', *Women's Studies International Forum,* 22(5).

Jahn, B. (ed.) (2006) *Classical Theory in International Relations* (Cambridge).

Jaquette, J. (1984) 'Power as Ideology: A Feminist Analysis', in J. H. Stiehm (ed.), *Women's Views of the Political World of Men* (Dobbs Ferry).

Jarvis, D. S. (2000) *International Relations and the Challenge of Postmodernism: Defending the Discipline* (Columbia, South Carolina).

Jay, M. (1973) *The Dialectical Imagination* (Boston).

Jeffery, L. A. (2002) *Sex and Borders: Gender, National Identity and Prostitution Policy in Thailand* (Basingstoke).

Jeffery, R. (2006) *Hugo Grotius in International Thought* (Basingstoke).

Jepperson, R., Wendt, A. and Katzenstein, P. J. (1996) 'Norms, Identity, and Culture in National Security', in Peter J. Katzenstein (ed.), *The Culture of National Security: Norms and Identity in World Politics* (New York).

Jervis, R. (1978) 'Cooperation Under the Security Dilemma,' *World Politics*, 30(2).

— (1998) 'Realism in the Study of World Politics', *International Organization*, 52(4).

— (2011) 'Force in Our Times', *International Relations*, 25(4).

Johnson, C. (2002) *Blowback*, 2nd edn (London).

Johnson, L. M. (1993) *Thucydides, Hobbes, and the Interpretation of Realism* (DeKalb).

Johnson, S. and Kwak, J. (2010) *13 Bankers* (New York).

Johnston, A. I. (1995) *Cultural Realism: Strategic Culture and Grand Strategy in Chinese History* (Princeton).

Jones, B. G. (2008) '"Tell No Lies, Claim No Easy Victories": Possibilities and Contradictions of Emancipatory Struggles in the Current Neocolonial Condition', in A. Ayers, (ed.) (2008) *Gramsci, Political Economy and International Relations Theory: Modern Princes and Naked Emperors* (Basingstoke).

Jones, C. (1999) *Global Justice: Defending Cosmopolitanism* (Oxford).

Jones, D. (1999) *Cosmopolitan Mediation? Conflict Resolution and the Oslo Accords* (Manchester).

— (2001) 'Creating Cosmopolitan Power: International Mediation as Communicative Action', in R. Wyn Jones (ed.), *Critical Theory and World Politics* (Boulder).

Jones, R. E. (1981) 'The English School of International Relations: A Case for Closure', *Review of International Studies*, 7(1).

Jørgensen, K. E. (2010) *International Relations Theory: A New Introduction* (New York).

Joseph, J. (2002) *Hegemony: A Realist Analysis* (London).

— (2006) *Marxism and Social Theory* (London).

Kabeer, N. (1994) *Reversed Realities: Gender Hierarchies in Development Thought* (London).

Kahler, M. (1997) 'Inventing International Relations: International Relations Theory After 1945', in M. W. Doyle and G. J. Ikenberry (eds), *New Thinking in International Relations Theory* (Boulder).

Kant, I. (1991) *Political Writings*, ed. H. Reiss, translated by H. B. Nisbet (Cambridge).

— (1999) *Metaphysical Elements of Justice*, ed. J. Ladd, 2nd edn (London).

Kaplan, R. (1994) The Coming Anarchy', *Atlantic Monthly*, February.

Kapoor, I. (2004) 'Deliberative Democracy and the WTO', *Review of International Political Economy*, 11(3).

Kapstein, E. and Mastanduno, M. (eds) (1999) *Unipolar Politics: Realism and State Strategies after the Cold War* (New York).

Kardam, N. (1991) *Bringing Women in: Women's Issues in International Development Programs* (Boulder).

— (2004) 'The Emerging Global Gender Equality Regime from Neoliberal and Constructivist Perspectives in International Relations', *International Feminist Journal of Politics*, 6(1).

Kassiola, J. J. (2003) 'Afterword: The Surprising Value of Despair and the Aftermath of September 11th', in J. J. Kassiola (ed.), *Explorations in Environmental Political Theory* (Armonk).

Katzenstein, P. J. (1996) *The Culture of National Security: Police and Military in Postwar Japan* (Ithaca).

— (1999) *Tamed Power: Germany in Europe* (Ithaca).

— (ed.) (2010) *Civilizations in World Politics: Plural and Pluralist Perspectives* (Abingdon).

— (2012a) *Sinicization and the Rise of China* (Abingdon).

— (2012b) *Anglo-America and Its Discontents* (Abingdon).

Katzenstein, P. J. and Okawara, N. (2001/2) 'Japan, Asian-Pacific Security, and the Case for Analytical Eclecticism', *International Security,* 26(3).

Kaufman, S. J. (1997) 'The Fragmentation and Consolidation of International Systems', *International Organization,* 51(2).

Kaufman, S., Little, R., and Wolhforth, W. C. (eds) (2007) *The Balance of Power in World History* (Basingstoke).

Kaufman-Osborn, T. (2005) 'Gender Trouble at Abu-Ghraib', *Politics and Gender,* 1(4).

Keal, P. (2003) *European Conquest and the Rights of Indigenous Peoples: The Moral Backwardness of International Society* (Cambridge).

Keck, M. and Sikkink, K. (1998) *Activist Beyond Borders* (Ithaca).

Keegan, J. (1993) *A History of Warfare* (New York).

Keeley, L. H. (1996) *War before Civilization: The Myth of the Peaceful Savage* (Oxford).

Keene, E. (2002) *Beyond the Anarchical Society: Grotius, Colonialism and Order in World Politics* (Cambridge).

— (2005) *International Political Thought: A Historical Introduction* (Cambridge).

Kelly, D. (2003) 'Karl Marx and Historical Sociology', in G. Delanty and E. Isin (eds) *Handbook of Historical Sociology* (London).

Kelsay, J. (2007) *Arguing the Just War in Islam* (Cambridge, MA).

Kennan, G. F. (1954) *Realities of American Foreign Policy* (Princeton).

— (1985) 'Morality and Foreign Policy,' *Foreign Affairs,* 64(2).

Keohane, R. O. (1984) *After Hegemony: Cooperation and Discord in the World Political Economy* (Princeton).

— (1986) 'Theory of World Politics: Structural Realism and Beyond', in R. O. Keohane (ed.), *Neo-Realism and Its Critics* (New York).

— (1988) 'International Institutions: Two Approaches', *International Studies Quarterly,* 32(4).

— (1989a) *International Institutions and State Power: Essays in International Relations Theory* (Boulder).

— (1989b) 'International Relations Theory: Contributions of a Feminist Standpoint', *Millennium,* 18(2).

— (2012) 'Twenty Years of Institutional Liberalism', *International Relations* 26(2).

Keohane, R. O. and Nye, J. (eds) (1972) *Transnationalism and World Politics* (Massachusetts).

— (1977) *Power and Interdependence: World Politics in Transition* (Boston).

Khalid, M. (2011) 'Gender, Orientalism and the Representation of the "Other" in the War on Terror', *Global Change, Peace and Security,* 23 (1).

Kier, E. (1997) *Imagining War: French and British Military Doctrine Between the Wars* (Princeton).

Kinsella, H. M. (2005) 'Securing the Civilian: Sex and Gender in the Laws of War' in M. Barnett and R. Duvall (eds), *Power in Global Governance* (Cambridge).

Kiser, E. and Hechter, M. (1991) 'The Role of General Theory in Comparative-Historical Sociology', *American Journal of Sociology,* 97(1).

— (1998) 'The Debate on Historical Sociology: Rational Choice Theory and its Critics', *American Journal of Sociology,* 104(3).

Kissinger, H. A. (1957) *A World Restored: Metternich, Castlereagh and the Problems of Peace, 1812–22* (Boston).

— (1977) *American Foreign Policy* (New York).

Klare, M. (2001) *Resource Wars: The New Landscape of Global Conflict* (New York).

Klein, B. (1994) *Strategic Studies and World Order: The Global Politics of Deterrence* (Cambridge).

Klotz, A. (1995) *Norms in International Relations: The Struggle Against Apartheid* (Ithaca).

Knei-Paz, B. (1978) *The Social and Political Thought of Leon Trotsky* (Oxford).

Kolko, G. (2006) *After Socialism: Reconstructing Critical Social Thought* (Abingdon).

Koontz, T. J. (1996) 'Christian Nonviolence: An Interpretation', in T. Nardin (ed.), *The Ethics of War and Peace: Religious and Secular Perspectives* (Princeton).

— (1997) 'Noncombatant Immunity in Michael Walzer's *Just and Unjust Wars*', *Ethics & International Affairs* 11(1).

Korac, M. (1998) 'Ethnic Nationalism, War and the Patterns of Social, Political and Sexual Violence against Women: The Case of Post-Yugoslav Countries', *Identities*, 5(2).

Koskenniemi, M. (2001) *The Gentle Civilizer of Nations: The Rise and Fall of International Law 1870–1960* (Cambridge).

— (2007) 'The Fate of Public International Law: between Technique and Politics', *Modern Law Review*, 70(1).

Koslowski, R. and Kratochwil, F. (1995) 'Understanding Change in International Politics: The Soviet Empire's Demise and the International System', in R. N. Lebow and T. Risse-Kappen (eds), *International Relations Theory after the Cold War* (New York).

Kothari, A. (1992) 'The Politics of the Biodiversity Convention', *Economic and Political Weekly*, 27(15-16).

Krasner, S. (1983) 'Structural Causes and Regime Consequences: Regimes as Intervening Variables', in S. D. Krasner (ed.), *International Regimes* (Ithaca).

— (1999) *Sovereignty: Organized Hypocrisy* (Princeton).

Kratochwil, F. (1988/9) 'Regimes, Interpretation and the "Science" of Politics: A Reappraisal', *Millennium*, 17(2).

— (1993) 'The Embarrassment of Changes: Neo-realism as the Science of Realpolitik Without Politics', *Review of International Studies*, 19(1).

— (2000) 'Constructing a New Orthodoxy? Wendt's "Social Theory of International Politics and the Constructivionist Challenge"', *Millennium: Journal of International Studies*, 29(1).

Kratochwil, F. and Ruggie, J. G. (1986) 'International Organization: A State of the Art on an Art of the State?', *International Organization*, 40(4).

Krippendorf, E. (1982) *International Relations as a Social Science* (Brighton).

Krook, M.-L. and True, J. (2012) 'Rethinking the Life Cycles of International Norms: The United Nations and the Global Promotion of Gender Equality', *European Journal of International Relations*, 18(1): 103–27.

Kubalkova, V. and Cruickshank, A. (1980) *Marxism-Leninism and the Theory of International Relations* (London).

Kuehls, T. (1996) *Beyond Sovereign Territory: The Space of Ecopolitics* (Minneapolis).

Kuper, A. (2005) *Global Responsibilities: Who Must Deliver on Human Rights?* (London).

Kurki, M. (2008) *Causation in International Relations: Reclaiming Causal Analysis* (Cambridge).

Kütting, G. and Lipschutz, R. (eds) (2009) *Environmental Governance: Power and Knowledge in a Local-Global World* (London)

Labs, E. J. (1997) 'Beyond Victory: Offensive Realism and the Expansion of War Aims', *Security Studies*, 6(4).

Lacher, H. (2006) *Beyond Globalization: Capitalism, Territoriality and the International Relations of Modernity* (Abingdon).

Laferrière, E. (1996) 'Emancipating International Relations Theory: An Ecological Perspective', *Millennium*, 25(1).

Laferrière, E. and Stoett, P. (1999) *Ecological Thought and International Relations Theory* (London).

— (2006) *International Ecopolitical Theory: Critical Approaches* (Vancouver).

Laffey, M. and Weldes, J. (1997) 'Beyond Belief: Ideas and Symbolic Technologies in the Study of International Relations', *European Journal of International Relations*, 3(2).

Latham, A. A. (2012) *Theorising Medieval Geopolitics: War and World Order in the Age of the Crusades* (Abingdon).

Lawson, G. (2007) 'Historical Sociology in International Relations: Open Society, Research Programme and Vocation', *International Politics*, 44(4).

Layne, C. (1993) 'The Unipolar Illusion: Why New Great Powers Will Arise', *International Security*, 17(4).

Lebow, R. N. (2003) *The Tragic Vision of Politics: Ethics, Interests and Orders* (Cambridge).

— (2010) 'The Past and Future of War', *International Relations*, 24(3).

Lee, K. (1993) 'To De-Industrialize – Is it so Irrational?', in A. Dobson and P. Lucardie (eds), *The Politics of Nature: Explorations in Green Political Theory* (London).

Lenin, V. (1964) *Collected Works*, volume 20 (Moscow).

— (1968)[1916] *Imperialism: The Highest Stage of Capitalism* (Moscow).

Levinas, E. (1969) *Totality and Infinity: An Essay on Exteriority* (Pittsburgh).

Levy, J. S. (1989) 'The Causes of War: A Review of Theories and Evidence', in P. E. Tetlock (ed.), *Behaviour, Society and Nuclear War* (New York).

Leysens, A. (2008) *The Critical Theory of Robert W. Cox: Fugitive or Guru?* (Basingstoke).

Ling, L. H. (2001) *Post-colonial IR: Conquest and Desire between Asia and the West* (London).

Linklater, A. (1990a) *Beyond Realism and Marxism: Critical Theory and International Relations* (London).

— (1990b) *Men and Citizens in the Theory of International Relations*, 2nd edn (London).

— (1992a) 'The Question of the Next Stage in International Relations Theory: A Critical Theoretical Point of View', *Millennium*, 21(1).

— (1992b) 'What is a Good International Citizen?', in P. Keal (ed.), *Ethics and Foreign Policy* (Canberra).

— (1993) 'Liberal Democracy, Constitutionalism and the New World Order', in R. Leaver and J. L. Richardson (eds), *Charting the Post-Cold War Order* (Colorado).

— (1997) 'The Achievements of Critical Theory', in S. Smith, K. Booth and M. Zalewski (eds), *International Theory: Positivism and Beyond* (Cambridge).

— (1998) *The Transformation of Political Community; Ethical Foundations of the Post-Westphalian Era* (Cambridge).

— (1999) 'Transforming Political Community: A Response to the Critics', *Review of International Studies*, 25(1).

— (2001) 'Citizenship, Humanity and Cosmopolitan Harm Conventions', *International Political Science Review*, 22(3).

— (2002a) 'The Problem of Harm in World Politics: Implications for the Sociology of States-Systems', *International Affairs*, 78(2).

— (2002b) 'Unnecessary Suffering', in K. Booth and T. Dunne (eds), *Worlds in Collision: Terror and the Future of Global Order* (London).

— (2007a) *Critical Theory and World Politics: Citizenship, Sovereignty and Humanity* (London).

— (2007b) 'Torture and Civilisation', *International Relations*, 21(1).

— (2011a) 'Process Sociology and International Relations', in N. Gabriel and S. Mennell (eds) *Norbert Elias and Figurational Research: Processual Thinking in Sociology*, Sociological Review Monographs (Oxford).

— (2011b) *The Problem of Harm in World Politics: Theoretical Investigations* (Cambridge).

— (2011c) 'Prudence and Principle in International Society Politics: Reflections on Vincent's Perspective on Human Rights', *International Affairs*, 87(5).

Linklater, A. and Mennell, S. (2010) 'Retrospective: Norbert Elias, The Civilizing Process: Sociogenetic and Psychogenetic Investigations', *History and Theory*, 49(3).

Linklater, A. and Suganami, H. (2006) *The English School of International Relations: A Contemporary Assessment* (Cambridge).

Lipschutz, R. D. (1997) 'From Place to Planet: Local Knowledge and Global Environmental Governance', *Global Governance*, 3(1).

Lisle, D. (2000) 'Consuming Danger: Reimagining the War/Tourism Divide', *Alternatives*, 25(1).

Litfin, K. (ed.) (1998) *The Greening of Sovereignty in World Politics* (Cambridge, MA).

Little, R. (2000) 'The English School's Contribution to the Study of International Relations', *European Journal of International Relations*, 6(3).

Locher, B. and Prügl, E. (2001) 'Feminism and Constructivism: Worlds Apart or Sharing the Middle Ground?', *International Studies Quarterly*, 45(1).

Lohmann, L. (2006) 'Carbon Trading: a Critical Conversation on Climate Change, Privatization and Power', *Development Dialogue* 48.

Long, D. and Wilson, P. (eds) (1995) *Thinkers of the Twenty Years' Crisis* (Oxford).

Low, N. and Gleeson, B. (1998) *Justice, Nature and Society* (London).

Luke, T. L. (1997) *Ecocritique: Contesting the Politics of Nature, Economy, and Culture* (Minneapolis).

— (2009) 'Situating Knowledges, Spatializing Communities, Sizing Contradictions: the Politics of Globality, Locality and Green Statism', in Kütting and Lipschutz (eds) *Environmental Governance: Power and Knowledge in a Local-Global World* (Abingdon).

Lukes, S. (1985) *Marxism and Morality* (Oxford).

Lynch, C. (1999) *Beyond Appeasement: Reinterpreting Interwar Peace Movements in World Politics* (Ithaca).

Lynch, M. (1999) *State Interests and Public Spheres: The International Politics of Jordanian Identity* (New York).

— (2000) 'The Dialogue of Civilisations and International Public Spheres', *Millennium*, 29(2).

Lynn-Jones, S. M. (1995) 'Offense-Defense Theory and Its Critics', *Security Studies*, 4(4).

Lynn-Jones, S. M. and Miller, S. E. (1995) 'Preface', in M. E. Brown, S. M. Lynn-Jones and S. E. Miller (eds), *The Perils of Anarchy: Contemporary Realism and International Security* (Cambridge).

Lyotard, J.-F. (1984) *The PostModern Condition: A Report on Knowledge* (Manchester).

— (1993) 'The Other's Rights', in S. Shute and S. Hurley (eds), *On Human Rights: The Oxford Amnesty Lectures* (New York).

MacBride, K. and Wibben, A. T. R. (2012) 'The Gendering of Counterinsurgency in Afghanistan', *Humanity* 3(2).

Machiavelli, N. (1970) *The Discourses* (Harmondsworth).

— (1985) *The Prince* (Chicago).

Mackenzie, M. (2012) *Female Soldiers in Sierre Leone: Sex, Security and Postconflict Development* (New York).

Mackie, V. (2001) 'The Language of Globalization, Transnationality, and Feminism', *International Feminist Journal of Politics*, 3(2).

Mackinder, H. J. (1919) *Democratic Ideals and Reality: A Study in the Politics of Reconstruction* (New York).

Maclean, J. (1981) 'Marxist Epistemology, Explanations of "Change" and the Study of International Relations', in B. Buzan and R. B. Jones (eds), *Change in the Study of International Relations: The Evaded Dimension* (London).

MacMillan, J. (1995) 'A Kantian Protest Against the Peculiar Discourse of Inter-Liberal State Peace', *Millennium*, 24(4).

— (1998) *On Liberal Peace: Democracy, War and International Order* (London).

MacPherson, C. B. (1973) *Democratic Theory* (Oxford).

— (1977) *The Life and Times of Liberal Democracy* (Oxford).

Magnusson, W. (1996) *The Search for Political Space: Globalization, Social Movements and the Urban Political Experience* (Toronto).

Maiguaschca, B. (2003) 'Introduction: Governance and Resistance in World Politics', *Review of International Studies*, 29 (Supplement).

Malcolm, N. (2002) 'Hobbes's Theory of International Relations', in N. Malcolm, *Aspects of Hobbes* (Oxford).

Mandalios, J. (2003) 'Civilizational Complexes and Processes: Elias, Nelson and Eisenstadt', in G. Delanty and E. Isin (eds) *Handbook of Historical Sociology* (London).

Mann, M. (1986) *The Sources of Social Power, vol. 1: A History of Power from the Beginning to 1760AD* (Cambridge).

— (1994a) 'In Praise of Macro-Sociology: Reply to Goldthorpe', *British Journal of Sociology*, 45(1).

— (1994b) *The Sources of Social Power, vol. 2: The Rise of Classes and Nation States, 1760–1914* (Cambridge).

Manning, P. (2003) *Navigating World History: Historians Create Global Past* (Basingstoke).

Mantle, D. (1999) *Critical Green Political Theory and International Relations Theory – Compatibility or Conflict,* PhD thesis, Keele University.

Maoz, Z. and Russett, B. (1993) 'Normative and Structural Causes of Democratic Peace, 1946–1986', *American Political Science Review,* 87(3).

Marchand, M. and Parpart, J. (eds) (1995) *Feminism/Postmodernism/ Development* (London: Routledge).

Marchand, M. and Runyan, A. S. (eds) (2000) *Gender and Global Restructuring: Sites, Sightings and Resistances* (New York).

Martin, R. and Reidy, D. A. (eds) (2006) *Rawls's Law of Peoples: A Realistic Utopia?* (Malden).

Marx, K. (1966) *The Poverty of Philosophy* (Moscow).

— (1973) *Grundrisse* (Harmondsworth).

— (1977a) 'Capital', 1, in D. McLellan (ed.), *Karl Marx: Selected Writings* (Oxford).

— (1977b) 'Theses on Feuerbach', in D. McLellan (ed.), *Karl Marx: Selected Writings* (Oxford).

— (1977c) 'Towards A Critique of Hegel's Philosophy of Right: Introduction', in D. McLellan (ed.), *Karl Marx: Selected Writings* (Oxford).

— (1977d) 'Economic and Philosophical Manuscripts', in D. McLellan (ed.), *Karl Marx: Selected Writings* (Oxford).

— (1977e) 'The Eighteenth Brumaire of Louis Bonaparte', in D. McLellan (ed.), *Karl Marx: Selected Writings* (Oxford).

Marx, K. and Engels, F. (1971) *Ireland and the Irish Question* (London).

— (1977) 'The Communist Manifesto', in D. McLellan (ed.), *Karl Marx: Selected Writings* (Oxford).

Mason, P. (2010) *Meltdown: The End of the Age of Greed* (London).

Mastanduno, M. (1991) 'Do Relative Gains Matter? America's Response to Japanese Industrial Policy', *International Security,* 16(1).

— (1997) 'Preserving the Unipolar Moment: Realist Theories and US Grand Strategy after the Cold War', *International Security,* 21(4).

Mattingly, G. (1956) *Renaissance Diplomacy* (Boston).

May, L. (2004) *Crimes against Humanity: A Normative Account* (Cambridge).

Mayall, J. (ed.) (1996) *The New Interventionism 1991–1994: United Nations Experience in Cambodia, Former Yugoslavia and Somalia* (Cambridge).

— (2000) *World Politics: Progress and its Limits* (Cambridge).

Mazlish, B. (1989) *The New Science: The Breakdown of Connections and the Birth of Sociology* (Oxford).

— (2006) *The New Global History* (Abingdon).

Mazlish, B. and Irigye, A. (eds) (2005) *The Global History Reader* (London).

McClure, K. (1992) 'The Issue of Foundations: Scientized Politics, Politicized Science and Feminist Critical Practice', in J. W. Scott and J. Butler (eds), *Feminists Theorize the Political* (New York).

McCracken, A. (2011) 'Beauty and the Quinceanera: Reproductive, Productive and Virtual Dimensions of the Global Political Economy of Beauty', in J. Ann Tickner and L. Sjoberg (eds) *Feminism and International Relations* (New York).

McGlen, N. E. and Sarkees, M. R. (eds) (1993) *Women in Foreign Policy: The Insiders* (New York).

McIntire, C. T. (ed.) (1979) *Herbert Butterfield: Writings on Christianity and History* (New York).

McMahan, J. (2009) *Killing in War* (Oxford).

McNeill, J. R. and McNeill, W. H. (2003) *The Human Web: A Bird Eye's View of World History* (New York).

McNeill, W. H. (1979) *A World History* (Oxford).

— (1986) *Mythistory and other Essays* (London).

— (1995) 'The Changing Shape of World History', *History and Theory,* 34(2).

Mead, W.R. (2012) 'The Once and Future Liberalism', *The American Interest,* 24 (January).

Meadowcroft, J. (2006) 'Greening the State', *Politics and Ethics Review*, 2(2).

Meadows, D. and Randers, J. (1992) *Beyond the Limits* (London).

Meadows, D., Randers, J. and Behrens, W. (1972) *The Limits to Growth* (London).

Mearsheimer, J. (1990) '"Back to the Future": Instability in Europe After the Cold War', *International Security*, 15(1).

— (1994/5) 'The False Promise of International Institutions', *International Security*, 19(3).

— (1995) 'A Realist Reply', *International Security*, 20(1).

— (2001) *The Tragedy of Great Power Politics* (New York).

Mearsheimer, J. and Walt, S. M. (2002) *Can Saddam Be Contained? History Says Yes*, Belfer Centre for Science and International Affairs, Harvard University (Massachusetts).

Mennell, S. (1990) 'The Globalization of Human Society as a Very Long-Term Social Process: Elias's Theory', *Theory, Culture and Society*, 7(3).

— (1994) 'The Formation of We-Images: A Process Theory' in C. Calhoun (ed.), *Social Theory and the Politics of Identity* (Oxford).

— (2007) *The American Civilizing Process* (Cambridge).

Merchant, C. (1980) *The Death of Nature: Women, Ecology and the Scientific Revolution* (San Francisco).

Micklewait, J. and Wooldridge, A. (2000) *A Future Perfect: The Challenge and Hidden Promise of Globalization* (New York).

Millennium: Journal of International Studies (1988), Special Issue: Women and International Relations, 17(3).

Miller, D. (2007) *National Responsibility and Global Justice* (Cambridge).

Miller, F. (1998) 'Feminisms and Transnationalism', *Gender and History*, 10(3).

Mishra, P. (2012) *From the Ruins of Empire: The Revolt against the West and the Remaking of Empire* (London).

Mitchell, R. (2006) 'Problem Structure, Institutional Design, and the Relative Effectiveness of International Environmental Agreements', *Global Environmental Politics*, 6(3).

Mitrany, D. (1948) 'The Functional Approach to World Organisation', *International Affairs*, 24(3).

Mitter, S. (1986) *Common Fate, Common Bond: Women in the Global Economy* (London).

Modelski, G. (1978) 'The Long Cycle of Global Politics and the Nation-State', *Comparative Studies in Society and History*, 20(2).

Mohanty, C. (1991) 'Under Western Eyes: Feminist Scholarship and Colonial Discourses', in C. Mohanty, T. A. Russo and L. Torres (eds), *Third World Women and the Politics of Feminism* (Bloomington).

Mol, A. (1996) 'Ecological Modernisation and Institutional Reflexivity: Environmental Reform in the Late Modern Age', *Environmental Politics*, 5(2).

Moon, K. (1997) *Sex Among Allies: Military Prostitution in US–Korea Relations* (New York).

Morefield, J. (2005) *Covenants without Swords: Idealist Liberalism and the Spirit of Empire* (Princeton).

Morgenthau, H. J. (1946) *Scientific Man Versus Power Politics* (Chicago).

— (1948/54/73) *Politics Among Nations: The Struggle for Power and Peace* (New York).

— (1951) *In Defense of the National Interest: A Critical Examination of American Foreign Policy* (New York).

— (1962) *Politics in the Twentieth Century, I: The Decline of Democratic Politics* (Chicago).

— (1970) *Truth and Power: Essays of a Decade, 1960–70* (New York).

Morton, A. (2007) *Unravelling Gramsci: Hegemony and Passive Revolution in the Global Political Economy* (London).

Mueller, J. (1989) *Retreat from Doomsday* (New York).

Myers, N. (1993) *Ultimate Security: The Environment as the Basis of Political Stability* (New York).

Nagel, T. (1986) *The View from Nowhere* (Oxford).

Nairn, T. (1981) *The Break-up of Britain* (London).

Nandy, A. (1983) *The Intimate Enemy: Loss and Recovery of Self under Colonialism* (Delhi).

Nardin, T. (1983) *Law, Morality, and the Relations of States* (Princeton).
— (2005) 'Justice and Coercion', in A. J. Bellamy (ed.), *International Society and Its Critics* (Oxford).
— (2006) 'The Question of Justice', *International Affairs*, 82(3).
— (2011a) 'Globalization and the Public Realm', *Critical Review of Social and Political Philosophy*, 12(2).
— (2011b) 'Middle-Ground Ethics: Can One Be Politically Realistic Without Being a Political Realist', *Ethics & International Affairs*, 25(1).
— (2011c) 'Political Philosophy in a Globalizing World', in G. Klosko (ed.), *The Oxford Handbook of the History of Political Philosophy* (Oxford).
— (2012) 'Justice and Authority in the Global Order', *Review of International Studies*, 37(5).
Nayak, M. and Selbin, E. (2010) *Decentering International Relations* (London).
Nayak, M. and Suchland, J. (2006) 'Gender Violence and Hegemonic Projects: Introduction', *International Feminist Journal of Politics*, 8(4).
Neal, A. (2009) *Exceptionalism and the Politics of Counter-Terrorism: Liberty, Security and the War on Terror* (London).
Nederveen Pieterse, J. (2004) *Globalization or Empire?* (London).
Nelson, B. (1973) 'Civilizational Complexes and Intercivilizational Encounters', *Sociological Analysis*, 34(2).
Neufeld, M. (1993) 'Interpretation and the "Science" of International Relations', *Review of International Studies*, 19(1).
— (1995) *The Restructuring of International Relations Theory* (Cambridge).
— (2000) 'Thinking Ethically – Thinking Critically: International Ethics as Critique', in M. Lensu and J.-S. Fritz (eds), *Value Pluralism, Normative Theory and International Relations* (London).
Newland, K. (1988) 'From Transnational Relationships to International Relations: Women in Development and the International Decade for Women', *Millennium*, 17(3).
Nexon, D. H. (2009) *The Struggle for Power in Early Modern Europe: Religious Conflict: Dynastic Empires and International Change* (Princeton).
Niarchos, C. N. (1995) 'Women, War, and Rape: Challenges Facing the International Tribunal for the Former Yugoslavia', *Human Rights Quarterly*, 17(4).
Niebuhr, R. (1932) *Moral Man and Immoral Society: A Study in Ethics and Politics* (New York).
— (1941) *The Nature and Destiny of Man: A Christian Interpretation, I: Human Nature* (New York).
— (1943) *The Nature and Destiny of Man: A Christian Interpretation, II: Human Destiny* (New York).
Nietzsche, F. (1969) *On the Genealogy of Morals, and Ecce Homo* (New York).
— (1990) *Twilight of the Idols/The Anti-Christ* (Harmondsworth).
Nisbet, R. A. (1966) *The Sociological Tradition* (London).
Norris, P. and Ingelhart, R. (2003) *Rising Tide: Gender Equality and Cultural Change Around the World* (Cambridge).
Nye, J. S. (1988) Neorealism and Neoliberalism', *World Politics*, 40(2).
— (2012) 'When Women Lead', *Project Syndicate*, February 8. http://www. project-syndicate.org/commentary/when-women-lead.
Nyers, P. (1999) 'Emergency or Emerging Identities? Refugees and Transformations in World Order', *Millennium*, 28(1).
Ohmae, K. (1995) *The End of the Nation State* (New York).
Okereke, C. (2008) *Global Justice and Neoliberal Environmental Governance* (London).
Ong, A. (1997) 'The Gender and Labor Politics of Postmodernity', in L. Lowe (ed.), *The Politics of Culture Under the Shadow of Capital* (Durham).
Onuf, N. (1989) *World of Our Making: Rules and Rule in Social Theory and International Relations* (Columbia).
Ophuls, W. (1977) *Ecology and the Politics of Scarcity* (San Francisco).

Organski, A. F. K. and Kugler, J. (1980) *The War Ledger* (Chicago).

O'Riordan, T. (1981) *Environmentalism*, 2nd edn (London).

Ostrom, E. (1990) *Governing the Commons: The Evolution of Institutions for Collective Action* (Cambridge).

Ó Tuathail, G. (1996) *Critical Geopolitics: The Politics of Writing Global Space* (Minneapolis).

Owen, J. M. (1994) 'How Liberalism Produces Democratic Peace', *International Security*, 19(2).

Owens, P. (2007) *Between War and Politics: International Relations and the Thought of Hannah Arendt* (Oxford).

Oye, K. (1985) 'Explaining Cooperation Under Anarchy: Hypotheses and Strategies', *World Politics*, 38(1).

Pagden, A. (ed.) (1987) *The Languages of Political Theory in Early-Modern Europe* (Cambridge).

Pangle, T. L. and Ahrensdorf, P. J. (1999) *Justice among Nations: On the Moral Basis of Power and Peace* (Lawrence, KS).

Parks, B. and Roberts, J.T. (2010) 'Climate Change, Social Theory and Justice', *Theory, Culture & Society*, 27(2–3).

Pasha, M. (2008) 'Islam, Soft Orientalism and Empire: A Gramscian Rereading', in A. Ayers, (ed.) *Gramsci, Political Economy and International Relations Theory: Modern Princes and Naked Emperors* (Basingstoke).

— (2009) 'Global Exception and Islamic Exceptionalism', *International Politics*, 46 (5).

— (2012) 'Global Leadership and the Islamic World: Crisis, Contention and Challenge', in S. Gill *Global Crises and the Crisis of Global Leadership* (Cambridge).

Pateman, C. (1986) 'Introduction', in C. Pateman and E. Gross, *Feminist Challenges: Social and Political Thought* (Sydney).

— (1989) *The Disorder of Women* (Stanford).

Paterson, M. (1999a) 'Overview: Interpreting Trends in Global Environmental Governance', *International Affairs*, 75(4).

— (1999b) 'Globalisation, Ecology, and Resistance', *New Political Economy*, 4(1).

— (2000) *Understanding Global Environmental Politics: Domination, Accumulation, Resistance* (Basingstoke).

— (2007) 'Environmental Politics: Sustainability and the Politics of Transformation', *International Political Science Review*, 28(5).

Paterson, M., Doran, P. and Barry, J. (2006) 'Green Theory', in D. Marsh, C. Hay and M. Lister (eds), *State Theory: Theories and Issues* (London).

Patomaki, H. (2007) 'Back to the Kantian "Idea for a Universal History"? Overcoming Eurocentric Accounts of the International Problematic', *Millennium*, 35(3).

Pattberg, P. (2007) *Private Institutions and Global Governance. The New Politics of Environmental Sustainability* (Cheltenham, UK).

Patton, P. (2000) *Deleuze and the Political* (London).

Peoples, C. (2010) *Justifying Ballistic Missile Defence: Technology, Security and Culture* (Cambridge).

Persram, N. (1994) 'Politicizing the Feminine, Globalizing the Feminist', *Alternatives*, 19(3).

Peters, J. and Wolper, A. (eds) (1995) *Women's Rights/Human Rights: International Feminist Perspectives* (New York).

Peterson, V. S. (1992a) 'Transgressing Boundaries: Theories of Gender, Knowledge and International Relations', *Millennium*, 21(2).

— (1992b) 'Security and Sovereign States: What is at Stake in Taking Feminism Seriously?', in V. S. Peterson (ed.), *Gendered States: Feminist (Re)visions of International Theory* (Boulder).

— (2003) *A Critical Rewriting of Global Political Economy: Integrating Reproductive, Productive and Virtual Economies* (New York).

Peterson, V. S. and Runyan, A. S. (2009) *Global Gender Issues in the New Millennium*, 3rd edn (Boulder).

Peterson, V. S. and True, J. (1998) 'New Times and New Conversations', in M. Zalewski and J. Parpart (eds), *The Man Question in International Relations* (Boulder).

Pettman, J. (1996) 'An International Political Economy of Sex', in J. Pettman (ed.), *Worlding Women: Towards a Feminist International Politics* (New York).

Philapose, E. (1996) 'The Laws of War and Women's Human Rights', *Hypatia,* 11(4).

Phillips, A. (2010) 'The Protestant Ethic and the Spirit of Jihadism-Transnational Religious Insurgencies and the Transformation of International Orders', *Review of International Studies,* 36(2).

— (2011) *War, Religion and Empire: The Transformation of International Orders* (Cambridge).

Philpott, D. (2001) *Revolutions in Sovereignty: How Ideas Shaped Modern International Relations* (Princeton).

Pietila, H. and Vickers, J. (1996) *Making Women Matter: The Role of the United Nations,* 3rd edn (London).

Pitts, J. (2006) *A Turn to Empire: The Rise of Imperial Liberalism in Britain and France* (Princeton).

Plumwood, V. (1993) *Feminism and the Mastery of Nature* (London).

Pogge, T. (2002) *World Poverty and Human Rights* (Cambridge).

— (2008) *World Poverty and Human Rights,* 2nd edn (Oxford).

Pogge, T. and Moellendorf, D. (2008) *Global Justice: Seminal Essays* (St Paul).

Polanyi, K. (1944) *The Great Transformation* (Boston).

— (1968) 'Our Obsolete Market Mentality', in G. Dalton (ed.), *Primitive, Archaic and Modern Economies* (New York).

Politics and Ethics Review (2006) 'Symposium on Robyn Eckersley's *The Green State'*, *Politics and Ethics Review,* 2(2).

Porritt, J. (1986) *Seeing Green* (Oxford).

Porter, G. and Brown, J. W. (1991) *Global Environmental Politics* (Boulder).

Porter, M. and Judd, E. (eds) (2000) *Feminists Doing Development: A Practical Critique* (London).

Pouliot, V. (2010) *International Security in Practice* (Cambridge).

Powell, R. (1994) 'Anarchy in International Relations Theory: The Neorealist-Neoliberal Debate', *International Organization,* 48(2).

Price, R. (1997) *The Chemical Weapons Taboo* (Ithaca).

— (ed.) (2008) *Moral Limit and Possibility in World Politics* (Cambridge).

Price, R. and Reus-Smit, C. (1998) 'Dangerous Liaisons: Critical International Theory and Constructivism', *European Journal of International Relations,* 4(3).

Princen, T. (2003) 'Principles for Sustainability: From Cooperation and Efficiency to Sufficiency', *Global Environmental Politics,* 3(1).

— (2005) *The Logic of Sufficiency* (Cambridge).

Programme of the German Green Party (1983) (London).

Prozorov, S. (2011) 'The Other as Past and Present: Beyond the Logic of "Temporal Othering" in IR Theory', *Review of International Studies,* 37(3).

Prügl, E. (2000) *The Global Construction of Gender* (New York).

— (2007) 'Gender and EU Politics' in K. E. Jørgensen, M. A. Pollack and B. Rosamond (eds), *The Handbook of European Union Politics* (Oxford).

Prügl, E. and Meyer, M. K. (eds) (1999) *Gender Politics and Global Governance* (Lanham).

Prügl, E., Gülay Ç. and Zwingel, S. (2012). *Feminist Strategies in International Governance* (New York).

Rae, H. (2002) *State Identities and the Homogenization of Peoples* (Cambridge).

Rai, S. M. and Waylen, G. (eds) (2008), *Global Governance: Feminist Perspectives* (New York).

Ralph, J. (2007) *Defending the Society of States: Why America Opposes the International Criminal Court and its Vision of World Society* (Oxford).

Ralston, D. B. (1990) *Importing the European Army: Introducing European Military Techniques and Institutions in the Extra-European Army, 1600–1914* (Chicago).

Ramraj, V. V. (ed.) (2008) *Emergencies and the Limits of Legality* (Cambridge).

Rao, A. (1995) 'Gender and Culture', in J. Peters and A. Wolper (eds), *Women's Rights/Human Rights: International Feminist Perspectives* (New York).

Rathergeber, M. (1995) 'Gender and Development in Action', in M. H. Marchand and J. L. Parpart (eds), *Feminism/Postmodernism/Development* (London).

Rawls, J. (1971) *A Theory of Justice* (Cambridge, MA).

— (1999) *The Law of Peoples* (Cambridge, MA).

Raymond, G. A. (1997) 'Problems and Prospects in the Study of International Norms', *Mershon International Studies Review*, 41(2).

Reanda, L. (1999) 'Engendering the United Nations: The Changing International Agenda', *European Journal of Women's Studies*, 6(1).

Regan, P. M. and Paskeviciute, A. (2003) Women's Access to Politics and Peaceful States', *Journal of Peace Research*, 40(3).

Reichberg, G. M., Syse, H. and Begby, E. (eds) (2006) *The Ethics of War: Classic and Contemporary Readings* (Malden).

Reid, J. (2003) Deleuze's War Machine: Nomadism against the State', *Millennium*, 32(1).

Rengger, N. (2008) 'The Ethics of Marxism', in C. Reus-Smit and D. Snidal (eds), *The Oxford Handbook of International Relations* (Oxford).

Rengger, N. and Thirkell-White, B. (2007) *Critical International Relations Theory After 25 Years* (Cambridge).

Reus-Smit, C. (1996) 'The Normative Structure of International Society', in F. Osler Hampson and J. Reppy (eds), *Earthly Goods: Environmental Change and Social Justice* (Ithaca).

— (1999) *The Moral Purpose of the State: Culture, Social Identity and Institutional Rationality in International Relations* (Princeton).

— (2000) 'In Dialogue on the Ethic of Consensus: A Reply to Shapcott', *Pacifica Review*, 12(3).

— (2002a) 'Imagining Society: Constructivism and the English School', *British Journal of Politics and International Relations*, 4(3).

— (2002b) 'The Idea of History and History with Ideas', in S. Hobden and J. M. Hobson (eds), *Historical Sociology and International Relations* (Cambridge).

— (2004a) *American Power and World Order* (Cambridge).

— (ed.) (2004b) *The Politics of International Law* (Cambridge).

Reus-Smit, C. and Snidal, D. (eds) (2008) *The Oxford Handbook of International Relations* (Oxford).

Ricardo, D. (1911 [1817]) *The Principles of Political Economy and Taxation* (London).

Richardson, J. L. (1997) 'Contending Liberalisms – Past and Present', *European Journal of International Relations*, 3(1).

Ripstein, A. (2009) *Force and Freedom: Kant's Legal and Political Philosophy* (Cambridge, MA).

Risse, T. (2000) '"Let's Argue!": Communicative Action in World Politics', *International Organization*, 54(1).

— (2004) 'Global Governance Communication Action', *Government and Opposition*, 39(2).

Roach, S. C. (2010) *Critical Theory of International Politics: Complementarity, Justice and Governance* (London).

Roberts, A. (1993) 'Humanitarian War: Military Intervention and Human Rights', *International Affairs*, 69(3).

Roberts, B. (1984) 'The Death of Machothink: Feminist Research and the Transformation of Peace Studies', *Women's Studies International Forum*, 7(4).

Robertson, G. (2006) *Crimes against Humanity: The Struggle for Global Justice* (New York).

Robinson, F. (1999) *Globalizing Care: Ethics, Feminist Theory, and International Relations* (Boulder).

— (2006) 'Methods of Feminist Normative Theory: A Political Ethic of Care for International Relations' in B. Ackerly, M. Stern and J. True (eds), *Feminist Methodologies for International Relations* (Cambridge).

Robinson, W. I. (2004) *A Theory of Global Capitalism: Production, Class and State in a Transnational World* (Baltimore).

Robinson, W. I., and Harris, J. (2000) 'Towards a Global Ruling Class? Globalization and the Transnational Capitalist Class', *Science and Society*, 64(1).

Rodin, D. (2002) *War and Self-Defense* (Oxford).

Rose, G. (1998) 'Neoclassical Realism and Theories of Foreign Policy', *World Politics*, 51(1).

Rosecrance, R. N. (1966) 'Bipolarity, Multipolarity, and the Future', *Journal of Conflict Resolution*, 10(3).

— (1986) *The Rise of the Trading State* (New York).

Rosenau, J. (1992) 'Governance, Order, and Change in World Politics', in J. N. Rosenau, and E.-O. Czempiel (eds), *Governance Without Government: Order and Change in World Politics* (Cambridge).

— (1993) 'Environmental Challenges in a Turbulent World', in K. Conca and R. Lipschutz (eds), *The State and Social Power in Global Environmental Politics* (New York).

Rosenau, J. and Holsti, O. (1982) 'Women Leaders and Foreign Policy Opinions', in E. Boneparth and E. Stoper (eds), *Women, Power, and Politics* (New York).

Rosenberg, J. (1994) *The Empire of Civil Society: A Critique of the Realist Theory of International Relations* (London).

— (2000) *The Follies of Globalization Theory: Polemical Essays* (London).

— (2006) 'Why is there no International Historical Sociology?', *European Journal of International Relations*, 12(3).

— (2007) 'International Relations – The Higher Bullshit: A Reply to the Globalization Theory Debate', *International Politics*, 44(4).

Rosenthal, J. H. (1991) *Righteous Realists: Political Realism, Responsible Power, and American Culture in the Nuclear Age* (Baton Rouge).

Rowlands, I.H. (1994) *The Politics of Global Atmosphere* (Manchester).

Ruggie, J. (1983) 'Continuity and Transformation in the World Polity: Toward a Neo-Realist Synthesis', *World Politics*, 35(2).

— (1986) 'Continuity and Transformation in the World Polity: Toward a Neorealist Synthesis', in R. O. Keohane (ed.), *Neorealism and Its Critics* (New York).

— (1993) 'Territoriality and Beyond: Problematizing Modernity in International Relations', *International Organization*, 47(1).

Runyan, A. S. and Peterson, V. S. (1991) 'The Radical Future of Realism: Feminist Subversions of IR Theory', *Alternatives*, 16(1).

Rupert, M. (1995) *Producing Hegemony: The Politics of Mass Production and American Global Power* (Cambridge).

— (2000) *Ideologies of Globalization: Contending Visions of a New World Order* (London).

— (2003) 'Globalising Common Sense: A Marxian–Gramscian (Re-vision) of the Politics of Governance/Resistance', *Review of International Studies*, 29 (supplement).

— (2006) 'Reading Gramsci in an Era of Globalising Capitalism', in A. Bieler and A. D. Morton, (eds) *Images of Gramsci: Connections and Contentions in Political Theory and International Relations* (Abingdon).

Rupert, M. and Solomon, M. S. (2005) *Globalization and International Political Economy: The Politics of Alternative Futures* (Lanhan).

Rupp, L. (1997) *Worlds of Women: The Making of an International Women's Movement* (Princeton).

Russell, F. H. (1975) *The Just War in the Middle Ages* (Cambridge).

— (2010) 'Just War', in R. Pasnau and C. Van Dyke (eds), *The Cambridge History of Medieval Philosophy*, vol. 2 (Cambridge).

Russell, G. (1990) *Hans J. Morgenthau and the Ethics of American Statecraft* (Baton Rouge).

Russett, B. (1993) *Grasping the Democratic Peace* (Princeton).

Rustin, C. (1999) 'Habermas, Discourse Ethics, and International Justice', *Alternatives*, 24(2).

Sachs, W. (ed.) (1992) *The Development Dictionary: A Guide to Knowledge as Power* (London).

— (1993) 'Global Ecology and the Shadow of "Development"', in W. Sachs (ed.), *Global Ecology* (London).

— (ed.) (1993) *Global Ecology* (London).

Said, E. (1979) *Orientalism: Western Conceptions of the Orient* (London).

Sajed, A. (2012) 'The Post Always Rings Twice? The Algerian War, Poststructuralism and the Postcolonial in IR Theory', *Review of International Studies*, 38(1).

Sale, K. (1980) *Human Scale* (San Francisco).

Sassen, S. (1991) *The Global City: New York, London, Tokyo* (Princeton).

— (1998a) 'Notes on the Incorporation of Third World Women into Wage Labor through Immigration and Offshore Production', in S. Sassen, *Globalization and its Discontents* (New York).

— (1998b) 'Toward a Feminist Analysis of the Global Economy', in S. Sassen, *Globalization and its Discontents* (New York).

Scarre, C. (ed.) (2005) *The Human Past: World Prehistory and the Evolution of Human Societies* (London).

Scheuerman, W. E. (2004) *Liberal Democracy and the Social Acceleration of Time* (Baltimore).

— (2008) 'Global Governance without Global Government: Habermas on Postnational Democracy', *Political Theory*, 36(1).

— (2009) *Morgenthau: Realism and Beyond* (Cambridge).

— (2011) 'Postnational Democracies without Postnational States? Some Skeptical Reflections', in R. Forst and R. Schmalz-Bruns (eds), *Political Legitimacy and Democracy in Transnational Perspective* (Oslo).

Schmidt, B. C. (1998) *The Political Discourse of Anarchy: A Disciplinary History of International Relations* (Albany).

Scholte, J.-A. (2000) *Globalization: A Critical Introduction* (Basingstoke).

Schumacher, E. F. (1976) *Small is Beautiful* (London).

Schwarzenberger, G. (1951) *Power Politics: A Study of International Society* (London/New York).

Schweller, R. L. (1994) 'Bandwagoning for Profit: Bringing the Revisionist State Back In', *International Security*, 19(1).

— (1997) 'New Realist Research on Alliances: Refining, Not Refuting, Waltz's Balancing Proposition', *American Political Science Review*, 91(4).

— (1998) *Deadly Imbalances: Tripolarity and Hitler's Strategy of World Conquest* (New York).

— (1999) 'Managing the Rise of Great Powers: History and Theory', in A. I. Johnston and R. S. Ross (eds), *Engaging China: The Management of an Emerging Power* (London).

— (2003) 'The Progressivism of Neoclassical Realism', in C. Elman and M. F. Elman (eds), *Progress in International Relations Theory: Appraising the Field* (Cambridge).

— (2006) *Unanswered Threats: Political Constraints on the Balance of Power* (Princeton).

Schweller, R. L. and Priess, D. (1997) 'A Tale of Two Realisms: Expanding the Institutions Debate', *Mershon International Studies Review*, 41(1).

Scott, J. W. (1988) *Gender and the Politics of History* (New York).

Selby, J. (2007) 'Engaging Foucault: Discourse, Liberal Governance and the Limits of Foucauldian IR', *International Relations*, 21(3).

Sen, A. (2001) *Development as Freedom* (New York).

Seth, S. (2009) 'Historical Sociology and Postcolonial Theory: Two Strategies for Challenging Eurocentrism', *International Political Sociology*, 3(3).

— (2011) 'Postcolonial Theory and the Critique of International Relations', *Millennium*, 40(1).

Shakman Hurd, E. (2004) 'The Political Authority of Secularism in International Relations', *European Journal of International Relations*, 10(2).

— (2008) *The Politics of Secularism in World Politics* (Princeton).

Shapcott, R. (1994) 'Conversation and Co-existence: Gadamer and the Interpretation of International Society', *Millennium*, 23(1).

— (2000a) 'Solidarism and After: Global Governance, International Society and the Normative "Turn"', *Pacifica Review,* 12(2).

— (2000b) 'Beyond the Cosmopolitan/Communitarian Divide: Justice, Difference and Community in International Relations', in M. Lensu and J.-S. Fritz (eds), *Value Pluralism, Normative Theory and International Relations* (London).

— (2001) *Justice, Community and Dialogue in International Relations* (Cambridge).

— (2010) *International Ethics: A Critical Introduction* (Cambridge).

Shapiro, M. J. (1988) *The Politics of Representation* (Madison).

— (1998) 'The Events of Discourse and the Ethics of Global Hospitality', *Millennium,* 27(3).

— (1999) *Cinematic Political Thought: Narrating Race, Nation and Gender* (Edinburgh).

— (2005) 'The Fog of War', *Security Dialogue,* 36(2).

— (2007) 'The New Violent Cartography', *Security Dialogue,* 38(3).

Sharoni, S. (1993) 'Middle-East Politics Through Feminist Lenses: Toward Theorizing International Relations from Women's Struggles', *Alternatives,* 18(1).

Sharp, G. (1973) *The Politics of Nonviolent Action* (Boston).

Shepherd, L. J. (2007) 'Victims, Perpetrators and Actors' Revisited: Exploring the Potential for a Feminist Reconceptualisation of (International) Security and (Gender) Violence', *British Journal of Politics and International Relations,* 9(1).

— (2008) 'Power and Authority in the Production of United Nations Security Council Resolution 1325', *International Studies Quarterly,* 52(2).

— (2010) *Gender Matters in Global Politics* (New York).

Sherman, D. and Nardin, T. (eds) (2006) *Terror, Culture, Politics: Rethinking 9/11* (Bloomington, IN).

Ship, S. J. (1994) 'And What About Gender? Feminism and International Relations Theory's Third Debate', in W. S. Cox and C. T. Sjolander (eds), *Beyond Positivism: Critical International Relations Theory* (Boulder).

Shiva, V. (1988) *Staying Alive: Women, Ecology and Development* (London).

— (1993) 'The Greening of the Global Reach', in W. Sachs (ed.), *Global Ecology* (London).

Shue, H. (1992) 'The Unavoidability of Justice', in A. Hurrell and B. Kingsbury (eds), *The International Politics of the Environment* (Oxford).

— (1995) 'Ethics, the Environment, and the Changing International Order', *International Affairs,* 71(3).

— (1999) 'Global Environment and International Inequality', *International Affairs,* 75(3).

Shue, H. and Rodin, D. (eds) (2007) *Preemption: Military Action and Moral Justification* (Oxford).

Simpson, G. (2004) *Great Powers and Outlaw States: Unequal Sovereigns in the International Legal Order* (Cambridge).

Singer, J. D. (1961) 'The Level-of-Analysis Problem in International Relations', *World Politics,* 14(1).

Singer, P. (2002) *One World: The Ethics of Globalization* (New Haven).

Sjoberg, L. (2006) 'Gendered Realities of the Immunity Principle: Why Gender Analysis Needs Feminism', *International Studies Quarterly,* 50(4).

— (2010) *Gender and International Security: Feminist Perspectives* (New York).

— (2012) 'Gender, Structure, and War: What Waltz Couldn't See', *International Theory,* 4(1).

Skinner, Q. (1969) 'Meaning and Understanding in the History of Ideas', *History and Theory,* 8(1).

Skocpol, T. (1979) *States and Social Revolutions: A Comparative Analysis of France, Russia and China* (Cambridge).

— (1984) 'Sociology's Historical Imagination', in T. Skocpol (ed.), *Visions of Historical Sociology* (Cambridge).

Slaughter, A.-M. (2004) *A New World Order* (Princeton).

Smith, D. (1990) *The Rise of Historical Sociology* (Cambridge).

Smith, K. (2012) 'India's Identity and its Global Aspirations', *Global Society,* 26(3).

Smith, L. T. (1999) *Decolonizing Methodologies: Research and Indigenous Peoples*, (London: Zed Books).

Smith, M. J. (1986) *Realist Thought from Weber to Kissinger* (Baton Rouge).

Smith, S. (1995) 'The Self-Image of a Discipline: A Genealogy of International Relations Theory', in K. Booth and S. Smith (eds), *International Relations Theory Today* (Cambridge).

— (1996) 'Positivism and Beyond', in S. Smith, K. Booth and M. Zalewski (eds), *International Theory: Positivism and Beyond* (Cambridge).

— (1997) 'Power and Truth: A Reply to Wallace', *Review of International Studies*, 22(4).

Smith, S., Booth, K. and Zalewski, M. (eds) (1996) *International Theory: Positivism and Beyond* (Cambridge).

Snidal, D. and Wendt, A. (2009) 'Why There is International Theory Now', *International Theory* 1(1).

Snyder, G. H. (1996) 'Process Variables in Neorealist Theory', *Security Studies*, 5(3).

— (1997) *Alliance Politics* (Ithaca).

— (2002) 'Mearsheimer's World: Offensive Realism and the Struggle for Security', *International Security*, 27(1).

Snyder, J. (1991) *Myths of Empire: Domestic Politics and International Ambition* (Ithaca).

Soguk, N. and Whitehall, G. (1999) 'Wandering Grounds: Transversality, Identity, Territoriality, and Movement', *Millennium*, 28(3).

Spaargaren, G., Mol, A. and Buttel, F. (eds) (2006), *Governing Environmental Flows: Global Challenges to Social Theory* (Cambridge MA).

Sparr, P. (ed.) (1994) *Mortgaging Women's Lives: Feminist Critiques of Structural Adjustment* (London).

Spegele, R. (1992) 'Richard Ashley's Discourse for International Relations', *Millennium*, 21(2).

Spretnak, C. and Capra, F. (1984) *Green Politics: The Global Promise* (London).

Spykman, N. J. (1942) *America's Strategy in World Politics: The United States and the Balance of Power* (New York).

Stalin, J. (1953) 'Marxism and the National Question', *Collected Works* (Moscow).

Standing, G. (1992) 'Global Feminization Through Flexible Labor', in C. K. Wilber and K. P. Jameson (eds), *The Political Economy of Development and Underdevelopment*, 5th edn (New York).

Stasiulis, D. and Bakan, A. B. (1997) 'Negotiating Citizenship: The Case of Foreign Domestic Workers in Canada', *Feminist Review*, 57(Autumn).

Steans, J. (2006) [1995] *Gender and International Relations*, 2nd edn (Cambridge).

Stearns, P. N., and Stearns, C. Z. (1985) 'Emotionology: Clarifying the History of Emotions and Emotional Standards', *American Historical Review*, 90(4).

Stern, M. (2005) *Naming Insecurity-Constructing Identity* (Manchester).

Steuernagel, G. A. (1990) 'Men do not do Housework! The Image of Women in Political Science', in M. Paludi and G. A. Steuernagel (eds), *Foundations for a Feminist Restructuring of the Academic Disciplines* (New York).

Stewart, C. (1997) 'Old Wine in Recycled Bottles: The Limitations of Green International Relations Theory', Paper presented to the BISA Annual Conference.

Stiehm, J. H. (2006) *Champions for Peace: Women Winners of the Nobel Peace Prize* (Lanham).

Stienstra, D. (1994) *Women's Movements and International Organizations* (Toronto).

Stiglitz, J.E. (2010) *Freefall: America, Free Markets, and the Sinking of the World Economy* (Norton).

Stivachtis, Y. (2010) '"Civilizing" the Post-Soviet/Socialist State: An English School Approach to State Socialisation in Europe: The Cases of NATO and the Council of Europe', *Perspectives: Review of International Affairs*, 18(2).

Strange, S. (1985) 'Protectionism and World Politics', *International Organisation*, 39(2).

— (1991) 'New World Order: Conflict and Co-operation', *Marxism Today*, January.

— (1996) *The Retreat of the State* (Cambridge).

— (1998) *Mad Money* (Michigan).

Stroeve, J., Serreze, M., Holland, M., Kay, J., *et al.* (2012) 'The Arctic's Rapidly Shrinking Sea Ice Cover: A Research Synthesis', *Climate Change*, 110 (3).

Suganami, H. (1989) *The Domestic Analogy and World Order Proposals* (Cambridge).

— (1996) *On the Causes of War* (Oxford).

Suh, J. J., Katzenstein, P. J. and Carlson, A. (2004) *Rethinking Security in East Asia: Identity, Power, and Efficiency* (Palo Alto).

Sylvester, C. (1987) 'The Dangers of Merging Feminist and Peace Projects', *Alternatives*, 8(4).

— (1990) 'The Emperors' Theories and Transformations: Looking at the Field through Feminist Lens', in D. Pirages and C. Sylvester (eds), *Transformations in the Global Political Economy* (London).

— (1992) 'Feminist Theory and Gender Studies in International Relations', *International Studies Notes*, 16(1).

— (1994a) *Feminist Theory and International Relations in a Postmodern Era* (Cambridge).

— (1994b) 'Empathetic Co-Operation: A Feminist Method for IR', *Millennium*, 23(2).

— (2001) *Feminist International Relations: An Unfinished Journey* (Cambridge).

Sznaider, N. (2001) *The Compassionate Society: Care and Cruelty in Modern Society* (Oxford).

Taliaferro, J. W. (2000/1) 'Security Seeking under Anarchy: Defensive Realism Revisited,' *International Security*, 25(3).

Tan, K.-C. (2000) *Toleration, Diversity, and Global Justice* (University Park).

— (2004) *Justice without Borders: Cosmopolitanism, Nationalism and Patriotism* (Cambridge).

— (2006) 'The Duty to Protect', in T. Nardin and M. S. Williams (eds), *Humanitarian Intervention* (New York).

Tannenwald, N. (1999) 'The Nuclear Taboo: The United States and the Normative Basis of Nuclear Non-Use', *International Organization*, 53(3).

Taylor, A. J. P. (1961) *The Origins of the Second World War* (Harmondsworth).

Taylor, B. (ed.) (1995) *Ecological Resistance Movements: The Global Emergence of Radical and Popular Environmentalism* (Albany).

Taylor, C. (1997) 'Interpretation and the Sciences of Man', in F. Dallmayr and T. McCarthy (eds), *Understanding and Social Inquiry* (Notre Dame).

Taylor, M. (1976) *Anarchy and Cooperation* (London).

— (1987) *The Possibility of Co-operation* (Cambridge).

Tellis, A. (1995/6) 'Reconstructing Political Realism: The Long March to Scientific Theory', *Security Studies*, 5(2).

Teschke, B. (1998) 'Geopolitical Relations in the European Middle Ages', *International Organisation*, 52(2).

— (2003) *The Myth of 1648: Class, Geopolitics and the Making of Modern International Relations* (London).

— (2008) 'Marxism', in C. Reus-Smit and D. Snidal, *The Oxford Handbook of International Relations* (Oxford).

Tessler, M., Nachtwey, J. and Grant, A. (1999) 'Further Tests of the Women and Peace Hypothesis: Evidence from Cross-National Survey Research in the Middle East', *International Studies Quarterly*, 43(3).

Tessler, M. and Warriner, I. (1997) 'Gender, Feminism and Attitudes toward International Conflict: Exploring Relationships with Survey Data from the Middle East', *World Politics*, 49(2).

The Ecologist (1972) *Blueprint for Survival* (Harmondsworth).

— (1993) *Whose Common Future? Reclaiming the Commons* (London).

Thomas, C. (1999) 'Where is the Third World Now?', *Review of International Studies*, 25 (Special Issue).

Thomas, S. (2001) 'Faith History and Martin Wight: The Role of Religion in the Historical Sociology of the English School of International Relations', *International Affairs*, 77(4).

Thompson, K. W. (1985) *Moralism and Morality in Politics and Diplomacy* (Lanham).

Thompson, K. W. and Meyers, R. J. (eds) (1977) *Truth and Tragedy: A Tribute to Hans Morgenthau* (Washington).

Thomson J. E. (1994) *Mercenaries, Pirates and Sovereigns: State-Building and Extraterritorial Violence in Early Modern Europe* (Princeton).

Thucydides (1982) *History of the Peloponnesian War* (New York).

Tickner, J. A. (1988) 'Hans Morgenthau's Political Principles of Political Realism: A Feminist Reformulation', *Millennium*, 17(3).

— (1991) 'On the Fringes of the World Economy: A Feminist Perspective', in C. Murphy and R. Tooze (eds), *The New International Political Economy* (Boulder).

— (1992) *Gender in International Relations* (New York).

— (2001) *Gendering World Politics: Issues and Approaches in the Post-Cold War Era* (New York).

— (2002) 'Feminist Perspectives on 9/11', *International Studies Perspectives*, 3(4).

Tierney, B. (1997) *The Idea of Natural Rights* (Atlanta).

Tilly, C. (1992) *Coercion, Capital and European States: AD 990–1992* (Oxford).

Towns, A. (2011) *Women and States: Norms and Hierarchy in International Society.* (Cambridge).

Trainer, F. E. (1985) *Abandon Affluence!* (London).

Treitschke, H. V. (1916) *Politics* (London).

Tronto, J. (1989) 'Woman, the State and War: What Difference Does Gender Make?', in V. S. Peterson (ed.), *Clarification and Contestation: A Conference Report* (Los Angeles).

— (2006) 'Is Peacekeeping Care Work?', paper presented at the Canadian Political Science Association, June.

True, J. (2003) *Gender, Globalization and Postsocialism: The Czech Republic After Communism* (New York).

— (2004) 'Feminism', in A. Bellamy (ed.), *International Society and its Critics* (Oxford).

— (2008a) 'Gender Mainstreaming and Regional Trade Governance in Asia Pacific Economic Cooperation (APEC)' in S. M. Rai and G. Waylen (eds), *Global Governance: Feminist Perspectives*, (New York).

— (2008b) 'The Unlikely Coupling of Feminism and Realism in International Relations' in A. Freyberg-Inan, E. Harrison and P. James (eds), *Rethinking Realism in International Relations: Between Tradition and Innovation* (Baltimore).

— (2009) 'Trading-off Gender Equality for Global Europe: The European Union and Free Trade Agreements', *European Foreign Affairs Review*, 14(4).

— (2012) *The Political Economy of Violence Against Women* (New York).

True, J. and Mintrom, M. (2001) 'Transnational Networks and Policy Diffusion: The Case of Gender Mainstreaming', *International Studies Quarterly*, 45(1).

True, J. and Parisi, L. (2012) 'Gender Mainstreaming Strategies in International Governance', in Prügl Elisabeth, Gülay Çaglar, Susanne Zwingel, *Feminist Strategies in International Governance* (New York).

Tuck, R. (1993) *Philosophy and Government 1572–1651* (Cambridge).

— (1999) *The Rights of War and Peace: Political Thought and the International Order from Grotius to Kant* (Oxford).

Tucker, R. W. (1977) *The Inequality of Nations* (New York).

— (1985) *Intervention and the Reagan Doctrine* (New York).

Tuhiwai Smith, L. (1999) *Decolonizing Methodologies: Research and Indigenous Peoples* (London).

United Nations (1992) *Framework Convention on Climate Change* (New York).

— (2000) *The World's Women's Progress* (New York).

United Nations Development Programme (UNDP) (1999) *Human Development Report 1999: Globalization with a Human Face* (Oxford).

Valentini, L. (2011) *Justice in a Globalized World: A Normative Framework* (Oxford).

Van der Pijl, K. (1998) *Transnational Classes and International Relations* (London).

— (2007) *Nomads, Empires, States: Modes of Foreign Relations and Political Economy, vol. 1* (London).

— (2010) *The Foreign Encounter in Myth and Religion: Modes of Foreign Relations and Political Economy, vol 2* (London).

Van Evera, S. (1998) 'Offense, Defense, and the Causes of War,' *International Security*, 22(4).

Van Krieken, R. (1998) *Norbert Elias* (London).

Van Parijs, P. (2007) 'International Distributive Justice', in R. E. Goodin, P. Pettit, and T. Pogge (eds), *A Companion to Contemporary Political Philosophy*, 2nd edn (Malden).

Vasquez, J. A. (1998) *The Power of Power Politics: From Classical Realism to Neotraditionalism* (Cambridge).

Vaughan-Williams, N. (2009) *Border Politics: The Limits of Sovereign Power* (Edinburgh).

Victor, D., Raustiala, K. and Skolnikoff, E. (eds) (1998), *The Implementation and Effectiveness of International Environmental Commitments: Theory and Practice* (Cambridge).

Victor, P. (2008) *Managing Without Growth: Slower by Design, Not Disaster* (Northampton, MA).

Vieira, K. (2012) 'Rising States and Distributive Justice: Reforming International Order in the Twenty-First Century', *Global Society*, 26(3).

Vincent, R. J. (1974) *Non-Intervention and International Order* (Princeton).

— (1984a) 'Edmund Burke and the Theory of International Relations', *Review of International Studies*, 10(3).

— (1984b) 'Racial Equality', in H. Bull and A. Watson (eds), *The Expansion of International Society* (Oxford).

— (1986) *Human Rights and International Relations* (Cambridge).

Vincent, R. J. and Wilson, P. (1994) 'Beyond Non-Intervention', in I. Forbes and M. Hoffman (eds), *Political Theory, International Relations and the Ethics of Intervention* (London).

Vogel, U. (2003) 'Cosmopolitan Loyalties and Cosmopolitan Citizenship in the Enlightenment', in M. Waller and A. Linklater (eds), *Political Loyalty and the Nation-State* (London).

Vogler, J. (1992) 'Regimes and the Global Commons: Space, Atmosphere and Oceans' in A. McGrew and P. Lewis (eds), *Global Politics: Globalization and the Nation-State* (Cambridge).

— (1995) *The Global Commons: A Regime Analysis* (London).

Vucetic, S. (2011) 'Genealogy as a Research Tool in International Relations', *Review of International Relations*, 37(3).

Wackernagel, M. and Rees, W. (1996) *Our Ecological Footprint: Reducing Human Impact on the Earth* (Gabriola Island).

Walker, R. B. J. (1987) 'Realism, Change and International Political Theory', *International Studies Quarterly*, 31(1).

— (1989) 'History and Structure in the Theory of International Relations', *Millennium*, 18(2).

— (1992) 'Gender and Critique in the Theory of International Relations', in V. S. Peterson (ed.), *Gendered States: Feminist (Re)visions of International Relations Theory* (Boulder).

— (1993) *Inside/Outside: International Relations as Political Theory* (Cambridge).

— (1995a) 'From International Relations to World Politics', in J. Camilleri, A. Jarvis and A. Paolini (eds), *The State in Transition: Reimagining Political Space* (Boulder).

— (1995b) 'International Relations and the Concept of the Political', in K. Booth and S. Smith (eds), *International Relations Theory Today* (Cambridge).

— (1999) 'The Hierarchalization of Political Community', *Review of International Studies*, 25(1).

— (2000) 'International Relations Theory and the Fate of the Political', in M. Ebata and B. Neufeld (eds), *Confronting the Political in International Relations* (London).

— (2010) *After the Globe, Before the World* (London).

Wall, D. (1994) 'Towards a Green Political Theory – In Defence of the Commons?', in P. Dunleavy and J. Stanyer (eds), *Contemporary Political Studies: Proceedings of the Annual Conference* (Belfast).

Wallace, W. (1996) 'Truth and Power, Monks and Technocrats: Theory and Practice in International Relations', *Review of International Studies*, 22(3).

Waller, M. and Linklater, A. (eds) (2003) *Political Loyalty and the Nation-State* (London).

Wallerstein, I. (1974) *The Modern World-System: Capitalist Agriculture and the Origins of the European World-Economy in the Sixteenth Century* (London).

— (1979) *The Capitalist World Economy* (Cambridge).

Walt, S. M. (1987) *The Origins of Alliances* (Ithaca).

Walter, A. (1996) 'Adam Smith and the Liberal Tradition in International Relations', in I. Clark and I. B. Neumann (eds), *Classical Theories of International Relations* (Oxford).

Waltz, K. N. (1959) *Man, the State and War* (New York).

— (1964) 'The Stability of a Bipolar World', *Daedalus,* 93(3).

— (1979) *Theory of International Politics* (Reading).

— (1986) 'Reflections on Theory of International Politics: A Response to My Critics', in R. O. Keohane (ed.), *Neo-Realism and Its Critics* (New York).

— (1990) 'Nuclear Myths and Political Realities', *American Political Science Review,* 84(3).

— (1991a) 'America as a Model for the World?', *PS: Political Science and Politics,* 24(4).

— (1991b) 'Realist Thought and Neo-Realist Theory', in R. L. Rothstein (ed.), *The Evolution of Theory in International Relations: Essays in Honor of William T. R. Fox* (Columbia).

— (1993) 'The Emerging Structure of International Politics', *International Security,* 18(2).

— (1996) 'International Politics Is Not Foreign Policy', *Security Studies,* 6.

— (2002) 'The Continuity of International Politics', in K. Booth and T. Dunne (eds), *Worlds in Collision: Terror and the Future of Global Order* (Basingstoke).

Walzer, M. (1977) *Just and Unjust Wars: A Moral Argument with Historical Illustrations* (New York).

— (1983) *Spheres of Justice: A Defense of Pluralism and Equality* (New York).

— (2004) *Arguing about War* (New Haven).

Wapner, P. (1996) *Environmental Activism and World Civic Politics* (Albany).

Warren, B. (1980) *Imperialism: Pioneer of Capitalism* (London).

Watson, A. (1982) *Diplomacy: The Dialogue between States* (London).

— (1987) 'Hedley Bull, States Systems and International Societies', *Review of International Studies*, 13(2).

— (1992) *The Evolution of International Society* (London).

WCED (1987) *Our Common Future – Report of the World Commission on Environment and Development* (Oxford).

Weber, C. (1994) 'Good Girls, Little Girls, and Bad Girls: Male Paranoia in Robert Keohane's Critique of Feminist International Relations', *Millennium,* 23(2).

— (1995) *Simulating Sovereignty: Intervention, the State, and Symbolic Exchange* (Cambridge).

— (1998) 'Performative States', *Millennium,* 27(1).

— (2002) 'Flying Planes Can be Dangerous', *Millennium,* 31(1).

— (2011) 'Interruption Ashley', *Review of International Studies,* 36(4).

Weber, Martin (2002) 'Engaging Globalization: Critical Theory and Global Political Change', *Alternatives,* 27(3).

— (2005) 'The Critical Social Theory of the Frankfurt School, and the "Social Turn" in IR', *Review of International Studies,* 31(1).

— (2006) 'IR Theory, Green Political Theory, and Critical Approaches', in Laferrière, E. and Stoett, P. (eds) *International Ecopolitical Theory: Critical Approaches* (Vancouver).

— (2007) 'The Concept of Solidarity in the Study of World Politics: Towards a Critical Theoretic Understanding', *Review of International Studies,* 33(4).

Weber, Max (1948) 'Social Psychology of the World Religions', in H. H. Gerth and C. Wright Mills (eds), *From Max Weber: Essays in Sociology* (London).

Weinstock, D. (2005) *Global Justice, Global Institutions* (Calgary).

Weiss, L. (1998) *The Myth of the Powerless State: Governing the Economy in a Global Era* (Cambridge).

Weiss, T. G. (2007) *Humanitarian Intervention* (Cambridge).

Welch, D. (1993) *Justice and the Genesis of War* (Cambridge).

Weldon, L. (2006) 'Inclusion, Solidarity and Social Movements: The Global Movement Against Gender Violence', *Perspectives on Politics*, 4(1).

Welsh, J. (2011) 'A Normative Case for Pluralism: Reassessing Vincent's Views on Humanitarian Intervention', *International Affairs*, 87(5).

Wendt, A. (1992) 'Anarchy is what States Make of it', *International Organization*, 46(2).

— (1994) 'Collective Identity Formation and the International State', *American Political Science Review*, 88(2).

— (1995) 'Constructing International Politics', *International Security*, 20(1).

— (1999) *Social Theory of International Politics* (Cambridge).

— (2003) 'Why a World State is Inevitable', *European Journal of International Relations*, 9(4).

Wendt, A. and Shapiro, I. (1997) 'The Misunderstood Promise of Realist Social Theory', in K. R. Monroe (ed.), *Contemporary Empirical Theory* (Berkeley).

Wheeler, N. J. (2000) *Saving Strangers: Humanitarian Intervention in International Society* (Oxford).

Wheeler, N. J. and Dunne, T. (1996) 'Hedley Bull's Pluralism of the Intellect and Solidarism of the Will', *International Affairs*, 72(1).

— (1998) 'Good International Citizenship: A Third Way for British Foreign Policy', *International Affairs*, 74(4).

Wheen, F. (1999) *Karl Marx* (London).

White, J. B. (1984) *When Words Lose their Meaning: Constitutions and Reconstitutions of Language, Character, and Community* (Chicago).

Whitworth, S. (1994) *Feminism and International Relations: Towards a Political Economy of Gender in Interstate and Non-Governmental Institutions* (London).

— (2001) 'The Practice, and Praxis, of Feminist Research in International Relations', in R. W. Jones (ed.), *Critical Theory and World Politics* (Boulder).

— (2004) *Men, Militarism and UN Peacekeeping: A Gendered Analysis* (Boulder).

Wibben, A. (2011) *Feminist Security Studies: A Narrative Approach* (New York).

Wight, M. (1966a) 'Why is there no International Theory?', in H. Butterfield and M. Wight (eds), *Diplomatic Investigations, Essays in the Theory of International Relations* (London).

— (1966b) 'Western Values in International Relations', in H. Butterfield and M. Wight (eds), *Diplomatic Investigations, Essays in the Theory of International Relations* (London).

— (1977) *Systems of States* (Leicester).

— (1991) *International Theory: The Three Traditions*, (ed.) G. Wight and B. Porter (Leicester).

— (1992) *International Theory: The Three Traditions* (New York).

Williams, B. (2005) *In the Beginning Was the Deed: Realism and Moralism in Political Argument* (Princeton).

Williams, J. (2002) 'Territorial Borders, Toleration and the English School', *Review of International Studies*, 28(4).

— (2006) *The Ethics of Territorial Borders: Drawing Lines in the Shifting Sand* (Basingstoke).

Williams, J. and Goose, S. (1998) 'The International Campaign to Ban Land Mines' in A. Maxwell, R. Cameron, J. Lawson and B. W. Tomlin (eds), *To Walk Without Fear: The Global Movement to Ban Landmines* (Toronto).

Williams, P. (2006) 'Social Constructivism, International Relations Theory, and Ecology', in Laferrière, E. and Stoett, P. (eds) *International Ecopolitical Theory: Critical Approaches* (Vancouver).

Wilson, P. (1998) 'The Myth of the First Great Debate', *Review of International Studies*, 24 (Special Issue).

Wohlforth, W. C. (1999) 'The Stability of a Unipolar World', *International Security*, 24(1).

— (2008) 'Realism', in C. Reus-Smit and D. Sindal (eds), *Oxford Handbook of International Relations* (Oxford).

Wohlforth, W. C., Little, R., Kaufman, S. J., *et al.* (2007) 'Testing Balance-of-Power Theory in World History', *European Journal of International Relations*, 13(2).

Wolfers, A. and Martin, L. W. (eds) (1956) *The Anglo-American Tradition in Foreign Affairs: Readings from Thomas More to Woodrow Wilson* (New Haven).

WWF (2010) *Living Planet Report 2010: Biodiversity, Biocapacity and Development* (Gland).

Wyn Jones, R. (2001) 'Introduction: Locating Critical International Relations Theory', in R. W. Jones (ed.), *Critical Theory and World Politics* (Boulder).

Yergin, D. (1990) *Shattered Peace*, rev. edn (London).

Young, M. (2011) *Responsibility for Justice* (Oxford).

Young, O. R. (1982) 'Regime Dynamics', *International Organization*, 36(2).

— (1989a) 'The Politics of International Regime Formation: Managing Natural Resources and the Environment', *International Organization*, 43(3).

— (1989b) *International Cooperation: Building Regimes for Natural Resources and the Environment* (Ithaca).

— (1994) *International Governance: Protecting the Environment in a Stateless Society* (Ithaca).

— (1997) 'Global Governance: Towards a Theory of Decentralized World Order', in O.R. Young (ed.), *Global Governance: Drawing Insights from the Environmental Experience* (Ithaca).

— (1999a) *Governance in World Affairs* (Ithaca).

— (ed.) (1999b), *The Effectiveness of International Environmental Regimes: Causal Connections and Behavioral Mechanisms* (Cambridge).

Young, R. (2004) *White Mythologies: Writing History and the West*, second edition (London).

Ypi, L. (2011) *Global Justice and Avant-garde Political Agency* (Oxford).

Zacher, M. W. and Matthew, R. A. (1995) 'Liberal International Theory: Common Threads, Divergent Strands', in C. W. Kegley, Jr (ed.), *Controversies in International Relations Theory* (New York).

Zahn, G. (1986) *In Solitary Witness: The Life and Death of Franz Jägerstätter* (Springfield, IL).

Zakaria, F. (1998) *From Wealth to Power: The Unusual Origins of America's World Role* (Princeton).

Zalewski, M. (1993) 'Feminist Standpoint Theory Meets International Relations Theory', *The Fletcher Forum for World Affairs*, 75(1).

— (1995) 'Well, What is the Feminist Perspective on Bosnia?', *International Affairs*, 71(2).

Zalewski, M. and Parpart, J. (eds) (1998) *The 'Man' Question in International Relations* (Boulder).

Zehfuss, M. (2003) 'Forget September 11', *Third World Quarterly*, 24(3).

Zimelis, A. (2009) 'Human rights, the Sex Industry, and Foreign Troops: Feminist Analysis of Nationalism in Japan, South Korea and the Philippines', *Cooperation and Conflict*, 44 (1).

Zolberg, A. (1981) 'Origins of the Modern World System: A Missing Link', *World Politics*, 33(2).

Index

Note: **bold type** = extended discussion or term emphasized in text.

absolute gains 40, 67
'absolute power' 235
'absolutist states' (Anderson) 145, 319
absorptive capacity **274**
Abyssinia 98
academic identity 224, 225
accountability 61, 305, 313
acid rain 183, 266, 278
Ackerly, B. A. 245, 263, **319**
actors
    political (pre-social, self-interested, rational) **220**
    social 220, **221**, 222, **226**, 233
    transnational 241
actors' interests
    endogenous to social interaction **226**
    exogenously determined 224, 226
Adler, E. 48, 239, 319
Adorno, T. 24, 29, 134, 142–3, 163, 179, 340
advocacy 313, 318
'aesthetic turn' (Bleiker) 194, 216, 322
Afghanistan 58, 63, 64, 83, 107, 252, 261, 262
Africa 292, 318
After Hegemony (Keohane, 1984) 219, 344
Agamben, G. **201–2**, 319
Age of Absolutism (1555–1848) 224–5
agency 192–3, 229, 230, 239, 242, 255–6, 263
agency problem 312
agents and structures,
    'mutually constituted (constructivism) **225**
aggression 48, 303–5, 307
'agonism' 191–2
aid/foreign aid 208, 246, 249, 309
AIDS 13, 183
Al-Ali, N. 241, 319
Al-Qaeda 13, 83, 85, 105, 109, 179
Algerian War 196
alienation (Marxist conception) 116–17, 173
alliances 43–4, 46, 366
alterity 213, 214–15
Amnesty International 13, 250
anachronism 315, 316, 318
'anarchical society' (Bull) 88–9, 325
'anarchist solution' (O'Riordan) 275–6, 352
'anarchocentrism' 148

anarchy 151, 279
    ordering principle 37
    see also international anarchy
'*anarchy problématique*' (Ashley) **197–9**, 209
Ancient Greece 93, 151, 163, 164, 214
Ancient Rome 147, 202, 299
Anderson, P. 129, 144, 145, 319
Annales school 155
Annenkov, G. 121
anomie 178
anthropocentrism 277, 279
anthropology 35, 238
'anti-foundationalism' (Hoffman) 221, 232
'anti-globalist Far Right' 131
Apartheid 70, 101, 344
'applied ethics' 292, 293
Aquinas, St Thomas 300
Arab Spring (2011) 59, 63, 92, 103, 106, 150, 211, 253
Archibugi, D. **182**, **320**
Archimedean perspective 18, 190
Arctic sea ice 274
Arendt, H. 318
'argumentative rationality' 183
aristocracy/nobility 60, 65, 146
    'lord and serf' 142
    'lords' (mediaeval) 156
Aristotle 55, 293
Ashley, R. K. 29, 168, 188–9, **320**, 361
    'dominant mode of subjectivity' (normalization) 207
    double reading of '*anarchy problématique*' **197–9**, 209
    post-structuralist ethics 213–14
    statecraft (post-structuralist interpretation) **207–9**
Asia Pacific Economic Cooperation (APEC) 78
Asian values 72
assumptions 18, 30, 42–5, 78, 92, 94, 105, 123, 128, 144, 146, 153, 169–70, 188, 192, 197–201, 203–5, 208, 216–17, 219, **220**, 222–4, 230, 234, 238, 243, 245, 248, 251, 253, 255, 257, 260–1, 265, 276, 286, 291–6, 318
    Hobbes **34–6**
    Marx and Engels 120
    Waltz 43

Athens 34
envoy to Melos 34, 48
and Sparta (bipolar system) 41
'Atlantic divide' **240**
'atomistic egoists' 226
atrocity **297–8**, 304
Australia 10, 331
Austro–Marxists 123, 126
autarky 60, 65
authoritarianism 62, 72, 150, 225, 228,
243, 275, 279, 282
authority 181, 184, **194**, 216
bio-environmentalism **275–6**
autocracy 21, 150
'autonomy of politics' (Morgenthau) 51
Axelrod, R. 219, 270, 320

Babylon 69
Bachelet, M. 247
Bäckstrand, K. 286, 320, 324
balance of power 12, **22**, 32, 63–4, 93, 98,
113, 136, 149, 233, 256, 307, 317,
343
military 218, 224
'realist conception' 235
balancing (Waltz) **37–9**, 40, 41, 45, 47,
96
Bali bombings 84, 103
Balkans 64
Bananas, Beaches, and Bases (Enloe, 1989)
243, 334
bandwagoning **37–8**, 40, 358
Bangladesh 247
'bare life' (Agamben) 201–2
Barkin, J. S. 152, 321
Barnett, J. 268, 321
Barnett, M. 48, 236, 319, 321
Barry, B. 309, 321
Barry, J. 284, 321
Bauer, O. 123
Beardsworth, R. 182, 215, 321
Behrens, W. **273–4**, 350
Beitz, C. 309, 310, 322
beneficence 43, 305, 311
Benjamin, W. 163
Berman, J. 242, 322
Bernauer, T. 271, 322
Beslan atrocity (2004) 84
Beyond the Limits (Meadows and Randers,
1992) 280, 350
Beyond Realism and Marxism (Linklater,
1990) 176, 346
'bi-multipolarity' 41
Bially Mattern, J. 239, 322
Bill of Rights (1689) 69
binary oppositions/dichotomies 196, 212,
213, 251, 259–61, 264
bio-environmentalism 267, 272, **273–9**,
280, 282, 284, 287
bio-regionalism 275

biodiversity 266, 278
biofuels 266, 274
biology 251, 258
bipolarity 38, 63, 91, 92, 98, 101, 112, 114,
256, 356
relative stability 41–2
Blanchard, J.-M. F. 45, 322
Bleiker, R. 188, 189, **194–5**, 210, **322–3**
Bloch, C. 7
Block, F. 129, 323
Blomert, R. 132, 323
'blowback' 84, 342
Bodansky, D. 266, 323
Bohman, J. 167, 168, 323
Bonaparte, N. 92
Bookchin, M. 282, 284, 323
Booth, K. 29, **323**
definition of 'emancipation' 171
'border politics' (Vaughan-Williams) 203,
364
Bosnia 190, 202, 326
'performatively constituted' 208–9
post-structuralist account **204–5**, 306
Boulainvilliers: H., Comte de 192
boundaries 199, **203–4**, 207, 210, 212–14,
293, 307, 317
feminist analysis 254
national ('increasing irrelevance') 75–6
'bounded communities' **176–7**
Bourdieu, P. 239
bourgeoisie 16, 113, 116, **118–21**, 124–5,
134, 137, 173
Brandenburg, E. 7
Braudel, F. 138, 144
Brazil 107, 112
Bretton Woods system 75, 79
Brincat, S. 29, 324
Britain *see* United Kingdom
British Committee for Study of International
Politics **151**
Bromley, S. 130, 324
Brundtland Commission (WCED, 1987)
281, 366
Brunkhorst, H. 180, 184, 324
Brunnee, J. 239, 324
Buck, S. J. 284, 324
Buddhist texts 69
Bukharin, N. 123–4, 324
Bulkeley, H. 278, 286, 324
Bull, H. 2, **3**, 5, 8, 18, 24, 28, 67, 72, **94–6**,
97, **98–9**, 151, 240, 302, **324–5**, 366,
367
human rights 100
'moral vision' in foreign policy 102
'most famous work' 88–9, 325
order and justice in international
relations **99–100**, 108
progress in international relations
108–11
protégé of Wight 90

rejection of white supremacism 101
revolt against West **103–7**
Burchill, S. **1–31**, 57–87, 252, 291, 294
bureaucratization 134, 141, 142
Burke, A. 215, 325
Burke, E. 314, 365
Burton, J. 289
Bush, G. W. 85, 91, 193, 236, 252, 341
Bush doctrine ('preventive war') 93
Butler, J. 193, 202, 251, 325
Buttel, F. 277, 284, 361
Butterfield, Sir Herbert 12, 33, 39–40, 55, 368
Buzan, B. 25, 26, 46, 88, 108, 110, 140, 147, 149, 150, 152, 159, **325–6**

Calvinism 142, 153
Cambodia 72, 73, 349
Vietnamese invasion (1978) 51, 73
Camilleri, J. A. 159, 326
Campaign for Nuclear Disarmament (CND) 250
'campaigns of compassion' 155
Campbell, D. **190–1**, 194, 195, 202–4, 208–9, 209–10, 213, **326**
containment **205–6**
post-structuralist ethics **214–15**
Canada 10, 114, 224
Caney, S. 307, 326
capabilities 37, 40, 41, 42, 43, 44, 47, 311
capital 68, 76, 124, 177
'sovereignty' 75
transnational 79–80, 130, 356
capital markets 80, 86
capital mobility 65, 76–7, 78
capitalism 21, 28–30, 57, 71, 74, 87, 116–18, 121–2, 127, 129, 141–7, 153, 160, 172, 173, 176, 178, 225, 243, 258, 265, 285, 290, 330, 335
'combined and uneven development' (Trotsky) 125
Green alternative 283
mode of production 114, 115
'prone to periodic crises' 114, 119–20, 124
world system 132
see also global capitalism
capitalist imperialism theory 125
capitalist mentality (Weber) 142
Capra, F. 274, 282, 361
Caprioli, M. 245, **326–7**
Carbon Disclosure Project 278
carbon markets 283, 347
care ethics 259–60
Carlyle, T. 142
Carnegie Institution 314
Carr, E. H. 1, 4, 7, 9, 27–8, 33, 34, 52, 54, 60, 65, 112, 115, 122, 124, 218, 235, 327
'carrying capacity' 273, **274**

Carter, A. 277, 282, 327, 359
Carthage–Rome (bipolar system) 41
cartography 204, 205, 213
'cash nexus' (Carlyle/Marx) 142
'casino capitalists' 13
Categorical Imperative (Kant) 179
causality/causation 12, 14, 17, 345
Central America 38, 105
Central Asia 62, 64
Central Europe 38
Certeau, M. de 238
Chakrabarty, D. 160, 206, 327
cheap labour 76, 77, 144, 246
Chechnya 250
child labour 71
children 13, 157, 248, 250, 293, 298, 310
Chile 247
Chin, C. B. 247, 328
China
'Ancient China' 94, 151, 152, 341
eighteenth century 103
'Middle Kingdom' 104
PRC era (1949–) 15, 44, 84, 91, 99, 112, 149, 342
pre-PRC 154, 342
rise to power 93, 107
tribute system 104
Chinese Revolution (1949) 147
Chomsky, N. 2, 15, 328, 339
Chou, M. 188, 322
Choucri, N. 273, 328
Christian monarchies 224–5
Christianity 55, 105, 117, 152, 154, 237
Christians 73
Augustinian 55
pre-Constantine 298
Christoff, P. 285, 326
Churchill, Sir Winston 307
cities/global cities 246, 317, 358
Cities for Climate Protection 286
citizens 172–3, 176, 180, 211, 302, 305, 313
citizenship 136, 182, 256
ecological 285, 287, 332
environmental 30
'good international' 101
city-states 93, 146, 151, 157
'*polis*' 164
civil law 293, 308
civil liberties 61, 85, 193
civil rights 301
civil society 4, 176–7, 178, 192, 302, 341
civilian casualties/fatalities 296, 297, 298
see also combatants
civilization 33, 120, 215, 317
civilizations 95, 104, 135, 157
nature **237**
'civilizing process' (Elias) 140, 156, 179, 333, 347, 350
Clapp, J. 266, 267, 273, 280, 284, 287, 328

Clark, H. 247

Clark, I. **96**, 102, 149, 150, 328

clash of civilizations (Huntington) 102–3, 105, 154, 179, 191, 237, 294, 341

class 14, 18, 71, 113, 126, 130, 132, 135–6, 171, 173, 261, 262, 294, 362, 364
    Marx **116–23**
    transnational 13

class conflict/struggle 16, 124, 128, 133, 145

classical realism/realists 33, 44, 49
    Hobbes **34–6**, 37

Claude, I. 218

Clausewitz, K. M. von 105, 192

climate change 67, 107, 150, **266**, 271, 274, 279, 289, 320, 324, 363

Climate Change and Biodiversity Alliance 278

Cobden, R. 61

coercion 133, 150, 153, 157, 262, 308, 309

cognitivism 271

Coke, Sir Edward 192

Cold War 9, 15, **38–9**, 47, 73, 85, 112, 114, 173, 205–6, 222, 235, 261
    bipolar system 41
    end 17, 229
    end (failure to predict) 49, 223
    not 'caused' by anyone 38

cold wars 205, 330

collective action 268, **269**

collective security 7, 90

Collège de France 192, 335

colonialism 66, **103–4**, 124, 150, 155, 196, 282, 317, 344
    feminist **261–2**, 351
    see also empire/s

'combatants' versus 'civilians' 258

commerce **65–6**, 118, 316

commodities 127, 281–2, 283

commons
    'already exists' **287**
    back to **282–4**
    enclosure 281

communication 120, 134, 225, **226**, 270

communicative action 184, 356

communism 38, 71, 85, 114, 335

Communist Manifesto (Marx and Engels) **120–1**, 135–6

communitarians 174, 310

community 141, 173, 215, 233, 283, 284
    see also global community

comparative advantage theory 65
    challenges **76–9**

'complex emergencies' (Dillon and Reid) 201, 331

'complex interdependence' (Keohane and Nye) 218

Comte, A. 143

conceptual oppositions (Derrida) 195

'concern, contractual environment, capacity' ('three Cs') 271

'concrete historical situation' (Horkheimer) 165

Confucianism 69, 72, 153

Connolly, W. 203–4, **213**, 328
    post-structuralist ethics 213–14

conscription 257, 298

consequentialism 306

'constitutionalism' 64, 184

constitutions 202

'constitutive outside' (Agamben) 202

constitutive theory 12

constraint **226**

constructivism 5, 11, 22, 25, **29–30**, 97, 103, 111, 146, 150–1, 152, 155, **217–40**, 241, 243, 254, 257, 264, 273, 285, 321, 324, 340, 345, 354, 368
    agents and structures ('mutually constitutive relationship') 217
    'analytical framework' rather than 'theory' 230
    'broad church' 235
    characteristics 217
    'chief contribution' (Price) 238
    'contingent generalizations' 230
    contrasts with rationalism **226–7**
    contribution **233–5**
    'conventional' versus 'critical' (Hopf) 232–3
    debate with rationalists (post-Cold War) 217, 229
    distinguished from first-wave critical theory 222
    'ethical veracity' 232
    feminist 248, 254
    green theory 270, 271
    'how' versus 'why' questions **233**
    ideas, beliefs, values 'have structural characteristics' 224
    interest-formation **225**
    'modernists' versus 'postmodernists' 224, **232–3**
    'new level of clarity and sophistication' 234
    'non-material structures' 224
    'one of principal theoretical approaches' 235
    practitioners 223
    recent developments **235–9**
    rise **222–3**, 229, 233, 235, 239
    'small-c' 175
    'stock in trade' 232
    'thin form' 231
    US mainstream 217, 223, 233, 234, 240
    US origins 240

constructivism: discontents **229–33**
    contribution to critical theory of IR 229, **232**

methodology (appropriate) 229, **231–2**
nature of theory 229, **230**, 232
relationship with rationalism 229,
    230–1, 232
constructivism: forms **227–9**
    holistic 30, **228–9**
    systemic 30, **227**, 228, 229, 230
    unit-level **227–8**
constructivists 110, 294
    classed as 'structurationists' 225, 238
    conventional-mainstream 237–8
    'core ontological propositions' 224
    'with critical inclinations' 238
    'modernists' versus 'post-modernists'
        224
    'placed sociological inquiry back at centre
        of discipline' 234, 239
containment, 'pivotal concept' 205–6
cooperation **39–40**, 47, 67–8, 110, 217,
    219–20, 233, 256, 270, 272, 283,
    302, 304, 320, 344, 353–4, 362, 368
    global social 310
'cooperation under anarchy' 28
Copenhagen talks (2009) 266, 333
core–periphery analysis 11, 13, 64–5, 71,
    115, 126–8, 132, 144, 149, 178
'corporate mercantilism' 78
corruption 303, 309
Cosmopolitan 243
'cosmopolitan culture of modernity' (Bull)
    95, 102
cosmopolitan democracy **182**, 286
'cosmopolitan education' 143
cosmopolitanism 90, 108, 109, 112, 118,
    120, 121, 125, 135, 139, 154, 158,
    163, 171, 179, **180–5**, 186, 293–4,
    302, 304, 307, 308, 310, 317, 320,
    321–2, 339
    'dialogical' (Linklater and Shapcott)
        181
    'international' justice 306
    'thin' (Linklater and Shapcott) **181–2**
Council of Women World Leaders 248
'counter-hegemonic movements' (Cox) 14,
    23, 130–2, 137, 178
counter-histories 189
counter-terrorism 67, 351
Cox, M. 92, 100, 329
Cox, R. W. **14–15**, 23, 29, 114, **130–1**, 135,
    175, **329**, 331, 346
    'critical theory' versus 'problem-solving
        theory' **166–8**
    'internationalization of state' 178
    'key issue' 177
    state and civil society 176–7
    theory 'always *for* someone' 23, 166
    theory of state **177**
Crawford, N. C. 150, 184, 329
credit ratings agencies 80

crime
    organized 67
    and punishment 157
    transnational 84
crimes against humanity 72–3, 298, 304
'crisis management' 11
critical constructivism 23–4
'critical international society' (Dunne and
        Wheeler) 111
'critical interpretivism' (modernists) 221
'critical political ecology' (Eckersley) 288
critical realism 299
critical theorists 223, 231, 294
    debate with rationalists (1980s) 217, 229
critical theory 4, 12, 20, 22–4, **29**, 30, 111,
    114, 118, 135–7, **162–86**, 201, 215,
    224, 241, 257, 264, 286
    challenge (to neo-realism, neo-liberalism)
        221–2
    common ground with Green theory 289,
        290
    contributions **185–6**
    'defining characteristic' 162
    'denaturalizing' critique 169
    emancipatory project 240
    'essentially a critique of dogmatism' 169
    first-wave 221, 222–3
    literature 321, 324, 331, 334, **336**,
        340–1, **346–7**, 349, 352, 354, 359,
        367
    'most pressing issues addressed' 162
    'must be self-reflective' **164**
    origins **163–6**
    'overall objective' 181
    problem-solving **166–70**
    purpose **165–6**
    relationship with constructivism **232**
    Reus-Smit usage 217
    social theory of state 176
    sociological analyses (purpose) 178
    task as emancipatory theory **170–1**
'critical-reflective participant' (Bohman) 168
Cuba 224
cultural imperialism 104–5
Cultural Norms and National Security
        (Katzenstein, 1996) 236, 343
Cultural Realism (Johnston, 1995) 236, 342
culture 4, 5, 22, 27, 58, 65, 71, 91, 95–6,
        103, 116, 123, 134, 143, 151, 153,
        154, 156, 176, 180, 230, 234, 239,
        240, 255, 256, 258, 262, 302, 307,
        310–11, 347
    indigenous 102
    constructivism (recent developments)
        236–7
    holistic understanding 236–7
'cultures of anarchy' (Wendt) 285
Cusack, T. R. 32, 329

Dalby, S. 205, 268, 277, 330

Dar al Harb (House of War) 104, 301
Dar al Islam (House of Islam) 104, 301
Dar al Suhl (temporary truce) 104
Darfur 50
Dauvergne, P. 267, 273, 280, 284, 287, 328
Davies, S. E. 260, 330
De Jure Belli ac Pacis (Grotius, 1625) 89
'de-territorialization' and 're-territorialization' **210–11**
debates
  communitarian-cosmopolitan 310
  constructivists versus critical theorists
    (post-Cold War) 217
  epistemology (1960s) 24
  global justice **313–14**
  humanitarian intervention **305–6**
  inter-paradigm (1970s, 1980s) 11
  'knowable reality' (1990s) 24
  'level of analysis' (1960s) 21
  neo-realist versus neo-liberal (1980s,
    1990s) 217, 229
  'pluralists' versus 'solidarists' **302–7**
  positivist-traditionalist 240
  rationalists versus constructivists (post-
    Cold War) 217, 229
  rationalists versus critical theorists
    (1980s) 217, 229
  realism-idealism ('first debate') 9, 90,
    240, 294
  'third debate' 166, 217, 243
decentralization 278, 287, 289, 290, 327
  social Green perspective **282–4**
decision-making **183–4**, 198, 248, 312,
  313
  contrasted with 'theorizing' 292
decolonization 329
  of European thought 196
deconstruction **135–6**, **195–6**, 199, 206,
  211, 216, 251
'defensive positionalists' (Grieco/Waltz) 44,
  219
defensive realism 44, 45
'deformalization' 312
Deleuze, G. 210, 330, 353, 355
'deliberate killing' **297**
democracy 8, 51, 57, 99, 200, 215, 249,
  258, 312, 313, 324, 333, 339
  cosmopolitan **182**, 286
  'de-territorialization' (Connolly) 213
  deliberative-discursive **285**, 287, 320
  ecological **286–7**
  global 313
  post-structuralist critique (Connolly)
    213, 328
  small-scale 284
  transnational 286
  treatment for 'disease' of war **61**
  see also liberal democracy
democratic deficit 82
democratic deliberation **286**

'democratic peace' theory 62, 64, 156
  'liberal-democratic peace' 12, 59, 60,
    61–2
  'liberal peace' 13, 17, 24, 28, 331, 348
democratic transition 228
'denaturalizing' critique (critical theory) 169
Denemark, R. 159, 330
dependency theory 115, 125–7, 130, 144,
  290
Der Derian, J. 111, 194, 330
Derrida, J. 29, **135–6**, 163, 165, 190, 194,
  204, 207, 221, 326, **330–1**, 338
  deconstruction **195–6**
  double-reading **196–7**
  post-structuralist ethics 214, 215
Deudney, D. 268, 331
Deutsch, K. W. 41, 331
developing countries 71, 77–8, 79, 107, 246
  'less-developed states' 309
development 281, 288, 290, 343, 357
  anti-ecological elements **281–2**
Devetak, R. **29**, **162–216**, 217, **331**
dialogic ideal (Diez and Steans) 180, 184,
  331
dialogue 6, 182, 183, 348
dictatorship of proletariat 136
Diez, T. 180, 331
difference 212, 260, 289, 303
Dillon, M. 200, 201, 203, 211, 326, 331
Dingwerth, K. 286, 332
diplomacy 7, 90, 92, 96, 106, 111, 136,
  149, 208, 239, 248, 293, 316, 317,
  330
'diplomatic culture' (Bull) 95
'diplomatic ethos' (Ashley and Walker) 214
diplomatic history (discipline) 6
  see also 'end of history'
diplomatic spouses 243
'disciplinary neo-liberalism' 130
Discipline and Punish (Foucault, 1977) 188,
  335
discourse 197, 316, 222, 315
  globalist 317
discourse ethics (Habermas) 135, **182–5**,
  357
  critique of political organization **185**
  'democratic' **183**
  features **183**
  'form of moral-practical reasoning' **183**
  implications for reconstruction of world
    politics **183–5**
  'inclusionary' **183**
  'procedural fairness' **183**
  procedure for regulating violent conflict
    184–5
discourse theory of morality (Habermas) 135
dissent 193, 198, **205–6**
  'transformed by globalization' **210–11**
'distant needy' 310
distributive justice 307, **309–11**

division of labour/specialization
    gender (internationalized) 246
    global 116, 121
    scholarly 140, 230
    social 156
Dobson, A. 267, 274, 277, 332
'domain apart' (Waltz) 25
domains (domestic and international)
        bridged (holistic constructivism)
        228–9
'domestic analogy' 90, 95, 293, 305, 306
domestic servants 246–7
domestic workers, international convention
        248
domestic–international divide 254, 259,
        289, 296, 307
dominance and dependence (global system)
        5, 11
dominant actors **13**
dominant relationships **13**
domination 18, 43, 44, 189–90, 221
dominion **151**
Donnelly, J. **27–8**, **32–56**, 218, **332**
Doran, P. 288, 332
'double effect' principle 296, 298
'double exclusion' (Ashley) 199
double reading 195, **196–9**
    '*anarchy problématique*' (Ashley) **197–9**
Doyle, M. 17, 24, 32, 59–62, 332
Dryzek, J. 276, 277, 284, 286, **332**
Dubash, N. K. 266, 333
Dunne, T. 88, 89, 92–3, 101, 108, 110, 111,
        333, 367
Durkheim, É. 142, 153
Dutch East India Company 315
duty **308**, **311–12**
Duvall, R. D. 236, 321

East Asia 58, 64, 71–2, 74
East Timor 50, 72
Eastern Europe 38, 58, 129
Eckersley, R. **277–8**, 279, **284–7**, 288, 290,
        321, 333, 354
eco-anarchism 278
eco-authoritarianism 269, 278, 285
eco-centrism **277–9**, 285, 290
    'core problem' 279
    'politically indeterminate' 279
ecological citizenship 285, 287, 332
'ecological debt' 275
ecological democracy **286–7**
'ecological footprints' (Wackernagel and
        Rees) 274–5, 365
ecological literature 323, 341, 350, 368
ecological modernization 285, 287, 326,
        338, 351
ecological movement 13
'ecological security' versus 'environmental
        security' 268
ecological unsustainability **288**

Ecologist 276, 283
    see also global ecology
economic determinism 124
    see also historical materialism
economic development 71–2, 79, 80, 81,
        105, 121, 126, 145
economic growth 99, 265, 273–4, 280, 281,
        284, 289
economic inequality 292, 307, 309
    intra-country 309
economic interdependency **68–9**
economic liberalism 57
    'dominant ideology' 73
economic power **147**
economic reductionism 28, 121, 133, 142,
        145, 148
    see also Marxism
economics 6, 14, 25, 173
    interdependencies with politics 146
    rationalist 217
Edkins, J. 189, 191, 201, **333**
education 10, 176, 246
egoism 32–3, 35–7, 39, 53, 275
Egypt 104, 150
Ehrlich, P. 268, 333
Eighteenth Brumaire of Louis Bonaparte
        (Marx, 1852) 119, 168, 349
Eisenstadt, S. N. 140, 333
Eleventh of September attacks (2011) 64,
        74, 83, 84, 101, 103, 105, 112, 114,
        162, 179, 199, 237, 241, 301
    feminist critique 258
    literature 325, 335, 341, 343, 363, 369
    post-structuralism **191**, **193**, 194, 215,
        216, 325, 369
    Zehfuss's analysis **193**, 369
Elias, N. 140, 143, 149, 159, 179, **333**, 347,
        350, 364
    'central question' 158
    'higher synthesis' **156–8**
    'elimination contests' (Elias) 156, 157–8
elites 45, 61, 68, 95, 102, 105, 130–2, 147,
        157, 244, 247, 255, 265, 309
    see also ruling class
Elman, M. F. 45, 333
Elshtain, J. 252, 255, 333–4
emancipation 70, 128, 137, 163, 164, 169,
        172, 175, 186, 221, 289, 290, 323
    definition (Booth) 171
    universal human 24
    'emancipation of species' 165
    'emancipation writ large' **277–8**
    'emancipatory counter-hegemonic' forces
        178
emancipatory politics 162, 232
emancipatory project **133–6**, 240
emancipatory theory 166
    critical theory **170–1**
emergencies 201–2, 301, 307, 312, 331
emissions 271, 273, 286

Emmanuel, A. 126, 334
emotionology 155, 361
emotions 30, **154–6**, 157, 158, 179, 239, 322, 329
empire/s 140, 146, 149, 151, 237, 294, 333
  'civilizing mission' 314
  idea 'denial of IR' **318**
  see also imperialism
empirical data 5, 12
empirical feminism **242, 244–51**, 260, 263, 264
'empirical idealism' 235
empirical inquiry **13**, 41, 44, 48, 239, 259, 295
empirical theory 26, 110, **295**
empiricism 15, 19, 53, 54, 175, 207, 214, 217, 219, 221, 229, 231, 238, 265, 277, 289
  constructivism **222–3**, 237
  terminology 'problematic' **295**
employment 118, 246, 247
enclosure **281**
'end of history' 294
  see also Fukuyama
Engels, F. 113, 115, 119–23, 132, 134–6, 349
  'interest in strategy and war' 120
English Common Law 69
English School 10, 11, 20, 22, 25, **28**, 67, **88–112**, 113, 128, 132, 150–1, 152, 217, 234, 239, 240, 260, 270, 294
  argument 108
  international society (from power to order) **93–7**
  literature 325, 334, 341, 347, 363
  order and justice in international relations **97–103**
  progress in international relations **108–12**
  revolt against West and expansion of international society **103–7**
Enlightenment 29, 57, 69, 113, 117, 127, 163, 171, **173**, 180–1, 290
Enloe, C. 30, 243, 245, 249, 253, 257, **271**, 334
'entrapment of politics' 204
environment 279, 337, 341, 352, 368–9
  global protection 220
  theorized within international relations **268–72**
environmental crisis, *problématique* 287
environmental degradation 68, 272–3, 280, 284, 286
  'political origins' 273
  political responses **275–6**
  spatial dimension **275–6**
environmental multilateralism 285, 287

environmental politics
  institutionalist accounts **269–72**
  see also global environmental politics
'environmental security' 268, 273, 330, 331
'environmentalism' versus 'ecologism' 267
Environmentalism and Political Theory (Eckersley, 1992) 286, 333
'epistemologico-juridical formation' (Foucault) 188
epistemology **6**, 12, 14, 24, 30, 110, 166, 194, 216–17, 221, 229–30, 233, 256, 263, 265, 290, 295, 299, 348
  feminist 242, **243–4**
  'feminist standpoint' **260–1**
equal opportunities law 248
equality 150, 172, 181, 186
  normative claims 119
equality assumption (Hobbes) 34, 35, 36
equality before law 61, 62
Escobar, A. 281, 282, 334
essentialism 237, 252
Esteva, G. 289, 334
ethical particularism **172–5**
'ethical peace' (post-structuralist) 215, 325
Ethics (discipline) 14
ethics **13**, 15, 17, 25, 27, 30, 50–4, 60, 63, 70–2, 85, 119, 134, 153, 169, 170, 221, 234–5, 238, 288, **292–3**, 329, 341, 356
  'anthropocentric' versus 'eco-centric' 277
  'de-territorialized' 214
  eco-centric 279, 286, 290
  as 'first philosophy' 214
  'middle ground' 302
  'moral' versus 'institutional' duties 293
  post-structuralist **213–16**
  realist 306
  transcultural 102
  'transgressive' 214
  see also global ethics
ethics of care 311
  feminist 255–6
'ethics and international affairs' 292
ethnic-cleansing 202, 205
ethnicity 18, 115, 126, 135, 137, 180, 262
Eurocentrism 128, 132, 143, 154, 340, 353, 359
Europe 26, 95, 103, 104, 107, 114, 121, 127, 148, 150, 156, 163, 196, 206, 215, 229, 242, 316, 317–18, 322, 338, 341, 362
  social theory 25
European Union 48, 66, 78, 248, 304, 313, 340
Everard, J. 203, 331
everyday life 138, 153, 197, 256, 263
evolutionary socio-biology 261
exceptionalism 202–3, 351
exclusion 203, 211–12, 216
  ethics **211–13**

'exemplary' models (Ashley) **207**
'exercise of judgment' (Bull) 240
'experts' (empowerment) 281–2
exploitation 116–19, 122–3, 125, 135–6, 288
extra-territoriality 104
extraordinary rendition 72

'factor endowments' 76, 77
facts **16–17**, 169
fact-value distinction 289
'failed states' 64, 107, 207, 339, 342
Falk, R. 159, 326
'false consciousness' 117
'False Promise of International Institutions' (Mearsheimer, 1994–5) 48, 350
famine 50, 201, 292
   'malnutrition' 100
Fay, S. B. 7
Febvre, L. 155
Federalist Papers (1788) 254
femininity 251, 252, 260–1
feminism 4, 11, 23–4, 25, 26, **30**, 136, 180, **241–65**, 281
   analytical **242**, **251–9**, 263, 264
   'broad church' 20
   common ground with Green theory 289, 290
   'constitutive theory' 241
   empirical **242**, **244–51**, 260, 263, 264
   'ethical principles' 241
   first-wave 242–3
   literature 319, 325–7, 330, 333, **334**, 335–7, 340–1, 344, 349–51, 353–60, **362**, **363–4**, 367–9
   'neo-feminism' 265
   'no high ground' **262–3**
   normative **242**, **259–63**, 264
   second-wave 243
feminist IR
   first generation (late 1980s) **243–4**
   second-generation **244**
feminists 16, 21–2, 25, 294, 311
'feminization of poverty' 246
Ferguson, Y. H. 140, 148, 159, 334
feudalism 118, 127, 141–2, 145, 146, 229, 335
Fierke, K. M. 169, 170, 334
Fiji 58
financial crisis (global, 2007–) 58, 74, 82, 87, 132, 236, 313236, 313
   'breathed new life into historical materialism' 114
   see also world economy
Finnemore, M. 110, 222, 321, 334
'first debate' (realists versus idealists) 90, 240, 294
Fischer, M. 145–6, 335
foedus pacificum (Kant) 62
food 246, 266, 274, 328

Forde, S. 32, 335
'foreign affairs' 317
Foreign Direct Investment (FDI) 79, 80
foreign exchange 79, 80, 247
foreign investment 77
   sovereignty and **79–83**
foreign ministers (women) 248
foreign policy 8, 11, 70, 100, 184, 205–6, 208, 242, 244, **248–9**, 294, 350
   'gender gap' 249
   moral norms **50–1**
   'moral vision' 182
   morality and **49–54**
Forest Stewardship Council 286
Forsyth, M. 316, 335
Foucault, M. 23, 29, 188, **192**, 199, 202, 221, 335
   'history of present' 193
foundationalism 290
   see also anti-foundationalism
frame analysis 264
France 44, 66, 92, 96, 98, 145, 360
   Napoleonic era 41
   social theory 22
France: Declaration of Rights of Man and Citizen (1789) 70
Frank, A. G. 126, 127, 144, 335
Frankfurt School 22, **29**, 30, 114, 115, 134, 142–3, 163, 165, 167, 179, 217, 221, 288, 337
   common ground with Green theory 290
free markets 85, 131
   free-market economies 59
   free-market environmentalism 267
free trade 28, **65–6**, 75, 124, 144, 225
   nature **76–9**
   treatment for 'disease' of war **61**
   see also trade
free trade zones 246
freedom 57, 70, 137, 165, 181, 186, 275, 311
   Marx's conception 120
   negative conception 171
   normative claims 119
   see also emancipation
French Revolution 147
Fromm, E. 163
Fukuyama, F. **57–60**, 63, 72, 73, 85, 254, 335
   see also history
functional differentiation (Waltz) 40
functions (Waltz) 37
future generations 13, 30

G8 78
G20 67
Gabriel, C. 263, 335
Gadamer, H.-G. 174, 359
Gaddafi, M. 73
Gallie, W. B. 122, 335

Gamble, A. 130, 325, 335
game theory 25, 67, 110, 327
'gap maximizers' 44
Gatens, M. 251, 336
Gellner, E. 18, 336
gender 5, 13, 18, 25, 30, 34, 123, 133, 137,
   180, **241**, 242–4, 249, 294, 297
   as concept (two main criticisms) **261–2**
   'culturally and historically constructed'
      262
   literature 325, 337, 340, 343, 355, 358,
      360–1, 363, 365, 367
   'social construction' 259
   'transformative' category **259**
gender analysis 253, 259, 265, 360
gender bias 251, 256
gender and development (GAD) 245
gender equality 265, 345
   international ranking of states 254
gender mainstreaming 247
gender persecution (AI) 250
'gender relations' (feminist concept) 251
genealogical method
   constructivist 232
   post-structuralist **189–94**, 199, 200,
      206–7, 216
   'systematic dissociation of identity'
      (Foucault) 192
generalizability (Kantian principle) 215
Geneva Convention Against War Crimes
   (1949) 250
genocide 70, 101, 174
geo-politics 18, 112, 113, 115, 120, 127,
   128, 131, 133, 137, 144–7, 149, 151,
   176, 177, 203–5, 317, 352, 362
George, J. 4, 336
Georgia [Caucasus] 250
Geras, N. 181–2, 336
Germany 38, 66, **227–8**, 316, 343
   Nazi era 92, 98, 129, 134, 143,
      201–2
Giddens, A. 63, 142, 176, 336
Gilbert, F. 339
Gill, S. 114, 118, 130, **178**, **336**
Gills, B. K. 127, 159, 330, 335, 336–6
Gilpin, R. 55, 149, 336
Gladstone, W. E. 73
Glaser, C. L. 47, 336
Gleeson, B. 289, 347
'global', usage 307, 308
global capitalism 125, 150, 287, 288
   'capitalist world economy' 114, 125,
      128, 131
   *see also Imperialism: Highest Stage of
      Capitalism*
global civil society 13, 264, 272, 312
'global commons' 324, 365
   'literally nonsensical' 284
'global community' 289
   'international community' 306, 311

'world community' 91
   see also community
global distributive justice
   requires 'shared meanings' 310
'global ecology' 281–2, 286, 288, 289
global environmental politics 108, 279, 280,
   285–6, 332
   institutional analyses (limits) **272–3**
   see also environmental politics
Global Environmental Politics (journal) 267
'global ethics' 5–6, 12, 110, 111, 128, 341
'global ethics of care' (Robinson) 170, 356
global governance 99, 163, 180, 184, 201,
   288, 293, **312**, 313
   literature 331, 353, 355–6, 369
   see also governance
global government 313
global justice 5–6, 19, 30, 73, 111, 112,
   131, 285, 291, 293, 303, 304,
   307–14, 317
   ambiguities **307–8**
   'global' versus 'international' **313**
   literature 326, 350, 360
   principles 308
   'thin' concept 302
   'two ideas' (towards conceptual
      coherence) **308**
   see also global justice
global politics 13, 203, 223, 266, 268, 277,
   278, 287, 322, 365
   feminist 251
   Green critique ('immanent' versus
      'transcendental') **284–7**
   Greening **284–7**, 321, 333, 354
   potential to be reshaped by ecological
      crises 267
   see also international politics
global polity 313
global public realm 313, 314
global space 194, 203, 352
global warming 284, 312
'globalism' 317
globalists 312
globalization 5, 20, 25–6, 57, 58, 86, 115,
   123, 125, 136, 138–9, 148, 159,
   181–4, 213, 234–5, 272, 279, 293,
   295, 312, 313, 317
   capitalist 113, **118**, 123
   economic 13, 114, 178, 242, 246
   liberalism and **74–6**
   literature 324, 330, 336–7, 346, 348,
      350, 353, 356–8, 365
   nineteenth century 113, 121, 142
   opposition movements 287
   restructuring of world order (Cox) 178
   transformation of dissent 210
globalization, financial system, and terrorism
   73–85
   liberalism and globalization **74–6**
   nature of 'free trade' **76–9**

non-state terrorism **83–5**
sovereignty and foreign investment
    79–83
Goldthorpe, J. 140, 337, 348
Gooch, G. P. 7
'good life' 10, 89, 99, 183
'good society' 96
Goodin, R. 277, 337
governance 58, 320, 369
global environmental 272, 278, 286, 347
    'institutionalized structures' 302
    multilevel 279, 286, 289
    private 272
    transnational 286, 289, 332
    see also global governance
governments 8, 15, 36, 61, 66, 71, 75, 77,
    80, 103, 106, 130, 250, 253, 305,
    306, 311, 312
    'primary obligation' 51
Graeco-Roman international society 94
Gramsci, A. 115, 129, 177, 320, 329, 336,
    351, 357
    'neo-Gramscian school' 130
'grand coalitions' 41
grand narratives 141, **158–60**, 294
    see also 'narrativization of reality'
Grant, R. 245, 255, 337
Gray, M. M. 242, 337
'great debates' *see* debates
great power hegemony 93
great power status 107
great powers 13, 36–8, 68, 92, 98, 100, 101,
    128, 144, 148, 228, 256, 341
    number **40–1**
    'rising' versus 'satisfied' 7, 41–2, 44
'great transformation' (modernity) 141, 143
Green politics/Green theory 11, 23–4, 25,
    26, **30–1**, 128, 241, 257, 264, **266–90**
    'central plank' 274
    challenge to world order **272–3**
    'critical' rather than 'problem-solving'
        288
    'cycles of concern' 266
    decentralist impulse **276–7**, 327
    'distinct political economy' 280
    electoral success and pragmatism 277
    ethical concerns 294
    explanatory and normative' 288
    explanatory concerns 289, 294
    'features in common with other critical
        approaches' **289–90**
    'four principal variants' 267
    'four principles' **275–6**
    global politics **284–7**
    institutionalist accounts **269–72**
    'key debate' (institutionalists versus bio-
        environmentalists and social greens)
        267–8
    literature 321–4, 326–8, 331–4, 337–45,
        347, 349–52, **353**, 354–61, 363–6,
        368–9

Paterson's usage 267
    theorizing environment within
        international relations **268–72**
Green State (Eckersley, 2004) **284–7**, 333,
    354
'greening of global reach' (Shiva) 280, 359
Greenland 274
Grieco, J. M. 32, 44, 337
'Grotian' community 228
Grotian theory 97, 217
'Grotian tradition' (Wight) 10, 89
Grotius, H. 69, 89, 294, **315**, 316, 342, 344
Guantánamo Bay (Cuba) 202
Guattari, F. 210, 330

Haacke, J. 184, 337
Haas, P. 270, 271, **337**
Habermas, J. 29, 164–5, 174, 180–1, 221,
    290, 303–4
    discourse ethics **182–5**
    Iraq War (2003) **184–5**
    literature 330, 331, **337–8**, 357
    'reconstruction of historical materialism'
        115, **134–5**
    'world's leading critical theorist' **162–3**
Hagey Lectures (1983) 108, 325
Hahn, R. W. 271, 338
Hajer, M. 285, 338
Hall, I. 103, 338
Halliday, F. **16–17**, 118, 129, 132–3, 329,
    338
Hamilton, A. 254
Hansenclever, A. 271, 338
Hapsburg–Bourbon bipolar system (C16) 41
Hardin, G. **268–70**, 272, 275, 283, 338
harm 162, **178–9**, 311, 312, 347
Harris, J. 131, 356
Harrison, N. 280, **338–9**
Harvey, D. 83, 339
Hay, C. 130, 339
Hechter, M. 139, 344
Hegel, G. W. F. 117, 119, 143, 163, 164,
    169
Hegelian movement 117
Hegelianism 131
'hegemonic discourse' 222
hegemonic gender identities 251
hegemonic powers 144
    see also great powers
'hegemonic social order' (Cox) 177
hegemonic stability 235
hegemony 40–1, 68–9, 93, 104, 148–9, **151**,
    219, 307
    Ashley **207**
    cultural 131
    global 14
    Gramsci 115, 129, 329
    'internal' centre (Ashley) 198
    literature 328, 329, 341, 343, 351, 357
    'preserved as much by consent as by
        coercion' 129, 130

Heins, V. 102, 111, 339
Held, D. 182, 183, 339
   cosmopolitan democracy **82–3**, 320, 339
Helman, G. B. 107, 339
Hempel, L., 279, 339
hermeneutics 170, 175
Herring, E. 15, 339
Herz, J. H. 33, 53, 339
heuristics 218–19, 223, 236, 242
'hidden transcripts' 211
hierarchy 33, 35, 36, 47, 64, 142, 151, 195,
   200, 214, 219, 221, 243, 252–3, 259,
   260, 275–6, 282, 304, 343, 363, 365
   'ordering principle' (Waltz) 37
Hinduism 69, 153
Hintze, O. 148, 339
historians 26, **292–4**, 296, 318
'historic blocs' (Gramsci) 130
historical materialism 113, 114, 123–5,
   128–33, 137, 146, 147, 319, 336
   'casts no light on international politics'
     (realist claim) 121–2
   'failure to recognize rivalries between
     absolutist states' 145
   'flawed theory of state' 129
   'pivotal theme' 117–18
   'reconstruction' (Habermas) 115, **134–5**
   'shed little or no light on state,
     nationalism, war' 136
   significance for IR 115–16
'historical and multicultural perspective'
   (Ferguson and Mansbach) 148
historical overview 140, 143
historical psychology (Febvre) 155
historical sociology 3, 11, 12, **19–20**, 25, 26,
   29, 102, **138–61**
   approaches 140
   'bounded communities' (Linklater)
     176–7
   'central question' 20
   definition 138
   grand narratives **158–60**
   'higher synthesis' **156–8**
   literature 325, 337, 340, 344, 346, 348,
     357, 359, 360, 363
   Marxist 145
   'multi-causal explanation' 145
   'one purpose' 142
   origins **141–3**
   'political' versus 'economic' forces 145
   'post-disciplinary' web 160
   power and production in **143–7**
   re-birth **234**
history 5, 7, 24, 35, 58, 94, 134, 177, 199,
   200, 206, 233, 252, 256, 279, 288,
   294
   'continuous transformation of human
     nature' (Marx) 118
   human intervention (Horkheimer) 165
   international (renewed interest) **234**, 239

international thought **314–18**
'journey from slingshot to a-bomb'
   (Adorno) 143
'journey from tribe to state' (St. Simon)
   142
literature 325, 358, 365, 369
military 297
narrative 14; *see also* grand narratives
post-structuralism **189–94**
'ritualistic recitation' (Reus-Smit) 234
see also universal history
History of Peloponnesian War (Thucydides)
   34, 363
'history of present' (Foucault) 193
Hitler, A. 38, 358
Hobbes, T. 33, **34–6**, 37, 234, 294, 314,
   315–16, 335, 348
'Hobbesian anarchy of enemies' (Wendt) 46
'Hobbesian fear' (Butterfield) 39–40
Hobbesian realism 192
   assessment **35–6**
Hobbesian state of nature **34–5**, 228
Hobden, S. 138, 144, 340
Hobsbawm, E. **82**, 84, 340
Hobson, J. 143, 340
Hobson, J. M. 144, 340
Hoffman, M. 170, 221, 280, 340
Holland *see* Netherlands
Hollis, M. 8, 12, 340
Holmes, S. 93, 340
Holsti, K. 5, 340
Homer-Dixon, T. 268, 273, 340
Homo Sacer: Sovereign Power and Bare Life
   (Agamben, 1998) **201–2**, 319
homosexuality 258
Honneth, A. 29, 163, 164, 184
Hopf, T. 232–3, 340
Horkheimer, M. 24, 29, 134, 163–7, 340
Hoskyns, C. 248, **340–1**
hospitality (Kantian ethic) 215
House of Islam (*Dar al Islam*) 104
House of War (*Dar al Harb*) 104
Hovden, E. 290, 341
Hui, V. T.-B. 152, 341
human emancipation 29, 117, 122–3
human nature 21, 33, 36, 60, 63, 118, 251,
   254
human rights 19, 57, 80, 91–2, 98–100,
   102, 105, 107, 182, 223, 225–6,
   248–9, 264, 292, 303–7, 311–12,
   317, 348, 365, 369
   universal 28, **69–73**
   women 250
human sciences 187, 188
human security 29, **143**
human species 139
   unification (economic/technological)
     118, 128
humanism 55, 110, 316
humanitarian duty 307

humanitarian intervention 13, 19, 28, 72–3, 86, 91, 92, 98, 99, 101, 110, 162, 182, 185, 249, 259–60, 292, 300, 311, 320, 323–4, 329, 349
  definition 305
  moral permissibility **305–6**
humanitarianism 50, 63, 156, **201**, 326
humanity 19, 159–60, 172–4, 178–80, 182, 185, 284, 306, 310, 311
  'most important issue' facing 290
humanity–nature dualism 273
Huntington, S. 103, 154, 237, 341
Hurrell, A. 88, 108, 270, 285, **341**
Hutchings, K. 166, 169, 170, **174**, 260, 341

'ideal state' (Fukuyama) 58
idealism 10, 16, 89, 90, 108, 275, 288, 316, 318
  'naivety' (Carr) 9, 112
idealists 8, 9
ideas 230, 233, 234–5, 239, 245, 316
ideational forces 152, 160
  see also normative and ideational structures
identity 5, 156, **192–3**, 199, **204–6**, 207–8, 210, 212, 214, 215, 217, 221, 224, 226, 230, 234–8, 249–50, 254
  'basis of interests' (Wendt) 225
  'boundedness' questioned 174–5
  literature 325, 326, 334, 352
  national 123
  social 184
identity politics 135
Ideologiekritik 170
ideology 7, **15–16**, 18, 38, 58, 71, 73, 75, 82, 91, 94–5, 97, 100, 109, 109, 129, 131, **147**, 164, 168, 177, 224, 254, 267, 273, 292, 357
'images' (Waltz) 21
imagination **225–6**
'immanent critique' 163, 169, 170
'immense process of integration' (Elias) 158
'immutability thesis' (Linklater) 170
imperial over-reach 45
imperialism 13, 16, 22, 106, 118, 136, 145, 159, 177, 215, 262, 280, 307, 317, 318, 324, 334
  theories **123–8**
  see also colonialism
Imperialism: Highest Stage of Capitalism (Lenin, 1916) 113, 124, 346
  see also industrial capitalism
'Indefinite Detention' (Butler, 2004) 202
India 44, 103, 107, 112
Indian Ocean tsunami (2004) 50
indigenous knowledge 260, 281, 360
indigenous peoples 93, 155, 343
individuals **92**, 98, 220, 226, 231, 253, 293, 312
  capacity for self-restraint 156–7

Indonesia 247
industrial capitalism 20, 115, 119, 124, 126, 128, 132–3, 136, 138, 143, 144, 150, 279
  'uneven and combined development' 146
  see also capitalism
industrialization 141, 142, 147, 176
inequality 91, 118, 131, 167, 180, 280, 281
  economic 292, 307, 309
  opportunities 14–15
  power 14–15, 35, 91
  status 91
injustice 165, 311, 313
  duty to resist 305–6
  'innocent people' **297–8**
inside-outside 213, 257, 259, 365
Inside/Outside (Walker, 1992) **212**, 365
institutions 47–9, 131, 135, 149, 151, 158, 177, 197, 219, 231, 253, 264, 282, 293, 310, 312
  global 316
  intergovernmental 50
  gendered processes and organizational cultures 247
  international 130, 183, 220, 233, 247, 270, 271, 278
  political 286
  social 211
  supranational 308, 313
  transnational 278
  see also international institutions
intellectual history 314
inter-disciplinarity 25
inter-relations **277**
inter-state anarchy 285, 287
  see also international anarchy
inter-state relations 5, 12
inter-war era 5, 53
  lessons of 1930s 17
interaction
  global–local 279
  Habermas 134
  'interaction capacities' 149
interconnectedness 120, 159, 160–1
  Elias **158**
  global 102, 139
interdependence 11, 57, **148–50**, 151, 153, 213, 218, 220
  economic 156, 310
  and liberal institutionalism **66–9**
  'interest formation' versus 'interest satisfaction' 230–1
interests 76, 168, 188, 234, 236–8, 271
'international'
  category 317
  usage 307
international anarchy 8, 10–11, 21–2, 25, 32–3, 35, 36–40, 42–3, 47–8, 50, 53, 59–60, 64, 67, 69, 90–1, 94, 111, 113, 128, 131, 145–6, 153, 175, 197,

international anarchy (*cont.*)
  200, 203, 208, 245, 252, 254–6, 272,
    288, 315–16, 318, 320, 353
  'remains a constant' (Axelrod and
    Keohane) 219
  'what states make of it' (Wendt) 29, 110,
    152
international association, two kinds (Kant)
  304
International Court of Justice (ICJ) 70, 72
International Covenant on Civil and Political
  Rights (1966) 70
International Covenant on Economic, Social
  and Cultural Rights (1966) 70
International Criminal Court (ICC, 2002–)
  72–3, 93, 250
international criminal law 28, 91, 102, 307
'international ethics' **292–3**
  terminology 293
international justice **302–7**
  theorizing 318
International Labour Organization (ILO)
  70, 248
international law 1, 50, 64, 73, 86, 89, 92,
    96, 98, 101, 109, 113, 131, 136, 149,
    176, 239, 255, 264, 293, 300, 313,
    315, 317–18, 324
  achievement of global justice **308–9**
  'constitutionalization' (Habermas) 182,
    184
  constructivist work 236
  customary 305
  foundational texts 314
  humanitarian intervention 305
  pluralist conception 302–4
'international legal theory' 318
international legitimacy (Wight) 96
International Monetary Fund (IMF) 78–9
international order/s 8, 152, 171, 229, 354
  'global order' 312
  'world order/s' 130, 172, **175–9**, 285
International Organization (journal) 267
international organizations 130, 149, 250,
    270
international political theory 3, 10, 11, 12,
    19, **31**, 128, **291–318**, 344, **351**
  character 'remains contested' 295
  versus 'IR theory' **295**
  questioning of assumptions 295–6
  terminology 293
  see also international thought
international politics 2, 9, 33, 113, 243,
    270, 334, 341
  'basic structure' 23
  'parsimonious' theory 47, 156
  'providing a good account' **26–7**
  theorizing **291–6**
  see also world politics
'international regime' 30, **270**, **271**, 275,
  338, 341, 345, 368

International Relations (upper case;
  academic discipline) 1, 2
  'Atlantic divide' **240**
  boundaries 'keenly contested' 26
  'central questions' 9, 157
  classic questions (rethinking in light of
    ecological challenge) 267
  'conceptual and empirical blindness' 265
  contested nature **5–6**
  'continuing dialogue and debate' (Wight)
    31
  debates 'important' **26**
  disciplinary preoccupations (recent times)
    13–14
  'emerging discipline' (snubbed by Wight)
    292
  'essential' to engage with all theoretical
    perspectives 31
  'failure as academic project' 141
  foundation of discipline **6–9**
  'historical concern' 294
  identity of discipline 9
  initial guidelines 8
  versus (lower case) 'international
    relations' (subject matter of discipline)
    1
  introduction **1–31**, 288, 289
  key concepts 'neither natural nor gender-
    neutral' 252
  Marxism (changing fortunes) **128–33**
  'moral' versus 'scientific' 294
  'no obviously correct theory' 31
  'ontological presuppositions' (Cox) 23
  politicized nature 16
  'practice turn' **238–9**
  reason for studying wide variety of
    theories 16
  sub-schools **20–1**
  subject matter **5**
'international relations' (lower case; subject-
  matter of IR discipline) 1
  'colliding billiard balls' versus 'cobwebs'
    218
  contested concept 13
  criteria of significance (Halliday) 17
  democratization 8
  'disappearance' 317
  'inside-out' approach **58–9**, 85
  liberal thinking 70
  Marx **116–23**
  order and justice **97–103**
  popular dissent (Bleiker) **210–11**
  power and interdependence **148–50**
  progress **108–12**
  pursuit of general theory 230
  structural context 184
  'systemic' features 60
  theorizing environment **268–72**
international relations theory 8, 11
  absence (Wight) 9–10, 25, 89, 368

'close connection with practice' 9
'intellectual and moral poverty'
        (contested) **291–2**
versus 'international political theory' **295**
'paucity' no longer 10
politics of knowledge **166–71**
'theory of survival' (Wight) 307
international society 22, 28, **88–93**, 112,
        179, 182, 227, 233, 234, 310, 315,
        318
    expansion **103–7**
    foundations (normative and ideational)
        232
    from power to order **93–7**
    Grotius 89
    'instrument of colonial domination' 106
    versus 'international system' (Bull) 94,
        97, 103, 111, 151
    literature 322, 325, 328, 343, 366
    long-term development 105–6
    medieval 108–9
    moral legitimacy 303
    'overlapping forms' (Linklater) 181
    'pluralist' versus 'solidarist' conceptions
        97–8, 100–2, 106, 107, 108, 110, 317
    see also society of states
International Studies Association: 'Theory
        Section' 295
international system 228
    'gender-hierarchical' (Sjoberg) 253
    nature 21
international thought
    'categorical problem' 318
    history **314–18**
    meaning and context **314–15**
international toleration
    'a central issue' **304**
internationalism 28, 276, 312, 316
    'liberal internationalism' 7, 275
interpretation **194–5**, 216
    Nietzsche 190
interpretive methodology 239–40, 295
'intersubjective meanings' 231
'intervening variables' 49
Iran 107
Iraq 58
Iraq War (2003–) 63, 83, 91, 97, 162, 258,
        261, 334
    Habermas critique **184–5**
    not supported by realists 15, 39, 85
Ireland 122
Irigye, A. 159, 349
Islam 55, 72, 103–6, 154, 224, 237, 258,
        300–1
    views of IR 104
Islamism 86, 105
Islamist terrorism 58, 63, 64, 74, 83, 103
    'jihadist terrorism' 152, 354
Israel 44, 84, 105, 250, 300
Italy 98

Jackson, R. 88, 91, 98, 101–3, 107, 342
Jackson, T. 274, 342
Japan 104, **227–8**, 343, 369
Jeffery, R. 89, 342
Jervis, R. 32, 149, 342
Jewish theology 214
Jews 73, 126
Johnston, A. I. 236, 342
Joseph, J. 116, 343
journals 244, 267–8
just cause (Aquinas) 300
'just life' (fairness) 164
just war 30, 258, 307, 316
just war theory 13, 19, 215, 294, 296, 298,
        302, 323–5, 333
    Aquinas **300**
    statist/legalist strand 301
justice 70, 85, 94, **97–103**, 106, 108, 111,
        112, 128, 171, 186
    different understandings 301
    as fairness (Rawls) 309–10
    'obscurity' 308
    retributive 307
    universal 175
    see also global justice
justice in war **296–301**

Kabeer, N. 247, 343
Kant, I. 60–1, 62, 65, 109–10, 163–4, 165,
        171, 173, 179, 185, 188, 215, 293–4,
        308, 313, 314, 318
    international association (two kinds) **304**
    literature 331, 332, 338, 353
    war 'dominant threat to creation of
        perfect society' 119
Kantianism 55, 182–3, 192, 348
    'neo-Kantian position' 59
Kaplan, R. 24, 268, 343
Katyn Forest massacre (1940) 297
Katzenstein, P. J. 236
    nature of civilizations **237**
    'unit-level constructivism' **227–8**, 343
Kaufman, S. J. 46, 149, 343
Kaufmann, C. 47, 336
Keal, P. 93, 343
Kelly, D. 138, 344
Kennan, G. F. 32, 52, 54, 344
Keohane, R. O. 4, 25, 33, 66-7, 68, 167,
        260, 269, 271, 320, 337, **344**, 366
    'liberal' 218
    cooperation under anarchy 219
    'neo-liberal institutionalist' 219
Keynesianism 75
kijich'on women 249
Kinsella, H. M. 258, 344
Kiser, E. 139, 344
Kissinger, H. 15, 360
Kittleson, M. C. 242, 337
Klare, M. 268, 344
Klein, B. 200, 344

Klotz, A. 231, 344
knowledge 185, 222, 224, 260, 262, 271, 347, 348
  'always constituted in reflection of interests' (Ashley) 168
  'conditioned by context' 164
  normative 265
  see also 'politics of knowledge'
knowledge claims 3, 221
knowledge formation
  political nature 171
knowledge and power 187–94, 216, 221, 288, 330, 332
  genealogy 189–94
Kosovo 50, 91, 162, 185
Krasner, S. D. 48,270, 345
Krasner, S. D. 270, 345
Kratochwil, F., 'holistic constructivism' 229, 231, 345
Krook, M.-L. 254, 345
Kuehls, T. 277, 345
Kütting, G. 279, 345
Kurki, M. 12, 17, 345
Kyoto Protocol on Climate Change (1997) 266, 340

labour 70, 134, 177, 178, 246
  bargaining power 'undermined' 75
labour aristocracy 124, 125
labour market 81, 248
labour-power 116, 117
Labs, E. J. 44, 345
Lacher, H. 118, 120, 346
Lakatos, I. 218, 219, 221
land 66, 268–9, 281
landmines 250
language 4, 18, 188, 231, 322
'languages' 316
Latham, A. A. 146, 153, 346
Latin America 58, 117, 131, 335
  'South America' 105
  Spanish conquest 314
law 6, 10, 24, 97–8, 104, 110, 131, 150, 308, 309, 313, 340
  obedience to 303
  versus 'policy' 312
  supranational 308
law of nations 69, 317
Law of Peoples (Rawls, 1999) 64, 302–5, 355
  'seeks middle ground' 310–11
Law of Sea 67
laws of war 258, 297–8, 344
Lawson, G. 141, 346
League of Nations 8, 98, 104
Lebow, R. N. 149, 346
'Left Academy' 114
Left Hegelians 117
legal-rational ties (Weber) 142

legitimacy 17, 23, 92, 101, 102, 111, 150, 152, 159–60, 183–5, 200, 225–6, 236, 247, 254, 294, 306, 328
  domestic political orders 59–60, 61–2, 69, 85
  moral 303–4, 305, 308–9
  narrow definition 303
'legitimate theoretical opinion' 16
legitimation 167, 192, 194, 206
Lenin, V. 113, 115, 123–6, 129, 346
lenses 18, 36
'lesser evil' doctrine 301
'lethality of group encounters' 159
'levels of analysis' 21, 289
Levinas, E. 214–15, 326
Levy, M. A., 271, 337
Leysens, A. 167, 346
'liberal capitalism' (Fukuyama) 58
liberal democracies 150
  conflicts with authoritarian states 62–3
liberal democracy 58–9, 82, 83, 85, 98–9, 202–3, 225, 226, 285–7, 303–4, 309, 348
  see also democracy
liberal democratic peace *see* 'democratic peace' theory
liberal egalitarianism 310–11
liberal institutionalism 1, 11, 25, 27, 57, 66–9, 269, 271–2, 278
  'institutionalism' 267, 288
  'neo-liberal institutionalism' 11, 28, 110, 167, 219, 252
  Paterson's usage 269
liberal institutionalists 9, 68, 270, 272–3
  non-rationalist 271
  'two types of question' (green theory) 271
'liberal principles' 303
liberalism 22, 28, 57–87, 224, 235, 264, 273–5, 294, 303, 332, 341
  'inside looking out' 59–60
  Kantian 192
  'left on back foot by unpredictable challenges' 87
liberals 5, 21, 90, 99, 174, 218
  'reductionism' (Waltz) 60
liberation theology 117
liberty 202, 351
Libya 63, 72, 91, 150, 258
life 201
  'solitary, poor, nasty, brutish, short' (Hobbes) 35, 36
'lifeboat ethics' 275, 338
Lilburne, J. 192
Lima, L. 29, 324
'limit-concept' (Nyers) 211
limits to growth 266, 275–6, 280, 282, 290
  physical 280
  social 280–2
Limits to Growth (Meadows, Randers, and Behrens, 1972) 273–4, 350

Linklater, A. **1–31**, 64, **88–161**, 217, 239,
    252, 260, 285–6, 289, 291, 294, 304,
    331, **346–7**, 366
  agenda-setting (critical theory) **172**
  critical project (three dimensions) **232**,
    346
  critical theory 162, 169–70, **171–2**, 174,
    185
  'dialogic ideal' 184
  harm (in IR/world politics) 162, **178–9**,
    347
  'one of foremost proponents of critical
    theory' 162
  praxeological dimension 180
Lipschutz, R. D. 277, 279, 345, 347
Lisle, D. 204, 347
List, F. 74
Little, R. 25, 26, 46, 88, 140, 147, 149, 150,
    159, 326, 347
Living Planet Report (WWF, 2010) 275,
    368
'living within nature's limits' 275
Locke, J. 69
'Lockean' rivals 46
'logic of anarchy' 129, 148, 156
'logic of rights' versus 'logic of power' 48
Lohmann, L. 283, 347
London 358
London School of Economics 89, 368
longue durée (Braudel) 138
Low, N. 289, 347
Lowenthal, L. 163
loyalty 17, 149, 181, 213, 317
Luke, T. L. 286, 347
Lynch, M. 184, 348
Lynn-Jones, S. M. 33, 44, 348
Lyotard, J.-F. 29, 159

Macdonald, L. 263, 335
Machiavelli, N. 33, 52, 53, 234, 299, 348
Maclean, J. 178, 348
MacMillan, J. 109, 348
MacPherson, C. B. 74, 348
macroeconomic theory **218–19**
Magna Carta (1215) 69
Maine, Sir Henry 141
Malaysia 247, 328
Malcolm, N. 316, 348
Man, State and War (Waltz, 1959) 21, 366
Mann, M. 63, 140, 147, 153, 159, 176, 348
Mansbach, R. W. 140, 148, 159, 334
Mantle, D. 290, 349
Marchand, M. 246, 349
Marcuse, H. 163, 290
'market civilization' 15, 98
market forces 74–5, 81–2, 87, 116, 142
  global 124
  'invisible hand' (Smith) 76–7
markets 114, 120, 130, 133
  competitive 41
  global/world 28, 68

Marx, K. H. 138, 139, 141–3, 145, 163–4,
    165, 171–3, 330, 344, **349**
  class, production, and international
    relations **116–23**
  'critique of heaven' versus 'critique of
    earth' 117
  'geo-political deficiency' 120
  'interpreting' versus 'changing' world 29,
    116, 139, 164
  people make own history, but not under
    circumstances of their own choosing
    119, 168
  writings on globalization 28
Marxism 7, 11, 14, 22, **28–9**, 30, 60, 177,
    235
  'broad church' 20
  'central flaw' (economic reductionism)
    121, 142, 148 (contested 133)
  changing fortunes in IR **128–33**
  'dominant version of critical theory until
    recently' 136
  ethics 132, 355
  'failings as secular theory' 117
  literature 324, 327, 335, 339, 343, 348,
    362
  'neo-Marxism' 5, 125–8, 144
  Western 123
'Marxism in power' 128–9
Marxism-Leninism 123
Marxists 5, 16, 21, 71, 224, 225, 294
  common ground with Green theory
    289–90
masculinity 30, 251–2, 254–5, 256, 258,
    260–1
Mastanduno, M. 44
materialism 233, 235, 236
'materialist interpretation of history' *see*
    historical materialism
Matthew, R. 268, 331
Mayall, J. 102, 349
Mayer, P. 271, 338
Mazlish, B. 159, 349
McCracken, A. 247, 349
McGlen, N. E. 248, 350
McNeill, J. R. 159, 350
McNeill, W. H. 159, 350
Meadowcroft, J. 287, 350
Meadows, D. **273–4**, 280, 350
means of production 118
  'mode of production' 120, 122
Mearsheimer, J. 33, 34, 44, 48, 51, 54, 63,
    360
media/mass media 210, 250
Melos 34, 48
Men and Citizens (Linklater, 1990) **172–3**,
    346
  'work of recovery' 173
Mennell, S. 156, 158, 347, 350
Mennonites 298
mentalities 155

mercantilism 65, 66, 68, 124
    'neo-mercantilism' 78
Merchant, C. 279, 350
Mesopotamia 146, 151
meta-theory 221–3, 229, 243
'metaBosnia' (Campbell) 208–9
'metalepsis' 192
'methodological conventionalism' 231, 232
methodologies 5, 14, 24–5, 26, 110,
    139–40, 163, 166–7, 169–70,
    216–17, 221, 223, 229, 239–40,
    243, 264, 360
    discontent within constructivism 231
    feminist 241, 245, 319
    interpretive 231
    Marx 119
    'no clearly identifiable Green' 288
    quantitative 232, 327
Mexico 247
microeconomic theory 220
Middle Ages/mediaeval era 150, 152, 156,
    157, 335, 362
Middle East 58, 62, 101, 103, 105, 106,
    150, 191, 319
migrant women 246, 358
migrants 210, 211
militarism 250, 288, 299
militarization 242, 249
military power 13, 144, 147, 151, 219, 235
'military state' 68
military-industrial complex 15, 304
Mill, J. S. 66, 314
Millennium (journal) 239, 244
Miller, D. 311, 350
Miller, S. E. 33, 348
Mills, C. W. 15
Milosevic, S. 73, 99
'minimal foundationalism' (Hoffman) 221,
    232
Mitchell, R. 271, 350
Mitrany, D. 66, 350
modernists 221, 290
modernity 154, 176, 200, 206, 215, 279,
    328, 346, 357
    'iron cage' (Weber) 142
modernization 105
    ecological 285, 287, 326, 338, 351
Mohanty, C. 261–2, 351
Mol, A. 277, 284, 285, 351, 361
monopoly 41, 131
Montesquieu: C. de S., Baron de la Brède et
    de 173
Moody's 80
Moon, K. 249, 351
'moral cartography' (Campbell) 213
moral community 70, 232, 317
moral conduct 294–5
moral norms/principles 90
    costs of compliance and violation 50–1
    universal 308

'moral pacifism' 298
'moral responsibility' 311
'moral scepticism' 299, 315
moral space
    superior–inferior (Campbell) 206
moral superiority assumption 71, 72
morality 20, 89, 92, 112, 134–5, 151,
    153–6, 158, 160, 176, 238, 295, 297,
    301, 316, 321, 341, 351, 354, 363
    'as you do unto me, I shall do unto you'
        153–4
    'in-group' versus 'out-group' (Weber)
        153–4, 157
morality and foreign policy 49–54
    costs of compliance and violation 50–1
    morality and moralism 53–4
    realism as prescriptive theory 51–2
    state pursuit of moral objectives 49–50
morality and moralism 53–4
More, Sir Thomas 89
Morgenthau, H. 1–2, 4–5, 9, 27–8, 32–4,
    39, 51–2, 54, 218, 254, 318, 351,
    357, 363
    six principles of power politics 256
Morton, A. 125, 131, 351
mothers 261
motives 42–5
    abstracting from versus assuming 43
    (re-)incorporating the state 43–5
Mubarak trial 73
Mueller, J. 63, 351
multiculturalism 97, 126, 213
multidisciplinarity 14, 25–6
Multilateral Agreement on Investments
    (MAI, 1995–8) 81
multinational corporations (MNCs) 218,
    246, 247, 272
    'transnational corporations' (TNCs) 13,
        75, 77, 78, 80, 84, 86
multipolar systems 41–2, 256, 356
murder 253, 298–9
'mutual coercion' (Hardin) 269
'mutual understanding' (Habermas) 135
My Lai (1968) 297
Myers, N. 268, 351

Nagel, T. 4, 351
Nardin, T. 31, 102, 324, 351
    international political theory 291–318
'narrativization of reality' (Campbell)
    190–1, 195
    see also grand narratives 294
'nation' 136, 204
nation-state 44, 58, 66, 71, 76, 80, 85, 90,
    95, 113, 114, 121, 128, 157, 174,
    204–5, 209–11, 247, 265, 279, 289,
    290, 336, 341, 365
    age of self-sufficiency 'over' 68
    'demise' 86–7, 352
    undermined by globalization 86

National Deconstruction (Campbell, 1998) 190, **204–5**, 326
national defence 298, 299, 307
national interest 52, 53, 70, 248, 254, 305
national security 38, 114, 122, **227–8**, 259, 343
national self-determination 126, 129
    see also self-determination
nationalism 26, 28, 65, 113, 116, 121–2, 136, 142, 154, 158, 224–5, 292, 369
    theories **123–8**
    under-estimation by Marx and Engels 115
'nationalist imaginary' (Campbell) 203
NATO 99, 162, 201
natural law 55, 69, 94, 173, 300, 308, 316, 317, 321
    see also human rights
natural sciences 2, 4, 24, 164, 167
nature/natural world 134, 281–2, 284, 288, 290, 341, 347, 350, 354
    power over 116, 138
Neal, A. 202, 351
'negative sovereignty' 107
neo-classical realism/realists 34, **44–5**, 47
neo-conservatives 85, 91
neo-liberalism 28, 73–8, 80, 84, 130–2, 217, 223, 229, 245, 265, 352
    challenged by critical theory **221–2**
    'dominant ideology' (1980s–) 15
    potential for sustained international cooperation **219–20**
    theory of international cooperation (Keohane) 219, 320
neo-liberals 67, 224, 231, 233
neo-realism 11, 14, 25, 28, 30, 33, 60, 67, 90, 108, 131, 137, 141, 145–6, 151, 153, 155–6, 217, 223, 229, 245, 252, 254, 257, 265, 299, 320, 345, 352, 357
    challenged by critical theory **221–2**
    critiques **22–3**
    elements incorporated by neo-liberals 219
    failure to predict end of Cold War 223
    origins **218–19**
    'problem-solving' purpose (Cox) 23
    'problem-solving theory' 167
    'reductionism' 133
    structural theory (rejected by feminists) 253
    see also structural realism
neo-realists 13, 20, 59, 69, 89, 112, 148, 150, 200, 220, 224–5, 230–1, 233
    'third-image' perspective 227
Netherlands 144
Neufeld, M. 170, 352
'new constitutionalism' 130
'new global history' 159

'new imperialism' 91
'new International' (Derrida) 135–6
'new international economic order' 309
New Right 75
new social movements 13, 178, 210
New York 358
New Zealand 247
Newland, K. 245, 255, 337
Nexon, D. H. 146, 352
Niebuhr, R. 32–34, 39, 54–5, 218, 352
Nietzsche, F. W. 163, 188–90, 193, 199, 322, 332, 335
    emphasis on struggle 192
Nimmo's War, Emma's War (Enloe, 2010) 261, 334
Nixon Administration 15
Nixon Doctrine 249
'no view from nowhere' (Nagel) 4
Nobel Women's Initiative 248–9
Noel-Baker, P. 7
nomadism 210, 211
'non-combatant immunity' 297
non-governmental organizations (NGOs) 102, 178, 278, 367
non-intervention principle 48, 100–1, 103, 106, 302
    qualification **305–6**
non-state actors 82, 210, 218, 223, 225, 241, 249
    women **249–50**
non-tariff barriers (NTBs) 78
'non-violence' (type of pacifism) 298
Nordic countries 48
normative approach/concerns 8, 18–20, 32, 50–1, 92, 97, 128, 134, 139, 143, 159, 164, 166, 168, 178, 183–5, 188, 212, 217, 221, 229, 232–3, 265, 271, 289, 293, 295
normative claims 24, 119, 279, 284
normative dimension (critical theory) **172–5**, 180
normative feminism **259–63**
normative forces, versus material forces (relative importance) 229
normative and ideational structures 224, **225–6**, 227, 229, 232
normative theory 267, 288, 356
    constructivism (recent developments) **237–8**
    reinvigorated by constructivism **234–5**
norms 153, 155–6, 181, 182–3, 225–6, 230, 233–5, 238, 240, 245, 264, 270, 283, 294–5, 308, 312, 363
    global 152
    institutionalized 231
    and institutions **47–9**
    social construction 22
    social and legal **227–8**, 236
North Africa 58
North American Free Trade Agreement (NAFTA) 78, 79, 247, 263, 335

North Korea 44
North–South (global) 127, 246
nuclear arsenals 10, 44, 47, 63–4, 68, 98,
    107, 257, 264, 266, 292, 301, 333
Nunes, J. 29, 324
Nuremberg trials 298
Nye, J. S. 66–7, 254, 344, 352
    'liberal' 218
Nyers, P. 211, 352

Ó Tuathail, G. 194, 203, 352
'object' versus 'subject' (separation) 164,
    167, 168
'object of inquiry' versus 'inquiry itself' 295
objectivity 5, 18, 24, 167, 169, 185, 188,
    190, 243–4, 254, 263–4
observation, 'inherent subjectivity' (critical
    theory) 221
Of Grammatology (Derrida, 1974) 194, 330
offensive positionalists (Mearsheimer) 44
offensive realism 44, 45, 48, 345, 360
Ohmae, K. 86, 352
Okereke, C. 280, 352
oligopoly 41
Omarska and Trnopolje (camps) 202
'one world' 317
ontology 14, **23**, 24, 166, 174–5, 192, 194,
    199–201, 209, 213–15, 217, 221,
    223–4, 227, 229, 240, 245, 252,
    255–6, 263, 276, 277, 323
'ontopology' (Campbell/Derrida) **204–5**,
    211, 213
Ophuls, W. 269, 275, 284, 352
optimism 158, 312
order **97–103**, 112, 128, 210
Organisation for Economic Co-operation
    and Development (OECD) 81
origins **189–90**
O'Riordan, T. 275, 352
Osama Bin Laden 193, 258
'Othering', spatial and temporal 206, 355
Ottoman Empire 145
'Out of Ivory Tower' (*Millennium* journal,
    2012) 239
'out there' 4, 15, 16, 18, 23, 26, 164, 252
Oye, K. 197, 353
ozone depletion 266, 271, 284

pacifism **298–300**
Paine, T. 61, 65, 173
Pakistan 107
Palestine 250
'paradigm of production' 128, 129
    beyond (implications for emancipatory
        project) **133–6**
'paradigm of sovereignty' (Ashley) 189
Parks, B. 280, 353
Parpart, J. 246, 349
Paterson, M. **30–1**, **266–90**, 320, **353**
Patomaki, H. 160, 353

patriarchy 16, 25, 136, 247, 252, 254, 256,
    279, 280
Pattberg, P. 286, 353
Patton, P. 210, 353
peace 7, 28, 35, 38, 89–90, 109, 122, 140,
    182, 186, 243, 249, 255, 288, 314,
    335, 356, 362
    gendered impact 241
    perpetual (Kant) 60, 119, 142
    'waging secret war' (Foucault) 192
    see also 'democratic peace' theory
peace prospects **60–5**
peacekeeping 260, 363
Pearl Harbor (1941) 191
perception 195, 253–4
Perpetual Peace (Kant, 1795) 318
Persian Gulf 64
'perspectivism' 190
pessimism/pessimists 156, 312
Peterson, V. S. 257, 259, **353–4**, 357
phenomenology 199
'phenomenology of ethical life' (Robinson)
    170
Philippines 247, 369
Phillips, A. 103, 152, 153, 354
philosophers/philosophy 6, 24, **292–4**, 318,
    336
Pin-Fat, V. 189, 333
Pinochet Ugarte, A. 73
Pitt the Younger 307
Plato,
    parable of cave 296
Plumwood, V. 279, 354
pluralism/pluralists 237, 289, 306, 317
    limits 304–5
    Rawls **302–5**
pluralistic security communities 48, 319
Pokrovsky, B. 7
Pol Pot 51
Poland 98, 122, 297
Polanyi, K. 74, 178, 354
polarity 37, **40–1**, 42, 48
policy-making 222, 312
policy-relevant analysis 5
political community 58, **172–85**, 201,
    204–5, 211, 212, 214, 286, 320, 365
    cosmopolitanism and discourse ethics
        172, **180–5**
    ethical particularism and social exclusion
        172–5
    normative dimension **172–5**
    'post-exclusionary form' (Linklater) 181
    praxeological dimension 172, **180–5**
    sociological dimension 172, **175–9**
    states, social forces, changing world
        orders 172, **175–9**
    'triple transformation' (Linklater) 180
political economy 58, 114, 136, 282, 290
    international/global 14, 125, 130, 136,
        244, 262, 341, 344, 357

political order/s 304, 307
political power 24, 120, 144, **147**, 216
'political prosaics' (Campbell) 210, 212, 326
political realism 298, 299, 301, 302, 315–16
  as ethical doctrine **306–7**
political space 203, 205, 348
political system
  'multi-tiered' (Eckersley) 278
  structure 21
political theorist
  'spectator, not participant' 295–6
  task 169–70
political theory 10, 11, 14, 25, 322
  global 326
  'opinion turned into ideology' 292
politics 54, 103, 110, 115, 119, 123, 134,
    136, 139, 141, 164, 173, 185, 200,
    215, **292–3**, 318
  domestic versus international 90, 96,
    157, 253
  interdependencies with economics 146
  'low' versus 'high' 307
  separation of domestic and international
    252
Politics and Ethics Review (2006) 284, 354
politics of identity 132, 326
politics of knowledge
  critical theory's task as emancipatory
    theory **170–1**
  problem-solving and critical theories
    166–70
'politics of memory' (Zehfuss) 193
Politics Among Nations (Morgenthau, 1948)
    1
polity 148, 237
pollution 272, 274
popular consent (Locke) 69
population 266, 268, 273–4, 280, 284, 333,
    343
Porritt, Hon. Sir Jonathon, 2nd Bt 274,
    354
'positive sovereignty' 107
positivism 2, 18, 168, 175, 180, 217, 242–3,
    263, 288, 289, 360
  characteristics 167
  'gold standard' 167
  'neo-positivism' 221–3, 231, 240
post-Cold War 20, 40–1, **57–9**, 63, 64, 72,
    73, 78, 84, 182, 217, 222, 234–5,
    236, 340
  rise of constructivism **222–3**
'post-colonial donors' 107
post-colonial era 22, 102
post-colonial scholars/writers 22, 106, 132,
    159–60, 282, 327, 359
post-colonial states/societies 48, 91, 103,
    105, 125
post-colonialism 25, 111, 112, 127, 136,
    154, 196, 215, 281, 309, 327
  feminist 262

'post-development' perspectives 280–1
post-modernism 4, 180, 217, 221, 240–1,
    251, 257, 260, 264, 281, 330, 348,
    349
'post-national democracies without post-
    national states' 180
post-positivism 2, 15, 217, 263
post-structuralism 4, 13, 18–19, **29**, 30,
    111, 127, 132, 136, 179, **187–216**,
    217, 243, 320, 326, 333
  chapter contention 187
  ethics **213–16**
  'ethos of political criticism' (Campbell)
    215
  'genealogy' **189–94**
  and Green theory (common ground) 289
  and Green theory (contrasts) 290
  'makes a substantial contribution' 216
  power and knowledge in international
    relations **187–94**
  sovereignty (spatial and temporal
    production) 203
  'theoretical innovations' 187
post-structuralism: textual strategies
    194–9
  Ashley's double reading of '*anarchy
    problématique*' **197–9**
  deconstruction **195–6**
  double reading **196–7**
post-structuralists **22–3**, 294
post-war era (1945–) 9, 51, 74, 75, 126,
    218–20
Pouliot, V. 239, 319, 354
poverty 71–2, 129, 245, 293, 314
  global/world 6, 311
poverty-alleviation of 303, 307, 310, 312
power 14–15, 18, 34–5, 91, 118, 137,
    148–50, 154–5, 160, 168, 171, 181,
    184, 200, 221, 226, 251, 271, 283,
    289, 309, 363
  'comes out of barrel of fun' (assumption
    dispelled) 243
  constructivism (recent developments)
    235–6
  feminist critique 243, **256–7**
  higher monopoly 156, 157–8
  historical sociology **143–7**
  limited (Linklater) 64
  'more holistic understanding'
    (constructivism) 236, 321
  new forms 24
  non-material sources (constructivism)
    236
  OED definition 40
  social 24
  see also political power
power asymmetry 119
power concentration 281
power configurations 151–2
'power of ideas' 235

power and knowledge **187–94**, 216, 221, 288, 330, 332
   genealogy **189–94**
'power over' 256, 259, 264
power politics 7, 32, 36, 53, 59, 129, 142, 192, 200–1, 243
   Ashley **197–9**
   definition 51
   Morgenthau's six principles (feminist critique) **256–7**, 362, 363
   'textual interplay' (Der Derian) 194
power relations 177, 188, 192, 241
   global configuration 169
power relativity 40
power structures 137, 280
power-maximization 44, 219, 235
'practice turn' (constructivism) **238–9**, 319, 322, 354
Prague 73
Prakash, M. S. 289, 334
Pratt, N. 241, 319
praxeological dimension **180–5**, 232
pre-capitalist societies 132–3, 146
   'post-capitalist societies' 123
pre-emption 83, 301
prediction 43, 45, 47, 48, 55, 120
'presentism' 20, 138, 148, 160
'preventive war' (Bush) 93
Pribram, A. F. 7
Price, R. 222, 232, 238, 354
Priess, D. 49, 358
Princen, T. 272, 354
Prisoners' Dilemma **39–40**, **269–70**
prisoners of war 297, 305
problem-solving 23, **166–70**, 184
process formations **46–7**
'process sociology' (Elias) **156–8**, 333
production 28, 150, 154–6, 160, 177–78, 183, 282–3
   historical sociology **143–7**
   internationalization 78
   in Marx's writings **116–23**
production systems 128, 130, 147
production–reproduction division 254, 255
productivism 276
productive capacity **274**
Programme of German Green Party (1983) 276, 355
progressivism 10, 89–90, 143
proletariat 113, 116, 118, 119, 124–5, 131, 134–5
   nationalism 121
proper authority (Aquinas) 300
prostitution 247, 249, 351, 369
protectionism 74, 76, 79
Protestantism 316
Provincializing Europe (Chakrabarty, 2000) 206, 327
Prozorov, S. 206, 355
Prügl, E. 248, 355

psychology/psychologists 21, 155, 261
public opinion 50, 62, 102, 314
'public realm' 312–13
'public reason' 303, 311
public spheres 184, 348
public–private division **252–3**, 254, 264, 286

Quakers 38, 298
qualitative measures 281
quantitative analysis 24, 241, 264, 273, 281, 295
quasi-phenomenology 199
quasi-philosophy 221
quasi-states 342

race 101, 104, 123, 133, 135, 137, 178, 261, 262
radical feminisms (1970s) 263
'radical interpretivism' (post-modernist) 221
Radical Islam 103, 105, 106
'radical' realists 34
Rajamani, L. 266, 333
Randers, J. 273–4, 280, 350
rape 250, 253, 255, 297
rational actor 248, 255, 257
rational choice theory 2, 25, 67, 269–70, 271
   Reus-Smit usage 217
Rational Ecology (Dryzek, 1987) 276, 332
'rational egoists' 25
rationalism 10, 109–10, **218–20**, 220–1, 223–4, 233, 240
   contrasts with constructivism 217, **226–7**, 229
   debate with critical theory (1980s) 217, 229
   'doubly insidious' 222
   relationship with constructivism **230–1**, 232
   Reus-Smit usage 217
rationalists 225, 230, 239
rationality 254, 259, 279
Ratner, S. R. 107, 339
Raustiala, K. 271, 364
raw materials 77, 127, 274
Rawls, J. 62–3, 64, **309–11**, 313
   international justice (pluralist conception) **302–5**, 355
   international distributive justice 309
   'key idea' (public reason) 311
Reagan era 85
'real world' 4, 15, 190–1, 194, 217, 268, 270
realism 11, 16, 20, 21, **27–8**, **32–56**, 91, 93, 95, 100, 105, 109, 113, 121, 133, 148, 152, 167, 171, 173, 175, 176, 252, 256, 268, 271, 273, 289, 294, 299, 316, 318
   'continuing relevance' 68

critics **54–6**
deconstruction and subversion **243–4**
definitions **32–4**
'does not comprehend *most* important
  things' 54–5
'dominant ideology' (Nixon era) 15
'dominant theory of IR' 218
'failure to account for end of Cold War'
  49
'geo-political reductionism' 130
'hegemonic discourse' 222
'inability to comprehend fundamental
  change in international relations' 49
lexicon 90
literature 332, 333, 335, 337, 342,
  357–8, 365, 367–8
motives (importance) **42–5**
'must be part of analytical toolkit' 56
power in international relations 235–6
as prescriptive theory **51–2**
'state-centrism' 89, 209
'sterility' (Carr) 9, 112
theoretical failures (three types) **42**
'two faces' 32
'realistic utopianism' (Carr) 235
realists 7, 9, 10, 13, 18, 62, 71, 83, 86, 112,
  137, 149, 200, 226, 270
  critique of Marxism **128–30**
  distinction between 'justice' and 'policy'
    307
  opposition to invasion of Iraq (2003) 15,
    39, 85
reality 3–4, 17, 18, **22–3**, 24, 26, 53, 114,
  115, 122, 134, 145, 175, 194, 245,
  343
Realpolitik 32
reason 9, 61, 188, 189, **200**, 215, 331
  instrumental 282
reason of state/*raison d'état* 51, 52, 197,
  301, 306, 316
'reclaiming the commons' 286
redistribution, rich to poor countries 309
reductionism 28, 60, 121, 130, 133, 142,
  145, 148, 254
Rees, W. 274–5, 365
refugees 201, 210, 211, 305, 331, 352
Reid, J. 201, 210, 331, 355
'relations of production' versus 'relations of
  exchange' **126**
'relative autonomy of state' 129
relative gains **39–40**, 45, 46–7, 67, 68
'relative power' 235
'relativism of patriotism' 301
religion 18, 58, 71, 97, 103, 114, 126, 142,
  147, 225, 255, 302, 354, 363, 364
  'opium of masses' (Marx) 117
  'tracklayer of history' (Mann) 153
  in world politics **237**
religious freedom 304
religious fundamentalism 102

Renewable Energy and Energy Efficiency
  Partnership 278
Rengger, N. 92, 100, 132, 329, 355
Renner, K. 123
Renouvin, P. 7
representative government 61, 62, 103
'Requirement' 105
resistance 118, 131–2, 137
'responsibility to protect' 101, 102, 306,
  311–12
'responsible sovereignty' principle 300
'retreat to barracks' 157
Reus-Smit, C. **29–30**, 46, 93, 97, 111, 152,
  153, 175, 285, 328, 354, **355–6**,
  368
  constructivism **217–40**
'revolt against West' (Bull) 71, 83, 84, 101,
  103–7, 132, 325
  economic 104
  five elements (Bull) 104
  legal, political, racial, economic, cultural
    104–5
  religious 105
revolutionism 90, 100, 109, 112
'revolutionists' (Wight) 10
revolutions (1848) 122
Ricardo, D. 65, 74, 76–7, 356
Richards, K. R. 271, 338
right intention (Aquinas) 300
'right to protect' (R2P) 73
Righteous Realists (Rosenthal, 1991) 51,
  357
Rights of Man (Paine, 1791) 61
Ripsman, N. R. 45, 322
Risse, T. 184, 356
Rittberger, V. 271, 338
Roberts, B. 251, 356
Roberts, J. T. 280, 353
Robinson, F. 170, 356
Robinson, M. 248
Robinson, P. 15, 339
Robinson, W. I. 131, 356
rogue states 68, 207
Rogues: Two Essays on Reason (Derrida)
  207, 215, 331
Rorty, R. M. 169
Rosecrance, R. N. 41, 68, 356
Rosenau, J. 278, 356–7
Rosenberg, J. 12, 114, 118, 125, 133, 146,
  357
Rosenthal, J. H. 51, 357
Rousseau, J.-J. 61, 69, 173, 314
Rowlands, I. H. 271, 357
Ruggie, J. 229, 231, 357
'rule of immanence' (Foucault) 188
rule of law 7, 62, 64, 69, 73, 90, 103, 173,
  182, 202, 312, 313
  'deformalization' and 'fragmentation'
    312
  domestic and international 304
rules of game 253

ruling class 61, 122, 129, 131
  see also elites
Runyan, A. S. 259, 357
Rupert, M. 131, 164, 173, **357**
Russett, B. 62, 357
Russian Federation 73, 84, 91
Russian Revolution 38, 147
  'Bolsheviks' 96
Rwanda 72, 101

Sachs, W. 281, 357
Saddam Hussein 73, 85, 99
Saint-Pierre, C. I. C., Abbé de 314
Saint-Simon, C. H. de R., Comte de 142
Sale, K. 275, 358
Sandholtz, W. 242, 337
Sarkees, M. R. 248, 350
Sassen, S. 246, 358
scale, bio-environmentalism **276–7**
Schmitt, B. 7
Schmitt, C. 201, 202
Schumacher, E. F. 276, 358
Schumpeter, J. A. 61
Schweller, R. L. 41, 45, 49, **358**
science 24, 25, 57, 260, 271, 279, 290,
  295
'science of ethics' (Durkheim) 153
'scientific realism' (Wendt) 230
scientism 294
scientists 296
Scott, J. W. 251, 358
'screen jockeys' 80
Second Cold War (Reagan era) 85
'sector integration' 149
'secular upper classes' (Elias) 157
secularism 103, 105, 237, 359
secularization 117, 237
security 186, 204–6, 208, 229, 241, 244,
  249, 289, 305, 326, 351, 354
  feminist critique **257–9**
  'international security' 162
'security dilemma' 40, 90
self and other 160, 174–5, 196, 204, **205–6**,
  212, 348, 355
  Other and Self (Levinas) 215
self-defence 63, 298, 300, 303, 306
self-determination 48, 172, 304
  Hutchings 174
  Marx 119
  see also national self-determination
self-interest 1, 34, 220
  constructivist approach 225
self-reflection (critical theory) 162
self-reflexivity 265
self-reliance 276
semi-peripheral areas 144
Sen, A. 246, 359
separate states **151**
Serbia 72, 99
Seth, S. 160, 206, 359

Sex Among Allies (Moon, 1997) 249, 351
sex trade (global) **262**
sex-tourism 247
sex-trafficking 242, 243, 247, 322
sexism 245
sexual and gender-based violence (SGBV)
  260, 330
sexual liberty 249
sexuality 258, 262
Shakman Hurd, E. 237, 359
Shapcott, R. 174, 181, **359**
Shapiro, I. 230, 367
Shapiro, M. J. 194, 206, 215, **359**
'shared meanings' **310**
Shepherd, L. J. 258, 359
Shiva, V. 280, 281, 359
Shue, H. 285, 360
simplistic approaches 7, 41
Singer, J. D. 24, 331, 360
Sinosphere 152
'situated knowledge' (Rupert) 164
Sjoberg, L. 241, **253**, 360
Skocpol, T. 129, 138, 360
Skolnikoff, E. 271, 364
slavery 70, 104, 118, 133, 150, 155
Smith, A. 65, 73–4, 76–7, 366
Smith, L. T. 260, 360
Smith, M. J. 32, 360
Smith, S. 2, 4, 8, 12, 27, 167, 340, 360
Snyder, G. H. 44, 46, **47–8**, 360
Snyder, J. 45, 361
social actors
  'atomistic egoists' 220, 221, 222, 233
  'inherently social' (critical theory) **221**
social agency, nature debated 229
social construction 175
social contract (Rousseau) 69
social development, 'endogenous models'
  (C19) 142
social ecology 267
social equity 178
social exclusion **172–5**, 180, 181
social greens 272, 273, 287
  back to commons **282–4**
  gap filled by 279
  social limits to growth **280–2**
'social inscription of global space' (Ó
  Tuathail) 203
social interaction 221, 226
  exogenous interests 220
  'not important determinant of interests'
  220
social learning (Marxism/Habermas) 134–5
social movements 348
social power (Mann) 140, 348
social sciences 2, 4, 115, 127–8, 132, 136–7,
  139, 141, 148, 187, 269, 323–4
  Lakatosian forms 221
  philosophical issues **14**
social space, inside–outside (Campbell)
  206

Social Theory of International Politics
    (Wendt, 1999) 230, 367
socialism 11, 113, 122, 123, 132, 134, 142,
    314
    'global phenomenon' (Marx) 118
'socialism in one country' 120, 128
socialist internationalism 123, 129, 136
socialist planning 119
socialization 208, 257
society 123, 130, 139, 141, 164, 165
    capabilities ('extensive' versus 'intensive')
        147
    constitutive realm (constructivism) **227**
    'cooperative venture for mutual
        advantage' (Rawls) 310
    'modern' 140
    'strategic domain' **224**
    'strategic realm' 220, 222, 227
    system and **150–2**
    transnational influences 147
'Society Must Be Defended' (lectures by
    Foucault, 1975–6) **192**, 335
'Society of Peoples' (Rawls) 64
society of states 10, 20, 22, 94–7, 100,
    108–9, 228, 239
    'anarchical' (Bull) 302
    'community of states' 224
    'European' versus 'universal' 101
    legitimacy 309
    multicultural 99
    'pluralist' (Linklater) 181
    'solidarist' (Linklater) 181
    see also world society
socio-ecology 266, 280, 282
sociological institutionalism 222, 334
sociology 25, 123, 132, 172, **175–9**, 186,
    333, 347
    broadening of horizons 140–1
    constructivist (critical theory) project
        232
    'placed back at centre of IR discipline' (by
        constructivists) 234
    states-system 180
    see also historical sociology
Soguk, N. 211, 361
soldiers **298**
solidarism 97–8, 100–2, 106–8, 110, 181,
    302–7
Solomon, M. S. 131, 357
Somalia 50, 64, 72, 107, 349
South Africa 70
South Korea 249, 369
Southeast Asia 38
Southern Africa 38
sovereign power (Agamben) **201–2**
sovereign rights 108, 309
sovereign state/s 96, 98, 120, 136, 148, 150,
    175, 181, 185–6, 192, 198, 215–16,
    218, 232, 278
    'by no means natural' 207

'democratically deficient nature' (Held)
    183
feminist perspective 260
'fetishized' (Marx) 172
'form anarchical society' (English School)
    88
'historically and politically conditioned'
    207
'naturalization' and 'dissemination' (post-
    structuralism) 207
'predicated on discourses of danger'
    (Campbell) 205
problem with 173–4
'rise and possible demise' 228–9
social identity (constructivism) 224
'territorial imperative' defied 211
    see also sovereignty
sovereign states: post-structuralist
    problematization **199–209**
    boundaries 199, **203–4**
    identity 199, **204–6**
    statecraft 199, **207–9**
    violence 199, **200–3**
sovereignty 46, 58, 72–3, 77, 90, 101, 103,
    106, 110, 128, 152, 157, 233, 277,
    293–4, 296, 300, 313, 333, 334
    antithesis of 'anarchy' (Ashley) **198–9**
    'constitutive principle' 189
    ethics of exclusion **211–13**
    and foreign investment **79–83**
    Hobbesian image 285
    judicial 176
    limits 69, 305
    'master signifier' (Edkins and Pin-Fat)
        189
    national economic 86
    spatial and temporal production (post-
        structuralism) 203
    territorial principle 71
    see also state sovereignty
sovereignty: beyond the paradigm
    (rethinking the political) **209–16**
    post-structuralist ethics **213–16**
    sovereignty and ethics of exclusion
        211–13
Sovereignty: Organized Hypocrisy (Krasner,
    1999) 48, 345
sovereignty-anarchy divide 259
'sovereignty contract' (Peterson) 257
Spaargaren, G. 277, 284, 361
Spain 103, 144, 145
Spanish colonists 105
Spanish Thomism 316
spirit of commerce **65–6**
Spretnak, C. 274, 282, 361
Spykman, N. J. 54, 361
stabilizations (stability-effects) (Derrida)
    196–7
Stalin, J. V. D. 123, 361
Stamnes, E. 260, 330

Standard & Poor's 80
starvation, freedom from (Vincent) 71, 92, 100
state, the 10, 26, 67, 113, 121, 122, 126, 128, 154, 185–6, 189, 284–5, 287, 322, 324, 331, 341
    capitalist 129
    and civil society (Cox) 176–7
    concept 136
    constant process of 'becoming-state' 209
    Cox's theory **177**
    Derrida 207
    'destructive fusion' (Linklater) 181
    evolution (Elias) 140
    'executive committee of bourgeoisie' 129
    feminist analysis 241, 242, 245, 246, 249, 250, 252, 253, 254, 262, 363
    'five monopoly powers' (Linklater) 176
    Green rejection 282
    historical materialism 'flawed theory' 129
    'inadequate for dealing with environmental change' 279
    'internationalization' (Cox) 178
    interpretation as 'subject on trial' (Weber) 209
    'made to appear as if it had an essence' 208
    monopoly of legitimate force 82, 86, 90, 129, 144, 176, 198, 201
    'moral purpose' 152
    'most important actor' 219
    'performatively constituted' **208–9**, 366
    'quasi-phenomenology' (post-structuralist) 199
    (re-)incorporation **43–5**
    'relative autonomy' 129
    social theory 176
    'totalizing project' (Linklater) 176, 180
    treated as 'unitary actor' (Wendt) 230
    welfare-nationalist 177
    see also territorial state
state identity (Wendt) **227**
state intervention (in economy) 74–5
state power 33, 121, 134, 143, 218, 228
    Kant 171
        limitations 57
        undermined by globalization (Hobsbawm) **82**
state sovereignty 83, 99, 157, 211–12, 213, 226, 278–9, 302–3
    'constitutive political practice' (Walker) 212
    moral rationale **305–6**
    see also sovereign state/s
'state is a state is a state' (Westphalian dogma) 175
state-building 148, 176
state-centrism 33, 211, 243, 293, 309
'state-form' (Deleuze and Guattari) 210

statecraft 188–9, 199, **207–9**, 242, 245
states 17, 18, 22, 43, **92**, 68, 130–1, 133, 218, 226, 234, 237, 268, 270–1, 293, 312
    communist 71
    'ecologically responsible' 30
    'essentially self-interested' (neo-realism) 219
    failure to cooperate 220
    good international citizens 249
    hegemonic 252
    identities and interests 228
    liberal 177
    'local agents of world common good' 108
    moral legitimacy **308–9**, 313
    ntological structuring 200–1
    'particularism' (Linklater) 180
    political legitimacy 306
    pursuit of moral objectives **49–50**
    rights (under global justice) 309
    rights and duties 313
    strong 48
    structural determinants of behaviour (Waltz) 219
    war-making (re-emergence) 200
    weak 38, 48
states, social forces, changing world orders 172, **175–9**
states-system/s 14, 20, 29–30, 114–15, 129, 140, 145, 149, 151–2, 155, 160, 167, 245, 256, 264, 285, 289, 294, 296, 307
    'harm' generated (Linklater) 179
    mediaeval 146, 148, 346, 352
    modern 146
    reification 284
    social theory 172
    sociology 180
statesmanship 33, 52, 53
statism 278, 301, 304
Steans, J. 30, 180, 361
Stern, M. 245, 319
Stoic-Christian ideal 173
Stoics 317
Stoll, R. J. 32, 329
strategic studies 10, 15
Strategic Studies and World Order (Klein, 1994) 200, 344
'strong' realists 34
structural adjustment policies (SAPs) 30, 79, 246
structural parasitism (Derrida) 195–6
'structural power' 235
structural predictions **41–2**
structural realism 33, **37–42**, **44**, 47, **149–50**, 299
    balancing **37–9**
    nature of structural predictions **41–2**
    polarity **40–1**

Prisoners' Dilemma, relative gain, cooperation 39–40
Waltzian structuralism 37
see also neo-realism
structuralism 152, 225, 229, 238
structure/s
definition 46
normative and ideational 224, 225–6, 227, 229, 232
'socially constructed' (Cox) 175
transnational 241
'struggle for equal sovereignty' (Bull) 104
struggle for power (and security) 1, 12, 14, 21, 26, 27, 29, 33, 48, 52, 59, 60, 71, 90, 91, 92, 95, 111–12, 113, 141, 144, 145, 148, 157, 158, 219, 235, 352, 360
'struggles for recognition' (Honneth) 184
style 188, 322
'subaltern history' (Chakrabarty) 206, 327
subjectivity 199–200, 203, 204, 211, 213, 215, 221, 250, 259, 264
hegemonic modes 207–8, 211–12
suffering 102, 122, 134, 138, 155, 158, 179, 311
'suffering humanity' (Dunne and Wheeler) 110
Suganami, H. 12, 17, 109, 110, 347, 362
Suharto, T. N. J. 73
suicide bombings 250, 301
sulphur emissions 271
superpowers 38, 47, 92, 98, 325
survival motive 43, 44, 48, 52, 55, 69, 89, 219, 233, 234, 307
'survival unit' (Elias) 157–8
sustainability 267, 275, 283–4, 286, 288, 353–4
sustainable development 280, 281–2
Sylvester, C. 30, 256–7, 262, 362
Syria 91, 150
System,
definition 46
system and society 150–2
system and structure 45–9
constancy and change 49
norms and institutions 47–9
process formations 46–7
systems theory 46, 47

Taliban 252
'taming of economic aristocracies' (Blomert) 132, 323
taxation 61, 86, 176
Taylor, M. 270, 362
technological innovation 121–2 149
technology 117, 268–9, 274, 282
Tellis, A. 33, 362
territorial conquest 66, 68, 85, 142, 314
territorial space 212

territorial state 149, 160, 206, 214, 303, 305, 309, 316
territoriality 157, 328
territorialization 213
territory 181, 204, 318
terrorism 68, 202, 228, 292, 301, 312
Islamist/jihadist 58, 63–4, 74, 83, 103, 152, 354
non-state 57, 83–5
nuclear fears 107
terrorist groups 93
terrorist states 207
Teschke, B. 12, 114, 120, 133, 140, 145–6, 146, 362
'text' (Derrida) 194
internal tensions (Derrida) 197
textual interplay 194, 195
textual strategies (post structuralism) 194–9
'textuality' (Derrida) 190, 194
Thailand 58
theoretical failures (three types) 42
'theoretical reflexivity' 168
theories and disciplines 9–16
theorizing 293, 296
theory
acquisition of disciplinary hegemony 15
'always *for* someone' (Cox) 23
'artful abstraction' (Donnelly) 36
'can be critical as well as explanatory' 294
diversity 2–5
'explanatory' versus 'constitutive' 16–19
'explanatory' versus 'constitutive' (Smith) 3
interdisciplinary 19–20
purposes 12, 17
'two conceptions' (Horkheimer) 164–5
theory: points of contestation 20–6
appropriate methodology 24–5
distinct area of intellectual endeavour 25–6
object of analysis and scope of enquiry 21–2
purpose of social and political enquiry 22–4
theory and practice 223
critical theory approach 222
theory construction (Lakatos' model) 218–19
theory evaluation 26–31
Theory of International Politics (Waltz, 1979) 22, 218–19, 366
'reinvigorated realism' 219
Theory of Justice (Rawls, 1971, rev. 1999) 309
'Theses on Feuerbach' (Marx) 164, 349
Thimme, F. 7
'think globally, act locally' (Green slogan) 276
'third debate' 166, 217, 243

'third way' (English School) 28
Third World 22, 101, 102, 107, 127, 178,
    246, 256, 334, 342, 358, 363
Third World feminism **261-2**, 351
Third World Marxism 125
Thomas, S. 103, 363
Thompson, K. W. 52, 363
Thompson, W. R. 159, 336
threat (Walt) 43-4
threats and dangers **204-6**, 347
Thucydides 34, 234, 294, 314, 315, 316
Tickner, J. A. 34, 256, 363
Tilly, C. 63, 146, 148, 363
time 41, 49, 208, 212
Tocqueville, A. de 328
Todorov, T. 174
Toennies, F. 141
Tokyo 80, 358
Toope, S. J. 239, 324
torture 70, 72, 179, 301
totalitarianism 143, 214, 215, 289
totality 196, 214-15
totalization 29, 211, 214-15, 216
totalizing logic 210
'totalizing project' (Linklater) 176, 180
tourism 204, 347
Towns, A. 254, 363
trade 11, 13, 65, 220, 316, 317, 318
    global 162, 247
    intra-firm transactions 77
    see also WTO
trade unions 81, 178
'trading state' (Rosecrance) 68, 356
'Tragedy of Commons' (Hardin, 1968)
    268-70, 272, 275, 276, 338
Trainer, F. E. 274, 363
Transformation of Political Community
    (Linklater, 1998) 176, **180-2**, 185,
    346
Transition Towns movement 278
transnational initiatives 278-9
'transnational moral entrepreneurs' 155
transnationalism 218, 344
'transversal struggles' (Ashley) 198
transversality 216, 361
Treaty of Berlin (1878) 73
Treaty of Kucuk-Kainardji (1774) 73
tripolar systems 41, 358
Tronto, J. 260, 363
Trotsky, L. D. B. 125, 128-9
True, J. 30, **241-65**, **319**, 345, 354
truth 190, 261
Turkey 104
Twenty Years' Crisis (Carr, 1939) 1, 9, 112

underdevelopment 126, 225
'unequal treaties' 104
Union of Soviet Socialist Republics (Soviet
    Union) 15, 92, 123, 128-9, 134, 143,
    205-6, 297

collapse 57-8, 98, 107, 114
collapse (failure to predict) 26; *see also*
    Cold War
relations with USA **38-9**
war in Afghanistan 261
unipolarity **40-1**, 63-4, 84, 93
United Kingdom 8, 10, 44, 75, 88, 97, 98,
    103, 114, 124, 144, 184-5, 193, 316
United Nations 85, 104, 184, 208, 246,
    247-8, 266, 304, 345, 359, 364
    UN Charter 305
    UN Deputy Secretary-General 247
    UN High Commissioner for Human
        Rights 247
    UN Secretary General 247
    UN Security Council Resolution No 1325
        (2000) 260
    UN Women (2011-) 247, 248
    UNDP 247
    UNESCO 247
    UNHCR 247
    UNICEF 247, 248
United States 1, 2, 8, 10, 25, 53-4, 59, 64,
    72-3, 75, 83-4, 93, 97-8, 109, 114,
    144, 154, 184-5, 193, 205-6, 217,
    222, 224, 252, 262, 295, 326
    balancing against threat rather than
        power 43-4
    'dominant player' which has 'framed the
        rules' 69
    foreign policy (post-11 September 2001)
        15
    'greatest threat to world order' 179
    origins of constructivism 240
    power limits 236
    relations with Canada 48
    relations with USSR 38-9
    relative power 219
    'unequal military alliance' with South
        Korea 249
    'unipolarity or 'hyperpower' unipolarity
        236
United States: Declaration of Independence
    (1776) 69-70
'units' versus 'levels of analysis' 45
'universal brotherhood' 154
Universal Declaration of Human Rights
    (1948) 70
'universal history'
    Fukuyama 58
    Kant/Marx 118, 353
    see also world history
universalism 171, 180-1
universality 28, **69-73**, 212, 214, 307-8,
    313, 317
    legal system 312
    versus local practices 314
University of Wales (Aberystwyth): Chair of
    International Politics 6, 7
University of Waterloo (Ontario) 108, 325

use of force 28, 89, 95–6, 105–6, 124,
    145–6, 150, 200, 249, 298
    'justified' versus 'unjustified' 299–300
    'necessary and proportionate' 299
    wrongful 302
'use value' versus 'exchange value' 283
utilitarianism 183, 306
utopianism 9, 10, 60, 82–3, 89, 90, 91, 92,
    93, 110, 112, 113, 169

value-neutrality 164–5, 168, 221
values 5, 15, 48, 91, 151, 153, 169, 188,
    190, 226, 233, 235, 239
    versus 'facts' 167, 168
    transcultural 102
    universal 212
    Western 102–3, 105, 106
    see also revolt against West
Van der Pijl, K. 114, 123, 131, 140, 147,
    159, 364
Van Evera, S. 47, 364
Van Krieken, R. 143, 364
variables 49
    endogenous/exogenous 36, 42, 85
    structural/non-structural 44
Vattel, E. de 98, 314
Vaughan-Williams, N. 203, 364
via media (middle way) tradition 89–90, 93,
    100, 112
Vico, G. B. 177, 331
Victor, D. 271, 364
Victor, P. 274, 364
victor's justice 99
Vietnam, invasion of Cambodia (1978) 51,
    73
Vietnam War 39, 292
'view from nowhere' 4, 190
Vincent, R. J. 28, 71, 88, 92, **100–1**, 110,
    329, 365
violence 48, 88–9, 95, 105–6, 109, 114–15,
    122, 124, 138, 146, 157–8, 179, 193,
    199, **200–3**, 204, 207, 215, 228, 258,
    303, 311, 325, 326, 328
    'both poison and cure' 200
    'duty to protect' from **305–6**
    'more structural' forms 262
    procedure for regulating (discourse
        ethics) **184–5**
    structural 245
violence against women 250, 253, 254, 255,
    260, 263, 367
'visible hand' 77
Vitoria, F. de 316
Vogler, J. 271, 272, 284, 365
von Wegerer, A. 7

Wackernagel, M. 274–5, 365
Walker, R. B. J. 182, 191, 204, 209, 212,
    320, **365**
    post-structuralist ethics 213–14

Wall Street 80
Wallerstein, I. 126, 127, 140, **144–5**, 366
Walt, S. M. **43–4**, 45, 366
Waltz, K. N. 5, 12, 14, 22, 25, 32–4, 45–7,
    54, 60, 67, 84, 108, 121, 128, 133,
    149, **218–19**, 230, 253–5, 320, 360,
    366
    abstracting from versus assuming motives
        43
    causes of wars **21**
    fears concerning unipolarity 63–4
    notion of power 256
    second- and third-image analyses 113
    structural realism **37–42**
Wapner, P. 277, 366
war 7–10, 18, 23, 33, 38–9, 43, 57, 89, 113,
    118, 121–2, 128, 131, 133–4, 136,
    140, 142–4, 146, 149, 151, 173, 245,
    248, 250, 253, 255, 257, 288, 303–4,
    316, 317
    'abolitionism' 298
    aggressive ('effective abolition') 48
        aggressors 301, 302
    causes **21**, 22, 242, 364
    'continuation of politics by other means'
        (Clausewitz) 105, 192
    culpability **298**
    'dominant threat to creation of perfect
        society' (Kant) 119
    gendered impact 241
    'just' versus 'unjust' (Grotius) 97–8
    'just on both sides' **301**
    justice in **296–301**
    'key cause' 252
    link with domestic gender inequality **249**
    literature 320, 327, 333–5, 346–7,
        359–60, 364
    'pre-emption' versus 'prevention' 301
    and tourism 204, 347
war of all against all (Hobbes) 35, 43
war crimes 72–3, 99, 298, 307
war, democracy and free trade **60–73**
    human rights **69–73**
    interdependence and liberal
        institutionalism **66–9**
    prospects for peace **60–5**
    spirit of commerce **65–6**
'war discourse' (Foucault) 192
'war system' (Paine) 61
war on terror/ism 72, 83–4, 93, 162, 179,
    191, 202, 301, 351
    causation 193
    feminist critique **258**
warfare 145, 148
    'Western way' 147
Washington Consensus 15, 79
water 273, 275, 281
Watson, A. 88, 91, 95, 101, 102, 140, 150,
    151, 159, 325, 366
    revolt against West **103–7**

'we-images' 156, 350
'weak and hedged' realists 34
wealth 65, 133, 235, 281
 'affluence' 310
 international inequality 309
weapons of mass destruction (WMD) 82,
 83, 85, 93, 107, 112, 223
Weber, C. 191, 194, 208–9, 233, 260
Weber, Martin 184, 290, 367
Weber, Max 129, 142, 144, 145, 163, 282,
 360, 367
 historical sociology **142**
 sociology of religion 153–4
Weldon, L. 263, 367
welfare 10, 129, 147
welfare state 75, 177
well-being 305, 306
'well-ordered peoples' (Rawls) 304
Wendt, A. 5, 29, 46, 55, **225**, 345, **367**
 attempted formulation of comprehensive
  social theory of international relations
  230
 power relations 235–6
 'supervening' power of structures 225
 'systemic constructivism' **227**
West, the 70, 85, 102, 118, 142, 143, 193,
 258, 261, 295, 301, 369
Western Europe 108, 127, 310
Westphalian era 140, 148, 175, 176, 178,
 181, 237, 346
Wheeler, N. J. 72, 88–9, 91–2, 98, 101–2,
 110, 111, 323, 333, 367
White, H. 190–1
white supremacism 104
Whitehall, G. 211, 361
Whitworth, S. 248, 367
WHO 247
*Whose Common Future? Reclaiming the
 Commons* (*The Ecologist*, 1993) **283**,
 363
 see also Brundtland Commission
'Why is There No International Theory?'
 (Wight, 1966) **9–10**, 25, 89, **291–2**,
 307, 368
Wibben, A. 241, 368
'wider universalities of discourse' 154
Wight, M. 5, 28, 31–2, 67, 88, **89**, 90, **94**,
 96, 100, 103, 108–11, 113, 140,
 151–3, 294, 318, 338, 363, **368**
 'fundamental political task' 92
 'snubbed' emerging IR discipline 292
 see also 'Why is There No International
  Theory?'
Williams, P. 285, 368
Wilson, President T. W. 73
'withering away of state' (Marx) 136
Wohlforth, W. C. 32, 149, 368
women 13, 70, 244, 297, 319, 334–5, 337,
 341, 350, 352, 358, 363–4
 primary care work 255

'support services for military activities'
 249
transnational organizing 263, 335
'Women in Black' 250
women in international development (WID)
 245
women world leaders 253
women's networks (transnational) **250**
workers, appendages to machine' (Marx)
 116
working class 122, 124
 see also proletariat
World Bank 78–9, 265, 278
World Economic Forum 265
world economy/global economy 69, 84,
 107, 131, 150
 anarchy 81–2
 material structure 224
 see also financial crisis (global)
World Food Programme 247
world government 90, 159, 182, 275, 318
 'central world authority' (lacking) 220
 'world state' 158, 269
world history 14, 25, 159, 350
 'global history' 119
 see also diplomatic history
world politics 13, 89, 111, 113, 128–30,
 176, 184, 218–19, 221, 226, 230,
 234–9, 241, 245, 252, 257, 289, 294
 approach **18–19**
 beyond paradigm of sovereignty **209–16**
 'central puzzle' (Waltz) 14
 constructivism 222–3
 constructivism (recent developments)
  236–7
 failure to predict events 265
 feminist perspective 244
 'foremost macropolitical trend'
  (Linklater) 60
 'harm' (Linklater) 162, **178–9**, 347
 Kantian conception 109
 literature 321, 329, 330, 347, 354, 356,
  359, 365, 367
 'transversal' nature (Campbell/Bleiker)
  210–11, 326
 women's location 261
 see also international politics
World Population Fund 247
world society 97, 102, 108, 120, 328
 see also international society
World Trade Organization (WTO) 13, 78,
 79
 see also free trade
World Values Survey 258
World War I ('Great War') 6, 121, 242, 314
 human cost 7
 search for cause/s 7–8, 16, 123–4
World War II 9, 202, 298
world-systems theory 115, 125, 126–7, 130,
 133, **144–5**, 247, 366, 369

'writing' 194, 326, 352
WWF 275, 368

xenophobia 158, 178

Yemen 107
Yergin, D. 15, 368
Young, O. R. 270–2, **368–9**
Young, R. 196, 369
Yugoslavia 101, 250, 258, 349

Zakaria, F. 44, 369
Zehfuss, M. 193, 369
zero-sum game 67–8, 219, 257
Zimelis, A. 249, 369
Zimmern, Sir Alfred 7, 11
Zolberg, A. 145, 369
'zone of indistinction' (Agamben) 202
zone of peace 62, 64–5, 73